Renner Learning Resource Center
Elgin Community College
Elgin, IL 60123

The Routledge International Companion to Multicultural Education

This volume is the first authoritative reference work to provide a truly comprehensive international description and analysis of multicultural education around the world. It is organized around *key concepts* and uses *case studies* from various nations in different parts of the world to exemplify and illustrate the concepts. Case studies are from many nations, including the United States, the United Kingdom, Canada, Australia, France, Germany, Spain, Norway, Bulgaria, Russia, South Africa, Japan, China, India, New Zealand, Malaysia, Singapore, Indonesia, Brazil, and Mexico. Two chapters focus on regions— Latin America and the French-speaking nations in Africa. The *Companion* is divided into ten sections, covering theory and research pertaining to curriculum reform, immigration and citizenship, language, religion, and the education of ethnic and cultural minority groups among other topics.

With 40 newly commissioned pieces written by a prestigious group of internationally renowned scholars, *The Routledge International Companion to Multicultural Education* provides the definitive statement on the state of multicultural education and on its possibilities for the future.

James A. Banks is the Kerry and Linda Killinger Professor of Diversity Studies and Founding Director of the Center for Multicultural Education at the University of Washington, Seattle. He is a past president of the American Educational Research Association (AERA) and the National Council for the Social Studies (NCSS). His books include the *Handbook of Research on Multicultural Education*; *Diversity and Citizenship Education: Global Perspectives*; and *Race, Culture, and Education: The Selected Works of James A. Banks* (Routledge).

Routledge International Handbook Series

The Routledge International Handbook of Lifelong Learning
Edited by *Peter Jarvis*

The Routledge International Handbook of Critical Education
Edited by *Michael W. Apple, Wayne Au, and Luis Armando Gandin*

The Routledge International Companion to Multicultural Education
Edited by *James A. Banks*

The Routledge International Companion to Multicultural Education

Edited by
James A. Banks

Routledge
Taylor & Francis Group
NEW YORK AND LONDON

First published 2009
by Routledge
270 Madison Avenue, New York NY 10016

Simultaneously published in the UK
by Routledge
2 Park Square, Milton Park, Abingdon, Oxon OX14 4RN

Routledge is an imprint of the Taylor and Francis Group, an informa business

© 2009 Routledge, Taylor and Francis

Typeset in Bembo by RefineCatch Ltd, Bungay, Suffolk
Printed and bound in the United States of America on acid-free paper by
Sheridan Books, Inc.

All rights reserved. No part of this book may be reprinted or
reproduced or utilized in any form or by any electronic, mechanical or
other means, now known or hereafter invented, including photocopying
and recording, or in any information storage or retrieval system,
without permission in writing from the publishers.

Trademark Notice: Product or corporate names may be trademarks
or registered trademarks, and are used only for identification
and explanation without intent to infringe.

Library of Congress Cataloging in Publication Data
The Routledge international companion to multicultural education / edited by James A. Banks.
  p. cm.—(Routledge international handbook series)
  1. Multicultural education.   2. Multicultural education—Cross-cultural studies.
  3. Multicultural education—Case studies.   I. Banks, James A.
LC1099.R685 2009
370.117—dc22
2008038494

ISBN10: 0–415–96230–7 (hbk)
ISBN10: 0–203–88151–6 (ebk)

ISBN13: 978–0–415–96230–8 (hbk)
ISBN13: 978–0–203–88151–4 (ebk)

Contents

List of figures	ix
List of tables	x
Editor, editorial research assistants, and international editorial advisory board	xi
Contributors	xii
Reviewers	xvii
Introduction	1

Part 1: Multicultural education: Theoretical perspectives and issues 7

1. Multicultural education: Dimensions and paradigms 9
   James A. Banks

2. Critical multiculturalism and education 33
   Stephen May

3. World population movements, diversity, and education 49
   Stephen Castles

4. Globalization, immigration, and schooling 62
   Marcelo M. Suárez-Orozco and Carola Suárez-Orozco

Part 2: Multicultural education and diversity across nations 77

5. Multicultural education in the United States: Historical realities, ongoing challenges, and transformative possibilities 79
   Sonia Nieto

CONTENTS

6 Multicultural education policy in Canada: Competing ideologies, interconnected discourses   96
   Reva Joshee

7 Multicultural education in Australia: Two generations of evolution   109
   Christine Inglis

8 Multicultural education in the United Kingdom   121
   Sally Tomlinson

9 From intercultural education to the inclusion of diversity: Theories and policies in Europe   134
   Cristina Allemann-Ghionda

10 Multicultural education in South Africa   146
    Crain Soudien

11 Multicultural education in Japan   159
    Yasumasa Hirasawa

Part 3: Race, intergroup relations, and schooling   171

12 Critical perspectives on race and schooling   173
    David Gillborn and Deborah Youdell

13 The nature and origins of children's racial attitudes   186
    Rebecca S. Bigler and Julie Milligan Hughes

14 Modifying children's racial attitudes   199
    Frances E. Aboud

15 Education programs for improving relations between Jews and Palestinians in Israel   210
    Zvi Bekerman

16 Multicultural education for young children   223
    Patricia G. Ramsey

Part 4: Culture, teaching, and learning   237

17 Cultural influences on learning   239
    Carol D. Lee

18 Socialization, literacy, and empowerment   252
    Thor Ola Engen

Part 5: The education of indigenous groups 263

19 Connecting the circle in American Indian education 265
    Donna Deyhle and Karen Gayton Comeau

20 Indigenous education in Peru 276
    María Elena García

21 The struggle to educate the Maori in New Zealand 288
    Wally Penetito

Part 6: Citizenship, immigration, and education 301

22 Diversity, group identity, and citizenship education in a global age 303
    James A. Banks

23 Education, integration, and citizenship in France 323
    Eva Lemaire

24 Citizenship education in France and England: Contrasting
    approaches to national identity and diversity 334
    Audrey Osler and Hugh Starkey

25 Democracy, antiracism, and citizenship education: European
    policy and political complacency 348
    Hugh Starkey and Audrey Osler

26 Diversity and citizenship education in Bulgaria 360
    Hristo Kyuchukov

Part 7: Language, culture, identity, and education 371

27 Language, culture, and identity across nations 373
    Suzanne Romaine

28 Language policies and language education in Francophone
    Africa: A critique and a call to action 385
    Hassana Alidou

29 Language education policy in multi-ethnic Malaysia 397
    Saran Kaur Gill

Part 8: Religion, culture, identity, and education 411

30 Cultural diversity, Muslims, and education in France and England:
    Two contrasting models in Western Europe 413
    Nasar Meer, Valérie Sala Pala, Tariq Modood, and Patrick Simon

31 Religion, culture, language, and education in India *Reva Joshee and Karen Sihra*	425
32 Islamic religious education and Muslim religiosity in Singapore *Mukhlis Abu Bakar*	437
33 Religion, ethnicity, and identity in Indonesian education *Joel C. Kuipers and Ella Yulaelawati*	449

Part 9: The education of ethnic and cultural minority groups in Europe — 461

34 Migrant minority groups in Germany: Success and failure in education *Sigrid Luchtenberg*	463
35 The education of ethnic, racial, and cultural minority groups in Spain *Teresa Aguado Odina*	474
36 Educational policies for ethnic and cultural groups in Russia *Isak D. Froumin and Andrei Zakharov*	486

Part 10: The education of ethnic and cultural minority groups in Asia and Latin America — 499

37 The education of ethnic minority groups in China *Gerard A. Postiglione*	501
38 Social inequality as a barrier to multicultural education in Latin America *Martin Carnoy*	512
39 Achieving quality education for Indigenous peoples and Blacks in Brazil *Petronilha Beatriz Gonçalves e Silva and Sonia Stella Araújo-Olivera*	526
40 The education of ethnic minority groups in Mexico *Sonia Stella Araújo-Olivera and Petronilha Beatriz Gonçalves e Silva*	540
Index	553

Figures

1.1	The Dimensions of Multicultural Education	15
1.2	Phases in the Development of Ethnic Revitalization Movements	18
1.3	The Total School Environment	27
1.4	Acculturation as a School Goal	28
1.5	Helping Students to Develop Identities and to Function in Cultural, National, and Global Communities	29
13.1	Processes Involved in the Formation of Social Stereotypes and Prejudice	189
13.2	Processes Involved in the Maintenance or Modification of Social Stereotypes and Prejudice	190
22.1	Types of Citizens, Defined by Four Levels of Participation	317
26.1	Results from Reading Comprehension Test	363
26.2	Spelling Mistakes Made by Roma Children	364
38.1	Trend Line of PISA 2003 and Imputed PISA 2003 Mean Mathematics Scores with Gross Domestic Product per Capita and Location of Latin American Students' Performance Relative to the Trend Line	514

Tables

1.1	Multicultural Education Paradigms	19
3.1	Types of Immigrants	51
3.2	Foreign-Born Population in Selected OECD Countries	52
24.1	Framing Questions on National Identity and Relations between Nations	337
24.2	Framing Questions on Social Cohesion and Social Diversity	342
33.1	Ethnic Groups in Indonesia, 2000	450
34.1	Percentages of Foreign Students in Types of Schools	469
34.2	Percentages of Germans and Non-Germans Earning Types of School-Leaving Certificates	469
35.1	Non-University Education: Number of Foreign Students According to Origin	478
35.2	Distribution of Numbers of Students According to Academic Year and Educational Model in Primary Education in the Basque Country	480
38.1	Latin America: Average Fourth-Grade Mathematics Score, School Average Socioeconomic (SES) Index, and SES Index Standard Deviation, 1997	516
38.2	Chile: Distribution of Students Across Schools, by Socioeconomic Class of Students and Average Socioeconomic Class of Students in Schools, 1998	517

Editor, editorial research assistants, and international editorial advisory board

Editor

James A. Banks, University of Washington, Seattle, USA

Editorial research assistants

Yuhshi Lee, University of Washington, Seattle, USA
Dennis Rudnick, University of Washington, Seattle, USA

International editorial advisory board

Cherry A. McGee Banks, University of Washington, Bothell, USA
Stephen Castles, University of Oxford, UK
Barry van Driel, Editor, *Intercultural Education*, The Netherlands
Peter Figueroa, University of Southampton, UK
Isak D. Froumin, The World Bank, Moscow, Russia
David Gillborn, Institute of Education, University of London, UK
Petronilha Beatriz Gonçalves e Silva, Federal University of São Carlos, Brazil
Yasumasa Hirasawa, Osaka University, Japan
Christine Inglis, University of Sydney, Australia
Jonathan D. Jansen, University of Pretoria, South Africa
Reva Joshee, Ontario Institute for Studies in Education, University of Toronto, Canada
Will Kymlicka, Queen's University, Canada
Leslie J. Limage, UNESCO (retired), Paris, France
Sigrid Luchtenberg, University of Duisburg–Essen, Germany
Tariq Modood, University of Bristol, UK
Sonia Nieto, University of Massachusetts, Amherst, USA
Audrey Osler, University of Leeds, UK
Gary Partington, Edith Cowan University, Australia
Suzanne Romaine, University of Oxford, UK
Sally Tomlinson, University of Oxford, UK
Wan Minggang, Northwest National University, China

Contributors

Frances E. Aboud is a professor at McGill University, Montreal, Canada. She conducts research on prejudice and cross-ethnic friendship among children. She also has an interest in programs to improve health and education for children in developing countries.

Teresa Aguado Odina is a professor in the faculty of education at the Distance University in Spain (UNED) and coordinator of the INTER Network. Her research focuses on intercultural education, teacher training, and school practice (European Commission).

Hassana Alidou is a professor of TESOL and cross-cultural studies, Graduate School of Education, Alliant International University, San Diego, California, USA. Her research interests are educational sociolinguistics, educational research, assessment and evaluation, and post-colonial and critical theories.

Cristina Allemann-Ghionda is a professor of comparative education and co-founder of the Center for Diversity Studies at the University of Cologne, Germany. Her main research fields are theory and policy issues in intercultural education, multilingual education, migration and school achievement, and comparative research on educational policy issues.

Sonia Stella Araújo-Olivera completed her doctoral studies in Latin American Studies under the supervision of Dr. Enrique Dussel at the National Autonomous University of Mexico. She is a professor in the Institute of Educational Sciences at the Autonomous University of the State of Morelos in Mexico.

Mukhlis Abu Bakar is an assistant professor at the Asian Languages and Cultures Academic Group, National Institute of Education, Nanyang Technological University, Singapore. He teaches courses on language, literacy, and culture. His research focuses on bilingualism and childhood literacy, as well as Islamic religious education.

James A. Banks is the Kerry and Linda Killinger Professor of Diversity Studies and founding director of the Center for Multicultural Education at the University of Washington, Seattle, USA. His research focuses on multicultural education and diversity and citizenship education in a global context.

Zvi Bekerman teaches anthropology of education at the School of Education and the Melton Center, Hebrew University of Jerusalem, Israel. He is also a research fellow at the Truman Institute for the Advancement of Peace, Hebrew University, and the editor of *Diaspora, Indigenous, and Minority Education: An International Journal* (Routledge).

Rebecca S. Bigler is a professor of psychology and women's and gender studies at the University of Texas at Austin, USA. Her research focuses on the development of social stereotypes and prejudice. She has also been active in developing and evaluating intervention programs to reduce racial and gender biases among children.

Martin Carnoy is the Vida Jacks Chair of Education at Stanford University, USA. He is a member of the National and International Academies of Education, on the American Educational Research Association (AERA) Grants Board, and on the scientific board of the National Institute of Educational Evaluation in Mexico.

Stephen Castles is a professor of migration and refugee studies at the International Migration Institute, which is attached to the James Martin 21st Century School and the Department of International Development, University of Oxford, UK.

Karen Gayton Comeau, now retired, was a professor of education at the University of Utah, USA, and Arizona State University, USA, and the first woman president of Haskell Indian Nations University. A member of the Standing Rock Sioux Tribe, Dr. Comeau (formerly Swisher) lives on the Standing Rock reservation in North Dakota.

Donna Deyhle is a professor of anthropology and education in the Department of Education, Culture, and Society and the coordinator of the American Indian Studies Program in the Ethnic Studies Program at the University of Utah, USA. Her major professional interests are anthropology and education, cultural conflict, racism, critical theory, and the education of American Indians and Navajos.

Thor Ola Engen is a professor of multicultural education at Hedmark University College, Hamar, Norway. He has been a member of a committee preparing the Norwegian Consensus Conference on Bilingual Education and of a committee that makes national policy proposals for the education of linguistic minority students.

Isak D. Froumin is a senior education specialist at the World Bank office in Moscow, Russia, and research supervisor of the Institute of Educational Policy at the Moscow Higher School of Economics.

María Elena García is an assistant professor in the Comparative History of Ideas Program at the University of Washington, Seattle, USA. Her book *Making Indigenous Citizens: Identities, Development, and Multicultural Activism in Peru* (Stanford University Press, 2005) examines indigenous politics and multicultural activism in Peru. Her work has been published in education, anthropology, and Latin American studies journals.

Saran Kaur Gill is a professor of sociolinguistics in multi-ethnic nations at the School of Language Studies and Linguistics, Universiti Kebangsaan Malaysia. She researches and publishes in the area of language policy and planning, with a focus on managing ethnic, national, and global identities. She is also deputy vice-chancellor for Industry and Community Partnerships.

David Gillborn is a professor of education at the Institute of Education, University of London, UK, and founding editor of the journal *Race, Ethnicity and Education*.

CONTRIBUTORS

Petronilha Beatriz Gonçalves e Silva is an associate professor in the Department of Teaching Methodologies of the Universidade Federal de São Carlos (Federal University of São Carlos) in the state of São Paulo, Brazil. She is an activist in the Black Movement in Brazil, and her research is linked to the interests of this social movement.

Yasumasa Hirasawa is a professor of education at the Graduate School of Human Sciences, Osaka University, and a visiting research fellow in the Kyoto Human Rights Research Institute, Japan.

Julie Milligan Hughes is an assistant professor of psychology at the College of New Jersey in Ewing, USA. Her research focuses on the consequences of racism awareness on the racial attitudes and political reasoning of children and adolescents.

Christine Inglis is director of the Multicultural and Migration Research Centre at the University of Sydney, Australia, where she is an honorary associate professor in the Department of Sociology and Social Policy.

Reva Joshee is an associate professor and chair in the Department of Theory and Policy Studies of the Ontario Institute for Studies in Education at the University of Toronto, Canada, where she teaches courses in multicultural education and policy analysis. Her research examines issues of diversity and policy in India, Canada, and the United States.

Joel C. Kuipers is a professor of anthropology and international affairs at the George Washington University in Washington, DC, USA.

Hristo Kyuchukov is an associate professor in Romani language and education at the University of Veliko Tarnovo, Bulgaria. He has published a number of books and articles related to Romani language, culture, and history.

Carol D. Lee is a professor of learning sciences at Northwestern University, USA. She is president of the American Educational Research Association (2009–2010), and has been president of the National Conference of Research on Language and Literacy, and a fellow at the Center for Advanced Study in the Behavioral Sciences at Stanford University.

Eva Lemaire has a Ph.D. in didactics of language and culture from Université Sorbonne Nouvelle – Paris III, France. She is a specialist in the education of separated children and teaches in the Department of Didactics at Université Marc Bloch – Strasbourg II, France.

Sigrid Luchtenberg has a Ph.D. in German linguistics and literature and a habilitation in multicultural education. She is a professor in the Faculty of Education at the University of Duisburg–Essen, Germany. Her work in multicultural and comparative education is underlined by her international connections, for example as a visiting professor at the University of Sydney, Australia.

Stephen May is Foundation Professor and chair of Language Education at the School of Education, University of Waikato, New Zealand. He is also a senior research fellow in the Centre for the Study of Ethnicity and Citizenship, University of Bristol, UK, and is the founding editor of the journal *Ethnicities*.

Nasar Meer is based in the Centre for the Study of Ethnicity and Citizenship, and the Department of Sociology, at the University of Bristol, UK. He has previously been a fellow with the W. E. B. Du Bois Institute for African and African-American Studies at

Harvard University, USA, and is currently engaged in European Union (EU)-funded research comparing citizenship programs across nine European countries.

Tariq Modood is a professor of sociology, politics, and public policy and the founding director of the Centre for the Study of Ethnicity and Citizenship at the University of Bristol, UK. His recent books include *Multiculturalism: A Civic Idea* (Polity, 2007); and, as co-editor, *Secularism, Religion and Multicultural Citizenship* (Cambridge University Press, 2008).

Sonia Nieto is professor emerita of language, literacy, and culture, University of Massachusetts, Amherst. She has written numerous books and journal articles on multicultural education, teacher education, and the education of students of culturally and linguistically diverse backgrounds. She has received many awards for her research, advocacy, and service.

Audrey Osler is a professor of education at the University of Leeds, UK, and director of the Centre for Citizenship and Human Rights Education. In 2007 she was a visiting scholar at the Center for Multicultural Education, University of Washington, Seattle, USA.

Wally Penetito is Maori, from the Tainui Confederation of tribes. He is a professor of education at the College of Education, Victoria University of Wellington, New Zealand. His research focuses on Maori education. He is also co-director of He Parekereke, the Institute for Research and Development in Maori and Pacific Education.

Gerard A. Postiglione is a professor and head of the Division of Policy, Administration and Social Science, Faculty of Education, University of Hong Kong. He is also editor of the journal *Chinese Education and Society*.

Patricia G. Ramsey is a professor of psychology and education at Mount Holyoke College in South Hadley, MA, USA. She is the author of *Teaching and Learning in a Diverse World* and co-author of *What If All the Kids Are White?*

Suzanne Romaine has been Merton Professor of English Language at the University of Oxford, UK, since 1984. She has received honorary doctorates from the University of Uppsala, Sweden, and the University of Tromsø, Norway, and in 2005–2006 was a resident fellow at the Center for Advanced Studies in the Behavioral Sciences in Stanford, California, USA.

Valérie Sala Pala is a lecturer in political science in the Department of Sociology, University of Saint-Etienne, France. She is a researcher at the Research Center for Public Administration of Saint-Etienne (CERAPSE).

Karen Sihra is a doctoral candidate in the Philosophy of Education Department at the Ontario Institute for Studies in Education at the University of Toronto, Canada.

Patrick Simon is director of research at Institut National d'Etudes Démographiques (INED) (National Demographic Institute), head of the International Migrations and Minorities research unit, and fellow researcher at the Centre d'Etude de la Vie Politique Française (CEVIPOF) (Center for the Study of French Political Life) in Paris, France.

Crain Soudien is a professor at the School of Education, University of Cape Town, South Africa. He writes on social difference, public history, and education policy. He is currently the president of the World Council of Comparative Education Societies and is heading a ministerial committee of enquiry into transformation in higher education in South Africa.

Hugh Starkey is a reader of education at the Institute of Education, University of London, UK, where he is co-director of the International Centre for Education for Democratic

Citizenship. He is program leader for a distance learning MA degree in citizenship and history education.

Carola Suárez-Orozco is professor of applied psychology at New York University's Steinhardt School of Culture, Education, and Human Development, and co-director of Immigration Studies.

Marcelo M. Suárez-Orozco is the Courtney Sale Ross University Professor at New York University, where he is also co-director of Immigration Studies.

Sally Tomlinson is emeritus professor of education at Goldsmiths College, University of London, UK, and a senior research fellow in the Department of Education, University of Oxford, UK. She has taught, researched, and published in the area of race, ethnicity, and education for over 30 years. She is also chair of trustees of the Africa Educational Trust.

Deborah Youdell is a senior lecturer in sociology of education at the Institute of Education, University of London, UK. She has published widely on issues of identity and inequality in education, including her recent book *Impossible Bodies, Impossible Selves: Exclusions and Student Subjectivities*.

Ella Yulaelawati, Ph.D., is director of the Equivalency Program in the Department of Education for the Republic of Indonesia.

Andrei Zakharov is an associate professor of education at the Moscow State Institute for Humanities and Education, Russia. He has a PhD in education.

Reviewers

Martine Abdallah-Pretceille
Universities of Paris VIII and Sorbonne
Nouvelle – Paris III
Paris, France

François Audigier
Université de Genève
Geneva, Switzerland

Harley D. Balzer
Georgetown University
Washington, DC, USA

Cherry A. McGee Banks
University of Washington
Bothell, WA, USA

Christine Bennett
Indiana University
Bloomington, IN, USA

Christophe Bertossi
Institut français des relations internationales
(IFRI)
Paris, France

Jill Bevan-Brown
Massey University
Palmerston North, New Zealand

Russell Bishop
University of Waikato
Hamilton, New Zealand

Christopher Bjork
Vassar College
Poughkeepsie, NY, USA

Vladimir Briller
Pratt Institute
New York, USA

Nazir Carrim
University of the Witswatersrand
Johannesburg, South Africa

Sveta Dave Chakravarty
Independent consultant
New Delhi, India

Kai-ming Cheng
University of Hong Kong
Hong Kong

Donna Christian
Center for Applied Linguistics
Washington, DC, USA

Serafin M. Coronel-Molina
Indiana University
Bloomington, IN, USA

Frank Darnell
University of Greenland – Ilisimatusarfik
Nuuk, Greenland

REVIEWERS

Maya Khemlani David
University of Malaya
Kuala Lumpur, Selangor, Malaysia

Hayley Delport
University of Jyväskylä
Jyväskylä, Finland

John Delport
University of Washington
Seattle, WA, USA

Nadine Dolby
Purdue University
West Lafayette, IN, USA

Barry van Driel
International Association for Intercultural Education
Amsterdam, The Netherlands

Peter Figueroa
University of Southampton
Southampton, UK

John Flint
Sheffield Hallam University
Sheffield, UK

Patricia Gándara
University of California
Los Angeles, CA, USA

Geneva Gay
University of Washington
Seattle, WA, USA

Encho Gerganov
New Bulgarian University
Sofia, Bulgaria

A. Lin Goodwin
Teachers College, Columbia University
New York, USA

Kris Gutierrez
University of California, Los Angeles
Los Angeles, CA, USA

Kenji Hakuta
Stanford University
Stanford, CA, USA

J. Mark Halstead
University of Huddersfield
Huddersfield, West Yorkshire, UK

Clive Harber
University of Birmingham
Birmingham, UK

Bob Hill
Charles Sturt University
Bathurst, NSW, Australia

Nancy H. Hornberger
University of Pennsylvania
Philadelphia, PA, USA

Christian Horst
Danish School of Education, University of Aarhus
Copenhagen, Denmark

Cynthia Hudley
University of California, Santa Barbara
Santa Barbara, CA, USA

Yasemin Karakasoglu
Bremen University
Bremen, Germany

Susan Roberta Katz
University of San Francisco
San Francisco, CA, USA

Seiji Kawasaki
Tokyo Gakugei University
Tokyo, Japan

Stephen T. Kerr
University of Washington
Seattle, WA, USA

Melanie Killen
University of Maryland
College Park, MD, USA

Gillian Klein
Trentham Books
London and Stoke-on-Trent, UK

Ryuko Kubota
University of North Carolina at Chapel Hill
Chapel Hill, NC, USA

Lai Ah Eng
Asia Research Institute, National University of Singapore
Singapore

Zeus Leonardo
University of California
Berkeley, CA, USA

Henry M. Levin
Teachers College, Columbia University
New York, USA

Jing Lin
University of Maryland
College Park, MD, USA

K. Tsianina Lomawaima
University of Arizona
Tucson, AZ, USA

Françoise Lorcerie
IREMAM-CNRS
Aix-en-Provence, France

Darren E. Lund
University of Calgary
Calgary, AB, Canada

Rong Ma
Peking University
Beijing, China

Glenda MacNaughton
University of Melbourne
Victoria, Australia

Beatriz Malik
Facultad de Educación, Universidad Nacional de Educación a Distancia
Madrid, Spain

Ifat Maoz
Hebrew University of Jerusalem
Jerusalem, Israel

Susan Martin
Georgetown University
Washington, DC, USA

Mark Mason
University of Hong Kong
Hong Kong

Clark McKown
Rush University Medical Center
Chicago, IL, USA

Luanna H. Meyer
Victoria University of Wellington
Wellington, New Zealand

Mark Miller
University of Delaware
Newark, DE, USA

Heidi Safia Mirza
Institute of Education, University of London
London, UK

Kogila Adam Moodley
University of British Columbia
Vancouver, BC, Canada

Stephen Murphy-Shigematsu
Stanford University
Stanford, CA, USA

Tania Ogay
University of Fribourg
Fribourg, Switzerland

Margarita del Olmo
Consejo Superior de Investigaciones Científicas
Madrid, Spain

Michael R. Olneck
University of Wisconsin-Madison
Madison, WI, USA

Olivette Otele
Université Paris XIII
Paris, France

REVIEWERS

Juliana Othman
University of Malaya
Kuala Lumpur, Malaysia

Patricia G. Ramsey
Mount Holyoke College
South Hadley, MA, USA

Fazal Rizvi
University of Illinois
Urbana-Champaign, IL, USA

Nicola Rollock
London Metropolitan University
London, UK

Janet Ward Schofield
University of Pittsburgh
Pittsburgh, PA, USA

Özlem Sensoy
Simon Fraser University
Burnaby, BC, Canada

Juan Carlos Silas
Instituto Tecnológico y de Estudios
Superiores de Occidente (ITESO)
Guadalajara, Mexico

Michael Singh
University of Western Sydney
Sydney, NSW, Australia

Christine E. Sleeter
California State University Monterey Bay
Seaside, CA, USA

Louise Derman Sparks
Pacific Oaks College
Pasadena, CA, USA

Nelly P. Stromquist
University of Maryland
College Park, MD, USA

Beth Blue Swadener
Arizona State University
Tempe, AZ, USA

Moshe Tatar
Hebrew University of Jerusalem
Jerusalem, Israel

Triadafilos Triadafilopoulos
University of Toronto
Toronto, Canada

Guadalupe Valdés
Stanford University
Stanford, CA, USA

Anand Valmiki
University of Washington
Seattle, WA, USA

Manka Varghese
University of Washington
Seattle, WA, USA

Michael Vavrus
Evergreen State College
Olympia, WA, USA

Robert Verhine
Universidade Federal da Bahia
Salvador, Bahia, Brazil

Jonathan W. Warren
University of Washington
Seattle, WA, USA

David Blake Willis
Soai University
Osaka, Japan

Tarajean Yazzie-Mintz
Indiana University
Bloomington, IN, USA

Daniel A. Yon
York University
Toronto, Canada

Joseph Zajda
Australian Catholic University
Melbourne, Australia

Mohamad Hassan Zakaria
Universiti Teknologi Malaysia
Johor, Malaysia

Introduction

A number of factors contributed to the rise and development of multicultural education around the world. The gap between ideals and realities in the Western democratic nations and the marginalized status of ethnic, cultural, and linguistic minorities stimulated the rise of ethnic revitalization movements in the 1960s and 1970s. These movements began in the United States when African Americans began a quest for political, economic, and cultural rights that was unprecedented in their history. The Black civil rights movement influenced other structurally excluded racial, ethnic, cultural, and linguistic groups in the United States as well as in other nations. Marginalized groups in Canada, Australia, the United Kingdom, and elsewhere also began movements that demanded that their histories, cultures, and languages be reflected in mainstream institutions and in the public and civic culture.

Schools, colleges, and universities were important targets of ethnic revitalization movements because they reflected and reinforced mainstream society and culture in their ethos, curriculum, and the languages and cultures they valued and sanctioned. The myriad responses to ethnic revitalization movements that schools implemented evolved into a series of phases that culminated in the development of multicultural education. The earliest phase of multicultural education consisted of the infusion of bits and pieces of ethnic and cultural content into the curriculum without changing it in significant ways. Over four decades and through several phases of development, multicultural education evolved into a transformative idea whose implementation requires substantial changes in all of the major variables of the school so that students from diverse racial, ethnic, cultural, language, and religious groups experience educational equality.

Multicultural education is a concept, an educational reform movement, and a process (Banks, 2007). It incorporates the idea that all students – regardless of their ethnic, racial, cultural, or linguistic characteristics – should have an equal opportunity to learn in school. Another important idea in multicultural education is that some students, because of their group characteristics, have a better chance to learn in schools as they are currently structured than do students who belong to other groups.

INTRODUCTION

The goals and development of the *Companion*

A companion is a single-volume reference work that gives an overview of the theory, research, and practice in a discipline or field. This *Companion* is designed to provide researchers, students, and educational practitioners with a one-volume reference that describes the research, concepts, theories, and practices in multicultural education within an international context. This volume also illustrates how multicultural education is a contested concept both within and across nations and how it reflects – in complex and nuanced ways – the national, social, and political context in which it is embedded. Another goal of this *Companion* is to advance theory, research, and practice in multicultural education by providing a source that researchers and educational practitioners can use to enrich their work with insights and findings from scholars and practitioners in other nations.

The first phase in the development of the *Companion* was the establishment of the International Editorial Advisory Board that consists of scholars in various parts of the world. After the Board was established, I constructed a working outline of the *Companion* that the Board reviewed critically. The Board was especially concerned that the *Companion* be inclusive and represent nations and cultures throughout the world. The revised outline, which incorporated the Board's comments, was substantially different from the original outline. It contained more chapters as well as chapters from a wider range of nations across the continents.

One of the most difficult problems with which the Board and I had to wrestle was how to represent a world that consists of 193 generally recognized nation-states (Martin & Zurcher, 2008) within a single-volume reference work that would have adequate depth and a logical organization that was helpful to readers. By reviewing the literature in the field and responding to the feedback from the Board, I decided to organize the *Companion* around *key concepts* and to use *case studies* from various nations to exemplify and illustrate the concepts. Consequently, the *Companion* consists of 10 parts organized around key concepts and case studies from nations in different parts of the world.

The organization of the *Companion*

Part 1 consists of four chapters that discuss cross-cultural issues, concepts, and theories in multicultural education. The first chapter describes the historical and contextual development of multicultural education and the dimensions and paradigms in the field. Chapters 2, 3, and 4 discuss critical multiculturalism, world population movements, and globalization, immigration, and schooling, respectively.

Multicultural education shares characteristics across nations but also reflects the national, cultural, and political context in which it is embedded. Part 2 consists of seven chapters that describe multicultural education within national contexts. The earliest phases of multicultural education developed in the US but first received official government sanction in policies of multiculturalism in 1971 in Canada and in 1978 in Australia. Some of the earliest phases of multicultural education in Europe were implemented in England in the 1970s to respond to the migrants who had started settling in the UK in significant numbers after World War II to fulfill labor needs. Multicultural education developed later in Asian nations such as Japan and India and has taken a unique path in South Africa because of that country's history of apartheid and reconciliation.

Race has been a powerful factor in all multiethnic and multicultural nation-states and societies since the development of Western imperialism, the construction of race to justify hegemony and slavery, and the spread of Western ideas about race throughout the world. Racial stratification and its consequences were by-products of colonization, the conquering of Indigenous peoples, and the construction of justifications for the taking of their lands and the destruction of their languages and cultures. The chapters in Part 3 examine institutional and structural racism from several perspectives. Chapter 12 analyzes structural and institutional racism and the ways in which it influences the schooling experiences of students. Chapters 13 through 16 describe research on the nature and origins of children's racial attitudes and how they can be modified with educational interventions.

To implement effective multicultural education, schools must help all students – including ethnic and language minority students as well as majority group students – to acquire the attitudes, knowledge, and skills needed for productive employment in a highly technological and global society, participate effectively in the political system, and take action to increase equity in society. Schools should also work to close the wide achievement gap that exists between middle-class mainstream students and low-achieving minority students. Research and theory grounded in the cultural difference paradigm indicate that if teachers incorporate the cultures and languages of diverse groups into instruction the academic achievement of these students will increase. The two chapters in Part 4 discuss research on ways in which culturally responsive teaching and improved home–school relationships can help students from diverse groups increase their academic achievement.

When nations in Western Europe established colonies in the Americas, Canada, Australia, the Caribbean, Africa, and other parts of the world, the cultures, religions, and languages of the Indigenous peoples were systematically destroyed by factors such as disease, war, and schooling. In the US, Canada, and Australia, Indigenous students were taken from their homes and sent to boarding schools where they were "civilized" by being stripped of their cultures, languages, and religions. The destruction of Indigenous cultures, languages, and religions left a poignant and challenging legacy in the US, Canada, Australia, the Caribbean, and Latin America. The three chapters in Part 5 are case studies that describe the legacy of colonization of Indigenous peoples and its effects on education in three nations: (1) the Maori in New Zealand, (2) the Indigenous people in Peru, and (3) the Native Americans in the United States.

Growth in international migration, increasing recognition of structural inequality within democratic nation-states, and growing recognition and legitimacy of international human rights have problematized citizenship and citizenship education in nation-states throughout the world, and especially in Western democracies. The near zero population growth in many of the Western developed nations and in Japan and the steady growth of the population in developing nations have created a *demographic divide* and a demand for immigrants to meet labor needs in the developed nations (Haub, 2007). The demographic divide and labor needs in developed nations have also stimulated acid debates about immigration and citizenship. The chapters in Part 6 examine immigration, citizenship, and education in selected nations. These chapters also describe the ways in which citizenship and citizenship education have changed to respond to the needs of Indigenous and immigrant groups. However, as several of the chapters in this volume point out, citizenship education is also being used in nations such as Australia, Canada, and the UK to promote a new form of assimilation called "social cohesion," which is a conservative response to immigration, radical Islam, and concerns about the fracturing of national identity and the maintenance of national unity.

In nations around the world, some languages have higher status than others, and students from language minority groups frequently experience alienation, low academic achievement, high dropout rates, and identity problems in schools. The chapters in Part 7 describe the status of various languages in selected nations, the extent to which students experience language inequality in school, and programs and practices that are being implemented to help language minority students experience academic success and educational equality.

The growth of the Muslim population in nations such as the United Kingdom, The Netherlands, and France and the rise of radical Islam around the world have evoked tension and Islamophobia in many nations. A string of terrorist events in different nations related to radical Islam has crystallized fear, stereotypes, and hostility toward all Muslims. These events include the bombing of the Pentagon and the World Trade Center in the US on September 11, 2001; the bombings of four commuter trains in Madrid, Spain, on March 11, 2004; the murder of the Dutch film director Theo van Gogh in Amsterdam on November 2, 2004; and the bombings in the London transportation system on July 7, 2005. In the United States as well as in the Arab world, religious fundamentalism is challenging democratic values. In nations such as the UK, France, and India religion has historically influenced education in significant ways. The chapters in Part 8 examine religious issues related to education in selected nations, the challenges and opportunities they create for schools, and how schools are responding to religious issues, tensions, challenges, and possibilities.

The experiences of groups such as Mexican Americans in the United States, Turks in Germany, African Caribbeans in the United Kingdom, Muslims in France, and Koreans in Japan are characterized by discrimination, marginalization, and the quest for inclusion and equality. Blacks and Indigenous groups in Brazil, and Indians in Mexico and Peru also experience poverty and educational inequality. China has 56 officially designated ethnic groups, most of whom experience educational challenges and do not attain the knowledge and skills needed to fully participate in mainstream Han society. The chapters in Parts 9 and 10 examine the educational problems that ethnic minority groups experience in schools and reforms that have been undertaken to respond to their educational needs.

Acknowledgments

I am deeply indebted to the members of the International Editorial Advisory Board, who provided wise counsel from the inception of the *Companion* project to its completion. They influenced significantly the conceptualization and contents of the *Companion*, helped me to identify authors to participate in the project, and gave me the encouragement that an editor of a volume of this magnitude needs to stay the course. Some members of the Board also wrote chapters for the *Companion*; others served as chapter reviewers. I am especially grateful to Will Kymlicka for his sage advice during the early phases of the *Companion* project and for helping me to identify authors in various parts of the world. Barry van Driel – the editor of *Intercultural Education*, published by the International Association for Intercultural Education (IAIE) – gave me excellent author recommendations, reviewed several chapters, and responded promptly to the countless e-mails I sent him seeking editorial advice. I shall be forever indebted to Barry for his help, encouragement, and friendship during the conceptualization and development of this *Companion*.

I am grateful to the contributing authors for preparing drafts of their chapters and revising them using input from the external reviewers. I wish to acknowledge with deep appreciation the significant contributions made by the external reviewers. They prepared perceptive, careful, and comprehensive reviews of the chapters, which enabled the authors to strengthen them for publication in the *Companion*. I am fortunate to have worked with such gifted and committed authors and reviewers from institutions in all parts of the world.

The *Companion* is a project of the Center for Multicultural Education at the University of

Washington, Seattle. As director of the Center, I have spent a significant part of my time during the last two years working on the *Companion*. Yuhshi Lee and Dennis Rudnick, research assistants at the Center, have worked diligently on the *Companion*. Yuhshi coordinated the 90-plus peer reviews of chapters completed for the project. Both she and Dennis worked on the chapters to make them consistent with the style requirements of the *Publication Manual of the American Psychological Association* (APA). During the final phase of manuscript preparation, Nicole Russell and Hui-Ching Yang – doctoral students in multicultural education at the University of Washington – helped Yuhshi and Dennis with the APA work on the manuscript. I wish to thank Kimberly McKaig for her editorial assistance when I was preparing the manuscript for submission to the publisher.

Several of my colleagues at the University of Washington consistently support the projects and work of the Center for Multicultural Education and help to make the Center and our College of Education stimulating intellectual communities. Geneva Gay, Walter Parker, Tom Stritikus, and Manka Varghese are valued colleagues and faculty associates of the Center. Patricia Wasley, dean of the College, and Mark Windschitl, chair of Curriculum and Instruction where the Center is housed, are friends and supporters of the Center. Jerry Purcell, assistant to the chair of Curriculum and Instruction, has helped with the preparation of this *Companion* in countless ways. I shall always be grateful for his professionalism, ingenuity, and friendship.

I would like to give special thanks to five colleagues who reviewed Chapter 1 and gave me prompt feedback within a tight deadline that helped me to strengthen it: Cherry A. McGee Banks, Peter Figueroa, Geneva Gay, Darren Lund, and Stephen Murphy-Shigematsu. Cherry and Walter Parker gave me helpful and constructive comments on this Introduction that I used to improve it.

I am grateful to Anna Clarkson, publisher at Routledge in the UK, for inviting me to edit the *Companion*, and to Catherine Bernard, my editor, for her editorial acumen, compassion, and support. I extend thanks to Heather Jarrow at Routledge for her professional help with various aspects of manuscript preparation, and especially for her work contacting authors. Richard Willis and Helen Moss of Swales & Willis handled the production of the *Companion* with grace, efficiency, and professionalism. I am especially indebted to Helen Moss, the copyeditor, for her stamina and keen and perceptive eye. Cherry A. McGee Banks, my wife and colleague, has supported and enriched my life and work during the four decades of our journey. My daughters, Angela and Patricia – two young college professors who have incorporated a social justice commitment into their work – give me hope for the next generation.

I hope the 48 authors and 90 external reviewers who contributed to the *Companion* project will take pride in their association with it and that this volume will advance theory, research, and practice in multicultural education and contribute to the attainment of social justice and equality for students around the world.

James A. Banks
Seattle, WA, USA

References

Banks, J. A. (2007). Multicultural education: Characteristics and goals. In J. A. Banks & C. A. M. Banks (Eds.), *Multicultural education: Issues and perspectives* (6th ed., pp. 3–30). Hoboken, NJ: Wiley.

Haub, C. (2007). Global aging and the demographic divide. *Public policy & aging report, 17*(4). Retrieved May 22, 2008, from http://www.prb.org/Articles/2008/globalaging.aspx

Martin, P., & Zurcher, G. (2008). Managing migration: The global challenge. *Population Bulletin, 63*(1), 1–20.

Part 1

Multicultural education

Theoretical perspectives and issues

1

Multicultural education

Dimensions and paradigms

James A. Banks
University of Washington, Seattle, USA

In nation-states around the world, there is increasing diversity as well as increasing recognition of diversity. Since the ethnic revitalization movements of the 1960s and 1970s, ethnic groups have articulated their grievances and pushed for equality and structural inclusion. The Black civil rights movement in the US – which echoed throughout the world (Painter, 2006) – stimulated the ethnic revitalization movements. The French and First Nations[1] in Canada, the West Indians and Asians in Britain, the Indonesians and Surinamese in the Netherlands, and the Aboriginal peoples in Australia joined the string of ethnic movements, expressed their rage and anger, and demanded that the institutions within their nation-states – such as schools, colleges, and universities – become more responsive to their needs, hopes, and dreams.

When the ethnic revitalization movements began in the 1960s and 1970s, the Western nations were characterized by tremendous ethnic, cultural, racial, religious, and linguistic diversity. This diversity resulted from several historical developments. The nations in Western Europe had longstanding linguistic and cultural minorities, such as the Basques in France and Spain, the Germans in Denmark, the Danes in Germany, and the Welsh, Scots, and Jews in the United Kingdom. Europe has historically been a crossroad and meeting ground – sometimes violent – of diverse cultural groups (Figueroa, 2008). Diversity in Europe was increased when thousands of migrants from colonial nations came to Europe to improve their economic and social status in the years after World War II.

Many of the nations in Asia have been diverse historically. Although the Han Chinese make up about 92% of the Chinese population, China has 56 officially designated ethnic groups (Postiglione, chap. 37, this volume). Malaysia is both ethnically and religiously diverse. Its population consists of approximately 50.4% Malay, 23.7% Chinese, 11% Bumiputera, 7.1% Indian, and 7.8% other ethnic groups (Hudson, 2007). Malaysia's religious groups include Muslim (53%), Buddhist (17.3%), Confucian and Taoist (11.6%), Christian (8.6%), and Hindu (7%). The Chinese (76.8%) are the largest ethnic group in Singapore, followed by the Malay (13.9%), and Indians (7.9%) (Hudson). Although Japan has historically viewed itself as a homogeneous and monoethnic nation-state (Murphy-Shigematsu, 2006), immigrants have lived in Japan for more than a century (Befu, 2006). Its minorities include the Ainu, Okinawans, Burakumin, Koreans, Chinese, and Taiwanese (Lie, 2001).

The United States, Canada, and Australia were diverse when the European explorers and settlers arrived in these distant lands. The diversity in these nations was enriched by the Indigenous peoples that the European settlers displaced, by Black people from Africa in the US, and by the large numbers of immigrants and refugees from nations around the world who settled in these three nations to realize their religious, political, and economic dreams. The US, Canada, and Australia have become more ethnically, racially, and linguistically diverse within the last 40 years. Although English was the most frequently spoken home language in Australia in 2006 (78.5%), the census indicated that more than 400 languages were spoken in homes, including Cantonese and Mandarin Chinese, Italian, Greek, and Arabic (Inglis, chap. 7, this volume).

In 2008, Canada's population was very diverse. Individuals of British Isles origin made up 28% of the population, 23% were of French origin, and 15% were other European. The other 34% of the population was made up of individuals of various ethnic groups and of mixed backgrounds (Statistics Canada, 2008). The US is experiencing its largest influx of immigrants since the late 19th and early 20th centuries. Most of the immigrants to the US today are coming from Asia and Latin America, whereas most came from Europe in previous centuries. The U.S. census (2007) projects that ethnic minorities will increase from one-third of the nation's population in 2006 to 50% in 2042. Ethnic minorities made up 100 million of the total U.S. population of just over 300 million in 2006. U.S. schools are more diverse today than they have been since the early 1900s when a flood of immigrants entered the US from Southern, Central, and Eastern Europe. In the 30-year period between 1973 and 2004, the percentage of ethnic minority students in U.S. public schools increased from 22% to 43% (Dillon, 2006).

Ethnic, racial, cultural, linguistic, and religious diversity is found in nations around the world. It extends far beyond the nations highlighted in the brief overview above. There is myriad diversity in Latin America and African nations, as the chapters in this *Companion* indicate. The educational challenges experienced by Indigenous and ethnic groups in Peru, Cuba, Brazil, and Mexico – and related educational reforms – are described in Chapters 20, 38, 39, and 40 respectively. Chapters 10 and 28 describe the educational challenges and reforms related to diversity in South Africa and in the Francophone nations in Africa.

Worldwide immigration and education

The movement of peoples across national boundaries is as old as the nation-state itself (Castles & Davidson, 2000). However, never before in the history of world migrations have the movement of diverse racial, cultural, ethnic, religious, and linguistic groups within and across nation-states been as numerous and rapid or raised such complex and difficult questions about citizenship, human rights, democracy, and education (Banks, chap. 22, this volume). In 2005, there were approximately 191 million migrants living outside the nation in which they were born, which was 3% of the world's population (Martin & Zurcher, 2008).

Many worldwide trends and developments are challenging the notion of educating students to function in one nation-state. They include the ways people are moving back and forth across national borders (Castles, chap. 3, this volume), the rights of movement permitted by the European Union, and the rights codified in the Universal Declaration of Human Rights. These trends indicate that we should be educating students to be cosmopolitan citizens in a global community (Appiah, 2006).

The assimilationist and liberal vision of society

The Western nations were characterized by myriad racial, cultural, ethnic, religious, and linguistic diversity when the ethnic revival movements emerged in the 1960s and 1970s. However, they were dominated by an *assimilationist* ideology. A major national goal in the US, Canada, and Australia was to create a nation-state in which one culture – the Anglo-Saxon or Anglo-Celtic – was dominant. The diverse groups that made up these nations were expected to forsake their original cultures and languages in order to become effective citizens of their nation-states. The older nation-states in Western Europe – such as the United Kingdom (Carby, 1982), France, Germany, and The Netherlands – were also dominated by an assimilationist ideology. Their goal was to maintain their national identities and the cultural hegemony of existing dominant groups.

The assimilationist and liberal ideology that dominated the Western nations envisioned a nation-state in which individuals from diverse groups are able to participate fully. However, the liberal-assimilationist believes that, in order for this kind of equitable, modernized society to emerge and flourish, individuals must surrender their ethnic and cultural attachments. Ethnic attachments and traditionalism, argues the liberal, are inconsistent with a modernized society and a civic culture. Traditional cultures promote historic prejudices, we–they attitudes, and cultural conflict (Porter, 1975). They also lead to the Balkanization of the nation-state. Traditionalism and cultural pluralism also stress group rights over the rights of the individual, and regard the group rather than the individual as primary (Patterson, 1977). In a modernized, equitable society, individual rights are paramount; group rights are secondary.

Liberals also argue that traditionalism promotes inequality, racial and ethnic awareness, group favoritism, and ethnic stratification. As long as attachments to cultural and ethnic groups are salient and emphasized, argues the liberal-assimilationist, they will serve as the basis for employment and educational discrimination as well as other forms of exclusion that are inconsistent with democratic ideals and values (Glazer, 1975). The solution to this problem, argues the liberal-assimilationist, is a common national culture into which all individuals are culturally and structurally assimilated and public policies that are neutral on questions of race and ethnicity.

The rise of ethnic revitalization movements

The scope and intensity of the ethnic protest movements during the 1960s and 1970s revealed that the liberal ideology that dominated Western social science and national policies had serious limitations and neither adequately explained nor predicted the course of events or the status of ethnic groups in modern democratic societies. Western social scientists studying race relations in the 1940s and 1950s viewed the assimilation of ethnic groups as both desirable and inevitable. They were heavily influenced by the writings of Park (1950), the noted sociologist at the University of Chicago who believed that the four basic processes of social interaction were *contact, conflict, accommodation,* and *assimilation.*

It was not only national policy makers and social scientists who endorsed an assimilationist ideology during the 1940s and 1950s. Most ethnic groups themselves, as well as their leaders, accepted assimilation into their national societies as a desirable goal and worked hard to achieve it. There were important exceptions of groups that pursued separatism, such as the French in Canada, the Euskadi Ta Askatasuna (ETA) quest for Basque independence in Spain, the Garvey movement in the United States, and other isolated separatist movements in Western nations that began prior to World War II. However, until the 1960s, most ethnic groups in the

Western nations worked to attain cultural assimilation and structural integration into their societies.

Ethnic groups tried to become assimilated into their national societies in large part because of powerful economic and political incentives. The strong appeal of attaining social mobility within the industrialized nation-states such as the United States, Canada, and Australia motivated many citizens of these nations to rid themselves of most aspects of their ethnic cultures and to become ashamed of their folk cultures and traditions. There has been historically – and continues to be – a cogent push toward assimilation in most nations because of the strong appeal of social and economic mobility.

The assimilationist and liberal ideology that has been dominant in Western nations such as the United States, Canada, and Australia has been successful for most White ethnic groups, who have achieved a significant degree of cultural and structural assimilation into their societies (Carr & Lund, 2007). However, the assimilationist ideology has worked much less well for non-White groups. Even when they are highly culturally assimilated, they may still experience high levels of structural exclusion. Although African Americans and the Indigenous groups in the United States (Native American and Alaska Natives) were expected to assimilate culturally, they were frequently denied the opportunity to attain a quality education, to vote, and to participate in the political process. The Canadian First Nations had a similar experience, as did the Australian Aboriginal peoples. The Western nations created expectations and goals for marginalized ethnic groups of color but often made it impossible for these groups to attain them. The structural exclusion of ethnic groups of color was a major cause of the ethnic revitalization movements that developed in the 1960s and 1970s.

Ethnic protest movements also arose in Western societies because ethnic groups that experienced discrimination and racism, such as African Americans in the United States and First Nations in Canada, internalized the egalitarian and democratic ideologies that were institutionalized within their nations and believed that it was possible for these ideals to be realized. While the conditions of these groups improved in the period after World War II, they still did not have many of the benefits enjoyed by the dominant groups in their societies. In the postwar period, their governments took steps to eliminate some of the most blatant forms of discrimination and to improve their social and economic status. However, these improved conditions created rising expectations. Rising expectations outpaced the improvement within the social, economic, and political systems. The disillusionment and shattered dreams that resulted from the historic quest for assimilation caused ethnic groups to demand structural inclusion and the right to retain important aspects of their cultures, such as their languages, religions, and other important ethnic characteristics and symbols.

The failure of Western nation-states to close the gap further between their democratic ideals and societal realities and the existence of discrimination and racism do not sufficiently explain the rise of ethnic revitalization movements in the 1960s and 1970s. The cultural and symbolic components of many of these movements indicate that they emerged in part to help individual members of ethnic groups to acquire the sense of community, moral authority, and meaning in life that highly modernized societies often leave unfulfilled. Writes Apter (1977), "[modernization] leaves what might be called a primordial space, a space people try to fill when they believe they have lost something fundamental and try to recreate it" (p. 75). As Apter points out, the liberal-assimilationist conception of the relationship between tradition and modernity is not so much wrong as it is incomplete, flawed, and oversimplified. It does not take into account the spiritual and community needs that ethnic cultures often help individuals to satisfy. The push toward assimilation in modernized societies is counterbalanced by the trenchant pull of primordialism, traditionalism, and the search for community. The quest for self-determination, equality, and inclusion are also important factors that drive ethnic revitalization movements (Figueroa, 2008).

The pursuit of independence by nations in Asia and Africa during the decolonization movement that followed World War II was another important factor that stimulated ethnic revitalization movements and motivated marginalized minority groups to seek autonomy and respect for their cultures, languages, and identities (Figueroa, 2008). The decolonization movement was especially active between 1945 and 1960, when many nations in Asia and Africa became independent from the UK and nations in Europe.

The rise and characteristics of multicultural education

The early phases of multicultural education developed first in the United States as a response to the civil rights movement. They developed subsequently in other nations, such as the United Kingdom, Canada, and Australia. Canada developed a multiculturalism policy in 1971; Australia in 1978. Multicultural education is an approach to school reform designed to actualize educational equality for students from diverse racial, ethnic, cultural, social-class, and linguistic groups. It also promotes democracy and social justice. A major goal of multicultural education is to reform schools, colleges, and universities so that students from diverse groups will have equal opportunities to learn. In most nations around the world, schools reflect and reproduce the racial and class stratification within society (Gillborn, 2008; Gillborn & Youdell, chap. 12, this volume; Gonçalves e Silva, 2004; Luchtenberg, 2004). The inequality that exists within society is reflected in the curriculum, textbooks, teacher attitudes and expectations, student–teacher interactions, languages and dialects spoken and sanctioned in the schools, and school culture.

Ethnic groups such as Mexican Americans in the United States, African Caribbeans and South Asians in the United Kingdom, the Aboriginal peoples in Australia, Algerians in France, and Indigenous groups in Mexico were experiencing academic and language problems in the schools when the early phases of multicultural education developed. A significant academic achievement gap existed between these groups and the mainstream racial, cultural, and linguistics groups within their societies. These groups demanded that the schools, colleges, and universities be reformed to reflect their cultures, identities, hopes and dreams, and to increase their academic achievement.

The early responses of schools in most nations to the ethnic revitalization movements were hastily conceptualized and implemented (Banks, 2006). An important goal of these early responses was to silence ethnic protest and discontent. There were few structural changes made within schools during the early phases of what became the multicultural education movement. The celebration of ethnic holidays and the insertion of ethnic units and courses at the primary level and of ethnic studies courses at the secondary level epitomized the responses of many schools in various nations. In Western European nations such as the UK and France, the achievement problems of immigrant groups were perceived first as mainly a language or dialect problem (Banks & Lynch, 1986). Consequently, the establishment of language education and bilingual education programs was a common early response to ethnic revitalization movements (Schools Council, 1970). Teachers from the original homelands of immigrant students were sometimes recruited to teach them.

When the achievement gap remained after superficial changes were made in the school curriculum, educators began to realize that deep structural changes were needed to increase the academic achievement of marginalized groups and to help all students to develop democratic attitudes and values. Consequently, the scope of the multicultural education movement broadened to include a focus on reform of all of the major variables in the school, such as teacher attitudes and expectations, testing and assessment, the language and dialects sanctioned by the schools, and school norms and values.

A significant degree of consensus exists within multicultural education about its major principles, concepts, and goals (Banks & Banks, 2004). However, specialists within the field emphasize different components and groups. A major goal of multicultural education is to restructure schools so that all students acquire the knowledge, attitudes, and skills needed to function in ethnically and racially diverse communities and nations, and in the world. Multicultural education seeks to actualize educational equality for students from diverse groups, and to facilitate their participation as critical and reflective citizens in an inclusive national civic culture.

Multicultural education tries to provide students with educational experiences that enable them to maintain commitments to their community cultures as well as acquire the knowledge, skills, and cultural capital needed to function in the national civic culture and community. Increasingly, multicultural education has a global component that seeks to help students develop cosmopolitan attitudes and become effective world citizens (Banks, 2008). Multicultural theorists view academic knowledge and skills as necessary but not sufficient for functioning in a diverse nation and world. They regard democratic racial attitudes and the knowledge and skills needed to function effectively within and across diverse groups as essential goals of schooling (Aboud, chap. 14, this volume; Ramsey, chap. 16, this volume; Stephan & Vogt, 2004).

Most multicultural theorists, researchers, and practitioners – within and across nations – accept the broad goals of multicultural education described above. However, there are variations within as well as across nations in the ways in which multicultural education is interpreted and implemented. In Western Europe, the movement is often referred to as *intercultural education*, a term used to recognize the desirability for people from different cultures to interact in dynamic and complex ways. *Antiracist education*, which emerged primarily in Britain but was influential in Canada, arose as a critique of multicultural education (Bonnett & Carrington, 1996; May, chap. 2, this volume).

In the 1970s and 1980s, antiracist educators argued that multicultural education did not promote an analysis of the institutional structures – such as racism, power, and capitalism – that keep ethnic and racial groups oppressed and victimized. Moodley wrote in 1995, "The shift from multicultural education to [antiracist] education is from a preoccupation with cultural difference to an emphasis on the way in which such differences are used to entrench inequality" (p. 812). The most significant ideas of antiracist education have been incorporated into mainstream multicultural education (Banks, 2006; Nieto & Bode, 2008; Sleeter, 2005). Consequently, the distinction between multicultural education and antiracist education is rarely heard in multicultural discourse today.

Although there is a significant degree of consensus about its goals among specialists and researchers in the field, multicultural education is a contested concept both within and across nations (James, 2005; Lund, 2006). There is debate within nations about the scope and boundaries of multicultural education, as the chapters in Part 2 of this volume indicate. In the United States as well as in other Western nations, multicultural education first focused on racial, ethnic, and language minority groups. In time and in response to protest movements by women and people with disabilities, multicultural education in the United States – at least among theorists – is slowly expanding to include issues related to gender and exceptionality. Gay rights advocates in the United States are making a compelling case that issues related to sexual orientation should be a part of multicultural education because of the discrimination that gay and lesbian youth experience in society and in the schools (Mayo, 2010). Authors of multicultural textbooks in the US are beginning to respond to their concerns (Gollnick & Chinn, 2009).

However, there is a significant gap between theory and practice in multicultural education in the United States as well as in other nations. There are few visible signs either within or across nations that schools are incorporating issues related to sexual orientation into the curriculum in meaningful ways.

The Dimensions of Multicultural Education

Banks (2004) developed the Dimensions of Multicultural Education to help educational practitioners and scholars to conceptualize and develop practices, theory, and research in the field. The five dimensions are: (a) content integration; (b) the knowledge construction process; (c) prejudice reduction; (d) an equity pedagogy; and (e) an empowering school culture and social structure (see Figure 1.1). Although each dimension is conceptually distinct, in practice they overlap and are interrelated. Each of the dimensions is defined and discussed below.

Content integration deals with the extent to which teachers use examples and content from a

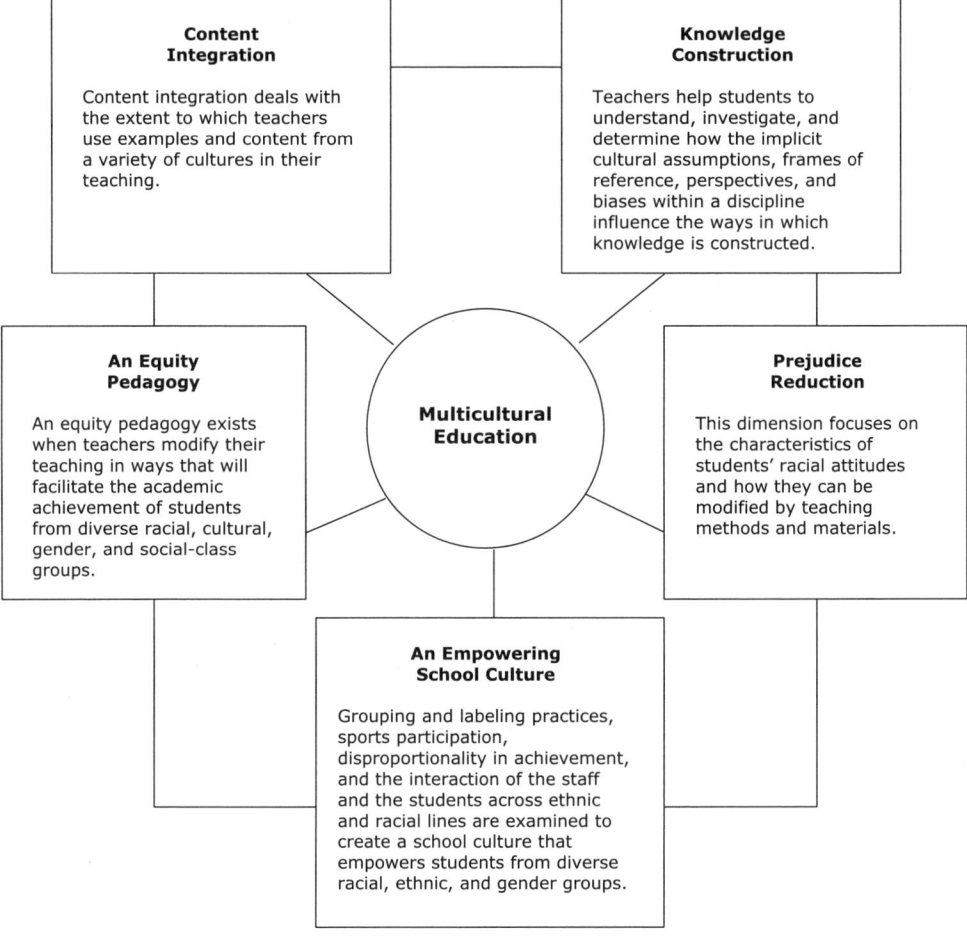

Figure 1.1 The Dimensions of Multicultural Education.
Copyright © 2009 by James A. Banks.

variety of cultures and groups to illustrate key concepts, principles, generalizations, and theories in their subject area or discipline. The infusion of ethnic and cultural content into a subject area is logical and not contrived when this dimension is implemented properly.

More opportunities exist for the integration of ethnic and cultural content in some subjects than in others. There are frequent and ample opportunities for teachers to use ethnic and cultural content to illustrate concepts, themes, and principles in the social studies, the language arts, and in music. Opportunities to integrate multicultural content into mathematics (Nasir & Cobb, 2007) and science (Harding, 1998) exist. However, they are less ample than they are in the social studies and the language arts. Content integration is frequently mistaken by school practitioners as constituting the whole of multicultural education, and is consequently viewed as irrelevant to instruction in disciplines such as mathematics and science.

The knowledge construction process describes teaching activities that help students to understand, investigate, and determine how the implicit cultural assumptions, frames of reference, perspectives, and biases of researchers and textbook writers influence the ways in which knowledge is constructed. Multicultural teaching involves not only infusing ethnic content into the school curriculum, but changing the structure and organization of school knowledge. It also includes changing the ways in which teachers and students view and interact with knowledge and helping students to become knowledge producers, not merely the consumers of knowledge produced by others (Banks, 1996).

The knowledge construction process helps teachers and students to understand why the cultural identities and positionality of researchers need to be taken into account when assessing the validity of knowledge claims. Multicultural theories believe that the values, personal histories, attitudes, and beliefs of researchers cannot be separated from the knowledge they create (Code, 1991; Harding, 1998). They consequently reject positivist claims of disinterested and distancing knowledge production. They also reject the possibility of creating knowledge that is not influenced by the cultural assumptions and positionality of the knowledge producer.

In multicultural teaching and learning, paradigms, themes, and concepts that exclude or distort the life experiences, histories, and contributions of marginalized groups are challenged. Multicultural pedagogy seeks to reconceptualize and expand the institutionalized curriculum canon, to make it more representative and inclusive of a nation's diversity, and to reshape the frames of reference, perspectives, and concepts that make up school knowledge.

The prejudice reduction dimension of multicultural education seeks to help students develop democratic racial attitudes (Stephan & Vogt, 2004). It also helps students to understand how ethnic identity is influenced by the context of schooling and the attitudes and beliefs of dominant groups. The theory developed by Allport (1954/1979) has significantly influenced research and theory in intergroup relations in the US and in nations around the world (see Bekerman, chap. 15, this volume). Allport theorized that contact between different groups would improve intergroup relations if the contact between these groups has these characteristics: (a) the individuals experience equal status, (b) they share common goals, (c) intergroup cooperation exists, and (d) the contact is sanctioned by authorities such as parents, teachers, and administrators – or by law or custom (cited in Pettigrew, 2004).

An equity pedagogy exists when teachers modify their teaching in ways that will facilitate the academic achievement of students from diverse groups. This includes using a variety of teaching styles and approaches that are consistent with the learning characteristics of various cultural and ethnic groups and being demanding but highly personalized when working with students such as Native Americans and Native Alaskans (Kleinfeld, 1975). It also includes using cooperative learning techniques in mathematics and science instruction to enhance the academic achievement of ethnic minority students (Cohen & Lotan, 1995).

An equity pedagogy rejects the *cultural deprivation paradigm* that was developed in the early 1960s. This paradigm posits that the socialization experiences in the home and community of low-income students prevent them from attaining the knowledge, skills, and attitudes needed for academic success. Because the cultural practices of low-income students are viewed as inadequate and inferior, cultural deprivation theorists focus on changing student behavior so that it is more congruent with mainstream school culture. An equity pedagogy – which exemplifies the *cultural difference paradigm* – assumes that students from diverse cultures and groups come to school with many strengths.

Cultural difference theorists describe how cultural identity, communicative styles, and the social expectations of students from marginalized racial and ethnic groups conflict with the values, beliefs, and cultural assumptions of teachers (Gay, 2000; Lee, 2007). The middle-class, mainstream culture of the schools creates a cultural dissonance and disconnect that privileges students who have internalized the school's cultural codes and communication styles.

Teachers practice culturally responsive teaching when an equity pedagogy is implemented (de Haan & Elbers, 2004; Gay, 2000; Ladson-Billings, 1995). They use instructional materials and practices that incorporate important aspects of the family and community cultures of students. Culturally responsive teachers also use the "cultural knowledge, prior experiences, frames of reference, and performance styles of ethnically diverse students to make learning encounters more relevant to and effective for them" (Gay, p. 29).

An empowering school culture involves restructuring the culture and organization of the school so that students from diverse groups experience equality. Members of the school staff examine and change the culture and social structure of the school. Grouping and labeling practices, sports participation, gaps in achievement among groups, different rates of enrollment in gifted and special education programs among groups, and the interaction of the staff and students across ethnic and racial lines are important variables that are examined and reformed.

An empowering school culture requires the creation of qualitatively different relationships among various groups within schools. Relationships are based on mutual and reciprocal respect for cultural differences that are reflected in schoolwide goals, norms, and cultural practices. An empowering school culture facilitates multicultural education reform by providing teachers with opportunities for collective planning and instruction, and by creating democratic structures that give teachers, parents, and the school staff shared responsibility for school governance.

Ethnic revitalization movements, the schools, and response paradigms

Structurally marginalized ethnic groups in the various Western nations demanded changes in a range of social, economic, and political institutions so that they could participate and exercise power in them. Much of the response to ethnic protest took place in schools, colleges, and universities, in part because these institutions included a range of constituencies (including ethnic groups) and in part because they were seen as powerful symbols and bastions of the status quo that had participated in the marginalization of ethnic groups (Williamson, 2008). They were consequently viewed as potentially significant vehicles that could play a pivotal role in their liberation.

The development of ethnic revitalization movements in Western democratic nations such as the United States, Canada, the United Kingdom, and Australia – and the responses that educational institutions have made to them since the 1960s and 1970s – reveal specific types and patterns of institutional responses. These patterns and prototypical responses are called *paradigms* in this chapter. Kuhn (1970) uses *paradigm* to describe the "entire constellation of beliefs, values, techniques, and so on shared by members of a given [scientific] community" (p. 175). The laws, principles, explanations, and theories of a discipline are also part of its paradigm. Kuhn states that, during the history of a science, new paradigms arise to replace older ones, which constitutes a "scientific revolution."

Educational paradigmatic responses do not necessarily occur in a linear or set order in any particular nation, although some of them tend to occur earlier in the development of ethnic revitalization movements than others. Thus the response paradigms relate in a general way to the various phases of ethnic revitalization movements. The *ethnic additive* and *self-concept development* paradigms, for example, tend to arise during the first or early phase of an ethnic revitalization movement. Single-explanation paradigms tend to emerge prior to multiple-explanation ones. While single-explanation paradigms usually emerge during the first phase of ethnic revitalization, multiple-explanation paradigms usually do not emerge or become popular until a later phase. The characteristics and cyclic quality of ethnic revitalization movements are illustrated in Figure 1.2.

A sophisticated *neoconservative* paradigm tends to develop during the later phase of ethnic

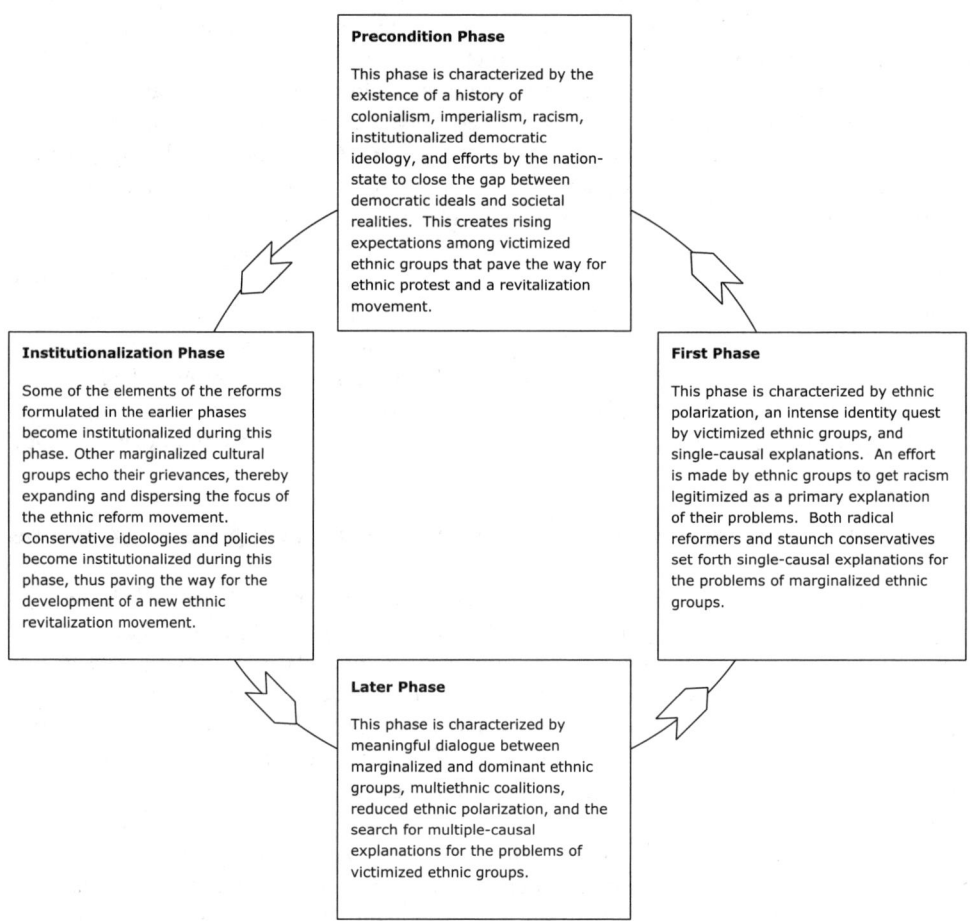

Figure 1.2 Phases in the Development of Ethnic Revitalization Movements.
Copyright © 2009 by James A. Banks.

revitalization, when the groups that are trying to institutionalize reforms related to diversity begin to succeed and those that are committed to assimilation and to maintaining the status quo begin to fear that the pluralistic reformers will institutionalize a new ideal and create new goals for the nation-state. The fears and concerns about multicultural education and other reforms related to diversity articulated by neoconservative scholars in the United States such as Glazer (1975) and Schlesinger (1991) epitomize this stance.

I will describe a number of response paradigms that develop when ethnic revitalization movements emerge (see Table 1.1). These paradigms might develop within a nation at different

Table 1.1 Multicultural Education Paradigms

Paradigm	Major Assumptions	Major Goals	School Programs and Practices
Ethnic Additive	Ethnic content can be added to the curriculum without reconceptualizing or restructuring it.	To integrate the curriculum by adding special units, lessons, and ethnic holidays to it.	Special ethnic studies units; ethnic studies courses that focus on ethnic foods and holidays; units on ethnic heroes.
Self-Concept Development	Ethnic content can increase the self-concept of ethnic minority students. Many ethnic minority students have low self-concepts.	To increase the self-concept and academic achievement of ethnic minority students.	Special units in ethnic studies that emphasize the contributions that ethnic groups have made to the building of the nation; units on famous ethnic individuals.
Cultural Deprivation	Many low-income and ethnic minority youth are socialized within homes and communities that prevent them from acquiring the cognitive skills and cultural characteristics needed to succeed in school.	To compensate for the cognitive deficits and dysfunctional cultural characteristics that low-income and ethnic minority youth bring to school.	Compensatory educational experiences that are behaviorist and intensive.
Cultural Difference	Ethnic groups such as African Americans, Mexican Americans, and American Indians have strong, rich, and diverse cultures.	To change the school so that it will respect and reflect the cultures of minority youths and use teaching strategies that are consistent with their cultural characteristics.	Culturally responsive and culturally sensitive teaching strategies.
Language	Linguistic minority students often achieve poorly in school because instruction is not conducted in their home and community languages.	To provide initial instruction in the student's home and community language.	Teaching English as a second language; bilingual-bicultural education programs.
Cultural Ecology	The low academic achievement of castelike or involuntary minorities is due primarily to their opposition to the mainstream culture in society.	To enable marginalized ethnic minorities to assimilate into the mainstream culture and to become structurally included.	Educational interventions that change the cultures of minority communities so that they are more consistent with the culture of the mainstream culture of society.

(*Continued Overleaf*)

Table 1.1 Continued

Paradigm	Major Assumptions	Major Goals	School Programs and Practices
Protective Disidentification	When individuals sense the possibility of conforming to a group stereotype or being judged in terms of the stereotype, it becomes threatening to their sense of self.	To reduce stereotypes for students who are members of marginalized groups and are vulnerable to stereotype threats.	Educational programs that reduce stereotype threat for students who are identified with academic subjects by creating environments that have high expectations for them.
Structural	Schools are limited in the role they can play to eliminate racism and discrimination and to promote equality for low-income and minority students. Structural changes are needed in the political economy to increase the academic achievement of low-income and minority students.	To help students and teachers to understand the structural factors in the political economy that impede economic and social mobility and to help them develop a commitment to radical social and economic change.	Educational programs that promote equality and that help students to understand the structural bases of racism and discrimination and how these structural issues might be addressed.
Antiracist	Educational inequalities of racialized groups are largely due to individual, cultural, social, institutional, and structural forms of racism.	To encourage teachers, schools, and students to understand and address each of these variables.	Prejudice reduction programs; analysis of cultural assumptions and their social and educational impact; appreciation of the strengths and limitations of different cultures and how we can learn from different cultures; understanding of group identity and of intra- and intergroup interactions, especially in the school setting; understanding of different aspects of institutional racism and how they may affect the school; understanding of how power in society and in the school might be related to racialized differences.

times or they may coexist at the same time. Each is likely to exist in some form in a nation that has experienced an ethnic revitalization movement. However, only one or two are likely to be dominant at any particular point in time. The leaders and advocates of particular paradigms compete in order to make their paradigms the most popular in academic, government, and school settings. Proponents of paradigms that can attract the most government and private support are likely to become the prevailing voices for multicultural education within a particular time or period.

Sometimes one dominant paradigm replaces another and something akin to what Kuhn

(1970) calls a scientific revolution takes place. However, what happens more frequently is that a new paradigm will emerge that challenges an older one but does not replace it. During the late 1960s in the United States the *cultural deprivation* paradigm dominated the theory, research, and practice related to educating low-income and minority groups (Bereiter & Engelmann, 1966). During the 1970s this paradigm was seriously challenged by the *cultural difference* paradigm (Baratz & Baratz, 1970). The cultural difference paradigm did not replace the cultural deprivation paradigm; the two paradigms coexisted. However, the cultural deprivation paradigm lost much of its influence and legitimacy, especially among a new generation of ethnic minority scholars and researchers. The cultural deprivation paradigm experienced a renaissance in the 1980s when a neoconservative movement developed and became influential in the United States. When it re-emerged, low-income and minority youth were referred to as "at-risk" students (Cuban, 1989).

The ethnic additive and self-concept development paradigms

Often the first phase of a school's response to an ethnic revitalization movement consists of the infusion of bits and pieces about ethnic groups into the curriculum, especially into courses in the humanities, the social studies, and the language arts. The teaching about ethnic heroes and the celebration of ethnic holidays are salient characteristics of the ethnic additive paradigm.

This paradigm usually emerges as the first one for a variety of reasons. It develops in part because ethnic groups demand that their heroes, holidays, and contributions be included in the curriculum during the first stage of ethnic revitalization. This paradigm also emerges because teachers usually have little knowledge about marginalized ethnic groups during the early phase of ethnic revitalization and find it much easier to add isolated bits of information about ethnic groups to the curriculum and to celebrate ethnic holidays than to integrate ethnic content meaningfully into the curriculum. Thus Black History Week, American Indian Day, and Asian and African Caribbean feasts and festivals become a part of the curriculum.

Another major goal expressed by educators during the first phase of ethnic revitalization is to raise the self-concepts of minority youths and to increase their group pride. This goal develops because leaders of ethnic movements try to shape new and positive ethnic identities and because educators assume that ethnic groups who have experienced discrimination and structural exclusion have negative self-concepts and negative attitudes toward their own racial and ethnic groups. Social science research in the US prior to the 1960s reinforced this belief (Clark & Clark, 1950); some leaders of ethnic movements also expressed it during the 1960s and 1970s. In the 1970s, many educators assumed that students needed healthy self-concepts in order to do well in school. They also assumed that curriculum content that includes ethnic heroes and the celebration of ethnic holidays would enhance the self-concepts and academic achievements of ethnic groups. In 1981, Stone – a lecturer at Surrey University in England – described the serious limitations of the self-concept paradigm. The influence of the additive and self-concept paradigms wanes as ethnic revitalization reaches its later phases.

The cultural deprivation paradigm

Cultural deprivation theories, programs, and research often develop during the first phase of an ethnic revitalization movement. Cultural deprivation theorists assume that low-income youths do not achieve well in school because of family disorganization, poverty, the lack of effective concept acquisition, and other intellectual and cultural deficits that these students experience during their first years of life. Cultural deprivation theorists assume that a major goal of school programs for culturally deprived youth is to provide them with cultural and other experiences that will compensate for their cognitive and intellectual deficits. Cultural deprivation theorists believe that low-income students can learn the basic skills taught by the schools, but that these skills must often be taught using intensive, behaviorally oriented instruction (Bereiter & Engelmann, 1966).

Programs based on the cultural deprivation paradigm require students to make major changes in their behavior. Teachers and other educators are required to make few changes in their behavior or in educational institutions. Such programs also ignore the cultures that students bring to school and assume that low-income and minority children are "culturally deprived" or "disadvantaged." The cultural deprivation paradigm also developed in other nations such as Canada and the UK during the 1970s. It usually evokes strong criticisms from ethnic minority scholars and researchers, such as Carby (1982) in England.

The cultural difference paradigm

Unlike the cultural deprivation theorists, cultural difference theorists reject the idea that low-income and ethnic minority youths have cultural deficits (Ladson-Billings, 1995; Lee, 2007). They believe that ethnic groups such as African Americans, Mexican Americans, and American Indians have strong, rich, and diverse cultures. These cultures, argue the cultural difference theorists, consist of languages, values, behavioral styles, and perspectives that can enrich the lives of all people. Ethnic minority youths, contend these theorists, fail to achieve in school not because they have deprived cultures but because their cultures are different from the school culture.

Cultural difference theorists believe that the school – rather than the cultures of minority students – is primarily responsible for their low academic achievement (de Haan & Elbers, 2004). The school must change in ways that will allow it to respect and reflect the cultures of low-income and minority youths and at the same time use teaching strategies that are consistent with their cultural characteristics. These kinds of teaching strategies will help ethnic minority youths to achieve at higher levels. The schools, argue these theorists, frequently fail to help ethnic minority students to achieve because schools often ignore or try to alienate them from their cultures and languages, and rarely use teaching strategies that are consistent with their learning characteristics. Cultural difference theorists cite research that shows how the cultures of the school and of ethnic minority youths differ in values, norms, and behaviors (Gay, 2000; Lee, 2007).

Cultural difference theorists are committed to helping low-income and ethnic minority youths experience educational equity and to protecting their rights to cultural democracy. Cultural democracy guarantees them the right to maintain ties with their ethnic families and communities and the right to retain their dialects and languages (Valdés, 2001), while at the same time developing competency in the national language or languages. Ramírez and Castañeda (1974) write:

> Cultural democracy, as we define it, states that an individual can be bicultural and still be loyal to American ideals. Cultural democracy is a philosophical precept which recognizes that the way a person communicates, relates to others, seeks support and recognition from his [or her] environment (incentive motivation), and thinks and learns (cognition) is a product of the value system of his [or her] home and community. Furthermore,

educational environments or policies that do not recognize the individual's right, as guaranteed by the Civil Rights Act of 1964, to remain identified with the culture and language of his [or her] cultural group are culturally undemocratic. (p. 23)

Cultural difference theorists maintain that every nation needs an overarching set of values and goals to which all members of the nation-state are committed and that there is a need for a national identity shared by all ethnic and racial groups. Members of all groups should also have the skills and attitudes needed to participate effectively in the political, economic, and social institutions of the nation-state, and should be given the opportunity to participate in these institutions. However, cultural difference theorists also recognize the need for Americans to maintain attachments to their ethnic communities. For many, especially those who are members of visible ethnic groups, their attachments to their ethnic families and communities are strong and important. It provides them with a sense of group identification, a sense of peoplehood, and psychological support. When members of these ethnic groups are provided the opportunities and skills to participate in the shared national culture and in their ethnic cultures and communities, they can make their maximum contributions to the civic culture because both their personal and their civic needs are being satisfied and are given the richest opportunities to develop.

The language paradigm

Often during the early phase of ethnic revitalization or when a large number of immigrants settle in a nation and enroll in the schools, educators view the achievement problems of these groups as resulting primarily from their language or dialect differences. When West Indians and Asians first enrolled in schools in England in significant numbers in the 1960s, many English educators believed that if they could solve the language problems of these youths they would experience academic success in English schools. The early responses by English educators to the problems of immigrant students were almost exclusively related to language (Schools Council, 1970). Special programs were set up to train teachers and to develop materials for teaching English as a second language to immigrant students. French educators also viewed the problems of the North African and Asian students in their schools in the late 1970s as primarily language related (Banks, 1978).

In the United States the low academic achievement of Puerto Ricans and Mexican Americans was often assumed to be rooted in language during the 1970s. Some proponents of bilingual education in the United States argued that, if the language problem of these students were solved, they would experience academic success in the schools. As bilingual programs were established in the United States, educators began to realize that many other factors, such as social class, learning characteristics, teacher attitudes and expectations, and motivation, were also important variables that influenced the academic achievement of Latino students.

The main focus of multicultural education in Japan today is language (Hirasawa, chap. 11, this volume). Multicultural education in Japan is driven by local groups, citizens, teachers, and activists who are keenly aware of the language and cultural problems with which newcomer immigrants are dealing (Murphy-Shigematsu, 2008). However, educational reforms to respond to the language needs of newcomer students have made only limited progress because of the strong assimilationist ideology in Japan and the propensity of the Japanese to view Japan as a monocultural and monolingual nation.

The experiences with programs based on the language paradigm in the Western nations teach us that an exclusive language approach to the educational problems of ethnic and immigrant groups is insufficient. Languages are integral parts of cultures. Curriculum interventions designed to educate students from diverse language and cultural groups must be comprehensive in scope, and focus on variables in the educational environment other than language. An exclusive language approach will not be effective in improving the academic achievement of language minority students.

The cultural ecology paradigm

Ogbu (2003; Fordham & Ogbu, 1986) hypothesized that the low academic achievement of African Americans was due primarily to their opposition to White mainstream culture and the fear of acting White. He distinguished between two types of racial minorities: *immigrant* or *voluntary* and *castelike* or *involuntary*. Voluntary immigrants come to a new nation because they view it as a land of opportunity and hope. Castelike minorities are Indigenous groups that have experienced institutionalized racism and discrimination in their homeland. Voluntary immigrants – such as immigrants from China, India, and Jamaica in the United States – are more academically successful than castelike minorities such as African Americans and Mexican Americans because they embrace U.S. mainstream values and behaviors that are normative in the schools.

Castelike minorities such as African Americans and Mexican Americans resist the academic values and behaviors institutionalized in the schools because of fictive kinship,[2] which causes them to reject mainstream institutions and values. Because they have been victimized by structural racism and discrimination in their society, castelike minorities have fictive kinship ties and a sense of peoplehood that are oppositional to the mainstream values and cultures of the nation-state. Ogbu (2003) believed that, in order for castelike minorities such as African Americans to experience academic success, significant changes had to be made within their cultures and communities.

A number of social scientists have described serious limitations in Ogbu's *cultural ecology* theory and the research that supports it (Carter, 2004; Tyson, Darity, & Castellino, 2004). Ogbu's theory essentializes what he calls castelike minorities and does not describe the wide variations within these groups. His theory also provides a rationale for educators to "blame the victim" for their educational problems (see Banks & Park [in press] for a discussion of the critiques of Ogbu's theory).

The protective disidentification paradigm

Steele (2004) uses an experimental approach to demonstrate a process of *protective disidentification* that occurs as a response to *stereotype threat*. His theory focuses on students who are particularly confident as well as competent in a domain such as mathematics or language arts and, as a result, identify with that domain. Stereotype threat applies to members of any stigmatized group, such as females, about whom a negative reputation or stereotype exists (e.g. that females are not as good as males in math). When individuals sense the possibility of conforming to the group stereotype or being judged in terms of the stereotype, it becomes threatening to their sense of self. In an attempt to protect their sense of self, individuals may respond to stereotype threat by disidentifying with the domain and consequently no longer allowing themselves to be vulnerable to the potential threat. Steele describes the detrimental effects that stereotype threat can have on students who are among "the academic vanguard of their group" (2004, p. 686).

Steele's (2004) protective disidentification paradigm suggests that well-intentioned remedial programs for minority students are likely to fail because they confirm the racial stereotypes that cause students to be at risk of failure. He recommends reducing stereotype threat for students who are identified with academic subjects by creating an environment that has high expectations for them and does not question their academic ability.

The structural paradigm

The *structural* paradigm tends to develop during the early or later stage of ethnic revitalization. Theorists with a variety of perspectives and points of view exemplify it, including neo-Marxists (Bowles & Gintis, 1976), critical theorists (McCarthy, 1988), antiracist theorists (Bonnett & Carrington, 1996), and critical race theorists (Ladson-Billings & Tate, 1995). These theories provide a structural and institutional analysis of the achievement problems of low-income and minority students. While the other paradigms assume that the school can successfully intervene to help ethnic minority youths to attain social, political, and economic equality, the structural paradigm assumes that the school is a part of the problem and plays a significant role in keeping ethnic groups marginalized. Thus, it is very difficult for the school to empower marginalized groups, because one of its central purposes is to educate students so that they will accept their assigned status in society. A primary role of the school is to reproduce the social-class stratification within society (Katz, 1975).

The structural paradigm stresses the limited role that schools can play to eliminate racism and discrimination and to promote equality for low-income and minority students. Jencks, a noted structural theorist in the United States, conducted – with his colleagues at Harvard University – an influential study that described the limited effects of schools in increasing social-class mobility (Jenks, Smith, Ackland, et al., 1972). He argued that the most effective way to bring about equality for low-income groups was to equalize incomes directly rather than to rely on the schools to bring about equality in the adult life of students. Jencks argued that the schooling route is much too indirect and will most likely result in failure. Bowles and Gintis (1976) wrote a neo-Marxist critique of schools in the United States that documented the way in which schools reinforce the social-class stratification within society and make students politically passive and content with their social-class status.

During the 1970s and 1980s some critical theorists in both England and the United States described what they viewed as the serious limitations of multicultural education. Some of them argued that multicultural education was a palliative to keep marginalized groups such as African Americans and African Caribbeans from rebelling against a system that promotes structural inequality and institutionalized racism (Carby, 1980; McCarthy, 1988). They also argued that schools do not provide interventions that will eliminate the structural and economic barriers that keep ethnic and racial groups oppressed and victimized. They maintained that, because multicultural education avoided serious discussion of class, institutionalized racism, power, and capitalism, it might divert attention from significant economic and structural problems and issues. These theorists stated that educators needed to focus on the institutions and structures of society rather than on the characteristics of minority students and cultural differences.

Most mainstream multicultural educators in the United States, Canada, and the United Kingdom have incorporated elements of the structural paradigm into their analyses (Banks,

2006; James, 2005; Lund, 2006; Nieto & Bode, 2008; Sleeter, 2005). Consequently, the criticisms of multicultural education by critical theorists are muted in these nations. However, the anti-racist theory is still viable and persistent, especially outside the US. Although they are limited in the extent to which they can change the structural factors in society, schools can implement reforms that can improve the academic achievement of students from diverse groups (Figueroa, 2008), as research in both the US (Brookover, Beady, Flood, Schweitzer, & Wisenbaker, 1979) and the UK has demonstrated (Rutter, Maughan, Mortimore, & Ouston, 1979).

The need for a multi-factor paradigm

Multicultural education is replete with single-factor paradigms that attempt to explain why low-income and minority students achieve poorly in school. Proponents of these paradigms often become ardent in their views and insist that one major variable explains the problems of minority students and that their educational problems can be solved if major policies, related to a specific explanation or paradigm, are implemented. Reforms related to culturally sensitive or responsive pedagogy are based on the cultural difference paradigm; cultural deprivation proponents view cultural enrichment as the most important variable influencing academic achievement; some structural theorists view the school as having little possibility of significantly influencing the life chances of low-income and minority students.

Experiences in the major nations around the world since the late 1960s and 1970s reveal that the academic achievement problems of students from diverse ethnic and social-class groups are too complex to be solved with reforms based on single-factor paradigms and explanations (Banks & Banks, 2004; de Haan & Elbers, 2004). Education is broader than schooling, and many of the challenges that students from diverse groups experience in the schools reflect the problems in the wider society. The critiques of schools by structural theorists are useful because they help educators to appreciate the limitations of formal schooling (Bowles & Gintis, 1976). However, structural explanations are limited because they do not provide educational practitioners with the guidelines needed to conceptualize and implement effective educational interventions.

When designing educational reform strategies, educators need to be keenly sensitive to the limitations of formal schooling that the structural theorists describe. However, they should be tenacious in their faith that the school can play a limited but significant role in bringing about equal educational opportunities for low-income and minority students (Noguera, 2003), and helping all students to develop cross-cultural understandings and competencies (Aboud, chap. 14, this volume). In order to effectively design school programs that will help low-income and ethnic minority youths to increase their academic achievement and to help all students to develop ethnic literacy and cross-cultural competency, educators need to conceptualize the school as a system in which all of its major variables and components are interrelated in complex ways (Figueroa, 1991).

A *holistic* paradigm, which conceptualizes the school as an interrelated whole, is needed to guide educational reform and intervention (see Figure 1.3). Viewing the school as a social system can help educators to derive an idea of school reform that can help all students to increase their academic achievement and to develop democratic attitudes and values. Both research and theory indicate that educators can successfully intervene to help students to increase their academic achievement (Lee, 2007) and to develop democratic attitudes and values (Banks & Banks, 2004; Stephan & Vogt, 2004).

Conceptualizing the school as a social system means that educators should formulate and

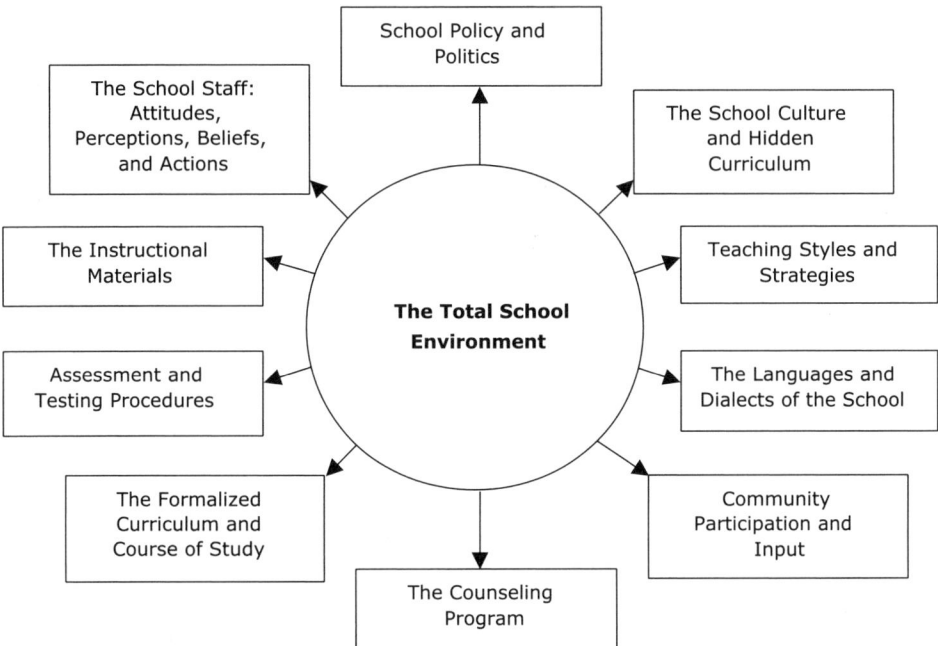

Figure 1.3 The Total School Environment.
Copyright © 2009 by James A. Banks.

initiate a change strategy that reforms the total school environment in order to implement multicultural education successfully. Reforming any one variable, such as curriculum materials and the formal curriculum, is necessary but not sufficient. Multicultural and sensitive teaching materials are ineffective in the hands of teachers who have negative attitudes and low expectations for various ethnic, cultural, and linguistic groups. Such teachers are likely to use multicultural materials rarely or to use them in a detrimental way when they do. Thus, helping teachers and other members of the school staff to develop democratic attitudes and values is essential when implementing multicultural programs and experiences.

When formulating plans for multicultural education, educators should conceptualize the school as a *microculture* that has norms, values, roles, stratifications, and goals like other cultural systems. The school has a dominant culture and a variety of subcultures. Most schools around the world are multicultural because many kinds of diversity exist within and across groups. Teachers in schools around the world also come from many different ethnic groups and cultures. Many teachers were socialized in cultures other than the dominant one, although these may be forgotten and repressed. The school is a microculture where the cultures of students and teachers meet. The school should be a cultural environment where acculturation takes place: both teachers and students should incorporate some of the views, perceptions, and ethos of each other as they interact (see Figure 1.4). This process will enrich both teachers and students, and the academic achievement of students from diverse cultures will be enhanced because their cosmos and ethos will be reflected and legitimized in the school.

Historically, schools in most societies have had assimilation rather than acculturation as their major goal. The students were expected to acquire the dominant culture of the school and society, but the school neither legitimized nor assimilated parts of the students' cultures.

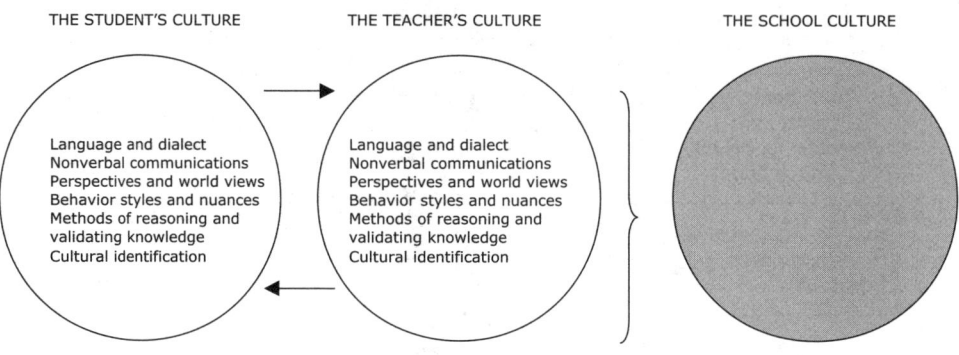

The school culture reflects the values, perspectives, and behaviors of the students and the teachers.

When the student incorporates elements of the teacher's culture and the teacher incorporates elements of the student's culture, the school becomes a synthesized cultural system that reflects the cultures of all it participants.

Figure 1.4 Acculturation as a School Goal.

Copyright © 2009 by James A. Banks. All rights reserved.

Assimilation and acculturation are different in important ways. Assimilation involves the complete elimination of cultural differences and differentiating group identification. When acculturation occurs, a culture is modified through contact with one or more other cultures but maintains its essence (Theodorson & Theodorson, 1969).

Both acculturation and accommodation should take place in schools in multicultural democratic societies. *When accommodation occurs, groups with diverse cultures maintain their separate identities but live in peaceful interaction.* It is essential that schools in democratic societies acculturate students rather than foster tight ethnic boundaries, because all students, including ethnic minority students, must develop the knowledge, attitudes, and skills needed to become successful citizens of their cultural communities, their nation-states, and the global community.

If they are to function successfully in their nation-states, ethnic minority students must develop competency in the national language or languages and acquire the skills needed to participate in the national civic culture. They must also develop a commitment to the overarching democratic ideals of their nation-state, such as equality and justice. Acquiring the knowledge, skills, and attitudes needed to participate in their nation-state and in the global community means that all students, including majority group students, will often find it necessary to assimilate cultural components that are not a part of their home and community cultures. However, ethnic minority students can assimilate essential aspects of the mainstream culture without surrendering the most important aspects of their first culture or becoming alienated from it. The school should help students to develop the knowledge, skills, and attitudes needed to function effectively in their community culture, in the mainstream national culture, and within and between other ethnic cultures (see Figure 1.5). The school should not require students to become alienated from their families and communities in order to acquire the knowledge, attitudes, and skills needed to function effectively in the national civic culture.

While students will find it essential to assimilate values, knowledge, and skills from the

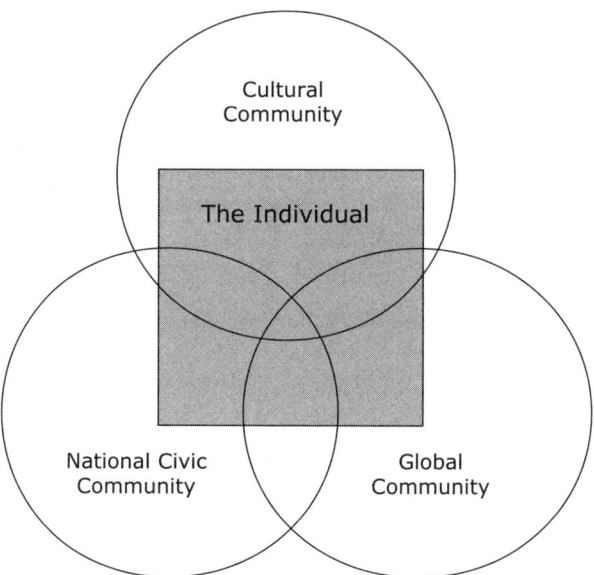

The school should help students to develop the knowledge, skills, and attitudes needed to function effectively in their community culture, in the mainstream national civic culture and community, and within and between other ethnic cultures and subsocieties.

Figure 1.5 Helping Students to Develop Identities and to Function in Cultural, National, and Global Communities.

Copyright © 2009 by James A. Banks.

mainstream culture, educators can gain valuable insights into their students' cultures by viewing the world from their perspectives, spending time in their students' homes and communities, and consequently gaining an understanding of the "funds of knowledge" in the worlds of their students (González, Moll, & Amanti, 2005). Viewing the world from the perspectives of their students and becoming aware of the complex knowledge, norms, and ethos in their communities and cultures will help educators to create a school culture that validates and legitimizes the cultures of their students as well as enriches their personal lives.

Notes

1 *First Nations* is a term used to describe the original peoples of Canada.
2 *Fictive kinship* is used by Ogbu (2003) to describe the strong sense of identity and affiliation that marginalized ethnic groups such as African Americans and Mexican Americans have with the members of their racial or ethnic groups that developed from a shared history of victimization and exclusion.

References

Allport, G. W. (1979). *The nature of prejudice* (25th anniversary ed.). Reading, MA: Addison-Wesley. (Original work published 1954)
Appiah, K. A. (2006). *Cosmopolitanism: Ethics in a world of strangers*. New York: Norton.

Apter, D. F. (1977). Political life and cultural pluralism. In M. M. Tumin & W. Plotch (Eds.), *Pluralism in a democratic society* (pp. 58–91). New York: Praeger.

Banks, J. A. (1978). Multiethnic education across cultures: United States, Mexico, Puerto Rico, France, and Great Britain. *Social Education, 42*, 177–185.

Banks, J. A. (Ed.). (1996). *Multicultural education, transformative knowledge, and action: Historical and contemporary perspectives.* New York: Teachers College Press.

Banks, J. A. (2004). Multicultural education: Historical development, dimensions, and practice. In J. A. Banks & C. A. M. Banks (Eds.), *Handbook of research on multicultural education* (2nd ed., pp. 3–29). San Francisco: Jossey-Bass.

Banks, J. A. (2006). *Race, culture, and education: The selected works of James A. Banks.* London & New York: Routledge.

Banks, J. A. (2008). Diversity, group identity, and citizenship education in a global age. *Educational Researcher, 37*(3), 129–139.

Banks, J. A., & Banks, C. A. M. (Eds.). (2004) *Handbook of research on multicultural education* (2nd ed.). San Francisco: Jossey-Bass.

Banks, J. A., & Lynch, J. (1986) (Eds.). *Multicultural education in Western societies.* London & New York: Holt, Rinehart & Winston.

Banks, J. A., & Park, C. (in press). Race, ethnicity, and education: The search for explanations. In P. H. Collins & J. Solomos (Eds.), *Handbook of race and ethnic relations.* Los Angeles: Sage.

Baratz, S. S., & Baratz, J. C. (1970). Early childhood intervention: The social science base of institutional racism. *Harvard Educational Review, 40,* 29–50.

Befu, H. (2006). Conditions of living together. In S. i. Lee, S. Murphy-Shigematsu, & H. Befu (Eds.), *Japan's diversity dilemmas: Ethnicity, citizenship, and education* (pp. 1–10). New York: iUniverse.

Bereiter, C. & Engelmann, S. (1966). *Teaching disadvantaged children in the preschool.* Englewood Cliffs, NJ: Prentice-Hall.

Bonnett, A., & Carrington, B. (1996). Constructions of anti-racist education in Britain and Canada. *Comparative Education, 32*(3), 272–288.

Bowles, S., & Gintis, H. (1976) *Schooling in capitalist America: Educational reform and the contradictions of economic life.* New York: Basic Books.

Brookover, W. B., Beady, C., Flood, P., Schweitzer, J., & Wisenbaker, J. (1979). *School social systems and student achievement.* New York: Praeger.

Carby, H. V. (1980). *Multicultural fictions* (Stenciled Occasional Paper, Race Series: SP No. 58). Birmingham, UK: University of Birmingham.

Carby, H. V. (1982). Schooling in Babylon. In Centre for Contemporary Cultural Studies (Ed.), *The empire strikes back: Race and racism in 70s Britain* (pp. 183–211). London: Hutchinson.

Carr, P. R., & Lund, D. E. (2007). Scanning whiteness. In P. R. Carr & D. E. Lund (Eds.), *The great white north? Whiteness, privilege, and identity in education* (pp. 1–15). Rotterdam, Netherlands: Sense.

Carter, P. L. (2004). Beyond ascription: Racial identity, culture, schools, and academic achievement. *Du Bois Review: Social Science Research on Race, 1*(2), 377–388.

Castles, S., & Davidson, A. (2000). *Citizenship and migration: Globalization and the politics of belonging.* New York: Routledge.

Clark, K. B., & Clark, M. P. (1950). Emotional factors in racial identification and preference in Negro children. *Journal of Negro Education, 19,* 341–350.

Code, L. (1991). *What can she know? Feminist theory and the construction of knowledge.* Ithaca, NY: Cornell University Press.

Cohen, E. G., & Lotan, R. A. (1995). Producing equal-status interaction in the heterogeneous classroom. *American Educational Research Journal, 32,* 99–120.

Cuban, L. (1989). The "at risk" label and the problem of school reform. *Phi Delta Kappan, 70*(10), 780–784, 799–801.

de Haan, M., & Elbers, E. (2004). Minority status and culture: Local constructions of diversity in a classroom in the Netherlands. *Intercultural Education, 15*(4), 441–453.

Dillon, S. (2006, August 27). In schools across U.S., the melting pot overflows. *New York Times,* pp. A7, A16.

Figueroa, P. (1991). *Education and the social construction of "race."* London & New York: Routledge.

Figueroa, P. (2008). Prepublication review of this chapter. Headley Down, Hampshire, UK.

Fordham, S., & Ogbu, J. U. (1986). Black students' school success: Coping with the burden of "acting White." *Urban Review, 18*(3), 176–206.

Gay, G. (2000). *Culturally responsive teaching: Theory, research, and practice.* New York: Teachers College Press.

Gillborn, D. (2008). *Racism and education: Coincidence or conspiracy?* London & New York: Routledge.

Glazer, N. (1975). *Affirmative discrimination: Ethnic inequality and public policy.* New York: Basic Books.

Gollnick, D. M., & Chinn, P. C. (2009). *Multicultural education in a pluralistic society* (8th ed.). Columbus, OH: Merrill.

Gonçalves e Silva, P. B. (2004). Citizenship and education in Brazil: The contribution of Indian Peoples and Blacks in the struggle for citizenship. In J. A. Banks (Ed.), *Diversity and citizenship education: Global perspectives* (pp. 185–217). San Francisco: Jossey-Bass.

González, N., Moll, L. C., & Amanti, C. (2005). *Funds of knowledge: Theorizing practices in households, communities, and classrooms.* Mahwah, NJ: Lawrence Erlbaum.

Harding, S. (1998). *Is science multicultural? Postcolonialism, feminisms, and epistemologies.* Bloomington: Indiana University Press.

Hudson, R. (Ed.). (2007). *Geographica world atlas and encyclopedia.* Milson Point, NSW, Australia: Random House Australia.

James, C. E. (Ed.). (2005). *Possibilities and limitations: Multicultural policies and programs in Canada.* Winnipeg, MB, Canada: Fernwood.

Jencks, C., Smith, M., Acland, H., Bane, M. J., Cohen, D., Gintis, H., et al. (1972). *Inequality: A reassessment of the effect of family and schooling in America.* New York: Basic Books.

Katz, M. B. (1975). *Class, bureaucracy, and schools: The illusion of educational change in America.* New York: Praeger.

Kleinfeld, J. (1975). Effective teachers of Eskimo and Indian students. *School Review, 83*, 301–344.

Kuhn, T. F. (1970). *The structure of scientific revolutions* (2nd ed.). Chicago: University of Chicago Press.

Ladson-Billings, G. (1995). Toward a theory of culturally relevant pedagogy. *American Educational Research Journal, 35*, 465–491.

Ladson-Billings, G., & Tate, W. F., IV. (1995). Toward a critical race theory of education. *Teachers College Record, 97*(1), 47–68.

Lee, C. (2007). *Culture, literacy, and learning: Taking bloom in the midst of the whirlwind.* New York: Teachers College Press.

Lie, J. (2001). *Multiethnic Japan.* Cambridge, MA: Harvard University Press.

Luchtenberg, S. (Ed.). (2004). *Migration, education and change.* London: Routledge.

Lund, D. E. (2006). Waking up the neighbors: Surveying multicultural and antiracist education in Canada, the United Kingdom, and the United States. *Multicultural Perspectives, 8*(1), 35–43.

Martin, P., & Zurcher, G. (2008). Managing migration: The global challenge. *Population Bulletin, 63*(1), 1–20.

Mayo, C. (2010). Queer lessons: Multiculturalism and sexual and gender minorities. In J. A. Banks & C. A. M. Banks (Eds.), *Multicultural education: Issues and perspectives* (7th ed.). Hoboken, NJ: Wiley.

McCarthy, C. (1988). Reconsidering liberal and radical perspectives on racial inequality in schooling: Making the case for nonsynchrony. *Harvard Educational Review, 58*(2), 265–279.

Moodley, K. A. (1995). Multicultural education in Canada: Historical development and current status. In J. A. Banks & C. A. M. Banks (Eds.), *Handbook of research on multicultural education* (pp. 801–820). New York: Macmillan.

Murphy-Shigematsu, S. (2006). Diverse forms of minority national identities in Japan's multicultural society. In S. i. Lee, S. Murphy-Shigematsu, & H. Befu (Eds.), *Japan's diversity dilemmas: Ethnicity, citizenship, and education* (pp. 75–99). New York: iUniverse.

Murphy-Shigematsu, S. (2008). Prepublication review of this chapter. Stanford University, Stanford, CA.

Nasir, N. S., & Cobb, P. (Eds.). (2007). *Improving access to mathematics: Diversity and equity in the classroom.* New York: Teachers College Press.

Nieto, S., & Bode, P. (2008). *Affirming diversity: The sociopolitical context of multicultural education* (5th ed.). Boston: Allyn & Bacon.

Noguera, P. (2003). *City schools and the American dream: Reclaiming the promise of public education.* New York: Teachers College Press.

Ogbu, J. U. (2003). *Black American students in an affluent suburb: A study of academic disengagement.* Mahwah, NJ: Lawrence Erlbaum.

Painter, N. I. (2006). *Creating Black Americans: African–American history and its meanings, 1619 to the present.* New York: Oxford University Press.

Park, R. E. (1950). *Race and culture.* Glencoe, IL: Free Press.

Patterson, O. (1977). *Ethnic chauvinism: The reactionary impulse.* New York: Stein & Day.

Pettigrew, T. F. (2004). Intergroup contact: Theory, research, and new perspectives. In J. A. Banks & C. A. M. Banks (Eds.), *Handbook of research on multicultural education* (2nd ed., pp. 770–781). San Francisco: Jossey-Bass.

Porter, J. (1975). Ethnic pluralism in Canadian perspective. In N. Glazer & D. P. Moynihan (Eds.), *Ethnicity: Theory and experience* (pp. 267–304). Cambridge, MA: Harvard University Press.

Ramírez, M., III, & Castañeda, A. (1974). *Cultural democracy, bicognitive development, and education.* New York: Academic Press.

Rutter, M., Maughan, B., Mortimore, P., Ouston, J. (with Smith, A.). (1979). *Fifteen thousand hours: Secondary schools and their effects on children.* Cambridge, MA: Harvard University Press.

Schlesinger, A. M., Jr. (1991). *The disuniting of America: Reflections on a multicultural society.* Knoxville, TN: Whittle Direct Books.

Schools Council. (1970). *Teaching English to West Indian children: The research stage of the project* (Schools Council Working Paper 29). London: Evans Brothers.

Sleeter, C. E. (2005). *Un-standardizing the curriculum: Multicultural teaching in the standards-based classroom.* New York: Teachers College Press.

Statistics Canada (2008). Summary tables. Retrieved July 27, 2008, from http://www40.statcan.ca/

Steele, C. M. (2004). A threat in the air: How stereotypes shape intellectual identity and performance. In J. A. Banks & C. A. M. Banks (Eds.), *Handbook of research on multicultural education* (2nd ed., pp. 692–698). San Francisco: Jossey-Bass.

Stephan, W. G., & Vogt, W. P. (Eds.). (2004). *Education programs for improving intergroup relations: Theory, research, and practice.* New York: Teachers College Press.

Stone, M. (1981). *The education of the Black child in Britain: The myth of multiracial education.* Glasgow, UK: Fontana.

Theodorson, G. A., & Theodorson, A. G. (1969). *A modern dictionary of sociology.* New York: Barnes & Noble.

Tyson, K., Darity, W., Jr., & Castellino, D. (2004). Breeding animosity: The "burden of acting White" and other problems of status group hierarchies in schools. Unpublished manuscript.

United States Census Bureau. (2007). *Statistical abstract of the United States* (126th ed.). Washington, DC: U.S. Government Printing Office.

Valdés, G. (2001). *Learning and not learning English: Latino students in American schools.* New York: Teachers College Press.

Williamson, J. A. (2008). *Radicalizing the ebony tower: Black colleges and the Black freedom struggle in Mississippi.* New York: Teachers College Press.

2

Critical multiculturalism and education

Stephen May
University of Waikato, New Zealand

In the 1990s, multiculturalism as public policy seemed to be in the ascendant. Some 30–40 years after the genesis of the multiculturalist movement, even its critics were acknowledging – albeit with an overtly wearied resignation – its increasingly significant influence on public policy, particularly within education. Nathan Glazer (1998), a long time skeptic of multiculturalism, did just that when he conceded, in the ironic title of his book, "we are all multiculturalists now." Multiculturalism, at least in his view, had finally "won" (p. 4) because the issue of greater public representation for minority groups was increasingly commonplace in discussions of democracy and representation in the civic realm (see, for example, Goldberg, 1994; Kymlicka, 1995; Taylor, 1994). It seemed that the notion of a pluralized public sphere – where cultural, linguistic, and religious diversity could be actively and positively accommodated – was becoming an increasingly accepted part of social and political life in modern nation-states.

How times have changed. In this first decade of a new century, and particularly post-9/11, we have seen a rapid and significant retrenchment of multiculturalism in a wide range of nation-states. In the US, decades of affirmative action and related civil rights advances for African Americans have been dismantled, most notably in relation to access to higher education (Kellough, 2006). The provision of bilingual education, particularly for Latino and Latina Americans, has also been severely circumscribed, and in some U.S. states actually proscribed, by legislation promoting a monolingual English language philosophy as a prerequisite for U.S. citizenship (May, 2008b). Meanwhile, across Europe, itself subject to the Madrid bombings of 2004 and the London bombings of 2005, multiculturalism as public policy is in apparent full retreat, as European states increasingly assert that minority groups "integrate" or accept dominant social, cultural, linguistic, and (especially) religious mores as the price of ongoing citizenship (Modood, 2007).

These arguments are not new – the "threat" of multiculturalism to social and political cohesion has long been a key trope of the Right (see, for example, Glazer & Moynihan, 1975; Schlesinger, 1992). However, they have clearly gained purchase in the increasingly securitized post-9/11 environment as both an explanation for, and a visceral rejection of, the apparent willful failure of minorities to accept dominant societal mores and values. As the recent polemics against multiculturalism by Barry (2000) and Huntington (2005) illustrate starkly, ongoing ethnic, cultural, linguistic, and religious differences are simply no longer to be tolerated if nation-states are to continue to make their way safely in the world, or so the story goes. And the role of education is often at the center of such attacks.

In this current "post-multicultural" environment, the observations made by Torres (1998) about the challenges still facing multiculturalism, at the time of its apparent ascendancy in the late 1990s, are thus highly prescient. As he argued then:

> The multitude of tasks confronting multiculturalism is overwhelming. They include the attempt to develop a sensible, theoretically refined, and defensible new metatheoretical and theoretical territory that would create the foundations for multiculturalism as a paradigm; the attempt to establish its epistemological and logical premise around notions of experience, narrative, voice, agency and identity; the attempt to pursue empirical research linking culture/power/knowledge with equality/inequality/discrimination; and the need to defend multiculturalism from the conservative Right that has demonized it as an unpatriotic movement. (p. 446)

Taken in reverse order, the challenges Torres (1998) highlights can be usefully paraphrased as:

- the ongoing critique of multiculturalism from the Right;
- the tendency of multiculturalism to concentrate on culture at the expense of structural concerns such as racism and socioeconomic inequality;
- the challenges that postmodernist understandings of identity present for multiculturalism;
- the urgent need to develop a multiculturalist paradigm that effectively addresses – and, where necessary, redresses – all of the above.

The challenge to multiculturalism from the Right, while a central contributing characteristic of its current international retrenchment, is not my immediate concern here. The wider sociopolitical circumstances that exist at present will inevitably require a significant social and political realignment if multiculturalism – and the related rights of minorities with their social, cultural, linguistic, and religious practices – is to re-emerge as acceptable public policy. It is not that this debate is not central or pivotal (it clearly is); it is just that it is beyond the scope of this chapter, with its particular focus on education (although for further discussion on these wider issues see Kymlicka, 2007; May 1999a, 2008a, 2008b; Modood, 2007).

However, for the purposes of this chapter, I do wish to review here the second and third challenges to multiculturalism identified by Torres (1998) – what might be termed the "culturalist" and "postmodernist" critiques, respectively – since these bear directly on the subsequent development of critical multiculturalism within education, my principal concern in what follows. In so doing, I will highlight key aspects of critical multiculturalism, and the implications attendant upon it. I will also argue that critical multiculturalism is an educational paradigm that, in Torres's words, is sufficiently "sensible, theoretically refined, and defensible" (p. 446) as to take us forward from here – particularly in light of, and indeed *despite*, the current sociopolitical circumstances that appear so antithetical to an ongoing commitment to public multiculturalism.

The problem of culture

For much of its history, multiculturalism has been plagued by an idealistic, naive preoccupation with culture at the expense of broader material and structural concerns. If only cultural differences could be recognized, so the story went, the prospects of a harmonious multi-ethnic society could then (more easily) be achieved. This strain of multiculturalism is most evident in the rhetoric of early forms of multicultural education, developed throughout the 1970s and 1980s (for useful critiques here, see Ladson-Billings & Tate, 1995; Modood & May, 2001). It is encapsulated by the British antiracist educator Hatcher's (1987) observation that:

> [While] culture is the central concept around which [this] multiculturalism is constructed, the concept is given only a taken-for-granted common sense meaning, impoverished both theoretically and in terms of concrete lived experience. It is a concept of culture innocent of class. (p. 188)

Hatcher's (1987) acerbic assessment formed part of a sustained assault by "antiracist" theorists in Britain in the 1980s and, subsequently, critical race theorists in the US in the 1990s, on what they perceived to be the endemic utopianism and naivety associated with the multicultural education movement of that era. This movement has since come to be described as "liberal multiculturalism" in the US and "benevolent multiculturalism" elsewhere (see May, 1994; Sleeter & Delgado Bernal, 2004). Antiracist critics of benevolent or liberal multiculturalism, notably the British antiracist educator Troyna (1993), have argued that such an approach constituted an irredeemably "deracialized" discourse, an approach which reified culture and cultural difference, and which failed to address adequately, if at all, *material* issues of racism and disadvantage, and related forms of discrimination and inequality. British commentators initiated this broad antiracist position – a result, in turn, of the British antiracist education movement's origins in a neo-Marxist critique of multiculturalism. However, it has since also been articulated forcefully in Canada (see, for example, Dei, 1996) and the US, the last most notably in the application of critical race theory to education (see, for example, Ladson-Billings, 1998; Ladson-Billings & Tate, 1995; McCarthy & Crichlow, 1993).

Despite the perspicacity of these criticisms, what antiracist and critical race theorists have consistently underestimated (or, simply, ignored) is the remarkably similar criticisms from more critical educators within the multiculturalist paradigm itself.[1] Thus, Kalantzis and Cope (1999), key proponents of multicultural education, can observe:

> Whilst mouthing good intentions about pluralism . . . this sort of multiculturalism can end up doing nothing either to change the mainstream or to improve the access of those historically denied its power and privileges. It need not change the identity of the dominant culture in such a way that there can be genuine negotiation with "minorities" about matters social or symbolic or economic. It need not change education in such a way that issues of diversity are on the agenda for all students. It need not change education so that diversity might become a positive resource for access rather than a cultural deficit to be remedied by affirmation of difference alone. (p. 255)

Multiculturalists have responded to this critique from both within and without by acknowledging more directly the role of unequal power relations and the inequalities and differential effects that ensue from them. As Berlak and Moyenda (2001) argue: "central to critical multiculturalism is naming and actively challenging racism and other forms of injustice, not simply recognizing and celebrating differences and reducing prejudice" (p. 92; see also Kincheloe & Steinberg, 1997; May, 1999a; McLaren, 1995, 1997; McLaren & Torres, 1999; Sleeter & Delgado Bernal, 2004). This more critical response – a central feature of "critical multiculturalism," as it has come to be known – acknowledges that the logic of much previous multiculturalist rhetoric failed

> to see the power-grounded relationships among identity construction, cultural representations and struggles over resources. . . . [Rather, it engaged] in its celebration of difference when the most important issues to those who fall outside the White, male and middle class norm often involve powerlessness, violence and poverty.
> (Kincheloe & Steinberg, 1997, p. 17)

In contrast, a more critical conception of multiculturalism

> takes as its starting point a notion of culture as a terrain of conflict and struggle over representation – conflict for which resolution may not be immediate and struggle that may not cease until there is a change in the social conditions that provoke it. Rather than present culture as the site where different members . . . coexist peacefully, it has to develop strategies to explore and understand this conflict and to encourage creative resolutions and contingent alliances that move [away] from interpreting cultures to intervening in political processes.
> (Mohan, 1995, p. 385)

However, in developing this broadly critical response, multiculturalists have also more recently come to face another, perhaps more intractable problem – a problem brought on to some extent by this very process of accommodation with antiracist theory. For example, the privileging of racism over other forms of discrimination in early conceptions of British antiracism resulted in an increasing preoccupation with "color racism" and the Black – White dichotomy (Modood & May, 2001). This, in turn, led to a *grand theory* approach which, in attributing racism as the primary modality in intercultural relations, came to be seen subsequently as both reductive and essentialist (see Modood, 1998a, 1998b). Such an approach subsumed other factors such as class, religion, sexuality, and gender, and failed to address adequately postmodernist accounts of identity as multiple, contingent, and subject to rapid change. These emphases in British antiracist theory also considerably understated both the multiplicity of racisms and their complex interconnections with other forms of inequality (for critiques along these lines, see Modood, 1998a, 1998b; Rattansi, 1999; although for a notable exception see Gillborn, 1995). As McLaren and Torres (1999) observe:

> [The] conflation of racialized relations into solely a Black – White paradigm has prevented scholars from engaging more fully the specificities of particular groups and from exploring more deeply comparative ethnic histories of racism and how these are linked to changing class relations in late capitalism. (pp. 45–46)

The preoccupation with color racism is also a feature of the parallel Canadian antiracist education movement, as well as critical race theory (CRT) as it has been developed in the US, and applied to education, over the last decade. Darder and Torres (2002), for example, in addressing CRT directly, are highly critical of the "overwhelming tendency" to focus on reified "notions of race" (p. 260). They argue instead for "a critical language and conceptual apparatus" that, while still foregrounding racism and racial inequality, simultaneously encompasses "multiple social expressions of racism" (Darder & Torres, p. 260). This would allow CRT advocates, as well as antiracist theorists, to better address the increasing articulation of new "cultural racisms," where race as a signifier is transmuted into the seemingly more acceptable discourse of "cultural differences" (Modood, 2007; Rattansi, 1999). In this process, essentialist racialized discourses are "disguised" by describing group differences principally in cultural and/or historical terms — ethnic terms, in effect — without specifically mentioning "race" or overtly racial criteria (Barker, 1981; Small, 1994). New racisms, in this sense, can be described as a form of *ethnicism* which, as Brah (1992) describes it,

> defines the experience of racialized groups primarily in "culturalist" terms: that is, it posits "ethnic difference" as the primary modality around which social life is constituted and experienced. . . . This means that a group identified as culturally different is assumed to be internally homogeneous . . . ethnicist discourses seek to impose stereotypic notions of common cultural need upon heterogeneous groups with diverse social aspirations and interests. (p. 129)

Such ethnicist discourses are increasingly articulated in the public domain in relation to minority groups. They are particularly evident in the public and academic discourses that explain and/or defend the abandonment of multiculturalism as public policy in these post-9/11 times.

Avoiding essentialism

But opponents of multiculturalism are not the only ones who homogenize groups and attribute to them fixed cultural characteristics. Ironically, the problems of cultural essentialism and the reification of group-based identities highlighted by Brah (1992) — and mobilized so effectively by new racist proponents — also continue to haunt much multicultural theory and practice. This is particularly evident within benevolent or liberal multicultural education, for example, where the regular invocation of "cultural difference" often presents culture as *sui generis*, as unique and unchanging, fixed, and final, and determined by ethnic origin (Hoffman, 1996; McCarthy, 1998). In the process, ethnicity is elided with culture and both come to be treated as "bounded cultural objects," to borrow a phrase from Handler (1988, p. 15), which are seen to attach unproblematically to particular individuals and/or groups. This naive, static, and undifferentiated conception of cultural identity and the allied notion of the incommensurability of cultures end up being not that dissimilar from the new racisms of the Right. Both appear to abandon universalist notions of individual choice, rights, and responsibility in order to revalorize closed cultures, roots, and traditions (Werbner, 1997b).

It is perhaps not surprising then that criticism of multiculturalism with respect to this issue comes predominantly from what one might term the "postmodernist/left" (see Phillips, 1997). The challenge posed by postmodernist/left critics is this: how can multiculturalism, based as it is on a notion of group-based identities and related rights, avoid lapsing into reification and essentialism? In effect, how can it codify without solidifying ethnic group identities, thus accounting for postmodernist understandings of voice, agency, and the malleable and multiple aspects of identity formation? Not easily is the short answer.

The principal problem for multiculturalism here is that any notion of group-based rights stands in direct contrast to much postmodernist theorizing on identit*ies* which — with its related concepts of hybridity, syncretism, creolization, and new ethnicities — highlights the "undecidability" and fluidity of much identity formation. Indeed, it is now almost de rigueur in this postmodernist age to dismiss *any* articulation of group-based identity as essentialist[2] — a totalizing discourse that excludes and silences as much as it includes and empowers (see, for example, Bhabha, 1994; Gilroy, 2000; Hall, 1992). Viewed in this way, multiculturalism's advocacy of group-based identities appears irredeemably passé.

Left/postmodernist critics are particularly exercised by, and skeptical of, any claims to the validity of distinct (ethnic) group identities, especially if such identities link cultural difference and identity ineluctably to a historical past of (supposed) cultural authenticity. Such critics argue that this form of "left-essentialist multiculturalism" (Kincheloe & Steinberg, 1997; McLaren, 1995), of which Afrocentrism is often seen as an exemplar (see Howe, 1998), may well be motivated by key concerns to acknowledge positively cultural difference, to address historical and current patterns of disadvantage, racism, and marginalization, and, from that, to effect the greater pluralization of the public sphere. However, it does so at the cost of overstating the importance of ethnicity and culture, and understating the fluid and dialogic nature of inter- and intragroup relations. In effect, communitarian conceptions of multiculturalism such as these are charged with operating a model of group membership that is at odds with the complexities of identity in the modern world. As Said argues, "no one today is purely one thing. Labels like Indian, or woman, or Muslim, or American are no more than starting points" (1994, p. 407).

This broad critique of "left-essentialist multiculturalism" is illustrated by two allied, although theoretically quite distinct, conceptions: cultural hybridity and the cosmopolitan alternative. Both celebrate the notion of cultural mixture and, concomitantly, disavow the validity of so-called "rooted" identities like ethnicity.

Cultural hybridity: The postmodernist critique

The articulation of cultural hybridity – and related concepts such as mestizaje and creolization – is a prominent feature of the work of British theorists Hall, Bhabha, and Gilroy, among others. Hall's (1992) discussion of "new ethnicities," Bhabha's (1994) celebration of creolization and subaltern voices from the margin, and Gilroy's (2000) discussions of a Black Atlantic – a hybridized, diasporic Black counter-culture – all foreground the "transgressive potential" of cultural hybridity. Hybridity is viewed as being able to subvert categorical oppositions and essentialist ideological movements – particularly ethnicity and nationalism – and to provide, in so doing, a basis for cultural reflexivity and change.

Within the discourses of hybridity, and of postmodernism more broadly, the new social agents are plural – multiple agents forged and engaged in a variety of struggles and social movements. Conversely, hybridity theory is entirely opposed to universalism, traditionalism, and any idea of ethnic or cultural rootedness. In line with postmodernism's rejection of totalizing metanarratives, exponents of hybridity emphasize the contingent, the complex, and the contested aspects of identity formation. Multiple, shifting, and, at times, nonsynchronous identi*ties* are the norm for individuals. This position highlights the social and historical constructedness of culture and its associated fluidity and malleability. It also posits contingent, local narratives – what Lyotard (1984) has described as *petits récits* – in opposition to the totalizing narratives of ethnicity and nationalism. The rejection of totality and foundationalism in hybridity theory, and its replacement by a plethora of local identities, thus lends itself at one level to a politics of difference that is commensurable with multiculturalism. Hybridity theorists, like multiculturalists, are fundamentally opposed to a static, closed sense of national identity where majoritarian (usually White) ethnicities come to be elided or equated with national ones, a position articulated most trenchantly by conservative opponents of multiculturalism

(Huntington, 2005; Schlesinger, 1992). Instead, and again like multiculturalists, they argue for a *differentiated* politics of representation in the public sphere.

However, where hybridity theorists differ from multiculturalists is in sharing with conservative commentators a view of ethnicity and nationalism as misconceived "rooted" identities. Similarly, these identities are almost always ascribed with the negative characteristics of essentialism, closure, and conflict. Postmodernists, like multiculturalists, may thus argue for the pluralization of the public sphere via a differentiated local politics, but they do so via a *rejection*, not a defense, of singular ethnic and cultural identities. Rather, as Bhabha (1994) argues, it is the "inter" and "in-between," the liminal "third space" of translation, which carries the burden of the meaning(s) of culture in this postmodern, postcolonial world. Others have described this process as one of "border crossing" (see Anzaldúa, 1987; Giroux, 1992).

Hybridity theory, as part of the wider postmodern critique, appears to offer us, among other things, a more contingent, situational account of identity and culture – a process which involves "decentering" the subject (Rattansi, 1999) and contesting essentialism wherever it is found. But there are also limits to hybridity. First, in arguing for the inter and in-between, hybridity is still predicated on the notion of (previous) cultures as complex wholes (Friedman, 1997). In juxtaposing the merits of the heterogeneous hybrid against the homogeneous ethnicist or nationalist, hybridity assumes that the liminal "third space" is replacing the bounded, closed ones that preceded it. Border crossing, in effect, assumes that (closed) borders were there to begin with. However, as Friedman points out, this simply perpetuates an essentialist conception of culture rather than subverting it since, as Lévi-Strauss (1994) has argued, *all* cultures are heterogeneous, arising out of cultural mixture. The juxtaposition of purity and hybridity, or authenticity and mixture, so central to hybridity theory, is thus fundamentally misconceived. In the end, hybridity is meaningless as a description of "culture" because it museumizes culture as "a thing" (Werbner, 1997b; see also Modood, 1998a).

Second, an advocacy of hybridity carries with it the imputation that all group-based identities are essentialist. This is most clearly demonstrated in the frequent conflation of ethnicity and nationalism with racism, which, as so-called rooted identities, are all treated with equal disparagement (see Gilroy, 1987). This is simply wrong. There are many examples of ethnic and national categorization which do involve the imputation of essentialized notions of racial and/or cultural difference, leading in turn to social and/or political closure, hierarchization, exclusion, and/or violence. The cultural racism of the New Right is an obvious example here. But, while ethnic and national categories may be essentialized in the same way as "race" categories have been historically, they need not always be. Nor are ethnic relations necessarily hierarchical, exploitative, and conflictual in the same way that "race relations" invariably are (Jenkins, 2008). Indeed, it has often been the case that the global impact of racism has overridden previously non-hierarchized ethnic categories (Fenton, 1999). In similar vein, Werbner (1997a) has argued that the politics of ethnicity, which objectifies communities situationally and pragmatically with regard to questions of redistributive justice in the public sphere, can be clearly distinguished from the violent essentializing of racism.

The failure to make these crucial distinctions points to a third weakness of hybridity theory: the considerable disparity between the intellectual celebration of hybridity and the reality of the postmodern world. This world *is* increasingly one of fractured – and fracturing – identities. But these identities are generally *not* hybrid: just the opposite, in fact. Nation-states, as conservatives will be the first to tell you, are facing a plethora of ethnic, regional, and other social and cultural minority demands, many of which are couched in singular, collectivist terms.

Given this, as Friedman (1997) argues, the valorization of hybridization is largely self-referential and self-congratulatory:

> Hybrids, and hybridization theorists are products of a group that self-identifies and/or identifies the world in such terms, not as a result of ethnographic understanding, but as an act of self-definition – indeed, of self-essentializing – which becomes definition for others via the forces of socialization inherent in the structures of power that such groups occupy: intellectuals close to the media; the media intelligentsia itself; in a sense, all those [and, one might add, *only* those] who can afford a cosmopolitan identity. (p. 81)

Ahmad (1995), in a similarly scathing critique, argues that articulations of hybridity fail to address adequately the social and political continuities and transformations that underpin individual and collective action in the real world. In that world, he argues, political agency is "constituted not in flux or displacement but in given historical locations" (p. 14). Moreover, it is sustained by a coherent "sense of place, of belonging, of some stable commitment to one's class or gender or nation" (p. 14).

Friedman's (1997) and Ahmad's (1995) critiques of hybridity accord here with two wider criticisms often leveled at postmodernist discourses. First, postmodernism is criticized for an overemphasis on aesthetics at the expense of politics, a preoccupation which, as Berman (1992) acerbically observes, has seen postmodernism appropriate the modernist language of radical breakthrough, wrench it out of its moral and political context, and transform it into a purely aesthetic language game. Second, and relatedly, postmodernism is attributed both with failing to describe accurately and with retreating from the (post)modern world as it actually is, thus offering little, if any, real hope of accomplishing any kind of radical, emancipatory, democratic change (Habermas, 1979). Developments post-9/11 suggest as much.

The cosmopolitan alternative

These arguments and counter-arguments with regard to hybridity theory are strongly echoed in debates within liberal political theory around the closely allied notion of the "cosmopolitan alternative" (Waldron, 1995). Waldron, in a trenchant critique of group-based rights (also known as multiculturalism), objects to the idea that our choices and self-identity are defined by our ethnicity and asserts, instead, the need for a cosmopolitan alternative. As he dismissively observes:

> Though we may drape ourselves in the distinctive costumes of our ethnic heritage and immure ourselves in an environment designed to minimize our sense of relation with the outside world, no honest account of our being will be complete without an account of our dependence on larger social and political structures that goes far beyond the particular community with which we pretend to identify. (p. 104)

On this view, people can pick and choose "cultural fragments" from various ethnocultural sources, without feeling an allegiance to any one in particular. Thus, Waldron (1995) argues, an Irish American who eats Chinese food, reads Grimms' *Fairy Tales* to their child, and listens to Italian opera actually lives in a "a kaleidoscope of cultures." While Waldron concedes that we need cultural meanings of some kind, he argues that we do not need *specific* cultural frameworks:

We need to understand our choices in the contexts in which they make sense, but we do not need any single context to structure our choices. To put it crudely, we need culture, but we do not need cultural integrity. (p. 108)

As with hybridity theory, Waldron (1995) proceeds on this basis to argue that any advocacy of group-based identities, and specific (multicultural) rights which may be seen to attach to these necessarily assume a homogeneous conception of ethnic groups (see Waldron, 1995, pp. 103–105). Likewise, he is particularly critical of notions of cultural "purity" and "authenticity," which, he asserts, are regularly employed by ethnic minority groups in support of differential treatment in the public sphere and, particularly, within education. These attempts at cultural delineation are manifestly artificial in his view and can only result in cultural stasis and isolationism.

However, as Kymlicka (1995, 2007) has countered, also from within liberal theory, the assertion of minority recognition and difference, and particular rights associated with this, is most often *not* based on some simplistic desire for cultural "purity." Advocates of multiculturalism are rarely seeking to preserve their "authentic" culture if that means returning to cultural practices long past. If it was, it would soon meet widespread opposition from individual members. Rather, it is the right "to maintain one's membership in a distinct culture, and to continue developing that culture in the same (impure) way that the members of majority cultures are able to develop theirs" (Kymlicka, 1995, p. 105). Cultural change, adaptation, and interaction are entirely consistent with such a position.

In a similar vein, Kymlicka (1989) asserts that minority rights "help to ensure that the members of minority cultures have access to a secure cultural structure *from which to make choices for themselves*, and thereby promote liberal equality" (p. 192, emphasis added). On this view, minorities continue to exercise their individual (citizenship) rights within their particular cultural (and linguistic) milieus and, of course, contextually, in relation to other cultural groups. The crucial element, however, is that members of the minority are themselves able to retain a significant degree of control over the process – something which until now has largely been the preserve of majority group members. The key issue thus becomes one of cultural *autonomy* rather than one of retrenchment, isolationism, or stasis.

In a related critique of Waldron's (1995) position, Margalit and Raz (1995) argue that people today may well adopt (and adapt) a varied range of cultural and social practices but that this does not necessarily diminish their allegiance to an "encompassing group" with which they most closely identify (see also Calhoun, 2003; Taylor, 1994). Moreover, if members of dominant ethnic groups typically value their own cultural membership, even if they don't articulate this as such, it is clearly unfair to prevent minority groups from continuing to value theirs. As Kymlicka (1995) again observes, "leaving one's culture, while possible, is best seen as renouncing something to which one is reasonably entitled" (p. 90).

Developing a critical multicultural paradigm

This brings us to the final challenge currently facing multiculturalism that I want to focus on here: what components are essential for multiculturalism to develop into a sensible, theoretically refined, and defensible paradigm, fit for the 21st century? In light of the above discussion, I want to suggest that the following key components of what has come to be known as "critical multiculturalism" constitute just such an educational paradigm.

Theorizing ethnicity

There is an obvious and ongoing tension that needs to be addressed more adequately in multicultural education theory and practice between, on the one hand, *recognizing* the significance of ethnicity and culture for (some) individuals and group identities, while, on the other hand, avoiding *essentializing* them. Critical multiculturalism attempts this difficult task. Indeed, unlike all the critiques of multiculturalism discussed in this chapter, from both the Left and the Right, critical multiculturalism aims to provide an adequate *understanding* and *theorization* of the ongoing collective purchase of ethnicity and the social and cultural practices that may be associated with it, in the (post)modern world. We may well demonstrate, as individuals, a considerable degree of latitude in our attachment to, and choice of, particular social and political identities. As such, ethnic choices and identifications may vary in their salience – both in themselves and in relation to other social identities – at any given time and place. Yet, at the same time, we need to acknowledge and explain why, "at the collective as opposed to the individual level, ethnicity remains a powerful, explosive and durable force" (Smith, 1995, p. 34).

One way this can be achieved is via Bourdieu's notion of *habitus* (Bourdieu, 1984; Bourdieu & Passeron, 1990; Bourdieu & Wacquant, 1992). The application of habitus to ethnicity and ethnic identity formation has been discussed at length elsewhere (see May, 2008a; Smaje, 1997). However, for my purposes, it is enough to say that the four key dimensions of habitus highlighted in Bourdieu's work – embodiment, agency, the interplay between past and present, and the interrelationship between collective and individual trajectories – provide us with a useful means by which the continuing purchase *and* malleability of ethnicity, in its particular contexts, can be critically examined (see May, 1999b, 2008a, for an extended discussion).

Another basis for theoretical analysis might be via a more Foucauldian approach to representation, discourse, and identity, of which hybridity theory is an obviously prominent component. If the limits to such an approach are acknowledged (see above), ethnicity can be usefully examined here in relation to other discursive constructions of identity – in terms both of their complex interconnections and, crucially, of their ongoing distinctions. The intersection of knowledge and power – that is, discourse as both a technique of power and the terrain on which identity and meaning are contested – is also usefully highlighted by such analysis (see, for example, Hall, 1997).

These examples are, of course, not meant to be taken as comprehensive – indeed, theoretical eclecticism is a prominent and welcome feature of critical multiculturalism (McLaren, 2001) – but they do point to the urgent need to theorize ethnicity, and its consequences, more adequately than we have hitherto. In so doing, both the durability and the malleability of ethnicity, its varied forms of cultural expression, and its complex interconnections with other forms of identity can be critically examined.

A critical multicultural approach can thus foreground sociological understandings of identity – the multiple, complex strands and influences that make up who we *are* – alongside a critical analysis of the structural inequalities that still impact differentially on so many minority groups: in other words, what such groups *face* or *experience*. Such an approach would, interestingly, also provide a theoretical complement to one of the most important developments in critical race theory, the use of (counter)stories to highlight the experiences of discrimination for so many minority students (Dixson & Rousseau, 2006; Ladson-Billings, 1998).

Acknowledging (unequal) power relations

To this end, a sensible and defensible theory of multiculturalism also requires a central recognition of unequal power relations – a feature at the heart of critical multiculturalism and one too often missing from earlier forms of "benevolent" or "liberal" multicultural education. Such recognition allows one to avoid the mistake made by many hybridity theorists (as well as liberal advocates of the cosmopolitan alternative) of "flattening out" differences, making them appear equal. This is both inadequate as theory and unreflective of practice, since it is clear that when it comes to ethnicity (or any other identity for that matter) some have more choices than others. In this respect, individual and collective choices are circumscribed by the ethnic categories available at any given time and place. These categories are, in turn, socially and politically defined and have varying degrees of advantage or stigma attached to them. Moreover, the range of choices available to particular individuals and groups varies widely. A White American may have a wide range of ethnic options from which to choose, both hyphenated and/or hybrid. An African American, in contrast, is confronted with essentially one ethnic choice – Black – irrespective of any preferred ethnic (or other) alternatives they might wish to employ.

The preceding example highlights the different ethnic choices available to majority and minority group members. In short, identities are not – indeed, *cannot* be – freely chosen and to suggest otherwise is to adopt an ahistorical approach which reduces life to the level of "a market, or cafeteria" (Worsley, 1984, p. 246). Rather, identity choices are structured by class, ethnic, and gender stratification, objective constraints, and historical determinations (McLaren, 1997). Put another way, individuals and groups are inevitably located, and often *differentially* constrained, by wider structural forces such as capitalism, racism, colonialism, and sexism. Both hybridity theory and the cosmopolitan alternative – as well as conservative critiques of multiculturalism – fail to recognize the often fundamental inequalities that ensue from these forces, particularly, in this context, for minority students within education.

Critiquing constructions of culture

When we do recognize this, we also recognize the need for culture to be understood as part of the discourse of power and inequality. In particular, attention needs to be paid here to the processes by which alternative cultural knowledges come to be *subjugated*, principally through the hegemonies and misrepresentations – what Bourdieu (1991) has termed, for instance, "méconnaissance" or "misrecognition" – which invariably accompany such comparisons (see Kincheloe & Steinberg, 1997; May, 1999b, 2008a). When this is grasped, alternatives become possible. For example, in critical multicultural pedagogy, previously subjugated cultural knowledges can be *re*valued and simultaneously employed as counter-hegemonic critiques of dominant forms of knowledge, along with the wider social, cultural, and material processes of domination to which the latter contribute (Kincheloe & Steinberg; Sleeter & Delgado Bernal, 2004).

But this may still not be enough, since the recognition and incorporation of ethnic and cultural differences within schools, even when allied to a critique of wider power relations, do not necessarily resolve or redress the problem of essentialism. Indeed, the problem may be compounded, since an emphasis on distinctive ethnic and/or cultural boundaries may lead in turn to a further (unhelpful) implication of ethnic and/or cultural *boundedness*. Certainly, in much of the actual educational practice of multiculturalism, including some of its more critical variants, minority ethnic groups have often come to be represented as being *contained* within their culture(s) and the discursive practices associated with them (Hoffman, 1996).

Maintaining critical reflexivity

Thus the final, and perhaps key, tenet of critical multiculturalism is the need to maintain at all times a reflexive critique of specific ethnic and cultural practices, one that avoids the vacuity of cultural relativism and allows for criticism (both internal and external to the group), transformation, and change (see Phillips, 1997). This reflexive position on culture and ethnicity is encapsulated by a distinction drawn by Bhabha (1994) between cultural *diversity* and cultural *difference*. The former, he argues, treats culture as an *object* of empirical knowledge: as static, totalized, and historically bounded, as something to be valued but not necessarily *lived*. The latter is the process of the *enunciation* of culture as knowledg*able*: as adequate to the construction of systems of cultural identification. This involves a *dynamic* conception of culture, one that recognizes and incorporates the ongoing fluidity and constant change that attend its articulation in the modern world. Likewise, Hall (1992) has argued that a positive conception of ethnicity must begin with "a recognition that all speak from a particular place, out of a particular history, out of a particular experience, a particular culture, *without being contained by that position*" (p. 258, emphasis added). In other words, the recognition of our cultural and historical situatedness should not set the limits of ethnicity and culture, nor act to undermine the legitimacy of other, equally valid forms of identity.

In the end, then, this kind of critical, reflexive multiculturalism must foster, above all, students (and teachers) who can engage critically with all ethnic and cultural backgrounds, including (and especially) their own. Such an approach would allow all participants to recognize and explore the complex interconnections, gaps, and dissonances that occur between their own and other ethnic and cultural identities, as well as other forms of social identity. At the same time, how ethnic and cultural identities differ in salience among individuals and across given historical and social contexts, and how these identities are situated in the wider framework of power relations, along with the value – or lack of value – that attends them, can also be highlighted.

This dual approach can involve for members of minority groups the retention of their ethnic and cultural identities, not by a retreat into traditionalism or cultural essentialism but by a more *autonomous* construction of individual and group identity (Kymlicka, 1995, 2007; May, 2008a). Put more simply, it provides minority groups, including minority students within schools, with more *scope* to continue to value their ethnic and cultural backgrounds as significant features of their identity, and to have them valued by others (teachers and students), without necessarily being wholly defined or delimited by them. For majority group members, this can involve in turn a critical interrogation of the normalization and universalization of majoritarian forms of identity – most notably Whiteness – and their subsequent "invisibility" in many discussions of benevolent or liberal multiculturalism and multicultural education.

The invisibility of Whiteness, most evident in "colorblind" approaches to education and wider public policy, is a key analytical focus of both critical race theory and critical multiculturalism (Dixson & Rousseau, 2006; McLaren & Torres, 1999). It is also, of course, a key pedagogical focus of critical pedagogy, which shares many of both critical race theory's and critical multiculturalism's principal concerns (see Darder, Torres, & Baltodano, 2002; Sleeter & Delgado Bernal, 2004, for further discussion).

Conclusion

These four components, in combination, constitute what has come to be known as "critical multiculturalism." Despite its detractors (see, for example, McLennan, 2001), critical multiculturalism offers, I believe, the most useful way forward in the contested arena that is multiculturalism and multicultural education. Critical multiculturalism combines both structural and culturalist concerns – linking culture to power, and multiculturalism to antiracism – in its advocacy of a greater politics of recognition and representation within education and the wider public sphere.

Critical multiculturalism engages actively with postmodernist conceptions and analyses of the contingent nature of identity, while still holding onto the possibility of an emancipatory, group-based politics – that we can actually *change* things for the better. In so doing, it manages to avoid the great limitation of postmodernism that, in Habermas's (1979) memorable riposte, is its tendency towards a politics of exhaustion.

And, perhaps most importantly, critical multiculturalism provides a defensible, credible, and critical paradigm that can still act as a template for the possibilities of a more plural, inclusive, and democratic approach to both education and wider nation-state organization in this new century. The fact that so much ground has been lost in the post-9/11 environment, with "integrationist" (read: assimilationist) public discourses increasingly in the ascendant, makes articulating and defending this critical multiculturalist alternative, both in education and in the wider society, all the more urgent.

Notes

1 Dixson and Rousseau's (2006) otherwise excellent account of critical race theory in education is a recent example of this continuing absence or omission.
2 *Essentialism* is taken to mean here the process by which particular groups come to be described in terms of fundamental, immutable characteristics. In so doing, the relational and fluid aspects of identity formation are ignored and the group itself comes to be seen as impervious to context and to processes of internal as well as external differentiation and/or change (Werbner, 1997a).

References

Ahmad, A. (1995). The politics of literary postcoloniality. *Race and Class*, 36(3), 1–20.
Anzaldúa, G. (1987). *Borderlands/La Frontera: The new mestiza*. San Francisco: Aunt Lute Books.
Barker, M. (1981). *The new racism: Conservatives and the ideology of the tribe*. London: Junction.
Barry, B. (2000). *Culture and equality: An egalitarian critique of multiculturalism*. Cambridge, MA: Harvard University Press.
Berlak, A., & Moyenda, S. (2001). *Taking it personally: Racism in the classroom from kindergarten to college*. Philadelphia: Temple University Press.
Berman, M. (1992). Why modernism still matters. In S. Lash & J. Friedman (Eds.), *Modernity and identity* (pp. 33–58). Oxford, UK: Basil Blackwell.
Bhabha, H. (1994). *The location of culture*. London: Routledge.
Bourdieu, P. (1984). *Distinction: A social critique of the judgement of taste*. Cambridge, MA: Harvard University Press.
Bourdieu, P. (1991). *Language and symbolic power*. Cambridge, MA: Polity Press.
Bourdieu, P., & Passeron, J. (1990). *Reproduction in education, society and culture* (2nd ed.). London: Sage.
Bourdieu, P., & Wacquant, L. (1992). *An invitation to reflexive sociology*. Chicago: Chicago University Press.
Brah, A. (1992). Difference, diversity and differentiation. In J. Donald & A. Rattansi (Eds.), *"Race," culture and difference* (pp. 126–145). London: Sage.
Calhoun, C. (2003). Belonging in the cosmopolitan imaginary. *Ethnicities*, 3(3), 531–553.
Darder, A., & Torres, R. D. (2002). Shattering the "race" lens: Towards a critical theory of racism. In

A. Darder, R. D. Torres, & M. Baltodano (Eds.), *The critical pedagogy reader* (pp. 245–261). New York: RoutledgeFalmer.

Darder, A., Torres, R. D., & Baltodano, M. (Eds.). (2002). *The critical pedagogy reader*. New York: RoutledgeFalmer.

Dei, G. (1996). *Anti-racism education: Theory and practice*. Black Point, NS, Canada: Fernwood.

Dixson, A. D., & Rousseau, C. K. (Eds.). (2006). *Critical race theory in education: All God's children got a song*. New York: Routledge.

Fenton, S. (1999). *Ethnicity: Racism, class and culture*. London: Macmillan.

Friedman, J. (1997). Global crises, the struggle for identity and intellectual porkbarrelling: Cosmopolitans versus locals, ethnics and nationals in an era of de-hegemonization. In P. Werbner & T. Modood (Eds.), *Debating cultural hybridity: Multicultural identities and the politics of antiracism* (pp. 70–89). London: Zed Books.

Gillborn, D. (1995). *Racism and antiracism in real schools*. Buckingham, UK: Open University Press.

Gilroy, P. (1987). *There ain't no Black in the Union Jack*. London: Hutchinson.

Gilroy, P. (2000). *Between camps: Nations, cultures and the allure of race*. London: Allen Lane/Penguin Press.

Giroux, H. (1992). *Border crossings: Cultural workers and the politics of education*. London: Routledge.

Glazer, N. (1998). *We are all multiculturalists now*. Cambridge, MA: Harvard University Press.

Glazer, N., & Moynihan, D. (1975). *Ethnicity: Theory and experience*. Cambridge, MA: Harvard University Press.

Goldberg, D. (1994). Introduction: Multicultural conditions. In D. Goldberg (Ed.), *Multiculturalism: a critical reader* (pp. 1–41). Oxford, UK: Basil Blackwell.

Habermas, J. (1979). *Communication and the evolution of society*. Boston: Beacon.

Hall, S. (1992). New ethnicities. In J. Donald & A. Rattansi (Eds.), *"Race," culture and difference* (pp. 252–259). London: Sage.

Hall, S. (Ed.). (1997). *Representation: Cultural representations and signifying practices*. London: Sage.

Handler, R. (1988). *Nationalism and the politics of culture in Quebec*. Madison: Wisconsin University Press.

Hatcher, R. (1987). Race and education: Two perspectives for change. In B. Troyna (Ed.), *Racial inequality in education* (pp. 184–200). London: Tavistock.

Hoffman, D. (1996). Culture and self in multicultural education: Reflections on discourse, text, and practice. *American Educational Research Journal, 33*, 545–569.

Howe, S. (1998). *Afrocentrism: Mythical pasts and imagined homes*. London: Verso.

Huntington, S. (2005). *Who are we? America's great debate*. New York: Free Press.

Jenkins, R. (2008). *Rethinking ethnicity: Arguments and explorations* (2nd ed.). London: Sage.

Kalantzis, M., & Cope, B. (1999). Multicultural education: Transforming the mainstream. In S. May (Ed.), *Critical multiculturalism: Rethinking multicultural and antiracist education* (pp. 245–276). London: RoutledgeFalmer.

Kellough, J. (2006). *Understanding affirmative action: Politics, discrimination, and the search for justice*. Washington, DC: Georgetown University Press.

Kincheloe, J., & Steinberg, S. (1997). *Changing multiculturalism: New times, new curriculum*. Buckingham, UK: Open University Press.

Kymlicka, W. (1989). *Liberalism, community and culture*. Oxford, UK: Clarendon Press.

Kymlicka, W. (1995). *Multicultural citizenship: A liberal theory of minority rights*. Oxford, UK: Clarendon Press.

Kymlicka, W. (2007). *Multicultural odysseys: Navigating the new international politics of diversity*. Oxford, UK: Oxford University Press.

Ladson-Billings, G. (1998). Just what is critical race theory and what is it doing in a *nice* field like education? *International Journal of Qualitative Studies in Education, 11*, 7–24.

Ladson-Billings, G., & Tate, W. (1995). Towards a critical race theory of education. *Teachers College Record, 97*, 47–68.

Lévi-Strauss, C. (1994). Anthropology, race, and politics: A conversation with Didier Eribon. In R. Borofsky (Ed.), *Assessing cultural anthropology* (pp. 420–429). New York: McGraw-Hill.

Lyotard, J.-F. (1984). *The postmodern condition: A report on knowledge* (G. Bennington & B. Massumi, Trans.). Manchester, UK: Manchester University Press.

Margalit, A., & Raz, J. (1995). National self-determination. In W. Kymlicka (Ed.), *The rights of minority cultures* (pp. 79–92). Oxford, UK: Oxford University Press.

May, S. (1994). *Making multicultural education work*. Clevedon, UK: Multilingual Matters.

May, S. (Ed.). (1999a). *Critical multiculturalism: Rethinking multicultural and antiracist education*. London: RoutledgeFalmer.

May, S. (1999b). Critical multiculturalism and cultural difference: Avoiding essentialism. In S. May (Ed.), *Critical multiculturalism: Rethinking multicultural and antiracist education* (pp. 11–41). London: RoutledgeFalmer.

May, S. (2008a). *Language and minority rights: Ethnicity, nationalism and the politics of language*. New York: Routledge.

May, S. (2008b). Bilingual/immersion education: What the research tells us. In J. Cummins & N. Hornberger (Eds.), *The encyclopedia of language and education* (2nd ed., Vol. 5, pp. 19–34). New York: Springer.

McCarthy, C. (1998). *The uses of culture: Education and the limits of ethnic affiliation*. New York: Routledge.

McCarthy, C., & Crichlow, W. (Eds.). (1993). *Race, identity and representation in education*. New York: Routledge.

McLaren, P. (1995). *Critical pedagogy and predatory culture: Oppositional politics in a postmodern era*. New York: Routledge.

McLaren, P. (1997). *Revolutionary multiculturalism: Pedagogies of dissent for the new millennium*. Boulder, CO: Westview Press.

McLaren, P. (2001). Wayward multiculturalists. *Ethnicities, 1*(3), 408–420.

McLaren, P., & Torres, R. D. (1999). Racism and multicultural education: Rethinking "race" and "whiteness" in late capitalism. In S. May (Ed.), *Critical multiculturalism: Rethinking multicultural and antiracist education* (pp. 42–76). London: Falmer Press.

McLennan, G. (2001). Can there be a critical multiculturalism? *Ethnicities, 1*(3), 389–408.

Modood, T. (1998a). Anti-essentialism, multiculturalism and the "recognition" of religious groups. *Journal of Political Philosophy, 6*(4), 378–399.

Modood, T. (1998b). Multiculturalism, secularism and the state. *Critical Review of International Social and Political Philosophy, 1*(3), 79–97.

Modood, T. (2007). *Multiculturalism: A civic idea*. Cambridge, UK: Polity Press.

Modood, T., & May, S. (2001). Multiculturalism and education in Britain: An internally contested debate. *International Journal of Educational Research, 35*, 305–317.

Mohan, R. (1995). Multiculturalism in the nineties: Pitfalls and possibilities. In C. Newfield & R. Strickland (Eds.), *After political correctness: The humanities and society in the 1990s* (pp. 372–388). Boulder, CO: Westview Press.

Phillips, A. (1997). Why worry about multiculturalism? *Dissent, 44*, 57–63.

Rattansi, A. (1999). Racism, "postmodernism," and reflexive multiculturalism. In S. May (Ed.), *Critical multiculturalism: Rethinking multicultural and antiracist education* (pp. 77–112). London: Falmer Press.

Said, E. (1994). *Culture and imperialism*. London: Vintage.

Schlesinger, A. (1992). *The disuniting of America: Reflections on a multicultural society*. New York: W. W. Norton & Co.

Sleeter, C., & Delgado Bernal, D. (2004). Critical pedagogy, critical race theory, and antiracist education: Implications for multicultural education. In J. A. Banks & C. A. M. Banks (Eds.), *Handbook of research on multicultural education* (2nd ed., pp. 240–258). San Francisco: Jossey-Bass.

Smaje, C. (1997). Not just a social construct: Theorising race and ethnicity. *Sociology, 31*, 307–327.

Small, S. (1994). *Racialised barriers: The Black experience in the United States and England in the 1980s*. London: Routledge.

Smith, A. D. (1995). *Nations and nationalism in a global era*. London: Polity Press.

Taylor, C. (1994). The politics of recognition. In A. Gutmann (Ed.), *Multiculturalism: Examining the politics of recognition* (pp. 25–73). Princeton, NJ: Princeton University Press.

Torres, C. (1998). Democracy, education, and multiculturalism: Dilemmas of citizenship in a global world. *Comparative Education Review, 42*, 421–447.

Troyna, B. (1993). *Racism and education: Research perspectives.* Buckingham, UK: Open University Press.

Waldron, J. (1995). Minority cultures and the cosmopolitan alternative. In W. Kymlicka (Ed.), *The rights of minority cultures* (pp. 93–119). Oxford, UK: Oxford University Press.

Werbner, P. (1997a). Essentialising essentialism, essentialising silence: Ambivalence and multiplicity in the constructions of racism and ethnicity. In P. Werbner & T. Modood (Eds.), *Debating cultural hybridity: Multicultural identities and the politics of antiracism* (pp. 226–254). London: Zed Books.

Werbner, P. (1997b). Introduction: The dialectics of cultural hybridity. In P. Werbner & T. Modood (Eds.), *Debating cultural hybridity: Multicultural identities and the politics of antiracism* (pp. 1–26). London: Zed Books.

Worsley, P. (1984). *The three worlds: Culture and world development.* London: Weidenfeld & Nicolson.

3

World population movements, diversity, and education

Stephen Castles
University of Oxford, UK

Multicultural education would not be an issue in a static world of closed-off nation-states. It has become important because populations are becoming increasingly mobile and diverse. Formal school education for all is a modern aspiration, connected with democracy, industrialization, and the construction of nation-states. Schooling has been a main instrument of nation-building, both in the older industrial countries and in post-colonial states. Not surprisingly, then, education has often been seen as an instrument for propagating a supposedly unitary national culture. That has always been problematic, because virtually no nation-state has ever actually been completely homogeneous and monocultural. National education has therefore often meant imposing a dominant culture, ignoring diversity, and devaluing (or even destroying) minority cultures.

Monocultural education models seem even more problematic in today's world of instant communication, easy travel, and growing population mobility. International migration has grown sharply since 1945, and shows every sign of continuing to do so. People move to seek economic opportunities, refuge from war and persecution, or just new ways of living. Many people move temporarily and then return home or go on to a new destination, but some always decide to stay on in a host country. These settlers have needs for education and vocational training, and this applies even more to their children (the so-called "second generation").

Immigration countries have therefore devised a range of strategies for the education of immigrants and ethnic minorities. These have changed over time. Where migrants were initially perceived as temporary "guest workers," educational policy focused on maintaining migrant languages and cultures so that migrants would be ready to go back home. Where, by contrast, migrants were expected to settle permanently, the approach was to ensure that children absorbed the culture and language of the receiving country and lost their cultural distinctiveness (Castles, 2004b).

However, by the 1970s, both these approaches became problematic, because immigrants were settling but often not assimilating: they could not assimilate because racial or ethnic discrimination and social disadvantage led to segregated work and housing situations; they did not want to assimilate because maintaining their language, religion, and customs was crucial to their identity. This led to the development of multicultural education to provide solutions to the special difficulties faced by immigrants and their children in finding ways of living in new socio-cultural contexts. Multicultural education takes different forms, but generally means recognizing cultural distinctiveness while at the same time providing children with the cultural tools needed to succeed in the host society.

The purpose of this chapter is to set the scene for analyses of multicultural education by outlining recent international population movements and their links to the other macro-trends that are collected under the label of "globalization": international economic integration, cultural change, transnational consciousness, and new forms of communication. Migration has consequences for education in many countries, but here the focus will be on immigrant-receiving countries in the OECD region (the Organisation for Economic Co-operation and Development, which embraces the rich countries of Europe, North America, Oceania, and Northeast Asia).

Human mobility in the age of globalization

International migration is an integral part of globalization. As less-developed countries in Africa, Asia, and Latin America are drawn into global economic linkages, powerful processes of social transformation are unleashed. Neo-liberal forms of international economic integration undermine traditional ways of working and living. Increased agricultural productivity displaces people from the land. Environmental change compels many people to seek new livelihoods and places to live. People move to the cities, but there are not enough jobs there, and housing and social conditions are often very bad. In addition, weak states and impoverishment lead to a lack of human security, and often to violence and violations of human rights. All these factors encourage emigration.

At the same time, globalization leads to social transformation in the OECD countries. Industrial restructuring means deskilling and early retirement for many workers. The new services industries need very different types of labor. But, owing to declining fertility, relatively few young nationals enter the labor market. Moreover, these young people have good educational opportunities and are not willing to do low-skilled work. Population aging leads to increased dependency rates and care needs. Developed countries have high demand for both high- and low-skilled workers, and need migrants – whether legal or not.

Globalization also creates the cultural and technical conditions for mobility. Electronic communications provide knowledge of migration routes and work opportunities. Long-distance travel has become cheaper and more accessible. Once migratory flows are established they generate "migration networks": previous migrants help members of their families or communities who wish to follow with information on work, accommodation, and official rules. Facilitating migration has become a major international business, including travel agents, bankers, lawyers, and recruiters. The "migration industry" also has an illegal side – smuggling and trafficking – which governments try to restrict. Yet the more governments try to control borders, the greater the flows of undocumented migrants seem to be. Governments remain focused on control of national models, while migrants follow the transnational logic of globalized labor markets (Castles, 2004a).

According to the United Nations Department of Economic and Social Affairs (UN/DESA), the world total of international migrants (defined as people living outside their country of birth for at least a year) grew from about 100 million in 1960 to 191 million in 2005 (UN/DESA, 2005). This sounds like a lot, but is just a small share of the world's 6 billion people. Only about 3% of the world's population are international migrants. It is important to realize that most people remain in their countries of birth. Indeed internal migration is much larger than international migration. Internal migration attracts far less political attention, but its social and cultural consequences can be important. For instance, in China, the "floating population" of people moving from the agricultural central and western provinces to the new industrial areas of the east coast numbers at least 100 million, and many of them experience legal disadvantage and economic marginalization very much like international migrants elsewhere.

Geographically, international migrants can be divided into four categories. As Table 3.1 shows, the largest flows are from the less-developed countries of the global South to the developed countries of the global North. These migrants are very diverse and include highly skilled specialists (medical doctors, international technology [IT] experts, engineers, and managers), as well as low-skilled workers, refugees, and family members. The second largest flows are between countries in the South. The third largest group consists of migrants moving between rich Northern countries. The smallest category is of people moving from North to South. South–North migration is the fastest-growing category, and has accounted for virtually all growth in international migration in the period of accelerated globalization since 1980.

Immigrants in developed countries

What makes migration such an important factor in social change is its regional and local concentration. According to the United Nations Population Division (UN/PD), by 2000, 63% of the world's migrants were in developed countries, where they made up 8.7% of the total population. By contrast, the share in developing countries had fallen to 37%, only 1.3% of total population (UN/PD, 2002). Table 3.2 shows the evolution of foreign-born populations in OECD countries. Some countries such as Canada, the USA, the UK, and Ireland show significant growth since 1995. Most rich countries have a large and growing share of foreign-born residents.

The main exceptions (not shown in the table owing to lack of data) are Japan, where foreign residents make up only 1.6% of the population, and South Korea, where they are 1% (but growing fast). However, many new industrial countries in Asia and the Middle East are also experiencing large-scale immigration: Malaysia, Hong Kong, Singapore, and Taiwan all rely

Table 3.1 Types of Immigrants

Type of Immigrant	Description	Number in 2005 (millions)
Move from global South to global North	Very diverse: highly skilled workers as well as low-skilled workers. The fastest-growing category of migrants	62
Move between countries in the global South	Highly diverse	61
Move between rich Northern countries	Highly skilled specialists and managers; non-economic migrants	53
Move from global North to global South	Business people, officials of international organizations, aid workers, journalists, and retirees	14

Source: UN/DESA (2005).

Note: All migratory flows include a range of migrants types. The description in the table refers to the most frequent types in each flow.

Table 3.2 Foreign-Born Population in Selected OECD Countries (thousands)

Country	1995	2000	2005	Share of Total Population 2005 (%)
Australia	4,164	4,417	4,826	23.8
Austria	–	843	1,101	13.5
Belgium	983	1,059	1,269	12.1
Canada	4,867	5,327	5,896	19.1
Czech Republic	–	434	523	5.1
Denmark	250	309	350	6.5
Finland	106	136	177	3.4
France	–	4,306[a]	4,926	8.1
Germany	9,378	10,256	10,621[b]	12.9[b]
Greece	–	–	1,122[c]	10.3[c]
Hungary	284	295	332	3.3
Ireland	–	329	487	11.0
Italy	–	–	1,147[c]	2.5[c]
Luxembourg	128	145	152	33.4
Netherlands	1,407	1,615	1,735	10.6
New Zealand	–	663	796	19.4
Norway	240	305	380	8.2
Poland	–	–	776[d]	1.6[d]
Portugal	533	523	661	6.3
Slovak Republic	–	119[c]	249	3.9[e]
Spain	–	–	2,172[c]	5.3[c]
Sweden	936	1,004	1,126	12.4
Switzerland	1,503	1,571	1,773	23.8
UK	4,031	4,667	5,842	9.7
USA	24,648	31,108	38,343	12.9

Sources: OECD (2006, p. 262; 2007, p. 330).

Notes: The term "foreign-born" includes resident foreign citizens as well as naturalized immigrants.
[a] Figure for 1999.
[b] Figure for 2003.
[c] Figure for 2001.
[d] Figure for 2002.
[e] Figure for 2004.

heavily on migrant labor, while in the Gulf oil states (Saudi Arabia, Kuwait, Dubai, etc.) the number of foreign workers often outnumbers the native populations. The governments of such countries reject the idea of permanent settlement (as European governments did back in the 1970s) and therefore refuse to allow migrants to bring in their families or become citizens. These cases will not be discussed here (see Castles & Miller, 2009, chaps. 6 and 7), but many observers believe that settlement processes are beginning, so that these nations too will need to think about long-term social, cultural, and educational consequences.

Processes of concentration also take place within host countries. Migrants and their descendants settle mainly in large cities: for example, 44% of the population in Toronto, 25% in London, and 29% in Brussels (Office of the United Nations High Commissioner for Refugees [UNHCR], 2006, p. 12). Migrants go where the jobs are, and immigration can be used as a barometer of the economic dynamism of cities, regions, and countries. Interestingly, local authorities of main migration destinations often complain about the strain put on resources, while the authorities of regions not popular with migrants – like Scotland or South Australia – try very hard to attract them. Migrants also go where they can join compatriots, who help them to find jobs and accommodation – the "network effect." These mechanisms reinforce each other and lead to residential clustering, especially in the early period of settlement of each group. This in turn puts pressure on inner-city schools, which often have to deal with sudden influxes of children with many different languages.

Migration leads to cultural and social change. In areas of origin, returnees may import new ideas that unsettle traditional practices and hierarchies. In receiving areas, migration is bringing about unprecedented cultural and religious diversity. Migrants are often seen as symbols of perceived threats to jobs, livelihoods, and cultural identities resulting from globalization. Campaigns against immigrants and asylum seekers have become powerful mobilizing tools for the extreme right.

Historically, nation-states have been based on ideas of common origins and culture. Most migrants moved with the intention either of permanent settlement or of a temporary sojourn in one receiving country. Today it is possible to go back and forth, or to move on to other countries. Increasingly, migrants see themselves as members of transnational communities: groups that live their lives across borders (Portes, Guarnizo, & Landolt, 1999). Many receiving countries have changed their nationality laws to help immigrants and their descendants to become citizens (Aleinikoff & Klusmeyer, 2001; Bauböck, Ershøll, Groenendijk, & Waldrauch, 2006a, 2006b). Rethinking community cohesion and solidarity to include people with diverse cultural and religious practices may be crucial for the future of democracy.

Inequality and the new labor force

The role of immigrants in the labor force of receiving countries is changing today, and this has important consequences for their position in society. The new migrations, which started after 1965 for the USA and from the 1980s for Europe, have led to much greater population diversity. Migrants come from all over the world, bringing with them varied skills as well as a multitude of cultural and religious backgrounds (see Castles & Miller, 2009, chap. 5).

In the case of the USA and Canada, most recent migrants come from Asia and Latin America, with predominantly irregular migration from Mexico playing a crucial role for the USA. For Europe, the former labor-source countries of the periphery (Southern Europe and Ireland) have experienced rapid economic growth – partly linked to European Union (EU) structural policies – and become major immigration destinations themselves (King, Lazaridis, & Tsardanidis, 2000; Reyneri, 2003). The former migrant-recruitment areas of Turkey and North Africa are being transformed into transit and immigration areas. After the end of the Cold War, Eastern and Central Europe became integrated into European migration circuits, especially after the EU accession of many of these states in 2004 and 2007. Seen initially as the solution to Western Europe's labor shortages, these countries are experiencing demographic shifts and economic growth that are turning them into new immigration zones.

From 1995 to 2005 there was sustained growth in OECD economies, leading to strong demand for labor. In the USA more than half of new jobs went to foreign-born persons, while migrants made up between one-third and two-thirds of new employees in most Western and Southern European countries. By 2005, foreign-born workers made up 44% of the labor force in Luxemburg, 25% in Switzerland, 20% in Austria and Germany, and around 12% in other Western European countries (Organisation for Economic Co-operation and Development [OECD], 2007, pp. 63–66).

New immigrants were vital not only because they filled jobs, but also because they brought skills with them. In Belgium, Luxembourg, Sweden, and Denmark, over 40% of the employed migrants who arrived from 1995 to 2005 had tertiary education. In France the figure was 35% and in the Netherlands 30%. In many cases, migrant workers had higher qualification profiles than local-born workers. Only in Southern European countries did low-skilled labor migration predominate (OECD, 2007, pp. 67–68). But, even in Western Europe, migrants are important for low-skilled jobs in agriculture, construction, hotels and catering, and other services. Some employers prefer migrants to locals because they are "more reliable, motivated and committed" and "more prepared to work longer and flexible hours" and "work harder" than domestic workers (Dench, Hurstfield, Hill, & Akroyd, 2006, p. iv).

Such qualities of migrant workers are often the result of their weak position due to lack of recognized qualifications, discrimination, or irregular legal status. Foreign-born workers tend to have lower occupational status and higher unemployment rates than non-migrant workers. Older migrant workers often seem to have got stuck in the manual manufacturing sectors for which they were originally recruited. Restructuring and recessions have led to displacement from the labor force or unemployment for such groups. One indication of this is the fact that migrants now have lower labor-force participation rates than natives in many countries. Unemployment rates of foreign-born workers are also much higher than for local workers – in Austria, Belgium, Denmark, Finland, Norway, Sweden, and Switzerland twice as high or more (OECD, 2007, pp. 62–95).

The second generation

A key issue for educationalists is the situation of the "second generation" (defined by the OECD as native-born persons with both parents foreign born). Since they have gained their education in the host country, it is valuable to compare their experience both with migrants of the same age group and with young people who do not have a "migration background" (native-born children of native-born parents). Studies of schooling in immigration countries during the early settlement period predicted that children of immigrants might inherit their parents' low socio-economic positions (Castles, Booth, & Wallace, 1984). Several national and international comparative studies (such as OECD's Programme for International Student Assessment – PISA) now make it possible to assess whether this has happened.

In general, the research shows that members of the second generation have better average educational outcomes than their parents. However, outcomes lag behind those of native-born young people without a migration background. The PISA study, which assessed performance of 15-year-olds in mathematics, science, reading, and cross-curricular competencies, found that, even after allowing for parental background, second-generation students remained at a substantial disadvantage. This applied particularly to former guest worker-recruiting countries, like Germany, Belgium, Switzerland, and Austria. Second-generation educational disadvantage was found to be insignificant in the cases of Sweden, France, Australia, and Canada (OECD, 2007, pp. 79–80). This makes it clear that the original mode of labor market incorporation can have effects that go across generations (see also Portes & Rumbaut, 2006, pp. 92–101).

The OECD research also revealed substantial gender differences. In all OECD countries studied (except the USA) second-generation young women did better than their male counterparts at school. This is particularly interesting in view of the fact that young immigrant women often have less education than young immigrant men (OECD, 2007, p. 81). Schooling in host countries seems to have an important emancipatory effect for second-generation women.

In the long run, the most important question for the second generation is whether they can get decent jobs. The OECD found that young second-generation members had a higher employment probability than immigrants in the same age group, but still suffered significant disadvantage compared with young people without a migration background. Worryingly, the disadvantage seemed greatest at the top end of the qualification scale, indicating the persistence of a "glass ceiling" for people of minority ethnicity or race. Native-born children of immigrants from African countries seemed to have the greatest labor market difficulties. Members of the second generation in Europe were up to twice as likely to be unemployed as young people without a migration background (OECD, 2007, pp. 81–85).

New forms of work

However, these OECD studies refer to legally employed migrants and their descendants. They leave out the growing numbers of migrants in irregular or informal employment. The labor force dynamics of contemporary economies are based on a proliferation of employment relationships that differentiate workers on the basis of ethnicity, race, gender, and legal status. Deregulation of the economy has meant polarization into high-level, well-paid jobs and low-level jobs with few rights and little protection. Casualization, sub-contracting, spurious self-employment, and informal employment affect natives and migrants alike, but there is a clear hierarchy, in which native workers tend to be best off, followed by long-established, legally resident ethnic minorities (with citizenship or at least permanent residence rights), and then by newer legal migrants, while irregular migrants are at the bottom with situations of rightlessness and insecurity (Düvell, 2005; Reyneri, 2003).

Contrary to neo-liberal theories of the labor market, which argue that variations in employment status are due to differing levels of human capital (Browne & Misra, 2003, p. 506), research shows the importance of race, gender, class, and sexual orientation in allocating positions. The specific (and usually disadvantaged) position of migrant women is crucial to certain types of enterprise (such as the UK garment industry). An analysis of European labor market statistics found marked differences between EU and "third-country" nationals (citizens of non-EU states), based on national origins, ethnicity, gender, and legal status. The majority of third-country nationals were employed in vulnerable, low-skilled, low-paid jobs. There were sharp differences in pay between men and women, owing to women's disproportionate representation in low-pay sectors (Ayres & Barber, 2006, p. 30).

Segmentation based on race, ethnicity, gender and national origins has been a feature of labor markets ever since the post-1945 boom, but its forms have changed fundamentally. A recent study of New York City provides a striking example. The 2000 census found that immigrants made up 2.9 million (36%) of New York City's 8 million people, but no less than 47% of the city's workforce. Moreover, immigrants made up 62% of the low-wage workforce (earning between U.S.$5.15 and U.S.$7.10 an hour). The new ethnic workforce was highly diverse, with newcomers from every continent. The worst jobs were done by undocumented migrants from the Dominican Republic, Mexico, and French West Africa, who competed for precarious and exploitative posts as garment makers, supermarket workers, delivery drivers, and kitchen workers (Ness, 2005; see also Portes & Rumbaut, 2006; Waldinger, 1996).

Diversity and belonging

A crucial question for receiving countries is how immigrants and their descendants can become part of society and the nation. A second question is how the state and civil society can and should facilitate this process. Answers have varied in different countries, and obviously education has a very important part to play. The key issue is whether immigrants should be incorporated into society as *individuals*, that is, without taking account of cultural difference or group belonging, or as *communities*, that is, ethnic groups which tend to cluster together and maintain their own cultures, languages, and religions.

The starting point for understanding incorporation is historical experiences of nation-state formation: the ways in which emerging states handled difference when dealing with internal ethnic or religious minorities, conquering new territories, incorporating immigrants, or ruling people in their colonies. "National models" for dealing with ethnicity and cultural difference emerged in various countries (see Bertossi, 2007; Brubaker, 1992; Favell, 1998), and these models helped to determine how states and the public later reacted to immigrants (Castles & Davidson, 2000). For example, England's history of conquering Wales, Scotland, and Ireland, and of dealing with religious diversity led to a politically integrated state, the United Kingdom, which required political loyalty, but accepted diverse group identities (Welsh or Scottish, Protestant or Catholic).

In France, the 1789 revolution established principles of equality that rejected group identity, and aimed to include individuals as equal political subjects. In both Britain and France, however, it was the expansion of the state that created the nation – political belonging came before national identity. Germany was different: it was not united as a state until 1871, and the nation came before the state. This led to a form of ethnic belonging that was not consistent with incorporation of minorities as citizens.

By contrast, the White settler societies of the Americas and Australia were built through the dispossession of indigenous peoples, and through immigration from Europe. Incorporation of immigrants as citizens was part of their national myths. This led to models of assimilation, such as the U.S. image of the "melting pot." Of course, it was thought that only White people could be assimilated: Australia, New Zealand, Canada, and the USA all had racially selective immigration laws.

When immigration started in the post-1945 boom, incorporation of the newcomers was not a major issue. The numbers were not expected to be large, and there was a strong belief in the "controllability of difference." The "classical immigration countries" (the USA, Canada, Australia, etc.) wanted only White settlers from their "mother countries" or other northwestern European countries, and saw no problem in assimilating them. Britain, France, and the Netherlands also expected to be able to assimilate fairly small groups of immigrants from their colonies and from other European countries. Germany and other "guest worker" importers (e.g. Austria and Switzerland) did not anticipate family reunion or settlement, and therefore pursued polices of temporary admission to the labor market. Migrants were granted work-related rights (health, accident, and unemployment insurance, the right to join trade unions), but were refused social and political rights (family reunion, long-term residence entitlements, access to citizenship). This approach can be termed "differential exclusion."

But the belief in the controllability of difference proved misplaced in all these cases. In the classical immigration countries, migrants from non-Western European backgrounds tended to have disadvantaged work situations and to become concentrated in specific neighborhoods. This led to community formation and the maintenance of minority cultures and languages. Since many immigrants had become citizens, they gained electoral clout in some inner-city areas. Assimilation had clearly failed, and new approaches were needed. In European host countries, similar trends were emerging. Even in the guest worker countries, settlement was taking place despite official denials, leading to social exclusion and an enduring link between class and ethnic background.

Assimilation was replaced (initially at least) by the principle of integration, which meant recognizing that adaptation was a gradual process that required some degree of mutual accommodation. Acceptance of cultural maintenance and community formation might be a necessary stage, but the final goal was still absorption into the dominant culture – integration was often simply a slower and gentler form of assimilation. Today, of all the highly developed immigration countries, France comes closest to the assimilationist model. Elsewhere, however, there was a shift to an approach that recognized the long-term persistence of group difference.

Multiculturalism meant that immigrants should be able to participate as equals in all spheres of society, without being expected to give up their own culture, religion, and language, although usually with an expectation of conformity to certain key values. There have been two main variants. In the USA, cultural diversity and the existence of ethnic communities are officially accepted, but it is not seen as the role of the state to work for social justice or to support the maintenance of ethnic cultures. The second variant is multiculturalism as a public policy. Here, multiculturalism implies both the willingness of the majority group to accept cultural difference and state action to secure equal rights for minorities. Multiculturalism originated in Canada, and was taken up in various forms between the 1970s and the 1990s in Australia, the UK, the Netherlands, and Sweden.

However, immigrant populations and their relationship with societies and nations have developed in complex and unexpected ways. All of the different approaches to incorporation have proved problematic in one way or another, so that by the early 21st century there appeared to be a widespread "crisis of integration." Starting in the 1990s, but much more obviously from the early 2000s, policies on incorporation of immigrants and minorities have been questioned and revised. The inescapable reality of permanent settlement has led to the abandonment of the differential exclusionary approach in Germany. Immigration and citizenship laws have been reformed. While multiculturalism is rejected at the national level, local provision of special social and educational services for minorities is widespread. However, there are limits to change: Germany still rejects dual citizenship and has introduced compulsory integration measures. Austria and Switzerland still cling to exclusionary policies, although these are modified by local integration efforts. Of course, differential exclusion remains the dominant approach to foreign workers in many of the new industrial countries of Asia and the Persian Gulf.

By the early 1990s, assimilation seemed to be on the way out everywhere, except France. Democratic civil societies were thought to have an inherent trend towards multiculturalism (Bauböck, 1996). That is no longer the case – there has been a widespread backlash against multiculturalism. Canada has maintained its multicultural principles, but watered down their implementation, and Australia has gone even further in this direction. Sweden, the Netherlands, and the UK have all re-labeled policies with much greater emphasis on "integration," "social cohesion," and "core national values." The Netherlands has had perhaps the most dramatic turn-around and seems to be on the way to a new assimilationism (Vasta, 2007). The policy measures that mark the shift from multiculturalism to social cohesion include the introduction of tests on the national language and values as a precondition for permanent residence status or citizenship (in Australia, France, Germany, the UK, and the Netherlands), extension of waiting times for applying for naturalization (from two to four years in Australia), high fees for naturalization (the UK), and a shift away from allowing dual citizenship (the Netherlands).

The backlash against multiculturalism has a number of causes. One is the growing awareness of the enduring social disadvantage and marginalization of many immigrant groups – especially those of non-European origin. The dominant approach is to claim that ethnic minorities are to blame by clustering together and refusing to integrate. Another factor is the growing fear of Islam and terrorism. Events like the bomb attacks on the transport system in Madrid (2004) and London (2005) and the murder of Theo Van Gogh (who had made a film highly critical of

Islam) in the Netherlands are seen as evidence of the incompatibility of Muslim values with modern European societies.

In this interpretation, recognition of cultural diversity has had the perverse effect of encouraging ethnic separatism and the development of "parallel lives" (Cantle, 2001). A model of individual integration – based if necessary on compulsory "integration contracts" and citizenship tests – is thus seen as a way of achieving greater equality for immigrants and their children. The problem for such views, however, is that the one country that has maintained its model of individual assimilation is also experiencing dramatic problems. The minority youth riots of 2005 and 2007 in France showed that the republican model of individual integration has failed to overcome inequality and racism.

All the different approaches to incorporation of immigrants thus seem problematic: differential exclusion is useless once settlement takes place; multiculturalism is accused by its opponents of leading to persistent separatism; while a policy of assimilation into a society marked by inequality and social divisions can perpetuate marginalization and conflict. This situation actually reflects the unwillingness of host societies to deal with two issues. The first is the deep-seated cultures of racism that are a legacy of colonialism and imperialism. In times of stress, such as economic restructuring or international conflict, racism can lead to social exclusion, discrimination, and violence against minorities. The second issue is the trend to greater inequality resulting from globalization and economic restructuring. Increased international competition puts pressure on employment, working conditions, and welfare systems. At the same time neo-liberal economic policies encourage greater pay differences and reduce the capacity of states to redistribute income to reduce poverty and social disadvantage.

Taken together these factors have led to a racialization of ethnic difference: that is, blaming situations of social exclusion and conflict on the behavior and culture of minorities. Minorities may have poor employment situations, low incomes, and high rates of impoverishment. This in turn feeds into patterns of concentration in low-income neighborhoods and growing residential segregation. The existence of separate and marginal communities is then taken as evidence of failure to integrate, and this in turn is perceived as a threat to the host society. The result, as Schierup, Hansen, and Castles (2006) argue for Europe, is a "dual crisis" of national identity and the welfare state. The attempt to resolve the crisis by blaming minorities does not provide a solution. Rather it threatens the fundamental values upon which democratic societies are based.

Challenges for education

Differing approaches to immigration and the incorporation of migrants and minorities have important consequences for education. Where politicians and the public perceive migrants as temporary sojourners, education may take two forms. In cases in which family reunion is prohibited (e.g. in many Middle Eastern and Asian countries), children who are brought in by their parents may have no right to education at all – the ultimate form of exclusion. However, teachers often make efforts to include migrant children in defiance of such rules. The second variant is to provide schooling for migrant children, but to focus on maintaining the language and culture of the origin country, as a preparation for return. This implies different educational goals and segregated classes for migrant and local children – as practiced in parts of Germany up to the 1980s (Castles, 2004b). This too is an exclusionary form of education, because migrant children have separate – and generally inferior – education compared with local children. The German education policies of the guest worker period seem to be a reason for the persistence of disadvantage in today's second generation.

By contrast, countries following assimilation policies are very concerned about integrating migrant children into regular schools. In France and the USA, for example, the school has been seen as the key to achieving equal opportunities in society, because it offers a free and equal education to all. However, the claim to equality is often ideological, because the quality of schools varies considerably according to location, and educational quality is strongly influenced by class and race. Migrant children are often concentrated at the lower end of the social hierarchy, owing to the disadvantaged position of many migrant parents. Equal chances in poor-quality schools do not generally offer a passport to social mobility.

Assimilationist schooling has another flaw: by ignoring children's cultural backgrounds it may isolate them and undermine the values and culture of their parents and communities. The result can be low self-esteem and failure. U.S. sociologists have pointed out that assimilation is not a general process of incorporation into society, but actually means assimilation into a specific segment, defined according to class and race (Zhou, 1997). For instance, Hispanic children whose ties to their own ethnic culture are loosened may end up becoming members of violent gangs that draw them into drug use and criminality, while unassimilated youth who maintain traditional family values may actually be better equipped to succeed (Portes & Rumbaut, 2001; Rumbaut & Portes, 2001). Thus equal individual treatment in the school system can lead to unequal outcomes for children from disadvantaged and stigmatized groups.

Multicultural education was developed in response to the shortcomings of both exclusionary and assimilationist forms of schooling. By combining the principles of recognition of cultural difference and working for equality, it takes account of differing group backgrounds and seeks to develop the full potential of all students. Specific examples of multicultural education will be discussed in other chapters, but it is worth pointing to some general issues here.

First, as Black teachers and parents pointed out when multicultural education was introduced in Britain in the 1960s and 1970s, it can give the impression that the problems of migrant children are based on cultural dissonance rather than on racist exclusion. Such educators therefore called for antiracist education, which stressed the need to address the attitudes of White students and their parents.

Second, multicultural education faces a serious practical problem. If too much emphasis is put on learning about cultural difference, this may take time away from working on the core subjects needed for later job success. Thus multicultural education risks producing graduates with lower levels of work-relevant cultural capabilities and skills. There is a potential contradiction between the goals of cultural recognition and working for equality, which has to be carefully negotiated by educators.

Third, multicultural education is generally premised on the idea that children of migrants will settle permanently in the host country – an assumption that was largely justified until recently. But the increasing ease of travel and communication resulting from globalization undermines this assumption. As more and more people perceive themselves as members of transnational communities, and maintain economic, social, political, and cultural relationships across borders, education needs to respond with new ways of conceptualizing citizenship and belonging.

Fourth, multicultural education models are still often focused almost exclusively on providing appropriate schooling for children of legal migrants, who have a right to send their children to school in the host country. They rarely take account of the new political economy (described above) of distinct and exploitative work patterns, often characterized by informality and illegality. Schools need to find ways of offering equal opportunities to children whose parents may lack legal residence rights, and who are therefore in a precarious and irregular situation. The challenge for multicultural educators is to make the school into a tool of social inclusion – even for those marginalized by neo-liberal economic policies.

Yet, despite such dilemmas, multicultural education is undoubtedly an important step forward compared with exclusionary or assimilationist approaches to schooling for children of migrants. Other chapters of this book provide detailed analysis of both the achievements and the challenges of multicultural education. But multicultural education is much more than a model for migrant education: to achieve its objectives, it must be an education for all children, whether of majority, minority, or migrant origin, and whatever their legal status. Multicultural education means helping to create a new awareness of the diversity of contemporary society for all young people. It can assist in overcoming histories of colonialism, racism, and xenophobia, and is therefore a vital instrument for change. But, to realize this potential, educationalists must address the very real problems still inherent in multicultural education models. Most important of all they need to respond to the current powerful challenges to multiculturalism, and the drift back towards assimilationism represented by the new discourses of social cohesion.

References

Aleinikoff, T. A., & Klusmeyer, D. (Eds.). (2001). *Citizenship today: Global perspectives and practices*. Washington, DC: Carnegie Endowment for International Peace.

Ayres, R., & Barber, T. (2006). *Statistical analysis of female migration and labour market integration in the EU* (Integration of Female Immigrants in Labour Market and Society Working Paper 3). Oxford: Oxford Brookes University.

Bauböck, R. (1996). Social and cultural integration in a civil society. In R. Bauböck, A. Heller, & A. R. Zolberg (Eds.), *The challenge of diversity: Integration and pluralism in societies of immigration* (pp. 67–131). Aldershot: Avebury.

Bauböck, R., Ershøll, E., Groenendijk, K., & Waldrauch, H. (Eds.). (2006a). *Acquisition and loss of nationality: Policies and trends in 15 European states: Vol. I. Comparative analyses*. Amsterdam: Amsterdam University Press.

Bauböck, R., Ershøll, E., Groenendijk, K., & Waldrauch, H. (Eds.). (2006b). *Acquisition and loss of nationality: Policies and trends in 15 European states: Vol. II. Country analyses*. Amsterdam: Amsterdam University Press.

Bertossi, C. (2007). *French and British models of integration: Public philosophies, policies and state institutions* (Working Paper 46). Oxford: Centre on Migration, Policy and Society. Retrieved July 8, 2008, from http://compas.ox.ac.uk/

Browne, I., & Misra, J. (2003). The intersection of gender and race in the labor market. *Annual Review of Sociology, 29*, 487–513.

Brubaker, R. (1992). *Citizenship and nationhood in France and Germany*. Cambridge, MA: Harvard University Press.

Cantle, T. (2001). *Community cohesion: A report of the independent review team*. London: Home Office.

Castles, S. (2004a). The factors that make and unmake migration policy. *International Migration Review, 38*(3), 852–884.

Castles, S. (2004b). Migration, citizenship and education. In J. A. Banks (Ed.), *Diversity and citizenship education: Global perspectives* (pp. 17–48). San Francisco: Jossey-Bass/Wiley.

Castles, S., Booth, H., & Wallace, T. (1984). *Here for good: Western Europe's new ethnic minorities*. London: Pluto Press.

Castles, S., & Davidson, A. (2000). *Citizenship and migration: Globalisation and the politics of belonging*. London: Macmillan.

Castles, S., & Miller, M. J. (2009). *The age of migration: International population movements in the modern world* (4th ed.). Basingstoke, UK: Palgrave-Macmillan.

Dench, S., Hurstfield, J., Hill, D., & Akroyd, K. (2006). *Employers' use of migrant labour: Summary report*. Retrieved July 1, 2008, from http://www.employmentstudies.co.uk/pubs/summary.php?id=rdsolr0406&style=print

Düvell, F. (Ed.). (2005). *Illegal immigration in Europe: Beyond control*. Basingstoke, UK: Palgrave-Macmillan.

Favell, A. (1998). *Philosophies of integration: Immigration and the idea of citizenship in France and Britain*. London: Macmillan.

King, R., Lazaridis, G., & Tsardanidis, C. (Eds.). (2000). *Eldorado or fortress? Migration in Southern Europe*. London: Macmillan.

Ness, I. (2005). *Immigrants, unions and the new U.S. labor market*. Philadelphia: Temple University Press.

Office of the United Nations High Commissioner for Refugees (UNHCR). (2006). *The state of the world's refugees 2006: Human displacement in the new millennium*. Oxford: Oxford University Press.

Organisation for Economic Co-operation and Development (OECD). (2007). *International migration outlook: Annual report 2007*. Paris: Author.

Portes, A., Guarnizo, L. E., & Landolt, P. (1999). The study of transnationalism: Pitfalls and promise of an emergent research field. *Ethnic and Racial Studies, 22*(2), 217–237.

Portes, A., & Rumbaut, R. G. (2001). *Legacies: The story of the immigrant second generation*. Berkeley: University of California Press.

Portes, A., & Rumbaut, R. G. (2006). *Immigrant America: A portrait* (3rd ed.). Berkeley: University of California Press.

Reyneri, E. (2003). Immigration and the underground economy in new receiving South European countries: Manifold negative effects, manifold deep-rooted causes. *International Review of Sociology, 13*(1), 117–143.

Rumbaut, R. G., & Portes, A. (2001). *Ethnicities: Children of immigrants in America*. Berkeley: University of California Press.

Schierup, C. U., Hansen, P., & Castles, S. (2006). *Migration, citizenship and the European welfare state: A European dilemma*. Oxford: Oxford University Press.

United Nations Department of Economic and Social Affairs (UN/DESA) (2005). *Trends in total migrant stock: The 2005 revision*. New York: Author.

United Nations Population Division (UN/PD) (2002). *International migration report 2002* (AT/ESA/SER.A/220). New York: Author.

Vasta, E. (2007). From ethnic minorities to ethnic majority policy: Multiculturalism and the shift to assimilationism in the Netherlands. *Ethnic and Racial Studies, 30*(5), 713–740.

Waldinger, R. D. (1996). *Still the promised city? African-Americans and new immigrants in postindustrial New York*. Cambridge, MA: Harvard University Press.

Zhou, M. (1997). Segmented assimilation: Issues, controversies, and recent research on the new second generation. *International Migration Review, 31*(4), 975–1008.

4

Globalization, immigration, and schooling

Marcelo M. Suárez-Orozco
New York University, USA

Carola Suárez-Orozco
New York University, USA

Globalization is the meta-context (Bronfenbrenner, 1977) for schooling in the 21st century. In today's schools immigration is the human face of globalization. Schools the world over, in cities large and small, from New York to Beijing, from Barcelona to Toronto, from Sydney to Reggio Emilia (in northern Italy), are being transformed by growing numbers of immigrant students. And, just as schools face the challenge of educating more linguistically, culturally, and racially diverse students, globalization imposes yet another challenge to education – requiring ever more complex skills of its students in order to equip them to be competitive in a globally interlinked economy (21st Century Workforce Commission, 2000; Levy & Murnane, 2004; M. Suárez-Orozco & Sattin, 2007; Süssmuth & Meier, 2008) while nurturing them to be globally conscious and engaged citizens of the 21st century (Banks, 2004; Boix-Mansilla & Gardner, 2007).

Globalization and immigration

During the first decade of the 21st century approximately 200 million transnational migrants are living beyond the countries of their birth – and hundreds of millions more are internal migrants within the confines of ever-changing nation states (United Nations Global Commission on International Migration, 2005). Globalization has increased immigration in a variety of ways. First, the post-national integration of production, distribution, and consumption of goods and services stimulates migration because where capital flows, immigrants follow (Massey, Durand, & Malone, 2002; Sassen, 1998). Second, the new information, communication, and media technologies not only further global economic production but also stimulate migration by generating new desires, tastes, consumption practices, and lifestyle choices (C. Suárez-Orozco & Qin-Hilliard, 2004). Would-be immigrants envision better lives elsewhere and with better information mobilize to achieve them. Third, globally integrated economies are increasingly structured around a voracious appetite for foreign workers (in Northwestern Europe and Japan due to demographic considerations: low fertility rates and rapidly aging populations) both in the well-remunerated knowledge-intensive sector and in the least desirable sectors of the economy (Myers, 2007; Saxenian, 1999). Fourth, the affordability of mass transportation has put the option of migration within the reach of millions who, heretofore, could not do so. Approximately 20 people cross an international border every second. Fifth, globalization has stimulated new migration because it has produced uneven results – wage differentials, when controlled for cost-of-living differences, are in the order of 10 to 1 in many North–South migration corridors. In short, globalization structures the new migratory flows by increasingly coordinating markets, economies, social practices, and cultural models.

In the field of global migration, remarkably, the well-being and future of the children of immigrants is all too often lost in the heated debates, specialized scholarly research, and policy-making (Fuligni, 1997; García-Coll & Magnuson, 1997; Lansford, Deater-Deckard, & Bornstein, 2007; C. Suárez-Orozco & M. Suárez-Orozco, 2001; C. Suárez-Orozco, M. Suárez-Orozco, & Todorova, 2008). Yet, in the United States, over 20% of youth (Rong & Preissle, 1998) are of immigrant origin, and it is projected that by 2040 over a third of all children will be growing up in immigrant households (Hernandez, Denton & Macartney, 2007; Landale & Oropesa, 1995). But globalization's demographic echo is not only a United States phenomenon. The children of immigrants are a fast-growing sector of the child and youth population in such countries as Australia, Canada, Germany, Italy, the Netherlands, Spain, Sweden, and others (Süssmuth, 2007). These new demographic realities have important implications for education and schooling in this global era.

The "new immigration"

Immigrant youth arrive in new destinations with distinct social and cultural resources: high aspirations for education, meta-cognitive advantages afforded by a dual frame of reference, well-honed skills for developing relationships to help them negotiate unfamiliar territories, and often the abilities needed to navigate across difficult circumstances (Centrie, 2000; García-Coll & Magnuson, 1997; C. Suárez-Orozco et al., 2008; Valenzuela, 1999; Zaal, Salah & Fine, 2007). Their optimism (Kao & Tienda, 1995), high aspirations (Fuligni, 1997; Portes & Rumbaut, 2001), dedicated hard work and positive attitudes towards school (C. Suárez-Orozco & M. Suárez-Orozco, 1995), and ethic of family support for advanced learning (Li, 2004) contribute to the fact that some immigrant youth educationally outperform their native-born peers (Hernández & Charney, 1998; Steinberg, Brown, & Dornbusch, 1996). Other immigrant youth, however, encounter a variety of challenges and struggle to gain their bearings in an educational system that often puts them on the path to downward assimilation (Portes & Zhou, 1993).

The United States as a paradigmatic country of immigration provides an important case study. It is one of a handful of advanced, post-industrial democracies where immigration is at once history and destiny. By the year 2008, the foreign-stock (the foreign born, plus the U.S.-born second generation) population of the United States was over 70 million people. By then, some 38 million were foreign born. Two dominant features characterize this wave of immigration: its *intensity* (immigrants grew 57% between 1990 and 2000) and the *shift in the sources* of immigration (until the mid-1960s, nearly 90% of immigrants were Europeans or Canadians) – by 2008, 54% of immigrants were Latin Americans and more than 25% were Asians, and 11 of the top 12 countries of origin were Asian, Caribbean, and Latin American.

Immigrants today are a heterogeneous population defying easy generalizations (C. Suárez-Orozco et al., 2008). They include highly educated, skilled individuals drawn by the growth in the knowledge-intensive sectors of the economy. They are more likely to have advanced degrees than the native-born population. They come to the United States and thrive. Immigrants originating in Africa and Asia are among the best-educated and skilled individuals in the United States. They are over-represented in the category of college graduates, professionals, and people with doctorates. Fully half of all entering physics graduate students in the late 1990s were foreign born. During California's Silicon Valley boom years, 32% of all the scientists and engineers were immigrants (Saxenian, 1999). Roughly a third of all Nobel Prize winners in the United States have been immigrants. In 1999, all (100%) U.S. winners of the Nobel Prize were immigrants. Never in the history of U.S. immigration have so many immigrants done so well so fast. Within a generation, these immigrants are bypassing the traditional trans-generational modes of status mobility and establishing themselves in the well-remunerated sectors of the U.S. economy.

At the same time, the new immigration also includes large numbers of poorly schooled, semi-skilled or unskilled workers, many of them in the United States without proper documentation (illegal immigrants). In 2007, approximately 29% of all immigrants had less than a high school education. Latinos, by far the largest immigrant group, face difficult educational journeys – very worrisome indeed because their numbers continue to grow. In 1995 the U.S. Latino population was 27,521,000; it had reached 44,252,278 by 2006 – two-thirds of them immigrants or the children of immigrants (C. Suárez-Orozco & Gaytán, 2009). In 2006, Latino youngsters represented approximately 20% of all public school students – a 55% increase from 1993. The enduring inequities in the U.S. education system augur problems ahead: recent data suggest that 51% of 8th-grade English language learners, the vast majority of them Latinos, lag significantly behind Whites in reading and math (Fry, 2007). In 2005, over 40% of all Latinos had not attained a high school education (U.S. Census Bureau, 2006). As the Latino school-age population continues to grow there is an urgent need to help ease the transition of Latino youth via schooling to citizenship and the labor market. It is important to note, however, that others who come with limited educational resources also face similar significant educational challenges (Lew, 2006; Louie, 2004).

Understanding varied pathways of academic outcomes among children of immigrants

Immigrant youth arrive from multiple points of origin, adding new threads of cultural, linguistic, religious, and racial difference to the American tapestry. Some are the children of educated professional parents, while others have illiterate parents. Some received excellent schooling, while others left educational systems that were in shambles. Some escape political, religious, or ethnic persecution; others are motivated by the promise of better jobs and better educational opportunities. Some are documented migrants, while others, nearly 2 million, are unauthorized young migrants (see Bean & Lowell, 2007). Some join well-established communities with robust social supports, while others move from one migrant setting to another, forcing students to change schools often. The social and educational outcomes of immigrant youth will vary substantially depending upon the specific constellation of resources and the settlement context (Portes & Rumbaut, 2001).

The global economy is largely unforgiving to those who do not achieve post-secondary education and beyond. More than ever, and all over the world, schooling processes and outcomes shape socio-economic mobility (Bloom, 2004; LeVine, 2007). Recent studies suggest that, while some children of immigrants are successfully navigating the American educational system (Kasitiz, Mollenkopf, Waters, & Holdaway, 2008; Portes & Rumbaut, 2001; C. Suárez-Orozco et al., 2008), large numbers struggle academically, leaving schools without acquiring the tools that will enable them to function in the globally competitive labor market (Portes & Rumbaut, 2001; C. Suárez-Orozco & M. Suárez-Orozco, 2001; C. Suárez-Orozco et al., 2008).

Academic trajectories and performance are multiply determined by an alchemy of family background variables, the kinds of schools that immigrant students encounter, second language acquisition challenges, student engagement, and relational supports that together serve to undermine or, conversely, bolster academic integration and adaptation. Data from the Longitudinal Immigrant Student Adaptation (LISA – see C. Suárez-Orozco et al., 2008) assessed the academic performance and engagement of approximately 400 recently arrived immigrant youth from Asia (born in China), the Caribbean (born in the Dominican Republic and in Haiti), and Latin America (born in Mexico and in various Central American countries), considering the constellation of factors mentioned above. A mixed-methods design was deployed longitudinally over the course of five years, using triangulated data taking into consideration student, parent, and teacher perspectives to document changes over time. Below we review the variables that had the strongest implications for the schooling performance and social adaptation of immigrant youth (C. Suárez-Orozco et al., 2008).

Family background

Parental education. Parental education mattered. Highly literate parents were better equipped to guide their children in studying and in accessing and making meaning of information, and were more likely to provide additional books, a home computer, Internet access, and tutors than less educated parents who had little idea how to navigate the educational system in the new land. Students with more educated parents often came from highly competitive, rigorous educational systems with sophisticated mathematical, test-taking, and study skills. In contrast, refugee youth could arrive with interrupted schooling, having missed years of classroom experience. Other immigrant students come with literacy challenges and are unable to read or write adequately in their native language. Such varied backgrounds will have implications for the educational transition. Unsurprisingly, youth arriving from families with lower levels of education tend to struggle academically, while those who come from more literate families and with strong skills often flourish (Kasititz et al., 2008; Portes & Rumbaut, 2001; C. Suárez-Orozco et al., 2008; Wilson, 1997).

Poverty. Large numbers of immigrants must face the challenges associated with poverty (Hernandez et al., 2007). Poverty frequently coexists with other factors that augment risks, such as single-parenthood, unsafe neighborhoods, and segregated, overcrowded, and understaffed schools (Luthar, 1999). Immigrant children are more than four times as likely as native-born children to live in crowded housing conditions and three times as likely to be uninsured (Hernandez et al., 2007). Children raised in circumstances of poverty are vulnerable to an array of psychological distresses, including difficulties concentrating and sleeping, anxiety, and depression (Luthar, 1999). Such a context of heightened stressors influences the educational outcomes of immigrant-origin youth (Fuligni & Yoshikawa, 2003).

Undocumented status. Today nearly 2 million immigrant youth live in the US without proper documentation – and an estimated 3.1 million are living in households headed by at least one undocumented immigrant (Passel, 2005). Further, undocumented students often arrive after multiple family separations and traumatic border crossings (C. Suárez-Orozco, Todorova, & Louie, 2002). Once settled, many experience fear and anxiety about being apprehended, separated from their parents, and deported (Capps, Castañeda, Chaudry, & Santos, 2007). Such psychological and emotional duress can take its toll on the academic experiences of undocumented youth. Undocumented students with dreams of graduating from high school and going on to college will find that their legal status stands in the way of their access to post-secondary education (C. Suárez-Orozco et al., 2008; M. Suárez-Orozco, 1989).

School contexts

Many immigrant-origin students attend segregated schools where the majority of their peers are other immigrant students. Immigrant segregation often involves race, poverty, and linguistic isolation – so-called triple segregation (Orfield & Lee, 2006). This triple segregation is linked to reduced school resources and negative educational outcomes: low expectations, linguistic isolation, lower achievement, greater school violence, and higher drop-out rates. Such school contexts typically undermine students' capacity to concentrate, sense of security, and the ability to form trusting relationships, and hence their ability to learn. When asked to relate their perceptions of school in the new country, many spoke of crime, violence, gang activity, weapons, drug dealing, and racial conflicts (C. Suárez-Orozco et al., 2008). Under such conditions, students are unable to concentrate or engage with the task of learning. In the LISA study, students who attended schools where they perceived such problems were more likely to disengage – low-achieving students and those whose performance precipitously declined over their time in U.S. schools reported experiencing the most school violence and problems. We also found a strong correlation between students' perceptions of school problems and a variety of objective indicators of school performance (C. Suárez-Orozco et al., 2008). Indicators of school inequality, including percentages of low-income students (eligible for free or reduced-price lunch), racial and ethnic segregation, percentages of inexperienced teachers (out-of-subject certification rate), greater-than-average school size, the drop-out rate, daily attendance, higher-than-average suspension and expulsion rates, percentage of students performing below proficiency on the state-administered English language arts and math standardized tests, and a significant achievement gap on the standardized exam between one or more ethnic groups that attend the school, were linked to lower student performance (C. Suárez-Orozco et al., 2008). As Orfield and Lee (2006) have established, there is a strong link between segregation and poverty and graduation rates. In the majority of schools, those that are highly segregated provide vastly unequal opportunities to their students.

The various academic performance trajectories of the LISA sample were linked to different levels of triple segregation and school inequalities. "Low achievers" and "precipitous decliners" attended the poorest and most racially segregated schools. "High achievers" were least likely to attend low-income and racially segregated schools; even so, a sizeable proportion did so (C. Suárez-Orozco et al., 2008). Indicators of school quality were consistent with poor performance on standardized tests. The LISA study found that fewer than one-third of all the students in low-quality schools reached proficiency level or higher on the English language arts exam. LISA students from different countries of origin attended schools that had different patterns of exam results. While Chinese students attended schools where 59% of the schools' students performed at the proficient or above level on the state English language arts standardized exam, only 37% of Haitians, 20% of Dominicans and Central Americans, and amazingly 16% of Mexicans did so. We found that a higher percentage of high-achieving immigrant students attended schools where more students pass the state exams (47%), whereas low achievers and precipitous decliners attended schools where only a small percentage of their students passed these tests (21% and 25%, respectively) (C. Suárez-Orozco et al., 2008).

We found a significant relationship between schools that were both poor and racially and linguistically segregated and achievement outcomes including both grades and students' Woodcock Johnson Test of Achievement scores (C. Suárez-Orozco et al., 2008). Segregation places students at a significant disadvantage as they strive to learn a new language, master the necessary skills to pass high-stakes tests, accrue graduation credits, get into college, and attain the skills needed to compete in workplaces increasingly shaped by the demands of the new global economy. Unfortunately, all too many schools that serve the children of immigrants, like schools that serve other disadvantaged students, are those that are designated to teach "other people's children" (Delpit, 1995). Such segregated, sub-optimal schools offer the very least to those who need the very most, structuring and reinforcing inequality (Oakes, 1985).

Language

Most immigrant youth are second language learners. Research has well documented that it takes 5 to 7 years of optimal academic instruction to develop academic second language skills comparative to native-born samples (Cummins, 1991). Yet immigrant students do not typically encounter robust second language acquisition educational programs. Revealingly, the National Assessment of Educational Progress (NAEP) data showed that 70% of English language learners (ELLs) tested in the 4th grade scored "below basic" in reading while 1% scored at the "advanced" level, and 71% of the ELLs in the 8th grade scored "below basic" while 0.1% scored at the "advanced" level (NAEP, 2008). LISA data revealed a similar reality: across all groups, after 7 years on average in the US, 7% of the sample had developed academic English skills comparable to those of their native-born English-speaking peers (Carhill, Suárez-Orozco, & Páez, in press; C. Suárez-Orozco et al., 2008).

Academic language difficulties present particular challenges for performance in the current context of educational tracking systems. Even when immigrant students are able to participate in mainstream classrooms, their academic language skills may still be developing. Many struggle with missing subtleties in lectures and discussions, reading more slowly than native speakers, and experiencing difficulty in academic writing. The Program for International Student Assessment (PISA) study quantified the comparative disadvantage of immigrant youth across 17 countries, showing that language-minority immigrant youth are on average one year behind their peers in various measures of academic achievement (Organisation for Economic Co-operation and Development [OECD], 2003).

For second language learners in the United States, high-stakes tests have become "de facto language policy," shaping their curriculum and daily instruction in a myriad of ways; many are tested before their skills are adequately developed (Menken, 2008). Second language acquisition issues can mask the actual skills and knowledge of immigrant youth. High-stakes tests such as the Regents exams in New York or the MCAS in Massachusetts and other tests have real implications for drop-out rates as well as college access.

With more time to develop academic language skills and more flexibility between educational tracks, however, immigrant students have been shown to sustain high achievement trajectories (Crul, 2007). The nearly exclusive focus on learning English and performance on high-stakes tests has led to a neglect of the immense opportunity immigrant youth have to contribute to a multilingual and multicultural society in the age of global interdependence. As a consequence of this neglect, immigrants typically lose their native language competencies by the second generation in the US (Portes & Hao, 1998). In a globalized economy where a second language has become a marketplace advantage, the US remains a "cemetery for languages" (Lieberson, 1981).

Student engagement

Certainly the challenges of poverty, segregation, and poor schools and the frustrations of learning a new language are daunting and can derail many a student. Beyond such structural contexts, how does individual agency matter? In recent years, a corpus of literature has pointed to individual level factors in considering the role of academic engagement in academic adaptation. Engagement is the extent to which students are connecting to what they are learning, how they are learning it, and who they are learning it with (Fredricks, Blumenfeld, & Paris, 2004). Highly engaged students are actively involved in their education, completing and internalizing the tasks required to perform well in school. Somewhat engaged students may be doing "good enough" work but not reaching their full potential. In cases of more extreme academic disengagement, a student's disinterest, erratic attendance, and missed or incomplete assignments can lead to failure in multiple courses, an outcome that often foreshadows dropping out of school (Rumberger, 2004). Academic disengagement may not be immediate but rather may occur over time in response to long-term difficulties in community, school, and family circumstances.

Engagement is a broad dimension that has been used in the social sciences in a variety of ways. Cognitive engagement is the degree to which the students are engrossed and intellectually involved in what they are learning (C. Suárez-Orozco et al., 2008). Cognitive engagement is the antithesis of "being bored" in school, and data show that attitudes toward school and academic self-efficacy are important in fostering student academic involvement (Schunk, 1991). LISA data revealed that cognitive engagement is a significant predictor of whether or not students put effort into their studies (C. Suárez-Orozco et al., 2008).

Relational engagement is the extent to which students feel connected to their teachers, peers, and others in schools. Such relationships are important for the academic adaptation of students (Levitt, Guacci-Franco, & Levitt, 1994). Social relations can provide a sense of belonging, emotional support, tangible assistance, guidance, role modeling, and positive feedback (Wills, 1985). The immigrant students who are most likely to adapt successfully to school are able to forge meaningful, positive relationships at school. Relationships in school can play a role in promoting socially competent behavior in the classroom and in fostering academic engagement and achievement. LISA data revealed that students who reported better school-based relations were more behaviorally engaged in their studies (C. Suárez-Orozco et al., 2008). Relational engagement also bolstered cognitive engagement. Students with better relationships in school found their academic work more interesting and engaging (C. Suárez-Orozco et al., 2008). Academic self-efficacy – a feeling of mastery over learning – was also highly related to greater relational engagement in the LISA study. The more meaningful, nurturing relationships students had with teachers and peers at school, the more they felt able to tackle learning (C. Suárez-Orozco et al., 2008).

Academic engagement and what we term "behavioral engagement" are often used somewhat interchangeably (Fredricks et al., 2004). Behavioral engagement, in our view, is a component of academic engagement that specifically reflects students' participation and efforts to perform academic tasks. When students do their best on class work and homework, turn in assignments on time, pay attention, behave appropriately in class, and maintain good attendance, they are behaviorally engaged.

We assessed whether the students completed the tasks necessary to be successful in school, including attending class, participating in discussions and classroom activities, and completing homework and course assignments (C. Suárez-Orozco et al., 2008). Behavioral engagement is highly correlated with grades (C. Suárez-Orozco et al., 2008). Longitudinally, LISA found a pattern of accelerating behavioral disengagement for the sample as a whole (C. Suárez-Orozco et al., 2008). There was little difference in the amount of effort boys and girls expended in their studies initially. Over time, however, girls maintained their levels of behavioral engagement while boys were more likely to disengage (C. Suárez-Orozco et al., 2008). High-achieving students were significantly more behaviorally engaged in school than were the low or precipitously declining performers.

Students with supportive school-based relationships were more likely to expend greater effort on their schoolwork. Cognitive engagement also contributed to behavioral engagement – when students were curious and interested in their schoolwork, they were more likely to try harder. As expected, school problems interfered with behavioral engagement – the greater the students' perceptions of school problems, the less engaged they were in their studies.

Social supports

From the time of arrival in their new country, social supports and networks of relations provide families with tangible aid, guidance, and advice, as well as emotional sustenance. These supports are critical for newcomers for whom the new environment can be disorienting. Positive relationships maintain and enhance self-esteem, while providing acceptance, approval, and a sense of belonging. During migration, extended family members – godparents, aunts, uncles, older cousins, and the like – are often important sources of tangible support. Family cohesion and the maintenance of a well-functioning system of supervision, authority, and mutuality can shape the well-being and social outcomes of children.

No family is an island, so wellness is enhanced when it is part of a larger community offering what Felton Earls termed "community agency" (Earls, 1997). For immigrant youth, community agency can inoculate against the toxic elements in their new settings (DeVos, 1992). In immigrant communities, these organizations are often associated with churches or religious organizations. Sociologist Min Zhou reports that community-based organizations serving Latino youth in the US often focus on problem behaviors such as gang interventions or pregnancy prevention. In contrast, however, community-based organizations serving Asian youth tend to emphasize proactive activities such as SAT preparation and math and English tutoring (Zhou & Li, 2004).

Peers can serve as both positive and negative social capital (Portes, 1998). Peers can encourage maladaptive behavior, promote drug use, and discourage competent academic engagement. In this case, peers serve to distract their classmates from performing optimally in school (Gibson, Gándara, & Koyama, 2004). Peers may contribute to unsafe school and community environments, which can undermine students' ability to concentrate, their sense of security, and their ability to experience trusting relationships in school. On the positive side, however, peer relationships can prove to be powerful role models, as they can provide a sense of belonging and tangible help (Gibson et al., 2004; Stanton-Salazar, 2004). For new immigrant students, the companionship of co-nationals is important as a source of information on school culture (C. Suárez-Orozco, Pimentel, & Martin, 2009). Peers can act as "vital conduits" (Stanton-Salazar, 2004) of information to disoriented newcomers. Peers not only buffer the loneliness new arrivals often experience but also can enhance self-confidence and self-efficacy, providing the sustenance that nourishes the development of new psychosocial competencies (C. Suárez-Orozco, Pimentel, & Martin, 2009).

Mentoring relationships are often important in the lives of immigrant youth (Crul, 2007; Rhodes, 2002; C. Suárez-Orozco et al., 2008). In stressed families with limited social resources, mentors serve to support healthier relationships by alleviating pressure on the family (Roffman, Suárez-Orozco, & Rhodes, 2003). Bicultural mentors can serve to bridge the old and new cultures (Crul, 2007). Bicultural mentors act as founts of information about the new cultural rules of engagement. Mentors can heal ruptures in relationships that have resulted from long immigrant separations and complicated reunifications. Since immigrant parents are often not available given their work schedules, the guidance and affection from a mentor serve to fill the void in the life of a youngster (Crul, 2007). Mentoring relationships have been shown to reduce substance abuse, aggressive behavior, and delinquency (Rhodes, 2002). Research suggests that college-educated immigrant-origin mentors help their protégés to perform better in school by helping them with homework, providing informed advice about access, and role modeling (Crul, 2007; C. Suárez-Orozco et al., 2008).

New skills for the global era

The next generation, immigrant and native alike, will need a new set of skills, competencies, and sensibilities to be fully engaged citizens in the economies and societies of the 21st century. The global workplace requires much more than simple rote memorization, following of hierarchical instructions, and steady work habits idealized in 20th-century education (Cheng, 2007). It demands the capacity to think analytically and creatively both within a single domain and in an interdisciplinary manner. Because globalization, far from homogenizing the world (Jenkins, 2004; Watson, 2004), is making difference normative, it requires the ability to work with people from diverse backgrounds and understand cultural, historical, and global patterns (Gärdenfors, 2007; Süssmuth, 2007). Formal education matters more than ever before (Bloom, 2004; LeVine, 2007). While a hundred years ago youth, including vast majorities of immigrant youth, could (and routinely did) drop out of school without hampering their futures, today the penalties for so doing are substantial.

The Gates Foundation (2006) has called for a reappraisal of the "three Rs" of education. Until the end of the last century, students needed to be grounded in reading, 'riting, and 'rithmetic. But in order to engage learners and prepare them for the new economy, schools must provide students with the new three Rs: *rigor* in challenging classes, *relevance* to engaging topics that "relate clearly to their lives in today's rapidly changing world," and *relationships* with adults "who know them, look out for them, and push them to achieve." We concur: all children should attend schools that are rigorous and engaging, as well as safe and welcoming. Schools need to maintain high standards and expectations for all students. Children now need the tools to learn how to learn so they may become the lifelong learners they need to be to succeed in the new knowledge-intensive economy.

The fortunes of youth growing up in different regions of the world will be demonstrably linked by ever more powerful global socio-economic, political, and demographic interconnections. In cities like Toronto, London, and Berlin, cross-cultural flows are increasingly normative. Every morning in New York City, youth from more than 190 countries get up to go to school, marking the first time in human history that one city represents practically every corner of the planet (Linares, 2006). Youth now interact and exchange ideas with peers around the corner or around the world, wear similar clothing, share tastes in music, and gravitate towards the same Web sites. New information, communication, and media technologies are the main tools youth use to connect with one another instantaneously. These tools shape new cognitive and meta-cognitive styles and social patterns of interaction.

These new tools and the digitalization of data have another global effect with deep consequences for formal education: They are putting a huge premium on knowledge-intensive work and making it possible for entire economic sectors to go global (Levy & Murnane, 2004). Data for a tax company in Boston can be entered in Bangalore; X-rays for a hospital in Brussels can be read and analyzed in Buenos Aires. Fewer jobs are strictly local now, as larger sectors of the economy outsource and offshore work to other regions of the world (Friedman, 2005).

Although much of the concern in the United States about globalization and education focuses on competition – how the country can, for example, maintain its global edge – competition is, in fundamental ways, the least of our problems. In today's globally interconnected world, issues that place youth at risk in China can lead to disaster in Toronto – for example, the severe acute respiratory syndrome (SARS) epidemic that originated in Guangdong Province, China, in November 2002 quickly spread globally, claiming victims half a world away including in Montreal, Canada.

As Bernard Hugonnier (2007) has noted, "with globalization some issues can no longer be solved at the national level" (p. 151). Today's challenge is collaborating to solve global problems that spill over national boundaries: global warming, environmental degradation, sustainability, deep poverty, infectious disease, refugee flows, and terrorism are thoroughly globalized problems. In order to lead engaged, fulfilled, ethical lives in the age of globalization, all students, immigrant and native alike, will need an array of new skills, competencies, and sensibilities.

Critical thinking skills

Levy and Murnane (2004) have argued that "expert thinkers" – those with the skills and sensibilities to solve "problems for which there are no rule-based solutions" – will have an edge in the global era (p. 167). The expert thinkers tomorrow must, *inter alia*, feel at ease working with mathematical and statistical tools that enable them to understand – and, in some cases, manage – complex data and ideas in multiple domains. For example, to comprehend how global warming rapidly became a threat students need a basic understanding of the chemistry and physics of gases, but also of the elementals of environmental science, population dynamics, and a general knowledge of development and the economics of growth. They need to master the concept of the scientific method in order to become informed consumers and in some cases practitioners of hands-on science (M. Suárez-Orozco & Sattin, 2007).

The complexity of challenges moving forward necessitates solutions that incorporate many different disciplinary perspectives. As Howard Gardner (2007) argues, the "synthetic mind" might turn out to be one of the most important minds for the future. While it is common for schools to link concepts from science and math and integrate social studies and language arts curricula, educators must begin to think about and elucidate connections among all four subject areas.

Communication skills

Students need to learn to effectively communicate and respectfully interact with people of different races, national origins, and religions (see Gärdenfors, 2007; Süssmuth, 2007). They should develop a familiarity with other cultures and religious traditions, values, kinship systems, systems of governance, and communication styles. Technology has opened up many avenues to link students in one classroom to another classroom across the globe, and assignments that require international collaboration, facilitating electronic pen pals, and setting up exchange programs, are just some of the ways schools can promote this kind of learning. Most importantly, students must use this knowledge to act ethically and in a globally conscious manner, and schools must take responsibility for helping students reflect on and understand their rights and responsibilities as citizens of an increasingly heterogeneous global society (Boix-Mansilla & Gardner, 2007; Hugonnier, 2007).

Language skills

Fluency in more than one language and culture is no longer an option – it is a prerequisite for global engagement (Süssmuth, 2007). Many schools, particularly in the United States, do students a disservice by providing inadequate foreign language training and shallow exposure to cultures outside the English-speaking world. School systems must train and attract high-quality language instructors, and provide a host of language options to equip students with the language skills and cultural awareness they need to live in a multicultural, multilingual, globally interconnected world. Immigrant-origin students and parents are a great resource and must be recognized as such: they add to the cultural and linguistic stock of the nation.

Collaborative skills

Working collaboratively in a variety of environments has never been more important both for securing a good job and for responsible citizenship (Cheng, 2007; Hugonnier, 2007; Levy & Murnane, 2004; Süssmuth, 2007). Group work and cooperative learning, in which the teacher becomes a facilitator rather than an instructor, need to play an ever-expanding role, replacing traditional "chalk and talk" pedagogical methods that confine students to their desks and dissuade them from interacting with peers in their own classroom or around the world.

Technology skills

Advanced technological skills are no longer optional for students in the 21st century. Schools must embed technology across the curriculum and view mastery of technology alongside literacy and numeracy as skills required of all graduates. In addition, schools need to take some responsibility for improving students' information literacy and helping them develop into discerning, savvy media consumers.

Thus, globalization requires that schools train ever more diverse students to greater levels of skills and competencies. Education for the global era is an education for lifelong cognitive, behavioral, and ethical engagement with the world (C. Suárez-Orozco et al., 2008). For diverse youth to develop the ethics, skills, sensibilities, and competencies needed for engagement, schools must rigorously nurture curiosity, cognitive flexibility, toleration of ambiguity, and cross-cultural skills (Süssmuth, 2007). From that alchemy will follow citizens who are culturally sophisticated and ethically grounded in the new global logic of the 21st century.

References

21st Century Workforce Commission (2000). *A nation of opportunity: Building America's 21st century workforce.* Retrieved February 1, 2000, from http://digitalcommons.ilr.cornell.edu/cgi/viewcontent.cgi?article=1003&context=key_workplace

Banks, J. A. (Ed.). (2004). *Diversity and citizenship education: Global perspectives.* San Francisco: Jossey-Bass.

Bean, F., & Lowell, L. (2007). Unauthorized migration. In M. C. Waters, R. Ueda, & H. B. Marrow (Eds.), *The new Americans: A guide to immigration since 1965* (pp. 70–82). Cambridge, MA: Harvard University Press.

Bloom, D. (2004). Globalization and education: An economic perspective. In M. Suárez-Orozco & D. Qin-Hilliard (Eds.), *Globalization* (pp. 56–77). Berkeley: University of California Press.

Boix-Mansilla, V., & Gardner, H. (2007). From teaching globalization to nurturing global consciousness. In M. M. Suárez-Orozco (Ed.), *Learning in the global era: International perspectives on globalization and education* (pp. 195–212). Berkeley: University of California Press.

Bronfenbrenner, U. (1977). Toward an experimental ecology of human development. *American Psychologist, 32*, 513–531.

Capps, R. M., Castañeda, R., Chaudry, A., & Santos, R. (2007). *The impact of immigration raids on America's children.* Washington, DC: Urban Institute.

Carhill, A., Suárez-Orozco, C., & Páez, M. (in press). Explaining English language proficiency among adolescent immigrant students. *American Educational Research Journal.*

Centrie, C. (2000). Free spaces unbound: Families, community, and Vietnamese high school students' identities. In L. Weiss & M. Fine (Eds.), *Construction sites: Spaces for excavating race, class, and gender among urban youth* (pp. 65–83). New York: Teachers College Press.

Cheng, K. (2007). The postindustrial workplace and challenges to education. In M. M. Suárez-Orozco (Ed.), *Learning in the global era: International perspectives on globalization and education* (pp. 175–191). Berkeley: University of California Press.

Crul, M. (2007). The integration of immigrant youth. In M. M. Suárez-Orozco (Ed.), *Learning in the global era: International perspectives on globalization and education* (pp. 213–231). Berkeley: University of California Press.

Cummins, J. (1991). Language development and academic learning. In L. M. Malavé & G. Duquette (Eds.), *Language, culture, and cognition* (pp. 161–175). Clevedon, UK: Multilingual Matters.

Delpit, L. (1995). *Other people's children: Cultural conflict in the classroom.* New York: New Press.

DeVos, G. (1992). *Social cohesion and alienation: Minorities in the United States and Japan.* Boulder, CO: Westview Press.

Earls, F. (1997, November/December). Tighter, safer, neighborhoods. *Harvard Magazine,* 14–15.

Fredricks, J. A., Blumenfeld, P. C., & Paris, A. H. (2004). School engagement: Potential of the concept, state of the evidence. *Review of Educational Research, 74*(1), 54–109.

Friedman, T. L. (2005). *The world is flat: A brief history of the twenty-first century.* New York: Farrar, Straus & Giroux.

Fry, R. (2007). *The changing racial and ethnic composition of U.S. public schools.* Washington, DC: Pew Hispanic Center.

Fuligni, A. (1997). The academic achievement of adolescents from immigrant families: The roles of family background, attitudes, and behavior. *Child Development, 69*(2), 351–363.

Fuligni, A. J., & Yoshikawa, H. (2003). Socioeconomic resources, parenting, and child development among immigrant families. In M. Bornstein & R. Bradley (Eds.), *Socioeconomic status, parenting, and child development* (pp. 107–124). Mahwah, NJ: Lawrence Erlbaum.

García-Coll, C., & Magnuson, K. (1997). The psychological experience of immigration: A developmental perspective. In A. Booth, A. C. Crouter, & N. Landale (Eds.), *Immigration and the family* (pp. 91–132). Mahwah, NJ: Lawrence Erlbaum.

Gärdenfors, P. (2007). Understanding cultural patterns. In M. M. Suárez-Orozco (Ed.), *Learning in the global era: International perspectives on globalization and education* (pp. 67–84). Berkeley: University of California Press.

Gardner, H. (2007). *Five minds for the future.* Cambridge, MA: Harvard Business School.

Gates Foundation. (2006). The 3Rs solution. Retrieved August 1, 2006, from www.gatesfoundation.org/Education/RelatedInfo/3Rs_Solution.htm

Gibson, M., Gándara, P., & Koyama, J. P. (2004). *School connections: U.S. Mexican youth, peers, and school adjustment.* New York: Teachers College Press.

Hernández, D., & Charney, E. (Eds.). (1998). *From generation to generation: The health and well-being of children of immigrant families.* Washington, DC: National Academy Press.

Hernandez, D., Denton, N., & Macartney, S. (2007). *Family circumstances of children in immigrant families: Looking to the future of America.* New York: Guilford Press.

Hugonnier, B. (2007). Globalization and education: Can the world meet the challenge? In M. M. Suárez-Orozco (Ed.), *Learning in the global era: International perspectives on globalization and education* (pp. 137–157). Berkeley: University of California Press.

Jenkins, H. (2004). Pop cosmopolitanism: Mapping cultural flows in an age of media convergence. In M. Suárez-Orozco & D. Qin-Hilliard (Eds.), *Globalization* (pp. 114–140). Berkeley: University of California Press.

Kao, G., & Tienda, M. (1995). Optimism and achievement: The educational performance of immigrant youth. *Social Science Quarterly, 76*(1), 1–19.

Kasitiz, P., Mollenkopf, J., Waters, M., & Holdaway, J. (2008). *Inheriting the city: The children of immigrants come of age*. Cambridge, MA and New York: Harvard University Press & Russell Sage Foundation.

Landale, N. S., & Oropesa, R. S. (1995). *Immigrant children and the children of immigrants: Inter- and intra-ethnic group differences in the United States* (Population Research Group [PRG] Research Paper 95-2). East Lansing: Michigan State University.

Lansford, J., Deater-Deckard, K., & Bornstein, M. (Eds.). (2007). *Immigrant families in contemporary society*. New York: Guilford Press.

LeVine, R. A. (2007). The global spread of women's schooling: Effects on learning, literacy, health, and children. In M. Suárez-Orozco (Ed.), *Learning in the global era: International perspectives on globalization and education* (pp. 121–136). Berkeley: University of California Press.

Levitt, M. J., Guacci-Franco, N., & Levitt, J. L. (1994). Social support and achievement in childhood and early adolescence: A multicultural study. *Journal of Applied Developmental Psychology, 15*, 207–222.

Levy, F., & Murnane, R. (2004). *The new division of labor: How computers are creating the next job market*. Princeton, NJ: Princeton University Press.

Lew, J. (2006). *Asian Americans in class: Charting the achievement gap among Korean American youths*. New York: Teachers College Press.

Li, J. (2004). "I learn and I grow big": Chinese preschoolers' purpose for learning. *International Journal of Behavioral Development, 28*(2), 116–128.

Lieberson, L. (1981). *Language diversity and language contact: Essays by Stanley Lieberson*. Stanford, CA: Stanford University Press.

Linares, G. (2006, December 9). *Findings from the mayor's office of immigrant affairs*. Paper presented at the conference on Race and Immigration: Challenges and Opportunities for the New American Majority, El Museo del Barrio, New York.

Louie, V. S. (2004). *Compelled to excel: Immigration, education, and opportunity among Chinese Americans*. Stanford, CA: Stanford University Press.

Luthar, S. (1999). *Poverty and children's adjustment*. Thousand Oaks, CA: Sage.

Massey, D. S., Durand, J., & Malone, N. J. (2002). *Beyond smoke and mirrors: Mexican immigration in an era of economic integration*. New York: Russell Sage Foundation.

Menken, K. (2008). *English learners left behind: Standardized testing as language policy*. Clevedon, UK: Multilingual Matters.

Myers, D. (2007). *Immigrants and boomers: Forging a new social contract for the future of America*. New York: Russell Sage Foundation.

National Assessment of Educational Progress (NAEP). (2008). *The nation's report card*. Retrieved March 11, 2008, from http://nces.ed.gov/nationsreportcard

Oakes, J. (1985). *Keeping track: How schools restructure inequality* (2nd ed.). Hartford, CT: Yale University Press.

Orfield, G., & Lee, C. (2006). *Racial transformation and the changing nature of segregation*. Cambridge, MA: Civil Rights Project at Harvard University.

Organisation for Economic Co-operation and Development (OECD). (2003). *Where students succeed: A comparative review of performance and engagement in PISA 2003*. Retrieved December 11, 2003, from http://www.oecd.org/document/44/0,3343,en_32252351_32236173_36599916_1_1_1_1,00.html

Passel, J. S. (2005). *Size and characteristics of the unauthorised migrant population in the U.S.* Pew Hispanic Center. Retrieved December 4, 2008 from http://pewhispanic.org/reports/report.php?ReportID=61

Portes, A. (1998). Social capital: Its origins and applications in modern sociology. *Annual Review of Sociology, 24,* 1–24.

Portes, A., & Hao, L. (1998). E pluribus unum: Bilingualism and loss of language in the second generation. *Sociology of Education, 71,* 269–294.

Portes, A., & Rumbaut, R. G. (2001). *Legacies: The story of the second generation.* Berkeley: University of California Press.

Portes, A., & Zhou, M. (1993). The new second generation: Segmented assimilation and its variants. *The Annals of the American Academy of Political and Social Science, 530*(1), 74–96.

Rhodes, J. E. (2002). *Stand by me: The risks and rewards of youth mentoring relationships.* Cambridge, MA: Harvard University Press.

Roffman, J., Suárez-Orozco, C., & Rhodes, J. (2003). Facilitating positive development in immigrant youth: The role of mentors and community organizations. In D. Perkins, L. M. Borden, J. G. Keith, & F. A. Villaruel (Eds.), *Positive youth development: Creating a positive tomorrow* (pp. 90–117). Brockton, MA: Kluwer Press.

Rong, X. L., & Preissle, J. (1998). *Educating immigrant students: What we need to know to meet the challenges.* Thousand Oaks, CA: Corwin Press.

Rumberger, R. (2004). Why students drop out of school. In G. Orfield (Ed.), *Dropouts in America: Confronting the graduation rate crisis* (pp. 131–156). Cambridge, MA: Harvard Education Press.

Sassen, S. (1998). *Globalization and its discontents: Essays on the new mobility of people and money.* New York: New Press.

Saxenian, A. (1999). *Silicon Valley's new immigrant entrepreneurs.* San Francisco: Public Policy Institute of California.

Schunk, D. H. (1991). Self-efficacy and academic motivation. *Educational Psychologist, 26,* 207–231.

Stanton-Salazar, R. S. (2004). Social capital among working-class minority students. In M. A. Gibson, P. Gándara, & J. P. Koyama (Eds.), *School connections: U.S. Mexican youth, peers, & school achievement* (pp. 18–38). New York: Teachers College Press.

Steinberg, S., Brown, B. B., & Dornbusch, S. M. (1996). *Beyond the classroom.* New York: Simon & Schuster.

Suárez-Orozco, C., & Gaytán, F. (2009). *Preface Latinos: Remaking America.* Berkeley: University of California Press.

Suárez-Orozco, C., Pimentel, A., & Martin, M. (2009). The significance of relationships: Academic engagement and achievement among newcomer immigrant youth. *Teachers College Record, 111*(3), 5–6. Retrieved September 26, 2008, from http://www.tcrecord.org (ID No. 15342)

Suárez-Orozco, C., & Qin-Hilliard, D. B. (2004). The cultural psychology of academic engagement: Immigrant boys' experiences in U.S. schools. In N. Way & J. Chu (Eds.), *Adolescent boys in context* (pp. 295–316). New York: New York University Press.

Suárez-Orozco, C., & Suárez-Orozco, M. (1995). *Transformations: Immigration, family life, and achievement motivation among Latino adolescents.* Stanford, CA: Stanford University Press.

Suárez-Orozco, C., & Suárez-Orozco, M. (2001). *Children of immigration.* Cambridge, MA: Harvard University Press.

Suárez-Orozco, C., Suárez-Orozco, M., & Todorova, I. (2008). *Learning a new land: Immigrant students in American society.* Cambridge, MA: Harvard University Press.

Suárez-Orozco, C., Todorova, I., & Louie, J. (2002). Making up for lost time: The experience of separation and reunification among immigrant families. *Family Process, 41*(4), 625–643.

Suárez-Orozco, M. (1989). *Central American refugees and U.S. high schools: A psychosocial study of motivation and achievement.* Stanford, CA: Stanford University Press.

Suárez-Orozco, M., & Sattin, C. (2007). Introduction: Learning in the global era. In M. M. Suárez-Orozco (Ed.), *Learning in the global era: International perspectives on globalization and education* (pp. 1–43). Berkeley: University of California Press.

Süssmuth, R. (2007). On the need for teaching intercultural skills: Challenges for education in a globalizing world. In M. M. Suárez-Orozco (Ed.), *Learning in the global era: International perspectives on globalization and education* (pp. 195–212). Berkeley: University of California Press.

Süssmuth, R., & Meier, J. (Eds.). (2008). *Immigrant students can succeed: Lessons from around the globe.* Berlin & Gütersloh: Bertelsmann Foundation.

United Nations Global Commission on International Migration. (2005). *Migration in an interconnected world: New directions for action.* Geneva: Switzerland GCIM Secretariat.

U.S. Census Bureau. (2006). Languages spoken at home. Retrieved May 12, 2006, from http://factfinder.census.gov/servlet/STTable?_bm=y&-geo_id=01000US&-qr_name=ACS_2006_EST_G00_S1601&-ds_name=ACS_2006_EST_G00_

Valenzuela, A. (1999). Gender roles and settlement activities among children and their immigrant families. *American Behavioral Scientist, 42*(4), 720–742.

Watson, J. L. (2004). Globalization in Asia: Anthropological perspectives. In M. Suárez-Orozco & D. Qin-Hilliard (Eds.), *Globalization* (pp. 141–172). Berkeley: University of California Press.

Wills, T. A. (1985). Supportive functions of interpersonal relationships. In S. Cohen & S. L. Syme (Eds.), *Social support and health* (pp. 61–82). Orlando, FL: Academic Press.

Wilson, W. (1997). *When work disappears: The world of the new urban poor.* New York: Vintage Books.

Zaal, M., Salah, T., & Fine, M. (2007). The weight of the hyphen: Freedom, fusion and responsibility embodied by young Muslim-American women during a time of surveillance. *Applied Developmental Sciences, 11*(3), 164–177.

Zhou, M., & Li, X. Y. (2004). Ethnic language schools and development of supplementary education in the immigrant Chinese community in the United States. In C. Suárez-Orozco & I. Todorova (Eds.), *Understanding the social worlds of immigrant youth: New directions for youth development* (Vol. 100, pp. 57–73). New York: Jossey-Bass.

Part 2

Multicultural education and diversity across nations

5

Multicultural education in the United States

Historical realities, ongoing challenges, and transformative possibilities

Sonia Nieto
University of Massachusetts, Amherst, USA

In the US cultural diversity (the coexistence of people of many different ethnic, racial, and social-class backgrounds) and pluralism (the need for them to live together with common ideals and in the best interests of the public good) have been both historic realities and ongoing challenges. In fact, the American creed of *E Pluribus Unum* (out of many one) is the very bedrock of U.S. society. This creed is based on the belief that the nation must be simultaneously supportive of pluralism and dedicated to unity. In spite of this ideal, how to handle diversity has been hotly contested throughout U.S. history.

From the idea that people of all backgrounds should become a "melting pot" to battles over whether English should be the official language, the history of the United States is replete with examples of vastly different approaches to what some have seen as the "problem" and others as the "promise" of diversity. The history of the United States has consequently been based on competing principles. One, the ideology of White supremacy, has been evident through a brutal history including the virtual extermination of Native people, the slavery of Africans, and other inequities suffered by immigrants and other marginalized groups. The second, the ideology of cultural pluralism and equality, has led to unparalleled advances, mainly as a result of sustained struggles, primarily on the part of those most directly affected, for the abolition of slavery, universal suffrage, workers' rights, disability equity, LGBTQI (lesbian, gay, bisexual, transgender, queer, questioning, and intersex) rights, and other human and civil advances (Feagin, 2002; Takaki, 1993; Zinn, 2005).

The "American dilemma" – the juxtaposition of the ideals of equality and fairness with the realities of slavery, racism, and other oppressive conditions – was eloquently articulated by Gunnar Myrdal (1944) in his comprehensive study of the lives of African Americans in the 1940s. This groundbreaking study powerfully captured the challenges of pluralism and unity and the need to confront the manifestations of inequality. The attempt to live by both diversity and unity provides the theoretical and moral foundations for cultural pluralism and social justice in the United States, and forms the basis for multicultural education as it developed in the United States.

Another defining ideal of the United States dating as far back as the mid-19th century has been the belief that public schools could be, in the words of Horace Mann (1868), the "great equalizer" (p. 669). Mann, a key player in the push for universal, free, and compulsory education, believed that students of all cultural backgrounds and social classes should share equally in the benefits of a public education (Mann, 1868). It can even be said that the quintessential battles over public schooling from the 19th century to the present have centered on questions of inequality, owing primarily to the demographics of the nation and its schools.

Since its very inception in the United States, a major goal of multicultural education has been to improve educational outcomes for students marginalized by society because of social and cultural differences. Given the nation's ethnic and cultural pluralism, and a fundamental belief in the power of schools to provide a level playing field for students of all backgrounds – as well as the many historic clashes over race, culture, language, and other differences – it is no surprise that multicultural education was first felt most strongly in the US rather than in other more homogeneous nations or in societies without a history of large-scale immigration and tensions around race and ethnicity.

From its origins in early African American intellectual thought, to the work of social scientists, to recent developments in feminism, critical race theory, postmodernism, and postcolonialism, multicultural education has undergone numerous changes in definition and approach. Yet it has remained true to its fundamental ideals. In this chapter, the roots and current status of multicultural education are briefly highlighted. Before reviewing the origins of multicultural education, however, some definitions are in order.

Definitions and parameters

What we now call multicultural education in the United States began in earnest in the early 1970s with names still familiar in the field, such as James Banks, Carlos Cortés, Geneva Gay, and Carl Grant (J. Banks, 2004b), and which today includes other prominent scholars (Bennett, 2007; Derman-Sparks & the A.B.C. Task Force, 1989; Gollnick & Chinn, 2006; Ladson-Billings, 1994; Nieto & Bode, 2008; Ramsey, 2006; Sleeter, 2006). Multicultural education is similar to what in other countries is called *intercultural education* (Santos Regó & Nieto, 2000), *antiracist education* (Gillborn, 1995), and *nonracial education* (South African Schools Act, 1996), as well as to what in the United States is also called *anti-oppressive education* (Kumashiro, 2000) or *social justice education* (Adams, Bell, & Griffin, 2007). There are, of course, both minor nuances and major differences among these variants throughout the globe, and it is for this reason that a brief discussion of how the field is generally defined in the United States is warranted. Although there is widespread agreement among U.S. scholars on the definition, parameters, and goals of multicultural education, there are also some differences. Geneva Gay (2004), a pioneer in the field, has described these differences as more semantic than substantive. Nevertheless, where divergence exists, it is most pronounced in practice, as we shall see further on.

James Banks, widely recognized as a leading scholar in the field as well as one of its founders, was among the first to define multicultural education, a definition that has remained remarkably stable over time. For Banks (J. Banks & C. Banks, 2007), multicultural education is

> an idea, an educational reform movement, and a process whose major goal is to change the structure of educational institutions so that male and female students, exceptional students, and students who are members of diverse racial, ethnic, language, and cultural groups will have an equal chance to achieve academically in school. (p. 1)

James Banks had begun to theorize and write about diversity as early as the late 1960s. His personal trajectory as a scholar, what he calls his "epistemological journey," closely matches the growth and development of multicultural education itself (J. Banks, 2006, p. 1). The field, and Banks's own scholarship, moved from ethnic studies to multiethnic education, and later to multicultural education. Each of these elements – particularly ethnic studies – is still a prominent feature of multicultural education in many universities and in K-12 curricula. Nevertheless, by the mid-1970s, the term *multicultural education* began to replace *multiethnic education* because it more accurately reflected the concerns of a wider range of social and human differences (J. Banks, 2006).

The insistence that multicultural education must be about more than what came to be known as "holidays and heroes" has had a pronounced influence in the field, most notably in its scholarship and theoretical constructs (Lee, Menkhart, & Okazawa-Rey, 1998). It is widely agreed that changes in institutional policies and practices are needed if multicultural education is to be a true and lasting reform. A watershed moment in this trajectory was Banks's typology of approaches to multicultural education, consisting of the *contributions, additive, transformative*, and *social action* approaches, a classification still widely used in multicultural education both in the United States and elsewhere (J. Banks, 1988).

Margaret Gibson (1976) also developed a typology of multicultural education early in the field's history. According to her, there are five general approaches to multicultural education: education of the culturally different (or benevolent multiculturalism); education about cultural differences (or cultural understanding); education for cultural pluralism; bicultural education; and multicultural education "as the normal human experience" (p. 15). This last approach, according to Gibson, differs from the others because it draws upon anthropological definitions of both education and culture, a connection that has been significant in both anthropological approaches to research and epistemological understandings of culture (Abrahams & Troike, 1972; Grant, Elsbree, & Fondrie, 2004; Heath, 2004; Spindler & Spindler, 1994; Wills, Lintz, & Mehan, 2004).

Christine Bennett's work in multicultural education has also been significant in this regard. In the first edition of her book *Comprehensive Multicultural Education* (1986), now in its sixth edition (2007), she described a number of conditions needed to promote cultural pluralism in schools, including an antiracist approach, positive teacher expectations, intercultural competence, an inclusive curriculum, and social action. Notably, as early as 1973 when the field was just emerging, Banks asserted that decision-making was at the heart of the social studies, the content area in which he developed many of his theories of multicultural education (J. Banks, 2006). This early stance inserted both teachers and students squarely within the democratic process that a multicultural education represents. Moreover, an antiracist approach was articulated early on and has remained constant in the field (Baker, 1973; J. Banks, 1975; Gay, 1977; Grant, 1975; Nieto, 1992; Sleeter & Grant, 1987).

In order to define multicultural education in both a more nuanced and a more comprehensive way, Banks developed what he called the *dimensions of multicultural education*, a typology that continues to have great resonance in the field (J. Banks, 1991). The dimensions include *content integration*, the extent to which content from a variety of cultures and groups is integrated into the curriculum; *knowledge construction*, the extent to which teachers and students understand how the perspectives, biases, and frames of reference in particular disciplines help shape knowledge in those disciplines; *prejudice reduction*, the way in which teachers help students develop positive and anti-biased attitudes about people of different backgrounds; *equity pedagogy*, in which pedagogical strategies are modified to help students of all backgrounds learn effectively; and *empowering school culture and social structure*, where the climate and organization of the school promote an equitable learning environment. These dimensions have been significant in defining the field, and they have led to the understanding that multicultural education is not just about tinkering with the curriculum.

Christine Sleeter and Carl Grant (1987), other early leaders in the field, helped define multicultural education through an influential typology first published in the *Harvard Educational Review*. In it, they classify multicultural education into five distinct types: teaching the exceptional and the culturally different; the human relations approach; the single-group studies approach; the multicultural education approach; and what they refer to as education that is multicultural and social reconstructionist. Although these types are neither necessarily incompatible nor exclusive, they define in clear and concrete ways particular goals and ideologies about multicultural education. The most transformative approach in the Sleeter and Grant typology is the fifth, because it challenges not only school curricula, organization, and policy, but also societal inequities. In practice, this approach revitalizes the curriculum and encourages students to take an activist pro-social justice stance.

Another widely used and comprehensive definition first developed by Sonia Nieto (1992; Nieto & Bode, 2008) situates multicultural education within a sociopolitical context. That is, given the underlying social, cultural, ideological, economic, and political context, the issue of power – who has it, how it is used, and who benefits from it – is articulated as a major concern of multicultural education. A deliberately adaptable collection of attributes rather than a fixed and static description, this definition focuses on seven basic characteristics of multicultural education as *antiracist, basic, important for all students, pervasive, education for social justice, a process*, and *rooted in critical pedagogy*. Influenced by the work of Paulo Freire (1970), this definition made critical pedagogy a prominent feature of multicultural education.

Regardless of definition, what is clear from this discussion is that multicultural education has a long history of advocating for equal and equitable education for students of all backgrounds, and that it goes beyond the classroom walls to implicate societal change as a fundamental goal. Tracing multicultural education from its beginnings will help illuminate this history.

The trajectory of multicultural education in the United States

Multicultural education in the United States as we know it today began in the mid-1970s. Nevertheless, it has deep roots, particularly through the activism and scholarship of African Americans in the late 19th and early 20th centuries. A number of decades later, scholars and activists of other cultural groups also contributed to the development of multicultural education. The intercultural education movement of the 1950s, as well as ethnic, gender, and disability studies and bilingual education (all of which followed in the 1960s), also influenced the development of multicultural education. A brief discussion of each of these influences follows.

The African American roots of multicultural education

The roots of multicultural education can be traced as far back as the final decades of the 19th century and first decades of the 20th in the work of scholars such as W. E. B. Du Bois (1935), Carter Woodson (1933), and other African American intellectuals whose work laid the foundation for the Civil Rights Movement of the 1950s that then led to ethnic studies and, later, multicultural education. The work of these intellectual giants focused on the inequality and oppression experienced by African Americans in education, the justice system, housing, health, and other public arenas as a result of slavery and, later, legal segregation and racism. Schools quickly became an important battlefield for activists and scholars. Calling for massive reforms in public education, among other institutions, Du Bois, Woodson, and others were in the forefront of demands for universal literacy, equitable school facilities, and a revamping of the curriculum to include the history of African Americans.

Educational inequality, particularly through segregated schooling, was a key matter for early African American scholars and activists. Especially repugnant was the doctrine of "separate but equal" in the U.S. South, whereby Black and White children were segregated in so-called "equal" schools that were in reality vastly unequal in materials and infrastructure. Although racially segregated schools were common in the South, these conditions were not confined to the South. Gloria Ladson-Billings (2004b), for instance, has documented the long history of African Americans' attempts to desegregate public schools beginning as early as 1849 in the Northeast, specifically in Boston, Massachusetts. The long struggle for desegregation led to the landmark 1954 *Brown v. Board of Education* decision, where schools were allegedly to be desegregated "with all deliberate speed." The desegregation was neither speedy nor deliberate, and public schools in all areas of the nation are today more segregated than at any time since the *Brown* decision (Orfield, 2001). Although no longer sanctioned by law, school segregation remains a reality, owing to housing patterns, historical tradition, and racism.

Contributions from other racial and cultural groups

Scholars and activists from other racial and cultural backgrounds were also engaged in the early development of the field, particularly through research and legal challenges to school desegregation and other forms of educational inequality. Segregated schools were evident in various areas of the country where children of racial and ethnic groups other than the dominant Anglo-Saxon population attended schools. Those denied an equal education, through either outright exclusion or segregation, included Chinese and Japanese children, primarily in California but in other states as well (Pang, Kiang, & Pak, 2004; Weinberg, 1977). The brutal history of boarding schools for Native Americans is also part of the story of the struggle for equal education (Archuleta, Child, & Lomawaima, 2000; McBeth, 1983).

Mexican Americans, the Latino group with the most extensive experience in the United States, also faced a long history of exclusion. George Sánchez (1940) was in the forefront of challenging the segregation, both de jure and de facto, of Mexicans in U.S. schools. The courts were an important arena for these challenges and led to watershed moments in the struggle for equal education for Mexican American and other Latino or Latina students. Yet few people, even educators, know about such cases as *Independent School District v. Salvatierra* in Texas (1930), protesting the segregation of Mexican children; the Lemon Grove incident in California that led to *Alvarez v. Owen* (1931), the first successful desegregation case in U.S. history; and *Méndez v. Westminster* in Orange County, California (1947), which ended the segregation of Mexican and other Latino children (the plaintiff, Gonzalo Méndez, was Mexican, and his wife, Felícitas, was Puerto Rican) in California schools. As a result, California became the first state in the nation to outlaw school segregation. Some of these cases, in fact, served as legal precedent for the 1954 *Brown v. Board of Education* decision.

Intercultural education

The intercultural movement that began in the late 1920s and lasted until the late 1950s is also a significant precedent to multicultural education (C. Banks, 2004). A broadly conceptualized reform movement that included curriculum improvement, program and professional development, and other institutional changes, it included at its zenith more than 200 organizations devoted to its cause (C. Banks, 2004). It is probable that this movement gained a great deal of credibility because some of the nation's major White social science scholars were actively involved in it (J. Banks, 2004b).

A response to the racial and ethnic tensions evident in the country at the time – tensions arising out of the tremendous increase in immigration, primarily from Europe, and internal migration, especially of African Americans moving from the agricultural South to the industrial North, in the late 19th and early 20th centuries – the intercultural movement is linked to contemporary multicultural education through its insistence on the need to reduce prejudice and create interracial and intercultural acceptance among students. By incorporating curricula and other materials that promoted intercultural understanding and respect, this movement was among the first educational attempts in the United States to acknowledge the multiracial and multicultural character of the nation. Its focus on democratic values as central in U.S. life became an important contribution to what would later be known as multicultural education.

Parallel movements

The ethnic studies, bilingual education, gender, and disability movements, which began in the 1960s, all emerged from the Civil Rights Movement. Accompanied by "high hopes, broken promises, and an uncertain future" (Nieto, 2005, p. 57), these movements were imbued with a deep sense of equity and social justice and with a commitment to improving the life chances, through education, of children of color and others who had been oppressed by their schooling. Although some of these movements were forerunners of multicultural education, they were at the same time parallel movements to it. Unlike intercultural education, which had largely disappeared by the 1960s, bilingual education, ethnic studies, gender studies, and disability rights have remained visible and viable fields in their own right.

Ethnic studies

The ethnic studies movement began with the recognition that African American children had long been educationally neglected and abused. By the 1960s, not only were they still attending overwhelmingly segregated and substandard schools, but African American people were also largely invisible in public school curricula. Soon, other groups also took up the banner of ethnic studies, demanding a place at the table of educational opportunity through more decision-making power, the improvement of facilities, and the inclusion of ethnic content in the curriculum. It was especially young people of African American, Mexican American, Puerto Rican, and Native American heritage in the nation's colleges and universities during the 1960s and early 1970s who demanded curricula related to their history and culture, and the recruitment of a more diverse faculty.

Banks has described the period of the early roots of multicultural education as the *monoethnic courses stage* (J. Banks, 2006). A significant landmark in K-12 ethnic studies was the publication of his *Teaching Strategies for Ethnic Studies* (J. Banks, 1975), a text that would define the field for many years. At the university level, ethnic studies remains strong and vibrant in many places throughout the nation. Some programs have consolidated to include groups with growing populations in the United States. For example, in some places African American studies have incorporated studies of the larger African diaspora, and some Puerto Rican and Chicano studies programs have taken on the broader categories of either Caribbean or Latino studies.

Bilingual education

Bilingual education in K-12 schools was another parallel movement to multicultural education (Crawford, 2004; García & Baker, 2007). The latest iteration of bilingual education started in the 1960s, but educating children through the use of their native language while they are also learning English has a much longer history in the United States. For instance, bilingual instruction in German and English was quite common in the Midwest in the 1800s, and by 1900 at least 600,000 children, or about 4% of students enrolled in public and parochial elementary schools, were being taught in German–English bilingual schools, with smaller numbers in Polish, Italian, Norwegian, Spanish, French, Czech, Dutch, and other languages (Crawford, 1992).

The struggle for bilingual education that began anew in the 1960s was based on the premise that teaching children in their native language can help turn around the abysmal educational outcomes that were traditional for many immigrants, particularly Latinos. As a result, from the 1960s to the 1990s, many advocates took to the streets, legislatures, and courts to advocate for bilingual education. The results can be seen in such cases as the 1974 *Lau v. Nichols* decision, and in such legislation as the 1968 Bilingual Education Act. In *Lau*, the U.S. Supreme Court recognized the connection between native language rights and equal educational opportunity by ruling unanimously that the civil rights of students who did not understand the language of instruction were indeed being violated.

Although bilingual education has generally been shown to be more effective than programs such as English immersion or English as a second language (ESL) without native language instruction, the public has always been deeply divided over this approach (Crawford, 2004; Cummins, 2001; Nieto, 2001). The fact that one of the fundamental goals of bilingual education is the learning of English often goes unmentioned by its opponents, who perceive using languages of instruction other than English as a threat to national unity and even as unpatriotic. As a result, U.S. language policies and practices have been inconsistent, ranging from "sink or swim" policies (i.e. immersing language-minority students in English-only classrooms to fend for themselves), to the imposition of English as the sole medium of instruction, all the way to allowing and even encouraging bilingualism (Crawford, 2000).

In recent years, there have been numerous instances of outright hostility towards native language instruction, no doubt owing in large part to growing immigration, particularly from Mexico. Examples of this hostility can be seen in California through Proposition 227 in 1998, which resulted in the elimination of bilingual education, and in similar propositions in Arizona (Proposition 203, 2000) and Massachusetts (Official Massachusetts information for voters, 2002).

Other parallel movements

Other parallel movements for equality during the 1960s and 1970s resulted in gender, queer, and disability studies. Student and activist demands led to gender studies programs in many colleges and universities, as well as to the inclusion of gender curricula in K-12 schools. Gender studies, which incorporates women, gay, lesbian, transgender, transsexual, and other groups formerly invisible in the curriculum, took hold most strongly in higher education (Schmitz, Butler, Guy-Sheftall, & Rosenfelt, 2004). Queer studies has also become a prominent feature at some universities and is a vibrant field in its own right (Spargo, 1999). In addition, legal precedents such as Title IX, guaranteeing equal access to girls' and women's sports and athletic facilities in schools and universities, were an outgrowth of the growing demands for equity in academic as well as nonacademic arenas.

The movement for disability rights also emerged from the Civil Rights Movement.

Although disability studies was much less common than gender studies as a field of study in either K-12 or higher education, results of disability rights activism are evident, for example, in the passage of the landmark federal Education for All Handicapped Children Act (Public Law 94–142) in 1975, the most recent iteration of which is the Individuals With Disabilities Education Act (IDEA) (2004).

These parallel movements – through their intellectual scholarship and the activism on which the scholarship is based – have been key catalysts in helping to broaden the parameters of multicultural education to be inclusive of many differences and oppressions not initially embraced in the early conceptions of the field.

Major controversies in multicultural education: A brief synopsis

In the United States, the history of multicultural education has closely mirrored the history of the struggle for equal education and for freedom in general. It has, thus, always been a contested terrain. "Multicultural education, like America itself," writes Gloria Ladson-Billings (2004a), "is about the expression of freedom, but notions of freedom and liberation almost always involve contestation" (p. 52). While it is beyond the scope of this brief chapter to articulate in any depth the major debates and controversies in multicultural education in the United States, it is important to know that, as a field, it has been criticized by both the Left and the Right (Nieto, 1995; Sleeter, 2001).

Most debates about multicultural education can be characterized in one of two ways: (a) that it is too radical (the conservative or Rightist position), or (b) that it is too conservative (the radical or Leftist position). By far the greatest number of critiques are from the Right, and they have been constant, although particularly evident beginning in the late 1980s and the early 1990s. These critiques have rarely discussed the actual scholarship or major scholars in multicultural education, but have instead focused on fringe scholars, or on such fears as the supposed shrinking of the Western canon, particularly at colleges and universities (Bloom, 1989), or on alarm that American common culture is being sacrificed at the altar of diversity, resulting in hatred of Whites and increased divisiveness (D'Souza, 1991; Hirsch, 1987; Ravitch, 1990). None of these grim predictions has come to pass.

On the Left, one major debate has centered on who is included in multicultural education. While most scholars in the field have in recent years broadened the scope of multicultural to include social class, gender, disability, and LGBTQI issues, among other social differences, others believe that being so inclusive diminishes the original purpose of multicultural education, which was to provide an equal education for marginalized students of color (Gay, 2003). In a review of research related to multicultural education, for instance, Carl Grant and his colleagues (2004) found that little attention had been paid to sexuality, "demonstrating perhaps that queerness is not yet accepted under the umbrella of multiculturalism" (p. 197). Yet even the major organization in multicultural education has embraced a broader perspective. For instance, according to the website of the National Association for Multicultural Education (NAME), "NAME believes that multicultural education promotes equity for all regardless of culture, ethnicity, race, language, age, gender, sexual orientation, belief system or exceptionality" (NAME, n.d.).

Another major critique from the Left is that the field has been undertheorized, leading to an idealistic and uncritical view of change as well as a static understanding of culture and identity, a serious charge given the hybridization in youth culture and massive changes due to globalization (Dolby, 2000). A related critique concerns the lack of analysis of institutionalized systems of oppression within the field. Hence, some on the Left have described multicultural education as a salve to neutralize African American demands for more substantive changes (McCarthy, 1988). Although it is certainly true that classroom practice has frequently been characterized by superficial approaches, academics in the field have long been grappling with issues of power and oppression, and there is now a deeper understanding of these issues than ever before (see Nieto, Bode, Kang, & Raible, 2008). At the same time, Christine Sleeter and Dolores Delgado Bernal (2004) have noted that, as more people have taken up multicultural education, it has come to be understood in a less critical way. For instance, in many cases, multicultural education is perceived as a psychological frame of mind or simply as the addition of Brown and Black heroes and holidays to the mainstream (White) curriculum, thereby avoiding the more critical matter of confronting and transforming institutional policies and practices.

Theory and research in multicultural education

Numerous theories have either influenced or emerged from – or both – the field of multicultural education. Research to substantiate these theories has grown in the past two decades. Given the constraints of space, only a small number of the theories will be mentioned below. Two excellent sources provide comprehensive reviews of research. One is the *Handbook of Research on Multicultural Education* (J. Banks & C. Banks, 2004), which includes reviews of research using quantitative methods (Padilla, 2004), qualitative methods (Heath, 2004), and ethnographic methods (Wills et al., 2004), as well as a review of research from 1990 to 2001 (Grant et al., 2004). Another is a conceptual mapping of the genres of research in multicultural education by Christine Bennett (2001). In it, she explores theories that have been influential in the field, clustered in four major areas: *curriculum reform, equity pedagogy, multicultural competence*, and *societal equity*. Bennett goes on to review numerous research studies related to each of the genres.

One of the early theories that influenced the emerging field of multicultural education is the *social contact theory*, based on the work of Gordon Allport (1954), which states that intergroup contact can either ameliorate or exacerbate prejudice. Allport theorized that positive outcomes would result when a number of conditions were met. These included equal status of the groups, shared goals, intergroup cooperation, and the support of those in authority. This theory has been the basis of much of the research supporting multicultural education, including the scholarship of Janet Ward Schofield on intergroup relations in schools (1989) and Elizabeth Cohen on collaborative group work (1986).

A related group of theories concerns ethnic identity development. First evident in the 1970s, these theories have had a significant influence on multicultural education research and practice. According to scholars in the field, individuals experience their ethnic and racial identity in different stages, and these are influenced by their personal experiences, social contacts, and sociopolitical realities. How people think about their identity and how their perceptions influence such matters as school achievement and interethnic relations are important questions in this field. William Cross (1991), Janet Helms (1990), and Beverly Daniel Tatum (1997) have been especially prominent in the area of ethnic identity development, and teacher education and intergroup relations have been greatly influenced by these ideas.

Learning style theories have also been significant in the field. In general, these theories are based on the assumption that culture – through child-rearing styles, ethnic family values, and early experiences in the home – has an impact on how people learn. The early work of Asa Hilliard (1989/1990), Wade Boykin (1979), and Manuel Ramírez and Alfredo Castañeda (1974) was especially significant in this area. Although these theories have been recognized as significant in the development of the field, they have also been criticized as sometimes overly deterministic (Gutierrez & Rogoff, 2003). According to Jacqueline Jordan Irvine and Darlene Eleanor York (2001), for example, because of problems related to its measurement and the complex relationship between culture and learning, "this body of research must be interpreted and applied carefully in classrooms of culturally diverse students" (p. 484). In practical terms, learning style theories have influenced such areas as curriculum development, teacher preparation, and school climate.

By the beginning of the 21st century, the enormous diversity of U.S. society, as well as complications arising from massive global immigration and the ensuing hybrid identities of many individuals and groups, meant that simple categories of race, gender, and social class were no longer sufficient to define the field of multicultural education. As a result, in recent years, postmodernism, postcolonialism, feminist scholarship, queer studies, and critical race theory (CRT) have become increasingly evident in the field as scholars, both novice and veteran, are retheorizing multicultural education, pushing it beyond its traditional parameters of curriculum integration and cultural awareness to include such matters as multiple identities and cutting edge epistemologies and methodologies (J. Banks, 1993; Nieto et al., 2008; Sleeter & Bernal, 2004).

Most scholars in multicultural education now understand identity as complex and situated in a multiplicity of contexts, a conception that has significant implications for the field. Consequently, the nature of research and practice in multicultural education is changing. Recent epistemological frameworks being used in the field include critical pedagogy, funds of knowledge, and CRT, which in turn are leading to new and innovative methodologies (Sleeter & Bernal, 2004). For instance, critical pedagogy has helped to clarify the political nature of education (Freire, 1970), placing issues of power and the voices of marginalized individuals and groups at the center of research (Morrell, 2008; Morrell & Duncan-Andrade, 2002). Feminism has focused on identity and positionality (Tetreault, 2007), leading to a keener focus on qualitative research and a rethinking of classroom practice (Grant et al., 2004). The funds of knowledge approach – where families of all backgrounds are respected for the wisdom and experience they possess and what they bring to their children's education – is also challenging traditional deficit views of nondominant families (Gonzalez, Moll, & Amanti, 2005). Critical race theory has resulted in such methodologies as *counterstories* and *storytelling* (Ladson-Billings & Tate, 1995), which in turn have led to innovative work by young scholars in which their communities' concerns are centered rather than marginalized (Brayboy, 2005; Yosso, 2006).

Another significant recent development is the globalization of the field. Although some scholars in multicultural education in the United States have for many years recognized the importance of international connections (J. Banks, 1992; Bennett, 1986), it has been only within the past decade that more serious attention has been paid to the educational implications of globalization and large-scale worldwide immigration. At the same time, the role of citizenship and democracy within this context has taken on even greater meaning (J. Banks, 2004a).

Multicultural teacher education

Because of the significance of preparing teachers for the growing diversity in the nation, by the 1970s teacher education had become an important component of multicultural education. It can be said that this sub-field began when, in 1972, the American Association of Colleges for Teacher Education (AACTE) released its far-reaching statement titled *No One Model American* (1972). The statement underscored the importance of multicultural education by stating that "multicultural education recognizes cultural diversity as a fact of life in American society, and it affirms that this cultural diversity is a valuable resource that should be preserved and extended" (n.p.). The statement urged schools and colleges of education to prepare educational personnel in settings "where a commitment to multicultural education is evident" and that this commitment "must permeate all areas of the educational experience provided for prospective teachers" (n.p.). Unlike any other declaration by a major educational organization up to that time, the *No One Model American* statement was to influence teacher education for many years.

Scholars such as Christine Sleeter, author of *Keepers of the American Dream* (1992), one of the first full-length studies on multicultural teacher education, and, more recently, a review of the research on preservice teacher preparation (Sleeter, 2000), and Geneva Gay (2000), whose work on culturally responsive teaching has been instrumental in making multicultural teacher education visible, have changed how schools and colleges of education prepare their students for diverse classrooms. Other influential scholars are Ana María Villegas and Tamara Lucas (2002), whose teacher education curriculum has helped schools of education prepare teachers for diversity. Jacqueline Jordan Irvine's (2003) work on the need for teachers to develop a culturally responsive pedagogy, or what she calls "seeing with a cultural eye," Kenneth Zeichner's (2003) research on recruiting and retaining teachers for diverse classrooms, and the research of Marilyn Cochran-Smith and her colleagues (Cochran-Smith, Davis, & Fries, 2004) in defining the parameters of the field of multicultural teacher education have also been considerable. All of these scholars have recognized the central role of preparing, recruiting, and retaining teachers for diverse classrooms, in the process making it clear that including a course in multicultural education in the teacher education curriculum is not enough. Instead, they insist that teachers need to develop the knowledge, awareness, dispositions, and interest to become effective teachers of all students, particularly those who have been least served by the public schools.

Much still needs to be done in preparing teachers for diversity. One recent study, for example, found that while 76% of new teachers said that teaching in ethnically diverse classrooms was "covered" in their teacher education courses, more than half still felt unprepared to teach students of diverse backgrounds (National Comprehensive Center for Teacher Quality and Public Agenda, 2008). Also, a review by Cochran-Smith and her colleagues found that very little has changed outside a small number of "local pockets of change" (Cochran-Smith et al., 2004, p. 964). Both the marginalization of teacher education and chronic underfunding for research help explain this situation.

Related to the focus on teacher preparation, another component of multicultural education in recent years is what has been variously called *culturally congruent, culturally relevant,* or *culturally responsive* education (Gay, 2000; Irvine, 2003; Ladson-Billings, 1994). With a focus on pedagogical practices that engage students of diverse backgrounds, culturally responsive pedagogy is a helpful response to the underachievement of many students of color in U.S. classrooms. According to Villegas and Lucas (2002), culturally responsive teachers must be socioculturally conscious (i.e. recognize that there are different ways of perceiving reality and that these are influenced by one's positionality), have affirming views of students of diverse backgrounds, view themselves as capable of bringing about educational change to benefit their students, understand how learners construct knowledge, be familiar with the lives of their students, and use their knowledge to design effective instruction.

Despite its usefulness, a culturally responsive framework can become problematic if culture is viewed as deterministic and static rather than as elastic and changeable. This challenge is being articulated by a number of young scholars in the field who, while supportive of the framework, caution against its potentially limited view of culture (Irizarry, 2007).

Multicultural education practice

An enduring dilemma in multicultural education has been the gulf between theories such as those articulated above and how these are realized in classroom practice. Geneva Gay (1995) expressed this dilemma over a decade ago, and it is still largely true. The result is that superficial changes in curriculum and materials often define a school's attempts to implement a multicultural perspective. Because the sociopolitical and transformative underpinnings of multicultural education are routinely neglected when translated into practice, few long-term institutional changes have taken root.

To be sure, today there are many so-called multicultural curricula, programs, and materials on the market in the US, but many of these do little more than reinforce stereotypes about marginalized groups by focusing solely on such matters as food, music, and holidays. Nevertheless, a growing number of resources successfully address the need to change larger institutional issues. The Center for Multicultural Education at the University of Washington, Seattle, for example, has produced school-friendly yet robust guidelines for improving school policies and practices (see, for example, J. Banks et al., 2001). In addition, a small but influential group of organizations is effectively tackling broader concerns such as racism, inequality, power, and globalization. These include the National Association for Multicultural Education (NAME), a professional organization that promotes the goals of multicultural education from P-16 and in higher education, especially in teacher education, and its various state chapters around the nation; Rethinking Schools, an organization that publishes a magazine and many antiracist and multicultural professional and curriculum resources written primarily for and by activist teachers; Teaching for Change, a progressive organization of educators that disseminates a wide array of critical multicultural classroom materials, professional resources, and children's books, and provides technical assistance to schools; Teaching Tolerance, the educational arm of the Southern Poverty Law Center, which publishes a teacher-friendly magazine with curriculum ideas (many written by classroom teachers), as well as posters, videos, and other resources that focus on inequality of all kinds; and the World of Difference (WOD), an educational project of the Anti-Defamation League (ADL) that develops materials for classrooms and schools concerning bias and discrimination and provides professional development for educators.

In addition to organizations, an increasing number of academic resources have been published in recent years on issues of equity and social justice. These include entire series such as the Multicultural Education Series, edited by James Banks, and the Teaching for Social Justice Series, edited by William Ayers, both from Teachers College Press; the Language, Culture, and Teaching Series, edited by Sonia Nieto, and the Teaching/Learning Social Justice Series, edited by Lee Bell, both from Routledge Publishers. The *Handbook of Research on Multicultural Education* (J. Banks & C. Banks, 1995, 2004) was a landmark in the field, and this *Routledge International Companion to Multicultural Education* represents another significant sign that multicultural education is strong not only in the United States but also in a number of other nations around the world. In addition, books written by classroom teachers are providing inspiring examples of K-12 multicultural education in action. These include Vivian Vasquez's *Negotiating Critical Literacies with Young Children* (2004) and Mary Cowhey's *Black Ants and Buddhists: Thinking Critically and Teaching Differently in the Primary Grades* (2006).

Final thoughts

The last four decades have witnessed tremendous changes in U.S. schools and society, including large-scale immigration, massive globalization, and radical changes in daily life. Multicultural education has both mirrored and addressed these changes. Although the field itself has undergone many changes in the intervening decades, its major focus, that is, the improvement of educational outcomes for students marginalized by society because of social and cultural differences, remains largely unchanged. As a result of the questions of inequality and lack of access at the heart of the field, many classroom teachers, administrators, scholars, and policymakers have modified their work. It is for this reason that James Banks has characterized multicultural education as transformative in its goals and approaches (J. Banks, 1996).

Newer epistemologies and methodologies are reinventing multicultural education in the 21st century. Although the terms may change and approaches may differ, given the rapidly changing demographics of U.S. society – where hybrid identities are becoming the order of the day and people of color (primarily of non-Anglo-Saxon background) are expected to constitute more than half of the nation's population by mid-century – multicultural education is here to stay. Despite the many controversies it has withstood over the years, the field has nevertheless endured because it is a project of hope: hope in the human spirit and hope in the promise of education to improve the lives of people both in the United States and around the globe.

References

Abrahams, R. D., & Troike, R. C. (1972). *Language and cultural diversity in American education*. Englewood Cliffs, NJ: Prentice-Hall.

Adams, M., Bell, L. A., & Griffin, P. (2007). *Teaching for diversity and social justice* (2nd ed.). New York: Routledge.

Allport, G. W. (1954). *The nature of prejudice*. Reading, MA: Addison-Wesley.

Alvarez v. Owen, No. 66625 (San Diego County Super. Ct. filed Apr. 17, 1931).

American Association of Colleges for Teacher Education (AACTE) (1972). *No one model American: A statement on multicultural education*. Washington, DC: Author.

Archuleta, M. L., Child, B. J., & Lomawaima, K. T. (2000). *Away from home: American Indian boarding school experiences, 1879–2000*. Phoenix, AZ: Heard Museum.

Baker, G. C. (1973). Multicultural training for student teachers. *Journal of Teacher Education, 24*(4), 306–307.

Banks, C. A. M. (2004). *Improving multicultural education: Lessons from the intergroup education movement*. New York: Teachers College Press.

Banks, J. A. (1975). *Teaching strategies for ethnic studies*. Boston: Allyn & Bacon.

Banks, J. A. (1988). Approaches to multicultural education. *Multicultural Leader, 1*(2), 1–3.

Banks, J. A. (1991). The dimensions of multicultural education. *Multicultural Leader, 4*, 5–6.

Banks, J. A. (1992). Multicultural education: Approaches, developments, and dimensions. In J. Lynch, C. Modgil, & S. Modgil (Eds.), *Cultural diversity and the schools: Vol. 1. Education for cultural diversity: Convergence and divergence* (pp. 83–94). London: Falmer Press.

Banks, J. A. (1993). Multicultural education: Historical development, dimensions, and practice. In L. Darling-Hammond (Ed.), *Review of Research in Education* (Vol. 10, pp. 3–49). Washington, DC: American Educational Research Association.

Banks, J. A. (1996). *Multicultural education, transformative knowledge, and action: Historical and contemporary perspectives*. New York: Teachers College Press.

Banks, J. A. (Ed.) (2004a). *Diversity and citizenship education: Global perspectives*. San Francisco: Jossey-Bass.

Banks, J. A. (2004b). Multicultural education: Historical developments, dimensions, and practice. In J. A.

Banks & C. A. M. Banks (Eds.), *Handbook of research on multicultural education* (2nd ed., pp. 3–29). San Francisco: Jossey-Bass.

Banks, J. A. (2006). *Race, culture, and education: The selected works of James A. Banks.* London & New York: Routledge.

Banks, J. A., & Banks, C. A. M. (Eds.). (1995). *Handbook of research on multicultural education.* New York: Macmillan.

Banks, J. A., & Banks, C. A. M. (Eds.). (2004). *Handbook of research on multicultural education* (2nd ed.). San Francisco: Jossey-Bass.

Banks, J. A., & Banks, C. A. M. (Eds.). (2007). *Multicultural education: Issues and perspectives* (6th ed.). Hoboken, NJ: John Wiley & Sons.

Banks, J. A., Cookson, P., Gay, G., Hawley, W. D., Irvine, J. J., Nieto, S., et al. (2001). Diversity within unity: Essential principles for teaching and learning in a multicultural society. *Phi Delta Kappan, 83*(3), 196–203.

Bennett, C. I. (1986). *Comprehensive multicultural education: Theory and practice.* Boston: Allyn & Bacon.

Bennett, C. I. (2001). Genres of research in multicultural education. *Review of Educational Research, 71*(2), 171–217.

Bennett, C. I. (2007). *Comprehensive multicultural education: Theory and practice* (6th ed.). Boston: Allyn & Bacon.

Bloom, A. C. (1989). *The closing of the American mind.* New York: Simon & Schuster.

Boykin, W. A. W. (1979). Psychological/behavioral verve: Some theoretical explorations and empirical manifestations. In A. W. Boykin, A. Franklin, & J. Yates (Eds.), *Research directions of Black psychologists* (pp. 351–367). New York: Russell Sage Foundation.

Brayboy, B. (2005). Toward a tribal critical race theory in education. *The Urban Review, 37*(5), 425–446.

Brown v. Board of Education of Topeka, 347 US 483 (1954).

Cochran-Smith, M., Davis, D., & Fries, K. (2004). Multicultural teacher education. In J. A. Banks & C. A. M. Banks (Eds.), *Handbook of research on multicultural education* (2nd ed., pp. 931–975). San Francisco: Jossey-Bass.

Cohen, E. G. (1986). *Designing groupwork: Strategies for the heterogeneous classroom.* New York: Teachers College Press.

Cowhey, M. (2006). *Black ants and Buddhists: Thinking critically and teaching differently in the primary grades.* Portland, ME: Stenhouse Publishers.

Crawford, J. (1992). *Hold your tongue: Bilingualism and the politics of "English only."* Reading, MA: Addison-Wesley.

Crawford, J. (2000). *At war with diversity: US language policy in an age of anxiety.* Clevedon, UK: Multilingual Matters.

Crawford, J. (2004). *Educating English learners: Language diversity in the classroom* (5th ed.). Los Angeles: Bilingual Education Services.

Cross, W. E., Jr. (1991). *Shades of Black: Diversity in African-American identity.* Philadelphia: Temple University Press.

Cummins, J. (2001). *Language, power, and pedagogy: Bilingual children in the crossfire.* Clevedon, UK: Multilingual Matters.

Derman-Sparks, L., & the A.B.C. Task Force (1989). *Anti-bias curriculum: Tools for empowering young children.* Washington, DC: National Association for the Education of Young Children.

Dolby, N. (2000). Changing selves: Multicultural education and the challenge of new identities. *Teachers College Record, 102*(5), 898–912.

D'Souza, D. (1991). *Illiberal education: The politics of race and sex on campus.* New York: Free Press.

Du Bois, W. E. B. (1935). *Black reconstruction.* New York: Harcourt Brace.

Education for All Handicapped Children Act, Pub. L. No. 94–142 (1975).

Feagin, J. R. (2002). *Racial and ethnic relations* (7th ed.). New York: Prentice-Hall.

Freire, P. (1970). *Pedagogy of the oppressed.* New York: Seabury Press.

García, O., & Baker, C. (Eds.). (2007). *Bilingual education: An introductory reader.* Clevedon, UK: Multilingual Matters.

Gay, G. (1977). Changing conceptions of multicultural education. *Educational Perspectives, 16*(4), 4–9.

Gay, G. (1995). Bridging multicultural theory and practice. *Multicultural Education, 3*(1), 4–9.

Gay, G. (2000). *Culturally responsive teaching: Theory, research, and practice.* New York: Teachers College Press.

Gay, G. (2003). The importance of multicultural education. *Educational Leadership, 61*(4), 30–35.

Gay, G. (2004). Curriculum theory and multicultural education. In J. A. Banks & C. A. M. Banks (Eds.), *Handbook of research on multicultural education* (2nd ed., pp. 30–49). San Francisco: Jossey-Bass.

Gibson, M. A. (1976). Approaches to multicultural education in the United States: Some concepts and assumptions. *Anthropology & Education Quarterly, 7*(4), 7–18.

Gillborn, D. (1995). *Racism and antiracism in real schools: Theory, policy, practice.* Berkshire, UK: Open University Press.

Gollnick, D. M., & Chinn, P. H. (2006). *Multicultural education in a pluralistic society* (7th ed.). New York: Prentice-Hall.

Gonzalez, N., Moll, L. C., & Amanti, C. (2005). *Funds of knowledge: Theorizing practices in households and classrooms.* Mahwah, NJ: Lawrence Erlbaum Associates.

Grant, C. A. (1975). Exploring the contours of multicultural education. In C. A. Grant (Ed.), *Sifting and winnowing: An exploration of the relationship between multi-cultural education and CBTE* (pp. 1–11). Madison, WI: Teacher Corps Associates.

Grant, C. A., Elsbree, A. R., & Fondrie, S. (2004). A decade of research on the changing terrain of multicultural education research. In J. A. Banks & C. A. M. Banks (Eds.), *Handbook of research on multicultural education* (2nd ed., pp. 184–207). San Francisco: Jossey-Bass.

Gutierrez, K. G., & Rogoff, B. (2003). Cultural ways of learning: Individual traits or repertoires of practice. *Educational Researcher, 32*(5), 19–25.

Heath, S. B. (2004). Ethnography in communities: Learning the everyday life of America's subordinated youth. In J. A. Banks & C. A. M. Banks (Eds.), *Handbook of research on multicultural education* (2nd ed., pp. 146–162). San Francisco: Jossey-Bass.

Helms, J. E. (1990). *Black and White racial identity: Theory, research, and practice.* New York: Greenwood Press.

Hilliard, A. G. (1989/1990, December/January). Teachers and cultural styles in a pluralistic society. *Rethinking Schools, 4*(2), 3.

Hirsch, E. D., Jr. (1987). *Cultural literacy: What every American needs to know.* New York: Houghton-Mifflin.

Independent School District v. Salvatierra, 33 S.W. 2d 790 (1930).

Individuals With Disabilities Education Act (IDEA), 20 U.S.C. §1400 (2004).

Irizarry, J. G. (2007). Ethnic and urban intersections in the classroom: Latino/a students, hybrid identities, and culturally responsive pedagogy. *Multicultural Perspectives, 9*(3), 1–7.

Irvine, J. J. (2003). *Educating teachers for diversity: Seeing with a cultural eye.* New York: Teachers College Press.

Irvine, J. J., & York, D. E. (2001). Learning styles and culturally diverse students: A literature review. In J. A. Banks & C. A. M. Banks (Eds.), *Handbook of research on multicultural education* (pp. 484–497). San Francisco: Jossey-Bass.

Kumashiro, K. (2000). Toward a theory of anti-oppressive education. *Review of Educational Research, 70*(1), 25–53.

Ladson-Billings, G. (1994). *The dreamkeepers: Successful teachers of African American children.* San Francisco: Jossey-Bass.

Ladson-Billings, G. (2004a). New directions in multicultural education: Complexities, boundaries, and critical race theory. In J. A. Banks & C. A. M. Banks (Eds.), *Handbook of research on multicultural education* (2nd ed., pp. 50–65). San Francisco: Jossey-Bass.

Ladson-Billings, G. (2004b). Landing on the wrong note: The price we paid for *Brown. Educational Researcher, 33*(7), 3–13.

Ladson-Billings, G., & Tate, W. E. (1995). Toward a critical race theory of education. *Teachers College Record, 97*(1), 47–68.

Lau v. Nichols, 414 U.S. 563 (1974).

Lee, E., Menkart, D., & Okazawa-Rey, M. (1998). *Beyond heroes and holidays: A practical guide to K-12 antiracist, multicultural education and staff development.* Washington, DC: Teaching for Change.

Mann, H. (1868). Twelfth annual report to the Massachusetts State Board of Education, 1848. In M. Mann (Ed.), *Life and works of Horace Mann* (Vol. 3, p. 669). Boston: H. B. Fuller.

McBeth, S. (1983). *Ethnic identity and the boarding school experience of west-central Oklahoma American Indians.* Washington, DC: University Press of America.

McCarthy, C. (1988). Rethinking liberal and radical perspectives on racial inequality in schooling: Making the case for nonsynchrony. *Harvard Educational Review, 58*(3), 265–279.

Méndez v. Westminster School District, 64 F. Supp. 544 (S.D. Cal. 1946), 161F, 2d 774 (9th Cir. 1947).

Morrell, E. (2008). *Critical literacy and urban youth: Pedagogies of access, dissent, and liberation.* New York: Routledge.

Morrell, E., & Duncan-Andrade, J. (2002). Promoting academic literacy with urban youth through engaging hip-hop culture. *English Journal, 9*(6), 88–92.

Myrdal, G. (1944). *An American dilemma: The Negro problem and modern democracy.* New York: Harper & Brothers.

National Association for Multicultural Education (NAME). (n.d.). *Welcome to NAME, the National Association for Multicultural Education!* Retrieved July 1, 2008, from http://www.nameorg.org/

National Comprehensive Center for Teacher Quality and Public Agenda. (2008). *Lessons learned: New teachers talk about their jobs, challenges and long-range plans.* Washington, DC: Author.

Nieto, S. (1992). *Affirming diversity: The sociopolitical context of multicultural education.* New York: Longman.

Nieto, S. (1995). From Brown heroes and holidays to assimilationist agendas: Reconsidering the critiques of multicultural education. In C. E. Sleeter & P. McLaren (Eds.), *Multicultural education, critical pedagogy, and the politics of difference* (pp. 191–220). Albany, NY: State University of New York Press.

Nieto, S. (2001). We speak in many tongues: Linguistic diversity and multicultural education. In C. P. Díaz (Ed.), *Multicultural education for the twenty-first century* (pp. 152–170). New York: Longman.

Nieto, S. (2005). Public education in the twentieth century and beyond: High hopes, broken promises, and an uncertain future. *Harvard Educational Review, 75*(1), 57–78.

Nieto, S., & Bode, P. (2008). *Affirming diversity: The sociopolitical context of multicultural education* (5th ed.). New York: Longman.

Nieto, S., Bode, P., Kang, E., & Raible, J. (2008). Identity, community, and diversity: Retheorizing multicultural curriculum for the postmodern era. In M. Connelly, M. Fang He, & J. Phillion (Eds.), *Handbook of curriculum and instruction* (pp. 176–197). Los Angeles: Sage Publishers.

Official Massachusetts information for voters: The 2002 ballot questions. (2002). Question 2: Law proposed by initiative petition: English language education in public schools. Retrieved July 1, 2008, from http://www.sec.state.ma.us/ele/elebq02/bq022.htm

Orfield, G. (2001). *Schools more separate: Consequences of a decade of resegregation.* Cambridge, MA: Civil Rights Project at Harvard University.

Padilla, A. M. (2004). Quantitative methods in multicultural education research. In J. A. Banks & C. A. M. Banks (Eds.), *Handbook of research on multicultural education* (2nd ed., pp. 127–145). San Francisco: Jossey-Bass.

Pang, V. O., Kiang, P. N., & Pak, Y. K. (2004). Asian Pacific American students. In J. A. Banks & C. A. M. Banks (Eds.), *Handbook of research on multicultural education* (2nd ed., pp. 542–563). San Francisco: Jossey-Bass.

Ramírez, M., & Castañeda, A. (1974). *Cultural democracy, bicognitive development, and education.* New York: Academic Press.

Ramsey, P. G. (2006). *Teaching and learning in a diverse world: Multicultural education for young children* (3rd ed.). New York: Teachers College Press.

Ravitch, D. (1990). E pluribus plures. *The American Scholar, 59*(3), 337–354.

Sánchez, G. I. (1940). *Forgotten people: A study of New Mexicans.* Albuquerque: University of New Mexico Press.

Santos Regó, M. A., & Nieto, S. (2000). Multicultural/intercultural teacher education in two contexts: Lessons from the United States and Spain. *Journal of Teaching and Teaching Education, 16*(4), 413–427.

Schmitz, B., Butler, J. E., Guy-Sheftall, B., & Rosenfelt, D. (2004). Women's studies and curriculum transformation in the United States. In J. A. Banks & C. A. M. Banks (Eds.), *Handbook of research on multicultural education* (2nd ed., pp. 882–905). San Francisco: Jossey-Bass.

Schofield, J. W. (1989). *Black and White in school: Trust, tension, or tolerance?* New York: Teachers College Press.

Sleeter, C. E. (1992). *Keepers of the American dream.* London: Falmer Press.

Sleeter, C. E. (2000). Epistemological diversity in research on preservice teacher preparation. *Review of Research in Education, 25,* 209–250.

Sleeter, C. E. (2001). An analysis of the critiques of multicultural education. In J. A. Banks & C. A. M. Banks (Eds.), *Handbook of research on multicultural education* (pp. 81–94). San Francisco: Jossey-Bass.

Sleeter, C. E. (2006). *Un-standardizing curriculum: Multicultural teaching in the standards-based classroom.* New York: Teachers College Press.

Sleeter, C. E., & Bernal, D. D. (2004). Critical pedagogy, critical race theory, and antiracist education: Implications for multicultural education. In J. A. Banks & C. A. M. Banks (Eds.), *Handbook of research on multicultural education* (2nd ed., pp. 240–258). San Francisco: Jossey-Bass.

Sleeter, C. E., & Grant, C. A. (1987). An analysis of multicultural education in the United States. *Harvard Educational Review, 7,* 421–444.

South African Schools Act, 1996. *Government Gazette of the Republic of South Africa,* N. 84 of 1996, v. 377, November 15, 1996.

Spargo, T. (1999). *Foucault and queer theory.* New York: Totem Books.

Spindler, G., & Spindler, L. (1994). *Pathways to cultural therapy with teachers and students.* Thousand Oaks, CA: Corwin Press.

Takaki, R. (1993). *A different mirror: A history of multicultural America.* New York: Little, Brown.

Tatum, B. D. (1997). *"Why are all the Black kids sitting together in the cafeteria?" and other conversations about race.* New York: HarperCollins.

Tetreault, M. K. (2007). Classrooms for diversity: Rethinking curriculum and pedagogy. In J. A. Banks & C. A. M. Banks (Eds.), *Multicultural education: Issues and perspectives* (6th ed., pp. 171–193). Hoboken, NJ: Wiley.

Vasquez, V. (2004). *Negotiating critical literacies with young children.* Mahwah, NJ: Lawrence Erlbaum Associates.

Villegas, A. M., & Lucas, T. (2002). *Educating culturally responsive teachers: A coherent approach.* Albany, NY: State University of New York Press.

Weinberg, M. A. (1977). *A chance to learn: A history of race and education.* Cambridge, UK: Cambridge University Press.

Wills, J. S., Lintz, A., & Mehan, H. (2004). Ethnographic studies of multicultural education in U.S. classrooms and schools. In J. A. Banks & C. A. M. Banks (Eds.), *Handbook of research on multicultural education* (2nd ed., pp. 163–183). San Francisco: Jossey-Bass.

Woodson, C. G. (1933). *The mis-education of the Negro.* Washington, DC: Associated Publishers.

Yosso, T. J. (2006). *Critical race counterstories along the Chicana/Chicano educational pipeline.* New York: Routledge.

Zeichner, K. (2003). The adequacies and inadequacies of three current strategies to recruit, prepare, and retain the best teachers for all students. *Teachers College Record, 105*(3), 490–519.

Zinn, H. (2005). *A people's history of the United States, 1492–present.* New York: Harper Perennial.

6

Multicultural education policy in Canada

Competing ideologies, interconnected discourses*

Reva Joshee
Ontario Institute for Studies in Education, University of Toronto, Canada

From the beginning of the 20th century elements of what we now call multicultural education have had a central role in the overall Canadian educational landscape. In the first part of the century, the key goal was to teach the English language and British ways to all those who were not of British or French origin, especially the original peoples of the land. Following the Second World War, recognition of and support for cultural diversity became increasingly important as part of a growing social justice infrastructure based on a Left liberal notion of human rights and intergroup understanding (Ungerleider, 1992). This multicultural model valued cultural diversity and implied a role for the state in developing a public sphere that accepted and accommodated it (Banting, 2005).

In the 1980s the neoliberal onslaught that affected much of the rest of the world began to take hold in Canada (Hyslop-Margison & Sears, 2006). However, the impact on multicultural education was not evident until the early 1990s (Joshee, 2007). As in other jurisdictions, neoconservative ideologies also became more prominent during the same era. Initially this turn to the Right included an explicit rejection of existing diversity policies in the province of Ontario, where antiracism and employment equity policies were repealed. Older policy discourses based in the liberal social justice ideology receded somewhat but did not completely disappear (Joshee, 2007). In more recent years there has been a return to the language of diversity and equity but within discourses inspired by the ideologies of neoliberalism and neoconservatism. This chapter outlines the ways in which the multicultural education policy sphere is currently being shaped by the interplay of neoliberal, neoconservative, and liberal social justice discourses. It explores the shift that has taken place in multicultural education policy in Canada by using specific examples from the province of Ontario.

The hallmark of neoliberalism is a belief in the supremacy of the free market system and an acceptance that society should operate as a marketplace (Mitchell, 2003). In Canadian education the influence of neoliberal ideology is most evident in the ever-increasing explicit connection between education and preparation for employment (Hyslop-Margison & Sears, 2006). Neoconservative ideology glorifies a particular vision of the past associated with the dominant group and its understanding of traditional values (Apple, 2006; Henderson, 2005). Neoconservatism also reinscribes a "we"/"they" dichotomy where the "we" – the dominant group – is considered to be hard working, decent, and virtuous, whereas the "they" – usually indigenous people, immigrants, women, and the poor – are considered lazy, immoral, and permissive (Apple, 2006). The dominant perspective guiding social policy development including multicultural education in Canada prior to the 1990s was closest to the recognitive paradigm of social justice (Gale, 2000) with a focus on "improving lives, relieving poverty, enhancing justice, creating opportunity" (Sears, 2005, p. 22). This approach to multiculturalism has been criticized as being more focused on containing diversity and constraining those groups seen to be "multicultural" (i.e. minoritized and racialized groups) than it is on creating a socially just and inclusive society (e.g. Dei, 1996; Lee & Cardinal, 1998). Nonetheless, it did create the space for a critical discussion of social justice and multiculturalism, which, in turn, has led to programs like the Africentric school in Toronto, the creation of a unit dedicated to addressing the concerns of African Canadians in Nova Scotia, and seven different bilingual education programs in Alberta.

National level policy discourses

The Council of Ministers of Education for Canada

Education in Canada is a responsibility of the provinces and territories. While there is some federal involvement in education, there is no federal department of education. Since the 1960s the Council of Ministers of Education for Canada (CMEC) has brought the provincial and territorial authorities responsible for education together in an attempt to provide some communication and coordination in education across the country. CMEC is also responsible for representing Canada in key international educational fora such as meetings of the Organisation for Economic Co-operation and Development (OECD). CMEC has been a significant institutional actor in propagating neoliberal discourses in education. The Joint Declaration of the Ministers for 1993 stated:

> We are all well aware of the challenges to the education systems posed by our rapidly changing world: globalization of the economy, openness with regard to other cultures, pressing needs for skilled labor, technological advances that are having an impact on our daily lives as well as the job market. These changes require constant adjustments to our educational practices to ensure high quality, accessibility, mobility and accountability.
>
> (CMEC, 2001, p. 1)

In this document CMEC was implying that the primary focus of education was to prepare students to participate in the global economy. A few years later, another CMEC document acknowledged that there were two competing visions of the goals of education. It defined the first as seeing "the school as the natural focal point for the delivery of social, health, psychological and nutritional services.... [and] as a fullservice public instrument whose role in social leveling is paramount" (CMEC, 1996, p. 11). The second vision was described as

> a concept of the school as a more narrowly focused centre of learning, with a critical mission to prepare students for the work world, for various educational futures, and for lifelong learning in an economy and society that is increasingly knowledge- and technology-based.
>
> (CMEC, 1996, p. 11)

Thus anyone who wanted to pursue social justice (or what CMEC called social leveling) was positioned as wanting schools to do everything, while advocates of the second vision were much more reasonable in wanting schools to concentrate on the core business of education.

By 1999, the goals of Canadian education were becoming more fully entrenched in a neoliberal framework. The Joint Statement of the Ministers of Education for 1999, for example, focused on the links between education and economic progress, nationally and internationally (CMEC, 1999). Neither diversity nor social justice (or even social leveling) was mentioned. Equity was seen only in relation to opportunities in education and training. It is not surprising then that by 2001 CMEC affirmed, "In recent years, we have seen a return to core subjects.... Themes of globalization, competitiveness, and productivity have guided many [provincial and territorial] administrations in this effort" (CMEC, 2001, p. 2).

In 2004 CMEC produced a report that was meant to address "education and gender equality [and] education for social inclusion" (CMEC, 2004, p. 9). After spending much of the report discussing inclusion and achievement of girls, First Nations[1] students, immigrant students, and students with disabilities, CMEC confirmed that education in Canada was officially concerned with "such issues as quality education, student success, partnerships, school-community links, transitions from school to work or higher education, and public accountability. The primary goal is the provision of quality education so that all can succeed" (CMEC, 2004, p. 45). This report affirms the importance of neoliberal goals rather than liberal social justice goals.

Federal discourses

One of the important ways in which the federal government has been engaged in education is through its responsibility in the areas of citizenship, official languages, multiculturalism, human rights, and relations with the original peoples of the land. Historically, the federal government has supported work in multicultural education through a number of its agencies working in these areas. A study conducted in 2004–2005 of diversity policy in Ontario revealed that there were six discourses evident in policy documents from both the federal and the provincial levels (Joshee, 2007). Through an examination of over 150 documents, 50 of which came from the federal departments of Canadian Heritage, Citizenship and Immigration, Justice, and Human Resources Development, and 72 of which came from a variety of Ontario government departments, the six discourses were identified. Of the six, four (equality as sameness, the business case, social cohesion, and equity of outcomes) reflected a neoliberal ideology and two (identity and rights) reflected a liberal social justice ideology. Since the time of the previous study a Rightist party, the Conservative Party, has formed the federal government. The major contribution of this party in terms of multicultural education policy has been to reaffirm the centrality of neoliberal ideology and introduce neoconservative ideology into the "policy web" (Joshee & Johnson, 2005).

For the sake of brevity, instead of providing an overview of all of the discourses present in the work of the complex of federal departments and agencies working in the area of diversity, the following discussion will focus on the Department of Canadian Heritage, which houses the federal Multiculturalism Program.

Given the ideological position of the Conservative government it is not surprising that a key goal of multiculturalism is to "leverage the benefits of diversity" (Department of Canadian Heritage, 2007, p. 26). This is accomplished, for example, through joint initiatives of the Department of Canadian Heritage and the Department of Foreign Affairs and International Trade "in areas of shared interest such as social cohesion, and pursuing priority activities such as the promotion of cultural exchanges in important markets like the United States as well as in key emerging markets like China and Brazil" (Department of Canadian Heritage, 2007, p. 26).

These same sentiments were reflected in a policy paper produced in 2004 tellingly titled *Developing the Business Case for Multiculturalism* (Burstein, 2004). Two of the key strategic concerns of multiculturalism were identified as "the need to capitalize on economic globalization. . . . [and] to manage actual and perceived threats to safety and security" (Burstein, 2004, pp. 9–10). In the interest of capitalizing on economic globalization, state-based policy actors are enjoined to pay attention to the link (or the potential link) between immigration and international trade and investment. Writes Burstein (2004), "To capitalize on these human assets, structural barriers and discrimination will need to be forcefully addressed" (p. 9). With regard to safety and security we are informed that

> multicultural policies have a palliative effect on both [international threats to security and backlash against minoritized groups in Canada]. The creation of an inclusive identity – where minority interests coincide with those of the larger community – increases the likelihood that minority groups will cooperate with police and intelligence agencies in their efforts to thwart external security threats.
>
> (Burstein, 2004, p. 10)

Thus addressing racism and exclusion is linked to creating international economic opportunities and ensuring security. These brief quotes provide examples of two central neoliberal diversity discourses: the business case and social cohesion (Joshee, 2007).

The business case discourse is based on the logic that multiculturalism (and diversity more generally) is valuable to the extent that it is a resource for international business and provides a strategy for managing workplace diversity. Within this discourse members of ethnocultural communities are constructed primarily, if not solely, as contributors to the economy, that is, as workers and consumers rather than citizens in a political and social sense (Fleras & Elliott, 1996). The social cohesion discourse is a response to the consequences of market-focused policies and programs. The competition and individualism inherent in the market model cause strains in the social and political realms of a society. Social cohesion is invoked as a corrective measure that can help to increase social solidarity and restore faith in the institutions of government (Jenson, 1998). Moreover, social cohesion is seen as a key to addressing real or perceived threats of terrorism (Jeannotte et al., 2002). It is based on the logic that if we can see past our differences and be nice to others then all will be well (Bernard, 1999). Multiculturalism, and diversity more generally, is cast as a problem, because any focus on difference is seen to pose "challenges to social cohesion" (Organisation for Economic Co-operation and Development [OECD], 2004).

Neoconservative ideology is reflected in a discourse of the tolerant Canadian. This thinking is evident in many of the Conservative government's messages about multiculturalism. For example, Prime Minister Stephen Harper has said that he "believes the characteristic that most defines Canadians is their openness. This openness was in evidence during the first encounters between the First Nations and the Europeans, and it has been a constant ever since through our evolution as a country" (Department of Canadian Heritage, 2006, p. xiv). The "we" in this case is the European group, which, we are told, has always shown tolerance and acceptance of others. The implication then is that any conflict, past or current, exists because "the Others" were not open, tolerant, and accepting.

The combination of neoliberal and neoconservative discourses has led to a reorientation of the federal multiculturalism program. In the early 1990s the program was defined by three key goals: encouraging civic participation, fostering the development of unique identities as part of a strong national identity, and addressing issues of social justice. Currently the Department of

Canadian Heritage defines its mandate as seeking "to contribute to a cohesive and creative Canada in which all Canadians have opportunities to participate in Canada's cultural and civic life" (Department of Canadian Heritage, 2007, p. 9). With regard to multiculturalism, the department focuses on "targeted measures for ethno-cultural and ethno-racial communities [to] assist these groups to more effectively participate into [sic] all aspects of Canadian life" (Department of Canadian Heritage, 2007, p. 67). Importantly the focus is not on addressing systemic or institutional barriers to participation but on helping minoritized groups to become more involved in the society as it is. While the Multiculturalism Program still acknowledges the existence of racism, the major initiative of the Conservative government for addressing racism is a program that recognizes historic injustices.

This has the effect of constructing racism as largely an issue of the past; any lingering evidence of racism is constructed as individual pathology. Finally, future directions for the program have been identified as addressing the supposed concerns of minoritized youth (no evidence is provided that young people themselves have identified these concerns) including economic integration, youth-at-risk, safety, and security (Department of Canadian Heritage, 2006). In short, the older agenda of citizenship, identity, and social justice has been subordinated to an agenda of economic participation and social cohesion.

Provincial discourses

Given that education is a provincial responsibility and that each province and territory has a somewhat unique approach to education, it is impossible to examine the full range of multicultural education policy discourses in Canada. Instead, this discussion will focus on Canada's largest province, Ontario. It must be understood that there are important differences across the 10 provinces and 3 territories and that there is interesting and important work being done in each jurisdiction. The example here provides an opportunity to understand how the policy web structures possibilities for action and activism. There are several different provincial ministries and agencies that play some role in multicultural education in Ontario, including the Ministry of Training, Colleges and Universities, the Ministry of Citizenship and Immigration, the Office of Francophone Affairs, the Ontario Human Rights Commission, and, of course, the Ministry of Education. Documents from all of these departments were analyzed as part of the 2004–05 study of diversity discourses mentioned above. The following discussion will focus on the specific discourses found in the work of the Ministry of Education.

In the mid-1990s, a Progressive Conservative government came to power in the province and quickly distanced itself from all work related to social justice. The Progressive Conservatives were defeated in 2003 by the Liberal Party, which was re-elected in 2007. The Liberal government has been far less hostile towards social justice than its predecessor, but it has not reinstated any of the policies or programs repealed by the Progressive Conservatives. The current government policy is firmly rooted in a neoliberal paradigm. The key neoliberal discourses present in the work of the Ministry of Education are social cohesion and equality of outcomes.

The social cohesion discourse is most evident in the specific policy work on safe schools and character development. The logic underlying policy statements on safe schools is that safety is a prerequisite for fulfilling the academic mandate of schools. The focus of the Safe Schools Act, which came into force in 2000, has been primarily reactive, that is, addressing violence after it occurs through lockdown procedures, suspensions, and expulsions. Although this area of policy was not initially identified as relating to multiculturalism or diversity, criticism of the act based on its disproportionate negative effect on students of First Nations origins, students with disabilities, and students from some racialized groups (Bhattacharjee, 2003) has resulted in revisions to the official policy. The current policy framework for safe schools makes explicit reference to the Ministry's Policy and Program Memorandum 119, a Policy on Anti-Racism and Ethnocultural Equity, and puts more focus on violence prevention, but true to the logic of social cohesion the focus of intervention is on specific individual behaviors, most particularly bullying (Safe Schools Action Team, 2006). As Policy and Program Memorandum 144 on Bullying Prevention and Intervention makes clear, bullying is seen as an act of one individual (or a group of individuals) against another individual and thus should be addressed by teaching students how to behave appropriately. Although there is an acknowledgement that bullying may be linked to issues of social diversity, there is no discussion of addressing systemic issues such as racism or sexism that are related to direct violence (Bickmore, 2005; Smith & Carson, 1998).

In a similar vein, the new character development strategy focuses on teaching students behaviors and attitudes that will contribute to "safe, healthy, and orderly school environments" (Ontario Ministry of Education, 2006, p. iii). In particular the focus is on helping students "to develop self discipline and the personal management skills that will make their communities, workplaces and lives the best that they can be" (Ontario Ministry of Education, 2006, p. 2). There is recognition that Ontario communities are culturally diverse and therefore that the mission of character development must be to "find common ground" and build consensus (Ontario Ministry of Education, 2006, p. 4). The message with regard to diversity is clear: it is a source of conflict and therefore we must move beyond it by focusing on commonalities. Focusing on social cohesion not only allows us to move beyond divisiveness but also helps to create a safe environment within which students will be able to concentrate on academic success.

The equality of outcomes discourse recognizes that inequalities exist and that the state has an obligation to intercede on behalf of disadvantaged members of society. The underlying logic of this discourse assumes that existing structures are fair and that all members of society want the same thing, namely to participate in the economy. As we see in the numerous initiatives designed to address "youth-at-risk," outcomes are defined in terms of a narrow understanding of academic achievement (mainly test scores). In addition, inclusive schools are defined "by the extent to which *all* students make successful transitions to the postsecondary destination of their choice" (Ontario Ministry of Education, 2005a, p. 2), and the legacy of educators is that their students "will take on the wide range of occupations and roles necessary to maintain thriving communities and prosperous provincial, territorial, and national economies" (Ontario Ministry of Education, 2005a, p. 4). Thus students are valued not for the people they are but for the workers they will become.

The consequences of neoliberal and neoconservative discourses

Despite some claims to the contrary, the cumulative effect of the neoliberal and neoconservative diversity discourses is to construct diversity as a problem to be addressed in limited ways. The terms *diversity* and *equity* are used to refer primarily, if not exclusively, to groups that are having trouble with the existing school system. As one report explains:

> Within every society there are vulnerable groups who, for a variety of reasons, require special attention, programs, and supports. In this report, the populations discussed in terms of social inclusion in the educational system are youth, immigrant students, and students with special needs.
>
> (CMEC, 2004, p. 21)

Thus diversity becomes understood only in terms of students who are having trouble succeeding. Programs are focused on them, to help them to fit in to the existing system. Minority students are the ones with the deficit; the gaze does not land on the system as deficient or inadequate. The system remains unchallenged.

The second consequence of this positioning is that if a group is succeeding academically then it is no longer seen as having legitimate concerns with regard to equity in education. We have seen this in the recent concerns over the achievement of boys in literacy tests. Girls got better scores; therefore they could have no legitimate complaints against the education system. Issues of harassment might be addressed as part of the larger set of concerns relating to safety, but equity goals for girls have been achieved and surpassed. The new equity issue has become "the challenge of improving the literacy skills of boys overall" (CMEC, 2004, p. 20). A similar situation appears to be developing in relation to racialized groups who are achieving academic success.

A third consequence of this particular framing of diversity is that the remedies are all focused on the individual, even though the individuals are constructed as members of minority groups. The individuals are viewed as needing special attention to be able to achieve success in school. This requires that additional resources and time be focused on those individuals. In a climate of cutbacks, efficiency, and accountability, resources and time are scarce commodities. Consequently, the students needing extra time and attention are seen as a drag on the system that can get in the way of the learning of other students. This then leads to the inevitable conclusion that it may not be worth the effort to try to address the needs of certain students or that it might be acceptable to exclude these students from school rather than to allow them to be a burden on their teachers and classmates.

Liberal social justice discourses

Notwithstanding the dominant ideologies discussed above, there are still reservoirs of social justice in Canadian education. The Canadian Studies Program of the Department of Canadian Heritage has continued to fund educational material that explores Canada's multicultural reality. Several of these projects reflect social justice discourses. For example, a section of the *Alberta Online Encyclopedia*, which the Canadian Studies Program has supported, examines issues of cultural diversity. One entry in the online encyclopedia is titled "Canadian Multiculturalism: An Inclusive Citizenship." Significantly, the entry appears in its entirety on the Department of Canadian Heritage Multiculturalism Program website. It begins by asserting that "Canadian multiculturalism is fundamental to our belief that all citizens are equal. Multiculturalism ensures that all citizens can keep their identities, can take pride in their ancestry and have a sense of belonging" ("Canadian Multiculturalism," n.d.). The final paragraph proclaims:

> Multiculturalism is a relationship between Canada and the Canadian people. Our citizenship gives us equal rights and equal responsibilities. By taking an active part in our civic affairs, we affirm these rights and strengthen Canada's democracy, ensuring that a multicultural, integrated and inclusive citizenship will be every Canadian's inheritance.
> ("Canadian Multiculturalism," n.d.)

What we see reflected in this educational resource are the discourses of identity, recognition, and rights. The identity discourse links multicultural education with valuing and developing particular ethnocultural identities. The discourse of recognition speaks to the need for all members of society to respect other people's identities and to include members of diverse communities in public life in ways that do not require them to dissociate from their cultural identities. Finally, the rights discourse "is closely linked to notions of human rights and therefore sees social, cultural, and economic justice, rather than economic benefit, as the rationale for supporting diversity" (Joshee, 2007, p. 182). While the discourse of recognition was not identified in the 2004–05 study, it was evident in a subsequent study of diversity policies in four Ontario school districts (Joshee, DeBeer, Goldberg, & Saunders, 2006).

At the provincial level, liberal social justice discourses are present in the very few antiracism and multiculturalism policies that were not repealed by the Progressive Conservatives, such as the Policy on Antiracism and Ethnocultural Equity (1993). This policy statement affirms that

> educational structures, policies, and programs have been mainly European in perspective and have failed to take into account the viewpoints, experiences, and needs of Aboriginal peoples and many racial and ethnocultural minorities. As a result, systemic inequities exist in the school system.
>
> (Ontario Ministry of Education, 1993)

Furthermore, the policy statement declares, "At all stages of implementation, a high priority shall be assigned to broadening the curriculum to include diverse perspectives and to eliminating stereotyping" (Ontario Ministry of Education, 1993). Here we see an explicit acknowledgment of the systemic character of racism as well as evidence of the need to recognize and respect cultural identities other than those of the dominant groups.

Perhaps more significantly, social justice discourses have recently reappeared in some of the work of the Literacy and Numeracy Secretariat of the Ministry of Education. The publication *Many Roots, Many Voices: Supporting English Language Learners in Every Classroom*, for example, draws on discourses of identity and recognition. Although the document begins by affirming that the goal of education is the success of every student (echoing the equality of opportunity discourse), it also speaks to the importance of focusing on first language development because first languages "help students preserve vital links with their families and cultural backgrounds and a solid sense of their own identity" (Ontario Ministry of Education, 2005b, p. 16). Additionally, the document encourages teachers to provide all students with "opportunities to share information about their languages, cultures, and experiences. In this way, they can develop an enriching awareness of both the differences and similarities among their cultures and languages, and all students can experience a sense of belonging" (Ontario Ministry of Education, 2005b, p. 17). One of the results of situating the discussion within the discourses of identity and recognition is that the definition of student success is expanded to include the development of mental flexibility and problem-solving skills, experiencing a sense of cultural stability and continuity, understanding their own cultural and family values, and becoming aware of the value of cultural diversity and multiple perspectives (Ontario Ministry of Education, 2005b, p. 16).

Mixing the old and new

We have now seen that neoliberal, neoconservative, and liberal social justice policy discourses coexist in the Canadian multicultural education policy arena. What becomes even more evident at the local level is that all of these sets of discourses can and do become embedded in particular initiatives. The final section of the chapter will provide an example from the Toronto

District School Board that illustrates the complexity of working for equity and diversity in the current policy context.

The Toronto District School Board (TDSB) was established in 1998 as the result of the amalgamation of seven distinct school districts, each of which had a different history with regard to equity and diversity. The TDSB now serves over 270,000 students, making it the largest school board in Canada and the fifth largest in North America. The website for the TDSB notes that approximately 45% of its students have a language other than English as their first language and about 12% of them arrived in Canada in the last three years.

Shortly after the amalgamation, work involving TDSB staff and members of diverse equity-seeking groups resulted in the creation of the Equity Foundation Statement and an accompanying set of procedures and guidelines (TDSB, 1999). This statement was followed by the Human Rights Policy (TDSB, 2000a), the Guidelines and Procedures on Religious Accommodation (TDSB, 2000b), and the Employment Equity Policy (TDSB, 2004). Together these four documents are the primary diversity policy statements for the TDSB. The discourses represented in these statements are largely social justice based, with a particular emphasis on recognition and rights. These four statements and related documents also introduce the discourses of equality of outcomes and social cohesion. Equality of outcomes can be seen, for example, on the web page that announces the TDSB commitment to equity in education as it affirms support for "a school climate that encourages all students to work to high standards, affirm the worth of all students, and help them strengthen their sense of identity and develop a positive self-image" (TDSB, n.d.). Social cohesion is evident especially in the Religious Accommodation document's focus on safety. For example, the first paragraph of the statement ends with a focus on a safe and respectful environment. The link to safety reappears in seven other places in the document, including three explicit references to the link between the Religious Accommodation policy and the Safe Schools policy.

Currently one of the key equity initiatives of the board is a program called Model Schools for Inner Cities. The program is meant to address the needs of students from economically disadvantaged backgrounds. Recognizing that economic poverty is often linked with other kinds of social disadvantage that influences school achievement, the TDSB has identified four essential elements of model schools:

1 *Equity*: Achieving fairness and equity to ensure the lives and realities of students are reflected and affirmed.
2 *Community*: The school becomes the heart of its community, with education and school resources acting as pillars of the neighborhood.
3 *Inclusiveness*: An inclusive culture that respects and reflects all aspects of the school, its community, students, and staff.
4 *Expectations*: Achievement enhances self-esteem, which in turn fuels achievement. Every child is expected to progress to the highest level of which they are capable, regardless of economic or cultural background. (TDSB, 2006, p. 2).

It is important to note that the starting point is one of disadvantage and that the key goal for students is academic achievement.

While the TDSB, and before it the Toronto Board of Education, has a long history of addressing inner-city education, this latest initiative arose from the work of the Model Schools for Inner Cities Task Force. This body, which included administrators, trustees (i.e. elected members of the school board), researchers, representatives of the provincial government, and one parent, was developed in 2004 with a mandate to identify effective models of inner-city education. Based on the advice of the task force, the TDSB committed itself to identifying and providing support for at least two schools that would become model inner-city schools. These model schools would help to provide models of best practice that could be emulated by other schools. The task force's vision was articulated in terms of the four essential elements highlighted above. These were more fully explained in the task force's proposal for the selection and support of model schools. Finally, the report also included an appendix that provided a fictionalized account of a day in the life of a model school.

The text of the report is replete with language reflecting liberal social justice discourses. For example, the schools the reader is asked to envision at the outset of the report are places where "newcomers to Canada are greeted in their native tongues, . . . social justice is the foundation for all teachable moments, . . . [and] all families are welcomed and learning starts the moment you walk through the front doors" (Model Schools for Inner Cities Task Force, 2005, p. 1). The report declares:

> Achieving fairness and equity are predicated on ensuring the lives and experiences of our students and their families are reflected and affirmed in the school curriculum and that relevant issues from various social justice perspectives are embedded in ongoing academic programs. Students are validated for who they are.
> (Model Schools for Inner Cities Task Force, 2005, p. 3)

Success is defined as students being able to critically question the world around them and understand the views of others (Model Schools for Inner Cities Task Force, 2005, p. 5).

Significantly, while the task force clearly stated that achieving equity and fairness would be predicated on a curriculum that addressed social justice issues and helped students to develop critical thinking skills, this aspect is not present in the current documentation on the program (TDSB, 2007). Also noteworthy is the fact that the narrative on the day in the life of a model school, which tells the story of a single-parent immigrant family, defines the family (and its individual members) largely in terms of deficit. The mother is someone who speaks limited English (Model Schools for Inner Cities Task Force, 2005, p. 27), cannot provide meals for her children (we are told on page 23 that when the children arrive they have a hot breakfast provided by the school, that they later have a hot lunch provided by "neighborhood assistants," and that in the evening they share a potluck meal prepared by the School Council), and needs assistance to access health care for her children (the school has arranged for a health and dental assessment for her youngest child and we are told on page 26 that the mother is "relieved she doesn't have to arrange the appointment herself due to her limited English").

The school helps her in all of these areas. The children are educationally challenged. For example, the oldest child and all of her classmates must attend remedial academic sessions after school (Model Schools for Inner Cities Task Force, 2005). The only skill the mother is depicted as having is the ability to read a story in Urdu to her youngest child, who is in the school-based day care (Model Schools for Inner Cities Task Force, 2005). The oldest child does help tutor younger students, which, in turn, fosters the image of a school where none of the children could possibly be academically successful without significant intervention and support. The oldest child intervenes in a conflict in the schoolyard, conjuring images of a school where violence is a problem and social cohesion becomes a priority. What is particularly important is that the cumulative effect of the narrative is to position the school as a benevolent caretaker rather than the hub of a respectful and inclusive community based on principles of social justice.

It is important to note that the schools that were part of the pilot project based on this report did include social justice inspired work as part of their agenda. For example, one school noted that it offered a Black Culture program (Firgrove School, 2007), and another offered heritage language classes in Tamil and Bengali (Willowpark School, 2007). Both of these schools, however, remained primarily focused on improving literacy and numeracy scores, improving the social skills of students, and working with "at-risk" youth.

Concluding remarks

Multicultural education policy in Canada is heavily influenced by neoliberal and neoconservative ideology. Consequently, diversity is being reframed in ways that stress that those groups identified as diverse are themselves the problem. They are seen as lacking what it takes to succeed and as a threat to social cohesion. Even though they are not the predominant discourses in the field, liberal social justice discourses do continue to influence the work of policy actors at the national, provincial, and local levels. What this analysis shows is that current multicultural education policy work, especially at the local level, can best be described as an ongoing dialogue where neoliberal and neoconservative discourses are modified by social justice discourses and vice versa. At the same time it is vital to understand that the overwhelming presence of neoliberal – and to a lesser extent neoconservative – discourses means that it is increasingly difficult to make arguments for social-justice-inspired visions of education. The current policy landscape is not as hospitable to critical multicultural education as it once was, but this does not mean that multicultural education has been forgotten in Canada. Quite clearly the struggle for social justice and equity continues.

Notes

* This chapter is in part based on research funded by the Social Sciences and Humanities Research Council of Canada.
1 *First Nations* is a term used to describe the original peoples of Canada.

References

Apple, M. (2006). Understanding and interrupting neoliberalism and neoconservatism in education. *Pedagogies: An International Journal, 1*(1), 21–26.
Banting K. G. (2005). The multicultural welfare state: International experience and North American narratives. *Social Policy and Administration, 39*(2), 98–115.
Bernard, P. (1999). *Social cohesion: A critique* (CPRN discussion paper No. F-09). Ottawa, ON: Canadian Policy Research Networks.
Bhattacharjee, K. (2003). *The Ontario Safe Schools Act: School discipline and discrimination.* Toronto, ON: Ontario Human Rights Commission. Retrieved March 19, 2005, from www.ohrc.on.ca
Bickmore, K. (2005). Teacher development for conflict participation: Facilitating learning for "difficult citizenship" education. *International Journal of Citizenship and Teacher Education, 1*(2). Retrieved April 2, 2007, from www.citized.info
Burstein, M. (2004). *Developing the business case for multiculturalism.* Ottawa, ON: Department of Canadian Heritage, Outreach and Promotion Directorate, Multiculturalism and Human Rights Branch.
Canadian multiculturalism: An inclusive citizenship. (n.d.). *Alberta Online Encyclopedia* (Celebrating multiculturalism). Retrieved December 19, 2007, from www.edukits.ca

Council of Ministers of Education for Canada (CMEC). (1996). *The development of education in Canada* (Report of Canada). Retrieved May 16, 2007, from www.cmec.ca

Council of Ministers of Education for Canada (CMEC). (1999). *Joint ministerial declaration: Shared priorities in education at the dawn of the 21st century: Future directions for the Council of Ministers of Education, Canada*. Retrieved March 18, 2007, from www.cmec.ca

Council of Ministers of Education for Canada (CMEC). (2001). *Learning content and strategies for living together in the 21st century* (Report of Canada). Retrieved March 20, 2005, from www.cmec.ca

Council of Ministers of Education for Canada (CMEC). (2004). *Quality education for all young people: Challenges, trends, and priorities* (Report of Canada). Retrieved March 18, 2007, from www.cmec.ca

Dei, G. S. (1996). *Anti-racism education: Theory and practice*. Halifax, NS: Fernwood Publishing.

Department of Canadian Heritage. (2006). *Annual report on the operations of the Multiculturalism Act, 2005–06*. Ottawa, ON: Minister of Supply and Services.

Department of Canadian Heritage. (2007). *Departmental performance report, 2006–07, Canadian Heritage*. Ottawa, ON: Minister of Supply and Services.

Firgrove School. (2007). *Firgrove School people*. Retrieved January 5, 2008, from www.tdsb.on.ca

Fleras, A., & Elliott, J. (1996). *Unequal relations: An introduction to race, ethnic and aboriginal dynamics in Canada* (2nd ed.). Scarborough, ON: Prentice-Hall Canada.

Gale, T. (2000). Rethinking social justice in schools: How will we recognize it when we see it? *International Journal of Inclusive Education, 4*(3), 253–269.

Henderson, D. (2005). What is education for? Situating history, cultural understandings and studies of society and environment against neo-conservative critiques of curriculum reform. *Australian Journal of Education, 49*(3), 306–319.

Hyslop-Margison, E., & Sears, A. (2006). *Neoliberalism, globalization and human capital learning: Reclaiming education for democratic citizenship*. Dordrecht: Springer.

Jeannotte, M. S., Stanley, D., Pendakur, R., Jamieson, B., Williams, M., & Aizlewood, A. (2002). *Buying in or dropping out: The public policy implications of social cohesion research*. Ottawa, ON: Department of Canadian Heritage.

Jenson, J. (1998). *Social cohesion: The state of Canadian research*. Ottawa, ON: Canadian Policy Research Networks. Retrieved January 27, 2005, from www.cprn.org

Joshee, R. (2007). Opportunities for social justice work: The Ontario diversity policy web. *The Journal of Educational Administration and Foundations, 18*(1 & 2), 171–199.

Joshee, R., DeBeer, Y., Goldberg, M. T., & Saunders, S. R. (2006). *Versions and subversions of diversity: Discursive struggles in Ontario school districts*. Paper presented at the annual meeting of the Canadian Society for Studies in Education, Toronto, ON.

Joshee, R., & Johnson, L. (2005). Multicultural education in the United States and Canada: The importance of national policies. In N. Bascia, A. Cumming, A. Datnow, K. Leithwood, & D. Livingstone (Eds.), *International handbook of educational policy* (pp. 53–74). Dordrecht: Kluwer Academic Publishing.

Lee, J.-A., & Cardinal, L. (1998). Hegemonic nationalism and the politics of feminism and multiculturalism in Canada. In V. Strong-Boag, S. Grace, A. Eisenberg, & J. Anderson (Eds.), *Painting the maple leaf: Essays on race, gender, and the construction of Canada* (pp. 215–241). Vancouver, BC: UBC Press.

Mitchell, K. (2003). Educating the national citizen in neoliberal times: From the multicultural self to the strategic cosmopolitan. *Transactions of the Institute of British Geographers, 28*(4), 387–403.

Model Schools for Inner Cities Task Force. (2005). *Model Schools for Inner Cities Task Force report*. Toronto, ON: Toronto District School Board.

Ontario Ministry of Education. (1993). *Antiracism and ethnocultural equity in school boards: Guideline for policy development and implementation*. Toronto, ON: Author.

Ontario Ministry of Education. (2005a). An educator's guide to program pathways (draft). Toronto, ON: Author.

Ontario Ministry of Education. (2005b). *Many roots, many voices: Supporting English language learners in every classroom*. Toronto, ON: Queen's Printer for Ontario.

Ontario Ministry of Education. (2006). *Finding common ground: Character development in Ontario schools, K-12*. Toronto, ON: Author.

Organisation for Economic Co-operation and Development (OECD). (2004). *OECD urges educators to address social cohesion risks*. Retrieved March 13, 2005, from www.oecd.org

Safe Schools Action Team. (2006). *Safe schools policy and practice: An agenda for action*. Toronto, ON: Ontario Ministry of Education.

Sears, R. V. (2005, March–April). The Left: From hope to sneers in only 25 years. *Policy Options*, 19–26.

Smith, D. C., & Carson, T. R. (1998). *Educating for a peaceful future*. Toronto, ON: Kagan and Woo.

Toronto District School Board (TDSB). (n.d). *Equity in the TDSB*. Retrieved June 12, 2007, from www.tdsb.on.ca

Toronto District School Board (TDSB). (1999). *Equity policy*. Retrieved June 12, 2007, from www.tdsb.on.ca

Toronto District School Board (TDSB). (2000a). *Human rights policy*. Retrieved June 12, 2007, from www.tdsb.on.ca

Toronto District School Board (TDSB). (2000b). *Guidelines and procedures on religious accommodation*. Retrieved June 12, 2007, from www.tdsb.on.ca

Toronto District School Board (TDSB). (2004). *Employment equity policy*. Retrieved June 12, 2007, from www.tdsb.on.ca

Toronto District School Board (TDSB). (2006). *Model schools for inner cities brochure*. Retrieved September 30, 2007, from www.tdsb.on.ca

Toronto District School Board (TDSB). (2007). *Inner city model schools: Research and review plan*. Retrieved January 5, 2008, from www.tdsb.on.ca

Ungerleider, C. (1992). Immigration, multiculturalism, and citizenship: The development of the Canadian social justice infrastructure. *Canadian Ethnic Studies*, *24*(3), 7–22.

Willowpark School. (2007). *Willowpark School profile*. Retrieved January 5, 2008, from www.tdsb.on.ca

7

Multicultural education in Australia

Two generations of evolution

Christine Inglis
University of Sydney, Australia

Australia is a nation of immigrants, with nearly one-quarter of its population born overseas while a further quarter, who were born in Australia, have at least one immigrant parent. Developing educational responses for this substantial number of immigrants and their children has involved major changes in Australia's educational institutions. This chapter outlines the changes and highlights how changes in Australian society and the international arena play a major part in that process of educational innovation.[1] In less than 50 years Australia has moved from being a society which expected immigrants to assimilate rapidly to one which, along with Canada, officially adopted multiculturalism as the model guiding policies relating to the incorporation of immigrant minorities and their children. Education was one of the main institutional areas which underwent significant changes as assimilation was replaced by a suite of responses which together constitute what in Australia is identified as multicultural education. Educational responses to diversity are, however, rarely static, and this chapter also traces how new developments since the 1980s have extended Australia's responses.

Australia's changing ethnic diversity and policy models

In 2006, Australia was a country of almost 20 million persons, of whom 70.9% were born in Australia (Australian Bureau of Statistics, 2007). Among the overseas born, the major countries of birth were England (4.3%), New Zealand (2.0%), China (1.0%), Italy (1.0%), and Vietnam (0.8%) (Australian Bureau of Statistics, 2007). Although this percentage of immigrants and their diversity resemble those at the time of Federation in 1901, they differ substantially from the situation in 1947, when Australia began its ambitious program to use immigration to increase its population by 1% a year. By 1947, after two world wars and the 1930s depression, the immigrant population was only 8.8% (Australian Bureau of Statistics, 1947). The majority of immigrants (66.0%) were from the United Kingdom (Australian Bureau of Statistics, 1947). The largest non-Anglo-Celtic background group were those born in Italy, who were 4.5% of the small proportion of overseas born in the total population of 7.6 million (Australian Bureau of Statistics, 1947).

In the second half of the 20th century, immigration was responsible for a substantial increase in Australia's population, as well as a major diversification in its ethnicity, with an increase in the percentages of those from continental Europe, Asia, and the Middle East. Associated with this growth has been increasing diversity in the languages spoken in Australian homes. By 2006, while English still remained the most common language spoken at home (78.5%), Cantonese and Mandarin Chinese were spoken by 2.3% of the population, Italian by 1.6%, Greek by 1.3%, and Arabic by 1.2%. In addition, the census recorded over 400 other languages spoken in homes. The impact of this language-based diversity varies between states. In New South Wales (NSW) and Victoria, the two most populous states, over a quarter of their populations speak languages other than English at home. For them, educational provisions for diversity have greater importance and involve somewhat different strategies than occurs in other states, with smaller non-English-speaking background populations ranging only from 8% to 14%. This diversity of languages and the absence of major residential concentrations of languages other than English have implications for the role of languages in Australian schools. Another significant change in the immigrant population is that selection policies since the mid-1980s have moved to greater preference to highly skilled migrants. In 2006–2007, two-thirds of all permanent immigrants to Australia were admitted under the skilled stream of immigrants (Department of Immigration and Citizenship [DIAC], 2008).

From the earliest days of British settlement, assimilation guided policy approaches to immigrant settlement and incorporation. However, by the late 1960s, its key assumption, that no adjustment in Australian institutions such as education was necessary to ensure immigrants' harmonious and peaceful incorporation into Australian society, was being challenged by the growing proportion of non-Anglo-Celtic immigrants. Teachers were increasingly finding students unable to speak English and who dropped out of school without completing their education. The growing role of educational professionals in formulating child-centered educational policies when combined with the increasing influence of voters of immigrant backgrounds was a major factor in the abandonment of assimilation policy and its replacement by the brief-lived policy of "integration." This policy was predicated on the view that, while immigrants needed to assimilate in public, they could retain their own culture in the private, home sphere (Martin, 1978). By the 1970s, the limitations of the integration model had led to increasing calls for an alternative policy of multiculturalism, which was predicated on the desirability of change within education and other Australian institutions.

Key policy milestones in the development of multiculturalism since then have included the Galbally Report (Galbally, 1978), which recommended that the Australian government should provide direct funding to ethnic organizations and other financial initiatives to assist those from non-English-speaking backgrounds (NESB). NESB replaced the earlier administrative term "immigrant" to refer to the group targeted for policy responses as it became evident that the descendants of immigrants continued to have distinctive policy needs extending beyond the first generation. Dissatisfaction with the term's inability to distinguish the wide range of diversity, its mixing of the relatively disadvantaged with those who were not, and its negative connotations led to a governmental decision in 1996 to replace it in official communication (DIAC, 1996). Now the most commonly used policy term is culturally and linguistically diverse (CALD). In 1989, the National Agenda for a Multicultural Australia (Office of Multicultural Affairs, 1989) was the first major summary of the policy initiatives which the Australian government was supporting.

Subsequently, with the election of a Liberal-National government in 1996 under the prime ministership of John Howard, who was widely seen as unsupportive of multiculturalism, many of the national institutional structures associated with multiculturalism, and the funding initiatives supporting proactive policies, disappeared. At the same time, many of the state-based institutions with local responsibility for ethnic minorities also changed their names, reflecting a shift away from "multiculturalism." In New South Wales, the state with the largest and most diverse population, the Ethnic Affairs Commission, which had published a groundbreaking 1978 report entitled *Participation* (Ethnic Affairs Commission of New South Wales, 1978), was renamed the Commission for Community Relations for a Multicultural New South Wales. In 2007, the word "Multicultural" was replaced by the word "Citizenship" in the name of the national government department with responsibility for immigration and settlement. Just prior to the November 2007 election which brought the Rudd government to office, the government's Human Rights and Equal Opportunity Commission (HREOC) prepared a position paper calling for a recommitment to multiculturalism (HREOC, 2007). While the new Rudd government had made a number of announcements concerning educational matters, by March 2008 there was none concerning "multiculturalism" apart from the title of the Parliamentary Secretary assisting the Minister for Immigration and Citizenship being changed from "Immigration and Citizenship" to "Multicultural Affairs and Settlement Services."

The abandonment of assimilation and redressing inequality in education

Up until the 1960s, Australian schools made no special provisions for students from non-English-speaking backgrounds, since the assimilation model considered this unnecessary, as it was assumed they would soon merge into the wider society. However, by the 1960s, these assumptions were being questioned, as Australian schools were catering for increased enrollments of students from non-English-speaking backgrounds whose own parents often came from rural areas and lacked extensive schooling. The classroom reality was that these students were failing to achieve on the same basis as their Australian-born peers, with many dropping out early from secondary school or being disruptive in the classroom.

The initial explanation for these problems was that students lacked fluency in English. This led to calls for special assistance in English, already available to adult migrants, to be extended to migrant children. In 1969, New South Wales commenced a pilot project, the Child Migrant Education Program, teaching English as a second language (ESL) in nine schools. The next year, 1970, the Australian Department of Immigration took over the funding for these programs. Since this time, ESL programs have been a mainstay of all Australian multicultural education provisions. With the realization that many Australian-reared or -born students could also benefit from ESL assistance, ESL programs have continued to develop. There is also a cadre of specialist ESL teachers with access to a professional career path.

In the latter part of the 1970s, the special difficulties facing adolescent immigrants adjusting to Australian schools led to the introduction of intensive English centers, where new arrivals are able to attend special secondary school centers where they receive intensive English assistance, studying the regular secondary curriculum and gaining knowledge of the Australian school's culture and organization. As their level of English improves, they are transferred into regular secondary schools, where they are supported by the school's ESL teachers.

The 1972 election of a reformist Labor government was promptly followed by a review of educational inequality in Australian schools (Interim Committee for the Australian Schools Commission, 1973). The 1973 Karmel Report identified a number of groups experiencing inequality, including those from migrant and working-class backgrounds, those from rural schools, and girls. Although often criticized for its reliance on using special funding to overcome disadvantage in schools, it was nevertheless important since it provided NESB students and their schools with additional funding. This allowed the development of ESL programs and the employment of additional teachers and teacher aides to address the needs of immigrant students and work with parents and community groups to overcome their lack of familiarity with the Australian educational system.

The focus on languages and cultural maintenance

Another early priority in programs to meet the educational needs of immigrant children concerned cultural maintenance and, in particular, mother-tongue language learning. Such languages came to be described as "community languages" to distinguish them from the traditional "foreign" languages, which at that time in Australia referred to languages such as Latin, French, German, Indonesian, and Chinese. These foreign languages dominated language teaching, which was concentrated in academically oriented secondary schools preparing students for university. Underlying the calls of lobby groups for opportunities for students to learn their mother tongue was a range of rationales. These included: social justice, the desirability of children becoming literate in their mother tongue to facilitate communication with their families and community, and pedagogical arguments that this would improve student performance in other school subjects, thereby overcoming educational inequality.

A number of practical difficulties affected initiatives to introduce a wider range of languages into schools. One of the major ones was that Australian schools typically catered for students from many different NESB backgrounds. This made the task of identifying the specific language(s) to be offered in the regular school curriculum, either at primary or at secondary level, extremely difficult. Without a critical mass of students in a particular language it was difficult to justify the selection of one language over another. It also meant there were often limited opportunities to continue studying a specific language from primary through to secondary level. This was because students were normally allocated to their neighborhood secondary school regardless of what languages it was offering in its curriculum. One response was to waive these zoning requirements. South Australia also established a specialist secondary school to teach a number of languages other than English (LOTEs). Resource issues also meant that the number of languages which could be accommodated within each school's timetable was limited. Despite these problems, NSW, like Victoria and South Australia, set up a special unit in its state education department with responsibility for developing curriculum, examination syllabi, and resource materials in a range of migrant languages.

Other innovatory delivery strategies were devised to increase the opportunities for language learning. The first involved government funding to support the teaching of migrant languages in after school hours "ethnic schools" operated by non-profit ethnic community organizations. Initially funded by state governments (NSW first provided funding in 1977), the initiative was subsequently funded by the national government on a per capita basis. This funding still continues but at a reduced level. Because of concerns about lack of government control of the content and general quality of these classes, which mainly catered for primary age children, by the late 1970s specialist community language teachers had begun to be appointed to regular primary schools with sufficient students from a particular language background. In 1978, the Galbally Report recommended that $5 million should be allocated to multicultural education. The NSW government used its share of this money to introduce the teaching of languages in selected primary schools. In 1981, the first 30 teachers funded under this program were appointed to NSW schools. These teachers had little preparation for their roles. While some schools used them to provide bilingual transitional programs, in others they team-taught with the regular classroom teachers and/or offered language classes to all students. Such programs still continue in NSW and other states such as Victoria, but they tend to be the exception rather than the rule.

Historically, the study of languages was seen in Australia as an elite enterprise more suited for students planning to attend university. Although examination syllabi were developed in a wide range of languages, the problems of identifying sufficient students to take individual language electives continued to bedevil the delivery of LOTEs at the secondary level. One response was to establish government-run Saturday schools which students could attend on Saturdays as part of their formal school attendance and where they could prepare for the public examinations in those languages not taught in their own school. The first of these schools in NSW was established in 1978. Today 26 languages are offered in 16 secondary schools in Sydney, Wollongong, and Newcastle. In Victoria, the comparable Victorian School of Languages offers courses in more than 40 languages in face-to-face classes and by distance education. Apart from studying languages such as Japanese, the majority of students in these classes are studying their own community language.

The rarest form of language provision in Australia is bilingual education. This is despite knowledge of the educational arguments supporting the intellectual advantages of bilingual education. Apart from public schools with community language programs, opportunities for bilingual study are almost entirely restricted to private schools catering to students from particular ethnic backgrounds. However, many of these schools teach specific languages rather than offering bilingual instruction. Where this is offered, it tends to involve transitional bilingual programs.

From migrant to multicultural education

The prominence of ESL and the expansion of official support for the teaching of immigrant languages inside and outside the formal school system speak to the importance of measures directly targeting the needs of immigrants and their children. However, a distinctive feature of Australian multicultural education is that integral to it are initiatives targeting the wider school culture and hidden curriculum. Another focus is on improving communication and understanding between the school and immigrant parents and providing opportunities for the latter to share their concerns, knowledge, and experiences with teachers, non-immigrant parents, and students. Language initiatives include the use of interpreters and the translation of school announcements and notices into community languages. Also popular is the inclusion of the culture of the immigrants in school concerts and activities. Sometimes derided as providing a simplistic acknowledgment of cultural diversity, these initiatives nevertheless provide an opportunity for the cultural background of immigrant groups to be presented in a positive light. This can be an important source of pride and self-esteem for parents and students in a situation where the Anglo-Celtic culture remains dominant in Australian schools and society.

Other important initiatives within the framework of multicultural education include a focus on providing a "multicultural perspective" and intercultural communication. The rationale for these initiatives is to produce positive relations between the diverse majority and minority groups by changing knowledge, attitudes, and actions. One strategy has been to change curriculum content to reflect better the diversity of experiences and practices of immigrants and their societies of origin. Curriculum areas as diverse as literature, history, social sciences, art, and music have been revised to reflect differences in knowledge and understanding between cultures. Examples range from having primary children discuss the different celebrations which are important in their family to studies, in the secondary curriculum, of literature or music which is outside the standard Western classical canon. Such initiatives directly address the issue of whose "culture" is embedded consciously, or unconsciously, in the school curriculum. Even in curriculum areas as solidly "fact" based as mathematics and science, teachers have opportunities to use material which highlights diversity, such as in the different systems of counting and the range of important scientific contributions made by Middle Eastern and Asian scholars.

The multifaceted nature of Australian educational responses to diversity is evident in the 1983 Multicultural Education Policy produced by the NSW State Department of Education. This report was a revision of the earlier 1979 *Multicultural Education Policy Statement*, which stated that multicultural education is "a process based on an acceptance of multiculturalism as a fundamental social value." The 1983 policy statement made the point that each school must choose those dimensions of the policy most relevant to its circumstances. Even those schools which lack large enough minority populations to warrant the provision of ESL teaching or the teaching of LOTEs are nevertheless required to implement those innovations targeting the whole school population. Such a policy initiative clearly sees that multiculturalism in the larger society requires changes from all sections of the population. Thus educational responses to diversity must shift from targeting only migrant students to ones which also target all students. These whole-of-school responses focus on the social dimensions of education and the classroom. Examples from the 21 non-language programs funded in 1983 by the Victorian Ministerial Advisory Committee on Multicultural and Migrant Education included funding for translations and interpreters and resources to develop a multilingual newspaper for a network of schools. Under the multicultural programs section, funding was given to a group performing multicultural drama programs and to a school preparing a cultural awareness program for parents and the school community, as well as to a publication for local communities identifying the difficulties faced by NESB students in studying mathematics (Ministerial Advisory Committee on Multicultural and Migrant Education, 1985).

By the mid-1980s, however, new areas of educational reform were competing for funding while the national government was seeking to reduce expenditure in all areas, including education. In its 1986 budget the national government proposed cutting out funding to various programs targeting minority groups. Although funding for ESL programs was saved, that for non-language initiatives such as the state multicultural advisory committees was not. These committees were a key source of funds for educational initiatives in non-language areas of the curriculum. Following these funding cuts the state governments soon ended their own discretionary funding to these areas, affecting resources for teacher development, support staff, and curriculum initiatives.

To the extent that the changes associated with the shift from migrant to multicultural education have been accepted into the standard operation of Australian schools and into major curriculum changes they remain as a critical, but often little noted, institutionalized feature of Australian multicultural education (Cahill, 1996; Eckermann, 1994; Foster, 1988; Hill & Allan, 2004). While the 1980s thus marks the high point in what was developed in Australia under the rubric of multicultural education, it has not meant the end of initiatives relating to ethnic and cultural diversity. New educational initiatives were developed in response to changes in the social and educational context.

Beyond multicultural education

Citizenship education

In the 1970s and 1980s, as Australian educational policies and practices changed in response to the increasing ethnic diversity of pupils, citizenship education was rarely discussed. This changed as a consequence of the 1988 celebrations of the bicentenary of European settlement, which generated debates about the place of the Indigenous population in Australian society and national identity. Further questions arose about Australian citizenship, the rights and responsibilities of citizens, and whether those of non-Anglo-Celtic, as well as Indigenous, backgrounds had access to the full social benefits of citizenship. The role of citizenship education in addressing these issues, including what it should consist of and how it should it be incorporated into the curriculum of Australian schools, was addressed in a major 1994 report, *Whereas the People . . .* (Civics Education Group, 1994).

The typical response in Australian schools is that, rather than being a separate subject, citizenship education occurs within established curriculum areas concerned with society and the environment. As elsewhere, concerns exist about whether what is provided within citizenship education tends to focus on the delivery of "facts" and the presentation of an overly celebratory view of Australian society. This is best exemplified by debates about the teaching of history. Especially under the Howard government, Australia has been embroiled in what have been called the "history wars" over the nature of Indigenous – European relations. In his last years in office, Prime Minister Howard played a leading role in seeking to reform the teaching of Australian history so that it would be more "factual" and include not only a revisionist view of Indigenous – White relations but greater prominence to the story of the Anzac soldiers at Gallipoli, which has become a potent symbol of Australian nationalism. These developments, together with the 2004 announcement that to be eligible to receive national government funding individual schools would need to have a "functioning flagpole" (Department of Education, Employment and Workplace Relations, 2004), the official specification of the values to be transmitted in Australian education, and the provision of funding for school chaplains, have been interpreted as indicating a return to a more nationalistic and assimilationist perspective about how diversity is to be incorporated into Australian education and society.

Antiracism

Among the most notable absences from the multicultural education policies were antiracism programs, which were seen as unnecessary given the emphasis on overcoming educational inequality and improving intercultural communication and understanding in multicultural education. This contrasted with the situation in the United Kingdom, where there were bitter debates between the advocates of antiracism and multicultural education as it was understood in the United Kingdom. By the 1990s, however, a variety of incidents in schools with both immigrant and Indigenous populations led New South Wales authorities to develop an antiracism policy and methods of addressing anti-social behavior in schools. What is noteworthy about this policy was that it for the first time was a policy addressing the needs of both immigrant and Indigenous minority students. The focus of the policy was on administrative responses to dealing with racist incidents occurring in the school and formulating responses designed to address the hidden curriculum. The extent of the problem of racism was evident in the nation-wide support given to the development of the on-line website *Racism No Way*, which contains a range of materials for use by teachers and students.

These educational initiatives coincided with increased society concerns about discrimination and prejudice. Following the 1996 election of the conservative Howard government, there were a range of attacks on multicultural initiatives. Howard had, himself, been involved in earlier criticisms of Asian immigrants, and he was known to be unsympathetic to both multiculturalism and efforts to address concerns of the Indigenous population. Elected at the same time was Pauline Hanson, who with her One Nation Party mounted a highly populist campaign against Indigenes and immigrants, especially those from Asia. This was associated with increased reports of verbal abuse and discrimination, as well as some violence directed to those of Asian background in Australia. Since the events of September 11, 2001 in the USA, reports of discriminatory and racist behavior involving Muslims have grown, so that now Muslims have replaced Asians as the major targets of hostility in Australia.

Highlighting the fragility of interethnic relations were the December 2005 riots on a major Sydney surf beach, Cronulla, involving attacks by youths from Anglo-Celtic backgrounds on young Muslim men and women. The background to the riots was rivalry for the use of the beach, which came to a head when Lebanese youths allegedly attacked a life-saver who admonished them for uncivil behavior. The situation was inflamed by radio "shock jocks" during the following week, and the circulation of SMS messages calling for action, which resulted in drunken youths draped in the Australian flag attacking men and women of Middle Eastern appearance who had ventured into the Cronulla area. Inevitably there was retaliatory action. The rioting occurred soon after the London Underground bombings and an increased emphasis by the Australian government on the potential dangers posed by Islamic fundamentalist terrorists and illegal Muslim "boat" people. As the riots highlighted, in such a climate the work undertaken in schools was insufficient to counter the discrimination and prejudice. Ironically the riots occurred only a week after the announcement of the most recent version of the New South Wales Antiracism Policy Statement for schools. Other educational pilot initiatives to address the interethnic tensions have focused on Muslim–non-Muslim relations. There have also been non-school-based initiatives, such as National Harmony Day, which aim to promote harmony and social cohesion.

Globalization

While the increasing focus on citizenship and antiracist education addresses issues of particular concern to those of non-English-speaking and Indigenous backgrounds, the impact of globalization on Australian education has affected all students, as it extends the educational responses from domestic multiculturalism to international multiculturalism.

In the mid-1980s the Australian government began a major restructuring of economic institutions in response to the perceived impact of economic globalization on Australia. Reflecting this economic emphasis the government's 1989 *National Agenda for a Multicultural Australia* included, as one of its three main principles, the right of all Australians to fully contribute their skills to the economic advancement of Australia. This recognition of the valuable economic contribution of migrants was also reinforced through promoting to the business community the concept of "productive diversity," which advocated the contribution of immigrants in developing trading initiatives with their homelands.

The most obvious impact of the engagement with globalization was a refocusing on LOTEs. The first major initiative in regard to debates about the role of languages in the curriculum was the 1987 *National Policy on Languages* (Lo Bianco, 1987). The report was a judicious attempt to balance the competing interests of those lobbying for more resources for migrant languages against those focusing on Australian economic and strategic needs reflected in the promotion of Asian languages. The impact of the report was relatively limited, since it was followed in 1991 by a Green Paper entitled *Australia's Language: The Australian Language and Literacy Policy* (Australia DEET, 1991). As its title indicated, its focus was on the importance of support for English as the dominant language in Australia rather than support for other languages.

Language programs continue to be offered in schools but there has been little impetus to develop them. While lack of resources to provide for additional language teachers and resources is a factor it is also evident that the demand for LOTEs from students and their families, including those from non-English-speaking backgrounds, is not as strong as it once was. This was noted by Cahill (1996) in his review of multicultural education undertaken in the mid-1990s. Underlying this apparent paradox is that many of the parents, despite their non-English-speaking backgrounds, have often gained their own education and current occupational status by virtue of their command of English. For them, it is often more important that their children gain high marks in their end-of-school examinations so that they can enter the most prestigious university programs in Australia or elsewhere. School study of the family's language in school is not necessarily seen as imperative to achieving this goal. Highly educated families also can provide their children with other ways to become literate in the family language where this is seen as important. In many of these families, language also is not necessarily seen as the key to retaining the family's cultural traditions and heritage.

The extent of the decline in enrollments in LOTE programs is documented in a recent report which notes that overall numbers of students studying languages as a proportion of the whole Australian school population had fallen from 50.9% in 2001 to 47.5% in 2005, with most language study occurring at primary and lower secondary levels. The six most popular languages remained Japanese, Italian, Indonesian, French, German, and Chinese (Research Centre for Languages and Cultures Education, University of South Australia, 2007). As this list indicates, Asian languages now are an important part of the school curriculum. This trend is likely to continue, as the new national government has reiterated its pre-election promise to expand the teaching of Asian languages and to place them under the aegis of the newly established National Curriculum Board. Underlying their prominence is the widespread acceptance among parents and students, as well as business people and other stakeholders, of the significance of the Asian region for Australia's future economic development. Also, because of extensive Asian immigration, Chinese has now become the major language spoken in Australia after English.

The future of educational provisions for diversity

After nearly four decades of specific educational programs designed to meet the needs of both immigrant minorities and Australian society as a whole, it is evident that these provisions cannot be assessed in terms of a static understanding of educational needs. The change of emphasis is evident in the 2005 New South Wales policy which replaced the earlier 1983 multicultural education policy. Renamed the *Cultural Diversity and Community Relations Policy: Multicultural Education in Schools*, the policy states that its objective is: "To ensure that schools' policies and practices respond to and reflect cultural, linguistic and religious diversity, and give students the opportunity to fully participate, achieve equitable educational outcomes, and develop skills and knowledge to be active citizens" (NSW Department of Education and Training, 2005). In setting out the key means through which this is done, there is a marked absence of the earlier policy's emphasis on cultural and linguistic maintenance, even though the statement has replaced "non-English-speaking background" by the newer phrase "culturally and linguistically different" (CALD). Instead, the emphasis is placed on harmony, tolerance, and being an active citizen.

The role of globalization in these changes cannot be overlooked. Since the 1970s, Australian society has changed dramatically, as indeed have immigrants and their home societies. One feature of globalization is far more extensive international mobility of individuals of immigrant and non-immigrant backgrounds. An effect of these changes is that they question many of the earlier educational responses based on the assumptions that all Australians will stay permanently in Australia. The rhetoric of developing educational responses to address Australia's and individuals' needs and objectives in this globalizing environment has been evident in Australia since the 1990s. Indeed it was one of the factors which led Cahill in his 1996 review of multicultural education to argue that it was now necessary to revisit what was understood by multicultural education (Cahill, 1996).

Just as the earlier emphasis on cultural maintenance has disappeared in the more recent Australian approaches to multicultural education, so, too, has the emphasis on overcoming educational inequality. One reason for this is that one of the outstanding achievements, which cannot be dissociated from Australia's early adoption of specific provisions to assist immigrant minorities, is that disparities between the second-generation immigrant population and those with three or more generations of residence are far less than in other comparable societies, apart from Canada (Heath & Cheung, 2007). Evidence from the 2003 Programme for International Student Assessment (PISA) survey indicates that Australia and Canada also stand out in the survey for the way in which there is little difference in the performance of native-born and immigrant students (Organisation for Economic Co-operation and Development [OECD], 2006). This finding supports the argument that the educational provisions for diversity in both countries have assisted in overcoming systemic educational inequality. Always there will be individual variation, but apart from the case of Indigenous students the ongoing existence of systemic educational inequality and disadvantage affecting specific ethnic groups does not appear to be a characteristic of Australian education.

While educational inequality is no longer a pressing issue requiring attention in implementing new Australian education responses to diversity, questions of identity and experiences of discrimination and prejudice in the schools and elsewhere remain to be resolved. While these experiences are a reflection of larger tensions and fault lines in Australian society, this does not absolve educators from seeking answers to address these issues, which are important if all Australians are to live harmoniously together. As the experience from earlier efforts to address diversity indicates, multifaceted educational provisions, whether termed multicultural or not, must continue to target both minority students and the whole school population, including teachers as well as pupils and community members.

Whether this will happen depends in large part on the role of governments. As state governments in Australia have constitutional responsibility for education, much depends on their assessment of the priority in educating students to live amidst domestic and international diversity. This is why New South Wales and Victoria, the states with far larger and more diverse populations, have been especially active in developing educational responses to diversity. However, even they are dependent for their educational funding on the national Australian government. This overview of changing policies and practices has shown the significant influence of the Australian government in education when it provides funding targeting (or ignoring) specific projects, whether they be ESL or citizenship education. Given that the 2007 elections brought to power a Labor government under Kevin Rudd with a mandate for change, it will be interesting to see what impact this has on the existing educational responses to diversity.

Note

1 Because of space limitations this chapter does not address the educational provisions for the Indigenous population, which have historically involved different institutional structures. These structures reflect the very different patterns of interethnic relations and circumstances of the Indigenous population, who are acknowledged to be the most socio-economically disadvantaged of all Australians (Inglis, 1986; New South Wales Aboriginal Education Consultative Group & New South Wales Department of Education and Training, 2004).

References

Australia DEET. (1991). *Australia's language: The Australian language and literacy policy*. Canberra: Australian Government Publishing Service.

Australian Bureau of Statistics. (1947). *Census of the Commonwealth of Australia, 30 June 1947*. Canberra: Author.

Australian Bureau of Statistics. (2007). *2006 census quick stats: Australia*. Canberra: Author.

Cahill, D. (1996). *Immigration and schooling in the 1990s*. Canberra: Bureau of Immigration and Multicultural and Population Research.

Civics Education Group. (1994). *Whereas the people . . . Civics and citizenship education: Report of the Civic Experts Group*. Canberra: Australian Government Publishing Service.

Department of Education, Employment and Workplace Relations. (2004). *Flagpole funding initiative overview*. Retrieved March 4, 2008, from http://www.dest.gov.au/sectors/school_education/programmes_funding/general_funding/capital_grants/flagpoles/

Department of Immigration and Citizenship (DIAC). (1996). *The guide: Implementing the standards for statistics on cultural and language diversity*. Retrieved January 5, 2008, from http://www.immi.gov.au/media/publications/multicultural/statistics_guide/03.htm

Department of Immigration and Citizenship (DIAC). (2008). *Population flows: Immigration aspects* (2006–07 ed.). Canberra: Author.

Eckermann, A. K. (1994). *One classroom, many cultures*. Sydney: Allen & Unwin.

Ethnic Affairs Commission of New South Wales. (1978). *Participation: Report to the Premier, June 1978*. Sydney: Author.

Foster, L. (1988). *Diversity and multicultural education*. Sydney: Allen & Unwin.

Galbally, F. (1978). *Review of post-arrival programmes and services for migrants*. Canberra: Australian Government Publishing Service.

Heath, A., & Cheung, S. Y. (Eds.). (2007). *Unequal chances: Ethnic minorities in Western labour markets*. Oxford: Oxford University Press for the British Academy.

Hill, B., & Allan, R. (2004). Multicultural education in Australia: Historical development and current status. In J. A. Banks & C. A. M. Banks (Eds.), *Handbook of research on multicultural education* (pp. 979–995). San Francisco: Jossey-Bass.

Human Rights and Equal Opportunity Commission (HREOC). (2007). *Multiculturalism: A position paper by the Acting Race Discrimination Commissioner*. Sydney: Author.

Inglis, C. (1986). Australia. *Education and Urban Society, 18*(4), 423–436.

Interim Committee for the Australian Schools Commission. (1973). *Schools in Australia: Report of the Interim Committee for the Australian Schools Commission, May 1973* (the Karmel Report). Canberra: Australian Government Publishing Service.

Lo Bianco, J. (1987). *National policy on languages*. Canberra: Australian Government Publishing Service.

Martin, J. (1978). *The migrant presence*. Sydney: Allen & Unwin.

Ministerial Advisory Committee on Multicultural and Migrant Education. (1985). *1983/84 annual report*. Melbourne: Author.

New South Wales Aboriginal Education Consultative Group & New South Wales Department of

Education and Training. (2004). *The report of the review of Aboriginal education: Yanigurra muya: Ganggurrinyma yaarri guurulaw yirringin.gurray, Freeing the spirit: Dreaming an equal future.* Sydney: Author.

NSW Department of Education and Training. (2005). *Cultural diversity and community relations policy: Multicultural education in schools.* Retrieved March 4, 2008, from https://www.det.nsw.edu.au/policies/student_serv/equity/comm_rela/PD20050234.shtml

Office of Multicultural Affairs. (1989). *National agenda for a multicultural Australia.* Canberra: Australian Government Publishing Service.

Organisation for Economic Co-operation and Development (OECD). (2006). *Where immigrant students succeed: A comparative review of performance and engagement in PISA 2003.* Paris: Author.

Research Centre for Languages and Cultures Education, University of South Australia. (2007). *An investigation of the state and nature of languages in Australian schools.* Canberra: Department of Education, Employment and Workplace Relations.

8

Multicultural education in the United Kingdom

Sally Tomlinson
University of Oxford, UK

By the first decade of the 21st century there was no longer any official education policy or curriculum activity in British schools referred to as multicultural education. In the early 1990s a survey of local education authorities in England carried out at the National Foundation for Educational Research had concluded that even by that time "the national educational and political climate was ideologically unpropitious for multi-cultural and antiracist education" (Taylor, 1992, p. 5). The incorporation of groups variously perceived by the White majority to be racially, ethnically, or culturally different into a society slowly coming to terms with the end of an Empire and a closer relationship with Europe had always raised antagonistic debate about a shared national identity, cultural heritage, and multiculturalism.

By the early 2000s the very notions of multiculturalism and a multicultural society were under sustained attack from a number of prominent political, media, and other groups. The chair of the Commission for Racial Equality, who in 2007 became chair of a merged Equality and Human Rights Commission, asserted a number of times that multiculturalism suggested separateness, and that by focusing on cultural difference the country had been "sleepwalking into segregation" (Phillips, 2005). The view of Britain as a disunited kingdom in which multiculturalism was the enemy was given wide publicity, particularly after the London bombings of July 7, 2005, when four young Muslim men, born and educated in the UK, killed themselves and 56 others. There were many suggestions that a once cohesive British society had been fractured by the presence of racial and ethnic groups and the arrival of newer economic migrants, refugees, and asylum seekers. A major political reaction was to focus on concepts of community cohesion and integration into an undefined "British" society, with little acknowledgement that the society had always been divided along lines of social class, wealth, gender, race, religion, and region. Yet there was also a recognition that Britain was and would continue to be a multicultural society, legislation continued to outlaw what was still described as racial discrimination, and both public and private institutions were required to implement race equality policies.

By 2007 some 21% of the school student body at primary level and 18% at secondary school level were officially described as of minority ethnic origin, as distinct from "White British," and over half of all schools included students from a variety of cultural and racial backgrounds. Education policy-makers at central and local level, eschewing the language of multicultural education, had adopted a language of diversity, equality, and inclusion, and under a 2006 Education Act all schools had a duty to promote inclusion and community cohesion. Teachers in training were required to take account of "a range of developmental, social, religious, ethnic, cultural and linguistic influences" affecting young learners (Training and Development Agency for Schools [TDA], 2007, p. 10), but there was little guidance on how to do this. In schools, teachers struggled with the realities of teaching young people with a variety of diverse origins, and citizenship education – compulsory in all schools from 2002 – was regarded as a major mode for teaching for diversity.

This chapter documents the rise and fall of activities described, from the 1960s to the 1990s, as multicultural and antiracist education, and the continuation into the 2000s of some of these under notions of diversity and citizenship education. The history and development of education in a British multicultural society has to be understood within the context of political and popular reactions to immigrant minorities over the years, and the changes in the education system from a public good in a welfare state to a market-oriented competitive enterprise where testing, and qualifications for employment dominate the curriculum and its assessment. Although the education systems in Scotland, Wales, and Northern Ireland are controlled separately from that in England, most of what follows applies to the whole of the UK, and the period in question is full of political, ideological, and policy contradictions. On the one hand, Britain, compared to other European countries, had been relatively successful in accommodating to racial, religious, and cultural diversity; on the other hand, there was continued hostility to settled citizens from the former British Empire, merged with antagonisms to refugees and asylum seekers, and to economic migrants from both outside and inside Europe. Policies encouraged labor migration but supported immigration control legislation. The education system was expected to incorporate migrants and minorities, while lacking political support. A rhetoric of inclusion and recognition of diversity was at odds with a competitive school system which excluded and disadvantaged many minority students.

The cultural politics of migration

After the Second World War the still extensive territories of the British Empire and legends of imperial triumphs formed the basis for nostalgia and notions of an unproblematic monocultural Britain in which a White Anglo-Saxon "race" was assumed to be the world's superior group – biologically, culturally, and linguistically (MacKenzie, 1986). The arrival and settlement of former colonial people, although invited by government, were mostly unwelcome to all social classes. The model of incorporation of migrant workers from the Caribbean, the Indian subcontinent, African countries, and Hong Kong assumed assimilation, a situation in which minorities supposedly relinquished their own cultures and languages and became indistinguishable from the majority – a view still urged in some popular and media understandings into the 2000s. But by the late 1960s a large-scale study reported that assimilation was not an option, and evidence of discrimination based on color was overwhelming (Rose et al., 1969). While labor migration for jobs White workers would not take was encouraged, a series of immigration control acts was passed from the 1960s onwards. In 1966 home secretary Roy Jenkins famously declared that the objective of policy was to be "equal opportunity accompanied by cultural diversity in an atmosphere of mutual tolerance." But tolerance was hard to detect, and race relations policy at this time was influenced by the civil rights movement in the US and by fear of possible civic unrest. Three Race Relations Acts outlawing racial discrimination were passed in the 1960s and 1970s, by which time the realities of color and cultural difference had penetrated official thinking and a language of integration, equal opportunity, and cultural pluralism superseded assimilation, with assertions that minority groups should be able to retain their own cultures, languages, and religions (Bullock, 1975). During this period education policy was largely based on a liberal democratic consensus that government should intervene to create equal opportunities, and a comprehensive school system was gradually replacing a selective system (Tomlinson, 2005).

By the 1970s and 1980s the settlement of immigrant minorities in areas where their labor was sought, discriminatory housing policies, and White flight had largely ensured spatial segregation. The presence of settlers bringing a variety of languages, religions, and cultural traditions was openly regarded as a racial threat to a British national identity. The arrival of Asians from East Africa, deported from Kenya, Uganda, and Malawi, together with Vietnamese refugees, and assertions of a militant Black identity, in particular by young people with Caribbean origins, led to what the Home Affairs Committee described as "a deteriorating state of race relations in Britain" (1981, p. vii). The acceptance of minorities into what was manifestly a multicultural and multiracial society, and their equal participation as citizens, became a major contested issue. Tensions continued between young Black males and the police, with race riots in major cities in 1980, 1981, and 1985. In 1987 the murder in his school playground of Ahmed Ullah, a 13-year-old boy of Bangladeshi origin, polarized views on racism in schools. An inquiry into the murder concluded that "it is crucial that schools declare unambiguously and openly what is their stance on racism, racial harassment and violence" (MacDonald, Kahn, Joh, & Bhavani, 1989, p. 365). Demands by Muslims during the 1980s made sure that religion was incorporated into debates on race, cultural identity, and nationalism. Much tension focused on the northern city of Bradford, with an altercation between Muslim parents and a White head teacher (Halstead, 1988), and the burning of Salman Rushdie's book *The Satanic Verses* (1988) in January 1989. The UK Parliament, having joined the European Economic Community in 1973, signed up to a Single European Act in 1986 and then the Maastricht Treaty of 1992, which transformed the Community into a European Union of then 15 (now 27) member states.

European citizens were given the right to live and work in other member countries. This treaty and a developing global economy considerably affected the movement and migration of people and their labor, and created more cultural convergences. However, while the Conservative government had from 1988 produced a National Curriculum which was Anglo-centric and anti-multicultural, a Labour Party document in 1989 claimed that "Britain is manifestly a multiracial society with a plurality of cultures. We believe the education system must ensure that all children develop an understanding and a sensitivity towards this plurality of cultures and traditions" (Labour Party, 1989, p. 2).

In the 1990s the first Persian Gulf war brought in refugees from Iraq, and asylum seekers arrived from civil wars in Sri Lanka, Somalia, Sudan, Sierra Leone, Afghanistan, Zimbabwe, and other places, to be joined after the collapse of the old Yugoslavia by Bosnians, Serbs, Croats, Albanians, and Roma from Eastern Europe. The new arrivals were greeted by much media denigration of refugees as "scroungers" or illegal immigrants, and legislation gradually removed the rights of asylum seekers to welfare benefits. The 1991 census was the first to include an "ethnic" question, asking for subjective identification by country of origin, color, or cultural affiliation, after which the geographical spread and extent of ethnic segregation became clearer. A fourth survey by the Policy Studies Institute, London, demonstrated that a "Black–White" divide was now more complex in a multicultural society and "the differences between minorities has become as important and significant to life chances as the similarities" (Modood et al., 1997, p. 8). Although some minority students were achieving well at schools and entering higher education, notably students of Indian (Sikh and Hindu) and Chinese origin, many others, especially with origins in the Caribbean, Pakistan, and Bangladesh, were negatively affected by the Conservative introduction of parental choice of school and the creation of a "diversity" of schools designed to promote competition.

Policies from this time increased the likelihood of separation of students by social class and ethnicity. Ministers largely ignored rising racial tensions in schools, refused an inquiry into the murder of 18-year-old Black student Stephen Lawrence in 1993, and made clear that any change to the National Curriculum to reflect a multicultural society was a "no-go area" (Graham, 1993, p. 32). Teacher training courses designed to promote understanding of multicultural and race issues gradually disappeared. Race, as U.S. scholar Michael Apple (1999) noted, had become an "absent presence" (p. 9). There was, however, a concentration on schools regarded as "failing" and some attention paid to the lower school achievements of Black and Muslim students.

Under a New Labour government, elected in 1997, race became a "present presence" again, with the new government eager to affirm the view of a modern national identity that valued cultural diversity and recognized the citizenship rights of settled minorities. The European Convention on Human Rights was incorporated into UK law in 1998, and an inquiry into the Stephen Lawrence murder set up (Macpherson, 1999), which resulted in a Race Relations (Amendment) Act in 2000. However, a commission set up to inquire into the future of multi-ethnic Britain had both its report and its recommendations ridiculed in the press as "attacking Britishness," and was disregarded by government (Parekh, 2000). This report had actually suggested that the government take a more active role in nurturing diversity while fostering a common sense of belonging and shared values among its citizens, a theme repeated in most of the subsequent official and academic literature. In the 2001 census, some 8% (4.5 million) of the population of the United Kingdom identified themselves as ethnic minority. Shortly after New Labour was elected for a second time in 2001 there were further race riots in English northern towns, and a Ministerial Group on Public Order and Community Cohesion was set up, with a Review Team asked to report on the disorders (Home Office, 2001). Best known as the Cantle Report, it strongly influenced government views that Britain now consisted of polarized communities living what it described as parallel lives, and duly recommended the promotion of community cohesion based on a greater sense of citizenship but with value placed on cultural difference. However, New Labour continued conservative policies of encouraging choice and competition between schools, including faith schools, which continued to separate students by class, ethnicity, and religion.

Government policy towards settled minorities and new migrants became more punitive after the attack on the World Trade Center in New York in September 2001 and the invasion of Afghanistan in 2001 and Iraq in 2003. A White Paper (Home Office, 2002) and a Nationality, Immigration and Asylum Act in 2002 required future British citizens to pass an English language and a citizenship test. During the decade there was continued antagonistic conflation of settled minorities, asylum seekers, and economic migration from the European Union, and there was much debate as to how government, social institutions, and society in general should treat minority citizens, migrants of all kinds, and especially the Muslim population. Some young Muslims had been drawn into radical Islamist groups from the early 1990s (Husain, 2007). The suicide bombing in London in July 2005 by four young men born and educated in Britain, and the attempted suicide attack on Glasgow airport in June 2007 by two highly educated men sparked further hostility against Muslims in general. Education policy-makers remained reluctant to perceive links between ongoing and new racial and cultural antagonisms and contradictions created by education policies. In particular, contradictions between competitive education policies and a rhetoric of community cohesion became more obvious. In 2004 a debate was sparked by the editor of *Prospect* magazine attacking "progressive liberals" for supporting diversity and multiculturalism and asserting that a society cannot incorporate both diversity and solidarity (Goodhart, 2004). There were claims that multiculturalism suggested separateness, with politicians and the media from both left and right arguing that Britain was becoming polarized by race, faith, and culture. It was left to the Queen, in her annual Christmas message to the nation in 2004, to make an impassioned plea for religious and cultural tolerance and for diversity to be recognized as a strength. While there were undoubtedly serious social problems in the society created by poverty, wealth disparities, wars abroad, terror attacks, religious bigotry from all faiths, and competition for good schools and employment, multiculturalism continued to be presented as a major problem. By August 2006 New Labour was being criticized for "stoking public fears" as Prime Minister Tony Blair announced that terrorism and immigration were the main public concerns, and other politicians criticized the Muslim community's supposed failure to integrate, with mode of dress, especially hijabs, niquabs, and jilbads, singled out (Tomlinson, 2008).

Official policy stressed integration, with an Advisory Committee on Integration and Cohesion for British Muslims, a Commission on Integration and Cohesion, and an Institute for Community Cohesion set up, and a former head teacher was asked to lead a curriculum review into diversity and citizenship (Ajegbo, 2007). Meanwhile the enlargement of the EU brought in what was estimated to be 600,000 mainly young workers from Poland, plus other European citizens. Universities were encouraged to recruit more international students, who brought in more cultural diversity and higher fees, and the number of languages spoken in schools increased, although there were cuts in funding for teaching English for speakers of other languages (ESOL). The government continued attempts to limit immigration flows on a selective basis, further reducing welfare benefits for some migrants, and from 2008 requiring migrants from outside the EU to demonstrate they could speak English before arrival. Political, media, and public debate continued to focus on complaints about the impact of "multiculturalism." Lord Tebbit, a former minister in Margaret Thatcher's government, complained in a national newspaper in January 2008 that "it is more than ten years ago that I argued that a multicultural society was a recipe for disaster . . . a society must have a dominant culture" (Tebbit, 2008, p. 11).

Multicultural education 1960–1980

Whereas in the US, multicultural education developed out of a civil rights movement and was grounded in a vision of democracy, social justice, and equality, and also served as a site for power struggles in the society (Banks, 1994; Sleeter, 1986), in the UK the activities described as multicultural education began as a pragmatic response to the arrival of children from former colonies. While education was initially regarded as a means to achieve assimilation, "a national system cannot be expected to promote the values of immigrant groups," as a 1964 Commonwealth Immigrants Advisory Committee report put it. There was no national policy to incorporate immigrant children and, responding to White parental fears, there was concern that too many minority children in any one school would be detrimental to the education of indigenous children. Some local authorities adopted one-way busing of minorities, a policy later ruled racially discriminatory, but those local education authorities (LEAs) incorporating minority children also began to produce positive policies. The only positive funding for minority children was made via section 11 of a 1966 Local Government Act. Although with hindsight it is easy to disparage the sometimes naive and patronizing response of educationalists to the incorporation of immigrant children into schools, historical credit should be given to Her

Majesty's Inspectorate (HMI), the old-style school inspectorate then independent of government, which produced pamphlets and encouraged research on teaching English, and organized conferences and courses, and to teacher and head teacher unions, which also supported research and information gathering. A survey at the end of the 1960s reported that schools regarded teaching English to non-English-speaking children, improved assessment techniques, home–school contacts, and teacher preparation as major tasks. While a majority of teachers at this time were well-meaning and liberal, evidence accumulated that they lacked knowledge of minority children and their backgrounds, were influenced by their racial beliefs derived from Empire, and also had lower expectations of children from immigrant backgrounds and from the manual working classes (Coard, 1971). But they were also aware that race, as defined by skin color and cultural difference, constituted a barrier to the incorporation of the children. Nandy (1971) commented that, while "assimilationist fervor" declined during the 1960s, teachers were aware of four major problems: the teaching of English; helping immigrant children adjust to a new society; understanding what it was like to belong to a minority group marked out by color, religion, or culture; and how to adapt to the educational needs of a multiracial, multicultural society.

There was also a growing awareness of tension between those who believed in an unproblematic British heritage and set of values which should be incorporated into the curriculum and those who believed it was time to reconsider a curriculum largely inherited from an imperial past. Immigrant parents, especially from the Caribbean, were already organizing to express their concerns about their children's education, setting up supplementary Saturday schools which were subject centered and incorporated the history and background of Black people. Worldwide during the 1970s the retention of minority group languages began to be regarded as crucial to the maintenance of a cultural identity, and a report produced by Lord Bullock's committee was influential in persuading government that children should not have to abandon their culture and language when they crossed the school threshold (Bullock, 1975, p 286). "Mother-tongue teaching" became a contested political issue, although the Department of Education and Science (DES) did sponsor two linguistic minority projects from 1979, and the National Union of Teachers suggested that schools should "make it clear by means of posters, notices, story books, library books and pictures that ethnic minority languages are held in equal regard to English" (1979, p. 6).

Between 1973 and 1981 a series of reports was produced by government committees, the Commission for Racial Equality, and academics making recommendations for improving the education of minority young people. Local authorities began to write multicultural policies and appoint multicultural advisors, and teachers in schools with minorities began to question the Anglo-centric curriculum. Central government eventually adopted a pluralist position, noting that "our society is a multicultural, multiethnic one and the curriculum should reflect a sympathetic understanding of the different cultures and races that now make up the society" (DES, 1977, p. 4).

Multicultural and anti-curriculum debates from the 1980s

By the early 1980s *multicultural education*, as Phillips-Bell (1981) noted, tended to be an umbrella term for a variety of changing practices in schools, including mother-tongue teaching, the provision of ethnic school dinners, the elimination of ethnocentricity in school subjects, and the inclusion of non-Christian religions. What followed in the 1980s was an avalanche of literature advocating commitment to a multicultural curriculum and a large literature critiquing this and supposed practices. An All London Teachers Against Racism and Fascism group argued that raising teachers' consciousness of their own racism should take precedence over curriculum change, and a number of left-oriented scholars claimed that multicultural education was assimilationist, tokenistic, and unsupportive of racial justice (Mullard, 1982; Troyna, 1986).

Others on the right attacked the "multiethnic brigade" as divisive (Hastie, 1986). What actually happened in schools was largely unrecorded, but there was much assumption and anecdote. A lack of clarification and national policy guidelines made attacks on any curriculum change easy, and there were heated debates about the removal of racially derogatory literature from classrooms and libraries (Klein, 1985). Despite this there were considerable advances in a multicultural direction during the 1980s. An interim report of the committee of inquiry into the education of children from minority groups discussed the issue of racism and discrimination in schools "both intentional and unintentional" (DES, 1981, p. 14) and noted the lack of leadership given by the DES in the field of multicultural education. The final report of this committee, chaired by Lord Swann, took the view that the aims of a multicultural and antiracist curriculum were synonymous with a good education designed to produce tolerant and knowledgeable citizens (DES, 1985, p. 324), and the report received wide publicity. Examining boards for the General Certificate of Secondary Education (GCSE), established in 1986, were required to have regard to cultural and linguistic diversity, money was made available through education support grants for curriculum projects in 120 predominantly White areas of England (Tomlinson, 1990), and by the end of the decade some two-thirds of local education authorities had produced multicultural and antiracist policies.

The issue of the educational performance of minority students and the way they were treated in schools was now on the agenda, and teacher preparation for teaching in a multicultural society improved with university and college education departments required to include such preparation. A Centre for Multicultural Education was set up at the Institute of Education in London, eventually becoming a Centre for Intercultural Studies (Gundara, 2000), although the term *intercultural* was never much used in the UK. However, any developments termed multicultural or antiracist, especially in local education authorities, continued to be presented as left-of-center egalitarianism, political subversion, and a threat to traditional British values (Palmer, 1986), and White parents continued to move their children away from schools attended by minorities.

The 1990s and the absent presence

The 1988 Education Reform Act impeded the equitable incorporation of minority children into the education system and brought to a halt much teacher discussion of a multicultural curriculum. An education market was proposed, with parents supposedly free to "choose" schools. Funding was to follow students, and competition between schools was encouraged. Parents and students were to become consumers of education, assisted by the publication of raw test scores of pupils, tested at ages 7, 11, 14, and 16, with newspapers quickly putting school scores into football-style "league tables." Research quickly established that school choice was affected by social class and ethnicity, and that racial and ethnic segregation was exacerbated (Gewirtz, Ball, & Bowe, 1995). The content of the curriculum was established by working groups appointed by the education secretary, there was much political interference in their work, and religious education was to be of a largely Christian nature. Prime Minister Margaret Thatcher objected that the history curriculum did not contain enough British history and recorded in her memoirs her distaste for multicultural education. A working group established to bring multicultural perspectives into the curriculum had its report censored (Thatcher, 1993; Tomlinson, 1993). David H. Hargreaves, professor of education at the University of Cambridge, recorded, "The 1988 Act could have looked forward with confidence and determination to a better multicultural, multilingual and multifaith Britain entering a new relationship with itself and the rest of the world, but it did not" (Hargreaves, 1993, p. viii).

In the early 1990s, under the government of John Major, race became an "absent presence" (Apple, 1999), as the government ignored higher exclusion rates of Black students, the lack of school places for some Muslim children in London, and the murder of Black student Stephen Lawrence by young White racists in 1993. The eventual inquiry into this murder in 1997 became a defining moment in the history of race in Britain, leading to an amended Race Relations Act (Macpherson, 1999). An overloaded National Curriculum was "slimmed down" in 1993, with lower tiers of entry to the GCSE examination at 16 being introduced, an issue later for Black students when it transpired that many of them were being entered for lower tiers without parental knowledge (Gillborn & Youdell, 2000). Although some minority groups began to perform well at school and in higher education entry, ethnic minorities continued on the whole to be part of lower socio-economic groups, and their social class and urban location continued to disadvantage them. Minority students were less likely to be selected by ability as measured by a test at 11 for remaining grammar schools, and all schools were encouraged to specialize in a curriculum subject, with 10% permitted selection by what was described as aptitude. It was noteworthy that schools specializing in technology attracted a high number of Asian applicants and those opting for a sports specialism were mainly inner-city schools with high numbers of Black students. With LEAs becoming marginalized and schools controlling their own funding and focusing on test results, overt concentration on activities referred to as multicultural or antiracist largely disappeared. Local authority policies were renamed as equal opportunity policies, and multicultural advisors and inspectors lost their jobs. The section 11 grant for funding minority education was reformed, refugee children were excluded from the grant, and in 1994 funding became part of a single regeneration budget for urban areas. Remaining staff formerly paid under section 11 were not encouraged to develop the curriculum in ways that might benefit minority or indeed any students. Teacher training was further centralized and overseen by a Teacher Training Agency with no special brief for developing courses relevant to a diverse society. Schools were to be inspected by a new, semi-privatized inspectorate with no initial requirement that inspectors be trained in issues relevant to a multicultural society. There was no response to 30 years of Black disquiet that the curriculum excluded their history and voice, and the Muslim Education Trust complained about the dominance of Christian education.

Hostility to Islam and a lack of recognition of Muslim needs had begun to radicalize some young Muslims, who were prepared to challenge their parents' moderate beliefs and become "anti-Western." By 1990 a school in Tower Hamlets, London, was becoming a place for the recruitment of radicalized young Muslims, unnoticed by teachers (Husain, 2007). Both initial and in-service training courses preparing teachers for a multiethnic society, which had begun to develop in universities, colleges, and local authorities, had more or less disappeared. John Major left office in 1997 declaring that "policies must be colour-blind, they must just tackle disadvantage" (Tomlinson, 2008, p. 124).

New Labour, citizenship, and cohesion

A New Labour government was elected in 1997, and Prime Minister Tony Blair asserted that his government was committed to education as a means to create a socially just society. This would embrace all backgrounds, creeds, and races, and "the attack on racial discrimination now commands general support, as does the value of a multicultural society" (Blair, 1998, p. 3). Positive moves included setting up a Social Exclusion Unit, which initially inquired into Black pupils' school exclusion, giving Muslim and other faiths the right to set up state-funded schools on a par with existing Anglican, Catholic, and Jewish schools, setting up an inquiry into the murder of Stephen Lawrence, putting in place a National Childcare Strategy and a Sure Start Programme for 0- to 3-year-olds which echoed the U.S. Head Start programs, replacing the section 11 grant with an ethnic minorities achievement grant (EMAG), and passing a Human Rights Act. Education action zones were set up mainly in inner cities, to bring schools, communities, and business closer together, with much encouragement of business studies in the curriculum. Eventually the action zones were subsumed into an "Excellence in Cities" program which was more clearly intended to reassure minority parents that attention would be focused on their children's school attainments and behavior. There were to be programs for the gifted and talented, learning support units for slow learners, and mentors for Black students.

The curriculum was once again subject to scrutiny by the Qualifications and Curriculum Authority (QCA), a body set up in 1997 with members appointed by the secretary of state for education. Changes included more concentration on literacy, numeracy, and information and communications technology, and all pupils were to respond to "changing employment and new work and leisure patterns resulting from economic migration and the continued globalisation of the economy and society" (Qualifications and Curriculum Authority/Department for Education and Employment [QCA/DfEE], 1999, p. 2).

Much faith was placed in the development of citizenship education (Figueroa, 2004) in order to produce what the QCA described as students "capable of positive participation in our ethnically diverse society" (QCA/DfEE, 1999, p. 2). The report of an advisory group on the teaching of citizenship and diversity in the National Curriculum (Crick, 1998) was followed up with guidance from the QCA and the 2002 introduction of citizenship into the National Curriculum. A major preoccupation post-2000 was on raising the educational achievements of minorities as measured by higher test and GCSE scores in the relatively unchanged curriculum subjects. A consultation paper, *Aiming High*, focused on improving the attainments of pupils of Caribbean and Pakistani backgrounds, those described as of mixed heritage, travelers or gypsies, and other "vulnerable" groups, although the paper appeared to blame the lower attainments of these groups on family and cultural backgrounds (Department for Education and Skills [DfES], 2003). The Teacher Training Agency produced guidelines in 2000 asserting that all trainee teachers needed to understand how to prepare pupils for life in a culturally diverse society, but there were few face-to-face courses apart from the occasional brief lecture. This organization, which became the Training and Development Agency in 2004, eventually set up a website for teachers which included information on ethnicity issues (www.multiverse.ac.uk) and a site for English as an additional language (www.naldic.org.uk), and the General Teaching Council set up an archive network in 2005 with a declared aim of preparing all pupils to live in a multiethnic and multicultural society.

Although the New Labour manifesto for a second term of office in 2001 referred to Britain as a multicultural, multiracial, and inclusive society, more race rioting in English towns in 2001 and 2005, plus the fear of internationally sponsored terrorism by radical Islamic groups, ushered in another round of examination of what constituted a British identity and conditions for citizenship and what was now referred to as community cohesion. A Home Office sponsored Community Cohesion Review Team, as part of a ministerial working group, was asked to consider how national policies could "promote better community cohesion, based on shared values and a celebration of diversity." The team was:

> struck by the depth of polarisation of our towns and cities with little attempt to develop clear values which focus on what it means to be a citizen of a modern multiracial Britain, rather than looking backwards to a supposedly monocultural society or a country of origin for a source of identity.
>
> (Home Office, 2001, p. 9)

There was some acknowledgment that education policies based on competition and choice and further development of faith schools could encourage community segregation, but the team could only suggest that the citizenship curriculum and cross-community school programs would produce more community cohesion. Faith-based schools receiving state funding included Church of England, Methodist, Catholic, and Jewish, with small numbers of Muslim, Hindu, Sikh, Greek Orthodox, and Seventh-day Adventist schools. However, over the next few years hostility to the Muslim population, particularly to modes of dress, and anxiety over possible youth indoctrination in mosques continued to take precedence over discussion of faith schools or curriculum contribution to cohesion. There was no publicity for a United Nations resolution in 2005 that all states should use education to understand religious and cultural conflict, extremism, and intolerance (Davies, 2008). In addition, politicians continued to blame Black communities for any lower student achievements. In August 2005 a Black college student was axed to death in Liverpool by White youths, yet Prime Minister Tony Blair claimed in a speech in his last year of office that youth violence in inner cities was caused by "Black culture" (Wintour & Dodd, 2007).

A book produced by academics and practitioners, *Tell It Like It Is: How Our Schools Fail Black Children*, was ignored by central government, although the mayor of London pointed out in the introduction that "the effects of years of failure to educate Black children has been catastrophic for these young people and their communities" (Livingstone, 2005, p. 15). The Commission on Integration and Cohesion (CIC), set up in September 2006, produced a 2007 report defining cohesion and integration as a process which ensured that different groups adapt to each other with a fair allocation of public services and community facilities. Its recommendations, largely avoiding references to conflict, put the onus for cohesion on local councils, with support for citizenship ceremonies and intercultural activities, and welcomed the new duty placed on schools to promote inclusion and community cohesion. However, this last recommendation appeared to be in contradiction to requirements in the 2006 Education Act that local authorities provide advisors and transport out of local communities to help parents "choose" schools. The government continued to support the development of academies, schools sponsored by business, faith, or other groups, which had the potential to fragment the education system and the school curriculum still further.

Education for a multicultural society

The July 2007 change of prime minister from Tony Blair to Gordon Brown led to ministerial reorganization, with a Department for Children, Schools and Families (DCSF) and a Department for Innovation, Universities and Skills (DIUS) replacing the former DfES. The word "education" disappeared from ministries, joining the disappearance of a language of multicultural education. However, political concern that education should help to create some kind of unity in a diverse multicultural society had not totally disappeared. Just as Joshee (2004) recorded, in reference to Canada, that each era of policy formation leaves a residue of practices and programs (2004, p. 51), so policy in Britain continued under a rubric of diversity and cohesion.

Ajegbo (2007), a former head teacher of a multiracial school, was asked to produce a report on diversity and citizenship. He suggested that a new element be introduced into the citizenship curriculum on "identity and diversity: living together in the UK," with a study of shared values and life in contemporary Britain (p. 97). Also, the National Foundation for Educational Research was commissioned to carry out a long-term study of the effects of citizenship education. A further reorganization of the National Curriculum was to be put in place from September 2008, with teachers allowed more input into course content and design. The history curriculum was to focus more on recent history in the UK, and a study of the British Empire and slavery was to be compulsory.

The inspectorate suggested that religious education in schools needed rethinking, in discussion with local standing committees on religious education, and there was some encouragement of teacher professional development courses in citizenship education. Right-wing groups, however, had not given up their attacks on curriculum developments, one group claiming in a pamphlet that "traditional subjects have been high-jacked to promote fashionable causes such as gender-awareness, the environment and anti-racism, while teachers are expected to achieve the government's social goals, instead of imparting a body of knowledge to their students" (Lawes, Ledda, McGovern, Patterson, & Standish, 2007, p. 2). In elections for local government in May 2008, five members of the fascist British National Party (BNP), a party which had always opposed multicultural education, were elected to the 28-member London Assembly.

Almost 30 years ago James (1981) argued that in Britain teachers "need to ask how far multiculturalism can be made a valid educational idea in a society whose institutions are not geared to tolerant pluralism" (p. 20). This chapter began by noting that, while in Britain there has always been antagonistic debate about a shared national identity and cultural heritage, by the early 21st century political hostility to multiculturalism, immigration, and diversity, combined with old-style post-imperial racism, had made the task of educating for a multicultural society very difficult. However, in a world more fractured than ever in terms of wealth and poverty, migration movements, and ethnic and religious conflict, it can now be recognized that policies and practices once described as multicultural and antiracist education did, despite hostility from many sides, lay the foundation for a wider project of equality, justice, and perhaps even community cohesion. It is slowly being understood that the task of government and educators is to construct a system sustained by common political and moral values, which still recognizes diversity and has the trust and understanding of all groups. What is now needed is political courage and leadership, and educators who look beyond a narrow National Curriculum to a global, intercultural curriculum which can prepare the next generation both with marketable skills and with knowledge and understanding of their multicultural, interdependent world.

References

Ajegbo, K. (2007). *Curriculum review on diversity and citizenship: The Ajegbo Report*. London: Department for Education and Skills (DfES).
Apple, M. W. (1999). The absent presence of race in educational reform. *Race, Ethnicity and Education, 2*(1), 9–16.

Banks, J. A. (1994). *An introduction to multicultural education.* Boston: Allyn & Bacon.

Blair, T. (1998). *The Third Way: New politics for a new century.* London: Fabian Society.

Bullock, A. (1975). *A language for life: The Bullock Report.* London: Her Majesty's Stationery Office (HMSO).

Coard, B. (1971). *How the West Indian child is made educationally subnormal in the British school system.* London: New Beacon Books.

Commission on Integration and Cohesion (CIC). (2007). *Our shared future.* London: Department for Communities and Local Government.

Commonwealth Immigrants Advisory Committee. (1964). *Second report.* London: Her Majesty's Stationery Office (HMSO).

Crick, B. (1998). *Education for citizenship and the teaching of democracy in schools: The Crick Report.* London: Department for Education and Skills (DfES).

Davies, L. (2008). *Educating against extremism.* Stoke-on-Trent, UK: Trentham Books.

Department of Education and Science (DES). (1977). *Education in schools: A consultative document.* London: Author.

Department of Education and Science (DES). (1981). *West Indian children in our schools: The Rampton Report.* London: Her Majesty's Stationery Office (HMSO).

Department of Education and Science (DES). (1985). *Education for all: The Swann Report.* London: Her Majesty's Stationery Office (HMSO).

Department for Education and Skills (DfES). (2003). *Aiming high: Raising the achievement of minority ethnic pupils.* London: The Stationery Office (TSO).

Figueroa, P. (2004). Diversity and citizenship education in England. In J. A. Banks (Ed.), *Diversity and citizenship education: Global perspectives* (pp. 219–244). San Francisco: Jossey-Bass.

Gewirtz, S., Ball, S. J., & Bowe, R. (1995). *Markets, choice and equity in education.* Buckingham, UK: Open University Press.

Gillborn, D., & Youdell, D. (2000). *Rationing education: Policy, practice, reform and equity.* London: RoutledgeFalmer.

Goodhart, D. (2004, February 24). Discomfort of strangers. *The Guardian,* pp. 24–25.

Graham, D. A. (1993). *Lesson for us all: The making of the National Curriculum.* London: Routledge.

Gundara, J. S. (2000). *Interculturalism, education and inclusion.* London: Paul Chapman.

Halstead, M. (1988). *Education, justice and cultural diversity: An examination of the Honeyford affair, 1984–1985.* London: Falmer Press.

Hargreaves, D. (1993). Preface. In A. S. King & M. J. Reiss (Eds.), *The multicultural dimension in the National Curriculum* (pp. vii–ix). London: Falmer Press.

Hastie, T. (1986). History, race and propaganda. In F. Palmer (Ed.), *Anti-racism: An assault on education and value* (pp. 61–73). London: Sherwood Press.

Home Affairs Committee. (1981). *Fifth Report: Racial disadvantage* (Vols. 1–4). London: Her Majesty's Stationery Office (HMSO).

Home Office. (2001). *Community cohesion: The Cantle Report.* London: Author.

Home Office. (2002). *Secure borders, safe haven: Integration with diversity in modern Britain.* London: The Stationery Office (TSO).

Husain, E. (2007). *The Islamist: Why I joined radical Islam in Britain, what I saw inside and why I left.* London: Penguin Books.

James, A. (1981). The "multi-cultural" curriculum. In A. James & R. Jeffcoate (Eds.), *The school in the multicultural society* (pp. 19–28). London: Harper & Row.

Jenkins, R. (1966, May 23). Address by the home secretary to a meeting of voluntary liaison committees. National Council for Commonwealth Immigration, London.

Joshee, R. (2004). Citizenship and multicultural education in Canada: From assimilation to social cohesion. In J. A. Banks (Ed.), *Diversity and citizenship education: Global perspectives* (pp. 127–156). San Francisco: Jossey-Bass.

Klein, G. (1985). *Reading into racism: Bias in children's literature and learning materials.* London: Routledge.

Labour Party. (1989). *Multi-cultural education: Labour's policy for schools.* London: Author.

Lawes, S., Ledda, M., McGovern, C., Patterson, S., & Standish, A. (2007). *The corruption of the curriculum.* London: Civitas.

Livingstone, K. (2005). Introduction. In B. Richardson (Ed.), *Tell it like it is: How our schools fail Black children* (pp. 14–16). Stoke-on-Trent, UK: Trentham Books.

MacDonald, I., Kahn, L., Joh, G., & Bhavani, R. (1989). *Murder in the playground: The Burnage Report.* Manchester, UK: Longsight Press.

MacKenzie, J. M. (1986). *Imperialism and popular culture.* Manchester, UK: Manchester University Press.

Macpherson, W. (1999). *The Stephen Lawrence Inquiry.* London: The Stationery Office (TSO).

Modood, T., Berthood, R., Lakey, J., Nazroo, J., Smith, P., Virdee, S., et al. (1997). *Ethnic minorities in Britain: Diversity and disadvantage* (Fourth national survey of ethnic minorities). London: Policy Studies Institute.

Mullard, C. (1982). Multiracial education in Britain: From assimilation to cultural pluralism. In J. Tierney (Ed.), *Race, migration and schooling* (pp. 120–133). London: Holt, Rinehart and Winston.

Nandy, D. (1971). Foreword. In J. McNeal & M. Rogers (Eds.), *The multi-racial school: A professional perspective* (pp. 7–11). Harmondsworth, UK: Penguin.

National Union of Teachers (NUT). (1979). *In Black and White: Guidelines on racial stereotyping in textbooks and learning materials.* London: Author.

Palmer, F. (Ed.). (1986). *Anti-racism: An assault on education and values.* London: Sherwood Press.

Parekh, B. (2000). *The future of multiethnic Britain: The Parekh Report.* London: Profile Books.

Phillips, T. (2005). Speech to Manchester Community Relations Council, Manchester, UK.

Phillips-Bell, M. (1981). Multicultural education: What is it? *Multiracial Education, 10*(1), 21–26.

Qualifications and Curriculum Authority/Department for Education and Employment (QCA/DfEE). (1999). *The review of the National Curriculum: The secretary of state's proposals.* London: Author.

Rose, E. J. B., Deakin, N., Abrams, M., Jackson, V., Peston, M., Vanags, A. H., et al. (1969). *Colour and citizenship: A report on British race relations.* London: Oxford University Press.

Rushdie, S. (1988). *The satanic verses.* London: Viking Books.

Sleeter, C. (1986). *Keepers of the American dream: A study of staff development and multicultural education.* London: Falmer Press.

Taylor, M. (1992). *Multicultural antiracist education after ERA: Concerns, constraints and challenges.* Slough, UK: National Foundation for Educational Research.

Tebbit, N. (2008, January 27). This much I know. *The Observer Magazine*, 11.

Thatcher, M. (1993). *The Downing Street years.* London: HarperCollins.

Tomlinson, S. (1990). *Multicultural education in White schools.* London: Batsford.

Tomlinson, S. (1993). The multicultural task group: The group that never was. In A. S. King & M. J. Reiss (Eds.), *The multicultural dimension in the National Curriculum* (pp. 21–31). London: Falmer.

Tomlinson, S. (2005). *Education in a post-welfare society* (2nd ed.). Berkshire, UK: Open University Press/McGraw-Hill.

Tomlinson, S. (2008). *Race and education: Policy and politics in Britain.* Berkshire, UK: Open University Press/McGraw-Hill.

Training and Development Agency for Schools (TDA). (2007). *Professional standards for teachers.* London: Author.

Troyna, B. (1986). Swann's song: The origins, ideology and implications of education for all. *Journal of Education Policy, 1*, 171–181.

Wintour, P., & Dodd, V. (2007, April 12). Blair blames spate of murders on Black culture. *The Guardian*, p. 12.

9

From intercultural education to the inclusion of diversity

Theories and policies in Europe

Cristina Allemann-Ghionda
University of Cologne, Germany

In this chapter, the evolution of the concept of intercultural education in Europe is outlined. Intercultural education is used as the original umbrella concept which includes some other related concepts such as multicultural education, antiracist education, the education of minorities, and further concepts which entered the scene later, including inclusion of diversity and citizenship education. In the first section, the origin of the concept and some of its central ideas will be described, along with the criticism that accompanied the theoretical debate from its beginnings. The second section is devoted to the evolution of the policies of European institutions in the field of intercultural education.

Based on some examples of policies in national states, it can be seen that a concept that claims to be universal is interpreted within national and local settings. Given the political and cultural as well as linguistic variety and complexity that characterize the European continent, this picture cannot be complete. There are 27 member states of the European Union and numerous other states which do not yet belong to the European Union. However, they participate in the scholarly and political debates on intercultural education and the treatment of diversity in education. Because of space limitations, I cannot give an exhaustive comparative history of three decades of intercultural education in Europe, nor can I describe systematically and analyze the present situation in detail. A few examples must suffice to illustrate some specific theory and policy patterns, within a sketch of general trends highlighting some differences and contradictions between the European policy in favor of intercultural education and interpretations of (or dissociations from) it in national educational policies. This contradiction represents the greatest challenge for an effective policy of recognition of intercultural issues and of diversity. The third section analyzes the structural conditions that favor or hamper the implementation of intercultural education and similar conceptions.

From intercultural education to integrating diversity: Approaches in research

In Western Europe, intercultural education has been a topic of discussion in educational sciences or pedagogy since the mid-1970s. Strictly speaking, a semantic distinction must be made between *multicultural* and *intercultural*. In multicultural education, the prefix *multi* describes the multiplicity of different cultures which live on the same territory and/or are taught in the same institution, for example in school or in higher education. In intercultural education the prefix *inter* underlines the interactive aspect. In the majority of European countries, the scholarly discourse uses the term *intercultural education*, but in some countries, for example the United Kingdom and the Netherlands, *multicultural education* seems to be more frequent than *intercultural education* (Leeman, 2008; Tomlinson, 2008). The term *antiracist education* may be seen as a specific discourse that is more used in some countries than in others: again, in the UK, and in Greece (Tsiakalos, 2000). Parallel to these concepts, other concepts have been and are used in some Western European countries, for example the education of minorities or the inclusion of diversity. In Eastern Europe, intercultural or multicultural education was not regarded as a significant issue until the collapse of the Soviet system, so the term and the idea were absent in the literature until the early 1990s. After 1990, empirical research and theoretical literature on the integration and education of ethnic minorities have been developing, but the term *intercultural education* is hardly present (Genov, 2005). The concept of intercultural education has been criticized from different points of views in Western Europe, as will be briefly described in this section, and gradually broadened its scope from a narrow culturalist perspective to one encompassing a multi-layered idea of diversity.

Origin

The origin of the concept intercultural education as it is used in Europe is manifold and can be seen as the result of several parallel and consecutive developmental lines. For the sake of simplicity, five main sources are described here as decisive.

First, a change of paradigm in social sciences in the 20th century results in the emerging importance and even pre-eminence of culture as an analytical category at the same level as social class, sex and gender, and age (Camilleri, 1995). Historical forerunners of a comparative and relativist view of cultures, languages, and religions are authors of the Enlightenment, for example Voltaire (1694–1778) or Wilhelm von Humboldt (1767–1835). In this line of thought, Taylor's (1994) theory of the politics of recognition represents a milestone in that it had a seminal influence for both the North American and the European discussion. From the late 1960s on, several disciplines discovered and analyzed the importance of cultural settings for different ways of interpreting the world and analyzing patterns of socialization and interpersonal communication. Theoretical reflection and empirical research in philosophy, cultural anthropology or ethnology, linguistics, literature, social psychology, cross-cultural and intercultural psychology, educational science (and the list is not yet complete) explored the intercultural dimension. Empirical research on intercultural communication, on multilingual development, and on intercultural education is an outcome of this radical change of interest in and appreciation of cultural difference based on a common epistemological foundation: the idea that cultures matter, and that they are equal (Dasen, 1997).

Second, social movements which took place in the United States in the 1960s and 1970s, especially the Civil Rights Movement, and the related ideas about equal dignity and rights of all cultures and groups, especially in the field of education, were followed with great interest in Europe (Steiner-Khamsi, 1992). The ways in which the cultural and ethnic facet, but also the gender aspect, of social inequality was discussed in the United States exerted a stimulating influence on the debate in Europe about what kind of theoretical model should be conceived to transform an education that had paid little attention to ethnic or language minorities until then, as well as not being particularly sensitive with regard to class and gender issues until the 1960s and 1970s.

Third, especially after World War II, migration was an increasingly important social reality in many countries in Western Europe. Especially in Germany, France, Switzerland, Belgium, the Netherlands, Luxembourg, Sweden, and the UK, from the 1950s, but much more intensely from the 1960s on, schools had increasing numbers of students coming from other countries and speaking other languages, which resulted in particular learning, teaching, and integration needs and tasks. Educationalists had to develop adequate theories and models. Pedagogical concepts that strove to compensate for deficits in areas such as language acquisition were generated. This was a response to the demands of schools consistent with the deprivation or deficit-driven and compensatory approaches that were dominant in the 1950s and 1960s (e.g. Bernstein, 1962). After a period of assimilation-driven pedagogy in which the cultures and languages of migrants were not considered as a matter of discussion, or if they were the aim was to prepare migrant students for reintegrating in their home countries (the 1960s until the mid-1970s), a first generation of intercultural education was very much concerned with developing a pedagogy based on the relativism of languages and cultures, on emancipation rather than on the compensation of deficits, and on the integration of migrant pupils rather than on their assimilation (Abdallah-Pretceille, 1990; Auernheimer, 1990). This shift from a deficit-oriented to a difference-oriented pedagogy can be observed, for example, in Germany (Faas, 2008). Developing a pedagogy of emancipation corresponded to similar trends in sociolinguistics (Labov, 1973) and in pedagogies designed in and for other continents (Freire, 1968/2007). Some countries in Southern Europe (especially Italy, Spain, Portugal, and Greece), which had provided the countries of northwestern Europe with labor and with students in the 1960s and 1970s, have increasingly become immigration countries since the 1980s. In these countries, intercultural education became an issue in educational sciences and in policies later than was the case in the traditional immigration countries (Alegre & Subirats, 2007; Portera, 1997).

In the countries which had been colonial powers (e.g. France, Belgium, the UK, the Netherlands), a considerable part of migration was composed of persons from the former colonies, so the educational needs of people from the former colonies and of first-, second-, and third-generation migrants from other countries represent two facets of the same challenge. In countries with a colonial past, the race issue is pre-eminent and inextricably linked to educational policies (Tomlinson, 2008). However, the ways of dealing with cultural difference, with the race issue, and more generally with diversity are different along a continuum that features the explicit mention of race and interactions related to it (the UK, the Netherlands) and at the other end the negation or minimization of cultural difference, the negation of the concept of race, and harsh criticism of racism in its biologistic and culturalist forms (France). In two of the countries which look back to a recent past of fascist dictatorship (Germany, Italy), the concept of race is considered as the extreme expression of essentialism and therefore harshly criticized and not considered as suitable for educational theory (Dittrich & Radtke, 1990).

Fourth, after World War II, an increasing consciousness of Europe's historical and present cultural and linguistic diversity as a resource was promoted by European institutions. Diversity has always been a characteristic of European countries and of Europe as a continent. But the consciousness that Europe (and every single individual) is culturally hybrid by definition was almost erased by the myth of supposedly pure national cultures, a myth cultivated especially in the course of the 19th century and until the end of World War II (Hobsbawm, 1990). At least in segments of the scholarly and of the political arena in single national states, from the 1957 Treaty of Rome on, European integration was to become a major issue in educational policies.

The idea of European integration rests on intercultural education and the acceptance of diversity. What may be called a second generation of intercultural education was developed from the 1990s on, based on the idea that the expressions of socio-cultural and linguistic plurality or diversity are multi-layered. Migration is the most visible and audible form of plurality and is perceived as the most challenging in many national educational discourses, both in research and in policy. But along with migration movements in the 20th and 21st centuries, European diversity is equally composed of a great number of historical ethnic and language majorities and minorities. The latter are citizens of the nations in which they live, but at the same time, as minorities, they are often not recognized as citizens and do not enjoy equal rights and equal educational opportunities. A discourse of intercultural education was developed within European institutions parallel to the scholarly debate and often in cooperation with scholars.

Fifth, the scholarly debate is more and more characterized by exchange and reciprocal influence within the international scientific community and with supranational organizations, especially the United Nations Educational, Scientific and Cultural Organization (UNESCO) in 1974, and the Organisation for Economic Co-operation and Development (OECD) in 1989. International associations like the International Association of Intercultural Education (IAIE), the Association pour la Recherche Interculturelle (ARIC), and the European Educational Research Association (EERA) organize conferences and publish journals. Research on intercultural education is more and more conceived in a comparative or at least in a global perspective. Criticism and new theoretical discourses are more and more embedded and developed in a transnational space.

Criticism

From its beginnings, intercultural education was criticized by some authors for its conceptual poverty (Abdallah-Pretceille, 1990). Before describing some of the arguments of critics, it must be said that criticism is not equally stern and does not address the same issues in all countries. In many cases, criticism cannot be applied to theories of intercultural education as such and as a whole, but rather to the particular kind of discourse that was or is dominant in one particular country. This was the case for years before the theoretical debate began to become more transnational, because many authors stayed within the boundaries of their own national discourse or, at best, within the limits of their own mother tongue, which in some cases was and is the language of several countries. In some ways criticism applies to a particular supranational pedagogical and cultural, language-bound discourse (e.g. English, French, German). In some cases, criticism applies more to reductive interpretations of intercultural education in practice than to elaborate theoretical concepts.

A second preliminary remark on criticism is that it comes both from a *conservative* perspective (cultural difference is of no value, assimilation is better than intercultural education) and from a *progressive* perspective (intercultural education is not enough to achieve equal rights and opportunities). Only the latter is considered here. With regard to this perspective, the following points appear to be most important:

1. Cultural reductionism (every difference or conflict is attributed to cultural reasons) and, closely related, essentialism (it is assumed that cultures are naturally closed and static systems) are criticized because they encapsulate the issue of cultural difference in a cage that is unrealistic, does not allow room for change, and contradicts the very basic idea of intercultural education (Dasen & Perregaux, 2002).
2. For some authors, it is necessary to analyze how society and educational institutions, in

some cases intercultural education, contribute to ethnicization, which is a form of reductionism and essentialism and contributes to discrimination (Lorcerie, 2004).
3 Intercultural education is seen by some educationalists as a pedagogy that neglects socio-economic factors; these, as opposed to cultural differences and to ethnicity, must be identified as responsible for poor school achievement and "institutional discrimination" (Gomolla & Radtke, 2002). Similar criticism of intercultural approaches comes from a sociological point of view (Demorgon, 2005).
4 A dichotomy between an intercultural education focused on migration and another intercultural education focused on European integration is denounced, whereas the intercultural dimension is claimed to be a common approach to migration and to European integration (Abdallah-Pretceille, 1997), as well as to the treatment and education of minorities in national states before the term *intercultural education* was even invented (Krüger-Potratz, 1997).

Main features and further developments

There is no complete survey of how intercultural or multicultural education is theoretically discussed in Europe, or of existing empirical research on its implementation or related questions. However, there are some studies which allow for comparing the state of the theoretical discussion and its correspondence in educational policies and in practice, at least in a number of European countries (Allemann-Ghionda, 2002, 2008b; Banks, 2004; Condet, 2008; Gomolla, 2005; Grant & Lei, 2001; Luchtenberg, 2004; Meunier, 2007).

In more than 30 years, the conception of intercultural education has changed. The present state of the theoretical debate is such that criticism has generated more awareness of the shortcomings and pitfalls of intercultural education. Intercultural education appears as too narrow if it is just about interactions between persons belonging to allegedly different cultures, although the criticism of earlier essentialist conceptions of intercultural education in which cultures appeared as static does not apply to more recent discourses. Its evolution can be described as a succession of stages from a narrow scope (focus on the interaction between cultures, especially between a given majority and ethnic minorities or migrants) to a broader perspective including several layers of socio-cultural plurality, and many facets of diversity including and beyond cultural or ethnic differences.

With some differences among countries and language and culture areas, the following issues are central in the conceptualization of intercultural education. First, the intercultural potential of multilingualism is a crucial issue in most European countries. Learning more than one language beyond one's mother tongue is seen as a way of opening one's mind to other cultural views. Fostering bilingual education, especially when migrants or ethnic minorities are concerned, is seen as a way of respecting their identities and their educational needs (Extra & Yagmur, 2004). Second, the way of including different religions or not in the curriculum is another central question. Closely linked is the question of relativism versus universalism in the realm of values, as well as the issue of laicism (or not) in public education (Doyle, 2006). Third, the integration and successful instruction and education of students with a migrant or ethnic minority background is a major preoccupation. Fourth, the intercultural or, in an enlarged perspective, the diversity dimension in the curricula of subject matters is preferred in most European countries and language areas to a subject "intercultural education" because it allows the design of an educational approach that overcomes and reaches beyond a narrow focus on migrants or minorities (Reich, Holzbrecher, & Roth, 2000).

Besides migration and European integration, the contemporary strategy to deal with a historical variety of languages or cultures, another dimension of international and intercultural relations, is increasingly seen as a social transformation that requires an education aware of intercultural facts and of diversity: international mobility and intercultural exchange in a physical and virtual sense. In the era of globalization, people are embedded and involved in a cross-cultural net that challenges them more than ever before, forcing them to take notice of language and cultural variety and to interact with it. The global dimension of human experience requires a conception of intercultural education that goes further than respecting the rights and needs of ethnic minorities and migrants, but encompasses and explores all aspects of the intercultural dimension (Abdallah-Pretceille & Porcher, 1996; Krüger-Potratz, 2005; Porcher & Abdallah-Pretceille, 1998). Attention has shifted towards the more general goal of integrating all forms of diversity (Dietz, 2007). Several intersecting lines of difference are described as components of diversity (Krüger-Potratz & Lutz, 2002). In some countries and for some authors, citizenship must be redefined, taking into account hybrid and changing identities and values and the diversity of humankind in a broader sense that goes beyond a narrow and static conception of cultural difference and of nation (Osler, 2008; Raveaud, 2007), in a similar way to that in the United States (Banks, 2008).

In each country, educational intercultural theories put the emphasis on those societal phenomena that are most relevant for educational institutional developments. In Eastern Europe the main focus continues to be on historical ethnic minorities, but there is more and more attention on the concept of citizenship education (which must deal with ethnic diversity) in the light of the democratization process (Froumin, 2004). The intercultural dimension of student mobility in the framework of European mobility programs is becoming an issue in which Western and Eastern Europe have common interests and projects. It becomes less and less relevant to identify distinct nationally or culturally based theories. Transnational similarities are increasing.

The European policy of intercultural education, and national interpretations of or dissociations from it

In the language of European institutions, *intercultural education* has a broad meaning that encompasses all the aspects discussed above, involving formal and informal education.

The Council of Europe was founded in 1949 and includes 47 European states. The European Union was constituted in a long process that began in 1957 with the Treaty of Rome. In 2008, it includes 27 member states. Its legislative organ is the European Parliament; its executive the European Commission.

The Council of Europe has introduced, developed, and disseminated the idea of intercultural education since the mid-1970s, starting from the assumption that migrants need support for their cultural development, but then enlarging the scope of the intercultural dimension (Porcher, 1981). Other European institutions, particularly those belonging or attached to the European Union, contributed to developing intercultural education. In a first phase, the European Commission concentrated on the issue of integrating migrants. A milestone of this commitment was the directive of the Council of European Communities (1977) which postulated that immigration countries foster the integration of migrant pupils by facilitating their learning of both their family languages (L_1) and the school language (L_2). Only since the 1990s has the concept of intercultural education appeared in reports and other publications by the European Commission at several levels and by the European Parliament. In a 2005 report by Portas, a member of the European Parliament, the importance of including the migrants' original languages in the school curricula and more effective programs of multilingual education are seen as means and ways to better integrate of migrant students, while contributing to an intercultural education for all students (Portas, 2005). European projects that operate with the term *intercultural* – not only in the framework of schools, but also in tertiary education, in non-governmental organizations (NGOs), and in society – as a dimension of non-formal and informal education are part of the strategies of European institutions to foster European integration. In 2008, the Year of Intercultural Dialogue program proposed a package of initiatives designed to disseminate and help implement this policy, which includes the European and international dimension in education (European Commission, n.d.). In this perspective, mobility programs like Comenius, Erasmus, and Erasmus Mundus are designed to promote intercultural understanding while enhancing the quality of education. For European institutions, diversity is currently a concept used parallel to intercultural education and includes the same comprehensive and multi-layered approaches that are found in the theoretical debate.

There is no doubt that all institutions belonging to or attached to the European Union are going in the same direction: socio-cultural diversity and multilingualism are features of all countries and societies and represent a cultural treasure, not to mention the economic value of diversity. European institutions encourage national states to adapt their educational policies to this principle. But how do European national states interpret and play out this vision?

According to a survey by Eurydice, the documentation center of the European Commission with descriptions of the educational systems and comparative information on special features in them, a focus on cultural diversity or on intercultural education is present in the educational policies of most member states of the European Union. Three main ways of conceptualizing this dimension of education are identified:

1 learning about cultural diversity in order to develop tolerance and respect among pupils, in some cases enhancing the fight against racism and xenophobia;
2 the international dimension, which should provide for an understanding of contemporary cultural diversity in its historical and social context;
3 the European dimension, which should enable pupils to develop a sense of European identity (European Commission, 2004, p. 57).

According to this survey, only Iceland and Bulgaria do not explicitly take account of intercultural education as a concept, or of integrating diversity in their curricula. In most countries multilingualism is mentioned as an important issue also with respect to the integration of migrant students, but the way in which the home languages of migrants are taught (or not) varies greatly. A more recent survey of this kind is not available, but the concept of *citizenship education* is being included in national educational policies more and more, and might be considered as a substitute for intercultural education when the latter is not compatible with national policies (European Commission, 2005).

While the theoretical debate is less and less marked by national traditions, owing to increasing reciprocal influences in the scientific community on the one side and between scholars and supranational organizations on the other, a comparison of the ways in which the European educational policy is interpreted in national policies demonstrates that different priorities are defined in each country according to the problems that a given society has to face, but obviously also following the political agenda of a government in a particular period. So a comparison of national policies of intercultural education or of an education inclusive of diversity will reveal distinct national ways and even some major discrepancies between European and national discourses and practices.

At one extreme of a conceptual continuum, we find policies in which differences are denied and assimilation is the explicit goal. Since the 1990s, policies in France and the United Kingdom have been following this tendency (Bleich, 1998). Different approaches in educational policies are closely linked to attitudes and general policies towards migration and cultural difference, and refer to underlying universal versus differentialist or particularist philosophies (Todd, 1994). At the other end, we find the official policy of European institutions, in which the differences between cultures, languages, and religions are explicitly mentioned as relevant issues for education. In most European countries, the dimension of intercultural education or of the inclusion of diversity in policies appears in some explicit way. The following classification may be helpful:

1. Intercultural education or the inclusion of diversity in educational systems that are structurally inclusive (e.g. Italy).
2. Intercultural education or the inclusion of diversity in educational systems that are structurally exclusive (e.g. Germany, Hungary).
3. The focus is mainly on migrants or ethnic minorities and on the interaction with them as well as on their specific educational needs, although policies declare that all students are concerned (most countries).
4. The focus is on all students, and the curricula of most subject matters include an intercultural or diversity dimension. In other words, the intercultural or diversity dimension is claimed to be transversal (e.g. Sweden, Germany).
5. Intercultural education is not part of the official policy, but an alternative concept like citizenship education is a specific statutory subject (e.g. the United Kingdom).

In many countries, a political and scholarly debate is taking place on the question of the success or failure of educational policies with regard to the education of migrants or minorities (Rijkschroeff, Dam & Duyvendak, 2005). The legitimacy of multicultural approaches is put in question from different sides, both in the scholarly and in the political debate. For example, in the same line of thought that informs Macedo's (2000) conception of civic competencies in a multicultural democracy, several national policies have been stressing more the ideal of national cohesion and of solidarity, while insisting on better second language learning and teaching and on assimilation rather than on the response to specific educational needs linked to the languages and cultures of origin.

So it appears that European policies in favor of intercultural dialogue and diversity are not shared by all official national policies. Europe is diverse, but an imagined homogeneity counteracts the implementation of intercultural education (Gaine, 2008). In most rhetoric of national educational policies the worth and the inclusion of diversity are celebrated, but social inequality is cultivated especially in those educational systems which are highly selective and segregating (Allemann-Ghionda, 2008a).

Implementing intercultural education and integrating diversity in practice: Structural conditions and perspectives

While comparing educational theories, policies, and practice in schools, several gaps appear evident: between European pro-diversity policies and some national policies; between educational intercultural theories and educational policies in single countries; and between national educational policies that are favorable to intercultural education or to the inclusion of diversity and their implementation in practice. Some examples of best practice or simply of practice have been described – sometimes in a comparative perspective. However, there is lack of extensive empirical research, especially of qualitative case studies. Despite this lack of data, there is enough evidence to indicate that intercultural education (or similar concepts) does not pervade the normal routine of schools. Major reasons for this are:

1. The problem of monitoring, controlling, and evaluating how intended curricula are applied is far from being satisfactorily solved.
2. In most institutions of higher teacher education, intercultural education is not included as a mandatory approach; prejudice and non-inclusive views about multicultural and intercultural issues are common among teachers (Edelmann, 2007; Moree, Klaassen, & Veugelers, 2008).
3. While analyzing the results of the first PISA survey, the OECD (2001) strongly recommended that students with a migration background should be better assisted in learning the host language (e.g. English, French, or German as a second language), while no attention is paid to the family or community languages. The routine practice of schools seems to prefer such suggestions to the intercultural proposals of European institutions. The consequence of it is a general shift towards neo-assimilationist policies and practice, in a flagrant contradiction of European pro-diversity policies.
4. Educational systems that are highly selective and organized according to a differentialist, segregating agenda reproduce social and ethnic selection to such an extent that ideas like intercultural education or the inclusion of diversity in the curriculum are neutralized by structures.

Perspectives

Without questioning the legitimacy of the basic assumption that respecting diversity is a human right, intercultural education or the inclusion of diversity should pay more attention to the issue of school achievement of minorities and migrants (Archer, 2008) and to the effectiveness of educational systems (Christensen & Stanat, 2007). Reducing failures (Field, Kuczera, & Pont, 2007) is a declared goal for the OECD, but this cannot be reached if education neglects the multilingual and multicultural background and thus the particular learning needs and competencies of an increasing number of students. Better educational achievement of less privileged parts of the population, especially of migrants and minorities, can be obtained only if the dilemma between integration and social cohesion on one side and taking identity seriously (Gewirtz & Cribb, 2008) on the other is tackled in a constructive way. In Europe, this must include multilingual education.

Intercultural education and the inclusion of diversity as transversal dimensions of the curriculum in all forms of education and teacher education (formal, informal, including teacher education) form a widely shared perspective in the current theoretical debate. The next stage of this evolution would be to emancipate from the minority versus majority dichotomy and from the narrow focus on cultural difference that still pervade some of the theories and much of the policy and practice adaptations. This enlarged perspective has a better chance to be effective if structural educational reforms in favor of inclusive pedagogies are decided and implemented. More empirical research is necessary, and the transnational exchange will benefit from scholarly and political networks in which the language barrier does not represent an obstacle anymore and in which more and more countries are involved.

References

Abdallah-Pretceille, M. (1990). *Vers une pédagogie interculturelle* [Towards an intercultural pedagogy] (2nd ed.). Paris: Publications de la Sorbonne.

Abdallah-Pretceille, M. (1997). L'interculturalisme comme mode de traitement de la pluralité [Interculturalism as a mode of treatment of plurality]. In C. Allemann-Ghionda (Ed.), *Multiculture et éducation en Europe* [Multiculture and education in Europe] (2nd ed., pp. 219–227). Berne, Switzerland: Peter Lang.

Abdallah-Pretceille, M., & Porcher, L. (1996). *Education et communication interculturelle* [Education and intercultural communication]. Paris: Presses Universitaires de France.

Alegre, M. À., & Subirats, J. (Eds.). (2007). *Educación e immigración: Nuevos retos para España en una perspectiva comparada* [Education and immigration: New challenges for Spain in a comparative perspective]. Madrid, Spain: Centro de Investigaciones Sociológicas.

Allemann-Ghionda, C. (2002). *Schule, Bildung und Pluralität: Sechs Fallstudien im europäischen Vergleich* [School, education and plurality: Six case studies on a European comparison] (2nd ed.). Berne, Switzerland: Peter Lang.

Allemann-Ghionda, C. (2008a). Für die Welt Diversität feiern: Im heimischen Garten Ungleichheit kultivieren? Von gegenläufigen Entwicklungen in der Politik, Theorie und Praxis der interkulturellen Bildung in Europa [Celebrating diversity for the world: Cultivating inequality at home? About opposite developments in policies, theories, and practice of intercultural education in Europe]. *Zeitschrift für Pädagogik* [Journal for Education], *54*(1), 15–33.

Allemann-Ghionda, C. (2008b). *Intercultural education in schools: A comparative study*. Brussels, Belgium: European Parliament, Policy Department: Structural and Cohesion Policies, Culture and Education, in cooperation with Deloitte Consulting.

Archer, L. (2008). The impossibility of minority ethnic educational "success"? An examination of the discourses of teachers and pupils in British secondary schools. *European Educational Research Journal*, *7*(1), 89–107.

Auernheimer, G. (1990). *Einführung in die interkulturelle Erziehung* [An introduction to intercultural education]. Darmstadt, Germany: Wissenschaftliche Buchgesellschaft.

Banks, J. A. (Ed.). (2004). *Diversity and citizenship education: Global perspectives*. San Francisco: Jossey-Bass.

Banks, J. A. (2008). Diversity, group identity, and citizenship education in a global age. *Educational Researcher*, *37*(3), 129–139.

Bernstein, B. (1962). Social structure, language and learning. *Educational Research*, *3*, 163–176.

Bleich, E. (1998). From international ideas to domestic policies: Educational multiculturalism in England and France. *Comparative Politics*, *31*(1), 81–100.

Camilleri, C. (1995). Sociétés pluriculturelles et interculturalité [Multicultural societies and interculturality]. In C. Camilleri (Ed.), *Différence et cultures en Europe* [Difference and cultures in Europe] (pp. 85–103). Strasbourg, France: Council of Europe.

Christensen, G., & Stanat, P. (2007, September). *Language policies and practices for helping immigrants and second-generation students succeed*. Berlin: Migration Policy Institute and Bertelsmann Foundation. Retrieved October 9, 2008, from http://www.migrationpolicy.org/pubs/ChristensenEducation091907.pdf

Condet, S. (2008). *Bibliographie: L'éducation interculturelle* [Bibliography: Intercultural education]. Retrieved May 27, 2008, from http://www.ciep.fr/bibliographie/Education_interculturelle.pdf

Council of European Communities. (1977). *Council Directive 77/486/EEC of 25 July 1977 on the education of the children of migrant workers*. Brussels, Belgium: Author.

Dasen, P. R. (1997). Fondements scientifiques d'une pédagogie interculturelle [Theoretical foundations of intercultural education]. In C. Allemann-Ghionda (Ed.), *Multiculture et éducation en Europe* [Multiculture and education in Europe] (2nd ed., pp. 263–284). Berne, Switzerland: Peter Lang.

Dasen, P. R., & Perregaux, C. (Eds.). (2002). *Pourquoi des approches interculturelles en sciences de l'éducation?* [Why intercultural approaches in educational sciences?] Brussels, Belgium: De Boeck Université.

Demorgon, J. (2005). *Critique de l'interculturel: L'horizon de la sociologie* [Critics of the intercultural: The horizon of sociology]. Paris: Economica-Anthropos.

Dietz, G. (2007). Keyword: Cultural diversity. A guide through the debate. *Zeitschrift für Erziehungswissenschaft* [Journal of Education], *10*(1), 7–30.

Dittrich, E. J., & Radtke, F.-O. (Eds.). (1990). *Ethnizität: Wissenschaft und Minderheiten* [Ethnicity: Research and minorities]. Opladen, Germany: Westdeutscher Verlag.

Doyle, A. (2006). Educational equality, religion and the education of Muslim pupils: A comparative study of France and England. In R. Griffin (Ed.), *Education in the Muslim world* (pp. 289–303). Oxford, UK: Symposium Books.

Edelmann, D. (2007). *Pädagogische Professionalität im transnationalen Raum: Eine qualitative Untersuchung über den Umgang von Lehrpersonen mit der migrationsbedingten Heterogenität ihrer Klassen* [Pedagogical professionalism in a transnational space: A qualitative inquiry on how teachers deal with the heterogeneity of classrooms as a consequence of migration]. Münster, Germany: LIT.

European Commission. (n.d.). *The European Commission proposes that 2008 be "European Year of Intercultural Dialogue."* Retrieved May 30, 2008, from http://ec.europa.eu/culture/portal/events/current/dialogue2008_en.htm

European Commission. (2004). *Integrating immigrant children into schools in Europe*. Brussels, Belgium: Eurydice.

European Commission. (2005). *Citizenship education at school in Europe*. Retrieved May 25, 2008, from http://www.eurydice.org/portal/page/portal/Eurydice/showPresentation?pubid=054EN

Extra, G., & Yagmur, K. (2004). European perspectives on immigrant minority languages at home and at school. In S. Luchtenberg (Ed.), *Migration, education and change* (pp. 140–166). Abingdon, UK & New York: Routledge.

Faas, D. (2008). From foreigner pedagogy to intercultural education: An analysis of the German responses to diversity and its impact on schools and students. *European Educational Research Journal*, *7*(1), 108–123.

Field, S., Kuczera, M., & Pont, B. (2007). *No more failures: Ten steps to equity in education*. Retrieved May 22, 2008, from http://www.oecd.org/document/5/0,3343,de_2649_201185_38692357_1_1_1_1,00.html

Freire, P. (2007). *Pedagogy of the oppressed*. New York: Continuum. (Original work published 1968)

Froumin, I. D. (2004). Citizenship education and ethnic issues in Russia. In J. A. Banks (Ed.), *Diversity and citizenship education: Global perspectives* (pp. 273–298). San Francisco: Jossey-Bass.

Gaine, C. (2008). Race, ethnicity and difference versus imagined homogeneity within the European Union. *European Educational Research Journal*, *7*(1), 23–38.

Genov, N. (Ed.). (2005). *Ethnicity and educational policies in South Eastern Europe*. Münster, Germany: LIT.

Gewirtz, S., & Cribb, A. (2008). Taking identity seriously: Dilemmas for educational policy and practice. *European Educational Research Journal*, *7*(1), 39–49.

Gomolla, M. (2005). *Schulentwicklung in der Einwanderungsgesellschaft: Strategien gegen institutionelle Diskriminierung in England, Deutschland und in der Schweiz* [Developing schools in a multicultural society: Strategies against institutional discrimination in England, Germany, and Switzerland]. Münster, Germany: Waxmann.

Gomolla, M., & Radtke, F.-O. (2002). *Institutionelle Diskriminierung: Die Herstellung ethnischer Differenz in der Schule* [Institutional discrimination: The construction of ethnic difference in school]. Opladen, Germany: Leske & Budrich.

Grant, C. A., & Lei, J. L. (Eds.). (2001). *Global constructions of multicultural education: Theories and realities*. Mahwah, NJ & London: Lawrence Erlbaum.

Hobsbawm, E. J. (1990). *Nations and nationalism since 1780: Programme, myth, reality*. Cambridge, UK: Cambridge University Press.

Krüger-Potratz, M. (1997). Interkulturelle Pädagogik in der Bundesrepublik: Fünf Skizzen. [Intercultural education in the Federal Republic: Five sketches]. In C. Allemann-Ghionda (Ed.), *Multiculture et éducation en Europe* [Multiculture and education in Europe] (2nd ed., pp. 229–242). Berne, Switzerland: Peter Lang.

Krüger-Potratz, M. (2005). *Interkulturelle Bildung: Eine Einführung*. [Intercultural education: An introduction]. Münster, Germany: Waxmann.

Krüger-Potratz, M., & Lutz, H. (2002). Sitting at a crossroads: Rekonstruktive und systematische

Überlegungen zum wissenschaftlichen Umgang mit Differenzen [Sitting at a crossroads: Reconstructive and systematic reflections on how differences are dealt with in research]. *Tertium Comparationis: Journal of International and Intercultural Comparative Education, 8*(2), 81–92.

Labov, W. (1973). *Studies in the Black English vernacular*. Philadelphia: University of Pennsylvania Press.

Leeman, Y. (2008). Education and diversity in the Netherlands. *European Educational Research Journal, 7*(1), 50–59.

Lorcerie, F. (2004). Discovering the ethnicized school: The case of France. In S. Luchtenberg (Ed.), *Migration, education and change* (pp. 103–126). Abingdon, UK, & New York: Routledge.

Luchtenberg, S. (Ed.). (2004). *Migration, education and change*. Abingdon, UK, & New York: Routledge.

Macedo, S. (2000). *Diversity and distrust: Civic education in a multicultural democracy*. Cambridge, MA: Harvard University Press.

Meunier, O. (2007). *Approches interculturelles en éducation: Etude comparative internationale* [Intercultural approaches in education: An international comparative study]. Retrieved May 22, 2008, from http://www.inrp.fr/vst/Dossiers/Interculturel/sommaire.htm

Moree, D., Klaassen, C., & Veugelers, W. (2008). Teachers' ideas about multicultural education in a changing society: The case of the Czech Republic. *European Educational Research Journal, 7*(1), 60–73.

Organisation for Economic Co-operation and Development (OECD). (1989). *One school, many cultures*. Paris: Author, Centre for Educational Research and Innovation.

Organisation for Economic Co-operation and Development (OECD). (2001). *Knowledge and skills for life: First results from PISA 2000*. Paris: Author, Centre for Educational Research and Innovation.

Osler, A. (2008). Citizenship education and the Ajegbo Report: Re-imagining a cosmopolitan nation. *London Review of Education, 6*(1), 9–23.

Porcher, L. (1981). *The education of the children of migrant workers in Europe: Interculturalism and teacher training*. Strasbourg, France: Council of Europe.

Porcher, L., & Abdallah-Pretceille, M. (1998). *Ethique de la diversité et éducation* [Ethics of diversity and education]. Paris: Presses Universitaires de France.

Portas, M. (2005). *Report on integrating immigrants in Europe through schools and multilingual education*. Brussels, Belgium: European Parliament, Committee on Culture and Education.

Portera, A. (1997). *Tesori sommersi: Emigrazione, identità, bisogni educativi interculturali* [Submerged treasures: Migration, identity, intercultural education needs]. Milan: Franco Angeli.

Raveaud, M. (Ed.). (2007). L'élève, futur citoyen [The student as a future citizen]. *Revue internationale d'éducation Sèvres* [International Review of Education Sèvres], *44*. Retrieved May 30, 2008, from http://www.ciep.fr/en/ries/ries44.php

Reich, H. H., Holzbrecher, A., & Roth, H.-J. (Eds.). (2000). *Fachdidaktik interkulturell: Ein Handbuch* [Intercultural teaching methods applied to subject matters: A handbook]. Opladen, Germany: Leske & Budrich.

Rijkschroeff, R., Dam, G. T., & Duyvendak, J. W. (2005). Educational policies on migrants and minorities in the Netherlands: Success or failure? *Journal of Educational Policy, 20*(4), 417–435.

Steiner-Khamsi, G. (1992). *Multikulturelle Bildungspolitik in der Postmoderne* [Multicultural educational policy in the postmodern era]. Opladen, Germany: Leske & Budrich.

Taylor, C. (1994). The politics of recognition. In A. Gutmann (Ed.), *Multiculturalism: Examining the politics of recognition* (pp. 25–74). Princeton, NJ: Princeton University Press.

Todd, E. (1994). *Le destin des immigrés: Assimilation et ségrégation dans les démocraties occidentales* [The destiny of migrants: Assimilation and segregation in Western democracies]. Paris: Seuil.

Tomlinson, S. (2008). *Race and education: Policy and politics in Britain*. Berkshire, UK: Open University Press/McGraw-Hill.

Tsiakalos, G. (2000). *Handbook of anti-racist education*. Athens, Greece: Ellinika Grammata.

United Nations Educational, Scientific and Cultural Organization (UNESCO). (1974). *Recommendation concerning education for international understanding, co-operation and peace and education relating to human rights and fundamental freedoms* (General Conference, 18th session). Paris: Author.

10

Multicultural education in South Africa

Crain Soudien
University of Cape Town, South Africa

Introduction

South Africa is one of the world's important social laboratories. It is a country in which the marks of conquest and subjugation, immigration and emigration, settlement and upheaval, occupation and dispossession, domination and oppression, integration and segregation, and conflict and reconciliation sit everywhere on its social and geographical landscape. "Race," predictably, is ubiquitous in the history of these experiences (Theal, 1897). But, as important commentaries have attempted to show (see Lekgoathi, 2004; No Sizwe, 1979), the motor forces behind the divisions, alliances, conflicts, and solidarities in the country, which often have been presented as manifestations of "race," are much more diverse in their nature. Towards a process of telling the history of South Africa in terms which acknowledge the pervasiveness of race but not its sovereignty, a more complex historiography of South Africa is emerging (see Davenport & Saunders, 2000; Hall, 1990; Reader's Digest, 1989). Critical themes of difference that are emerging in these new "tellings" of the South African story include:

1 *the social*, reflecting issues such as language, "race," ethnicity, social class, income levels, religion, educational status, political orientation, gender, and sexual preference (see Hoad, Martin, & Reid, 2005; Seekings & Nattrass, 2005);
2 *the historical or temporal*, drawing attention to the ways in which differences between "traditional" and modern and that which is of "apartheid" and "post-apartheid" (see Comaroff & Comaroff, 1991, 1993) continue to influence people's perceptions of the world;
3 *the spatial*, referring in particular to the ways in which regional and global differences and one's urban or rural status mark people as being either insiders or outsiders (Mamdani, 1996); and, somewhat controversially,
4 *the epidemiological*, referring to one's age, disability, and health status in relation to diseases such as tuberculosis and HIV/AIDS (see Watermeyer, Swartz, Lorenzo, Schneider, & Priestley, 2006), which determine one's degree of social acceptability.

There are, of course, many countries in the world where these issues, in one combination or another, have existed and continue to exist and have consequences for everyday life. There are few, however, where they have come together in the synchronous, recursive, and compounding way in which they do in South Africa. Obvious countries which offer themselves as comparisons include the United States of America and to a lesser extent Brazil. Neither, however, has had to contend, or at least to the same degree, with – for example – the perplexing phenomena of the mind such as "tradition" and modernity, both for the subjects themselves and for social analysts (see Joubert, 2008, p. 3), or those of the body such as HIV/AIDS (see Baxen, 2006). The upshot of this is that many South Africans are enmeshed in what are perceived as deep challenges – *gifts* though for others – of working out what and who they are. At the level of the everyday, key among these are those of living together, accepting each other's differences, treating each other with respect, understanding and engaging with the histories and myths about themselves that individuals and groups bring to their relationships with one another, and, critically, considering how this diversity can be crafted into a resource. Among intellectuals, the challenges have been no less intense. How they should name, describe, and analyze the social landscape before them has seen scholars of all stripes taking positions and arguing over the nature of social difference in the country, about its primordial essence or its constructed character, and about whether terms such as "race" are admissible, and in the process disagreeing, as an illustration, over whether terms such as "Black" and "White" should be capitalized, rendered in inverted commas, or neither (Adhikari, 2005; Alexander, 2002; Habib & Bentley, 2008, p. xii). The applicability of concepts such as "integration" and "multiculturalism" – essentially because of their North American provenance – has also been an intense question (Christie, 1990; Soudien, 2004).

Paradoxically, the processes and events through which South Africa became a democracy in 1994, instead of facilitating the resolution of these challenges, deepened their complexity. Having recently emerged from the experiment of apartheid – that form of social organization in which race was used not only to separate and hierarchize people but to actually *order* social difference – the country became, needless to say, preoccupied with the question of race and its uses. This preoccupation yielded a raft of regulatory, policy, and other kinds of initiatives at all levels of society. The single most important development in the country was the adoption of a new Constitution (Republic of South Africa [RSA], 1996a), which powerfully expressed itself against all forms of discrimination. Progressive as this document is – and widely lauded as its promulgation was as a leading global charter of human rights – its making was unable to escape the contextual politics of the time in which it came into being. Central in this context was the compromise made between the African National Congress, the leading liberation movement, and the National Party, the party of apartheid, to respect each other's cultural institutions, implicated as those were in the essential character of White supremacy (Modisha, 2008). A consequence of this compromise was that the Constitution was and remains amenable to interpretations which have catalyzed and even magnified opportunities for schismatic differences, even on grounds of race. With respect to education, for example, it says that "everyone has the right to establish and maintain, at their own expense, independent educational institutions that . . . do not discriminate on the basis of race" (RSA, 1996a, p. 14), but elsewhere, with respect to language and culture, it says that "everyone has the right to use the language and to participate in the cultural life of their choice" (RSA, 1996a, p. 15). This constitutional provision made possible the re-appropriation of racial privilege through particular groups' abilities to practice what they came to present as "their own culture." And, eminently reasonable as this right was, it projected culture in essentialist and uncritical ways.

Against this background the purpose of this chapter is to provide a description of how the field of education has engaged with questions of social difference. The difficulties of talking about social difference without essentializing it, and particularly race, should be noted. While, therefore, the chapter is underpinned by a deep belief in the vacuousness of the concept of race, it remains deeply alert to the ideological complexity of racism. The major challenge for writing and reflecting on race in any context is being aware of how the language of social science, which is now almost universally underpinned by concepts such as social construction, continues to be contradicted by the ways individuals and groups in their lived experience, even by the very proponents of the idea of social constructionism, continue to reify the meaning of race.

A limitation of this chapter is that it does not deal with multicultural education approaches in the classroom in any detail. Because of limitations of space it is unable to describe the problems and the innovations of the changes that have taken place in schools over the last 15 years. This chapter, towards the project of unpacking the durability of this process of reification of race, begins with a quick summary of the history of how schools have officially and unofficially dealt with these questions and a description of what the field looks like in terms of this major social vector of difference, that is, race. It then looks at the most important developments with respect to difference over the last 30 years and focuses on the issues that are emerging in relation to these.

The history of education and social difference in South Africa

The first formal school in South Africa was established in 1658, making formal education in South Africa 350 years old in 2008. The first 150 years of this history were dominated by the experience of slavery. Framed as slavery was by racial signification, importantly religion and simply contingency modulated race sufficiently to make this early experience of schooling one which was marked by a certain degree of fluidity. One regularly saw, for example, children who would have been deemed not to be European sitting alongside their White peers and, as interestingly, the frequent presence of former slave schoolmasters in White schools. After the arrival of the British in 1806, schooling was provided more systematically for children in the country, and, while the children of the White colonists were given preference, the fluidity that marked the social organization of the school in the first 150 years of its history persisted until 1953, when the Bantu Education Act was passed and formal apartheid was introduced in South Africa (Christie & Collins, 1984; Soudien et al., in press).

The significance of apartheid for understanding formal schooling in South Africa is great. One of the major purposes of the apartheid school was to induct young people into and to teach them racial identity. Challenged as it was by young people from 1976 onwards in the great student uprisings that essentially led to the attainment of democracy in 1994, as a racialization project apartheid was extremely effective. Students classified African, White, Colored, and Indian were schooled in their separate racial education systems and, except where their teachers actively organized to bring young people together in cultural and sports activities (for the story of the non-racial school sports organization, see Peterson, 2006; Smith, 2006), and where they themselves established student organizations such as the Congress of South African Students (COSAS) (Cross, 1999; Hyslop, 1999), had little to do with each other. Racial identification in this period hardened.

The opening up of schools in South Africa

The first real moves to change this situation, which meant actively defying the apartheid state, began in 1976 in church schools at the height of the student uprising. Thereafter, school integration moved through three significant phases from 1976 to the present, namely 1976 to 1990, 1990 to 1994, and 1994 to the present. Important to note about this periodization is that it is essentially based on the White school experience. The reason for basing this periodization on the White school experience is that the most significant attempts at developing an approach and a practice towards multicultural education happened in these schools. The argument made in this chapter is that the state did not develop a practical integration and multicultural policy for schools and that this had the consequence of change with respect to social difference becoming a concern of the former White school sector only. Because of this approach the former African schools remained untouched and remained much as they had been under apartheid. There has been, as a result, no substantive work on diversity, issues of difference, and multicultural education in former African schools. Unlike former White, Colored, and Indian schools, they face no pressure to engage with the challenges of multiculturalism. While, as indicated elsewhere in the chapter, one sees significant changes made in their approach to race and racism by individual Colored and Indian schools, it is in former White schools that the most important deliberate efforts – some of which are thoughtful and others less so – are undertaken with respect to multicultural education.

The first phase of Integration

The earliest substantial attempts at integration were made by the Anglican and Catholic churches. The first real initiative was taken by the Anglican Church with the establishment of St. Barnabas College in Johannesburg. Established in 1963, it was the country's first self-declared non-racial school (Chisholm, 1999). Ten years later this initiative was followed by the Catholic Church, responding to pressure brought from the Black Consciousness Movement (Christie, 1990; Flanagan, 1982; Soudien, 2007b). There were also Colored and Indian schools making moves to open their admission to children who were classified as African at the time. In fact, there were schools, such as Livingstone High School in the Western Cape, officially under the aegis of the Coloured Affairs Department, which stopped admitting African children only under extreme pressure from the government. While the Catholic Church agreed to open its schools, it did so for limited numbers of children of color and then, more significantly, largely on assimilationist terms. There were key individuals and schools in this first phase that argued for a deeper reflection on what a new South African school might look like, and while this initiative never became ascendant they briefly opened up a space in the wider society for an intense discussion around notions of "self" and "other." This moment is almost unparalleled in the history of the White community in South Africa. These leaders raised questions of White consciousness and its relationship to the "other." What does it mean, they asked, to be White in South Africa and what might it take for White people to see themselves as part of, instead of standing at the head of, humanity? In the wake of this development key role players in the church took a view to a growing discussion about the admission of Black children to White private schools that was keenly aware of the critique of culture and power that was then circulating in Black theological circles. An important player, Sister Michael, urged an approach to integration that would keep these issues in mind (cited in Christie, 1990):

> Do we mean by integration the admission of a few numbers of other races into existing White schools, expecting them to conform to the way of life of the White pupil, to adopt his attitudes and values? If we do, then we should think more deeply on this matter. . . . There is another possibility of course. The creation of a completely new type of school . . . where each race meets the other [quoting James Cone, a Black American theologian]

"on equal footing with no race possessing the power to assert the rightness of its style over the other." (p. 22)

Importantly, this perspective did not prevail. It did, however, introduce into the integration debate a powerful awareness among some school people in the church of the problems of assimilation and what came to be known as *enculturation*. The most significant elaboration of this approach was made by Brother McGurk, a Marist brother and for a period of time the headmaster of Sacred Heart College, in a series of interventions that drew attention to the "mechanisms of protection of 'this culture' [of domination] [which] are mainly psychological, but [also] tied to power and privilege" (McGurk, 1990, p. 24). At the core of McGurk's argument were a number of propositions which sought to challenge the teleological inevitability of a modernity framed in the hegemony of the White experience. The work of McGurk was translated into innovative curriculum materials which dealt with issues of difference in inclusive ways (Potenza, 1992).

As suggested above, this radical line of thought of Brother McGurk and Sister Michael – radical in relation to the context – during this phase of integration did not hold sway. Hegemonic voices in the Catholic Church not only resisted them but succeeded in pushing them to the side. The outcome of this contest was that this first phase of integration was essentially managed on assimilationist premises, central to which were assumptions "that open schools would offer white standards of education to a small and select number of black pupils" (Christie, 1990, p. 25). The materials that were developed in schools and the pedagogies around them, especially in subjects such as history, remained informed by assumptions of White superiority (Bam & Visser, 1996). Exceptions to this were found in Catholic schools where themes of South African difference in literature, history, and geography were treated with a great deal more sensitivity (Potenza, 1992).

The second phase of integration

Significantly, the second phase of integration took a decidedly different turn. School integration moved, in this phase, from a discussion of what was happening in private schools to the public school sector. During the late 1980s many public schools began to admit children of color, in defiance of government warnings that they were doing so illegally. Much of this initiative had to do with their falling enrollments and the danger that under-utilized schools would be closed. To bring a semblance of order to the process, the apartheid government placed three options in front of White schools in 1991. These options, which came to be known as "models," gave schools the option of becoming independent (Model A) and so taking control over themselves entirely, or choosing between two versions of state control (Models B and C), which allowed them to remain public schools with limited degrees of latitude with respect to their student admissions (Botha, 1991). Most schools chose to become Model C schools, which permitted them to admit students of color up to no more than half of their enrollment (Folb, 1991). In order for schools to assume this status they had to obtain the consent of more than two-thirds of their parent community.

While public debate during this phase was vigorous and heated, in contrast to the first phase of the integration process, it lacked the introspection urged by McGurk (1990) and, critically, also, a sensitivity about the particularity of South Africa's racial history. The discussion, as the argument below attempts to make clear, took direction from mainstream and conventional approaches to multiculturalism and never quite came to grips with the politics of the larger social context of South Africa (Carrim & Sayed, 1991). The form of "knowing" the Black "other" – how Black people are described and understood – that emerged in this phase was clothed in the language of tolerance that characterized the international multicultural discourse, but was essentially animated by old colonial-style narratives of White paternalism. In these approaches schools were encouraged to make space for the cultures of what were perceived to be minority groups. These concessions, moreover, occurred on the periphery of school life. Special cultural days were organized and ethnic histories were encouraged. But nowhere was the power of White dominance challenged. The apparent generosity surrounding White schools' invitation to Black people masked deep anxieties about the dangers that come with closer proximity to them. Grant and Tate (1995, p. 146) describe this kind of multiculturalism as the human relations approach, an approach, they argue, that glosses over real conflict. Teaching during this time, as work conducted by the author (Soudien, 1994) in a number of Model C schools showed, was characterized by anxiety on the part of teachers to address controversial subjects such as racism.

Important as this period was as a stage in undoing the racial separation of White and Black children, it was surrounded by a politics of anxiety and the consolidation of the form of "knowing" the "other" that had been inherited from the apartheid era. Unlike the situation in the earlier period, when participants in the debate used the opportunity to subject White identity to scrutiny, the preoccupation of White parents appeared to be about preserving their social advantage. As Folb (1991) explained, parents were concerned, *inter alia*, that their traditions should be preserved, that a racial balance in favor of Whites should be protected, that there should be strict admission criteria applied, and that Black children should be admitted from only the neighborhood of the schools. Difference in this discourse, as Troyna (1982, 1987, 1993), Apple (1996), and Goldberg (2002) argued, continued to be premised on essentialist racial and cultural terms. The concepts of race and culture were not understood as social constructions. Taking its cue from mainstreamed policy initiatives around race in the UK and the USA, a similar pluralist South African multicultural discourse, in a very short period of time, was to be heard everywhere. Schools were encouraged to adopt the language of tolerance and to accept all cultures, religions, and backgrounds.

The third phase of integration

A distinctly ambivalent moment in South Africa's history was 1994, the year in which democratic elections in South Africa were held for the first time. It was of course a break from, but at the same time also characterized by, continuity with the old. It is important to note two features of this ambivalence. First, the agreement between the African National Congress and the National Party left the bureaucratic apparatus of the state largely intact (Department of Education, 1995). While the personnel structure of this bureaucracy was gradually overhauled through processes of early retirements and restructuring after 1994, the residue of people, modes of operation, and policies inherited from the apartheid state within it was sufficiently influential to destabilize the new welfare project of the post-1994 government. This fact, in the context of the social nature of the country remaining largely intact, marked as it is by an obdurate social topography articulated by race and class, meant that, while the new government worked hard to reposition itself ideologically, it had to adapt to the reality that social differentiation within the country continued to operate largely on the terms of the old order. Second, revealing the full complexity of the period (and related to the last observation in the previous sentence), White people were no longer in political control (Alexander, 2002). The loss of this political control for former White schools elevated the importance of other forms of control. Cultural dominance began to find new forms of expression and new justifications. Taken together, these two points modified the kind of assimilation pursued during this period.

Schools are central in the struggle between the old and the new. For the new government, they represented the premier site for the reconfiguration of social relations. However, for many White communities, their schools constituted a terrain on which to defend their positions of privilege. An intense process of struggle ensued between the new government and former White schools as a result (Soudien, 2004). Initially, what was at stake in this struggle was by no means clear to everybody concerned. At one level, as the discussion below will make clear, it was about access, but at several other levels it had to do with the racial and cultural character of the school and the standards assumed to signify this character.

The role played by the new government, in attempting to give character and shape to the schooling system, was crucial. It assumed control over the system by passing the South African Schools Act (SASA) in 1996 (RSA, 1996b) and introducing a new curriculum, Curriculum 2005 (C2005), which has now become known, as a result of its revision, as the National Curriculum Statements (NCS). The act, following the constitution, outlawed discrimination and obliged schools to open their admission procedures to all. At the same time as declaring all schools open, it did however – and this reflects the compromise of 1994 – give schools the right to determine their own media of instruction, their cultural character, their policies with respect to extra-mural activities, and also the power to shape their teaching staff and to raise school fees to supplement the subsidy they received from the state. The NCS, as C2005, was launched in March 1997 by the minister of education, Professor Bhengu. It was described as a strategy for moving away from a racist, apartheid, rote-learning model of learning and teaching to a liberating, nation-building, learner-centered, outcomes-based one. Based on constructivist principles which came to be interpreted as learner-centeredness, it committed the new education system to the values of democracy, non-racialism, and non-sexism. In an outcomes-based curriculum, these values were incorporated into what were called the "critical cross-field outcomes" of the curriculum. These included teaching citizenship, anti-sexist, and antiracist values.

Interesting as the politics of these developments was, critical for our purposes here is how schools in general – governed as they were by this new policy framework – dealt with the process of integration (Soudien & Sayed, 2004). Integration had, in the meanwhile, become a distinct feature of the character of most former White English-speaking schools, and also those which were formerly Colored and Indian (Soudien, 2004). Those that were formerly Afrikaans-speaking White, simply because they were Afrikaans, received very few students of color. African schools, also, largely because of their perceived inferior status, received no children from outside their legacy communities.

School responses to the new policy landscape

How then did these measures seeking to promote inclusion come to be taken up in schools? The evidence from the Soudien and Sayed (2003) study in three provinces suggests that the entry of schools into the new phase under the policy leadership of the government was marked by passivity, especially within the Black community, and a grudging compliance on the part of the White community. This passivity among Black people was of course not unique to education. It was manifested in many areas of social activity, where a form of demobilization of civil society took place. In this demobilization, organizations not only ceded their authority to the new government, but assumed that the government would take the lead in shaping the social agenda (Mare, 2003). Most schools simply accepted the new policy framework. In contrast to earlier phases of the integration process, there was very little public debate about the future direction schools should take. In Black schools, in particular, the general orientation was effectively to work with the directions they were given by government. As the work of the author (Soudien, 1996) has attempted to show, there were Colored and Indian schools that deliberately addressed the challenges of racism and put in place antiracist practices at their schools. Schools such as these (and a number continue to operate in Cape Town) used the curriculum to show how race was structured into the knowledge-making process and introduced to their learners a sophisticated language about the commonality of human beings. Many of the teachers in these schools would have been members of teacher organizations such as the South African Democratic Teachers' Union and the Teachers' League of South Africa.

By contrast, in the majority of historically Black schools and in many former White schools – while there was a sense of compliance – there was also innovation and struggle. A few former White schools (Soudien, 2007b) went to great lengths to democratize their classrooms, to introduce new attitudes in the playgrounds and in the classrooms, and to draw parents into conversations about the kind of schools a non-racial society ought to have. One powerful example was, and still is, the Grove Primary School in Cape Town. This school, through the active leadership of its principal and its school governing body, worked hard to build a new civic identity in its teaching, extra-mural activities, and community relationships. It came close to the self-consciousness that the Catholics such as McGurk (1990) had sought for their schools in the 1980s.

In most other schools, intense struggle against the new thinking in the country was and remains the order of the day. While maintaining postures of compliance, they worked the spaces provided them by the legislation and proceeded to develop novel forms of resistance to the new political authority. The author has argued elsewhere (Soudien & Sayed, 2004) that this resistance was made possible by the SASA policy of decentralization. Decentralization made it possible for the local school to embark lawfully on a range of oppositional courses of action to the broad objectives of the state. In many former White schools one saw the legitimation of race-recidivist-type activities, such as the entrenchment of their cultural characters through the formal and the informal curriculum, such as language use. When these initiatives were challenged by the government, because it perceived the initiatives to be exclusionary, they used the policy of decentralization to defend themselves. They mounted, for example, a number of influential court actions against the state to defend their actions.

In one such notable action a former White Afrikaans school in the Western Cape Province, Mikro Primary, took the state to court because it had been ordered to admit English-speaking children of color and to teach them through the medium of English. The school argued that the Constitution and the SASA entitled it to choose its medium of instruction and to preserve its cultural character. In *Mikro v. the State* (Soudien, 2005), the judge found in favor of the school, stating that it had a constitutional right to define itself as an Afrikaans school and therefore the power to withhold admission rights to English-speaking children. There are currently more than 15 legal cases being fought in the country between the new government and former White schools (Soudien, 2007b). The approach of the state to its own legislation has effectively been to take a defensive posture and, in some ways by default, to look to the courts for the legitimation of its policy intentions ("Race and Reason," 2001). White schools have become aware of this and have assembled strong legal capacity in their school governing bodies and come, in the process, to produce a whole new terrain of education law practice.

Similar struggles took place around the NCS. Harley and Parker (1999), important critics of the NCS, saw in the document the praiseworthy imperative of inclusion premised on the ideal that all children could learn: "there are no pupil deficits" (p. 190). They argued, however, that the NCS misread the South African context. The policy depended on the availability of knowledgeable teachers. These, Harley and Parker said, did not exist, and it was in this essential flaw that the whole project of inclusivism stood imperiled. The teachers imagined in the policy, even those with strong professional histories in middle-class schools, did not correspond with the de-professionalized and under-prepared corps operating in the schools. More critically, the pupils themselves were socially and culturally not the autonomous subjects imagined in the constructivist ideals of C2005. They were, especially those in the schools of the poor, children who had been denied opportunity in the past. The NCS, they suggested, addressed a middle-class context, which is certainly what the majority of the country's children were not. The outcome was that the NCS was observed in form in former Black schools but seldom, because both teachers and pupils struggled with it, practiced as it was intended.

Significantly, as the school-based work of Sayed, Subrahmanian, Soudien, and Carrim (2007) has shown, former White schools thrived using the new curriculum, while poor and mostly Black schools struggled to make it work. The author (Soudien, 2007a) has argued that the policy has, contrary to its intentions, come to constitute an important new discriminatory force on the education landscape. In the work of Sayed et al. (2007), it became clear that the NCS enabled schools to use the argument of standards, the standard of the curriculum in particular, to control the entry and manage the progress of children in schools. It kept Black children back when they could not perform grade-appropriate tasks, without providing them with the requisite kinds of assistance and help. It merely assumed that these children would, and indeed should, simply find their way through the complexity of the curriculum. In the process, English in English-medium schools was used to differentiate between those who could manage the curriculum and those who could not, and Afrikaans in Afrikaans-medium schools was used simply to keep children of color out.

Conclusion

Two related interpretations with respect to the government's policy for integration and multiculturalism can be made. The first is that, in not driving through a practical integration and multicultural policy that deliberately included former Black schools, it effectively left that sector of the education landscape out of a structured program for delivering a policy of change. The consequence of this was that integration and multicultural education became, largely, a concern of former White schools only. The second is that in configuring its policies in ways that devolved authority down to school levels, it allowed many former White schools to develop approaches to the challenges of integration and multiculturalism which insufficiently problematized the country's history of White privilege. Without proper guidance from the government, what these schools began to do, not unexpectedly, was to work with what they knew, and what they knew, unfortunately, was only that form of multiculturalism which they had inherited from their past. The approach they took to integration and contact was based on the inherited but untroubled assumptions which governed relationships between White and Black people. While it is true (Soudien, 2007b) that new relationships were and are being forged between White and Black children in schools, their parents continue to define the conditions of these relationships. In many White schools these relationships continue to be based on paternalistic attitudes toward Black children. Black children continue to be projected and managed as deficient subjects.

In bringing this discussion to a close, it is quite clear that the politics of difference in the South African school have been and are being configured in important new ways which we need to understand. Central is the emergence of important trends which draw on the following realities:

- In coming to power the African National Congress government developed a set of anti-discrimination policies. These policies were circumscribed, however, by the compromise made between the opposing parties in the reconciliation process. The central effect of this compromise was to deliver a governance package for schools based on decentralization which left power in the hands of schools' legacy communities.
- These legacy communities, White and Black in the main, approached the new policy environment in which they found themselves formed in different ways. In the absence of strong, centrally driven campaigns, most former Black schools largely accepted the new policy, while White schools engaged with it. The latter, in engaging with the policy, however, realize that they can no longer speak in the language of White supremacy.

What these realities have produced is a newly contoured landscape in which privilege has been reconfigured. Central in understanding this reconfiguration is asking what has happened to race. In describing the struggles between the state and the schools, as described above, it is clear that race remains central to privilege, hierarchy, and division in schools. It is, however, not the same phenomenon that one saw under apartheid. White schools are intensely aware that they can no longer use the argument of race to justify privilege. What they have done, it is important to recognize, is to use the new policy but to recruit it for the purposes of defending many of the features of the old apartheid order. Using the discourse of standards, they have extracted themselves from what they describe as the mediocrity of South African education and presented themselves as examples of world-class excellence (for an interesting discussion about the situation in the USA, see Macedo & Gounari, 2006; for the South African manifestation of this, see Dolby, 2001).

Dominance is extrapolated from its local context and from the politics that hold it in place and is re-instantiated as a globalizing project. "Knowing" continues to mean reading the "other" in deficit terms, but is prosecuted now on the basis of a universalized cosmopolitanism. Instead of the political authority of the state, the White school now turns to the authority of the global market. Its strategy in this process is to argue for the retention of what it does because its cultural orientation and the habits and relationships it fosters are consonant with the requirements of what it perceives to be the identity of the globalized subject. The interesting outcome of this is that former White schools remain sites of assimilation and that stereotyping forms of multiculturalism continue to be the order of the day.

References

Adhikari, M. (2005). *Not White enough, not Black enough: Racial identity in the South African Coloured community*. Athens, OH: Ohio University Press.

Alexander, N. (2002). *An ordinary country: Issues in the transition from apartheid to democracy in South Africa*. Pietermaritzburg, South Africa: University of Natal Press.

Apple, M. (1996). *Cultural politics and education*. Buckingham, UK: Open University Press.

Bam, J., & Visser, P. (1996). *A new history for a new South Africa*. Cape Town, South Africa: Kagiso Press.

Baxen, M. (2006). *An analysis of the factors shaping teachers' understandings of HIV/AIDS*. Unpublished doctoral dissertation, University of Cape Town, Cape Town, South Africa.

Botha, V. (1991). *Draft discussion document: Education for a new South Africa*. Cape Town, South Africa: Centre for Intergroup Studies.

Carrim, N., & Sayed, Y. (1991). Open schools: Reform or transformation. *Work in Progress, 74*, 28–29.

Chisholm, L. (1999). Change and continuity in South African education: The impact of policy. *African Studies, 58*(1), 87–103.

Christie, P. (1990). *Open schools: Racially mixed Catholic schools in South Africa, 1976–1986*. Johannesburg, South Africa: Ravan Press.

Christie, P., & Collins, C. (1984). Bantu education: Apartheid ideology and labour reproduction. In P. Kallaway (Ed.), *Apartheid and education: The education of Black South Africans* (pp. 160–183). Johannesburg, South Africa: Ravan Press.

Comaroff, J., & Comaroff, J. (1991). *Of revelation and revolution: Christianity, colonialism and consciousness in South Africa*. Chicago: University of Chicago Press.

Comaroff, J., & Comaroff, J. (Eds.). (1993). *Modernity and its malcontents: Ritual and power in post-colonial Africa*. Chicago: University of Chicago Press.

Cross, M. (1999). *Imagery of identity in South African education, 1880–1990*. Durham, NC: Carolina Academic Press.

Davenport, T., & Saunders, C. (2000). *South Africa: A modern history*. Basingstoke, UK: Macmillan.

Department of Education. (1995). *White Paper on education and training*. Cape Town: Parliament of the Republic of South Africa. Retrieved October 20, 2008, from http://www.info.gov.za/whitepapers/1995/education1.htm

Dolby, N. (2001). *Constructing race: Youth, identity and popular culture in South Africa*. Albany: State University of New York Press.

Flanagan, B. (1982). Education, policy and practice. In A. Prior (Ed.), *Catholics in apartheid society* (pp. 83–96). Cape Town, South Africa: David Philip.

Folb, P. (1991, April). *The open schools movement in South Africa, 1986–1990: Social revolution or epiphenomenon?* Paper presented at the Centre for African Studies Africa seminar, University of Cape Town, South Africa.

Goldberg, D. T. (2002). *The racial state*. Oxford, UK: Blackwell.

Grant, C., & Tate, W. (1995). Multicultural education through the lens of the multicultural education research literature. In J. Banks & C. Banks (Eds.), *The handbook of research on multicultural education* (pp. 145–168). New York: Macmillan.

Habib, A., & Bentley, C. (Eds.). (2008). *Racial redress and citizenship in South Africa*. Cape Town, South Africa: Human Sciences Research Council Press.

Hall, M. (1990). *Farmers, kings and traders: The people of Southern Africa, 200–1860*. Chicago: University of Chicago Press.

Harley, K., & Parker, B. (1999). Integrating differences: Implications of an outcomes-based national qualifications framework for the roles and competencies of teachers. In J. Jansen & P. Christie (Eds.), *Changing curriculum: Studies on outcomes-based education in South Africa* (pp. 181–202). Kenwyn, Cape Town, South Africa: Juta.

Hoad, N., Martin, K., & Reid, G. (Eds.). (2005). *Sex and politics in South Africa*. Cape Town, South Africa: Double Storey Books.

Hyslop, J. (1999). *The classroom struggle: Policy and resistance in South Africa, 1940–1990*. Pietermaritzburg, South Africa: University of Natal Press.

Joubert, P. (2008, May 16–22). Back to the dark days. *Mail & Guardian, 24*(20), p. 3.

Lekgoathi, S. (2004). Some reflections on early African and South African history: An historiographical essay. In Institute for Justice and Reconciliation and the South African History Project (Eds.), *Turning points in history: Ancient civilisations and global trade* (Vol. 1, pp. 52–63). Parktown, South Africa: STE Publishers.

Macedo, D., & Gounari, P. (2006). Globalization and the unleashing of new racism: An introduction. In D. Macedo & P. Gounari (Eds.), *The globalization of racism* (pp. 3–35). Boulder, CO: Paradigm.

Mamdani, M. (1996). *Citizen and subject: Contemporary Africa and the legacy of late colonialism*. Claremont, Cape, South Africa: David Philip.

Mare, G. (2003). The state of the state: Contestation and race re-assertion in neo-liberal terrain. In J. Daniel, A. Habib, & R. Southall (Eds.), *State of the nation: South Africa, 2003–2004* (pp. 25–52). Cape Town, South Africa: Human Sciences Research Council Press.

McGurk, N. J. (1990). *I speak as a White: Education, culture and nation: A collection of contemporary papers on education, culture, and the national question in South Africa from a theological perspective.* Marshalltown, South Africa: Heinemann.

Modisha, G. (2008). Affirmative action and cosmopolitan citizenship in South Africa. In A. Habib & K. Bentley (Eds.), *Racial redress and citizenship in South Africa* (pp. 153–178). Cape Town, South Africa: Human Sciences Research Council Press.

No Sizwe (1979). *One Azania, one nation: The national question in South Africa.* London: Zed Press.

Peterson, H. (2006). School sport organisations and education, 1960s–1990s. In C. Thomas (Ed.), *Sport and liberation in South Africa: Reflections and suggestions* (pp. 120–137). Alice, South Africa: University of Fort Hare, National Heritage and Cultural Studies Centre.

Potenza, E. (1992). *The broken string: An integrated approach to Southern African history.* Houghton Estate, Johannesburg, South Africa: Heinemann-Centaur.

Race and reason (Supplement). (2001, September). *Cape Argus*, p. 6.

Reader's Digest. (1989). *Illustrated history of South Africa: The real story.* Cape Town: Reader's Digest Association of South Africa.

Republic of South Africa (RSA). (1996a). *The Constitution of the Republic of South Africa.* Pretoria, South Africa: Government Printer.

Republic of South Africa (RSA). (1996b). *South African Schools Act of 1996.* Cape Town, South Africa: Government Printers.

Sayed, Y., Subrahmanian, R., Soudien, C., & Carrim, N. (2007). *Education exclusion and inclusion: Policy and implementation in South Africa and India.* London: Department for International Development.

Seekings, J., & Nattrass, N. (2005). *Race, class and inequality in South Africa.* Scottsville, South Africa: University of KwaZulu-Natal Press.

Smith, A. (2006). The invisible factor: Women in the non-racial sports movement. In C. Thomas (Ed.), *Sport and liberation in South Africa: Reflections and suggestions.* Alice, South Africa: University of Fort Hare, National Heritage and Cultural Studies Centre.

Soudien, C. (1994). Dealing with race: Laying down patterns for multiculturalism in South Africa. *Interchange, 25*(3), 281–294.

Soudien, C. (1996). *Apartheid's children: Student narratives of the relationship between experiences in school and perceptions of racial identity in South Africa.* Unpublished doctoral dissertation, State University of New York at Buffalo.

Soudien, C. (2004). "Constituting the class": An analysis of the process of "integration" in South African schools. In L. Chisholm (Ed.), *Changing class: Education and social change in post-apartheid South Africa* (pp. 89–114). Cape Town, South Africa: Human Sciences Research Council Press.

Soudien, C. (2005). Racial discourse in the Commission on Native Education (Eiselen Commission), 1949–1951: The making of a "Bantu" identity. *Southern African Review of Education, 11*, 41–58.

Soudien, C. (2007a, April). *Structural discrimination in South African schooling.* Symposium conducted at Princeton University, Princeton, NJ.

Soudien, C. (2007b). *Youth identity in contemporary South Africa: Race, culture and schooling.* Cape Town, South Africa: New Africa Books.

Soudien, C., Chisholm, L., Cross, M., Kallaway, P., Morrow, S., Maabe, B., et al. (in press). *The Amersfoort legacy: The history of 350 years of formal schooling in South Africa.* Cape Town: South African History Online.

Soudien, C., & Sayed, Y. (2003). Integrating South African schools? Some preliminary findings. *Institute of Development Studies (IDS) Bulletin, 34*(1), 29–42.

Soudien, C., & Sayed, Y. (2004). A new racial state? Exclusion and inclusion in education policy and practice in South Africa. *Perspectives in Education, 22*(4), 101–115.

Theal, G. (1897). *The history of South Africa.* London: Swan Sonnenschein.

Troyna, B. (1982). The ideological and policy response to black pupils in British schools. In A. Hartnett

(Ed.), *The social sciences in educational studies: A selective guide to the literature* (pp. 127–143). London: Tavistock.

Troyna, B. (1987). *Racial inequality in education.* London: Tavistock.

Troyna, B. (1993). *Racism and education: Research perspectives.* Buckingham, UK: Open University Press.

Watermeyer, B., Swartz, L., Lorenzo, T., Schneider, M., & Priestley, M. (Eds). (2006). *Disability and social change: A South African agenda.* Cape Town, South Africa: Human Sciences Research Council Press.

11
Multicultural education in Japan

Yasumasa Hirasawa
Osaka University, Japan

Multicultural Japan

We now live in the era of globalization, and a multicultural reality is rapidly evolving throughout the world. Japan is no exception. However, multicultural education is a relatively recent phenomenon in Japan, because Japan has long identified itself as a homogeneous nation with one ethnicity, one language, and one culture (Hirasawa, 1997; Murphy-Shigematsu, 2004). It was after a large number of newcomer foreigners (or Newcomers) settled in Japan in the 1990s that terms such as *multicultural* and *multicultural education* became popular.

The most recent national census indicates that Japan has approximately 2.15 million foreign nationals, accounting for 1.69% of the total population, which is about 128 million people (Homusho, 2008). Their percentage may still be quite small compared to that of other countries, but the rate of increase and the social impact of the foreign population have been significant. When the percentage of foreign nationals exceeded 1% in 1993 – a decade and a half ago – it made big national news in Japan.

Before 1990, when the government revised the immigration laws significantly, the majority of foreign nationals in Japan were resident Koreans. In the past, Koreans made up more than 80% of the non-Japanese population. In 1984 Koreans were 82% of the population of foreign nationals in Japan (0.68 million out of 0.83 million). Most resident Koreans are descendants of individuals who were forcibly brought to Japan as a result of the Japanese occupation of Korea beginning in the early 20th century. Under Japan's military rule, those Koreans were compelled to speak Japanese, use Japanese names, and acquire Japanese manners and customs. Immediately after World War II, they were deprived of Japanese citizenship, but circumstances necessitated that most of them remain in Japan. They have since suffered discrimination, because Japanese society has treated them as second-class citizens. Today they are often called "Oldcomers," along with long-term-resident Chinese, in contrast to "Newcomers."

A multicultural reality already existed in Japan before the visible influx of Newcomers in the 1990s. However, resident Koreans were not generally perceived as creating cultural diversity or multiculturalism because they mostly looked and behaved like mainstream Japanese. Assimilation-oriented government policies and social environments in Japan have given them an ambiguous identity as "outsiders within."

The number of foreign nationals in Japan almost doubled between 1984 (0.83 million) and 1994 (1.64 million). The population of foreign nationals has increased by 47.3% since 1996, and their national and ethnic backgrounds have become quite diverse (representing 190 countries and areas). Currently, Chinese account for 28.2% of the foreign national population, Koreans 27.6%, Brazilians (mostly of Japanese descent) 14.7%, and Filipinos 9.4% (Homusho, 2008). The number of Brazilians and Peruvians of Japanese descent has increased rapidly since 1990 because the revised immigration law of 1990 gave them special status and allowed them to work in Japan based on the principle of *jus sanguinis* (right of blood). Between 1986 and 1992, the number of Japanese Brazilians and Japanese Peruvians increased 68-fold and 55-fold respectively.

Most Newcomers have settled in Japan as factory workers, field workers, entertainers, and wives of Japanese husbands. Because of globalization, an increasing number of non-Japanese businesspersons, professionals, and students have come to live in Japan. These Newcomers have settled throughout Japan. The majority of foreign nationals (including both Oldcomers and Newcomers) are concentrated in five metropolitan prefectures: Tokyo (17.8%), Aichi (10.3%), Osaka (9.8%), Kanagawa (7.6%), and Saitama (5.3%) (Tokyo, Kanagawa, and Saitama are in eastern Japan, Aichi is in central Japan, and Osaka is in western Japan). These prefectures have major industrial areas and big businesses, particularly those related to the automobile industry, which employs a large number of Newcomers.

In addition to Oldcomers and Newcomers, there are several categories of "others" or "outsiders within," which make Japan multicultural (Lee, Murphy-Shigematsu, & Befu, 2006; Willis & Murphy-Shigematsu, 2008). There are, for instance, Buraku people (a caste-like Japanese minority population), Ainu people (an indigenous minority population that used to inhabit Japan's northernmost island of Hokkaido), and children of international marriage including Amerasians (those who were born to a U.S. military father and an Asian mother).

Okinawans from the southwestern islands of Japan used to face severe discrimination in Japanese society. However, they are perceived rather positively now because contemporary Japanese people have come to enjoy their music and find new value in their ways of living harmoniously with nature. This example indicates the possibility that the power relations and boundaries between majorities and minorities can change as the general socio-political and cultural contexts evolve and as new advocacies develop. The same observation applies to the situation of other categories of "outsiders within."

History of multicultural education in Japan

In the 1980s, when the Japanese economy was growing rapidly in the world market, a number of new policy directions were proposed to "internationalize" Japanese education. For example, the Final Report of the Prime Minister's Council for Educational Reform (Rinkyoshin, 1987) outlined six major policies for this purpose:

1. to accommodate and meet the needs of Japanese returnee students from abroad effectively and to create schools that are open to the world;
2. to improve institutional arrangements in order to accommodate more exchange students from other countries;
3. to improve foreign language education;
4. to improve Japanese language education;
5. to reform higher education from a global perspective;
6. to help develop self-directed thinking skills and attitudes among Japanese students.

Looking back, these policies had much to do with the issues and concerns of multicultural education. However, because the view of culture in Japan was generally constructed in terms of visible difference (by race, ethnicity, and language), the concept of multicultural education first appeared in Japanese education as a foreign idea.

The theories and practices as well as the historical contexts of multicultural and intercultural education in other countries – particularly the United States, Canada, Australia, France, Germany, and the United Kingdom – began to be introduced to Japanese researchers and educators beginning in the late 1980s. However, it was only after the 1990s, against the backdrop of the increasing and visible influx of Newcomers, that multicultural education became a popular concern among Japanese educational researchers, educators, and the public.

In the comprehensive theoretical study of multicultural education first published in Japan, Kobayashi (1985), after referring to the development and issues of multicultural education in the world, stated:

> Lastly, regarding Japan, it remains to be a future issue whether we can introduce the concept of multicultural education meaningfully in Japan. . . . Japan achieved its national unification following the model of 19th-century Europe, and it appears that the sense of "one nation, one state" is becoming stronger in the context of growing nationalism these days. In this context, it may not be easy to acknowledge properly the existence of non-Japanese people in Japan and guarantee their children's education, and to teach Japanese children to live harmoniously with other people. In that sense, we can regard the education of resident Korean children as the most urgent issue of multicultural education in Japan because Koreans have accounted for the vast majority of the non-Japanese populations and because we have had the deepest relations with them in the past. (pp. 345–346)

Multicultural education in Japan has been "discovered" and constructed as an independent genre of educational practice and research in the wake of the "massive emergence" of Newcomer students. However, even before the 1990s, "de facto" approaches to multicultural education could be found in various educational practices and movements in Japan (Hirasawa, 1987; Nakajima, 1998). They are: 1) the education of Japanese returnee students; 2) Dowa education (an educational movement against Buraku discrimination); and 3) the education of resident Korean students.

Education of Japanese returnee students

Interest in education for international understanding grew in Japan as the Japanese economy began to globalize in the late 1970s through the 1980s. An increasing number of Japanese children went abroad with their parents and were socialized in different cultures. As of May 1995, for instance, the number of Japanese elementary and junior high school students staying overseas reached almost 50,000, and about 13,000 returnee children came back annually after a significantly lengthy stay in other countries. Because they had acquired different ways of thinking, feeling, and behaving, they were perceived and treated as "strange Japanese" in schools within the context of the dominant view of Japan as a homogeneous nation. The returnee students often faced bullying and harassment because of their cultural differences, and were subject to strong pressures for assimilation and group conformity. Rather than being proud of themselves as they were, many returnees were compelled to disguise their differences in order to become part of mainstream society.

However, as the trend for globalization increased, the independent attitudes and critical thinking skills of returnee students began to be perceived as positive human resources in Japanese society. As a result, the general perception of returnee students gradually shifted from "strange" to "unique" (Sato, 2003). A number of important tenets of multicultural education can be found in the process of this historical transition.

Dowa education

Dowa education – or the educational movement against Buraku discrimination – has been one of the most influential grassroots initiatives for democracy and social justice in Japanese education (Hirasawa, 1997; Hirasawa & Nabeshima, 1995). Buraku people are a caste-like minority (based on descent or social origin), and they are the largest minority population in Japan. Excluded from mainstream economic and social relations for centuries, Buraku people have not only suffered from various forms of educational inequalities but perceive the future as limited and view outsiders as untrustworthy. As a result, Buraku children have continued to experience lower academic achievements despite decades of Buraku improvement measures that have been implemented by central and local governments since the late 1960s. Their rate of enrollment in colleges and universities is less than half the national average. One popular explanation for this achievement gap derives from Ogbu's (1978) cultural ecology theory, which maintains that historically oppressed minorities tend to resist school goals and to develop cultures that are oppositional to the mainstream society.

Buraku discrimination is symbolic of Japanese society and culture because it is deeply rooted in the dominant Japanese belief system that places a high value on blood relations and family ties and that emphasizes group conformity. Buraku people have often been regarded as "filthy" or as people of different blood, and have experienced marriage- and employment-related discrimination. Non-Buraku people have tried to secure their place in Japanese society by not associating with Buraku people. Therefore, complete elimination of Buraku discrimination, in theory, requires a thorough democratization of Japanese society and the value system as well as improvement in human rights protection systems and public awareness of human rights.

An increasing number of Buraku students have recently entered mainstream society by acquiring more highly regarded academic careers. There are more diverse and successful role models among Buraku people today. Discrimination against them is gradually declining. However, it will take quite a while for it to be eliminated.

Historical studies have revealed that among the ancestors of Buraku people were pioneering creators of traditional Japanese cultural forms such as Noh and Kabuki plays and Japanese gardens. Also, their liberation movement founded the Leveler's Association (*Suiheisha*) and adopted its Declaration in 1922, which is often referred to as the first human rights declaration in Japan. In this sense, societal discrimination not only discouraged Buraku people but also inspired them to create and enrich a culture of democracy and human rights as well as Japan's traditional culture.

Dowa education has dealt with these various aspects of Buraku reality through decades of empowering educational practices that were built on the slogan "Learning from the Reality of the Discriminated-Against" (Nakano, Ikeda, Nakao, & Mori, 2000). Its concerns and perspectives overlap significantly with theories and practices of multicultural education and human rights education.

Education of resident Korean students

Students of Korean background have been subject to discrimination and second-class treatment in Japanese society (Umakoshi, 1986). In the 1970s, anti-discrimination educators began to develop an educational strategy that encourages Korean students to be proud of their cultural background and to use their Korean names. These educators learned a great deal from the experience of Dowa education, especially as implemented in the case of western Japan. They also tried to teach mainstream Japanese students to understand critically the history of Japan's military rule of Korea and the series of oppressive incidents that later occurred.

However, it was only after the 1990s that the education of Korean students began to be discussed in the context of education for multicultural living-together, along with growing concerns for the education of Newcomer students. Today, educational authorities and grassroots organizations of educators in many parts of Japan are trying to promote the education of Korean and Newcomer students increasingly within the framework of multicultural education.

The identity of resident Koreans is not monolithic in contemporary Japanese society. Fukuoka (1993) revealed through his field research that there are at least four or five different types of self-identifications among young resident Koreans in Japan. Before 1984, children who were not born to a Japanese father could not obtain Japanese nationality. However, the revised Nationality Law of 1984 permits children who were born to a Korean father and a Japanese mother to choose Japanese nationality. As a result, most children born with a Japanese and a Korean parent choose Japanese nationality (more than 80% of resident Koreans marry a Japanese today). In addition, about 10,000 Koreans naturalize as Japanese citizens every year. This means that there are increasingly more Japanese children with Korean heritages.

In this context, the validity of a group category-based approach, which was dominant in the education of Korean students in the 1970s and 1980s, has been critically interrogated because it had a strong tendency to depict resident Korean children as a monolithic group. A new approach based on a comprehensive theory of multicultural education and with clear focus on multiple identities is now essential.

Education of Newcomer students

The education of Newcomer students has evolved from the educational practices discussed above and from the new social environment that has recently developed in Japan. In 1991, the Ministry of Education began to collect statistics on non-Japanese children who need special Japanese language instruction. These children receive Japanese as second language (JSL) instruction in order to succeed in public schools. According to the most recent statistics (as of September 1, 2006), the total number of such students (in public elementary and secondary schools, and special schools for the handicapped) was 22,413 (an 8.3% increase from 2005).

These students were enrolled in 5,475 schools (a 3.7% increase from 2005). Their mother tongues were Portuguese (8,633), Chinese (4,471), Spanish (3,279), and other languages (6,030). Their geographical distribution was greatly varied. In Aichi Prefecture, there were 4,089 students in need of JSL. In order of student numbers, the figures were: 2,404 (Kanagawa Prefecture), 2,343 (Shizuoka Prefecture), 1,762 (Tokyo), 1,118 (Mie Prefecture), and 1,117 (Osaka Prefecture). In Wakayama Prefecture (south of Osaka), there were only 9 students in need of JSL. In 24 prefectures (out of 47 prefectures) in 2006, there were fewer than 100 JSL students in each.

Those students whose mother tongues are Portuguese, Chinese, or Spanish accounted for more than 70% of JSL students in 2006. Over 80% of these children attended schools where the number of such students was less than five. The students who speak Portuguese are from Brazil, and most of them are of Japanese descent. Those who speak Spanish are mainly from Peru and other South American countries, and most of them are also of Japanese descent. They came to Japan because the revised immigration law of 1990 gave their parents special status as immigrant workers because of their Japanese blood. The students who speak Chinese are mainly those whose parents were orphaned in China during World War II.

In 1991, the total number of JSL students was 5,463. They were enrolled in 1,973 schools, and their mother tongues were Portuguese (1,932), Chinese (1,624), Spanish (596), and other languages (1,311). This means that the number of students who need special JSL instruction has almost quadrupled in the 15 years from 1991 to 2006. This is quite a drastic increase compared to the rate of increase in the total population of foreign nationals during the same period of time (from 1.2 million to 2 million).

These figures indicate only the number of Newcomer students who seriously need JSL. The number of Newcomer students who face difficulties in daily and school life is much larger. An important issue is that, even when these students appear to have become relatively fluent in Japanese in daily conversations, they often have difficulty understanding school lessons because their mastery of academic Japanese language is still poor.

The significant number of these Newcomer students and the difficulties they encounter in Japanese society and schools have compelled central and local governments as well as education authorities to take new actions to accommodate them in public schools. JSL classes are among the various special measures that have been implemented. However, it has not been easy for JSL students to settle comfortably in Japanese schools for several reasons. First, the Japanese government has not regarded the provision of public schooling for non-Japanese children as its legal obligation. These children are not entitled by law to receive compulsory education in Japan. They are only "allowed" to go to school as long as they wish and other conditions permit.

Second, Japanese education has traditionally been designed to nurture Japanese nationals. Group conformity and consumption of official knowledge have been encouraged in Japanese schooling, and many non-Japanese students have found it difficult to conform and accept official Japanese knowledge uncritically and to assimilate into the existing school system. Japanese school culture has often hindered non-Japanese students from receiving an empowering education (Shimizu & Shimizu, 2001). Ohta (2000) argues that the mother tongue and culture of Newcomer students should be more properly respected in Japanese schools in order to support their positive identity development and that Japanese public schools should be changed from "schools for only Japanese" to "schools for both non-Japanese and Japanese students" (p. 187).

Third, there are differences among non-Japanese children in their perception of the significance of schooling. Many families from Brazil came to work in Japan expecting to return to Brazil after a temporary stay. A significant proportion of their children have not enrolled in Japanese schools. There are about 90 schools (enrolling about 9,000 students) in Japan set up and run by Brazilians to provide education following the school curriculum in Brazil. Most of these children did not feel comfortable in Japanese schools and chose to attend Brazilian schools. Returnee children from China have more or less tried to make their way in the Japanese school system because they envision their future life in Japan or between China and Japan. A "bridge model" has been quite popular among returnee children from China, and a number of them have pursued their careers in the image of a bridge between two societies as an interpreter, as a trader, or as a business coordinator.

Common to these different forms of educational reforms are the key elements and characteristics of multicultural education, namely: pursuit of equity and social justice; critical interrogation of oppressive elements of the educational system and school culture; challenging mainstream education from the perspective of minorities; respecting transformative potentials in the life and culture of minorities; and developing critical pedagogy and a human rights–oriented curriculum. Examined in this way, there have been diverse approaches to and practices of multicultural education in Japan, even if they are not generally perceived as such. In addition, educational transformation has been advocated for the benefit not only of minority students but also of mainstream Japanese students.

Education for multicultural living-together and multicultural education

Kawasaki City (near Tokyo) was the first local government in Japan to use the term *multicultural living-together (tabunka kyosei kyoiku)* in its official publication in 1993. Immediately after the Great Hanshin-Awaji Earthquake (1995), the Center for Multicultural Living-Together was founded in Osaka to provide needed support to multinational residents. Gunma Prefecture launched a research project for multicultural living-together in 2002, and Hyogo Prefecture set up a children's center for multicultural living-together in 2003. Miyagi Prefecture enforced regulations titled Ordinance to Promote the Formation of Society for Multicultural Living-Together in 2007. Throughout Japan, local governments and grassroots organizations began to take new initiatives to promote policies and actions for "multicultural living-together" in the past 15 years. Among central government ministries, Homusho (Ministry of Justice) was the first to use the term *multicultural living-together* officially in proposing the Program for Promoting Multicultural Living-Together in March 2006.

As these recent developments indicate, *multicultural living-together* is often an official term employed by government authorities in many parts of Japan. Similarly, in the field of education, *education for multicultural living-together* rather than *multicultural education* is preferred by many educational authorities and educators. It is partly because the expression *education for multicultural living-together* clearly implies peaceful coexistence of differences and social harmony while the term *multicultural education* conveys a vague image to the general public and is frequently misunderstood as "teaching about many different cultures."

The Japanese word *kyosei* can also be translated as symbiosis, with a strong biological connotation, and some people argue that *education for multicultural living-together* should be called *multicultural education* and that its original orientations toward social transformation should be deliberately emphasized. However, *multicultural living-together* continues to be a popular term among policy makers and educators, and advocates of multicultural education sometimes define and propose *education for multicultural living-together*, strategically using the language of critical multicultural education.

Among educational researchers, interest in education for multicultural living-together as well as multicultural education has been increasing. For example, the Japanese Society for the Study of Adult and Community Education published its annual bulletin titled *Multicultural and Multiethnic Living-Together and Lifelong Learning* in 1995, and outlined its perspectives and research findings. Other academic organizations such as the Japan Association for International Education, the Intercultural Education Society of Japan, the Japan Society of Educational Sociology, and the Japanese Educational Research Association have shown increasing interest in education for multicultural living-together and multicultural education.

Current situation in Japan and future challenges

Recently, there has been a growing trend of neo-conservatism and neo-liberalism in Japan, and the government implemented a firm initiative to revise the Fundamental Law on Education in December 2006. The law had been regarded as a basis for democratic education since the end of World War II. Even though a number of conservative government administrations had tried to change the law in the past, they had not been successful. However, the law was finally revised to put more emphasis on promoting nationalistic orientations through education. "Nurturing patriotism" is a symbolic aim of the revised law. Past efforts to bring more attention to human rights, peace, and gender sensitivities in schooling are often criticized as "bad traditions" by neo-conservatives. A next anticipated action by the government is to change the Constitution of Japan itself, particularly Article 9, which stipulates: "Aspiring sincerely to an international peace based on justice and order, the Japanese people forever renounce war as a sovereign right of the nation and the threat or use of force as a means of settling international disputes." Since the end of World War II, Article 9 has been regarded as the symbol of Japan's peace-loving stance.

Multicultural education has been advocated as a powerful challenge to the long-held myth of "homogeneous Japan" and to promote education for democracy, social justice, peace, diversity, and human rights. Actions by local governments and grassroots organizations to support the education and life of non-Japanese and minority populations have been growing. In general, diversity in society is increasingly regarded as a vital social resource and strength rather than as a problem.

Many local governments have implemented policies to assist and empower non-Japanese and minority populations by providing supportive measures and services and by collaborating with grassroots organizations. Yamawaki (2005) maintains that local governments with a significant size of non-Japanese populations have taken more progressive measures compared to the central government. He classifies these local governments into two major types: "international-oriented" and "human rights oriented." Among "international-oriented" local governments are Hamamatsu City (Shizuoka Prefecture) and Aichi Prefecture, and among "human rights-oriented" local governments are Osaka Prefecture and Osaka City. Yamawaki regards Kawasaki City as an "integrated" type: having both "human rights" and "international" orientations.

However, this classification does not mean that the "international-oriented" type pays little attention to human rights. The "human rights-oriented" type has generally evolved from preceding policies and grassroots movements strongly concerned with discrimination against resident Koreans, whereas the "international-oriented" type usually emerged with growing concerns about Newcomers. In other words, both types pay sufficient attention to "internationalization" and "human rights." However, the evolution process and the place of emphasis differ.

A case study: Human rights-oriented approach in Osaka

In the following discussion, I illustrate and examine a "human rights-oriented" approach to multicultural education whose aim is to promote the broad goals of education for social justice, diversity, and critical citizenship.

In Japan, both governmental and community organizations tend to use the term *human rights education* today as an umbrella concept that includes anti-discrimination education, gender equity education, multicultural education, education for international understanding, environmental education, and global education. This trend has become more evident in the last decade as a large number of local governments as well as the central government of Japan set up action plans to promote the United Nations Decade for Human Rights Education (1995–2004) (Hirasawa, 2005).

Several prefectural governments in western Japan such as Osaka, Kyoto, Nara, Hyogo, and Fukuoka, for example, have given much emphasis to human rights education and education for multicultural living-together in terms of human and financial resource allocation and development of specific guidelines and curriculum. This is particularly because anti-discrimination movements have been strong politically in the western parts of Japan.

In this context, a case study of a "human rights-oriented approach" in Osaka may be informative. Osaka is the second largest metropolitan area in Japan. Both Osaka Prefecture and Osaka City have been known as local governments promoting policies and measures that respect human rights and diversity. Both have their specific policies and guidelines to support non-Japanese populations and students.

Osaka has a human rights museum (Liberty Osaka), a human rights center (Osaka Human Rights Center), a peace center (Peace Osaka), a center for gender issues (Dawn Center), a regional human rights information center (Asia-Pacific Human Rights Information Center), and facilities for human rights-oriented nonprofit organizations (NPOs) (e.g. pia NPO). These have been significantly funded and supported by Osaka Prefectural and City governments. In schools in Osaka, compared to other areas, there are more teachers with non-Japanese backgrounds, particularly Koreans, as well as a range of special measures to support non-Japanese students and minority students.

Osaka has the highest ratio of foreign nationals among all prefectures in Japan (2.43%; 214,630 out of 8,832,242 residents as of December 2007). Among them, Koreans account for 66.2% (142,112), and Chinese 19.9% (42,630). In other words, the ratio of Oldcomers is quite high in Osaka as compared to other prefectures in Japan. Almost a quarter (23.8%) of resident Koreans in Japan live in Osaka.

In Osaka, all public school students are supplied with a supplementary textbook titled *Ningen* (human being) for teaching peace, diversity, and human rights. Both Osaka Prefectural and Osaka City boards of education have adopted policies to create human rights-conscious schools and to nurture human rights-conscious educators. Human rights education is promoted in many schools in Osaka by teaching issues related to peace, international understanding, gender, and disability, as well as Buraku discrimination. Because the Buraku liberation movement has been quite strong politically in Osaka, and through its networking with other grassroots movements and effective negotiations with local governments, the unique history of human rights and diversity-conscious policies has been developed. These policies and measures have benefited non-Japanese populations and other minorities as well as mainstream populations and students.

Given these backgrounds, the grassroots movement to promote education for multicultural living-together and diversity has grown significantly in Osaka. The movement began with the initiative by resident Koreans to fight the discrimination they experienced. The organized movement of Koreans in Osaka resulted, through its negotiations with the local governments in Osaka, in the official provision of Korean ethnic classes in public schools. As of June 2004, among 431 public schools (elementary and junior high) in Osaka City, 98 had ethnic classes providing after-school programs (studying language, history, and Korean culture) for Korean students as well as Japanese students. Osaka City Board of Education has designated eight elementary and junior high schools in the city as "center schools" to provide special educational programs for Newcomer students. In Osaka, official measures have been implemented to meet the needs of both Oldcomer and Newcomer students as well as to raise awareness among Japanese students so that they become future citizens who can appreciate diversity and respect human rights.

Osaka-Fu Zainichi Gaikokujin Kyoiku Kenkyu Kyogikai (Osaka Prefectural Association for the Education of Non-Japanese Students) has demonstrated a clear example of the transition from a major focus placed on Koreans to a new initiative to promote multicultural education. The association published a booklet in 1998 and outlined its strategies for promoting effective education for multicultural living-together based on its past decades of educational movement to improve education for resident Koreans in Osaka. The association has learned from the theories and practices of multicultural education in the US and other countries as well as from human rights education theories and practices in the world, particularly those advocated by the United Nations (Osaka-Fu Zainichi Gaikokujin Kyoiku Kenkyu Kyogikai, 1998).

A good example of an increasing concern for promoting awareness of human rights and diversity is also shown in popular teaching materials for adults in Osaka. A booklet produced by the Office of Human Rights, Osaka Prefectural Government, in 2006 is titled *Minna Chigatte Minna Ii* (There is beauty in diversity) (Osaka-Fu Jinken Shitsu, 2006). The office produces similar booklets every year (40,000 copies) to raise awareness among the 8 million residents of Osaka. They are generally intended to describe the current situation of various human rights issues in Osaka faced by minority and non-mainstream populations such as Buraku people, women, people with disabilities, foreign nationals, children, elderly people, people with HIV, homeless people, and sexual minorities. The perspective of diversity here is not limited to foreign nationals but includes other categories of non-mainstream populations. The beginning pages of the 2006 booklet described several key concepts that are vital for respecting human rights, such as human dignity and diversity, breaking stereotypes, raising self-esteem, being assertive, and appreciating the value of life. The booklet clearly conceptualizes human rights awareness and citizenship by focusing on the need to respect and appreciate diversity.

The discussion above has focused on the case study of Osaka, where respect for human rights and appreciation of diversity have been translated into concrete policy guidelines and implementation. The developments have been significantly driven by grassroots movements for human rights and diversity, and the experiences of Osaka have become important models for other local initiatives in Japan.

Toward education for diversity and critical citizenship

In the globalizing world today, it is vital to educate for civic knowledge, attitudes, and skills that make critical and active citizens (Hirasawa, 2005). It is important to define clearly the knowledge, attitudes, and skills needed by citizens to appreciate diversity, read the world, and change it to promote peace and social justice (Freire, 1973). Many educators, researchers, and activists in Japan who are concerned deeply about discrimination and human rights issues are now working to create a vision of education for diversity and critical citizenship by learning from past experiences of multicultural and human rights education in Japan and the world.

References

Freire, P. (1973). *Pedagogy of the oppressed*. New York: Seabury Press.
Fukuoka, Y. (1993). *Zainichi Kankoku Chosen-Jin: Wakai Sedai No Aidentiti* [Resident Koreans in Japan: Identities of the young generation]. Tokyo: Chuo Koron Sha.

Hirasawa, Y. (1987). Kokusaika no Shiza to Kaiho Kyoiku [Perspectives of internationalization and education for liberation]. *Buraku Kaiho Kenkyu* [Bulletin of Buraku liberation], *58*, 141–154.

Hirasawa, Y. (1997). Intercultural education in Japan. In D. Coulby, J. Gundara, & C. Jones (Eds.), *World yearbook of education 1997: Intercultural education* (pp. 132–141). London: Kogan Page.

Hirasawa, Y. (2005). *Jinken Kyoiku no Tame no Sekai Puroguramu* [World program of human rights education]. Osaka: Kaiho Shuppansha.

Hirasawa, Y., & Nabeshima, Y. (Eds.). (1995). *Dowa education: Educational challenge toward a discrimination-free Japan*. Osaka: Buraku Liberation Research Institute.

Homusho [Japanese Ministry of Justice]. (2008). *The number of registered foreigners in Japan (as of December 31, 2007)*. Retrieved June 24, 2008, from http://www.moj.go.jp/PRESS/080601-1.pdf

Kobayashi, T. (1985). Sokatsu: Tabunka Kyouiku no Kadai [Summing up: Issues of multicultural education]. In T. Kobayashi & K. Ebuchi (Eds.), *Tabunka Kyoiku no Hikaku Kenkyu* [A comparative study of multicultural education] (pp. 337–359). Fukuoka: Kyushu Daigaku Shuppankai.

Lee, S. I., Murphy-Shigematsu, S., & Befu, H. (Eds.). (2006). *Japan's diversity dilemmas: Ethnicity, citizenship, and education*. New York: iUniverse.

Murphy-Shigematsu, S. (2004). Expanding the borders of the nation: Ethnic diversity and citizenship education in Japan. In J. A. Banks (Ed.), *Diversity and citizenship education: Global perspectives* (pp. 303–332). San Francisco: Jossey-Bass.

Nakajima, T. (1998). Tabunka Kyoiku Kenkyu no Shiten [Perspectives of research in multicultural education]. In T. Nakajima (Ed.), *Tabunka Kyoiku: Tayousei no Tame no Kyoikugaku* [Multicultural education: Pedagogy for diversity] (pp. 13–32). Tokyo: Akashi Shoten.

Nakano, R., Ikeda, H., Nakao, K., & Mori, M. (2000). *Dowa Kyoiku eno Shotai* [Invitation to Dowa education]. Osaka: Kaiho Shuppansha.

Nihon Shakai Kyoiku Gakkai [Japan Society for the Study of Adult and Community Education]. (1995). *Tabunka-Minzoku Kyosei Shakai to Shogai Gakushu* [Multicultural and multiethnic living-together and lifelong learning]. Tokyo: Toyokan Shuppansha.

Ogbu, J. U. (1978). *Minority education and caste: The American system in cross-cultural perspective*. New York: Academic Press.

Ohta, H. (2000). *Nyu Kamah no Kodomo to Nihon no Gakko* [Newcomer children and Japanese schools]. Tokyo: Kokusai Shoin.

Osaka-Fu Jinken Shitsu [Office of Human Rights, Osaka Prefectural Government]. (2006). *Minna Chigatte Minna Ii* [There is beauty in diversity]. Osaka: Osaka-Fu.

Osaka-Fu Zainichi Gaikokujin Kyoiku Kenkyu Kyogikai [Osaka Prefectural Association for the Education of Non-Japanese Students]. (1998). *Nijyu-Isseiki wo Tembosuru Tabunka Kyosei Kyoiku no Koso* [A vision of education for multicultural living-together toward the 21st century]. Osaka: Author.

Rinkyoshin [Prime Minister's Council for Educational Reform] (1987). *Saishu Toshin* [Final report]. Tokyo: Ohkurasho Shuppan-Kyoku.

Sato, G. (2003). *Kokusaika to Kyoiku* [Internationalization and education] (Rev. ed.). Tokyo: Nihon Hoso Shuppan Kyokai.

Shimizu, K., & Shimizu, M. (2001). *Nyu Kamah to Kyoiku* [Newcomers and education]. Tokyo: Akashi Shote.

Umakoshi, T. (1986). The education of Korean children in Japan. In D. Rothermund & J. Simon (Eds.), *Education and the integration of ethnic minorities* (pp. 36–47). London: Frances Pinter.

Willis, D. B., & Murphy-Shigematsu, S. (Eds.). (2008). *Transcultural Japan*. London & New York: Routledge.

Yamawaki, K. (2005). Tabunka Kyosei no Tobira [Window to multicultural living-together]. *Jichitai Kokusaika Foramu* [Forum on internationalization of local authorities], *187*, 34–37.

Part 3
Race, intergroup relations, and schooling

12

Critical perspectives on race and schooling

David Gillborn
Institute of Education, University of London, UK

Deborah Youdell
Institute of Education, University of London, UK

Although there are up to 1 million words in the English language (McCrum, Cran, & MacNeil, 1992, p. 1), writers frequently use the same word for very different approaches. Designations of *critical* and prefixes of *post* are two such terms that frequently recur in contemporary social science but with different meanings. In this chapter we use both terms as we offer a brief guide to critical approaches to race and schooling. In particular we explore the central elements of Marxist analyses; the emerging field of critical race theory in education; and post-structural and post-structural feminist approaches to race politics and raced identity.

We outline a series of key ideas that might be conceived as a series of conversations – sometimes these are clearly linked and at other times they seem to be talking past each other. These conversations are concerned with the relative importance of (and interactions between) social class, race, gender, and sexuality. Along the way, fundamental questions are raised about contemporary identities, the significance of culture, and the nature of power.

We conclude by considering the promise of hybrid critical approaches, taking forward a call to *intersectionality* that insists that we do not automatically foreground any single marker of identity or axis of inequality and that we further develop our theorization and analyses of the connections across these categories as they shape contemporary lives and inequities.

Structuralism, critical theory, and post-structuralism

In simple terms *structural* approaches involve a focus on deep social structures of class formation as the basis for social inequality, while *post*-structural approaches are more concerned with discourses and the way these are implicated in the making of social inequalities. However, there is no single "structural" approach to race, racism, and inequality that sits in contrast to a "post-structural" approach. There are important continuities between these approaches as well as internal variations. Furthermore, the *post*- indicates new ways of thinking and understanding that add to and change, but do not erase or entirely abandon, structural approaches. Despite these enduring connections there *are* important distinctions between structural and post-structural approaches that shape their concerns. At the heart of these distinctions are understandings of power and its operation; the place and influence of economics; the nature of race identity; and the forms of political action that might achieve significant social change.

Structural approaches to race theory

Structural approaches to race theory take a number of forms and combine a concern with race inequality with analyses of capital and class relations, language, and how language shapes social and gender relations.

The Marxist theory of class domination is the foundation of much critical theory. This approach offers a critique of capitalism and the inequalities necessary to the operation of capitalist societies. Structural approaches to race frequently extend previous Marxist analyses of the exploitation of the working-class majority for the profit of the ruling class, by adding a further layer of analysis of how capitalist economies were built on and continue to be sustained by the exploitation of African American, Indigenous, and other minoritized people.

The theory of linguistics developed by Saussure (1974) highlights the absence of any concrete connection between things, words, and meanings and instead explores the structure of the relationships between them. This assertion of the arbitrariness of the relationship between things, words, and meanings is a fundamental part of the theoretical movement that has rejected essentialism and insisted that raced bodies, hierarchies, and inequalities are social or cultural constructions and not biological facts. These approaches suggest instead that the meaning of race or ethnicity (and particular race or ethnic designations) is culturally made and specific to historical and social contexts (Jacobson, 1998). Indeed, this claim to the *situatedness* of race and ethnicity has led to thinking about how the "hybridity" of identities such as race, ethnic, and other markers of identity come together in new ways as a result of global migrations and "diaspora" (Hall, 1996).

Black feminism and post-colonial feminism, emerging out of African American, Indigenous, and other minority ethnic women's engagements with feminism, have insisted that what is, in effect, *White* feminism listens to and takes account of the material conditions as well as the particular experiences, concerns, and allegiances of minority ethnic women and women of color. The influence of Black feminist writers such as hooks (1990), Spillers (1987), and Collins (2000) has worked in a series of directions. It has led feminist theory and practice to recognize that women are heterogeneous, that they experience different material conditions, that they have different life experiences and concerns, and that their political priorities might be in tension. It has led race theory to recognize that the political concerns of women cannot be collapsed into those of men and that – within race or ethnic groups – women's lives and experiences may well be quite different from men's. It has insisted that analyses of race inequality pay attention to the "private sphere," that is, those spheres of life that are populated predominantly by women, such as the home. And it has demanded an engagement with how gender, race, and class work together to locate people and groups in particular ways – an approach often referred to as "intersectional" (Collins, 2000; Crenshaw, 1991).

Taken together as a single (but internally diverse) intellectual and political movement these approaches are often understood as *critical*.

Critical theory and critical pedagogy

Foster (2005) has described critical theory as focusing on the "structures of domination of nations... examining how these systems exert direct or indirect control over their members" and exposing the roots of inequality "that are often hidden" (p. 175). There are many different strands to critical theory: some of the best-known critical work in education draws on a class-based perspective. This work views education as part of the apparatus by which the state maintains its control of the masses in the interests of the ruling class (Freire, 1993; McLaren, 1995, 2005). There are many different versions of this approach, with more or less direct citation of Marx (1818–1883) as the key philosophical touchstone for their analyses. A traditional Marxist perspective tends to view other axes of oppression, such as race and gender, as complicating factors that detract attention from the fundamental class inequalities that, ultimately, are seen to lie at the heart of the system. This has led to the accusation that Marxism has "a white blind spot" (Ayers, 2006). McLaren, probably the leading contemporary Marxist theorist in education, responds to this critique as follows:

> I am not saying "class is everything" and "forget race".... I do stress the explanatory primacy of class for analyzing the structural determinants of race, gender and class oppression. Not for analyzing their psychological aspects, or their phenomenological or cultural dimensions. But, and I will repeat this again, for analyzing their structural determinants.
> (McLaren, 2007)

Although McLaren wants to take seriously the lived realities of racist and sexist oppression, this position maintains that those oppressions arise, ultimately, from a class conflict at the heart of capitalism. He argues that antiracist and anti-sexist action is vital but that significant change can come only through addressing class exploitation: "Class includes a state apparatus whose conquests and regulations create races and shape gender relations. You have to abolish a class-defending state if you want to make real headway in eliminating racism and patriarchy" (McLaren, 2007).

Apple (1979, 1993, 2006) – a leading critical theorist – has sought to move beyond Marxist orthodoxy. Like McLaren, Apple has worked closely with the Brazilian philosopher and activist Paulo Freire. However, Apple's work increasingly focuses on the multiple cross-cutting and contradictory ways in which class, gender, and race exploitation work in, through, and sometimes against each other. Apple is highly critical of the rhetorical posturing of some writers in both the Marxist and the post-structuralist camps, emphasizing instead the absolute necessity of critical work that connects to contemporary struggles in order to "illuminate the ways in which educational policy and practice are connected to the relations of exploitation and domination in the larger society" (Apple, 2006, p. 681).

Apple's (2006) conceptual position is influenced by the work of the Italian revolutionary Antonio Gramsci (1971), who – while devoting his life to the goal of socialist revolution (he died shortly after release from a fascist prison) – argued for a critique of capitalism that gave greater weight to the importance of ideas, ideology, and cultural factors (Gramsci was born in 1891 and died in 1937). As Jones (2006) argues: "Instead of seeing the economy as determining culture and politics, Gramsci argues that culture, politics and the economy are organized in a relationship of mutual exchange with one another, a constantly circulating and shifting network of influence" (p. 5).

Central to this perspective is a recognition of the importance of popular culture in shaping or creating views of the world that act in the interests of the powerful, not merely as a reflection of a deeper economic structure but as a realm that has relative autonomy from the economic base. Writes Jones (2006):

> Gramsci's highly original understanding of power sees it as something actively lived by the oppressed as a form of common sense . . . in part drawn from "official" conceptions of the world circulated by the ruling bloc, in part formed out of people's practical experiences of social life. . . . Gramsci argues that this is not inevitable. Official and practical conceptions can be dismantled in order to show how they serve the interests of a ruling power. (pp. 4–9)

This is where critical *theory* informs critical *pedagogy*, in creating an approach to teaching that aims to equip students to actively deconstruct and resist dominant forms of oppression. Unfortunately, despite a great deal of rhetoric, critical pedagogy is by no means a simple set of approaches and, in practice, can be difficult if not impossible to discern from its more oppressive counterpart, especially where White students articulate their frustration, anger, and resentment at being identified – sometimes for the first time in their lives – as the beneficiaries of a racist system (see Dlamini, 2002; Leonardo, 2002). Apple (2006), long seen as one of the pioneers of critical theory, has noted that so many different interpretations are now attached to the term *critical pedagogy* that discerning any definite meaning is virtually impossible.

Apple's early works (1979, 1986, 1993) included a detailed analysis of the power of school curricula to encode particular class-biased perspectives. This is now a familiar theme in critical theory, exposing the means by which the taken-for-granted elements in much educational work actually have particular consequences for the legitimation of elite interests and perspectives. Apple's most recent work (2001, 2006) develops this approach still further, including an analysis of the home-schooling movement and the impacts of "accountability" and "standards" discourses which promise improvements for all but are used in practice as a means of attacking public (state-funded) schooling and ensuring that a market in education is available to further cement existing inequalities (Apple, 2001; see also Ball, 2008). Race inequality has become a particularly important element in this work. As he argues, the rhetorical commitment to diversity in the official "story" of the USA erases the true and racist historic roots – and contemporary reality – of the nation:

> While all too many textbooks in our schools construct the history of the United States as the story of "immigrants," such a story totally misconstrues the different conditions that existed . . . some "immigrants" came in *chains*, were enslaved, and faced centuries of repression and state-mandated apartheid. Others were subjected to death and forced enclosure as official policies.
>
> (Apple, 2001, p. 207, original emphasis)

Textbook illusions of a common past, therefore, might appear superficially progressive but often erase the systematic racial discrimination that characterizes U.S. history and ignore what Ladson-Billings (2006) has termed the *education debt*, that is, the centuries of exploitation and oppression that are reflected today in the continuing achievement gap. Ladson-Billings is a pivotal figure in the attempt to break away from the dominant role of class analyses in U.S. critical theory by drawing on a radical tradition of work that emerged from U.S. legal studies in the 1970s and 1980s known as critical race theory (CRT).

Critical race theory

CRT began as a radical alternative to dominant perspectives in U.S. legal scholarship. It grew in opposition to both the conservative "mainstream" and the ostensibly radical tradition of *critical legal studies*, which, despite its rhetoric, actually gave little serious consideration to the role of race and racism (see Crenshaw, 2002). Key foundational CRT scholars include Derrick Bell, Richard Delgado, and Kimberlé Crenshaw. Gloria Ladson-Billings and William Tate (1995) first introduced CRT into education, and since then a growing number of educators have begun working with these ideas.

There is no single dogmatic statement of CRT, but the approach is broadly characterized by a focus on the central importance of White racism and the need for active struggle towards greater equity. Write Crenshaw, Gotanda, Peller, and Thomas (1995):

> Although Critical Race scholarship differs in object, argument, accent, and emphasis, it is nevertheless unified by two common interests. The first is to understand how a regime of white supremacy and its subordination of people of color have been created and maintained.... The second is a desire not merely to understand the vexed bond between law and racial power but to change it. (p. xiii)

The phrase *White supremacy* is used here in a way that is very different to its common meaning: the term usually refers to individuals and groups who engage in the crudest, most obvious acts of race hatred. But for critical race theorists the more important, hidden, and pervasive form of White supremacy lies in the operation of forces that saturate the everyday, mundane actions and policies that shape the world in the interests of White people. Writes Ansley (1997):

> A political, economic, and cultural system in which whites overwhelmingly control power and material resources, conscious and unconscious ideas of white superiority and entitlement are widespread, and relations of white dominance and non-white subordination are daily reenacted across a broad array of institutions and social settings. (p. 592)

White supremacy, understood in this way, is as central to CRT as the notion of capitalism is to Marxist theory and patriarchy to feminism (Mills, 2003, p. 182; Stovall, 2005, p. 247). This perspective on the nature and extent of contemporary racism is one of the key defining elements of critical race theory. CRT views racism as more than just the most obvious and crude acts of race hatred: it focuses on the subtle and hidden processes which have the effect of discriminating, regardless of their stated intent. Write Delgado and Stefancic (2000): "CRT begins with a number of basic insights. One is that racism is normal, not aberrant, in American society. Because racism is an ingrained feature of our landscape, it looks ordinary and natural to persons in the culture" (p. xvi).

When White people hear the word "racism" they tend to imagine acts of conscious and deliberate race hatred: discrimination is assumed to be an abnormal and relatively unusual facet of the education system. In contrast, CRT suggests that racism operates much more widely, through the routine, mundane activities and assumptions that are unquestioned by most practitioners and policymakers: what Delgado and Stefancic (2000) call "business-as-usual forms of racism" (p. xvi). For example, racism is figured in the selection and training of teachers (where minoritized teachers tend to have less secure jobs and to teach less advanced classes); in the identification of "ability" (where both formal and informal types of assessment encode the assumptions and experiences of White people, thereby disadvantaging minoritized students); and through the selection of curricula (that celebrate a false notion of society as colorblind, where anyone can succeed on the basis of their individual merit) (see Gillborn, 2008; Tate, 1997). This is part of what is sometimes called CRT's *critique of liberalism*: "CRT portrays dominant legal claims of neutrality, objectivity, color blindness, and meritocracy as camouflages for the self-interest of powerful entities of society" (Tate, 1997, p. 235).

CRT is not critical of the *idea* of a meritocracy (a place where people rise solely according to their efforts and talents), but rather it attacks the *ideology* of meritocracy, that is, the false belief that such a state actually exists in places like the US and the UK. In these systems, characterized by deep and recurring race inequity, the pretense of a meritocracy disguises the continued benefit that White people draw from racism and allows race inequities to be presented as just and necessary, as a mere reflection of the deficiencies of the people who suffer racism (Delgado & Stefancic, 2001).

In addition to a focus on racism, CRT is also distinguished by certain other themes. For example, there is a *call to context* which challenges researchers to pay attention to the historical location of particular events and, in particular, to recognize the experiential knowledge of people of color. CRT does not assume that any group of people can simply read off one "true" view of reality, but there is a belief that people who experience racism are uniquely positioned to understand certain elements of its operation and power (Tate, 1997).

Another distinctive CRT theme is its revisionist critique of civil rights laws as fundamentally limited as a means of addressing inequality. Detractors have sought to present CRT as disrespectful of civil rights campaigns and victories, but this is a misrepresentation. CRT is not critical of the campaigns, nor the people who sacrificed so much to advance race equality (see Crenshaw et al., 1995, p. xiv). Rather, CRT looks at the limits to law and policymaking, and shows how even apparently radical changes are reclaimed and often turned back over time. A key element here is the concept of *interest convergence* (Bell, 1980). Put simply, this view argues that advances in race equality come about only when White elites see the changes as in their own interest. Bell (2004), the leading African American legal scholar, coined the idea of interest convergence and has summarized the notion like this:

Justice for blacks vs. racism = racism
Racism vs. obvious perceptions of white self-interest = justice for blacks (p. 59)

Bell (2004) argues that a study of the civil rights movement reveals that time and again the "perceived self-interest by Whites rather than the racial injustices suffered by Blacks has been the major motivation in racial-remediation policies" (Bell, 2004, p. 59). For example, the moves to outlaw segregation in the 1960s are usually presented as a sign of growing enlightenment, but they have to be understood within the context of the Cold War and the fact that the US was having difficulty soliciting the help of friendly African states to safeguard U.S. influence in the region when Soviet interests could point to the forms of apartheid that operated in the Southern US. As the distinguished African American scholar W. E. B. Du Bois noted of the famous *Brown vs. Board of Education* desegregation case: "No such decision would have been possible without the world pressure of communism," which made it "simply impossible for the United States to continue to lead a 'Free World' with race segregation kept legal over a third of its territory" (cited in Bell, 2004, p. 67). The obvious signs of segregation have gone – such as separate toilets and lunch counters – but the reality continues in economic, residential, and educational terms.

Similarly, in the UK, the racist murder of Stephen Lawrence (a Black teenager stabbed by a White gang as he waited for a London bus) is widely hailed as a landmark case that changed race relations forever. An official inquiry into the police's failure to prosecute Stephen's killers revealed gross incompetence, disregard, and deep-rooted racism. Much of the inquiry was held in public, and the nightly coverage in the news media meant that the catalogue of police errors and racism was broadcast nationally, initially to a skeptical public but eventually to a growing sense of outrage. When the inquiry report was published, in 1999, the revelations about the police's arrogance, incompetence, and racism were such that inaction by policymakers was inconceivable (Macpherson, 1999). The prime minister, Tony Blair, promised changes in the law and said that the report signaled "a new era in race relations . . . a new more tolerant and more inclusive Britain" (*Hansard*, 1999, col. 380–381).

Radical changes were made to race relations legislation; more than 45,000 public bodies faced a new legal duty to proactively ensure race equality. All state-funded schools had to design a race equality policy, monitor achievements for signs of bias, and publicly plan to eradicate any signs of race inequity. On paper these are some of the most far-reaching equality duties anywhere on Earth, but in practice they have been largely ineffective because most schools have ignored their duties, while the national education department has paid lip-service to race equality but continued to press ahead with key reforms (such as expanding the use of hierarchical teaching groups and promoting a national "gifted and talented" scheme) that have *increased* the institutional barriers to success facing most Black students in school (Gillborn, 2005, 2008; Gillborn & Youdell, 2000; Tomlinson, 2008).

The Stephen Lawrence case in the UK, like the *Brown* decision in the US, exemplifies the way in which apparently radical civil rights breakthroughs have uncertain consequences in practice. Delgado and Stefancic (2001) argue that such events can be seen as "contradiction closing cases" which heal the gulf between the reality of racism in practice and the public rhetoric of equal opportunities and social justice: "after the celebration dies down, the great victory is quietly cut back by narrow interpretation, administrative obstruction, or delay. In the end, the minority group is left little better than it was before, if not worse" (p. 24).

Critical race theory represents a dramatic break with previous approaches to studying racism in education and is being taken up by a growing array of scholars on both sides of the Atlantic (Dixson & Rousseau, 2006; Gillborn, 2008; Hylton, 2008; Yosso, 2006). However, the approach goes a good deal further than previous perspectives by placing White racism at the center of its analysis and, for this reason, faces criticism from both sides of the political spectrum. Writes Taylor (1998): "CRT's usefulness will be limited not by the weakness of its constructs but by the degree that many whites will not accept its assumptions; I anticipate critique from both left and right" (p. 124).

Contrary to the caricature of CRT contained in some of its detractors' accounts, the approach does not view all Whites as *uniformly* privileged and racist: all Whites do not benefit equally from White supremacy, but all Whites are beneficiaries of the system to some degree, whether they like it or not. White working-class youth suffer multiple educational inequalities, for example, but their interests and cultural identities remain valorized in mainstream politics and culture. In the UK, for example, White students are considerably less likely to be expelled from school than their Black peers (Gillborn, 2005), are not automatically assumed to be the product of lone parents and chaotic households (Rollock, 2007), and are free from the oppressive focus on "cohesion" and "integration" which has become a hallmark of public policy that now views any sign of minoritized identity as a potential threat to national culture and, post-9/11 and the 2005 London bombings, as a threat to security (Gillborn, 2008).

Post-structural theory and race

Across structural approaches there is an understanding of power that sees it as being held by those in positions of relative advantage over others. Whether these are long-standing social elites or a newly expanded middle class – themselves marked by race, ethnicity, and citizenship – they are seen as using their power to perpetuate their own advantage, even if this advantage is in part reproduced through the circulation of hegemonic meanings. Structural approaches also tend to accept an understanding of the person whose "identity" is made up of a collection of identity categories pertaining to their race, ethnicity, gender, sexuality, social class, and so on, who is seen as complete and (relatively) constant over time, who knows her/himself and her/his motivations, and who has "agency" to act to achieve her/his desired ends. What sort of account of power is foregrounded and whether this person is seen always in existence or as a product of biology, psychology, society, culture, or discourse are important coordinates for locating particular authors and their work in relation to structural and post-structural theory.

Post-structural approaches problematize the understandings of power, identity, and agency that are at the heart of structuralism. Post-structural approaches commonly focus on power as it circulates through the "micro-circuits" of prevailing ideas or "discourses," consider "subjectivity" rather than "identity," understanding this as an illusion created over and over again by these prevailing discourses, and understand agency as simultaneously made possible and reined in by discourse. Discourse, then, is a central concept in post-structural theory, and this is why post-structuralism is often said to be characterized by the "turn to discourse," a notion we will consider shortly. Here we focus on the contribution of three key contemporary philosophers – Michel Foucault, Judith Butler, and Jacques Derrida – whose work has been taken up and had a significant influence on theorizing race and race politics.

Productive power, discourse, and race

A Foucauldian understanding of "disciplinary" or "productive" power and discourse is an important starting point. Foucault argues that as well as understanding the power embedded in the law (judicial power) and the power of the state or monarch to impose their will (sovereign power) we should also take account of the power that circulates in the knowledges, processes, and practices of institutions, communities, and people, that is, disciplinary power. Disciplinary power works through institutionalized practices, or "technologies," that make the person visible and knowable to others as well as to her/himself. This opening up of the person to "surveillance" and "self-surveillance" simultaneously provokes the person to act and think in particular ways, to make themselves and others as particular sorts of persons: in this sense it is *productive* (Foucault, 1990, 1991). Discourse is central to these processes. For Foucault, discourses are multiple and shifting systems of knowledge with varied and potentially porous status, ranging from what is taken as a self-evident truth (a "regime of truth") through to what is unspeakable or ridiculous ("disavowed" or "subjugated" knowledges). Discourses are not seen as descriptive but as *creative*; they have the potential to *produce* and *regulate* the world in their own terms as if they were true. Disciplinary power circulates through discourses and, in this sense, power, knowledge, and discourse are inseparable. It is important to recognize that discourse, in this sense, refers to much more than speech alone: discourses are cited by and circulate in speech and writing as well as visual representations, bodily movements or gestures, and social and institutional practices.

The notion of discourse and its productive force is a central concept for thinking about race not as biologically or culturally fixed but as the *product* of prevailing discourses (regimes of truth) that *make* race and ethnicity *as if* they were biologically or culturally fixed. The turn to discourse, then, allows us to see how classificatory systems of physiognomic races that were dominant scientific ideas in the 19th and 20th centuries are, in fact, regimes of truth that function to produce race in these terms (see Jacobson, 1998; Youdell, 2003, 2006a). An important example of the usefulness of a Foucauldian account of discourse can be found in the work of Said (2003), who has examined the way that discourses work historically and in the present to simultaneously produce and delineate Same/Other, West/East, and Occident/Orient binaries, processes that Said refers to as "Orientalism."

Subjectivation and race

One of the key sites in which the post-structural turn to discourse is found is in relation to subjectivity and work that interrogates the constitutions of gender, sexuality, social class, ability, and disability, as well as race, ethnicity, culture, religion, and nationality. Another idea drawn from the work of Foucault is important here: "subjectivation" (Foucault, 1982). Subjectivation, which builds on Althusser's (1971) notion of subjection, is centrally concerned with the person's relationship to power and to the social world. According to Foucault, the person is *subjectivated* – through the productive force of circulating discourses people are made as social subjects and subjected to relations of power. Speaking of the "subject" (rather than the self or the person) reminds us that the subject is inextricably connected to *productive power*. In this sense raced subjects are not self-evident, already existing, and subsequently subjected to and in uneven relations of power. Rather, subjects are made recognizable as subjects, as people, in part through the ascription of race designations *at the same time* as these ascriptions position the social subjects in prevailing race discourses and their embedded hierarchies (see Youdell, 2006b).

The performativity of race

Judith Butler (1990, 1993, 1997, 2004) takes up Foucault's ideas of the productive force of discourse and subjectivation and brings these together with the idea of "performativity" to explore how particular sorts of people (subjects) are made. The idea of the performative is borrowed from linguistics, where it is a word or phrase that has the potential to do or create the thing that it states. Judith Butler, who developed these ideas in her work related to gender, suggests that designations such as "boy" and "girl" are performative. That is, they *create* gendered subjects but do this appearing to just *describe* them. Extending this thinking to the analysis of race suggests that designations such as "White," "Black," "African American," and "Latino" or "Latina" are not simply descriptions of pre-existing race or ethnic identities, but are part of ongoing processes that create or *discursively constitute* these categories and the people allocated to them. This does not mean that race or ethnic positions can simply be taken up by "choice" – in order for a performative to work it must make sense, that is, it must be situated in and cite those discourses through which race and ethnicity are made meaningful. Given the endurance and force of the discourse of racial phenotypes, for instance, it is unlikely that naming or claiming a race that directly contradicted these would "work" – in the constraints of prevailing discourse a person designated and recognized as "White" cannot simply name her/himself "Black"; this would not be intelligible (Youdell, 2003). Maintaining the notion of subjectivation when thinking about performative processes underscores the conceptual claim that performatives, and the subjects they constitute, are not neutral, but are invested in enduring relations of discursive, productive power.

The politics of deconstruction and strategic provisionality

Understanding hierarchically raced subjects as being subjectivated through discourse suggests that a key political challenge is to constitute race discourses, and so raced subjects, differently. Foucault (1982), Butler (1990), and Derrida (1978) offer tools for thinking how this might be done. As we showed above, the idea that the performatives that subjectivate raced and ethnicized subjects "work" because they cite enduring discourses and so "make sense" means that we cannot simply put down one raced subjectivity and take up another. Yet this does not mean that raced or ethnicized subjectivities are determined in advance by discourse – recognizable subjectivities are constrained but, as discourses are not fixed, the subjectivities that are constituted through them are not fixed either.

A particularly important idea here is Derrida's (1978, 1988) notion of deconstruction, which is concerned with the *reversal and displacement* of those embedded hierarchical binaries that he argues are intrinsic to the inscription of power relations. This reversal and displacement is a viable ambition because, as Derrida points out, any performative is open to misfire; its location in chains of historically and contextually mediated meanings means that a performative might sometimes make meaning that is unintended or unexpected. Similarly, Foucault's (1990) account of discourse insists that no discourse is guaranteed: while particular discourses prevail in some contexts and endure, there remains the potential for the meanings to shift and/or be unsettled by subordinate discourses.

Butler (1997) reminds us that subjects who are constituted in discourse have "discursive agency" (p. 127) and so can act with intent and make things happen: discourse and its effects might exceed the intent or free will of an agent, but the performatively constituted subject can still deploy discursive performatives that have the potential to be constitutive. Gay, lesbian, bisexual, and transgender politics' reinscription of "queer," disability studies' reinscription of "crip," and the Black Power movement's insistence that Black is beautiful might all be understood as examples of such performative politics in action. This has important implications for critical accounts of race and education, because it insists that nobody is necessarily anything and so what it means to be a teacher, a student, White, or of color might be opened up to radical rethinking. What these approaches suggest is that, rather than take up the sort of "strategic essentialism" that is explored by Gayatri Chakravorty Spivak (1988), we take up a position of "strategic provisionality" (Butler, 2007), endlessly refusing to be pinned down, located, or made a subject who stands in and acts her/his "place" in discourse.

Conclusions

> Arguing across conference tables is useless. For those of us who are concerned with the social justice project in education, our work will be done on the frontline with communities committed to change . . . neither race nor class exists as static phenomena.
> (Stovall, 2005, p. 257)

In this chapter we have briefly sketched some of the key developments in Marxist cultural and feminist structural theory, critical race theory, and post-structural theory. Each of these approaches lays claim to a *critical* character, but how far is it possible to reconcile these different perspectives? Some writers believe that reconciliation is not only difficult but actually unhelpful: Marxist critics, for example, have argued that "it is impossible to enliven or extend the debate on educational policy with its inherent inequalities by using the language of 'race' "

(Darder & Torres, 2004, p. 100). In response, some critical race theorists view Marxism's insistence on placing class center-stage as merely reinforcing the regime of White supremacy (Allen, 2006; Gillborn, 2008; Mills, 2003).

Post-structural approaches to understanding the subject and power are relatively new to CRT, but the usefulness of these to the collection of conceptual tools that CRT draws on is evident. CRT's critique of liberal reform, for instance, might be usefully augmented by a Foucauldian understanding of disciplinary power. A rejection of race categories from a CRT perspective might use notions of the performative and subjectivation to explain how race continues to appear as "natural" or "self-evident." And attention to discourse might illuminate the processes through which "business-as-usual" racism identified by CRT operates (Gillborn, 2008; Youdell, 2006b).

Our aim here has been to review a range of approaches that recognize the significance and severity of material inequalities and the ways these are reproduced through macro-policy processes, social structures, and institutions, common sense, and the micro-processes and practices of everyday life. One approach is to view these as conceptual *tools* that can be worked with in combination (albeit a tense combination), variously taken up and set aside as demanded by the analysis and the problems with which we are grappling. At this level, the critical perspectives we have reviewed are, at least, united by their determination to expose and oppose the usually hidden and taken-for-granted means by which oppression and inequity are normalized and legitimated.

The notion of *intersectionality* may be useful here. Collins (2000) suggests that, within a "matrix of domination," "cultural patterns of oppression are not only interrelated, but are bound together and influenced by the intersectional systems of society" (p. 42). A call to intersectionality requires us to do better than map the difficulties and complexities of this project; it asks us to detail these complexities and account for *how* categories and inequalities intersect, through what processes, and with what impact and implications. Intersectionality incites us to pay attention to more than one axis of subordination and inequality, more than one category of identity, and to attend to the relationships between inequalities, between identities, and between inequalities and identities.

The notion of intersectionality is increasingly being embraced, especially by minoritized feminist writers (see Brah & Phoenix, 2004). However, it is important to recognize that to *claim* intersectionality is not necessarily to *accomplish* it. Just as Marxists can be accused of a form of "class-plus" thinking (always beginning with class and then adding a dimension or two), so critical race theorists might be viewed as operating in a "race-plus" fashion, while the feminist turn to intersectionality often becomes "gender-plus" theorizing. There is no easy way to reconcile these issues. As David Stovall (2005) argues, the best test of our ability as critical theorists may be the measure of our impact as anti-oppressive agents. Kimberlé Crenshaw argues that "intersectionality might be more broadly useful as a way of mediating the tension between assertions of multiple identity and the ongoing necessity of group politics" (Crenshaw, 1991, p. 1296). It is important to retain the sense that critical theory should not be merely a dry, cerebral activity: fundamentally, critical theory is theory with a purpose, and that purpose is to challenge inequality and bring about social change.

References

Allen, R. L. (2006). The race problem in the critical pedagogy community. In C. A. Rossatto, R. L. Allen, & M. Pruyn (Eds.), *Reinventing critical pedagogy* (pp. 3–20). Lanham, MD: Rowman & Littlefield.

Althusser, L. (1971). Ideology and ideological state apparatuses. In B. Brewster (Trans.), *Lenin and philosophy, and other essays* (pp. 170–186). London: Monthly Review Press.
Ansley, F. L. (1997). White supremacy (and what we should do about it). In R. Delgado & J. Stefancic (Eds.), *Critical White studies* (pp. 592–595). Philadelphia: Temple University Press.
Apple, M. W. (1979). *Ideology and curriculum*. London: Routledge & Kegan Paul.
Apple, M. W. (1986). *Teachers and texts: A political economy of class and gender relations in education*. London: Routledge.
Apple, M. W. (1993). *Official knowledge: Democratic education in a conservative age*. London: Routledge.
Apple, M. W. (2001). *Educating the "right" way: Markets, standards, God, and inequality*. London: Routledge.
Apple, M. W. (2006). Rhetoric and reality in critical educational studies in the United States. *British Journal of Sociology of Education, 27*(5), 679–687.
Ayers, W. (2006). *Notes from a self-realizing, sensuous, species-being (I think)*. Retrieved February 4, 2008, from http://billayers.wordpress.com/2007/04/25/a-review-of-capitalists-and-conquerors-and-an-exchange/
Ball, S. J. (2008). *The education debate*. Bristol: Policy Press.
Bell, D. (1980). *Brown v. Board of Education* and the interest convergence dilemma. *Harvard Law Review, 93*, 518–533.
Bell, D. (2004). *Silent covenants*. New York: Oxford University Press.
Brah, A., & Phoenix, A. (2004). Ain't I a woman? Revisiting intersectionality. *Journal of International Women's Studies, 5*(3), 75–86.
Butler, J. (1990). *Gender trouble: Feminism and the subversion of identity*. London: Routledge.
Butler, J. (1993). *Bodies that matter: On the discursive limits of "sex."* New York: Routledge.
Butler, J. (1997). *Excitable speech: A politics of the performative*. London: Routledge.
Butler, J. (2004). *Precarious life: The powers of mourning and violence*. London: Verso.
Butler, J. (2007, October). *Sexual politics: The limits of secularism, the time of coalition*. Speech presented at the London School of Economics and Political Science, London.
Collins, P. H. (2000). *Black feminist thought* (2nd ed.). New York: Routledge.
Crenshaw, K. (1991). Mapping the margins: Intersectionality, identity politics, and violence against women of color. *Stanford Law Review, 43*, 1241–1299.
Crenshaw, K. W. (2002). The first decade. *UCLA Law Review, 49*, 1343–1372.
Crenshaw, K., Gotanda, N., Peller, G., & Thomas, K. (Eds.). (1995). Introduction. *Critical race theory: The key writings that formed the movement* (pp. xiii–xxxii). New York: New Press.
Darder, A., & Torres, R. D. (2004). *After race: Racism after multiculturalism*. New York: New York University Press.
Delgado, R., & Stefancic, J. (2000). Introduction. In R. Delgado & J. Stefancic (Eds.), *Critical race theory: The cutting edge* (2nd ed., pp. xv–xix). Philadelphia: Temple University Press.
Delgado, R., & Stefancic, J. (2001). *Critical race theory: An introduction*. New York: New York University Press.
Derrida, J. (1978). *On writing and difference*. London: Routledge.
Derrida, J. (1988). Signature event context. In J. Derrida (Ed.), *Limited Inc* (pp. 1–23). Evanston, IL: Northwestern University Press.
Dixson, A. D., & Rousseau, C. K. (Eds.). (2006). *Critical race theory in education*. London: Routledge.
Dlamini, S. N. (2002). From the other side of the desk: Notes on teaching about race when racialised. *Race, Ethnicity and Education, 5*, 51–66.
Foster, M. (2005). Race, class and gender in education research. In Z. Leonardo (Ed.), *Critical pedagogy and race* (pp. 175–183). Oxford: Blackwell.
Foucault, M. (1982). The subject and power. In H. L. Dreyfus & P. Rabinow (Eds.), *Michel Foucault: Beyond hermeneutics and structuralism* (pp. 208–226). Brighton: Harvester.
Foucault, M. (1990). *The history of sexuality: An introduction* (Vol. 1). London: Penguin.
Foucault, M. (1991). *Discipline and punish: The birth of the prison*. London: Penguin.
Freire, P. (1993). *Pedagogy of the oppressed*. New York: Continuum.
Gillborn, D. (2005). Education policy as an act of White supremacy. *Journal of Education Policy, 20*, 485–505.
Gillborn, D. (2008). *Racism and education*. London: Routledge.

Gillborn, D., & Youdell, D. (2000). *Rationing education*. Buckinghamshire, UK: Open University Press.

Gramsci, A. (1971). *Selections from the prison notebooks*. New York: International Publishers. (Written 1929 to 1935)

Hall, S. (1996). Who needs "identity?" In S. Hall & P. D. Gay (Eds.), *Questions of cultural identity* (pp. 1–17). London: Sage.

Hansard (1999, February 24). Prime Minister's questions (col. 379–387). Retrieved May 3, 2007, from http://www.publications.parliament.uk/pa/cm199899/cmhansrd/vo990224/debtext/90224-20.htm#90224-20_spmin0

hooks, b. (1990). *Yearning: Race, gender and cultural politics*. Boston: South End Press.

Hylton, K. (2008). *"Race" and sport: Critical race theory*. London: Routledge.

Jacobson, M. F. (1998). *Whiteness of a different color: European immigrants and the alchemy of race*. Cambridge, MA: Harvard University Press.

Jones, S. (2006). *Antonio Gramsci*. London: Routledge.

Ladson-Billings, G. (2006). From the achievement gap to the education debt. *Educational Researcher, 35*(7), 3–12.

Ladson-Billings, G., & Tate, W. F. (1995). Toward a critical race theory of education. *Teachers College Record, 97*, 47–68.

Leonardo, Z. (2002). The souls of White folk. *Race, Ethnicity and Education, 5*, 29–50.

Macpherson, W. (1999). *The Stephen Lawrence Inquiry* (No. CM 4262-I). London: The Stationery Office.

McCrum, R., Cran, W., & MacNeil, R. (1992). *The story of English*. New York: Penguin.

McLaren, P. (1995). *Critical pedagogy and predatory culture*. London: Routledge.

McLaren, P. (2005). *Capitalists and conquerors: A critical pedagogy against empire*. Oxford, UK: Rowman & Littlefield.

McLaren, P. (2007). *Peter McLaren responds to Bill Ayers: Bad faith solidarity*. Retrieved February 6, 2008, from http://www.tcrecord.org/Discussion.asp?i=3&vdpid=2695&aid=2&rid=12888&dtid=0

Mills, C. W. (2003). *From class to race: Essays in White Marxism and Black radicalism*. New York: Rowman & Littlefield.

Rollock, N. (2007). *Failure by any other name?* London: Runnymede Trust.

Said, E. (2003). *Orientalism*. London: Penguin.

Saussure, F. de. (1974). *Course in general linguistics*. London: Fontana.

Spillers, H. J. (1987). Mama's baby, papa's maybe: An American grammar book. *Diacritics, 17*(2), 65–80.

Spivak, G. C. (1988). *In other words: Essays in cultural politics*. New York: Routledge.

Stovall, D. (2005). Forging community in race and class. *Race, Ethnicity and Education, 9*, 243–259.

Tate, W. F. (1997). Critical race theory and education: History, theory, and implications. In M. W. Apple (Ed.), *Review of research in education* (Vol. 22, pp. 195–247). Washington, DC: American Educational Research Association (AERA).

Taylor, E. (1998). A primer on critical race theory. *Journal of Blacks in Higher Education, 19*, 122–124.

Tomlinson, S. (2008). *Race and education*. Maidenhead, UK: Open University Press.

Yosso, T. J. (2006). *Critical race counterstories along the Chicana/Chicano educational pipeline*. New York: Routledge.

Youdell, D. (2003). Identity traps or how Black students fail. *British Journal of Sociology of Education, 24*, 3–20.

Youdell, D. (2006a). *Impossible bodies, impossible selves: Exclusions and student subjectivities*. Dordrecht: Springer.

Youdell, D. (2006b). Subjectivation and performative politics – Butler thinking Althusser and Foucault: intelligibility, agency and the raced-nationed-religioned subjects of education. *British Journal of Sociology of Education, 27*(4), 511–528.

13

The nature and origins of children's racial attitudes

Rebecca S. Bigler
University of Texas, Austin, USA

Julie Milligan Hughes
The College of New Jersey, Ewing, USA

The nature and origins of children's racial attitudes

Racial diversity is increasing at unprecedented rates around the globe. In the US, for example, Latino Americans and African Americans now constitute 12% and 13% of the population respectively, and those numbers are expected to grow to 24% and 15% by 2050 (Census Bureau, 2004). In contrast, European Americans, who currently constitute 69% of the U.S. population, are expected to make up just 50% of the population by the year 2050. Similar trends of cultural diversification exist in nations around the world. It is imperative, therefore, that children develop positive racial attitudes and are able to interact respectfully and harmoniously within racially diverse societies.

A great deal of psychological literature indicates, however, that youth in the US and abroad continue to endorse racial stereotypes (i.e. assign characteristics to others solely on the basis of race) and hold racial biases (e.g. show more positive affect toward racial ingroup than outgroup members; see Aboud & Doyle, 1995, 1996; Bar-Tal, 1996; Bigler & Liben, 1993; Black-Gutman & Hickson, 1996; Cameron, Rutland, Brown, & Douch, 2006; Doyle, Beaudet, & Aboud, 1988; Masson & Verkuyten, 1993). Some research suggests that a lessening of racial biases has occurred; children typically do not, for example, approve of the exclusion of others solely on the basis of race (Killen, Lee-Kim, McGlothlin, & Stangor, 2002). Other work, however, suggests that low levels of explicit bias among some children are the result of social desirability concerns rather than internalized views of racial equality (see Katz, Johnson, & Parker, 1970; Rutland, Cameron, Milne, & McGeorge, 2005) and that many children continue to show evidence of strong, sometimes unconscious, biases (Baron & Banaji, 2006; Wittenbrink, Judd, & Park, 1997). Within the past five years, for example, several schools across the US have been temporarily closed because of racial hostilities among students. The numerous negative consequences of racial bias make it imperative to understand the origins of racial attitudes.

Developmental and social psychological research conducted over the last 50 years has gained significant ground in uncovering the roots of racial prejudice among children. The relevant literature is enormous, and space constraints prevent us from covering this work in depth. Excellent reviews of the literature are available (see Levy & Killen, 2008; Quintana & McKown, 2008). In this chapter, we instead apply a new major theoretical model of social stereotyping and prejudice, developmental intergroup theory (DIT) (Bigler & Liben, 2006, 2007), to the nature and origins of children's racial attitudes.

The chapter is divided into three major sections. The first section presents a brief overview of developmental intergroup theory and the theoretical work on which it is based. The second section applies the component processes of developmental intergroup theory to understanding racial stereotyping and prejudice. The third and final section proposes directions for future work.

Developmental intergroup theory

DIT (Bigler & Liben, 2006, 2007) provides a constructivist model of the formation and maintenance of stereotyping and prejudice among children. The theory outlines the processes and rules by which children single out groups as targets of stereotyping and prejudice, and by which they develop the stereotypic attributes and affective prejudices that are associated with those groups in their culture. The theory seeks to explain stereotyping and prejudice (a) across multiple domains, (b) within a developmental framework, and (c) as a function of interactions between organismic and environmental factors. DIT is named for its grounding within, and integration of, two theoretical perspectives: intergroup theory (Tajfel, Billig, Bundy, & Flament, 1971; Tajfel & Turner, 1986) and cognitive-developmental theory (Piaget, 1970). Although many developmental researchers have begun to adopt intergroup perspectives (see Levy & Killen, 2008), we use the phrase *developmental intergroup theory* to refer to the specific theoretical model outlined by Bigler and Liben (2006, 2007).

Theoretical foundations

Intergroup theory. This is a term given to a group of social psychological theories aimed at explaining the origins of intergroup biases, including social identity theory (Tajfel & Turner, 1986) and self-categorization theory (Turner, 1987). The fundamental hypothesis of intergroup theory is that individuals are motivated to maintain a positive and distinct identity, and that they use group identities as sources of positive identity development and maintenance. To that end, individuals favor social ingroups and disfavor social outgroups (Tajfel, 1982; Tajfel & Turner, 1986).

Empirical findings related to intergroup relations have proliferated in recent decades, and intergroup theories have increasingly been applied to racial attitudes. Some empirical work is supportive of the utility of social identity and self-categorization theories for understanding children's ethnic and racial attitudes (see Barrett & Davis, 2008). For example, European American children perceive greater similarity within than between races (e.g. Doyle & Aboud, 1995), and individual differences in children's perceptions of between-race similarity are related to levels of prejudice (Aboud & Mitchell, 1977; Doyle & Aboud, 1995; Katz, Sohn, & Zalk, 1975). Furthermore, European American children with higher self-esteem show greater racial ingroup bias than their peers with lower self-esteem (see Davis, Leman, & Barrett, 2007).

Intergroup approaches are, however, marked by important limitations. One limitation is that these theories fail to address issues of development. Implicitly, the individual is conceived of as a static entity, assumed to respond to social categorization consistently across the life course. A second limitation is that such theories fail to address the specific environmental conditions under which individuals with differing cognitive competencies might come to categorize others as ingroup and outgroup members on the basis of some particular attribute (such as race). Bigler and Liben's (2006) developmental intergroup theory sought to address these limitations.

Cognitive-developmental theory. Given that cognitive processes are involved in the formation of stereotypes about social groups, cognitive-developmental change is likely to affect stereotyping and prejudice. DIT draws upon Piagetian theory (see Piaget, 1970), as well as other contemporary accounts of cognitive development (e.g. Gelman, 2003), in predicting age-related changes in social stereotyping and prejudice.

Bigler and Liben draw heavily on two aspects of cognitive-developmental theory to predict age-related changes in children's stereotyping and prejudice. The first relevant aspect of Piagetian theory is its analysis of the ways that children's logical skills change with development. Although most commonly studied in relation to children's educational achievements (e.g. progress in mathematics and science), changes in logical reasoning skills are also likely to shape children's thinking about, and behavior toward, social groups. Aboud and her colleagues (Aboud, 1984, 1988; Bigler & Liben, 1993; Doyle & Aboud, 1995; Doyle et al., 1988) were among the first researchers to apply Piagetian principles to understanding racial attitude change across childhood. Aboud argued that cognitive constraints characterizing the early elementary school years (e.g. centration, perception-bound reasoning) limit the flexibility with which children think about members of racial groups. Bigler and Liben extend this line of reasoning, arguing that classification skills (e.g. sorting, reclassification, multiple and hierarchical classification skills) affect the formation and revision of social stereotyping and prejudice.

The second relevant aspect of Piagetian theory for understanding stereotyping and prejudice concerns constructivism. Piagetian theory views children as actively assimilating experience into existing knowledge structures and modifying those structures to accommodate new information rather than passively absorbing information from their environment (Piaget, 1970). Thus, Bigler and Liben argue that children will interpret information about race based on their existing knowledge of race; at times children will modify their concepts of race to accommodate new information, and at other times children will assimilate new information about race to match existing knowledge structures (see Bigler & Liben, 1993).

Core components of the formation and maintenance of racial stereotypes and prejudice

According to DIT, four basic processes are involved in the formation and maintenance of stereotypes and prejudice. Three of the component processes are relevant to the *formation* of social stereotypes and prejudice (see Figure 13.1). The fourth component process is relevant to the *maintenance* or modification of stereotypic views and prejudice (see Figure 13.2). These four processes include (a) establishment of the psychological salience (EPS) of person attributes, (b) categorization of encountered individuals (CEI) by salient dimension, (c) development of stereotypes and prejudices (DSP) concerning salient social groups, and (d) application of a stereotype filter (ASF) to encountered individuals. Empirical evidence in support of the basic component processes comes from studies of novel social groups (e.g. Bigler, 1995; Bigler, Brown, & Markell, 2001; Patterson & Bigler, 2005, 2006; Yee & Brown, 1992), as well as the literatures on stereotyping within specific domains (e.g. gender, race, age). In the next section of the chapter, we describe each component as it applies specifically to racial stereotyping and prejudice.

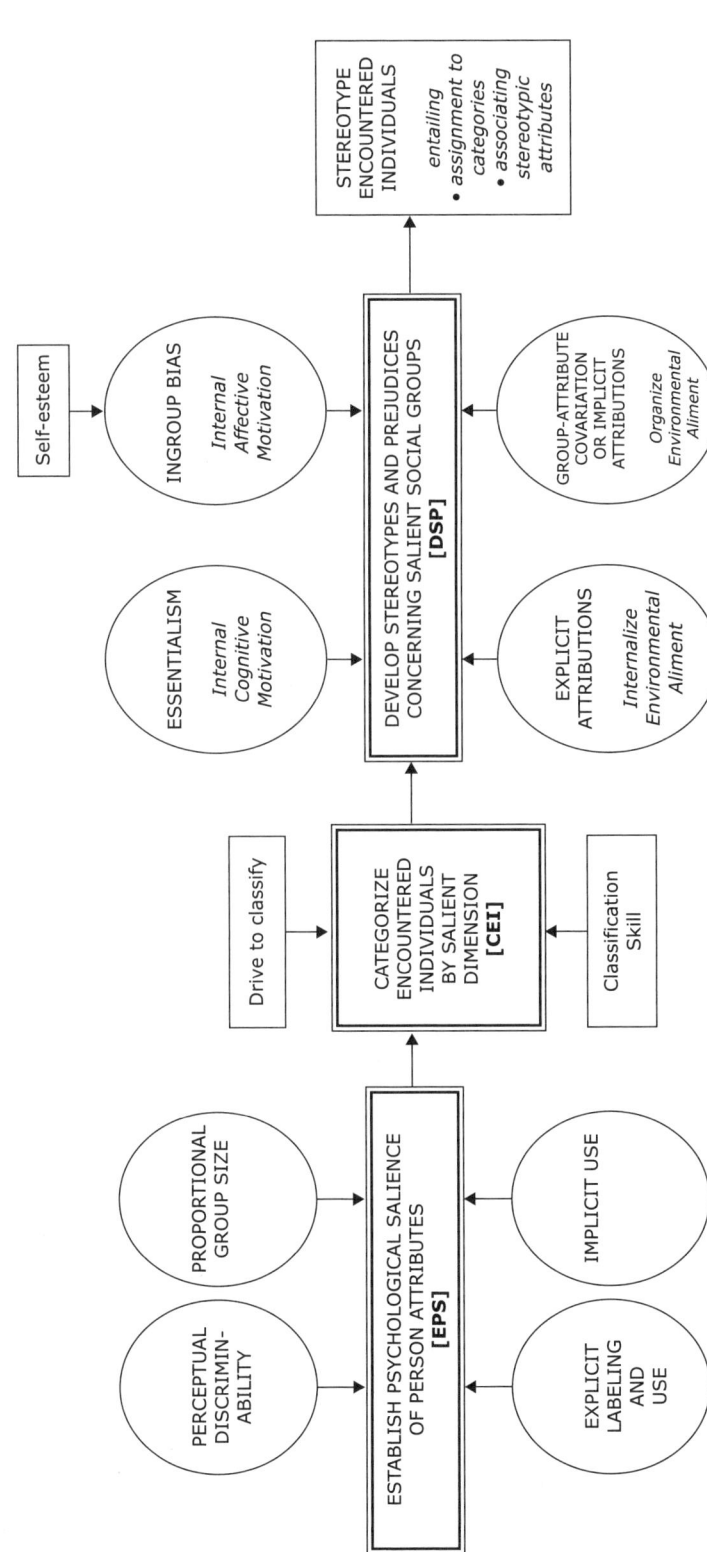

Figure 13.1 Processes Involved in the Formation of Social Stereotypes and Prejudice. Reprinted with permission of the publisher from Bigler & Liben (2006).

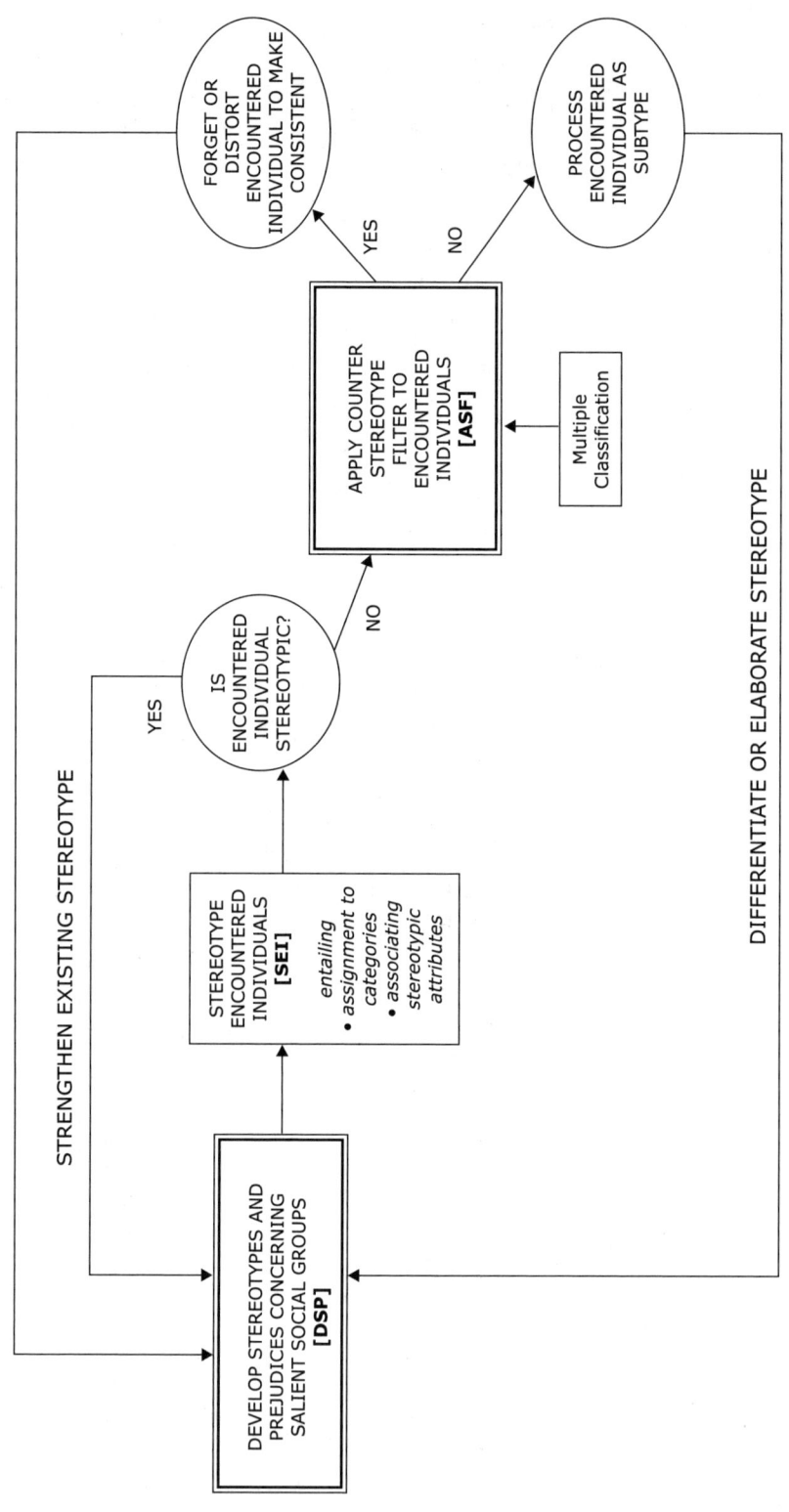

Figure 13.2 Processes Involved in the Maintenance or Modification of Social Stereotypes and Prejudice. Reprinted with permission of the publisher from Bigler & Liben (2006).

Establishment of the psychological salience of race

Developmental intergroup theory, like intergroup theory and cognitive-developmental theory, proposes that racial stereotyping and prejudice depend on children's categorization of individuals by race. There are, however, almost endless bases on which children might parse individuals into groups. How and why do children come to view *race* as a meaningful dimension along which to sort individuals?

The first component of DIT depicted in Figure 13.1 (see EPS rectangle) addresses the process by which some person attributes become salient for categorization. To understand this component of DIT, it is useful first to note that DIT differs from other major theories of racial stereotypes in several important ways. First, race is not viewed as a "privileged" dimension. Race-based classification does *not* occur reflexively as a result of an innate predisposition. Instead, we argue that culture and children's cognitive skills interact to make children deem race to be significant. Second, we argue that classification on the basis of some particular dimension is not primarily the result of an individual's history of reinforcement or punishment for the use of this dimension, or an individual's imitation of adults' expression of stereotyping and prejudice on the basis of this dimension, as proposed in traditional and social learning theories (Allport, 1954; Bandura, 1977; Skinner, 1969). Instead, we posit that children search for categories that are appropriate to, and useful within, their culture. The environment provides children with information that (a) serves to make race a *salient* basis for classification and (b) provides the aliment from which children *construct* the meaning of race. That is, environmental input plays an important role in shaping children's racial attitudes because it serves to make race salient and leads children to devise hypotheses about the meaning of race.

DIT posits that four factors contribute to the psychological salience of race: perceptual discriminability, unequal racial group size, explicit labeling of racial group membership, and implicit racial segregation.

Perceptual discriminability. One factor that contributes to the psychological salience of race is its perceptual discriminability. Novel group studies with children (e.g. Bigler, Jones, & Lobliner, 1997) have demonstrated that intergroup biases form most readily when children are able to visually discriminate among social group members. There is mounting evidence that infants as young as 3 months are able to categorize faces according to race (e.g. Bar-Haim, Ziv, Lamy, & Hodes, 2006; Kelly et al., 2007). Because many of the markers for race are perceptually discriminable (skin color, hair color and texture, physiognomy), infants and young children are capable of categorizing others on the basis of their racial group membership.

Proportional group size and minority status. A second factor theorized to contribute to the psychological salience of race is proportional group size. Within most societies, racial groups are represented in unequal numbers. Theoretical and empirical work within social psychology indicates that proportionately smaller social groups are more distinctive than proportionately larger social groups (Mullen, 1991; Mullen & Hu, 1989). Furthermore, those individuals who are members of proportionately smaller groups experience their group membership as more salient than those who are members of proportionately larger groups (Brewer & Brown, 1998). Individuals who have been the *sole* members of their race within some setting readily attest to the increased salience of their category membership. Many individuals also report that the experience of being a member of a numeric minority group is negative. Illustrative data come from three studies in which minority groups were created experimentally by, for example, having only two or three children wear blue shirts while all others in their classroom wore yellow shirts (Brown & Bigler, 2002). Children assigned to minority groups were typically less happy with their group assignment than their majority group peers.

Explicit labeling and use. DIT proposes that the extent to which children's environments explicitly draw attention to race will also affect the psychological salience of race. In novel group studies, children form intergroup biases more readily when authority figures label and use social groups to organize the environment (e.g. "Good morning, reds and blues," or "The blue group may line up; the red group may line up") than when these groups are ignored (Bigler et al., 1997; Bigler et al., 2001). Such conditions characterized most of U.S. history (e.g. the presence of "White" and "Black" public facilities). Consistent with DIT tenets, levels of explicit racial prejudice among children have been very high in the US, as documented by classic research such as Clark and Clark's work (1939, 1950), and have declined as such conditions (i.e. de jure segregation) were removed. Indeed, in response to the notion that labels trigger attention to race, many parents and educators have adopted "colorblind" (or "color-mute") approaches (Pollock, 2004). It is important to note, however, that, although the routine labeling of race is likely to increase racial stereotyping and prejudice, strict adherence to colorblind approaches is also undesirable because it prevents explicit discussion of racial issues, including racial inequality and discrimination (see Hughes, Bigler, & Levy, 2007).

Implicit use. The two mechanisms discussed above provide *explicit* markers of adults' judgments about groups' distinction. DIT also posits that there are *implicit* mechanisms that children take as important markers of which social categories adults view as important. One particularly important implicit mechanism is racial *segregation*, which continues to characterize neighborhoods, schools, and community organizations within the US (Orfield & Yun, 1999). DIT posits that children notice such implicit sorting by race and infer that race groups are segregated *because* they differ in important and non-obvious ways (Patterson & Bigler, 2005). Thus segregation increases the psychological salience of race to children and, in turn, their categorization of others by race. Environments that are racially integrated, by corollary, may decrease the psychological salience of race and subsequent racial categorization. This may be the reason, for example, that children with higher levels of cross-race contact hold less biased racial attitudes than other children (e.g. Crystal, Killen, & Ruck, 2008; Killen, Sinno, & Margie, 2007).

Categorization of encountered individuals by race

The second major process in the formation of racial prejudices and stereotypes is the categorization of individuals by race. Developmental intergroup theory is similar to many other theoretical accounts of the origins of racial attitudes in its emphasis on racial categorization (e.g. Aboud, 1988; Allport, 1954; Nesdale, Durkin, & Maass, 2004; Tajfel & Turner, 1986; Turner, 1987). DIT proposes that the racial categorization process will be moderated by children's classification skills. Thus, although infants appear able to categorize faces by race under some circumstances (Kelly et al., 2007), the ability to categorize others by race is likely to continue to develop across the preschool years (see Aboud, 1988). The mere act of categorization triggers, according to DIT, processes involved in the construction of social stereotypes and prejudices.

Development of racial stereotypes and prejudices

According to DIT, the process of categorization is hypothesized to result in constructivist cognitive-developmental processes that serve to attach meaning to social groups in the form of beliefs (i.e. stereotypes) and affect (i.e. prejudice) (see DSP rectangle in Figure 13.1). This process is facilitated both by internal mechanisms and by external mechanisms, described below.

Essentialism. Essentialist thinking is characterized by the belief that category members share important, internal (or non-obvious), and permanent characteristics (Gelman & Taylor, 2000).

Hirschfeld (1996) was among the first researchers to argue that essentialist thinking about race fuels the development of racial stereotypes and prejudices. Empirical work indicates that children are especially likely to describe race as defined by physical or genetically inherited traits (Quintana, 1994, 2008; Quintana & Vera, 1999) and to believe that members of one racial group automatically share important, internal qualities that are not shared with members of other racial groups. Indeed, there is evidence that children's essentialist thinking about race increases perceptions of differences across racial groups and perceptions of similarities within racial groups (Hirschfeld, 1996), which is tantamount to racial stereotyping (Aboud, 1988).

Ingroup preference. A second internal mechanism that facilitates the development of racial prejudice and stereotyping is ingroup bias. A great deal of social psychological research indicates that the mere act of categorizing individuals into social groups ("minimal groups") is sufficient to produce intergroup prejudice and discrimination (Tajfel & Turner, 1986). Applied to race, DIT posits that children will view racial ingroup members more positively than racial outgroup members as a consequence of the psychological salience of race and children's categorization of themselves and others according to racial group membership.

Ingroup preference is also likely to facilitate the formation of racial stereotypes, which in turn strengthen racial prejudice. Positive views of one's racial ingroup will guide children's attention and memory to positive attributes of their ingroup and to negative attributes of their outgroups. Thus, children's stereotypes about their racial ingroup are likely to be positive, and their stereotypes of racial outgroups are likely to be negative. For example, although adults from a variety of racial backgrounds rate "snobby" and "smart" as equally strongly associated with European Americans, European American children more strongly associate their ingroup with "smart" (a positive trait) than with "snobby" (a negative trait) (Hughes & Bigler, 2007). In other words, European American children's ingroup racial stereotypes tend to be more positive than negative as a result of ingroup bias.

Explicit attributions. Developmental intergroup theory also proposes external factors that fuel the formation of racial prejudices and stereotypes. One of these external factors is explicit information from parents, peers, the media, or other sources, describing the attributes of various racial groups. DIT proposes that children will integrate these messages into their racial group concepts. Racially stereotypic messages might include such statements as "Blacks are good at basketball." Although research suggests that such blatant stereotypic statements are uncommon in the US today, it is possible that overt expressions of racial stereotypes are more common outside of research settings, when adults are less self-conscious about their speech (see Pollock, 2004), and are more common among children, who may make such remarks out of the earshot of adults. Very little research is available to determine the extent and consequences of explicit racial attributions in children's environments, but DIT proposes that children exposed to such attributions are likely to hold rigid racial stereotypes and prejudices.

Group-attribute covariation or implicit attributions. Beginning in infancy, children learn about the attributes of various categories of people through their detection of implicit group-attribute covariation (see Spelke & Kinzler, 2007). Implicit information linking race to social roles or traits is thus also theorized to promote the formation of racial stereotyping and prejudice. Within many cultures, for example, race is correlated with occupational roles (e.g. Brown et al., 2003). Children to whom race is psychologically salient, and who categorize individuals according to race, are likely to construct an understanding of race that includes these associations between race and occupational roles. For example, a child who encounters five doctors, four of whom are European American, is likely to stereotype doctors as European American (see Hughes & Bigler, 2007). Children also encounter implicit messages about the links between race and attributes in adult- and child-directed media (Calvert, 1999) and in the *nonverbal behavior* that adults (e.g. parents, teachers) direct toward members of social groups, or show in response to the presence of group members. So, for example, European American parents may become nervous or socially withdrawn in the presence of African Americans, perhaps as the result of automatic or implicit racial prejudice. Although little evidence is available documenting the causal effects of implicit messages on children's racial attitudes, Bigler and Liben (2006) argue that children are very likely to be aware of these links, and this information informs their racial prejudices and stereotypes.

Application of stereotype and prejudice filter to encountered individuals

Developmental intergroup theory proposes that the final process in the formation and expression of children's racial prejudices and stereotypes is the application of their racial stereotypes and prejudices in new situations. The consequences of the application of this racial attitude filter are twofold. The first consequence is that children will base judgments about unfamiliar others on their existing racial stereotypes and prejudices. For example, racially biased children will prefer to play with racial ingroup members over racial outgroup members given no other information about those individuals. The second consequence is that children's prejudice and stereotype filters will guide information processing to remember attitude-consistent information and to forget or distort attitude-inconsistent information. For example, while learning about the life of an African American leader such as George Washington Carver, children who endorse racial stereotypes may forget his intellectual accomplishments (attitude-inconsistent information) but remember that he was born a slave (attitude-consistent information).

There is empirical support for the hypothesis that children will behave according to their existing racial prejudices and stereotypes in unfamiliar situations. For example, children with negative attitudes toward racial outgroups are less likely than their non-biased peers to have cross-race friendships (Aboud, Mendelson, & Purdy, 2003). Children who are aware of occupational stereotypes of African Americans and European Americans apply these stereotypes to their judgments about the status of completely unfamiliar occupations (Bigler, Averhart, & Liben, 2003). Furthermore, children who endorse racial stereotypes are likely to distort counter-stereotypical information about racial group members so that it is stereotype consistent (e.g. misremembering an African American story character who was a ballerina as a maid instead; Bigler & Liben, 1993).

The application of racial stereotype and prejudice filters to new situations is likely to promote the maintenance of these stereotypes and prejudices. For example, children whose racial prejudices lead them to prefer same-race play partners are likely to engage in more friendship activities with racial ingroup members than with racial outgroup members. Spending more time with same-race friends than with cross-race friends is likely to promote and maintain children's preference for same-race individuals. Furthermore, children's tendency to distort counter-stereotypic information to be consistent with their existing racial stereotypes helps to maintain these stereotypes and may explain why interventions aimed at revising children's racial stereotypes by providing counter-stereotypical models sometimes result in *increased* racial stereotyping (see Bigler, 1999).

Conclusions and future directions

Children are driven to understand their world, and this drive is manifested in their tendency to categorize natural and non-natural stimuli, and to search the environment for cues about which of the great number of potential bases for categorization are important. The first step in the process of racial stereotype and prejudice formation is, therefore, the establishment of the psychological salience of race. Four factors are hypothesized to establish the psychological salience of race: (a) perceptual discriminability, (b) minority status, (c) explicit use, and (d) implicit use of racial groups. Perceptually discriminable person characteristics are more likely than other characteristics to become the basis of stereotyping, but perceptual discriminability alone is insufficient to trigger psychological salience. Thus, for example, young children's ability to detect race does not mean that race will inevitably become the basis of stereotypes and prejudice. Instead, children are especially likely to view race as a salient feature of interpersonal variation if racial groups are characterized by minority status, group labeling, or implicit or explicit racial segregation. Without these environmental conditions, children should be less likely to attend to race and, thus, less likely to form racial prejudices and stereotypes.

Once race becomes salient, we propose that children categorize newly encountered individuals along this dimension. The act of categorization then triggers the process of racial stereotyping and prejudice formation. Four factors are hypothesized to affect the formation of racial stereotypes and prejudice: (a) essentialism, (b) ingroup bias, (c) explicit links between attributes and racial groups, and (d) implicit race-attribute covariation. The strengthening (or weakening) of any of these four factors should accordingly influence children's levels of racial prejudice and stereotyping.

If the tenets of DIT are correct, there would be important implications for social, educational, and legal policies related to social groups. We noted, for example, ways in which race is made psychologically salient (e.g. the use of labels, segregated conditions). Importantly, factors such as these are largely under societal control, that is, institutions and individuals can choose whether to label and to use race routinely within children's environments. There are similar decisions to be made about whether to prevent or permit various forms of racial segregation. Our hope is that DIT will ultimately prove valuable not only for understanding the development of racial stereotypes and prejudices in children but for guiding interventions aimed at preventing the development of racial stereotypes and prejudices.

There is still much to be learned concerning the nature of children's racial attitudes. Remaining questions include the role of racial socialization and racism awareness on children's racial prejudices and stereotyping (see Hughes, 2003; Hughes et al., 2007). Children's incorporation of moral reasoning and lay theories (e.g. colorblind ideals) into their views of race should also be further examined (see Levy & Killen, 2008). Finally, the developmental trajectory of children's views about race from early childhood through adolescence and early adulthood has yet to be outlined fully. It is our hope that the field of racial attitude research can move toward more integrative and comprehensive approaches to understanding this very important topic.

References

Aboud, F. E. (1984). Social and cognitive bases of ethnic identity constancy. *Journal of Genetic Psychology*, 145, 217–230.

Aboud, F. E. (1988). *Children and prejudice*. New York: Blackwell.

Aboud, F. E., & Doyle, A. B. (1995). The development of in-group pride in Black Canadians. *Journal of Cross-Cultural Psychology*, 26, 243–254.

Aboud, F. E., & Doyle, A. B. (1996). Parental and peer influences on children's racial attitudes. *International Journal of Intercultural Relations*, 20, 371–383.

Aboud, F. E., Mendelson, M. J., & Purdy, K. T. (2003). Cross-race peer relations and friendship quality. *International Journal of Behavioral Development*, 27, 165–173.

Aboud, F. E., & Mitchell, F. G. (1977). Ethnic role taking: The effects of preference and self-identification. *International Journal of Psychology, 12*, 1–17.

Allport, G. W. (1954). *The nature of prejudice*. Reading, MA: Addison-Wesley.

Bandura, A. (1977). Self-efficacy: Toward a unifying theory of behavioral change. *Psychological Review, 84*, 191–215.

Bar-Haim, Y., Ziv, T., Lamy, D., & Hodes, R. M. (2006). Nature and nurture in own-race face processing. *Psychological Science, 17*, 159–163.

Baron, A. S., & Banaji, M. R. (2006). The development of implicit attitudes: Evidence of race evaluations from ages 6 and 10 and adulthood. *Psychological Science, 17*, 53–58.

Barrett, M., & Davis, S. C. (2008). Applying social identity and self-categorization theories to children's racial, ethnic, national, and state identifications and attitudes. In S. M. Quintana & C. McKown (Eds.), *Handbook of race, racism, and the developing childhood* (pp. 72–110). Hoboken, NJ: Wiley.

Bar-Tal, D. (1996). Development of social categories and stereotypes in early childhood: The case of "the Arab" concept formation, stereotype and attitudes by Jewish children in Israel. *International Journal of Intercultural Relations, 20*, 341–370.

Bigler, R. S. (1995). The role of classification skill in moderating environmental influences on children's gender stereotyping: A study of the functional use of gender in the classroom. *Child Development, 66*, 1072–1087.

Bigler, R. S. (1999). The use of multicultural curricula and materials to counter racism in children. *Journal of Social Issues, 55*, 687–705.

Bigler, R. S., Averhart, C., & Liben, L. S. (2003). Race and the workforce: Occupational status, aspirations, and stereotyping among African American children. *Developmental Psychology, 39*, 572–580.

Bigler, R. S., Brown, C. S., & Markell, M. (2001). When groups are not created equal: Effects of group status on the formation of intergroup attitudes in children. *Child Development, 72*, 1151–1162.

Bigler, R. S., Jones, L. S., & Lobliner, D. B. (1997). Social categorization and the formation of intergroup attitudes in children. *Child Development, 68*, 530–540.

Bigler, R. S., & Liben, L. S. (1993). A cognitive-developmental approach to racial stereotyping and reconstructive memory in Euro-American children. *Child Development, 64*, 1507–1518.

Bigler, R. S., & Liben, L. S. (2006). A developmental intergroup theory of social stereotypes and prejudice. In R. V. Kail (Ed.), *Advances in child development and behavior* (Vol. 34, pp. 39–89). San Diego, CA: Elsevier.

Bigler, R. S., & Liben, L. S. (2007). Developmental intergroup theory: Explaining and reducing children's social stereotyping and prejudice. *Current Directions in Psychological Science, 16*, 162–166.

Black-Gutman, D., & Hickson, F. (1996). The relationship between racial attitudes and social-cognitive development in children: An Australian study. *Developmental Psychology, 32*, 448–456.

Brewer, M. B., & Brown, R. J. (1998). Intergroup relations. In D. T. Gilbert, S. T. Fiske, & G. Lindsey (Eds.), *The handbook of social psychology* (4th ed., Vol. 2, pp. 554–594). New York: McGraw-Hill.

Brown, C. S., & Bigler, R. S. (2002). Effects of minority status in the classroom on children's intergroup attitudes. *Journal of Experimental Child Psychology, 83*, 77–110.

Brown, M. K., Carnoy, M., Currie, E., Duster, T., Oppenheimer, D. B., Schultz, M. M., et al. (2003). *White-washing race: The myth of a color-blind society*. Berkeley, CA: University of California Press.

Calvert, S. L. (1999). *Children's journeys through the information age*. New York: McGraw-Hill.

Cameron, L., Rutland, A., Brown, R., & Douch, R. (2006). Changing children's intergroup attitudes toward refugees: Testing different models of extended contact. *Child Development, 77*, 1208–1219.

Census Bureau (2004). *Projected population of the United States, by race and Hispanic origin: 2000 to 2050*. Washington, DC: U.S. Census Bureau. Retrieved January 3, 2008, from http://www.census.gov

Clark, K. B., & Clark, M. P. (1939). Segregation as a factor in the racial identification of Negro preschool children. *Journal of Experimental Education, 8*, 161–163.

Clark, K. B., & Clark, M. P. (1950). Emotional factors in racial identification and preference in Negro children. *Journal of Negro Education, 19*, 341–350.

Crystal, D. S., Killen, M., & Ruck, M. (2008). It is who you know that counts: Intergroup contact and judgments about race-based exclusion. *British Journal of Developmental Psychology, 26*, 51–70.

Davis, S. C., Leman, P. J., & Barrett, M. (2007). Children's implicit and explicit ethnic group attitudes, ethnic group identification, and self-esteem. *International Journal of Behavioral Development, 31*, 514–525.

Doyle, A. B., & Aboud, F. E. (1995). A longitudinal study of White children's racial prejudice as a social-cognitive development. *Merrill-Palmer Quarterly, 41*, 209–228.

Doyle, A. B., Beaudet, J., & Aboud, F. (1988). Developmental patterns in the flexibility of children's ethnic attitudes. *Journal of Cross-Cultural Psychology, 19*, 3–18.

Gelman, S. A. (2003). *The essential child.* New York: Oxford University Press.

Gelman, S. A., & Taylor, M. G. (2000). Gender essentialism in cognitive development. In P. H. Miller & E. Kofsky Scholnick (Eds.), *Toward a feminist developmental psychology* (pp. 169–190). Florence, KY: Taylor & Francis/Routledge.

Hirschfeld, L. A. (1996). *Race in the making: Cognition, culture, and the child's construction of human kinds.* Cambridge, MA: MIT Press.

Hughes, D. (2003). Correlates of African American and Latino parents' messages to children about ethnicity and race: A comparative study of racial socialization. *American Journal of Community Psychology, 31*, 15–33.

Hughes, J. M., & Bigler, R. S. (2007, March). *Development and validation of new measures of racial stereotyping and prejudice.* Poster presented at the biennial meeting of the Society for Research in Child Development, Boston.

Hughes, J. M., Bigler, R. S., & Levy, S. R. (2007). Consequences of learning about historical racism among European American and African American children. *Child Development, 78*, 1689–1705.

Katz, P. A., Johnson, J., & Parker, D. (1970). Racial attitudes and perception in Black and White urban school children. *Proceedings of the Annual Convention of the American Psychological Association, 5*, 311–312.

Katz, P. A., Sohn, M., & Zalk, S. R. (1975). Perceptual concomitants of racial attitudes in urban grade-school children. *Developmental Psychology, 11*, 135–144.

Kelly, D. J., Liu, S., Ge, L., Quinn, P. C., Slater, A. M., Lee, K., et al. (2007). Cross-race preferences for same-race faces extend beyond the African versus Caucasian contrast in 3-month-old infants. *Infancy, 11*, 87–95.

Killen, M., Lee-Kim, J., McGlothlin, H., & Stangor, C. (2002). How children and adolescents evaluate gender and racial exclusion. *Monographs of the Society for Research in Child Development, 67*(4).

Killen, M., Sinno, S., & Margie, N. G. (2007). Children's experiences and judgments about group exclusion and inclusion. In R. V. Kail (Ed.), *Advances in child development and behavior* (Vol. 35, pp. 173–218). New York: Elsevier.

Levy, S. R., & Killen, M. (2008). *Intergroup attitudes and relations in childhood through adulthood.* New York: Oxford University Press.

Masson C. N., & Verkuyten, M. (1993). Prejudice, ethnic identity, contact and ethnic group references among young Dutch adolescents. *Journal of Applied Social Psychology, 23*, 156–168.

Mullen, B. (1991). Group composition, salience, and cognitive representations: The phenomenology of being in a group. *Journal of Experimental Social Psychology, 27*, 297–323.

Mullen, B., & Hu, L. (1989). Perceptions of ingroup and outgroup variability: A meta-analytic integration. *Basic and Applied Social Psychology, 10*, 233–252.

Nesdale, D., Durkin, K., & Maass, A. (2004). Group status, outgroup ethnicity and children's ethnic attitudes. *Journal of Applied Developmental Psychology, 25*, 237–251.

Orfield G., & Yun, J. T. (1999). *Resegregation in American schools.* Cambridge, MA: Civil Rights Project, Harvard University. (ERIC Document Reproduction Service No. ED445171)

Patterson, M. M., & Bigler, R. S. (2005, April). *The formation of intergroup attitudes in young children.* Poster presented at the biennial meeting of the Society for Research in Child Development, Atlanta, GA.

Patterson, M. M., & Bigler, R. S. (2006). Preschool children's attention to environmental messages about groups: Social categorization and the origins of intergroup bias. *Child Development, 77*, 847–860.

Piaget, J. (1970). Piaget's theory. In P. H. Mussen (Ed.), *Carmichael's manual of child psychology* (pp. 703–732). New York: Wiley.

Pollock, M. (2004). *Colormute: Race dilemmas in an American school.* Princeton, NJ: Princeton University Press.

Quintana, S. M. (1994). A model of ethnic perspective-taking ability applied to Mexican-American children and youth. *International Journal of Intercultural Relations, 18*, 419–448.

Quintana, S. M. (2008). Racial perspective taking ability: Developmental, theoretical, and empirical trends. In S. M. Quintana & C. McKown (Eds.), *Handbook of race, racism, and the developing child* (pp. 16–36). Hoboken, NJ: Wiley.

Quintana, S. M., & McKown, C. (2008). *Handbook of race, racism, and the developing child.* Hoboken, NJ: Wiley.

Quintana, S. M., & Vera, E. M. (1999). Mexican American children's ethnic identity, understanding of ethnic prejudice, and parental ethnic socialization. *Hispanic Journal of Behavioral Sciences, 21*, 387–404.

Rutland, A., Cameron, L., Milne, A., & McGeorge, P. (2005). Social norms and self-presentation: Children's implicit and explicit intergroup attitudes. *Child Development, 76*, 451–466.

Skinner, B. F. (1969). *Contingencies of reinforcement: A theoretical analysis.* New York: Appleton-Century-Crofts.

Spelke, E. Z., & Kinzler, K. D. (2007). Core knowledge. *Developmental Science, 10*, 89–96.

Tajfel, H. (1982). Social psychology of intergroup relations. *Annual Review of Psychology, 33*, 1–39.

Tajfel, H., Billig, M. G., Bundy, R. P., & Flament, C. (1971). Social categorization and intergroup behaviour. *European Journal of Social Psychology, 1*, 149–178.

Tajfel, H., & Turner, J. C. (1986). The social identity theory of intergroup behaviour. In S. Worchel & W. G. Austin (Eds.), *Psychology of intergroup relations* (2nd ed., pp. 7–24). Chicago: Nelson-Hall.

Turner, J. C. (1987). *Rediscovering the social group: A self-categorization theory.* Oxford, UK: Blackwell.

Wittenbrink, B. J., Judd, C. M., & Park, B. (1997). Evidence for racial prejudice at the implicit level and its relationship with questionnaire measures. *Journal of Personality and Social Psychology, 72*, 262–274.

Yee, M. D., & Brown, R. (1992). Self-evaluations and intergroup attitudes in children aged three to nine. *Child Development, 63*, 619–629.

14

Modifying children's racial attitudes

Frances E. Aboud
McGill University, Canada

Systematic attempts to modify children's racial attitudes have aroused interest among parents, teachers, the media, and society at large. At one time, most people assumed that children were not prejudiced, but rather were curious about people from different ethnic and racial groups. However, children are sometimes prejudiced if we define it as "holding derogatory social attitudes . . . towards members of a group on account of their membership of that group" (R. Brown, 1995, p. 8) as expressed through emotions and evaluations. Although their prejudice is rarely strongly negative or hateful, attitudes toward other racial groups are frequently less positive and more negative than attitudes toward their own group. It is this bias in racial attitudes (i.e. more positive to own and more negative to other) that serves to isolate children in an increasingly diverse world.

In recent years, our understanding that children hold negative attitudes toward others has been complemented by evidence on the developmental course of bias. Initially it was assumed that children gradually learn attitudes from parents. Consequently, racial attitudes were expected to become more negative with age. However, many studies identified 4 to 7 years of age as the time when children showed the greatest bias – they held exaggerated positive attitudes toward their ingroup and negative or less positive attitudes toward others. While children are capable of learning attitudes from parents, particularly from parents who overtly express their prejudice, the attitudes of children in North America frequently do not match those of their parents (Aboud & Doyle, 1996; Ritchey & Fishbein, 2001). In fact, tolerant parents are sometime shocked to discover how prejudiced their children are. A parallel finding in the sex role literature showed that children frequently hold highly biased sex role stereotypes in the absence of parental support. Thus, modifying children's attitudes by indirectly targeting parents was not sufficient.

Understanding how children acquire prejudice in the first place would help us design programs to prevent prejudice in young children but not necessarily help us modify existing attitudes. Very few preventive programs exist for 3-year-olds, and fewer still have been evaluated. Preventive programs are to be used with children who are not already biased. Typically they introduce children to the positive qualities of diverse racial groups and to multiculturalism, in the hopes of instilling respect and tolerance (e.g. National Association for the Education of Young Children website; Robertson, 1999; Teaching Tolerance website and magazine).

Unfortunately, many White (or majority) children are already biased by 5 years of age. Consequently, these programs are well intentioned but inadequate, as this review will show.

Modifying attitudes among children, particularly White children, who are already biased poses a greater challenge. Interventions to modify children's attitudes must have a dual objective, namely to overcome their currently held bias and to add more positive attitudes. The currently held bias presents an obstacle because it blocks contradictory information about people who disconfirm the bias. Bigler and Liben (1993) demonstrated this clearly in a study where children were unable to recall information about people who did not fit the stereotype; sometimes information was even distorted to fit the stereotype. If counter-bias information cannot be retained mentally, then it has no chance to create and become incorporated into a new, positive attitude. Children over 7 years of age possess greater mental flexibility and are more likely to process and retain counter-bias information. Consequently it is now recognized that the child's age and corresponding mental capabilities must be considered when designing an intervention to modify attitudes.

Overcoming the cognitive barriers of children under 7 years who are already biased presents an unsolved dilemma. Children of this age who lack the ability to differentiate, as evidenced by their non-conservation, egocentrism, and dichotomous categorization, find it difficult to process simultaneously positive and negative attributes of the same person. Consequently, they are unable to adopt positive attitudes toward persons or groups who are initially seen as negative. Promising solutions might be to modify the underlying cognitive barrier itself at least temporarily while new attitude information is introduced (e.g. Rogers, 1990), or to provide real, vicarious, or virtual friends and only later make their group affiliation salient (to be described later).

In addition to a cognitive barrier to attitude change, young children also have a normative barrier. The normative barrier refers to their belief that there is general consensus about prejudice (Augoustinos & Rosewarne, 2001). Egocentrically assuming that most people are prejudiced leads young children to dismiss the tolerant attitudes of a parent or teacher. While older children possess fewer cognitive constraints and fewer normative barriers, they still might want to conform to the norms of their agemates. Older children are also more influenced by their peers than younger ones. Consequently, in addition to considering age as a factor in attitude modification, we must also consider the socializer of the intervention, namely who delivers the message. Whether the socializer is an adult or a peer from the ingroup or an outgroup may matter (Mackie & Wright, 2001).

Modifying children's attitudes thus requires attention to the child (e.g. race/ethnicity, age, mental capability), to the socializer who delivers the attitude-changing intervention, and to the message itself. The message varies according to the intervention. We have chosen to discuss three, although others can be found in previous reviews (e.g. Aboud & Levy, 2000; Pfeifer, Brown, & Juvonen, 2007; Stephan & Stephan, 2001). (a) Multicultural education is often in the form of information about the lives, culture, and history of different racial groups. Here we have selected media interventions that deliver information via books, television, or instructional material. (b) Integrated schooling provides opportunities to interact with peers from your own and other racial groups. The message is the individual and racial attributes of students and teachers from these groups and the social relationships that emerge from contact. (c) Behavior-change interventions provide the models and social support to counter everyday forms of prejudice, such as name-calling. The studies selected here for review and evaluation typically use field settings to implement programs designed for homes and schools. They go beyond the one-off laboratory experiment, but yet spotlight the actual attitudinal outcomes of programs. By identifying the conditions for an effective intervention, we may eventually develop a blueprint for the means to modify children's racial attitudes.

Along with the social conditions constructed by the intervention are psychosocial mediators that make it work. Mediators help explain why and how a social condition translates into attitude change. To identify mediators, we have used past research on cognitive, emotional, and behavioral processes that reduce prejudice. These include, but are not limited to, five experiences or information that (a) personalize members of other groups without masking their group membership (Aboud & Fenwick, 1999; Katz & Zalk, 1978), (b) strengthen perceptions of between-group similarity by creating additive or inclusive identities (Aboud & Sankar, 2007; Houlette et al., 2004); (c) reduce anxiety and distrust (Corenblum & Stephan, 2001), (d) increase empathy and intimacy (Finlay & Stephan, 2000; Vescio, Sechrist, & Paolucci, 2003), and (e) alter social cognitive or behavioral skills (Bigler, 1995).

The chapter builds on the framework presented by Bigler and Liben (2006) which integrates environmental conditions and developmental capabilities to explain both the formation and the modification of prejudice. Because children's early cognitive constraints lead them to seek environments that fit their mindset or to distort environments that do not, attempts to modify attitudes must create environmental inputs that will not be distorted or will remove or bypass the cognitive constraints. Here we address environmental inputs such as the socializer and the message, and cognitive skills such as perspective taking, empathy, and multiple classification. The recent programs to be described here add to the impressive list compiled by Pfeifer, Brown, and Juvonen (2007).

Multicultural media interventions

Many educational interventions use media such as television or print to communicate information and attitudes. This strategy is particularly useful when there are no opportunities for direct contact with a diverse group of children. Sometimes the communication is soft-sell in that realistic information about racial groups is expected to reduce ignorance and provide detailed exposure. Less often the communicator aims to persuade the audience to adopt a new attitude or behavior. The soft-sell approach, evaluated in a number of New Hampshire preschools, produced preschoolers who could identify more similarities and differences between pairs of diverse children, but who held no more unbiased attitudes than preschoolers without such a program (Perkins & Mebert, 2005). Schools that use their own homemade programs are often unsuccessful because they are not constructed on what we know about the mediators of attitude change and the developmental constraints of children. Our strategy here is to describe how specified book and television programs were used more or less successfully to change children's attitudes.

A number of studies have examined the effectiveness of reading storybooks to young children (Wham, Barnhart, & Cook, 1996) or showing diversity-loaded television shows with an anti-prejudice message to young children (Persson & Musher-Eizenman, 2003). Despite the number of exposures, children did not change their attitudes. We might expect that the stories would convey positive and variable attributes of the group members, thus helping to personalize children's possibly uninformed or stereotyped view. The stories might furthermore reduce perceived differences if the listening children heard about play activities were similar to their own favorites, while enhancing positive emotions toward the protagonists. None of these mediators were measured, but in any case the outcome indicated a lack of effectiveness. One reason is that young children have a number of cognitive and normative barriers to accepting an anti-bias message and integrating it into their repertoires of attitudes. The intended anti-bias message might have been distorted or, worse still, gone unnoticed and been replaced by a perceived unintended message that all adults are prejudiced. Consequently, after such exposure, children need extensive discussions led by an adult to overcome these barriers.

A more recent intervention modified existing storybooks in several theoretically directed ways and engaged primary school students actively during the shared group reading (Cameron, Rutland, Brown, & Douch, 2006). Stories featured the friendship of an ingroup child with an outgroup child, thus creating a vicarious situation of indirect contact. It was indirect in that the reader identified with the ingroup story character and thereby experienced indirectly his/her friendship with the outgroup character. When direct contact is not feasible, indirect contact has been shown experimentally to be associated with lower prejudice (Wright, Aron, McLaughlin-Volpe, & Ropp, 1997). In addition, students heard repeatedly about the common group membership of the two friends, namely their school, as well as their separate group memberships, in this case English and refugee. It was expected that this would enhance between-group similarities as well as differences. Reminding children about the two distinct social categories is considered necessary for the positive friend relationship to generalize to other refugees, in this case. Three storybooks were read over six weekly sessions, with the post-test conducted two weeks after.

Attitudes here were measured in terms of both positive and negative evaluations. The main finding was that those who heard the stories were more positive to outgroup members than those who did not hear the stories. They were more positive even than students who heard the stories without group membership reminders, emphasizing only the individual attributes of the protagonists. Outgroup attitudes were most positive among those who also said they felt close to outgroup members. Closeness could be said to represent perceived similarity. So students who heard and read the stories about the two friends felt closer to refugees and this accounted for their more positive attitudes. The children were between 5 and 11 years of age, but the story reading affected them all equally. Although students had high levels of ingroup identification, the story intervention had stronger effects on students at the lower end of the range.

Why did this intervention work when previous ones have not? One reason is that the socializer in this case was not only the adult who came with the books and read the stories, but also the students in the reading group, who spontaneously reacted positively or negatively to the story as it was read. In other words there were several age-appropriate socializers: younger students might have been more influenced by the adult while older students could have been more attentive to their peers' reactions. Contact with an outgroup refugee was indirect rather than direct because it was vicariously experienced by identifying with an ingroup child who had exciting experiences with an outgroup friend. All the potential benefits of indirect contact, such as reduced anxiety, personalized information, and between-group perceived similarity, were available to the students. Furthermore, the major obstacle of contact, namely generalizing to outgroup members beyond the friend, was explicitly overcome by repeating the outgroup label, in this case "refugee." There were several limitations of this study, but it does provide encouragement and a strong evaluation design for future research on the use of media to modify racial attitudes.

Another strategy is more direct in its attempt to address prejudice by talking openly about and strengthening the cognitive underpinnings of prejudice. Our study on the effectiveness of fifth-grade instructional materials, "More than Meets the Eye," showed that high-prejudice children became less so after the program, compared to controls (Aboud & Fenwick, 1999). The program provided opportunities for the children in large and small groups to discuss why members of different ethnic groups are more similar than they look and why people do not often fit the stereotype. Not only were students told about differences of others but they had to learn the personal qualities of a parallel class of students from several racial groups. The 11-week program provided motivating activities for them to practice the skills for processing individual differences, multiple classification, and reconciliation. Subsequently, Clark (2004) created an interactive DVD called "All That We Are" to help children develop these skills with computer activities that they perform individually.

This section on media points to features of programs that succeed in modifying attitudes and ones that are unsuccessful. Successful ones go beyond the simple pedagogical truth that active, multimedia routes to learning about different racial groups are useful. They are largely insufficient for children above 5 years who are already biased. Rather the cognitive and social underpinnings of prejudice must be directly addressed.

Racially integrated schooling: Contact and cooperative learning

A great deal has been written about integrated schooling and the common finding that simply putting students together in the same school does not reduce prejudice (Stephan & Stephan, 2001). Intergroup contact, at the sociological level, works more powerfully when the contact meets Allport's (1954/1979) criteria, namely equal status, common goals, cooperation, authority support, and opportunities for friendship (Pettigrew & Tropp, 2006). In other words, the contact is close and personalized, namely when students become friends (Kenworthy, Turner, Hewstone, & Voci, 2005). Friendship is considered the gold standard of contact because it provides the context for necessary emotional, cognitive, and behavioral changes. This includes: intimacy, empathy, and anxiety reduction on the emotional side; personalized individual difference information about the friend and a perception of between-group similarities on the cognitive side; and behavioral skills in cooperation and conflict reduction. The experience in youth makes it more likely that one will have cross-race friends in subsequent years (Patchen, 1982). Positive attitudes and similarities tend to increase with the duration of a friendship. Furthermore, if the friend's ethnicity or race is made salient by visits to their home and family and by contacts with ingroup friends of the friend, then positive attitudes are more likely to generalize to other members of that group. Without the salience of ethnicity or race, the contact is unlikely to generalize (Cameron et al., 2006; Kenworthy et al., 2005).

Cooperative learning is the most popular form of classroom contact that incorporates Allport's criteria. Slavin (e.g. Slavin, Hurley, & Chamberlain, 2003) has done most work on this program, showing that it changes students' behaviors such as helping and liking, while maintaining school achievement. It does not necessarily change attitudes toward the outgroup as a whole (Weigel, Wiser, & Cook, 1975), especially when the contact is not equal status (Cohen & Lotan, 1995) and does not turn into friendship. The cooperative learning procedure is now being used in many countries, including Israel (Shachar & Shmuelevitz, 1997).

Friendship may be an important mediator for cooperative learning to yield positive racial attitudes. White children at an integrated elementary school in Montreal had more positive attitudes if they hung around with more outgroup classmates and if they had a high-quality outgroup friend, including qualities of loyalty, companionship, and intimacy (Aboud, Mendelson, & Purdy, 2003). Furthermore, in a series of descriptive studies, Turner, Hewstone, and Voci (2007) found that British students had more positive explicit as well as implicit attitudes if they had South Asian friends with whom they were intimate (self-disclosing) and when their anxiety about contact was low. It also helped if they had friends and family who also had South Asian friends. Because having direct friends and having indirect contact were highly correlated, it would seem that the indirect contact (friends of friends) may have added to the direct friendship by providing validating and normative information, i.e. that it is good and common to have such friends. Because simply providing opportunities for contact is not sufficient for generating friendships, schools need to arrange for curricular or extra-curricular activities to bring students of like mind together – activities such as dyadic class assignments and after-school playgroups.

The need for schools to provide many cooperative opportunities for friendship was apparent in our studies of integrated bilingual education. Some schools in Montreal and in California bring together students from two language groups (French and English or Spanish and English) and instruct them at least part time using the two languages. Instruction in the outgroup's language can potentially provide the communication and cultural skills that reduce anxiety about contact; it may also raise the status of the language and the group that speaks that language. Wright and Tropp (2005) found some positive influences of these programs on students' perceived similarity and attitudes (see also Tropp & Prenovost, 2007). However, we looked more closely at many forms of contact, including hanging around with others, indirect contact, and close friendship, and we examined several programs around Montreal. Some schools simply housed French- and English-speaking students in the same building and provided instruction in the other's language, without any arranged intergroup activities. Although the students took recess and lunch at the same time and location, there were very few cross-ethnic indirect contacts or friends. Only children who played and worked together in the after-school program managed to develop close friends. Other schools fully integrated students in the same classroom and instructed them in one language for half the week and in the other language for the other half. These children had considerably more cross-ethnic friends, and the friendships were of high quality (Aboud & Sankar, 2007).

Not all schools have the opportunity to integrate children from different ethnic and racial groups with equal status. However, those that do show strong benefits in terms of attitudes and friendships. Why does this form of contact work? According to Kenworthy et al. (2005) and the research, cross-race friendships confer emotional (anxiety, empathy), cognitive (identification, perceived similarity), and behavioral (cooperation, conflict reduction) benefits that translate into lasting attitudes. Indirect contact has similar benefits but for different reasons; knowing that your friends have cross-race friends creates a different norm about the acceptability of having such friends (Castelli, De Amicis, & Sherman, 2007; Turner, Hewstone, Voci, Paolini, & Christ, 2007). Despite the benefits of cross-race friendships, their actual frequency is much lower than expected. Students who come together from neighborhoods where there is little mixing will not inevitably develop cross-race friends and positive attitudes. Moreover, although attitudes do tend to become more tolerant with age, friendships in many settings decline as children enter puberty. Reasons for the decline are not clear, though it could be related to identity or dating concerns. Consequently, schools need to make a concerted effort to provide opportunities for friendship.

Behavior-change strategies to counter prejudice

Biased and discriminatory behavior occurs in the schoolyard and sometimes in the classroom. This often takes the form of name-calling and other types of bullying. Nasty name-calling is the most common form of bullying (e.g. Aboud & Joong, 2007; C. Brown & Bigler, 2005), experienced in particular by ethnic and racial minority children but also by majority children (Verkuyten, 2002). Regardless of the name used, intergroup name-calling is perceived as a form of racial discrimination. The name-caller may not be more prejudiced than others in the schoolyard, but recognizes that singling out someone for abuse will have the desired effect of dominating and controlling. Such aggressive children are often perceived to be popular even though they are not actually popular or liked by many (Cillessen & Mayeux, 2004). Because most children witness intergroup bullying, but rarely observe anyone intervening to stop it, they come to accept and tolerate it. This results in a high level of acceptance of public discrimination from the early grades through high school (Wessler & De Andrade, 2006).

Derman-Sparks and Phillips (1997) advocate teaching students the skills to counter racial prejudice within their sphere of influence such as the schoolyard. Slaby (1999) reported his evaluation of a school program to encourage witnesses of prejudice to intervene when they witnessed intergroup bullying. He succeeded in increasing students' self-efficacy, but there was no attempt to teach or assess specific skills. Acquiring and using verbal skills to address name-callers is important, as it is known that, despite their good intentions to stop name-calling, students do not act on these. Their dilemma is not bystander apathy but rather an approach-avoidance conflict that pits anger at the bully against fear of retaliation and distress at being ineffectual. Bystanders might be more likely to intervene if they were encouraged to consider effectiveness in terms of expressing their anti-bias sentiment. At the same time, they would counter the schoolyard norm of tolerating public displays of discrimination.

Simulations and exposure to simulations of discrimination may provide a context for raising empathy and observing peer models who take a public stand against discriminatory acts in the schoolyard. One televised program, called *La Leçon de Discrimination* (Société Radio–Canada, 2006), involved third-grade students who had discussed discrimination and then experienced it for two days, once as the lower-status group and once as the higher-status group. Despite the warning, students acted in a discriminatory manner toward their fellow classmates. A follow-up meeting with the students allowed children to express their emotions and understand how the anxiety arising from their lower status made their classroom performance worse than usual. The program, lasting 30 minutes, does not directly teach skills but it allows students to identify prejudice and the emotions it arouses in them. Students discuss social norms that allow prejudice to continue unchecked, and develop intentions to stop it with the social support of their peers.

Research on training anti-bias behavior is relatively new. Two programs of research exist. One, by Aboud (Aboud & Joong, 2007; Aboud & Miller, 2007), examined modeling and practice in the context of inter-racial name-calling; the second, by Bigler (Lamb, Bigler, Liben, & Green, under review), compared modeling against practice in a school program to reduce sexist remarks. The paradigm used by Aboud examined how age and intergroup context influenced the students' anti-bias response to a name-caller. Individual children heard an audiotape scenario of a typical name-calling episode along with a peer or adult model's low- and high-confrontational responses to the bully. Some also heard a psychological and moral rationale for not calling names. It was assumed that, when children had the opportunity to respond, they would co-construct a verbal retort that fit their personal and developmental proclivity.

Children might prefer to intervene to stop bias with a low or high level of confrontation according to their age. Levels of confrontation were derived from theoretical and empirical research on socializing transgressors (e.g. Grusec & Goodnow, 1994; Hawkins, Pepler, & Craig, 2001): low confrontation levels consist of questioning or disagreeing with the bully ("Why are you calling her that? She's not that way"), whereas higher levels state the behavioral rule and value (e.g. "Stop calling names; it's mean and rude"). In our research, peer and adult models used both low and high levels of confrontation in their anti-bias retorts to name-callers. Our findings reveal the levels students choose to use. Intergroup in contrast to intragroup name-calling was more likely to provoke the use of a higher level of confrontation along with a moral rationale for stopping. Younger students chose to use higher levels of confrontation and a psychological rationale, whereas older elementary students preferred lower levels of confrontation and a moral rationale. Younger students were more influenced to intervene by an adult model, whereas older ones were more influenced by a peer model. The latter were also influenced by descriptive and prescriptive peer norms, manipulated by listening to a tape of a fictitious focus group discussion. Because students rarely used the exact words of the model, their co-constructions revealed the words they considered appropriate for the context and felt comfortable using. Students' self-efficacy for intervening was high, unrealistically so given the actual number who chose to intervene. Finally, older children felt less efficacious in stopping the bully than younger students, but both felt strongly that their intervention expressed their feelings and supported the victim.

The Bigler anti-bias program taught students specific phrases to use in the face of sexist remarks (Lamb et al., under review). Six 20-minute classroom lessons in kindergarten through grade 3 provided children with the opportunity to create skits that used these phrases (e.g. "You can't say that boys [girls] can't play!"). While these children practiced the phrases, a parallel class of students heard stories in which the phrases were modeled in response to a sexist incident. At a 6-month post-test, children in the practice program were more likely than those in the story model condition to challenge a confederate peer's sexist remark with a verbal response and showed less bias on a test of sex typing. Therefore, the opportunity to practice responding to racist and sexist bullying is essential. Practicing in a group context not only teaches the verbal skill but also establishes a new group norm for countering intergroup discrimination, so students realize they are supported by their peers when responding to bullies, whether they are the victim or the bystander. It may be reasonable to teach specific phrases to younger students, but older elementary students are more likely to take their cue from peer models and to co-construct phrases that suit them and the protagonists. For good reasons, both of these programs teach anti-bias responses to a bully rather than to the victim. When students are seen to intervene in the schoolyard, it is most likely to the bully, possibly because victims are generally not well liked (thus selected as victims).

Conclusion

In conclusion, a number of interventions have been demonstrated to work in reducing prejudice, especially in White children who have the highest levels. Multicultural media interventions using books or television may work only if they incorporate some post-exposure discussion. They must also include specific features that address cognitive and social underpinnings of prejudice relating to friendship, identity, and norms. Likewise, contact works better if it entails some form of friendship, namely a direct high-quality friendship or an indirect connection through a friend. Once again, these forms of friendship work because they reduce intergroup anxiety, increase intimacy and trust, expand one's identification, and inform about norms of acceptance. Finally, students themselves may help to modify their colleagues' attitudes by countering prejudice whenever it is witnessed in the schoolyard. Verbal and social bullies are not necessarily the most prejudiced students on the schoolyard, but their public displays of prejudice lead to a passive acceptance that influences everyone. The most promising strategies must provide good models, a well-publicized social norm, and rehearsal for bystanding students, who otherwise do not act. All of these interventions emphasize the need to do more than talk to children. Thoughtful programs incorporate evidence-based messages, from a trustworthy socializer, with attention to the cognitive and normative barriers that make children resistant to change.

References

Aboud, F. E., & Doyle, A. B. (1996). Parental and peer influences on children's racial attitudes. *International Journal of Intercultural Relations, 20,* 371–383.

Aboud, F. E., & Fenwick, V. (1999). Exploring and evaluating school-based interventions to reduce prejudice in preadolescents. *Journal of Social Issues, 55,* 767–785.

Aboud, F. E., & Joong, A. (2007). Intergroup name-calling and conditions for creating assertive bystanders. In S. R. Levy & M. Killen (Eds.), *Intergroup attitudes and relations in childhood through adulthood* (pp. 249–260). Oxford, UK: Oxford University Press.

Aboud, F. E., & Levy, S. R. (2000). Interventions to reduce prejudice and discrimination in children and adolescents. In S. Oskamp (Ed.), *Reducing prejudice and discrimination* (pp. 269–293). Mahwah, NJ: Erlbaum.

Aboud, F. E., Mendelson, M. J., & Purdy, K. T. (2003). Cross-race peer relations and friendship quality. *International Journal of Behavioral Development, 27,* 165–173.

Aboud, F. E., & Miller, L. (2007). Promoting peer intervention in name-calling. *South African Journal of Psychology, 37,* 803–819.

Aboud, F. E., & Sankar, J. (2007). Friendship and identity in a language-integrated school. *International Journal of Behavioral Development, 31,* 445–453.

Allport, G. W. (1979). *The nature of prejudice.* Cambridge, MA: Perseus Books. (Original work published 1954).

Augoustinos, M., & Rosewarne, D. L. (2001). Stereotype knowledge and prejudice in children. *British Journal of Developmental Psychology, 19,* 143–156.

Bigler, R.S. (1995). The role of classification skill in moderating environmental influences on children's gender stereotyping: A study of the functional use of gender in the classroom. *Child Development, 66,* 1072–1087.

Bigler, R. S., & Liben, L. S. (1993). A cognitive-developmental approach to racial stereotyping and reconstructive memory in Euro-American children. *Child Development, 64,* 1507–1518.

Bigler, R. S., & Liben, L. S. (2006). A developmental intergroup theory of social stereotypes and prejudice. In R. V. Kail (Ed.), *Advances in child development and behavior* (Vol. 34, pp. 39–89). San Diego, CA: Elsevier.

Brown, C. S., & Bigler, R. S. (2005). Children's perceptions of discrimination: A developmental model. *Child Development, 76,* 533–553.

Brown, R. (1995). *Prejudice: Its social psychology.* Cambridge, MA: Blackwell.

Cameron, L., Rutland, A., Brown, R., & Douch, R. (2006). Changing children's intergroup attitudes toward refugees: Testing different models of extended contact. *Child Development, 77,* 1208–1219.

Castelli, L., De Amicis, L., & Sherman, J. (2007). The loyal member effect: On the preference for ingroup members who engage in exclusive relations with the ingroup. *Developmental Psychology, 43,* 1347–1359.

Cillessen, A. H. N., & Mayeux, L. (2004). From censure to reinforcement: Developmental changes in the association between aggression and social status. *Child Development, 75,* 147–163.

Clark, K. (2004). *All that we are: Interactive program to reduce racial bias* [CD-ROM]. Eugene, OR: University of Oregon, Oregon Center for Applied Science.

Cohen, E. G., & Lotan, R. A. (1995). Producing equal-status interaction in the heterogeneous classroom. *American Educational Research Journal, 32,* 99–120.

Corenblum, B., & Stephan, W. G. (2001). White fears and Native apprehensions: An integrated threat theory approach to intergroup attitudes. *Canadian Journal of Behavioural Science, 33,* 251–268.

Derman-Sparks, L., & Phillips, C. B. (1997). *Teaching/learning anti-racism: A developmental approach.* New York: Columbia University, Teachers College.

Finlay, K. A., & Stephan, W. G. (2000). Improving intergroup relations: The effects of empathy on racial attitudes. *Journal of Applied Social Psychology, 30,* 1720–1737.

Grusec, J. E., & Goodnow, J. J. (1994). Impact of parental discipline methods on the child's internalization of values: A reconceptualization of current points of view. *Developmental Psychology, 30,* 4–19.

Hawkins, D. L., Pepler, D. J., & Craig, W. M. (2001). Naturalistic observations of peer interventions in bullying. *Social Development, 10,* 512–527.

Houlette, M., Gaertner, S. L., Johnson, K. M., Banker, B. S., Riek, B. M., & Dovidio, J. F. (2004). Developing a more inclusive social identity: An elementary school intervention. *Journal of Social Issues, 60*, 35–55.

Katz, P. A., & Zalk, S. R. (1978). Modification of children's racial attitudes. *Developmental Psychology, 14*, 447–461.

Kenworthy, J. B., Turner, R. N., Hewstone, M., & Voci, A. (2005). Intergroup contact: When does it work and why? In J. F. Dovidio, P. Glick, & L. Rudman (Eds.), *On the nature of prejudice: Fifty years after Allport* (pp. 278–292). Malden, MA: Blackwell.

Lamb, L. M., Bigler, R. S., Liben, L. S., & Green, V. A. (under review). When children bully peers for sex "inappropriate" behavior: Theoretical and practical implications of anti-bullying interventions.

Mackie, D. M., & Wright, C. L. (2001). Social influence in an intergroup context. In R. Brown & S. L. Gaertner (Eds.), *Blackwell handbook of social psychology: Intergroup processes* (pp. 281–300). Malden, MA: Blackwell.

National Association for the Education of Young Children website. http://www.naeyc.org/

Patchen, M. (1982). *Black–White contact in schools: Its social and academic effects.* West Lafayette, IN: Purdue University Press.

Perkins, D. M., & Mebert, C. J. (2005). Efficacy of multicultural education for preschool children: A domain-specific approach. *Journal of Cross-Cultural Psychology, 36*, 497–512.

Persson, A., & Musher-Eizenman, D. R. (2003). The impact of a prejudice prevention television program on young children's racial attitudes and knowledge. *Early Childhood Research Quarterly, 18*, 530–546.

Pettigrew, T. F., & Tropp, L. R. (2006). A meta-analytic test of intergroup contact theory. *Journal of Personality and Social Psychology, 90*, 751–783.

Pfeifer, J. H., Brown, C. S., & Juvonen, J. (2007). Teaching tolerance in schools: Lessons learned since *Brown vs. Board of Education* about development and reduction of children's prejudice. *Social policy report: Giving child and youth development knowledge away, 21*(2), 3–23.

Ritchey, P. N., & Fishbein, H. D. (2001). The lack of an association between adolescent friends' prejudices and stereotypes. *Merrill-Palmer Quarterly, 47*, 188–206.

Robertson, J. P. (1999). *Teaching for a tolerant world, grades K–6.* Urbana, IL: National Council of Teachers of English.

Rogers, V. (1990). *All the colours of the rainbow.* Vancouver: Pacific Educational Press.

Shachar, H. & Shmuelevitz, H. (1997). Implementing cooperative learning, teacher collaboration and teachers' sense of efficacy in heterogeneous junior high school. *Contemporary Educational Psychology, 22*, 53–72.

Slaby, R. G. (1999). *Above prejudice and beyond tolerance: A bystander approach to reducing prejudice and improving intergroup relations.* Final report to Carnegie Foundation, Newton, MA.

Slavin, R. E., Hurley, E. A., & Chamberlain, A. (2003). Cooperative learning and achievement: Theory and research. In W. M. Reynolds & G. E. Miller (Eds.), *Handbook of psychology: Educational psychology* (Vol. 7, pp. 177–198). Hoboken, NJ: Wiley.

Société Radio-Canada (2006). *La leçon de discrimination* [A lesson in discrimination] [DVD and Petit Guide Pédagogique]. Montreal: Radio-Canada.

Stephan, W. G., & Stephan, C. W. (2001). *Improving intergroup relations.* Thousand Oaks, CA: Sage.

Teaching Tolerance website. http://www.tolerance.org/teach

Teaching Tolerance magazine. Montgomery, AL: Southern Poverty Law Center. http://www.tolerance.org/teach/magazine/index.jsp

Tropp, L. R., & Prenovost, M. A. (2007). The role of intergroup contact in predicting children's interethnic attitudes: Evidence from meta-analytic and field studies. In S. R. Levy & M. Killen (Eds.), *Intergroup attitudes and relations in childhood through adulthood* (pp. 236–248). Oxford, UK: Oxford University Press.

Turner, R. N., Hewstone, M., & Voci, A. (2007). Reducing explicit and implicit outgroup prejudice via direct and extended contact: The mediating role of self-disclosure and intergroup anxiety. *Journal of Personality and Social Psychology, 93*, 369–388.

Turner, R. N., Hewstone, M., Voci, A., Paolini, S., & Christ, O. (2007). Reducing prejudice via direct and extended cross-group friendship. *European Review of Social Psychology, 18*, 212–255.

Verkuyten, M. (2002). Perceptions of ethnic discrimination by minority and majority early adolescents in the Netherlands. *International Journal of Psychology, 37*, 321–332.

Vescio, T. K., Sechrist, B., & Paolucci, M. P. (2003). Perspective taking and prejudice reduction: The mediational role of empathy arousal and situational attributions. *European Journal of Social Psychology, 33*, 455–472.

Weigel, R. H., Wiser, P. L., & Cook, S. W. (1975). The impact of cooperative learning experiences on cross-ethnic relations and attitudes. *Journal of Social Issues, 31*, 219–244.

Wessler, S. L., & De Andrade, L. L. (2006). Slurs, stereotypes, and student interventions: Examining the dynamics, impact, and prevention of harassment in middle and high school. *Journal of Social Issues, 62*, 511–532.

Wham, M. A., Barnhart, J., & Cook, G. (1996). Enhancing multicultural awareness through storybook reading experience. *Journal of Research and Development in Education, 30*, 1–9.

Wright, S. C., Aron, A., McLaughlin-Volpe, T., & Ropp, S. A. (1997). The extended contact effect: Knowledge of cross-group friendships and prejudice. *Journal of Personality and Social Psychology, 73*, 73–90.

Wright, S. C., & Tropp, L. R. (2005). Language and intergroup contact: Investigating the impact of bilingual instruction on children's intergroup attitudes. *Group Processes and Intergroup Relations, 8*, 309–328.

15

Education programs for improving relations between Jews and Palestinians* in Israel

Zvi Bekerman
The Hebrew University of Jerusalem, Israel

I cannot do justice to all the theoretical and empirical studies which are available for review because of the limited space provided for this chapter. The studies chosen follow both from personal and theoretical preferences which will hopefully do justice to what is becoming an important field of research and practice in Israel. The need to limit the review to those activities which are organized for Palestinians and Jews within the internationally recognized borders of the state of Israel slices the field to be covered in a justifiable way. The encounters conducted among Jews and Palestinians in the state of Israel take place between national groups which share the same citizenship and the same social, economic, and educational systems, living generally in peaceful, non-violent relations.

The encounters conducted among Jews and Palestinians in the Palestinian Authority are conducted among members of two separate and relatively autonomous national entities living under conditions of acute conflict. Yet at the same time the delimitation leaves aside many activities and findings which, because of the nature of the conflict and the intricate connections among mainly the Palestinian populations in Israel and in the Palestinian Authority, could contribute to a more complex and richer picture of the educational scene.

I will divide the review into two parts: the first will deal with research findings on short-term intergroup encounters for which most of the existing research has been conducted; and the second will attend to a new and scant but growing research corpus on the integrated Palestinian–Jewish schools in Israel. These schools (only five in 2007) are a new development on the Israeli educational scene, and the findings on them might carry significant relevance for the readers of this volume because they are very similar to traditional school-based multicultural initiatives around the world. The review, thus, should not be seen as a definitive study but instead as a catalyst for further study and dialogue in this important field of research and educational activity.

After a short section in which I offer some insights into the past and present complexities of the Palestinian–Jewish conflict in Israel and the complexities of the status of the Palestinian minority I will (a) describe four main approaches adopted in peace education in Israel, (b) review the main findings of the research in the field of short-term intergroup encounters, (c) describe the new integrated bilingual initiative and review the main findings of the research in this field, and (d) conclude the review, offering some critical insights on the educational activity.

The socio-historical context

The Israeli–Palestinian conflict can be traced to the beginning of Zionist colonialization of Palestine, claimed by Jews as the land of their birthright towards the end of the 19th century. The seemingly intractable conflict resulted out of at least two dominant ideological discourses (one Jewish, one Palestinian) on the control of the land and recognition of group sovereignty. Historically, the region was never autonomously controlled, having a long history of colonial and imperial rule (Khalidi, 1997). The 1948 war, called the War of Independence by the Israelis and the Naqbe (the Catastrophe) by the Palestinians, was the first open military clash between the Zionist and Palestinian nationalist movements. Palestinians in Israel (20%) can be viewed as a distinct national minority (Palestinian), as well as an ethnic (Arab), religious (Muslim, Christian, and Druze), and linguistic (Arabic) group who formed the majority in Palestine (two-thirds of the population) until 1947.

The ongoing violent Israeli occupation of the Gaza Strip and the West Bank since 1967 and the Intifada outbreaks in 1997 and 2000 brought about events which shattered the optimism for a peaceful solution that emerged after the Oslo agreements between the Israeli government and the Palestine Liberation Organization in 1993. It remains to be seen whether the recent disengagement from the Gaza Strip holds any future promises; the 2006 second Lebanese war and the recent takeover by Hammas of the Gaza area of the Palestinian Authority leave little possibility for optimism.

Since its inception and as is clearly stated in its Declaration of Independence made on May 14, 1948, Israel has been committed to full political and social equality for all its citizens irrespective of their religion or ethnic affiliation. Yet even the Israeli government agrees that it has not been fully successful in implementing this ideal and has, for the most part, implemented segregationist policies towards its non-Jewish minorities, policies which only recently are starting to be challenged in the courts of justice (Gavison, 2000). In general the Palestinian Israeli population is geographically segregated and institutionally and legally discriminated against (Al-Haj, 1995; Kretzmer, 1992).

In spite of Israel's declared goals of offering equal opportunity to all its citizens through the educational system, the gap between the Jewish and Palestinian sectors remains significant. For example, in 1991, 45.4% Palestinian and 67.3% Jewish children earned a matriculation diploma, while in 2001 the percentage increased to 59.1% and 69.7%, respectively (Israel Central Bureau of Statistics, 2002).

Not only are the school systems segregated, but so too are the curricula. Israel has no official multicultural educational policies. The Jewish curriculum focuses on national Jewish content and Jewish nation-building, and the Palestinian curriculum is sanitized of any national Palestinian content (Rouhana, 1997). While Jewish students are called to engage in the collective Jewish national enterprise, Palestinian students are called on to accept the definition of Israel as a Jewish democratic state (Al-Haj, 2005). All in all, the Palestinian educational system in Israel lacks the preferential support given by the government to the Jewish educational system, thus creating an enormous gap and leaving the Palestinian educational system behind.

The theoretical foundations and educational models that support intergroup dialogic encounters

In Israel it was only in the mid-1980s that intergroup encounters, designed to overcome distrust and hostility and contribute to coexistence, were initiated (Helman, 2002). The immediate stimulus seems to have been the publication of a survey (Zemach, 1980) disclosing anti-democratic attitudes and feelings among Jewish Israeli youth towards the Palestinian minority. This disclosure fanned fears that Israeli society might reject its democratic character (Katz & Kahanov, 1990; Maoz, 2000b) and brought about the formation of what Rabinowitz (2000) defined as the "coexistence sector," which focused on the development of formal and informal educational dialogue activities, geared towards the recognition of otherness and coexistence (Maoz, 2000c, 2002; Suleiman, 1997). In the 1990s, the efforts towards educational coexistence activity were guided primarily by dedicated non-government organizations (NGOs) strengthened with the Oslo Accords. Their activities focused mainly on questions of the conflictual relations among the national groups and the possibility of coexistence and reconciliation (Bar & Bargal, 1995).

Most of the first efforts towards establishing intergroup dialogues in Israel were grassroots initiatives that were not based on scholarly theoretical approaches. However, most of the intergroup encounters in Israel were apparently organized around two main explanations for the emergence of human conflict. The first was a more psychological perspective which emphasizes internal mental processes, and the second was more societal but still within the psychological realm (Bar & Eady, 1998; Bargal, 1990). Psychoanalytic models build on Freudian conceptions which find aggression imprinted in the human psyche, while more cognitive perspectives refer to processes of categorization and ethnocentrism. Societal models point at socializing processes and social forces and their influences on shaping human conflicts.

These foundational perspectives allow for the organization of intergroup encounters as they have evolved in Israel into a variety of models, the main two being the contact and the psychodynamic models. The first and the most popular draws its inspiration from Allport (1954), the leading figure in the "contact hypothesis" tradition, who supported social change through extensive integration towards the achievement of social stability and harmony. Allport's influential initial articulation has throughout the years evolved into a complex taxonomy of conditions for "good contact" to be possible. The main prescriptions recommended in the contact literature include the following: contact should be regular and frequent; it should involve a balanced ratio of in-group to out-group members while allowing for a genuine "acquaintance potential"; it should occur between individuals who share equality of status, and while being institutionally sanctioned it should be organized around cooperation toward the achievement of superordinate goals. The second model emphasizes the need to deal with problems which touch upon personal psychodynamic processes (Ben-Ari & Amir, 1988), while trying to expand personal experiences and feelings towards alterity (Katz & Kahanov, 1990).

More recently other theoretical perspectives have entered the scene and allowed for the expansion of available working models. One of these chooses to approach the encounter as taking place between two national groups rather than individuals, while assuming that the encounters represent a microcosm of the reality outside (Halabi & Sonnenschein, 2004). This approach treats the group as representing the collective unconscious of its members. It stresses group identities and asymmetric power relations at the expense of diminishing opportunities to create close personal relationships of trust and friendship among participants of the group (Suleiman, 1997). This strategy attempts to achieve the goals of empowering members of the minority group and helping the dominant group develop new insights into its ambivalence and power orientation (Halabi, 2004).

Perhaps the most recent model developed is the one that traces its roots to narrative perspectives (Bruner, 2002; Polkinghorne, 1988), which assumes that one of the main influences on groups in conflict is their perceived histories and memories as tools for building their own collective identities at the expense of delegitimizing the "others" (Bar-Tal & Harel, 2002).

Narrative approaches not only emphasize the collective but also look for an outlet of personal memories and recollections. Narrative approaches assume that the sharing of personal narratives will enhance the participants' ability to develop empathy towards the others and to understand their experience (Bar-On & Kassem, 2004; Salomon, 2004b).

The research and theory reviewed above reveal that one of the central dilemmas that often appear in planned peace- or reconciliation-aimed contacts between members of groups in conflict is the problem of identity and identifications. Thus another way of organizing the existent approaches to intergroup encounters is one which points at the moves or negotiations between two poles of identity and identification: (a) high emphasis on individual identity with low emphasis of national or ethnic group identification; and (b) high emphasis on national or ethnic group identity with low emphasis of individual identity. A few studies have indeed described contact situations as characterized by tension between individual and group identities and as moving between interpersonal and intergroup interactions (Bar-On, 1999; Suleiman, 1997).

Main research findings

As is the case for many other unresolved issues in the social sciences, research results on educational efforts towards coexistence, conflict resolution, and peace education in Israel are not only not definitive but also scant (Nevo & Brem, 2002; Salomon, 2004a; Walter & Paul, 2004).

During the decade of the 1980s substantial research was conducted on a variety of short-term intergroup encounters programs through numerous quantitative and action research methods (Hertz-Lazarowitz, Kupermintz, & Lang, 1998). Most of the findings of this research replicate research conducted in the decade of the 1970s on casual meetings of Palestinians and Jews in Israeli universities (Amir, 1976; Hertz-Lazarowitz, Kupermintz, & Lang). This research indicated that, while the groups involved in the encounter expressed a high level of readiness for social contact, the Palestinian group desire was consistently shown to be higher than the one for the Jewish group.

In the last two decades, since the eruption of the first Intifada, the educational efforts geared towards peace have grown and the Palestinian Jewish conflict has also escalated. Maoz (2000a), in a study which examined intergroup encounters in the post-Oslo era using a mix methods approach, found that youth from both groups come to the encounters with a very limited acquaintance with each other, while holding negative mutual stereotypes. Against the background of these mutual negative emotions the qualitative analysis undertaken shows that the dialogical encounters enable youth to change their initial perceptions of each other. The comparison of the pre-post quantitative measures shows similar results. After participating in the workshops, each group's perceptions of the other became significantly more favorable on a variety of dimensions such as "considerate" and "tolerant," indicating that transformative practices can still be effective in the context of a harsh sociopolitical context.

A more recent study (Bar-Natan, as cited in Salomon, 2004a) partially replicates these findings. Bar-Natan carried out her study with youth participating in a 3-day encounter program. She examined whether interpersonal friendships emerge among Jews and Palestinians during the encounter and generalize to become greater acceptance of members of the other group and to an at least partial legitimization of the other group's collective narrative. The study yielded consistent positive correlations for both the Jewish and the Palestinian groups in the number of intergroup personal friendships developed during the encounter and in pre- to post-changes in their willingness for closer contact with members of the other group. Friendships seem to have also contributed to the legitimization of the Palestinian group narrative for the Jewish group, an effect not found for the Palestinian cohort.

A study by Rosen (2006) examined the possible differential changes in central and more peripheral beliefs as a function of Jewish-Israeli and Palestinian-Israeli youngsters' participation in initiated encounters. In contrast with other studies that have examined the changes in attitudes as a function of participation in such programs, this study dealt with the differentiation between central and peripheral beliefs about the conflict, while also examining the durability of the impact.

The study showed that peace education programs can effectively influence youngsters' peripheral attitudes and beliefs (e.g. stereotypes, prejudices, and negative emotions), while the roadblocks of peace education pertain to the core beliefs that stand in the center of the groups' collective narratives. However, peripheral attitudes and beliefs that are more easily affected by peace education programs changed back as easily by adverse social and political influences, yet they can be rehabilitated by the use of role-play "induced compliance" activities.

Qualitative studies have been slowly developing; although some critical perspectives have evolved within this approach, still some optimism remains. Tracking university students participating in intergroup encounter courses, researchers have uncovered and discussed the dominance of Jewish participants in Jewish–Palestinian dialogues, describing it as linked to the efforts of these participants to focus on the interpersonal level of the dialogue while avoiding confrontation with the Palestinians on issues related to conflict and national identity (Halabi & Sonnenschein, 2004).

Bekerman (2002) has exposed the discursive resources adopted by participants in the dialogue encounters that shape national majority–minority rhetoric in the context of the nation-state, and seem also to guide and shape the encounters' communicational exchange while co-constructing the participants' ethnic or national identities as essentialized. Helman's (2002) interpretative analysis shows how dialogic encounters between groups positioned in contexts of domination and structural inequality reproduce monological discourses of culture and identity, turning them into tools which ultimately legitimize power differentials and structural inequality.

Maoz (2002) illustrates the dynamics of a "good enough" dialogue that fulfills the basic purposes of such an intervention in conflictual contexts, describing the dialogues as a developing drama of intergroup interaction, an experience through which the participants can come to view themselves and others in a different way. In a later study, Maoz, Bar-On, Bekerman, and Jaber-Massarwa (2004) describe what could be called a "bad enough" dialogue that clearly fulfills none of the above purposes, though the conversation still goes on. In that sense, a "totally bad" dialogue would mean that the dialogue disintegrated or could not even be maintained. Together these studies help us understand the dialogical strategies and practices which can support fruitful intergroup encounters.

It is worth mentioning one of the few longitudinal studies conducted on participants in short-term encounters. The study (Litvak-Hirsh & Bar-On, 2007) describes the results of a 4-year longitudinal, qualitative study of a group of Jewish and Palestinian university students who initially took part in a year-long encounter group workshop that was based on a narrative/life story model. The students were interviewed immediately before and after the intergroup encounter and also 3 years later. The study concludes that there appears to be agreement between the Jewish and Arab interviewees with regard to the meaningful contribution of the narrative life story model as a means for personal enrichment, and for the creation of a listening environment and communication on both the interpersonal and the group levels. The interviews make it apparent that there was a change in perception of the "other" by both the Jewish and the Arab participants, which indicates an enhancement of the understanding of the inherent complexity of these issues, particularly as a result of hearing the familial stories in the workshop.

Hammack's (2006) study of a mix group of Israeli Jews and Palestinians and Palestinians from the Palestinian Authority (the only study of its kind reported here for it might point at the possible commonalities among the Palestinian cohorts) presents ambivalent results. On the one hand the participants seem to be able to construct a new narrative, thus transcending their initial dominant polarized identity discourse which serves to reproduce the existing conflict, but on the other identity accentuation was a common outcome for the participating adolescents up to 2 years following participation. The study reveals that the process of identity intervention is not always clearly linear and that it allows for a host of variables to affect the ultimate narrative outcome.

The above review indicates that the initiated encounters efforts are partially effective but that their effects are possibly limited because they are short-term interventions which do not transform the existing social context characterized by asymmetrical relations of power and deep social segregation. The following section describes the case of the integrated bilingual schools which try to overcome some of these problems.

The integrated bilingual schools in Israel

There were five integrated bilingual bicultural schools in Israel in 2007. The schools serve a population of over 1,000 students representing, for the most part, the middle to upper-middle strata of the liberal Jewish and Palestinian population in Israel. The Neveh Shalom elementary school opened its doors in 1984, having as its aim the fostering of egalitarian Palestinian–Jewish cooperation in education, primarily through the development of a bilingual and multicultural curriculum. In 1998 two new schools guided by similar principles were initiated by the Hand in Hand Center, one in Jerusalem and the other in the Upper Galilee. A third school was opened in 2004 in Kfar Karah, the first to be established in a Palestinian village, and in this sense it truly revolutionized basic Israeli perspectives which might be able to accept integrated schools in Jewish majority settlements but have difficulties in considering sending Jewish children to a segregated Palestinian area. A new school opened in Beer-Sheva in the 2007–08 academic year.

The schools are recognized as non-religious schools supported by the Israeli Ministry of Education. They use, for the most part, the standard curriculum of the state non-religious school system, the main difference being that both Hebrew and Arabic are used as languages of instruction. These educational initiatives have to confront what Spolsky and Shohamy (1999) have characterized as being a Type 1 monolingual society: one in which a sole language (in this case Hebrew) is recognized as associated with the national identity while another language (i.e. Arabic), though officially recognized as a second language for education and public use (Koplewitz, 1992; Spolsky, 1994), has been marginalized.

Research on these schools has brought about a welcomed shift in the traditional research paradigms applied. While research in short-term encounter programs has been mostly dominated by psychological interests and perspectives, the research in the integrated bilingual schools, though yet scarce, has brought about the inclusion of educational considerations and perspectives into the research scene. The challenges involved in educating children together while actively trying to sustain their separate group identities, one of the main goals of these schools, have become an important subject that preoccupies researchers in this field.

The first qualitative study was conducted by Feuerverger (2001). The study gathers a significant amount of data, the analysis of which highlights the complexities of bilingual, bicultural, and binational education in its attempt to respect differences, sustain dialogue, and inspire a moral vision in the framework of an ever changing political reality, a reality which constantly confronts and problematizes the participants' efforts to reshape the boundaries that divide their existence. The school is approached as an example of a moral community evolving within extremely conflictual conditions. In particular, it focuses on the community's growing awareness of the powers of language (bilingualism) and the need to narrow the gap between linguistic practices and educational discourse so as to alleviate binational tensions inherent in the context within which the educational initiative develops.

The study also describes how current political events at the time, such as the 1991 Persian Gulf war, invade the school arena, introducing a multiplicity of moral issues which teachers need to be aware of and confront, not only in order to elucidate the way these events should shape the curriculum but, first and foremost, to clarify how they themselves are shaped by the events. According to the study, the school has opened a space for reshaping pedagogical processes and has made it possible for the participants at the school to become "border crossers" and thus challenge the limitations created by hegemonic domination. These processes are supported by the creation of new pedagogical relationships among teachers and students and textual materials characterized by an emancipatory discourse of cultural and linguistic equality.

Gavison (2000) conducted research on the Neve Shalom/Wahat-al-Salam School (NS/WAS) as a part of her broader investigation into the question of whether equality requires integration. The Neve Shalom/Wahat al-Salam School was the first integrated school to open in Israel, in 1984, 3 years after the first integrated Catholic–Protestant school opened in Northern Ireland in 1981. Considering the number of different kinds of schools that exist in the Israeli educational system serving different ideologies and different sectors of the population, Gavison is concerned about the state's ability to educate its citizens towards a common civil identity. She examines the NS/WAS School's approach towards Jewish and Palestinian historical narratives in order to see if it might serve as a model that the state could use to inculcate among its citizens a common civil identity, while enabling (or encouraging) different groups to cultivate different cultural identities. Under present circumstances, she indicates, the only way to be inclusive is to add a layer of shared and common interests (like humanity and civic identity) to the wish to stress the plurality and equal worth of particular national, religious, and linguistic identities.

Gavison (2000) proposes that, if the school wants to move beyond the two-narratives approach for the particular identities, it must think creatively of the ways in which a shared narrative can be produced that will be credible not only to the students but to the teachers as well. Naturally, she admits, Palestinians should be permitted and even encouraged to include such cultural elements in their curriculum. Yet the context of the conflict does raise an issue for separate Palestinian cultural education in the schools. Israel, she believes, has the right and the duty to see to it that this autonomy is not used in ways which may weaken the civic connection of Palestinians to their country. She shows that inherent in some versions of the Palestinian narrative is a deep reluctance to concede the legitimacy of Israel as the state in which Jews exercise their right to self-determination. It follows that Arabs who adhere to this narrative, by definition, have an instrumental relationship to Israel. They abide by its laws because they must. But their struggle is not exhausted by the wish to gain (the elusive) equality. It is a struggle for justice as seen by them – the return to the situation in which they were the masters of their own homeland in its entirety.

Youngsters educated under this narrative, she fears, may feel that the only dignified option they have is one of struggling against their state and challenging its right to exist as a place where Jews may exercise self-determination (Gavison, 2000). This is not a message conducive to peace or to dialogue. It will make equality and integration of the Palestinians into Israel even more difficult. More important, it may weaken or undermine the conditions of peace and order which are crucial for any serious political dialogue about how to balance better the implications of the Jewish nation-state and full equality to all its citizens. Though Gavison's (2000) critique is tinted by a very particular Zionist ideological perspective, it needs to be seriously considered, for it reflects issues which substantiate the Jewish and Palestinian fears that stand at the basis of the conflict.

Glazier (2003) looks at how children in one of the Jewish–Arab schools develop what she calls "cultural fluency," or the ability to step back and forth between cultures. Following the progress of their cooperation in the classroom, Glazier finds that the Jewish and Palestinian children and teachers gradually learn to appreciate and respect differences of the other's culture while learning to embrace their own culture.

In her ethnographic study, Glazier (2003) uncovers the practices teachers implemented for cross-cultural interaction and learning. Some of these practices left students at the edge of contact (pair assignment which did not lead to any cooperation, e.g. computer work), while others moved them into company (cooperative drawing and guided dialogue). The overlap of the experiences is what was most transformative, contributing to the development of cultural fluency. Activities in which students were committed to the project, as well as to one another, while producing shared texts, proved to be the ones conducive, through "company," to cultural fluency. Teachers' reflective and continuous involvement in the activities is shown to be central to students' cross-engagement, even in tasks in which language literacy becomes a barrier. The teacher's role in moving into company is critical. Though it was common for students to segregate themselves on the playground and play in homogeneous groups, there were also instances of children initiating cross-cultural company, borrowing from "official" classroom experiences, mostly in the second part of the school year. The study underlines that contact alone will not allow, all by itself, for cultural fluency. Individuals must engage in ongoing, meaningful, and shared tasks across borders. Such an engagement is facilitated through curriculum and pedagogy, two critical components often left out of the group contact equation.

Bekerman (2003, 2004, 2005; Bekerman & Horenczyk, 2004; Bekerman & Shhadi, 2003) has conducted the most comprehensive research work on Jewish–Palestinian bilingual education. He examined the connection between power relations in Israeli society and the difficulties of creating a truly bilingual educational program for Jews and Palestinians in Israel (Bekerman, 2005). He demonstrates how the different social realities of Jews and Palestinians influence the families' motivation to send their children to the Jewish–Palestinian schools and how the different status of Hebrew and Arabic in Israeli society influences each group's motivation to acquire the language of the other. He finds that the practical importance of Hebrew language acquisition is clear to Palestinian children and to their families. As a minority group the Palestinians need Hebrew in order to advance academically and professionally in the country, and they regularly need Hebrew in order to communicate on the street in Israeli society. The Jewish parents on the other hand generally hope that their children will learn Arabic, but there is no apparent price that the children will pay if they fail to acquire the language. Without a practical need for the language, the Jewish pupils' level of Arabic comes nowhere near the Palestinians' level of Hebrew, despite the great educational effort invested in the bilingual program. Amara (2005) presented similar findings regarding the place of language and the challenge of Arabic language acquisition.

Bekerman (2003) examines how the multicultural goals of the schools shape religious and national narratives. He shows how parents and teachers see culture and religion as areas in which mutual understanding can help to bridge the gaps that separate the populations in Israel. Parents put the stress on getting to know and understand the other's culture better, and believe that the schools are achieving this goal. Teachers emphasize similar goals and educational activities or celebrations around these issues that appear to be conducted with ease and in fruitful collaboration.

These celebrations carry a strong religious emphasis. In fact, it could be said that religious aspects are disproportionately emphasized given that the majority of the Jewish parents belong to secular sectors of Israeli society and the Muslim populations, though more traditional, are also mostly non-religious. While Jewish parents sometimes express concerns and ambivalence about this religious emphasis, they also seem to find solace in the religious underpinning of cultural activities given their (mostly unarticulated) fear that their children's Jewish identity will be eroded as a result of participation in a binational program.

The ethnographic data also suggest that issues of national identity have become the ultimate educational challenge for parents and educational staff alike. National issues are compartmentalized into a rather discrete period in the school year corresponding, in the Jewish Israeli calendar, to Memorial Day and Israel's Independence Day and, in the Palestinian calendar, to the Day of the Naqbe. In accordance with the policy of the Ministry of Education, all three schools hold a special ceremony for the Jewish cohort on Memorial Day which the Palestinian cohort does not attend. Depending on the schools' (complex) relations with the surrounding community and the Ministry of Education's supervision, a separate ceremony is conducted for the Palestinians in commemoration of the Naqbe. For the Palestinian group, tensions are apparent, particularly among the teachers, who see themselves at the forefront of the struggle to safeguard the Palestinian national narrative, which remains unrecognized by the Israeli educational officialdom. For most liberal Jews, Israeli Palestinian cultural and religious expression in school is legitimate. However, national identification with the Palestinian Authority is not welcomed, and neither are perspectives which would in any way try to deny the right of Israel to be a Jewish state.

The research shows that school activities, at the intergroup level, are working well. While knowing and clearly recognizing their own ethnic, religious, or national affiliation, the children seem able to create and sustain social interactional spheres where identity is not necessarily attended to. This facility of children stands in sharp contrast to the adult stakeholders' tendency to adopt a purely categorized identity approach, based on the premise that strengthening ethnic and national identities is the path to achieving its aims. The research suggests that the adoption of a categorized approach needs to be critically considered and revised if the schools wish not to replicate the discourse of accentuated identities which is central to the present conflictual situation.

Conclusions and challenges

We should not expect peace or coexistence educational initiatives to be able to offer solutions to longstanding and bloody conflicts whose roots are to be found in a very material unequal allocation of resources. Unfortunately societies and/or governments often find it easier to support such initiatives rather than work hard towards structural change. Hoping this is not the situation in Israel, the question becomes what can be realistically expected from such initiatives. Salomon's (2004a) thesis sounds partially true when affirming that though peace education cannot resolve intractable conflicts it can prepare the ground for desirable political change. What needs to be clarified is what type of educational interventions can prepare the ground.

I have already stated that for the most part present interventions are guided by psychological perspectives and lack educational theorizing. I believe that the psychological premises which presently substantiate and guide peace educational efforts need to be critically reviewed and that educational insights – specially those following from socio-historical perspectives – need to be accounted for when planning intercultural encounters. Future research and educational efforts into coexistence and reconciliation processes should pay special attention to the strong connection between the concepts of identity and culture and the coming into being of the political organization of the nation-state (Billig, 1995; Gellner, 1983; Reicher & Hopkins, 2001). It is to this political organization that we owe the powerful machinery in the shape of massive educational efforts aimed at homogenizing populations through the invention of primordial identities and cultures (Anderson, 1983; Elias, 1998; Porter, 1997). These categories and the institutions which established them seem to be the ones which molded the problems that well-intentioned educators want to overcome. Overlooking these processes might posit serious obstacles to our understanding of the developments I have presented in this review.

Adopting socio-historical perspectives will guide us in a similar direction, for they position cognition in social interaction and are attentive to their development through time, while emphasizing collusional detailed activities. Peace education needs to look beyond dominant curricula and the reproduction of existing knowledge and problematize the politics of identity around issues of justice and coexistence. Pedagogies that wish to disrupt the normalizing politics of identity must teach critical resistance and not sustain it or repress it. Critical practices which work towards the subversion of dichotomies around identity or culture are crucial to pedagogies that wish to disrupt fear, hatred, and resentment. Bekerman and Maoz (2005) suggest that goals such as peace and coexistence education may be better achieved if the emphasis on separate identity and culture is somewhat relaxed. Relaxing this emphasis means working against present hegemonic national powers, which might not be easy, but any other choice might just not work.

Many of the findings reported above seem to be related to these paradigmatic quandaries. At times they guide the inquiring eyes of researchers, blinding them to multiple other possible research questions, and at times they guide the educational activity, which turns itself into a tool which supports the present situation instead of helping it to become an emancipatory device.

Freeing the imagination to take new educational paths or research approaches might imply adopting the old Hippocratic adage "Cura te ipsum" (Take care of yourself first) while struggling to confront our paradigmatic perspectives so as to expose and try to overcome the structures and practices which have established the present conflictual situation and their functional categories.

Note

* *Palestinian Israelis* in recent years has become the preferred denomination for what were traditionally known as Arab Israelis; thus I use this term in this chapter.

References

Al-Haj, M. (1995). *Education, empowerment, and control: The case of the Arabs in Israel*. Albany, NY: State University of New York Press.

Al-Haj, M. (2005). National ethos, multicultural education, and the new history textbooks in Israel. *Curriculum Inquiry, 35*(1), 48–71.

Allport, G. W. (1954). *The nature of prejudice.* London: Addison-Wesley.

Amara, M. H. (2005). *Summary report: The bilingual model.* Jerusalem: Hand in Hand – The Center for Arab Jewish Education in Israel.

Amir, Y. (1976). The role of intergroup contact in change of prejudice and ethnic relations. In P. A. Katz (Ed.), *Towards the elimination of racism* (pp. 245–308). New York: Pergamon.

Anderson, B. (1983). *Imagined communities: Reflections on the origin and spread of nationalism.* London: Verso.

Bar, H., & Bargal, D. (1995). *Living with conflict: Encounters between Jewish and Palestinian Israeli youth.* Jerusalem: Jerusalem Institute for Israeli Studies.

Bar, H., & Eady, E. (1998). Education to cope with conflicts: Encounters between Jews and Palestinian citizens of Israel. In E. Weiner (Ed.), *Handbook of interethnic coexistence* (pp. 514–534). New York: Continuum.

Bargal, D. (1990). Contact is not enough: The contribution of Lewinian theory to inter-group workshops involving Palestinian and Jewish youth in Israel. *International Journal of Group Tensions, 20,* 179–192.

Bar-On, D. (1999). *The "other" within us: A sociopsychological perspective on changes in Israeli identity.* Beer-Sheva, Israel: Ben-Gurion University.

Bar-On, D., & Kassem, F. (2004). Storytelling as a way to work through intractable conflicts: The German-Jewish experience and its relevance to the Palestinian–Israeli context. *Journal of Social Issues, 60*(2), 289–306.

Bar-Tal, D., & Harel, A. S. (2002). Teachers as agents of political influence in the Israeli high schools. *Teaching and Teacher Education, 18*(1), 121–134.

Bekerman, Z. (2002). The discourse of nation and culture: Its impact on Palestinian–Jewish encounters in Israel. *International Journal of Intercultural Relations, 26,* 409–427.

Bekerman, Z. (2003). Reshaping conflict through school ceremonial events in Israeli Palestinian–Jewish co-education. *Anthropology & Education Quarterly, 34*(2), 205–224.

Bekerman, Z. (2004). Multicultural approaches and options in conflict ridden areas: Bilingual Palestinian–Jewish education in Israel. *Teachers College Record, 106*(3), 574–610.

Bekerman, Z. (2005). Complex contexts and ideologies: Bilingual education in conflict-ridden areas. *Journal of Language Identity and Education, 4*(1), 1–20.

Bekerman, Z., & Horenczyk, G. (2004). Arab–Jewish bilingual coeducation in Israel: A long-term approach to intergroup conflict resolution. *Journal of Social Issues, 60*(2), 389–404.

Bekerman, Z., & Maoz, I. (2005). Troubles with identity: Obstacles to coexistence education in conflict-ridden societies. *Identity, 5*(4), 341–358.

Bekerman, Z., & Shhadi, N. (2003). Palestinian Jewish bilingual education in Israel: Its influence on school students. *Journal of Multilingual and Multicultural Development, 24*(6), 473–484.

Ben-Ari, R., & Amir, Y. (1988). Promoting relations between Arab and Jewish youth. In J. Hofman (Ed.), *Arab–Jewish relations in Israel: A quest in human understanding* (pp. 249–270). Bristol, IN: Wyndham Hall Press.

Billig, M. (1995). *Banal nationalism.* London: Sage.

Bruner, J. (2002). *Making stories.* New York: Farrar, Strauss and Giroux.

Elias, N. (1998). Civilization, culture, identity: " 'Civilization' and 'culture': Nationalism and nation state formation:" An extract from *The Germans.* In J. Rundell & S. Mennell (Eds.), *Classical readings in culture and civilization* (pp. 225–240). New York: Routledge.

Feuerverger, G. (2001). *Oasis of dreams: Teaching and learning peace in a Jewish–Palestinian village in Israel.* New York: RoutledgeFalmer.

Gavison, R. (2000). Does equality require integration? *Democratic Culture, 3,* 37–87.

Gellner, E. (1983). *Nations and nationalism.* Oxford, UK: Basic Blackwell.

Glazier, J. A. (2003). Developing cultural fluency: Arab and Jewish students engaging in one another's company. *Harvard Educational Review, 73*(2), 141–163.

Halabi, R. (Ed.). (2004). *Israeli and Palestinian identities in dialogue: The school for peace approach* (D. Reich, Trans.). New Brunswick, NJ: Rutgers University Press.

Halabi, R., & Sonnenschein, N. (2004). The Jewish Palestinian encounter in a time of crisis. *Journal of Social Issues, 60*(2), 373–387.

Hammack, P. L. (2006). Identity, conflict, and coexistence: Life stories of Israeli and Palestinian adolescents. *Journal of Adolescent Research, 21*(4), 323–369.

Helman, S. (2002). Monologic results of dialogue: Jewish–Palestinian encounter groups as sites of essentialization. *Identities: Global Studies in Culture and Power, 9*, 327–354.

Hertz-Lazarowitz, R., Kupermintz, H., & Lang, J. (1998). Arab–Jewish student encounter: Beit Hagefen coexistence program. In E. Weiner (Ed.), *The handbook of international coexistence* (pp. 565–584). New York: Continuum.

Israel Central Bureau of Statistics. (2002). *Statistical abstract of Israel, 2001.* Jerusalem: Author.

Katz, L., & Kahanov, M. (1990). A survey of dilemmas in moderating Jewish–Arab encounter groups in Israel. *Megamot, 33*, 29–47.

Khalidi, R. (1997). *Palestinian identity: The construction of modern national consciousness.* New York: Columbia University Press.

Koplewitz, I. (1992). Arabic in Israel: The sociolinguistic situation of Israel's linguistic minority. *International Journal of the Sociology of Language, 98*, 29–66.

Kretzmer, D. (1992). The new basic laws on human rights: A mini-revolution in Israeli constitutional law? *Israel Law Review, 26*(2), 238–249.

Litvak-Hirsh, T., & Bar-On, D. (2007). Encounters in the looking glass of time: Longitudinal contribution of a life story workshop course to the dialogue between Jewish and Arab young adults in Israel. *Peace and Conflict Studies, 14*(1), 19–42.

Maoz, I. (2000a). An experiment in peace: Processes and effects in reconciliation aimed workshops of Jewish-Israeli and Palestinian youth. *Journal of Peace Research, 37*(6), 721–73.

Maoz, I. (2000b). Multiple conflicts and competing agendas: A framework for conceptualizing structured encounters between groups in conflict – The case of a coexistence project of Jews and Palestinians in Israel. *Journal of Peace Psychology, 6*(2), 135–156.

Maoz, I. (2000c). Power relations in intergroup encounters: A case study of Jewish–Arab encounters in Israel. *International Journal of Intercultural Relations, 24*, 259–277.

Maoz, I. (2002). Conceptual mapping and evaluation of peace education programs: The case of education for coexistence through intergroup encounters between Jews and Arabs in Israel. In G. Salomon & B. Nevo (Eds.), *Peace education: The concept, principles and practices around the world* (pp. 185–197). Mahwah, NJ: Lawrence Erlbaum.

Maoz, I., Bar-On, D., Bekerman, Z., & Jaber-Massarwa, S. (2004). Learning about "good enough" through "bad enough:" The story of a planned dialogue between Israeli Jews and Palestinians. *Human Relations, 57*(9), 1075–1101.

Nevo, B., & Brem, I. (2002). Peace education programs and the evaluation of their effectiveness. In G. Salomon & B. Nevo (Eds.), *Peace education: The concept, principles, and practices around the world* (pp. 271–282). Mahwah, NJ: Lawrence Erlbaum.

Polkinghorne, D. E. (1988). *Narrative knowing and the human sciences.* Albany, NY: State University of New York Press.

Porter, R. (1997). Introduction. In R. Porter (Ed.), *Rewriting the self histories from the Renaissance to the present* (pp. 1–17). London: Routledge.

Rabinowitz, D. (2000). Postnational Palestine/Israel? Globalization, Diaspora, transnationalism, and the Israeli–Palestinian conflict. *Critical Inquiry, 26*, 757–772.

Reicher, S., & Hopkins, N. (2001). *Self and nation.* London: Sage.

Rosen, Y. (2006). *The effects of peace education programs on changing central versus peripheral attitudes and beliefs.* Unpublished doctoral dissertation, University of Haifa, Haifa, Israel.

Rouhana, N. (1997). *Palestinian citizens in an ethnic Jewish state.* New Haven, CT: Yale University Press.

Salomon, G. (2004a). Does peace education make a difference in the context of an intractable conflict? *Journal of Peace Psychology, 10*, 257–274.

Salomon, G. (2004b). A narrative-based view of coexistence education. *Journal of Social Issues, 60*(2), 273–287.

Spolsky, B. (1994). The situation of Arabic in Israel. In Y. Suleiman (Ed.), *Arabic sociolinguistics: Issues and perspectives* (pp. 227–236). Richmond, UK: Curzon Press.

Spolsky, B., & Shohamy, E. (1999). Language in Israel society and education. *International Journal of the Sociology of Language, 137,* 93–114.

Suleiman, R. (1997). The structured encounter between Jewish and Palestinian Israelis as a microcosm: A social psychological approach. *Observations in Education* (New series), *1,* 71–85.

Walter, S. G., & Paul, V. W. (2004). *Education programs for improving intergroup relations: Theory, research, and practice.* New York: Teachers College Press.

Zemach, M. (1980). *Attitudes of the Jewish majority in Israel towards the Arab minority.* Jerusalem: Van Leer Foundation.

16

Multicultural education for young children

Patricia G. Ramsey
Mount Holyoke College, USA

From the earliest days of the multicultural movement, the early childhood field embraced multicultural principles for a number of reasons. First, ever since the Clarks' seminal research in the 1940s (Clark & Clark, 1947), researchers in the USA and other countries had noted that young children readily absorb racially prejudiced views (e.g. Aboud, 1988; Goodman, 1964; Katz, 1982; Troyna & Hatcher, 1992; Williams & Morland, 1976). Second, multicultural principles meshed well with some of the philosophical underpinnings of early childhood education, namely teaching the whole child and developing close relationships with families and communities (Kendall, 1983; Ramsey, 1982; Williams, DeGaetano, Harrington, & Sutherland, 1985).

Early childhood multicultural education, however, has a distinct history and frames of reference. First, the field of early childhood has been heavily influenced by the research and theories of developmental psychology, which have identified phases of cognitive, social, and emotional development. Many studies based on this orientation have shown that preschool and early elementary school children (ages 3–8 years) tend to think in concrete ways and have difficulty grasping abstract or hypothetical ideas, understanding nuances of meaning, or imagining and connecting with experiences different from their own. These patterns have been observed in young children's responses to people from different groups and life experiences. For example, MacNaughton and Davis (2001) observed that Anglo-Australian preschoolers' recollections of information about Aboriginal people were often limited to concrete facts about artifacts and activities such as how they made fires in the past. Moreover, the children viewed Indigenous Australians as exotic and historic "others" who were completely different from themselves.

Young children also tend to organize information in broad categories that are often rigid and dichotomous and often see extremes rather than gradations (e.g. dividing the world into strict gender roles or seeing the world as "good guys" versus "bad guys"). As a result, they often make sweeping assumptions about different groups and enact gender and race roles and cultural assumptions that reflect the social, political, and economic histories in their respective communities and countries (Connolly, 2000, 2006; Connolly, Fitzpatrick, Gallagher, & Harris, 2006; MacNaughton & Davis, 2001).

Although the capabilities of young children pose constraints on the complexity of material that they can introduce, many early childhood teachers have the freedom to develop an emergent curriculum in response to children's interests and experiences and are not as constrained by specific curriculum guidelines as are their colleagues in the higher grades. Moreover, play traditionally has been the primary learning mode in early childhood classrooms, and it offers a fluid and imaginative sphere in which to introduce and explore issues with young children. Also, in the course of their play, children sometimes reveal beliefs that reflect biases and power inequities (MacNaughton, 1993, 2000; Van Ausdale & Feagin, 2001). These revelations provide teachers with insights that they can use to engage children in conversations and activities to challenge their assumptions (MacNaughton, 2000). Unfortunately, as high-stakes testing becomes more widely implemented (in the USA and other countries), some early childhood educators are losing this flexibility and are spending more time teaching specific academic skills rather than facilitating children's in-depth explorations of real-life experiences and concerns (Olfman, in press).

Another distinctive characteristic of early childhood education is the close relationships between families and schools. Family members (particularly those with preschoolers) frequently talk with teachers on a daily basis and often participate in the classroom. Programs that serve low-income families often have family outreach workers who also support the connection between families and schools. These relationships are critical for integrating children from different backgrounds, because teachers have ongoing access to information about their families' cultural backgrounds, childrearing priorities, and current situations. However, forming and maintaining these close ties can be challenging. First, they may be undermined if teachers or other staff members have difficulty understanding or accepting parental values, lifestyles, and childrearing methods that differ from their beliefs or professional guidelines about "parenting skills." Even when teachers are open to families and eager to engage them, they sometimes fail to understand the complexity of their situations (Kroeger, 2001).

Second, some parents are very protective of their children and may object to any information that they fear will be upsetting, such as images and discussions about poverty and racism or even unfamiliar cultural practices. Neubert and Jones (1998) described how some European American parents resisted a curriculum on el Dia de los Muertos that the teachers had planned collaboratively with Mexican families in the school and the local community. They feared that the discussions about death and images of skeletons would scare their children. These concerns may also have reflected (unspoken) negative feelings toward Mexicans. Likewise, Lakey (1997) reported how parents who had previously supported the multicultural program at a school vehemently protested the inclusion of any images, stories, or discussion about gay and lesbian families – some temporarily boycotting the school, and one family withdrawing altogether. In both of these cases, parents and teachers engaged in fruitful discussions and eventually reached compromises that all could accept. However, these examples show how parent resistance can have a chilling effect on implementing multicultural education, especially if teachers avoid or withdraw from difficult conversations. Many early childhood teachers go to great lengths to avoid contentious issues (Connolly et al., 2006) because they want to maintain harmonious relationships for the good of the children and to conform to the early childhood culture that tends to define conflict as problematic. In centers that are financially dependent on tuition, some teachers and administrators worry that raising issues that challenge affluent families' beliefs and privilege may have financial consequences.

Trends of multicultural education for young children

In many countries, multicultural education has shifted from surface portrayals of cultural diversity to deeper analyses of power and oppression, a focus on the intersections of gender, race, culture, and social class, and advocacy for radical social and economic change. Because early childhood curriculum is built largely on stories, arts and crafts, and music, it was particularly easy for the initial multicultural efforts to focus on holidays, foods, crafts, and music of disparate cultures – often inadvertently reinforcing stereotypes and "exoticizing" others. This superficial approach was reinforced by the influx of commercial "multicultural" products – plastic foods, dolls, posters, puzzles – depicting different racial groups and cultural practices in varying degrees of authenticity and overgeneralization. These materials have the potential to create learning environments that reflect the experiences of a wider range of children, including those of newly arrived immigrants. They also can challenge children's assumptions that everyone lives the same way as they do. However, often teachers simply place them in classrooms and fail to provide contexts or to monitor and challenge children's reactions that sometimes reflect bias (e.g. White children refusing to play with the darker-skinned baby dolls).

Louise Derman-Sparks and colleagues (1989), in the *Anti-Bias Curriculum: Tools for Empowering Young Children*, boldly criticized these superficial approaches as "tourist curricula." They also advocated shifting from the focus on cultural diversity to an anti-bias approach, which embodies a critique of discrimination in all its forms – race, social class, gender, sexual preference, and abilities – and engagement in social activism to respond to these injustices. This broader definition and critical stance had a profound effect on early childhood multicultural education, and teachers and teacher educators in many countries re-cast their work as anti-bias teaching.

The emergence of critical race theory (CRT) has led to an increased awareness of the effects of racial stratification and unequal power among families and communities and concerns that White children are developing a sense of racial superiority that undermines their willingness to respect and connect with different and/or less advantaged groups. After observing preschoolers' conversations and play in a racially diverse preschool for a year, Van Ausdale and Feagin (2001) noted that many White children often assumed that they were racially superior and imposed subordinate roles on their classmates of color. Thus, supporting White children to develop identities that encompass antiracist – rather than racist – images is an emerging priority and critical to the development of predispositions to appreciate and respect unfamiliar groups and to resist injustice (Derman-Sparks & Ramsey, 2006).

The Reconceptualizing Early Childhood Movement also has had a profound influence on early childhood multicultural education. As part of the postmodernist movement, it has challenged predetermined truths and, in particular, the theories and research of developmental psychology. One point made by many reconceptualists (e.g. Cannella, 1997; MacNaughton, 2000; Skattebol, 2003) is that most developmental theories are based on European or European American children and are not relevant to children from different backgrounds. Writers have also raised questions about the whole notion of childhood and the value of creating programs that are "developmentally appropriate" (Grieshaber & Cannella, 2001). Silin (1995) likewise has challenged the attachment to developmental stages and the tendency to protect children's innocence and asks whether we are simply trying to distance children from the "disquieting material realities in which they live" (p. 104). Instead of focusing on children's developmental limitations, reconceptualists advocate that teachers and researchers recognize the complexities and biases in society and the enactment of power differentials in the classroom, genuinely collaborate with families, children, and communities to design programs, and constantly re-examine values and practices for their impact on who is being served, excluded, or disqualified (Cannella & Grieshaber, 2001). As part of this movement authors encourage teachers not to limit their perspectives and roles to the confines of developmental theories and practice but instead to recognize that their work and identities are inherently political (Boutte, 2000) and situated within historical, political, and economic contexts (Ryan, Ochsner, & Genishi, 2001).

Another current trend is the increasing awareness of the connections between oppression and the destruction of the natural environment (Bowers, 2001; Cowhey, 2006; Derman-Sparks, Edwards, & the AB Task Force, in press; Lalley, in press; Ramsey, 2004; Running Grass, 1994). As is evident in the ongoing protests at World Trade Organization (WTO) meetings, people all over the world are concerned that global capitalism is "paving over" not only the rainforests but also workers' rights, environmental protections, and the traditional livelihoods and cultures of many groups. A further connection between the multicultural and ecological issues is the disparity between the environmental degradation in poor and affluent countries and communities. For example, three out of the five largest hazardous waste facilities in the United States are located in African American and Latino American communities (Fruchter, 1999).

An additional theme that represents a convergence of social class and environmental concerns is a critical look at consumerism (Derman-Sparks et al., in press; Pelo, in press-a; Ramsey, 2004; Vasquez, 2004). Over the past two decades, young children have become the targets of relentless advertising campaigns and have joined their older peers in pressuring family members to buy media-inspired clothing and toys, low-nutrition fattening foods, and an endless array of video and computer games. Aside from the financial pressures on families and the resulting exacerbation of social-class differences, these fascinations reinforce stereotyped images and roles (MacNaughton, 2000). For example, boys tend to gravitate toward hyper-masculine (usually White) male superheroes. Conversely, many preschool girls now have "make-over parties" so that they can look like their favorite (usually White) elegantly attired Disney "princess." This obsession with possessions also generates competition among children and potentially undermines their willingness to care for others (Ramsey, 2004).

Environmental and consumerist concerns provide early childhood teachers with many opportunities to raise multicultural issues because they are often manifested in ways that are familiar and meaningful to young children. For example, if a low-income neighborhood is suffering from the fumes of a nearby plant, the children can smell and see the problem and understand viscerally how the interests of low-income communities often are disregarded. They also can engage in meaningful activities to try to effect change (e.g. posting signs of protest in the neighborhood, writing letters to the local newspaper, the company, or local Environmental Protection Agency officials). Consumerist issues also come up frequently in classrooms, with children either showing off new possessions or talking longingly about getting them. These are opportune moments for teachers to engage children in critical thinking and conversations about advertisements and how they stereotype groups, make children want things they do not need, and cause tensions in families, especially those that have less money. Pelo and Davidson (2000), Ramsey (2004), Derman-Sparks and Ramsey (2006), and Vasquez (2004) describe many examples of these possibilities.

Purpose and goals of multicultural education for young children

The purpose and practice of early childhood multicultural education vary across schools, communities, and countries but usually include efforts to ensure that children from all backgrounds have a successful start in school and a strengthened sense of themselves and their abilities, to weave into the earliest school experiences information and skills that will help children navigate societal contradictions and ambiguities related to race, social class, culture, gender, sexual preference, and abilities, and to support children to recognize and challenge the injustices that divide and diminish their world (Derman-Sparks & the A.B.C. Task Force, 1989; Kendall, 1996; Ramsey, 2004). The following goals are derived from this overall purpose but may vary in their relevance according to the cultural, historical, and political contexts of particular groups:

- developing culturally responsive practices that enable all children from a range of backgrounds to have a successful start in school and to participate fully in early childhood programs;
- encouraging children to develop positive and realistic identities that embody their race, culture, gender, and abilities, and their personal, family, and social histories;
- broadening children's perspectives so that they learn to recognize, respect, and appreciate commonalities and differences among people in their communities, country, and the world and develop a sense of solidarity with all people and with the natural environment;
- engaging children in critically examining their own assumptions and inequities in their immediate environment and the larger world;
- encouraging and supporting children to gain the confidence and skills to be activists for social change.

Each of these goals will be discussed in more detail below.

Culturally responsive teaching is critical because many countries are experiencing a dramatic increase in the number of immigrant families whose children are struggling to bridge the gap between their home cultures and languages and those of the mainstream schools. Moreover, as a consequence of worldwide migrations and economic polarization, rising numbers of families are coping with temporary or chronic poverty. It is also increasingly clear that culturally responsive early childhood education can play a pivotal role in the academic success of these children (Espinosa, 2005). The well-known Kamehameha Elementary Education Project (KEEP) demonstrated how adapting classroom practices to be more compatible with children's culture yielded significant academic gains (Au, 1980; Tharp & Gallimore, 1988). Igoa (1995) documented specific techniques such as making filmstrips and using photographs and artifacts to create familiar spaces in the classroom that helped immigrant children in her classrooms adjust to life and schools in the United States. Ritchie (2001) described Te Whāriki, an early childhood curriculum in New Zealand that is based on collectivism rather than individualism and is more compatible with the Māori traditions. Quintero (2004) reported how teachers successfully engaged young refugee children using storybooks and conversations and investigations. Likewise, Purnell, Ali, Begum, and Carter (2007) identified ways that literacy and arts activities can bridge gaps between children's home lives and school. See Pelo's edited volume *Rethinking Early Childhood Education* (in press-b) for more examples of ways that teachers connect with families who might otherwise feel alienated from schools because of cultural and language differences, poverty, and sexual orientation.

In an overview of many dimensions of culturally responsive teaching, Espinosa (2005) offers guidelines for designing and implementing a curriculum for children who have particular disadvantages entering school, such as experiencing cultural discontinuities between home and school, living in poverty, learning English as a second language, and managing disabilities.

Nieto points out (chap. 5, this volume) that culturally responsive education is not effective if teachers base their understanding of children's culture on outdated and static views. Early childhood teachers can potentially avoid this pitfall if they use their close ongoing contacts with families to gather current information about individual children and the evolving cultural values of their specific families and communities. Many books include suggestions for ways to generate productive and mutually learning conversations with family members (e.g., Brown, 2001; Derman-Sparks & the A.B.C. Task Force, 1989; Derman-Sparks et al., in press; Ramsey, 2004). To be responsive, teachers need to be aware of their own backgrounds and how their personal history may bias their perceptions and expectations of children (Adler, 2001; Ramsey, 2004). In particular, they should avoid seeing their young charges as "at risk" but rather as "at promise" (Swadener, 1999, p. 4).

To make schooling more accessible and to ease the burdens on families, some early childhood centers are integrated into a wider range of services for young children and their families, such as family literacy centers, health screening, and weekend activities for families. One example is Toronto First Duty, which includes "a universal program of seamless care, early learning, and parenting support" (Pelletier & Corter, 2005, p. 30). It has been successful in serving families from a wide range of cultural and economic backgrounds.

Encouraging children to develop comprehensive and realistic identities requires that teachers "nurture each child's construction of a knowledgeable, confident self-concept and group identity by creating early childhood programs that encourage all children to deepen their ties with their families and communities and to know and appreciate their unique attributes" (Derman-Sparks & Ramsey, 2009, p. 137). This goal builds on early childhood education's core philosophic commitment to nurturing children's self-concepts. It is critical to keep in mind that identities are complex, fluid, and ever-changing (Grieshaber & Cannella, 2001; Skattebol, 2003).

To meet this goal, all children in a program should be equally visible throughout the classroom and the curriculum (Derman-Sparks & the A.B.C. Task Force, 1989; Derman-Sparks & Ramsey, 2009; Ramsey, 2004). Teachers can display photographs of children and their families and encourage children to share their ideas, life experiences, and feelings through talking, singing, drawing, and writing. One cautionary note, however, is that some identity- or self-esteem-oriented activities can take on a tone of "I am special" or "All about me" that is counterproductive, especially for children who may already feel superior to other children (Derman-Sparks & Ramsey, 2006). Furthermore, teachers should be prepared to challenge children who are enacting roles and identities that reflect misinformation or assumptions about hierarchies and power (MacNaughton, 1993, 2000).

Wasson-Ellam and Li (1999) found that efforts to enhance young children's ethnic identities were often overwhelmed by peer pressures to fit images of White consumerist culture. However, they noted that teachers were able to use "culturally conscious books . . . that aim to open children's minds and hearts so that they learn to understand and value both themselves and others' perspectives" (p. 30) to encourage children to talk about and appreciate their own and others' cultural backgrounds and personal histories.

Broadening perspectives and developing a sense of solidarity with all people and the natural world is challenging, because young children often are wary of unfamiliar languages, appearances, or behaviors and draw conclusions that appear to be prejudiced and polarized. They often see others as totally different, with no connection to their own lives (MacNaughton & Davis, 2001). Children growing up in homogeneous settings are particularly at risk of developing negative attitudes about unfamiliar groups, because they have no direct experiences with which they can challenge misinformation and fears (McGlothlin & Killen, 2005, 2006), whereas White children growing up in heterogeneous communities are more likely to develop positive cross-group attitudes (Rutland, Cameron, Bennett, & Ferrell, 2005). Thus, integrating children from a range of racial, cultural, and socioeconomic backgrounds is probably the most effective strategy for raising children with less bias (Aboud, chap. 14, this volume). However, because communities tend to be racially and economically segregated, many early childhood settings are relatively homogeneous. Moreover, even in integrated classrooms, teachers need to monitor cross-group interactions to ensure that societal divisions and power inequities are not simply being replicated (Cohen, 1977; Emihovich, 1981; MacNaughton, 1993; Mednick, 2008; Sapon-Shevin, 1983; Van Ausdale & Feagin, 2001).

To help children expand their perspectives, teachers often provide activities, images, and objects that depict a wide range of human appearances and activities (e.g. Barrera, 2005; Swiniarski, 2006). There is, however, some controversy about this point. On one hand, there is ample evidence that young children are well aware of racial, gender, and cultural differences. For example, studies have shown that children notice racial cues during infancy (Kelly et al., 2007) and that, by the age of 3 or 4, most children have a rudimentary concept of race (Katz, 1982; Katz & Kofkin, 1997; Ramsey & Williams, 2003; Van Ausdale & Feagin, 2001).

On the other hand, researchers (Bigler & Hughes, chap. 13, this volume; Bigler & Liben, 2007; Patterson & Bigler, 2006) have found that, when differences are psychologically salient, the potential for stereotyping and in-group bias increases. These latter findings suggest that minimizing or blurring differences might be a better strategy than exposing children to them. In fact, many educators uphold the ideal of "colorblindness," that is, ignoring differences and denying that social divisions define individuals or influence others' perception of them.

One way to reconcile these two different perspectives is to include images of a wide range of people but to emphasize that similarities and differences are continua, not polarities, and that we all share a combination of common and unique traits and experiences. For example, children can learn that most people have the same senses (e.g. sight, hearing) and feel similar emotions but that faces may vary by skin color and physiognomy and that individuals may express feelings in different ways. Quintero (2004) describes how teachers can use stories about different groups and life experiences to stretch young children's awareness – even when they are as young as infants and toddlers.

One challenge is the paucity of materials that authentically represent different groups. In a comprehensive critique of children's books, Mendoza and Reese (2001) point out that stories can serve as mirrors for children to see themselves and their families and as windows to learn about the rest of the world. However, if information is distorted or omitted, then these books only perpetuate stereotypes. Even some popular award-winning picture books that have been hailed as "multicultural" have misappropriated and misrepresented material from marginalized groups. Mendoza and Reese (2001) point out that this pattern is perpetuated because publishers often overlook authors and illustrators from underrepresented groups and rely on well-known ones who may have only superficial information about the groups they are portraying. Boutte (2002) urges teachers to scrutinize books for their implicit and explicit agendas and to encourage children to be critically aware of underlying messages and perspectives.

There is also the question of what children learn when they are exposed to images and materials depicting human similarities and differences. Aboud and Levy (2000) reviewed several studies done in the 1970s that revealed that simply exposing children to books and televised images about other groups did not change their views. The authors concluded that, to reduce prejudice, teachers cannot simply provide materials but also need to discuss and model alternative attitudes. Day (1995) and Lee and Lee (2001) reached similar conclusions after observing young children's reactions to multicultural materials – dolls, props, clothing, and food items – representing different cultural groups. Although the children (especially the girls) played enthusiastically with the new items, they appeared to be mostly attracted by the novelty of the materials and did not connect them with different cultures or other multicultural themes.

In some of the very few systematic studies of the effects of the multicultural curriculum, Connolly et al. (2006) and Connolly and Hosken (2006) have had more encouraging results in programs developed in Northern Ireland. In one study (Connolly & Hosken, 2006), a dramatic presentation and follow-up activities had a positive effect on young children. Compared to the control group, those who participated in the activities increased their ability to recognize social exclusion, their willingness to include others, and their awareness of commonalities they shared with unfamiliar children. Interestingly, however, children did not become more accepting of different racial groups. The authors concluded that, to achieve this change, activities would need to be focused explicitly on race. Connolly et al. (2006) also developed a large-scale intervention in Northern Ireland using short televised cartoons that encouraged young children to be socially inclusive. Based on child interviews and teacher reports, this approach seemed to be effective in helping children to become more aware of exclusionary behavior and its effect on others and more willing to include peers.

A number of practitioners and researchers attest to the effectiveness of persona dolls in engaging children to think and care about individuals from unfamiliar backgrounds and life experiences (Brown, 2001; Derman-Sparks & the A.B.C. Task Force, 1989; Pelo & Davidson, 2000; Whitney, 1999). These life-sized cloth dolls, depicting a range of racial groups, "belong" to the teacher, who introduces each doll to the children by creating and describing his or her life story. Over time, the teacher creates ongoing stories about the dolls to introduce, personalize, and explore aspects of diversity. For instance, a story about a persona doll being rejected because her family is living in a homeless shelter might encourage children to discuss how they would feel and what they could do about it. Because the children "know" the dolls, they readily empathize and learn about a broader range of life experiences in a meaningful and emotionally connected way.

Another way to emphasize connections among all people is to provide concrete examples of how we all live on the same planet, breathe the same air, drink the same water, and share an interest in conserving our resources. Many time-honored early childhood practices of observing nature and growing plants can be expanded to incorporate this awareness. Nimmo and Hallett (2008) report how working in the school garden helped children to learn about different cultural practices and environmental issues and to connect with individuals of different ages and abilities. Likewise, Satterlee and Cormons (2008) describe how a family-based nature program in a low-income rural community enhanced children's learning and family participation in the school.

Critical thinking is a challenge for young children, who often feel small and helpless because they live in a world largely determined by adults. At the same time, they can identify injustices in their immediate world, such as biased beliefs and behavior of peers, stereotyped messages in books, materials, and electronic media, and school and community policies and practices that are unfair and/or environmentally destructive (Pelo & Davidson, 2000; Vasquez, 2004; Walters, in press). MacNaughton and Davis (2001) note that, although many of the Anglo-Australian children they interviewed had superficial and stereotyped concepts of Aboriginal people, others had more critical perspectives and were aware of the colonialism and oppression that still affect many Indigenous Australians. However, they also point out that teachers need to recognize and deliberately address children's nascent attitudes and the misinformation that they are learning. Skattebol (2003) reports several conversations that show how teachers cannot simply respond to children's comments in a neutral way but need to explicitly challenge assumptions about different groups and relative positions of power.

Many educators testify to the positive effects of engaging children in conversations in which they can explore and challenge their assumptions and the inequities in the world around them. Aboud and Doyle (1996) found that children with high levels of prejudice moderated their positions after talking about race with low-prejudiced peers. In another study (Reeder, Douzenis, & Bergin, 1997), five high-prejudiced second-graders participated in a series of counselor-led discussions about racial similarities and differences and social skills. Classroom observations and pre- and post-tests revealed that, after these discussions, the children felt more comfortable with different-race classmates and were less likely to make racially biased comments. An observational study (Levine, 1993) showed how a kindergarten – first-grade teacher was able to create a safe space for all children in the classroom to express and compare their perspectives and to challenge the "authority" of the written word and social conventions. De Marquez (2002) described discussion groups in which the children raised and challenged each other about social justice issues, demonstrating that, under appropriate conditions, young children can understand and discuss complex concerns. Marsh (1992) documented how the children in her racially mixed kindergarten participated in a number of anti-bias activities and, as a result, became more aware of injustices and began to take actions (e.g. protesting the lack of African American crossing guards at the school). In a study designed to pinpoint the effects of specific multicultural activities, Lee, Ramsey, and Sweeney (2008) found that some activities, particularly games and simulations, led to in-depth discussions about racial and economic misinformation and inequities. Chafel, Flint, Hammel, and Pomeroy (2007) used books to encourage children to engage in meaningful conversations about issues such as poverty and inter-group antagonisms. They learned that, when children were allowed to weave their own experiences into classroom discussions, they were more actively engaged and readily generated ideas about how to challenge inequities. Quintero (2004) illustrated how a problem-posing method engaged children in critical discussions about their lives and the world around them.

Engaging children in social activism has to be done thoughtfully so that their actions are meaningful to them. Experience has shown that teachers can effectively engage children as young as 4 years old in activism if the projects emerge from real incidents or issues in their lives, are simple and direct, have a clear, tangible focus, and are geared to the children's experiences rather than achieving a particular outcome. These activities should not be about changing the world from an adult's perspective, but rather about children making their own "worlds" a little fairer (Cowhey, 2006; Derman-Sparks & Ramsey, 2006; Hoffman, 2004; Pelo & Davidson, 2000).

In one case, Hoffman (2004) describes how a group of children noticed the lack of diversity in the images of children in a new calendar and, after much discussion, wrote a letter to the company. When they did not get a response, they circulated a petition and sent that to the company as well. Vasquez (2004) reports how her kindergarteners identified, protested, and changed several discriminatory school policies (e.g. the kindergarteners were excluded from a bookmark contest, the food at the school barbecue did not include any vegetarian dishes). Lalley (in press) describes the principles that one program in Seattle follows to engage children, families, and teachers in social activism. Pelo and Davidson's volume (2000) offers many detailed examples of children identifying issues in their everyday worlds (e.g. gender-stereotyped assumptions of peers, vandalized trees in a local park, local people who are homeless, racist images in books) and how teachers worked with the children and families to learn more about these issues and to take actions to address them.

Conclusion

As we move toward the second decade of the 21st century, the numbers of immigrant families are rapidly increasing in nations around the world, as is the gap between affluent and low-income individuals and groups. Early childhood teachers need to be aware, flexible, and creative as they respond to increasingly complex social, political, and economic challenges – from supporting children who are the targets of racial and economic discrimination to challenging those who are immersed in expectations of privilege. Because of the young age of the children, the close relationships between families and schools, and the emphasis on play and an emergent curriculum, early childhood educators are uniquely situated to advance the goals of multicultural education.

At the same time, this potential is often undermined because in many countries (particularly the USA) early childhood programs are woefully under-funded and often seen as expendable. Many poorly paid but highly committed early childhood educators have tirelessly and creatively moved the field to and through many phases of multicultural education. As we face the future, we must fight for funding for early childhood education so that all children throughout the world have access to well-equipped centers and highly trained teachers who have the time and resources to fulfill the many promises of multicultural education for young children.

References

Aboud, F. (1988). *Children and prejudice*. London: Blackwell.
Aboud, F. E., & Doyle, A. (1996). Does talk of race foster prejudice or tolerance in children? *Canadian Journal of Behavioural Science, 28*, 161–170.
Aboud, F. E., & Levy, S. R. (2000). Interventions to reduce prejudice and discrimination in children and adolescents. In S. Oskamp (Ed.), *Reducing prejudice and discrimination* (pp. 269–293). Mahwah, NJ: Lawrence Erlbaum.
Adler, S. M. (2001). Racial and ethnic mirrors: Reflections on identity and voice from an Asian American educator. In S. Grieshaber & G. S. Cannella (Eds.), *Embracing identities in early childhood education: Diversity and possibilities* (pp. 148–157). New York: Teachers College Press.
Au, K. (1980). Participation structures in a reading lesson with Hawaiian children. *Anthropology and Education Quarterly, 11*(2), 91–115.
Barrera, R. (2005). Visit the world with young children. *Scholastic Early Childhood Today, 20*, 36–40.
Bigler, R. S., & Liben, L. S. (2007). Developmental intergroup theory: Explaining and reducing children's social stereotyping and prejudice. *Current Directions in Psychological Science, 16*, 162–166.
Boutte, G. (2000). Multiculturalism: Moral and educational implications. *Dimensions of Early Childhood, 28*(3), 9–16.
Boutte, G. (2002, Spring). The critical literacy process: Guidelines for examining books. *Childhood Education*, 147–152.
Bowers, C. A. (2001). *Educating for eco-justice and community*. Athens, GA: University of Georgia Press.
Brown, B. (2001). *Combating discrimination: Persona dolls in action*. Sterling, VA: Trentham Books.
Cannella, G. S. (1997). *Deconstructing early childhood education: Social justice and revolution*. New York: Peter Lang.
Cannella, G. S. & Grieshaber, S. (2001). Conclusion: Identities and possibilities. In S. Grieshaber & G. S. Cannella (Eds.), *Embracing identities in early childhood education: Diversity and possibilities* (pp. 173–180). New York: Teachers College Press.
Chafel, J. A., Flint, A. S., Hammel, J., & Pomeroy, K. H. (2007). Young children, social issues, and critical literacy: Stories of teachers and researchers. *Young Children, 62*(1), 73–81.
Clark, K. B., & Clark, M. P. (1947). Racial identification and preference in Negro children. In T. M. Newcomb & E. L. Hartley (Eds.), *Readings in social psychology* (pp. 169–178). New York: Free Press.
Cohen, S. (1977). Fostering positive attitudes toward the handicapped: New curriculum. *Children Today, 6*(6), 7–12.
Connolly, P. (2000). Racism and young girls' peer-group relations: The experiences of South Asian girls. *Sociology, 34*, 499–519.
Connolly, P. (2006). The masculine habitus as "disturbed cognition": A case study of 5- to 6-year-old boys in an English inner-city, multi-ethnic primary school. *Children and Society, 20*, 140–152.
Connolly, P., Fitzpatrick, S., Gallagher, T., and Harris, P. (2006). Addressing diversity and inclusion in the

early years in conflict-affected societies: A case study of the Media Initiative for Children–Northern Ireland, *International Journal for Early Years Education, 14*, 263–278.

Connolly, P. and Hosken, K. (2006). The general and specific effects of educational programmes aimed at promoting awareness of and respect for diversity among young children. *International Journal of Early Years Education, 14*, 107–126.

Cowhey, M. (2006). *Black ants and Buddhists: Thinking critically and teaching differently in the primary grades.* Portland, ME: Stenhouse.

Day, J. A. E. (1995). Multicultural resources in preschool provision: An observational study. *Early Child Development and Care, 110*, 47–68.

de Marquez, T. M. (2002). Stories from a multicultural classroom. *Multicultural Education, 9*, 19–20.

Derman-Sparks, L., & the A.B.C. Task Force. (1989). *Anti-bias curriculum: Tools for empowering young children.* Washington, DC: National Association for the Education of Young Children.

Derman-Sparks, L., Edwards, J. O., & the AB Task Force. (in press). *Anti-bias education: Tools for empowering children and ourselves.* Washington, DC: National Association for the Education of Young Children.

Derman-Sparks, L., & Ramsey, P. G. (2006). *What if all the kids are White? Engaging White children and teachers in multicultural education.* New York: Teachers College Press.

Derman-Sparks, L., & Ramsey, P. G. (2009). A framework for culturally relevant, multicultural, and anti-bias education in the 21st century. In J. Johnson & J. Roopnarine (Eds.), *Approaches to early childhood education* (5th ed., pp. 120–146). Columbus, OH: Merrill.

Emihovich, C. A. (1981). Social interaction in two integrated kindergartens. *Integrated Education, 19*, 72–78.

Espinosa, L. M. (2005). Curriculum and assessment considerations for young children from culturally, linguistically, and economically diverse backgrounds. *Psychology in the Schools, 42*, 837–853.

Fruchter, J. (1999). Linking social justice concerns with environmental issues. *ZPG Recorder* (Special Issue on Kid-Friendly Cities), *31*(4), 10–11.

Goodman, M. E. (1964). *Race awareness in young children.* New York: Collier.

Grieshaber, S., & Cannella, G. S. (2001). From identity to identities: Increasing possibilities in early childhood education. In S. Grieshaber & G. S. Cannella (Eds.), *Embracing identities in early childhood education: Diversity and possibilities* (pp. 3–22). New York: Teachers College Press.

Hoffman, E. (2004). *Magic capes, amazing powers: Transforming superhero play in the classroom.* St. Paul, MN: Redleaf Press.

Igoa, C. (1995). *The inner world of the immigrant child.* New York: St. Martin's Press.

Katz, P. A. (1982). Development of children's racial awareness and intergroup attitudes. In L. G. Katz (Ed.), *Current topics in early childhood education* (pp. 17–54). Norwood, NJ: Ablex.

Katz, P. A., & Kofkin, J. A. (1997). Race, gender, and young children. In S. Luthar, J. Burack, D. Cicchetti, & J. Weisz (Eds.), *Developmental perspectives on risk and pathology* (pp. 51–74). New York: Cambridge University Press.

Kelly, D. J., Liu, S., Ge, L., Quinn, P. C., Slater, A. M., Lee, K., et al. (2007). Cross-race preferences for same-race faces extend beyond the African versus Caucasian contrast in 3-month-old infants. *Infancy, 11*, 87–95.

Kendall, F. (1983). *Diversity in the classroom: Multicultural approaches to the education of young children.* New York: Teachers College Press.

Kendall, F. (1996). *Diversity in the classroom: Multicultural approaches to the education of young children* (2nd ed.). New York: Teachers College Press.

Kroeger, J. (2001). A reconstructed tale of inclusion for a lesbian family in an early childhood classroom. In S. Grieshaber & G. S. Cannella (Eds.), *Embracing identities in early childhood education: Diversity and possibilities* (pp. 73–86). New York: Teachers College Press.

Lakey, J. (1997). Teachers and parents define diversity in an Oregon preschool cooperative: Democracy at work. *Young Children, 52*(4), 20–28.

Lalley, J. (in press). An interview with Hilda Magana. In A. Pelo (Ed.), *Rethinking early childhood education.* Milwaukee, WI: Rethinking Schools.

Lee, C. E., & Lee, D. (2001). Kindergarten geography: Teaching diversity to young people. *Journal of Geography, 100*, 152–157.

Lee, R., Ramsey, P. G., & Sweeney, B. (2008). Engaging young children in conversations about race and social class. *Young Children* (November).

Levine, L. (1993). "Who says?" Learning to value diversity in school. In F. Pignatelli & S. W. Pflaum (Eds.), *Celebrating diverse voices: Progressive education and equity* (pp. 87–111). Newbury Park, CA: Corwin Press.

MacNaughton, G. (1993). Gender, power and racism: A case study of domestic play in early childhood. *Multicultural Teaching, 11*, 12–15.

MacNaughton, G. (2000). *Rethinking gender in early childhood education.* London: Paul Chapman.

MacNaughton, G., & Davis, K. (2001). Beyond "othering": Rethinking approaches to teaching young Anglo-Australian children about Indigenous Australians. *Contemporary Issues in Early Childhood, 2*, 83–93.

Marsh, M. M. (1992). Implementing antibias curriculum in the kindergarten classroom. In S. Kessler & B. B. Swadener (Eds.), *Reconceptualizing the early childhood curriculum: Beginning the dialogue* (pp. 267–288). New York: Teachers College Press.

McGlothlin, H., & Killen, M. (2005). Children's perceptions of intergroup and intragroup similarity and the role of social experience. *Applied Developmental Psychology, 26*, 680–698.

McGlothlin, H., & Killen, M. (2006). Intergroup attitudes of European American children attending ethnically homogeneous schools. *Child Development, 77*, 1375–1386.

Mednick, L. G. (2008). Peers, power, and privilege: The social worlds of a second grade. *Rethinking Schools, 23*(1), 27–31.

Mendoza, J., & Reese, D. (2001). Examining multicultural picture books for the early childhood classroom: Possibilities and pitfalls. *Early Childhood Research & Practice, 3*(1), 1–38.

Neubert, K., & Jones, E. (1998). Creating culturally relevant holiday curriculum: A negotiation. *Young Children, 53*(5), 14–19.

Nimmo, J., & Hallett, B. (2008). Childhood in the garden: A place to encounter natural and social diversity. *Young Children, 63*(1), 32–38.

Olfman, S. (in press). What about play? In A. Pelo (Ed.), *Rethinking early childhood education.* Milwaukee, WI: Rethinking Schools.

Patterson, M. M., & Bigler, R. S. (2006). Preschool children's attention to environmental messages about groups: Social categorization and the origins of intergroup bias. *Child Development, 77*, 847–860.

Pelletier, J., & Corter, C. (2005). Toronto First Duty: Integrating kindergarten, childcare, and parenting support to help diverse families connect to schools. *Multicultural Education, 13*, 30–37.

Pelo, A. (in press-a). Bringing earth home: Professional development on ecology. In A. Pelo (Ed.), *Rethinking early childhood education.* Milwaukee, WI: Rethinking Schools.

Pelo, A. (Ed.). (in press-b). *Rethinking early childhood education.* Milwaukee, WI: Rethinking Schools.

Pelo, A., & Davidson, F. (2000). *That's not fair: A teacher's guide to activism with young children.* St. Paul, MN: Redleaf Press.

Purnell, P. G., Ali, P., Begum, N., & Carter, M. (2007). Windows, bridges, and mirrors: Building culturally responsive early childhood classrooms through the integration of literacy and the arts. *Early Childhood Education Journal, 34*, 419–424.

Quintero, E. P. (2004). *Problem-posing with multicultural children's literature: Developing critical early childhood curricula.* New York: Peter Lang.

Ramsey, P. G. (1982). Multicultural education in early childhood classrooms. *Young Children, 37*(2), 13–24.

Ramsey, P. G. (2004). *Teaching and learning in a diverse world* (3rd ed.). New York: Teachers College Press.

Ramsey, P. G., & Williams, L. R. (2003). *Multicultural education: A resource book* (2nd ed.). New York: Routledge.

Reeder, J., Douzenis, C., & Bergin, J. J. (1997). The effects of small group counseling on the racial attitudes of second-grade students. *Professional School Counseling, 1*, 15–18.

Ritchie, J. (2001). Reflections on collectivism in early childhood teaching in Aotearoa/New Zealand. In S. Grieshaber & G. S. Cannella (Eds.), *Embracing identities in early childhood education: Diversity and possibilities* (pp. 133–147). New York: Teachers College Press.

Running Grass, R. (1994). Towards a multicultural environmental education. *Multicultural Education, 2*, 4–6.

Rutland, A., Cameron, L., Bennett, L., & Ferrell, J. (2005). Interracial contact and racial constancy: A multi-site study of racial intergroup bias in 3–5 year old Anglo-British children. *Applied Developmental Psychology, 26,* 699–713.

Ryan, S., Ochsner, M., & Genishi, C. (2001). Miss Nelson is missing! Sightings in research on teaching. In S. Grieshaber & G. S. Cannella (Eds.), *Embracing identities in early childhood education: Diversity and possibilities* (pp. 45–59). New York: Teachers College Press.

Sapon-Shevin, M. (1983). Teaching young children about differences: Resources for teaching. *Young Children, 38*(2), 24–32.

Satterlee, D. J., & Cormons, G. D. (2008). Sparking interest in nature–family style. *Young Children, 63*(1), 16–20.

Silin, J. G. (1995). *Sex, death, and the education of children: Our passion for ignorance in the age of AIDS.* New York: Teachers College Press.

Skattebol, J. (2003). Dark, dark and darker: Children's negotiations of identity in an early childhood setting. *Contemporary Issues in Early Childhood, 4,* 149–166.

Swadener, B. B. (1999). Research as praxis: Unlearning oppression and research journeys. In C. Grant (Ed.), *Multicultural research: A reflective engagement with race, class, gender and sexual orientation* (pp. 212–227). Florence, KY: Taylor & Francis.

Swiniarski, L. B. (2006). Helping young children become citizens of the world. *Scholastic Early Childhood Today, 21,* 36–42.

Tharp, R. G., & Gallimore, R. (1988). *Rousing minds to life: Teaching, learning, and schooling in social context.* Cambridge, UK: Cambridge University Press.

Troyna, B., & Hatcher, R. (1992). *Racism in children's lives: A study of a mainly White primary school.* London: Routledge.

Van Ausdale, D., & Feagin, J. R. (2001). *The first R: How children learn race and racism.* Lanham, MD: Rowman & Littlefield.

Vasquez, V. M. (2004). *Negotiating critical literacies with young children.* Mahwah, NJ: Lawrence Erlbaum.

Walters, S. (in press). Fairness first: Learning from Martin Luther King and Ruby Bridges. In A. Pelo (Ed.), *Rethinking early childhood education.* Milwaukee, WI: Rethinking Schools.

Wasson-Ellam, L., & Li, G. (1999). Identity-weaving in the places and spaces of a cross-cultural classroom. *Canadian Children, 24,* 23–34.

Whitney, T. (1999). *Kids like us: Using persona dolls in the classroom.* St. Paul, MN: Redleaf Press.

Williams, J. E., & Morland, J. K. (1976). *Race, color, and the young child.* Chapel Hill, NC: University of North Carolina Press.

Williams, L. R., DeGaetano, Y., Harrington, C. C., & Sutherland, I. R. (1985). *Alerta: A multicultural, bilingual approach to teaching young children.* Menlo Park, CA: Addison-Wesley.

Part 4

Culture, teaching, and learning

17
Cultural influences on learning

Carol D. Lee
Northwestern University, USA

Core propositions about learning and their relevance to culture

Researchers in cognitive science have accumulated substantive knowledge about how people learn. Effective and generative learning involves:

- *the coherent organization of knowledge* about domains and topics by structuring what we pay attention to and what salience we attribute to particular features of problems we seek to understand (Bransford, Brown, & Cocking, 1999; Nasir, Rosebery, Warren, & Lee, 2006);
- the development and deployment of *strategies appropriate to targeted problems* (Collins & Ferguson, 1993), but equally important are adaptive strategies (Hatano & Inagaki, 1986; Spiro, Feltovich, Jackson, & Coulson, 1991) that help learners tackle new problems that may be far removed from the kinds of problems for which they have developed routine competence (Griffin, Case, & Capodilupo, 1995; Singley & Anderson, 1989);
- *the activation of prior knowledge* that may be relevant to new problems encountered (Walker, 1987; Yekovich, Walker, Ogle, & Thompson, 1990), with the understanding that some forms of prior knowledge may potentially constrain new learning (e.g. as with naive conceptions and misconceptions) (Clement, Brown, & Zietsman, 1989);
- *monitoring one's reasoning* and understanding through metacognitive processes through which one regulates attention, activates prior knowledge, and makes predictions, particularly when faced with uncertainty (Flavell, 1981; White & Frederickson, 1998). This includes not only metacognitive knowledge, but the willingness to engage with uncertainty (Lee, 2006; Perkins, 1995).

Cognitive orientations have traditionally focused on individuals as agents of learning, but now increasingly acknowledge the fundamentally social nature of learning; that is, humans learn in social settings, in interactions with other people, and with cultural artifacts that embody the ideas and beliefs of other humans (Perkins, 1993; Saxe, 1999). This chapter focuses on culture as represented by ethnicity, race, and nationality. It also acknowledges cultural practices based on gender, age cohort, religion, sexual orientation, and disability. Thus, the discussion addresses the cultural implications of these core, agreed-upon propositions about learning in terms of ethnicity, race, and nationality, primarily within the U.S. context.

In the US, attention to culture and learning has been characterized by deficit orientations (Deutsch & Brown, 1964). These deficit orientations have a long history that goes back to European intellectual traditions and the foundations of modern psychology (Muschinske, 1977). However, current research on culture and cognition provides a generative orientation that accounts for variation in learning outcomes and modes of learning as different adaptations to ecological niches. Current research also recognizes the complex reasoning that is embedded in everyday and blue-collar workplace activities (Rogoff & Lave, 1984; Super & Harkness, 1986; Weisner, 2002).

A focus on cognition within particular ecological niches reveals both how displays of knowledge are situated and the multiple dimensions of learning that go beyond the cognitive structure of domains of knowledge. These multiple dimensions include the emotions that propel or constrain our efforts to learn (Dai & Sternberg, 2004; Zajonc & Marcus, 1984), which are influenced partly by how we appraise the situation, the task, and the people (Eccles, Wigfield, & Schiefele, 1998), whether the tasks are relevant to our goals or not (i.e. functionally relevant, relevant to short- or long-term interests), and whether the tasks are doable or not in terms of perceptions of our abilities as well as the costs (mental, emotional, social, material) attached to participation (Dweck, 1999, 2002). These attributions that influence our emotional responses are influenced by the history of our participation in prior cultural practices through experiences in families (including daily routines), peer and other social networks, and institutional practices such as schooling, religion, and macro-level belief systems (e.g. with regard to ethnicity, race, gender, disability, and particular domains, such as "Mathematics is hard," "You are born good at math or not," "Women aren't good at mathematics," or "Math is for nerds") (Graham & Hudley, 2005; Nasir & Saxe, 2003).

On the cognitive side, there is increased research on the structure of knowledge constructed out of everyday experience in academic domains, such as mathematics, science, and multiple literacies, and their relevance for school-based learning (Barton & Hamilton, 1998; Lee, 2007; Rogoff & Lave, 1984). These everyday settings are culturally constructed spaces that include forms of social organization that are culturally inherited and culturally negotiated in real time. These everyday settings are also part of broader cultural ecologies, networks of settings, and people that often share broad belief systems.

The next section of this chapter offers specific examples in the domain of mathematics, science, and literacy, situating everyday practices within their broader social ecologies and their relevance to school-based learning. These are not intended as comprehensive syntheses, but rather as illustrative cases of the role that culture plays in learning within disciplines. These are examples of research that examines conceptual and pedagogical relationships between everyday and disciplinary knowledge, with a particular focus on everyday knowledge constructed in the routine practices of ethnic and linguistic minority communities. This body of research is significant not only for its implications for youth whose educational opportunities have historically been restricted based on societal stigmatization and persistent patterns of poverty, but equally for the evolution of robust theories which help us understand that learning does not have a singular pathway of progression (Lee, 2008; Rogoff, 2003)

Mathematics

Perhaps the most direct cultural link to mathematics learning is the field of ethnomathematics (Ascher, 1991). Ethnomathematics documents practices that embody mathematical thinking within everyday practices (counting systems, games, art, architecture, practical engineering, etc.) across a wide range of cultural communities, historical and contemporary. While such everyday practices embody mathematical ideas, there are controversies about whether the ideas constitute mathematics as an academic discipline that reifies abstract versus practical reasoning (Dowling, 1990). However, there are pedagogical efforts to help youth make connections between concepts, problem-solving strategies, and dispositions constructed in the context of everyday cultural practices and their extensions and applications in the formal mathematics taught in schools. Efforts to make such pedagogical connections are emergent and represent new conceptions of culturally relevant pedagogy. These new conceptions move beyond simple recognition of mathematical contributions from diverse cultural communities in the past.

A classic body of work in this area is the studies of Brazilian candy sellers. Nunes, Schliemann, and Carraher (1993) and Saxe (1991, 1999; Saxe & Esmonde, 2005) have in separate studies conducted long-term cognitive ethnographies of low-income children in Brazil who have little schooling but successfully sell candy on the streets of Recife, Brazil. These studies have documented the children's ability to calculate sums and make change mentally. Their calculations involve mental representations of what in school-based algorithms would include borrowing and carrying. Saxe expands these observations by documenting the broader ecological system in which these children develop a sequence of competencies over time.

As the children get older and more experienced, they learn to calculate street prices on the basis of wholesale prices, to group items for sale in ways that minimize the cognitive load of making change, and to adjust street prices on the basis of the exchange rate for the foreigners to whom they typically sell. The ecological supports include the wholesalers, older sellers helping younger children, and a system of routine practices through which the buying and selling take place. Saxe (1991, 1999) also compared the conceptual understanding and strategy use of school children with and without selling practice. He found candy sellers who attended school did adapt their street mathematical strategies to school-based problem solving. However, Saxe and colleagues have not developed specific pedagogical interventions to apply these findings to the teaching of school mathematics.

Several scholars have continued this line of research and have documented the mathematical reasoning involved in the everyday activities of African American youth living in urban centers in the US. Nasir (2000; Nasir, Rosebery, Warren, & Lee, 2006; Nasir & Saxe, 2003) has conducted studies of African American youth routinely engaged in playing dominoes on the West Coast of the US and of African American adolescents who routinely play basketball. In both cases, like Saxe (1991, 1999), she documents the ecological environments that support children's mathematical learning in these contexts, including the nature of supports from the structure of the practices themselves, adults, and more expert-like peers, and culturally rooted norms for talk and participation. Like Saxe, she has documented developmental trajectories from novice to more expert levels of practice. Taylor (2005) has documented the number sense and computational abilities of African American young children living in Oakland, California, as they routinely engage in buying candy after school. Taylor too has demonstrated the complex ecological supports for children's developing competencies, including supports from the adult seller, and how the complexity of children's mathematical goals is influenced by the specifics of the contexts; in this case, children who have to shop quickly in order to catch the school bus that will take them home develop less complex purchases and purchasing strategies than children who live in the neighborhood, walk home from school, and thus have more time to reason about how much they can purchase for their money. As with the Brazilian candy sellers, these computations are all mental. Nasir (Nasir, Hand, & Taylor, 2008; Nasir & Saxe, 2003) has added another dimension to this tradition of research by focusing on the nature of the social and emotional supports that help youth to set goals and to persist in the face of challenges.

There are, however, also programs of research in the US that have developed pedagogical interventions based on helping students make connections between their engagement with mathematics out of school and targeted school-based mathematics. Jerry Lipka (Lipka, 1991) and colleagues have developed a mathematics curriculum that draws on traditional mathematical practices among the Yup'ik Eskimo communities in Alaska. Moll and Gonzalez (2004), who developed the Funds of Knowledge Project (FOK), have done similar work based on community-based practices in Mexican American communities in Arizona. The FOK Project involves teachers and researchers conducting interviews with parents and community residents and doing in-depth community-based observations to determine the range of activities in which adults in children's families and neighborhoods routinely engage that might serve as resources for academic learning. Marta Civil (Civil, 2001, 2002) has spearheaded the work in mathematics for the project.

The Algebra Project (AP) is among the few such projects operating at the middle and high school levels (Moses & Cobb, 2001; Moses, Kamii, Swap, & Howard, 1989; Silva, Moses, Rivers, & Johnson, 1990). Developed by civil rights activist and mathematician Robert Moses, the AP has developed an intervention to teach algebra in schools across seven states in the US. The AP posits that learning higher mathematics is the civil right of the 21st century because robust mathematics training is a prerequisite for science, technology, engineering, and mathematics (STEM) careers. Moses and colleagues use what some have called bridging analogies (Clement, 1993), representations, and anchors, or what Lee (2007) calls "cultural data sets." These are practices that require disciplinary-like reasoning with which students have deep, but tacit, understandings. The logic is that students' conceptual understanding can be facilitated by helping them to examine how they reason about these everyday problems or practices.

This work is accompanied by pedagogical strategies that articulate how these everyday understandings map on to the formal features of disciplinary problem solving. It includes making connections to new features and strategies that are less directly related to the target formal discipline-based problem. For example, Moses argues that one of the major conceptual challenges in the transition from arithmetic to algebra is children's thinking of numbers as only about quantity. In order to help middle and high school students understand the concept of integers – having the properties of both quantity and directionality – the AP uses urban youth's intuitive understandings about navigating the urban transit system: moving from point A (the Harvard Street Station) to point B (the Kendall Street Station) as entailing x number of stops in y direction. Students actually take rides on the train, then develop problems involving moving along the transit system in their own words (including their home languages – African American English, Hmong, Spanish, etc.), and then progressively translate those problems into the symbolic representations of algebraic algorithms.

The AP has been quite successful. Similar work has been carried out with regard to the linguistic resources of students for whom English is a second language, documenting how reasoning in youth's native language, drawing on linguistic cognates and on the ways that particular languages linguistically represent number families, has also proven successful (Cocking & Mestre, 1988; Fuson, Smith, & LoCicero, 1997; Gutiérrez, 2000; Moschkovich, 1999, 2002; Stevenson & Stigler, 1992).

Science

While there is a substantive body of research on the cultural foundations of mathematics learning, there is less in the area of school science. While cognitive psychologists have documented that very young children develop fundamental understandings of number (Canfield & Smith, 1996; Case, 1992; Gelman & Gallistel, 1978; Starkey & Gelman, 1982) as well as biological and physical causality (Baillargeon, 1995; Bertenthal, 1993; Massey & Gelman, 1988; Schilling & Clifton, 1998) across cultural contexts, little research has investigated how to scaffold youth's everyday scientific understandings for teaching formal school science. Indeed, some research has demonstrated that children and adults develop both naive conceptions and misconceptions about forces in the natural world that can interfere with learning scientific concepts, particularly in the area of physics, that are counterintuitive to what we are able to naturally observe in the real world (Clement, 1982; Clement, Brown, & Zietsman, 1989; DiSessa, 1982). For example, studies have shown that even college engineering students who have studied gravitation and force in college physics classes still retain misconceptions (Clement, 1982). Some educational projects stress inquiry processes by providing students with rich data sets (Edelson & Reiser, 2006); others build on the kinds of routine misconceptions that experienced teachers have observed (Hunt & Minstrell, 1994). However, few explicitly scaffold everyday knowledge, particularly that of youth from ethnic and linguistic minority groups (Barton, Ermer, Burkett, & Osborne, 2003).

The Cheche Konnen Project designs interventions that scaffold displays of scientific reasoning among diverse groups of students in the Boston, Massachusetts school district, including African Americans, Haitians, Cape Verdeans, and Eritreans (Rosebery, Warren, Ballenger, & Ogonowski, 2005; Rosebery, Warren, & Conant, 1992; Warren, Ballenger, Ogonowski, Rosebery, & Hudicourt-Barnes, 2001; Warren & Ogonowski, 1998, 2001; Warren & Rosebery, 1996). This project is a unique contribution to the broader efforts of scaffolding everyday knowledge to support disciplinary learning. The project staff works closely with groups of teachers – typically from elementary, especially primary, grades – to examine practice through videotapes of their instruction, similar in some ways to the tradition of lesson study in Japan (Lewis, Perry, & Murata, 2006). Through the joint problem solving of experienced teachers (many of whom are themselves members of the cultural communities of their students) and Cheche Konnen researchers, the problems of practice in which children display non-canonical forms of scientific reasoning are identified. They warrant claims about the significance of these non-canonical displays by examining both the history of science and the practices of real scientists. The project staff argue that there are a number of problem-solving resources that have been historically and are currently used by scientists, particularly when they are investigating phenomena about which the field knows little that are not represented in our traditional approaches to the teaching of scientists.

These include processes like embodied cognition, embodied imagining, narrativizing one's reasoning, and the use of analogies (Lakoff & Nunez, 2000; Nemirovsky, Tierney, & Wright, 1998; Varela, Thompson, & Rosch, 1991; Wilson, 2002). The researchers and teachers then together design instructional practices that elicit and support these modes of reasoning and in so doing help teachers to recognize these practices as they emerge in classroom activities. These non-canonical forms emerge from children's everyday practices and are not explicitly taught in school. The researchers have further demonstrated how culturally rooted linguistic practices facilitate engagement in scientific problem solving in school contexts. For example, they have illustrated how a form of argumentation in Haitian communities called *bay odyans* invites multiple-party talk that entails the use of claims, evidence, and warrants (Nasir, Rosebery,

Warren, & Lee, 2006). The researchers have empirical evidence that this form of cultural scaffolding, or what Lee (2007) calls *cultural modeling*, can improve performance on formal assessments of scientific knowledge; but, more importantly, they have demonstrated robust forms of scientific reasoning in classrooms with culturally diverse students from low-income communities where such cultural scaffolding is routine practice.

Another important program of research in science focuses on the knowledge of botany and biological and ecological systems among the Menominee Indians of Wisconsin in the US. Medin and colleagues have conducted longitudinal cognitive ethnographies of Menominee practices, including fishing and gardening (Atran & Medin, 2008; Bang, Medin, & Atran, 2007; Medin & Atran, 1999). Using a combination of observational, survey, and quasi-experimental designs, Medin and colleagues have documented that Menominee youth, adults, and elders have a rich storehouse of knowledge about the natural world, and that these routine everyday practices entail epistemological assumptions that differ from those of a working-class White community in a town in Wisconsin near the Menominee reservation. For example, fishing is a routine practice in both communities, but the meaning they ascribe to the practice and the attributes about the natural world from which they work are quite distinct. Bang (Bang, Medin, & Atran, 2007) has extended this research by examining the similarities and differences in terms of epistemologies and scientific knowledge of the natural world between Menominee who live on the reservation and Menominee and other American Indians who live in Chicago.

Literacy

In literate societies, reading, writing, and speaking take place in a wide variety of settings (Resnick & Resnick, 1977). In out-of-school environments, reading and speaking are a result of goal-directed behaviors largely driven by interest and practical needs. School, however, demands forms of reading and writing that are connected to the academic disciplines and may differ in significant ways from the kinds of reading and writing associated with everyday practices (Lee & Spratley, in press; O'Brien, Stewart, & Moje, 1995). Workplace settings also often demand specialized ways of reading and writing. Linguistic knowledge is central to acts of reading and writing, regardless of setting. For decades in the US, the language practices of peoples of color and low-income people have been deemed as barriers to academic reading and writing. This includes language practices based on dialect differences and first languages other than English. In this section, I describe programs of research that articulate a paradigm that stresses resources and talent rather than deficits. In this paradigm, the everyday reading, writing, and speaking practices of communities of color in the US serve as resources for academic reading and writing (Lee, 1997, 2005a).

I describe cultural modeling because it offers a framework for analyzing how culturally rooted everyday knowledge can scaffold disciplinary learning. The cultural modeling framework provides a model for examining relationships between everyday practice and academic reasoning, with empirical research that addresses literacy practices specifically (Lee, 1993, 1995a, 1995b, 2000, 2003, 2005b, 2007). This framework requires an analysis of the problem-solving demands of the academic domain in question and of everyday routine practices in communities. It targets everyday practices that entail concepts, modes of reasoning, types of problems, and/or declarative knowledge that is also embodied in disciplinary reasoning in a given domain. The reasoning of everyday practice is often tacit. In cultural modeling, the design of instruction to scaffold the points of convergence between everyday and academic reasoning involves what are called "metacognitive instructional conversations" (Lee, 2007). Here, students are supported in making public and explicit how they reason about the everyday problem. Canonical problems are then introduced and sequenced in such a way as to bridge the introduction of new features of the problem type that may not be captured in the everyday practice, but where students now have initial contact inside the domain. This may be a point of leverage based on strategies, declarative knowledge, or epistemologies.

The early research in cultural modeling will be used to illustrate its basic principles. Signifying is a form of talk in African American English that involves double entendre and a high use of figurative language. Despite the fact that African American English has been viewed as restricting learning, cultural modeling has documented how the tacit reasoning strategies employed by youth who are speakers of African American English in producing and comprehending signifying are similar to the strategies used to interpret such comprehension problems in literary narratives (Lee, 1993, 1995a, 1995b, 2007). Cultural modeling involves students analyzing the strategies they use to comprehend signifying and then applying those strategies to problems of figuration in canonical texts. Pre-post assessments have shown improvement in narrative comprehension by scaffolding this everyday linguistic knowledge. More recent studies have documented the ways that youth examine literary problems such as symbolism, irony, satire, and unreliable narration in everyday texts such as rap lyrics, videos, and film (Fisher, 2003; Morrell, 2002; Morrell & Duncan-Andrade, 2002). Research in cultural modeling has shown how these tacit strategies can be leveraged to help struggling adolescent readers learn to interpret complex canonical literature (Lee, 2007).

Other research has focused specifically on African American cultural resources that support academic writing. Composition studies have examined relationships between oral practices in minority communities and academic composing. Ball (1992, 1995) documented preferred expository writing styles among adolescents that are rooted in African American linguistic traditions. She has documented the rhetorical qualities of these preferred expository styles. Smitherman (1977, 1994, 2000a, 2000b) showed that what she calls African American rhetorical features characterized those writing samples from several years of the National Assessment of Educational Progress with the highest scores. This was a post hoc analysis. These studies illustrate conceptual links between everyday oral practices and academic composing, as well as the pedagogical implications of such links.

Other studies have examined how everyday linguistic practices can serve as effective modes of communication in academic contexts, or how inattention to such practices may constrain opportunities to learn in classrooms. Au and colleagues (Au, 1980; Tharp & Gallimore, 1988) designed a program of research in schools serving native Hawaiian children on the island that strategically used a linguistic genre called *talk story*. Talk story is an indigenous oral tradition. It re-defines the roles that students can play in modes of argumentation. Studies show significant improvement in reading comprehension when talk story was used as a medium of instructional conversations. Norms for talk in American Indian communities have been shown to involve different rules for entering conversations than is typically expected in U.S. classrooms (John-Steiner, 1984; Phillips, 1983). Studies have shown that participation patterns in classroom dialogue among American Indian students may be misconstrued as indicating not knowing when students have different expectations about entering instructional conversations than teachers.

Another important body of research addresses the role of differences between the national languages of home and school. While bilingual issues are relevant to instruction across disciplines, the centrality of reading, writing, and speaking to learning in schools makes literacy and bilingualism a particularly important area in countries around the world (Valdes, 1996). Sometimes immigrants speak other languages than the national language at home. In other cases, such as South Africa, countries are themselves multilingual. In the case of South Africa, post-apartheid instruction continues to take place predominantly in English, while students at home may speak a variety of African languages (Ball, 2000).

Studies have shown a variety of ways in which a second language may serve as a resource for learning. Explicit support for thinking through reading comprehension problems in one's first language has been shown to improve performance (Garcia, 1998, 2000; Jimenez, Garcia, & Pearson, 1995). Careful attention to reading competencies in the first language, particularly when youth have had schooling in their countries of origin, is important for assessing reading competence. Distinguishing between decoding abilities in the second language and comprehension in the second language has implications for text selection and sequencing (Garcia, 1991, 1998, 2000; Gutierrez, Baquedano-Lopez, & Tejeda, 1999; Jimenez, Garcia, & Pearson, 1995, 1996; Langer, Bartolome, Vasquez, & Lucas, 1990; Moll, Estrada, Diaz, & Lopes, 1980; Valdes, Bunch, Snow, & Lee, 2005).

Conclusion

The role of culture in learning is complex and fundamental. Our work in education should be informed by theories that account for the variation in pathways for learning across cultural communities. This variation must include patterns of both continuity and difference within communities. One way to address this continuity and difference is to examine the everyday routine practices of cultural communities, with the understanding that there will be variation in such patterns of activity (Gutierrez & Rogoff, 2003). Examining conceptual and pedagogical links between everyday and disciplinary knowledge expands opportunities for more youth to learn academic problem solving, especially those from ethnic minority, immigrant, and low-income communities.

This work illustrates how the social organization of routine practices (in and out of school) can influence goals, effort, and the structure and deployment of knowledge, as well as how people see themselves in relation to practice. The research described here provides a foundation for future work that should be transnational. The challenges of conceptualizing this complexity and its implications for teaching and learning are perhaps more important than at any other point in history. These challenges are made all the more difficult by the history of hegemonic beliefs that inform institutional practices and societal organization in most nations, especially those involving systems of Western education. However, the research base about how culture can be strategically leveraged to support learning provides important guidance for our efforts.

References

Ascher, M. (1991). *Ethnomathematics: A multicultural view of mathematical ideas*. Pacific Grove, CA: Brooks/Cole Publishing Company.

Atran, S., & Medin, D. L. (2008). *The native mind and the cultural construction of nature*. Cambridge, MA: MIT Press.

Au, K. H. (1980). Participation structures in a reading lesson with Hawaiian children: Analysis of a culturally appropriate instructional event. *Anthropology and Education, 11*(2), 91–115.

Baillargeon, R. (1995). Physical reasoning in infancy. In M. S. Gazzaniga (Ed.), *The cognitive neurosciences* (pp. 181–204). Cambridge, MA: MIT Press.

Ball, A. F. (1992). Cultural preferences and the expository writing of African-American adolescents. *Written Communication, 9*(4), 501–532.

Ball, A. F. (1995). Text design patterns in the writing of urban African-American students: Teaching to the strengths of students in multicultural settings. *Urban Education, 30,* 253–289.

Ball, A. F. (2000). Teachers developing philosophies in literacy and their use in urban schools. In C. D. Lee & P. Smagorinsky (Eds.), *Vygotskian perspectives on literacy research: Constructing meaning through collaborative inquiry* (pp. 226–255). New York: Cambridge University Press.

Bang, M., Medin, D. L., & Atran, S. (2007). Cultural mosaics and mental models of nature. *Proceedings of the National Academy of Sciences, 104,* 13868–13874.

Barton, A. C., Ermer, J. L., Burkett, T. A., & Osborne, M. D. (2003). *Teaching science for social justice.* New York: Teachers College Press.

Barton, D., & Hamilton, M. (1998). *Local literacies: Reading and writing in one community.* London: Routledge.

Bertenthal, B. I. (1993). Infants' perception of biomechanical motions: Intrinsic image and knowledge-based constraints. In C. E. Granrud (Ed.), *Carnegie Mellon symposia on cognition: Visual perception and cognition in infancy* (pp. 175–214). Hillsdale, NJ: Lawrence Erlbaum.

Bransford, J., Brown, A., & Cocking, R. (1999). *How people learn: Brain, mind, experience and school.* Washington, DC: National Academy Press.

Canfield, R. L., & Smith, E. G. (1996). Number-based expectations and sequential enumeration by 5-month-old infants. *Developmental Psychology, 32,* 269–279.

Case, R. (1992). *The mind's staircase: Exploring the conceptual underpinnings of children's thought and knowledge.* Hillsdale, NJ: Lawrence Erlbaum.

Civil, M. (2001). Mathematics instruction developed from a garden theme. *Teaching Children Mathematics, 7*(7), 400–405.

Civil, M. (2002). Culture and mathematics: A community approach. *Journal of Intercultural Studies, 23*(2), 133–148.

Clement, J. (1982). Student preconceptions of introductory mechanics. *American Journal of Physics, 50,* 66–71.

Clement, J. (1993). Using bridging analogies and anchoring intuitions to deal with students' preconceptions in physics. *Journal of Research in Science Teaching, 30*(10), 1241–1257.

Clement, J., Brown, D., & Zietsman, A. (1989). Not all preconceptions are misconceptions: Finding anchoring conceptions for grounding instruction on students' intuitions. *International Journal of Science Education, 11,* 554–565.

Cocking, R. R., & Mestre, J. P. (1988). *Linguistic and cultural influences on learning mathematics.* Hillsdale, NJ: Lawrence Erlbaum.

Collins, A., & Ferguson, W. (1993). Epistemic forms and epistemic games: Structures and strategies to guide inquiry. *Educational Psychologist, 28*(1), 25–42.

Dai, D. Y., & Sternberg, R. (2004). *Motivation, emotion, and cognition: Integrative perspectives on intellectual functioning and development.* Mahwah, NJ: Lawrence Erlbaum.

Deutsch, M., & Brown, B. (1964). Social influences in Negro–White intelligence differences. *Journal of Social Issues, 20,* 24–35.

DiSessa, A. (1982). Unlearning Aristotelian physics: A study of knowledge-base learning. *Cognitive Science, 6,* 37–75.

Dowling, P. (Ed.). (1990). *Mathematics versus the national curriculum.* Bristol, PA: Falmer Press.

Dweck, C. S. (1999). *Self-theories: Their role in motivation, personality, and development.* Philadelphia: Psychology Press.

Dweck, C. S. (2002). Beliefs that make smart people dumb. In R. Sternberg (Ed.), *Why smart people can be so stupid* (pp. 24–41). New Haven, CT: Yale University Press.

Eccles, J. S., Wigfield, A., & Schiefele, U. (1998). Motivation to succeed. In W. Damon & N. Eisenberg (Eds.), *Handbook of child psychology* (5th ed., Vol. 3, pp. 1017–1095). New York: Wiley.

Edelson, D., & Reiser, B. (2006). Making authentic practices accessible to learners: Design challenges and strategies. In K. Sawyer (Ed.), *Cambridge handbook of the learning sciences* (pp. 335–354). New York: Cambridge.

Fisher, M. T. (2003). Open mics and open minds: Spoken word poetry in African diaspora participatory literacy communities. *Harvard Educational Review, 73*(3), 362–389.

Flavell, J. H. (1981). *The development of comprehension monitoring and knowledge about communication.* Chicago: University of Chicago Press.

Fuson, K., Smith, S., & LoCicero, A. (1997). Supporting Latino first graders' ten-structured thinking in urban classrooms. *Journal for Research in Mathematics Education, 28,* 738–760.

Garcia, G. E. (1991). Factors influencing the English reading test performance of Spanish-speaking Hispanic children. *Reading Research Quarterly, 26*(4), 371–392.

Garcia, G. E. (1998). Mexican-American bilingual students' metacognitive reading strategies: What's transferred, unique, problematic? *National Reading Conference Yearbook, 47,* 253–263.

Garcia, G. E. (2000). Bilingual children's reading. In M. Kamil, P. Mosenthal, P. D. Pearson, & R. Barr (Eds.), *Handbook of reading research* (Vol. 3, pp. 813–834). Mahwah, NJ: Lawrence Erlbaum.

Gelman, R., & Gallistel, C. R. (1978). *The child's understanding of number.* Cambridge, MA: Harvard University Press.

Graham, S., & Hudley, C. (2005). Race and ethnicity in the study of motivation and competence. In A. J. Elliot & C. S. Dweck (Eds.), *Handbook of competence and motivation* (pp. 392–413). New York: Guilford Press.

Griffin, S. A., Case, R., & Capodilupo, A. (1995). Teaching for understanding: The importance of the central conceptual structures in the elementary mathematics curriculum. In A. McKeough, J. Lupart, & A. Marini (Eds.), *Teaching for transfer: Fostering generalization in learning* (pp. 123–151). Hillsdale, NJ: Lawrence Erlbaum.

Gutierrez, K., Baquedano-Lopez, P., & Tejeda, C. (1999). Rethinking diversity: Hybridity and hybrid language practices in the third space. *Mind, Culture, and Activity, 6*(4), 286–303.

Gutierrez, K., & Rogoff, B. (2003). Cultural ways of learning: Individual traits or repertoires of practice. *Educational Researcher, 32*(5), 19–25.

Gutiérrez, R. (2000). Advancing African American, urban youth in mathematics: Unpacking the success of one mathematics department. *American Journal of Education, 109*(1), 63–111.

Hatano, G., & Inagaki, K. (1986). Two courses of expertise. In H. W. Stevenson, H. Azuma, & K. Hakuta (Eds.), *Child development and education in Japan* (pp. 262–272). New York: Freeman.

Hunt, E., & Minstrell, J. (1994). A cognitive approach to the teaching of physics. In K. McGilly (Ed.), *Classroom lessons: Integrating cognitive theory and classroom practice* (pp. 51–74). Cambridge, MA: MIT Press.

Jimenez, R. T., Garcia, G. E., & Pearson, P. D. (1995). Three children, two languages, and strategic reading: Case studies in bilingual/monolingual reading. *American Educational Research Journal, 32,* 31–61.

Jimenez, R. T., Garcia, G. E., & Pearson, P. D. (1996). The reading strategies of Latina/o students who are successful English readers: Opportunities and obstacles. *Reading Research Quarterly, 31*(1), 90–112.

John-Steiner, V. (1984). Learning styles among Pueblo children. *Quarterly Newsletter of the Laboratory of Comparative Human Cognition, 6,* 57–62.

Lakoff, G., & Nunez, R. (2000). *Where mathematics comes from: How the embodied mind brings mathematics into being.* New York: Basic Books.

Langer, J., Bartolome, L., Vasquez, O., & Lucas, T. (1990). Meaning construction in school literacy tasks: A study of bilingual students. *American Educational Research Journal, 27*(3), 427–471.

Lee, C. D. (1993). *Signifying as a scaffold for literary interpretation: The pedagogical implications of an African American discourse genre.* Urbana, IL: National Council of Teachers of English.

Lee, C. D. (1995a). A culturally based cognitive apprenticeship: Teaching African American high school students skills in literary interpretation. *Reading Research Quarterly, 30*(4), 608–631.

Lee, C. D. (1995b). Signifying as a scaffold for literary interpretation. *Journal of Black Psychology, 21*(4), 357–381.

Lee, C. D. (1997). Bridging home and school literacies: A model of culturally responsive teaching. In J. Flood, S. B. Heath, & D. Lapp (Eds.), *A handbook for literacy educators: Research on teaching the communicative and visual arts* (pp. 330–341). New York: Macmillan.

Lee, C. D. (2000). Signifying in the zone of proximal development. In C. D. Lee & P. Smagorinsky (Eds.), *Vygotskian perspectives on literacy research: Constructing meaning through collaborative inquiry* (pp. 191–225). New York: Cambridge University Press.

Lee, C. D. (2003). *Cultural modeling and pedagogical content knowledge: The case of the teacher of literature.* Paper presented at the Annual Meeting of the American Educational Research Association, Chicago, IL.

Lee, C. D. (2005a). Culture and language: Bi-dialectical issues in literacy. In P. L. Anders & J. Flood (Eds.), *Literacy development of students in urban schools: Research and policy* (pp. 241–274). Newark, DE: International Reading Association.

Lee, C. D. (2005b). Double voiced discourse: African American vernacular English as resource in cultural modeling classrooms. In A. F. Ball & S. W. Freedman (Eds.), *New literacies for new times: Bakhtinian perspectives on language, literacy, and learning for the 21st century* (pp. 129–147). New York: Cambridge University Press.

Lee, C. D. (2006). The educability of intellective competence. In E. W. Gordon & B. L. Bridglall (Eds.), *The affirmative development of academic abilities* (pp. 155–188). Boulder, CO: Rowman & Littlefield.

Lee, C. D. (2007). *Culture, literacy, and learning: Taking bloom in the midst of the whirlwind.* New York: Teachers College Press.

Lee, C. D. (2008). The centrality of culture to the scientific study of learning and development: How an ecological framework in educational research facilitates civic responsibility. *Educational Researcher, 37*(3), 267–279.

Lee, C. D., & Spratley, A. (in press). *Reading in the disciplines and the challenges of adolescent literacy.* New York: Carnegie Foundation of New York.

Lewis, C., Perry, R., & Murata, A. (2006). How should research contribute to instructional improvement? A case of lesson study. *Educational Researcher, 35*(3), 3–14.

Lipka, J. (1991). Toward a culturally based pedagogy: A case of one Yup'ik Eskimo teacher. *Anthropology and Education Quarterly, 22,* 3203–3223.

Massey, C. M., & Gelman, R. (1988). Preschoolers decide whether pictured unfamiliar objects can move themselves. *Developmental Psychology, 24,* 307–317.

Medin, D. L., & Atran, S. (Eds.). (1999). *Folkbiology.* Cambridge, MA: Bradford.

Moll, L., Estrada, E., Diaz, E., & Lopes, L. M. (1980). The organization of bilingual lessons: Implications for schooling. *The Quarterly Newsletter of the Laboratory of Comparative Human Cognition, 2*(3), 53–58.

Moll, L., & Gonzales, N. (2004). Engaging life: A funds of knowledge approach to multicultural education. In J. A. Banks & C. A. M. Banks (Eds.), *Handbook of research on multicultural education* (2nd ed., pp. 699–715). New York: Jossey-Bass.

Morrell, E. (2002). Toward a critical pedagogy of popular culture: Literacy development among urban youth. *Journal of Adolescent & Adult Literacy, 46*(1), 72–78.

Morrell, E., & Duncan-Andrade, J. (2002). Promoting academic literacy with urban youth through engaging hip-hop culture. *English Journal, 91*(6), 88–93.

Moschkovich, J. (1999). Supporting the participation of English language learners in mathematical discussions. *For the Learning of Mathematics, 19*(1), 11–19.

Moschkovich, J. (2002). A situated and sociocultural perspective on bilingual mathematics learners. *Mathematical Thinking and Learning, 4*(2/3), 189–212.

Moses, R. P., & Cobb, C. E. (2001). *Radical equations: Math literacy and civil rights.* Boston: Beacon Press.

Moses, R. P., Kamii, M., Swap, S. M., & Howard, J. (1989). The algebra project: Organizing in the spirit of Ella. *Harvard Educational Review, 59*(4), 423–443.

Muschinske, D. (1977). The nonwhite as child: G. Stanley Hall on the education of nonwhite peoples. *Journal of the History of the Behavioral Sciences, 13*(4), 328–336.

Nasir, N. (2000). "Points ain't everything": Emergent goals and average and percent understandings in the play of basketball among African American students. *Anthropology and Education, 31*(1), 283–305.

Nasir, N., Hand, V., & Taylor, E. (2008). Culture and mathematics in school: Boundaries between "cultural" and "domain" knowledge in the mathematics classroom and beyond. *Review of Research in Education, 32,* 187–240.

Nasir, N., Rosebery, A. S., Warren, B., & Lee, C. D. (2006). Learning as a cultural process: Achieving equity through diversity. In K. Sawyer (Ed.), *Handbook of the learning sciences* (pp. 489–504). New York: Cambridge University Press.

Nasir, N., & Saxe, G. (2003). Emerging tensions and their management in the lives of minority students. *Educational Researcher, 32*(5), 14–18.

Nemirovsky, R., Tierney, C., & Wright, T. (1998). Body motion and graphing. *Cognition and Instruction, 16*(2), 119–172.

Nunes, T., Schliemann, A. D., & Carraher, D. W. (1993). *Street mathematics and school mathematics.* New York: Cambridge University Press.

O'Brien, D., Stewart, R., & Moje, E. B. (1995). Why content literacy is difficult to infuse into the secondary school: Complexities of curriculum, pedagogy, and school culture. *Reading Research Quarterly, 30,* 442–463.

Perkins, D. (1993). Person-plus: A distributed view of thinking and learning. In G. Salomon (Ed.), *Distributed cognitions: Psychological and educational considerations* (pp. 88–110). New York: Cambridge University Press.

Perkins, D. (1995). *Outsmarting IQ: The emerging science of learnable intelligence.* New York: Free Press.

Phillips, S. U. (1983). *The invisible culture: Communication in classroom and community on the Warm Springs Indian Reservation.* New York: Longman.

Resnick, D., & Resnick, L. (1977). The nature of literacy: An historical exploration. *Harvard Educational Review, 43,* 370–385.

Rogoff, B. (2003). *The cultural nature of human development.* New York: Oxford University Press.

Rogoff, B., & Lave, J. (1984). *Everyday cognition: Its development in social context.* Cambridge, MA: Harvard University Press.

Rosebery, A. S., Warren, B., Ballenger, C., & Ogonowski, M. (2005). The generative potential of students' everyday knowledge in learning science. In T. Romberg, T. Carpenter, & D. Fae (Eds.), *Understanding mathematics and science matters* (pp. 55–80). Mahwah, NJ: Lawrence Erlbaum.

Rosebery, A. S., Warren, B., & Conant, F. R. (1992). Appropriating scientific discourse: Findings from language minority classrooms. *The Journal of Learning Sciences, 2*(1), 61–94.

Saxe, G. (1991). *Culture and cognitive development: Studies in mathematical understanding.* Hillsdale, NJ: Lawrence Erlbaum.

Saxe, G. (1999). Cognition, development, and cultural practices. In E. Turiel (Ed.), *Culture and development: New directions in child psychology* (pp. 19–35). San Francisco: Jossey-Bass.

Saxe, G., & Esmonde, I. (2005). Studying cognition in the flux: A historical treatment of Fu in the shifting structure of Oksapimin mathematics. *Mind, Culture and Activity, 12,* 171–225.

Schilling, T. H., & Clifton, R. K. (1998). Nine-month-old infants learn about a physical event in a single session: Implications for infants' understanding of physical phenomena. *Cognitive Development, 133,* 165–184.

Silva, C. M., Moses, R. P., Rivers, J., & Johnson, P. (1990). The Algebra Project: Making middle school mathematics count. *Journal of Negro Education, 59*(3), 375–392.

Singley, K., & Anderson, J. R. (1989). *The transfer of cognitive skill.* Cambridge, MA: Harvard University Press.

Smitherman, G. (1977). *Talkin and testifyin: The language of Black America.* Boston: Houghton Mifflin.

Smitherman, G. (1994). The blacker the berry, the sweeter the juice: African American student writers. In A. Dyson & C. Genishi (Eds.), *The need for story: Cultural diversity in classroom and community* (pp. 80–101). Urbana, IL: National Council of Teachers of English.

Smitherman, G. (2000a). African American student writers in the NAEP, 1969–1988/89 and "The blacker the berry, the sweeter the juice." In G. Smitherman (Ed.), *Talkin that talk: Language, culture and education in African America* (pp. 163–194). New York: Routledge.

Smitherman, G. (2000b). *Talkin that talk: Language, culture and education in African America.* New York: Routledge.

Spiro, R., Feltovich, P. L., Jackson, M. J., & Coulson, R. L. (1991). Cognitive flexibility, constructivism, and hypertext: Random access instruction for advanced technology acquisition to ill-structured domains. *Educational Technology, 31*(5), 24–33.

Starkey, P., & Gelman, R. (1982). The development of addition and subtraction abilities prior to formal schooling. In T. Carpenter, J. M. Moser, & T. Romberg (Eds.), *Addition and subtraction: A developmental perspective* (pp. 99–116). Hillsdale, NJ: Lawrence Erlbaum.

Stevenson, H. W., & Stigler, J. W. (1992). *The learning gap: Why our schools are failing and what we can learn from Japanese and Chinese education.* New York: Simon & Schuster.

Super, C., & Harkness, S. (1986). The developmental niche: A conceptualization at the interface of child and culture. *International Journal of Behavioral Development, 9,* 545–569.

Taylor, E. (2005). *Low-income African-American first- and second-grade students' engagement in currency exchange: The relationship to mathematical development.* Unpublished doctoral dissertation, University of California, Berkeley.

Tharp, R., & Gallimore, R. (1988). *Rousing minds to life: Teaching, learning, and schooling in social context.* New York: Cambridge University Press.

Valdes, G. (1996). *Con respeto: Bridging the distances between culturally diverse families and schools.* New York: Teachers College Press.

Valdes, G., Bunch, G. E., Snow, C., & Lee, C. (2005). Enhancing the development of students' language(s). In L. Darling-Hammond & J. Bransford (Eds.), *Preparing teachers for a changing world: What teachers should learn and be able to do* (pp. 126–168). San Francisco: Jossey-Bass.

Varela, F., Thompson, E., & Rosch, E. (1991). *The embodied mind: Cognitive science and human experience.* Cambridge, MA: MIT Press.

Walker, C. H. (1987). Relative importance of domain knowledge and overall aptitude on acquisition of domain-related knowledge. *Cognition and Instruction, 4,* 25–42.

Warren, B., Ballenger, C., Ogonowski, M., Rosebery, A. S., & Hudicourt-Barnes, J. (2001). Rethinking diversity in learning science: The logic of everyday sense-making. *Journal of Research in Science Teaching, 38,* 529–552.

Warren, B., & Ogonowski, M. (1998). *From knowledge to knowing: An inquiry into teacher learning in science.* Newton, MA: Education Development Center.

Warren, B., & Ogonowski, M. (2001, April). *Embodied imagining: A study of adult learning in physics.* Paper presented at the meeting of the American Educational Research Association, Seattle, WA.

Warren, B., & Rosebery, A. S. (1996). "This question is just too, too easy!": Perspectives from the classroom on accountability in science. In L. Schauble & R. Glaser (Eds.), *Innovations in learning: New environments for education* (pp. 97–125). Hillsdale, NJ: Lawrence Erlbaum.

Weisner, T. S. (2002). Ecocultural understanding of children's developmental pathways. *Human Development, 174,* 275–281.

White, B. Y., & Frederickson, J. R. (1998). Inquiry, modeling, and metacognition: Making science accessible to all students. *Cognition and Science, 16,* 90–91.

Wilson, M. (2002). Six views of embodied cognition. *Psychonomic Bulletin & Review, 9*(4), 625–636.

Yekovich, F. R., Walker, C. H., Ogle, L. T., & Thompson, M. A. (1990). The influence of domain knowledge on inferencing in low-aptitude individuals. In A. C. Graesser & G. H. Bower (Eds.), *The psychology of learning and motivation* (pp. 175–196). New York: Academic Press.

Zajonc, R. B., & Marcus, H. (1984). Affect and cognition. In C. E. Izard, J. Kagan, & R. B. Zajonc (Eds.), *Emotions, cognition and behavior* (pp. 73–102). Cambridge, UK: Cambridge University Press.

18

Socialization, literacy, and empowerment

Thor Ola Engen
Hedmark University College, Norway

Like many Western societies, Norway has experienced Program for International Student Assessment (PISA) shock (Hvistendahl & Roe, 2004; Roe, Linnakylä, & Lie, 2003). This shock has created a new consensus among school authorities and politicians that a stronger focus on academic learning is needed. This consensus is inspired by the Organisation for Economic Co-operation and Development (OECD) slogan: "Quality education is one of the most valuable assets that a society and an individual can have" (OECD, 2008; see also Baker, 2006). An explicit implication of this consensus is that skills are key factors for productivity, economic growth, and better living standards (Gurria, 2008). Consequently, rather strong measures have been taken to make sure that educational programs focus strongly on fundamental skills – especially in reading, but also in writing and mathematics (Undervisnings- og Forskningsdepartementet [Ministry of Education and Research], 2003).

As far as linguistic minority students are concerned, mainstreaming and majority language teaching have been encouraged at the expense of models of bilingual teaching (Oslo Kommune [Municipality of Oslo], 2004a, 2004b). School authorities have accepted the widespread assumption that majority language literacy is the opportunity by which minority language students are given the means to increase their chances of prosperity, power, and prestige (Baker, 2006). The marked shift of mentality that has taken place (Haug & Bachmann, 2007) – in Norway as in other Western countries – presumably has been justified by arguing that the focus on fundamental skills empowers students and gives them access. Even if the primary concern has been to give linguistic minority students more equal access to the labor market, an accompanying assumption has been that a skills approach will enhance cultural cohesion through social integration of linguistic minorities and thereby empower them as citizens.

However, Norwegian schools have for a long time been practicing a unilateral, mainstreaming approach (Engen, 2003a). The results of a recent international study concerned with linguistic minority adolescents' psychological and sociocultural acculturation suggests that the strategy may have rather paradoxical and unexpected outcomes (Berry, 2006). An ethnic-oriented category of linguistic minority youths – consisting of 29.5% of the sample – was largely embedded within the youths' own cultural milieu, endorsing a separation attitude, with low scores on assimilation, national identity, and contacts with the national group and little involvement with the larger society. Instead the members showed a clear orientation toward their own ethnic group, with high ethnic identity, ethnic language proficiency and usage, high ethnic peer contacts, and well-above-average support for family relationship values.

Another category, consisting of 27.4% of the sample, reported low proficiency in the national language and somewhat low national identity and national peer contacts. At the same time, the category reported high proficiency and usage of the ethnic language, but also low ethnic identity. This group endorsed assimilation as well as marginalization and separation, a contradictory pattern suggesting that the members were uncertain about their place in society. As they seemed to lack a direction or purpose in their lives and often were socially isolated, their profile is diffuse (Berry, 2006).

Only one group of the sample showed the national acculturation profile. The adolescents in this category were proficient in the national language and used it predominantly. Their peer contacts were largely with members of the national group, and they showed low support for family obligations. Further, they were high on national identity and very low on ethnic identity. This group of "nationals" seems to exemplify the idea of assimilation, indicating a lack of retention of their own ethnic culture in terms of identity, language, peer contacts, or values (Berry, 2006). In spite of the dominating mainstreaming approach in schools, they formed only 14.6% of the sample.

A final category (28.5% of the sample) shared most of the characteristics of the "nationals;" they were high on national identity, had high involvement in the national culture, reported high national language proficiency, and had peer contacts with the national group. At the same time, however, they were also high on ethnic identity, with a relatively high involvement in their ethnic culture, reported average ethnic language proficiency, and also had peer contacts with their own group. This group appeared to be comfortable in both ethnic and national contexts in terms of identity, language, peer contacts, and values. They strongly endorsed integration and thought less favorably of assimilation, as well as separation and marginalization (Berry, 2006).

These acculturation profiles may be closely correlated with the academic success of adolescents in school (Engen, 2003a). It may well be assumed that most of the students in the national group had been academically successful. Further, both theoretical and empirical evidence (Cummins, 2000; Øzerk, 2003) suggests that the bicultural and bilingual profile of the integration group must be actualized through the joint efforts of the home and the school. The ethnic-oriented group may be interpreted as segregated, because many must have been excluded through relative school failure (Engen, 2003a; Hvistendahl & Roe, 2004; Roe et al., 2003), but also as separated, because withdrawal for some may have been voluntary. The contradictory pattern of the diffuse group suggests that the members perhaps wanted to be part of the larger society but lacked the interpersonal skills to make contacts because of school failure (Berry, 2006).

The hypothesis

On the background of Berry's (2006) results, a hypothesis of work division between the home and the school formulated by Engen (2003a) may be reintroduced: A monolingual mainstreaming strategy may lead to integration, but only when the school's unilateral majority cultural influence is balanced by parents who are in a position to compensate for, supplement, and mediate the schools' effort with home cultural perspectives. When a majority of linguistic minority students fail academically, making segregation, separation, or marginalization the most probable outcome, it is because most linguistic minority parents are unprepared to meet the challenge involved. Assimilation is the least probable outcome of socialization, because it is reserved for students who manage to succeed without decisive support from the home.

According to this hypothesis, it is disputable whether a mainstreaming approach has the power to supply linguistic minority students with the fundamental literacy skills needed for equal access to the labor market (i.e. empowerment in a narrow sense of the concept). Further, as empowerment in a more extended sense of the concept implies a process of transition from lack of control to the acquisition of control over one's life and immediate environment (Delgado-Gaitan & Trueba, 1991; see also Banks, 2008), the hypothesis gives little reason to assume that such an outcome will occur from a mainstreaming skills approach. At this point the hypothesis is supported by critics who claim that a skills approach threatens not only to undermine the development of self-understanding and value commitment (Løvlie, 2005; Telhaug, 2005), but also to replace the idea of the educated citizen by that of the isolated individual responsible for his/her own life (Carlgren, Klette, Myrdal, Schnack, & Simola, 2006; see also Banks, 2008). Thus, there is little support for the assumption that a mainstreaming skills approach has the potential to bridge the achievement gap between minority and majority linguistic students (Collier & Thomas, 2002; Thomas & Collier, 2002).

In this chapter, this hypothesis will be elaborated and substantiated by a general theory of socialization introduced by Hoëm (1978; Darnell & Hoëm, 1996). Hoëm argues that the tasks of a narrow and extended empowerment are closely interrelated, but also that it is only optimal conditions for extended empowerment that secure instrumental learning and empowerment in the narrow sense. Hoëm's theory then contradicts the assumption that extended empowerment will follow automatically as long as optimal conditions for instrumental learning are secured. Further, especially in a diverse society where many parents are quite unfamiliar with the expectations and traditions of the school, the task of extended empowerment cannot be left to the homes alone. Before this theoretical argument is outlined, however, it will be introduced and illustrated by the case of early literacy teaching.

Fundamentals of early literacy teaching

According to Fillmore (1986, p. 661), by reading we refer to the act of reconstructing the meaning of a text and through this process gaining access to the information that is encoded in the text. What the reader applies in this constructive process is knowledge that is not encoded by the written word: knowledge of the language, of conventions of its use, of the real world, and of topics treated in the text. However, for reading to function as a reconstructive process, the learner must be able to focus all attention on the *meaning* of the text. And for that to occur decoding must become automatized to such a degree that it can be taken for given; that is, decoding has to become orthographic and fluent, caused by a paradigmatic change of reference – from the sound system of oral speech to the sign system of written speech.

Until beginning readers have developed fluent, automatized decoding, however, it is fundamental that they are allowed to take *comprehension* as a given, precisely of knowledge that is not encoded by the written word. Only in such a case will elementary texts open a "world" behind the words that is rich and varied enough to mobilize both motivation and relevant cognitive processes so that decoding can become integrated with comprehension in much the same way as salt is dissolved in water. Thus, the student must experience spontaneous comprehension in order to be able to focus all attention on the acquisition of *technical* decoding skills (Elsness, 2003; Fillmore, 1986; Gardner & Lambert, 1972; Ricoeur, 1973; Uppstad & Solheim, 2005; Vygotsky, 1987).

When comprehension does not occur spontaneously, however, it will require attention and time of its own, interrupting the task of technical training as well as slowing down progression. In the worst of cases, lack of spontaneous comprehension threatens to isolate decoding from comprehension, reducing it to a more or less mechanical skill. For as long as the learner has to be consciously concerned with the technical aspects, reading will hardly become orthographic and fluent enough for the learner to focus all attention on the *meaning* of the text. In such a case, the development of orthographic reading – which is a presupposition for academic learning in subsequent stages of school – will not only be retarded but perhaps hardly be developed at all. Further, and just as crucial, the student will not be able to acquire the fairly high level of knowledge of the language and the culture which is a prerequisite for true reading (Engen, 2003b).

As this argument clearly indicates, decoding and comprehension are closely interrelated. But for as long as promoting decoding skills is the aim, spontaneous comprehension has to function as a type of profound and autonomous cultural decoding. This may be one reason why basal books such as the "easy readers" do not function very well, even if they are designed with a special concern for academically weak students, in order to improve their reading – that is, decoding – skills (Baker, 2006). Their simplified majority language is unfavorable for the spontaneous comprehension of students with linguistic minority backgrounds. At best, they will decode a different meaning, but "easy readers" may also threaten to isolate the task of decoding from comprehension, turning it into a purely mechanical skill.

With a high correspondence between reading material and the child's preconceptions, linguistically and culturally, however, the conditions for elementary reading development are enhanced, not only as far as breaking the reading code is concerned, but also for preparing a foundation for a paradigmatic change of reference: from the sound system of oral speech to the sign system of written speech. When there is a high correspondence between reading material and the students' preconceptions, students will gradually be enabled to use reading as a powerful instrument in subsequent knowledge acquisition, not least when it comes to the establishment of reading strategies and metacognitive awareness.

This is why the case of elementary literacy teaching illustrates a more general argument that the correspondence between the students' preconceptions and the cultural and linguistic characteristics of the learning material is of crucial importance for learning (Baker, 2006). Even if all students are equipped with a certain cultural capital when they come to school, they are dependent upon its recognition to profit optimally from instruction (Bourdieu & Passeron, 1990). Hoëm (1978), based on extensive empirical research on the indigenous Sami population, suggested that, when the students' cultural capital is rejected, the home–school relation is characterized by a conflict of values that will lead to de-socialization, re-socialization, or shielded socialization. Accordingly, the students' cultural capital should be recognized in order to prepare a commonality of values between the home and the school, so that a sufficient basis for a course of reinforcing socialization is constituted.

Reinforcing socialization

Hoëm's (1978) argument substantiates on a more general basis that a close correspondence between the students' preconceptions and the cultural and linguistic characteristics of the learning material creates optimal conditions for restricted empowerment in terms of instrumental learning. In addition, however, Hoëm anticipates the arguments of Taylor (1994) and Ricoeur (2004) on the fundamental pedagogical importance of recognition for extended empowerment. Like Taylor and Ricoeur, he argues that recognition both constitutes a relation of mutual respect and is a main premise for dialogue between a cultural majority and minorities, while lack of recognition undermines any dialogue and leads to indignation, contempt, and a feeling of exclusion.

Hellesnes (1975) argues that recognition prepares a foundation for a process of localization that promotes a deeper understanding and awareness of the social and cultural world in which students belong, while they also learn to understand themselves as social individuals (Freire, 1970). A process of localization is central also to reinforcing socialization. But for it to correspond to empowerment in the extended sense of the word, two additional characteristics are needed. If recognition is interpreted narrowly as identity confirmation alone, the cultural context of the learning material will easily be granted, so that students may remain largely unaware of their cultural predispositions. Secondly, and in such a case, the learning material may even be demagogic, indoctrinating, or counter-indoctrinating, so that the school systematically tries to make students understand their situation by means of the thoughts of others, making them an object for control. In both cases *adaptation* is the outcome, meaning that students are socialized in such a way that one takes for granted the social conditions within which one exists. The well-adapted individuals are dutiful students who perform whatever functions are assigned without thinking much about which power relations and social processes they are confirming and preserving. They have become blind to historical change and have learned to perceive any given historical state as *the* state, as natural and obvious (Hellesnes, 1975, 1984).

Adaptation may be a central aspect of empowerment in the restricted sense. But to exceed adaptation and realize empowerment in the extended sense the school must be concerned with the personal reflection of students so that they can begin to trust their own experiences. The teacher's task is to provide clarifying concepts and theoretical perspectives, and to help students gain confidence in their own rationality, for, if one has rationality and truth on one's side, there is no need for indoctrination. Instead one should argue and give reasons (Hellesnes, 1975).

To exceed adaptation and to realize empowerment in the extended sense, the academic subjects – according to Hoëm (1978) – have to be treated according to their true nature (i.e. the logical and argumentative quality of scientific texts, or the esthetic or artistic – sometimes also moral and ethical – quality of humanistic texts). The word limitation for this chapter prevents a discussion of the full implications of this argument. Consequently, a brief illustration will be given. While "easy readers" by means of a simplified language do not function very well to develop instrumental skills, their fundamental problem still remains if they are redesigned for the purpose of identity confirmation and spontaneous comprehension. As their artistic or esthetic quality remains a secondary concern, their justification and internal quality also remain instrumental. As Baker (2006) points out, real books are always written by authors, while basal books are made to teach reading.

The descriptive concept of culture

When we speak of culture in everyday conversation, there is often a certain scale of values implied. If we, for example, refer to something as developed or underdeveloped, civilized or uncivilized, an absolute or normative culture concept is reflected, with its given hierarchy of values more or less presupposed. The same is often the case when the argument is in favor of a certain canon in school. Cultural scientists, however, have introduced a concept of culture which is relative to definite or absolute citations (Frykman & Löfgren, 1994). Culture is defined in descriptive terms as the knowledge, evaluations, and perspectives that a certain group of people share, implying that their collective forms of consciousness cannot be explained in isolation from their social context. Further, culture is something people use to systematize, explain, and legitimize the world which surrounds them. The term *world view* is often used to signal that culture – as underlined also by Bourdieu's *habitus* concept (Bourdieu & Passeron, 1990) – includes both ideological and substantial premises for how we think and act, and that our ways of thinking and perceiving are deeply rooted in our subconscious.

By organizing its learning program according to a descriptive concept of culture, the school will be concerned with the *external cultural quality* of the learning material, and have a suitable tool both to realize recognition and to establish a commonality of values in relation to students' homes. Part of this commonality will be related to phenomena which both parties are consciously aware of, for example conceptions of religious belief or the legitimacy and status of religion. More fundamentally, however, as illustrated by the case of initial reading instruction, a commonality of values should be based on the world view of the parties – or unarticulated knowledge – that is, the students' habitus on the one hand and the school's silent and articulate curriculum on the other (Engen, 1989; Hoëm, 1978).

A commonality of interests

A commonality of values is necessary, but not sufficient, for reinforcing socialization. According to Hoëm (1978), a supplementary commonality of interests is also needed, implying that the school and the home have a common belief that what knowledge the school has to offer is advantageous as far as the students' restricted empowerment is concerned. When the knowledge has instrumental value for both parties, a type of motivation which is external in relation to the learning material – and therefore instrumental – is constituted. But as conceptions of what knowledge has most instrumental value vary between subgroups, even instrumental motivation is of course culturally embedded. This is why the classic question "What knowledge is most important?" is reframed to "*Whose* knowledge is most important?"

A commonality of interests may also occur in combination with a conflict of values. Parents may be concerned that their children have access to the instrumental advantages of school knowledge, while at the same time they want their children to identify with and belong to their particular culture. A commonality of interests and a conflict of values combined will therefore tend to move the focus of instruction and learning towards the potential instrumental advantages of education and towards adaptation and restricted empowerment. According to Hoëm (1978), such a relation promotes either de-socialization or re-socialization.

De-socialization

De-socialization occurs when students succeed in acquiring the school's instrumental knowledge without at the same time changing their cultural belonging and identity. Even if de-socialization is successful, its empowering potential is restricted, as the term also suggests. To the extent that identity formation still takes place, it will be strictly related to the instrumental motive and lead to adaptation. Indirectly – perhaps also in an unreflected way – the students will learn to consider themselves, society, and culture in a reductive, instrumental manner, and their conceptions of the good, the beautiful, and the true will be tied to commercial values and market prices. Even if the students earn high marks, they will have a weak commitment to general ethical, moral, and esthetic perspectives and arguments (Engen, 1989).

Re-socialization

De-socialization should therefore be supplemented by re-socialization, which is also based on a combination of commonality of interests and conflict of values. At the same time as initial cultural belonging is weakened, however, a new sense of belonging and self-understanding gradually emerges – based on the value foundation of the school. Whether de-socialization or re-socialization will be the ultimate outcome most fundamentally requires that the academic subjects are treated according to their true nature. As conditions for recognition are missing in the case of value conflict, a meaningful context and horizon for instrumental learning need another foundation.

Secondly, however, re-socialization also presupposes sustained instrumental success, operationally communicated to students and the home by good grades (Engen, 1975). Only gifted children manage to succeed when parents are not in a position to mediate the school's unilateral influence, even if they are highly motivated (Engen, 2003a). In Berry's (2006) study, therefore, none of the four categories seem to be re-socialized. The integrated group develop their profile partly through the effort of the home and can hardly be perceived as re-socialized. The group with a strong majority cultural orientation should primarily be understood as de-socialized, especially in a system with a strong skills orientation. As the category members are both adapted and assimilated, it is clear that de-socialization has unwanted outcomes even when it succeeds.

De-socialization, however, may just as well fail, because academic success based on a fragile commonality of interests and instrumental motivation alone is hard to achieve (Engen, 1975). In Berry's (2006) study, only 15% of adolescents may be considered successfully de-socialized. For those who fail (who according to the data of Berry represent the majority of adolescents), the alternatives are either withdrawal to the ethnic network, as in the case of the ethnic youths, or segregation or marginalization, as in the case of the diffuse group. Even if the ethnic youths experience a perfectly satisfactory psychological acculturation, they are at best adapted (to their own ethnic group) but certainly not empowered in the extended sense of the word. To the diffuse group, empowerment in both senses of the word is unattainable.

Shielded socialization

For both groups, withdrawal from the school's influence is the option, an alternative Hoëm (1978) characterizes as shielded socialization. As most linguistic minority children are instrumentally motivated, shielded socialization is most often based on an initial commonality of interests combined with a conflict of values. When the experiences of students convey that their hopes and aims are unrealistic because they fail academically, instrumental motivation and the commonality of interests wane, and a conflict of values predominates.

Discussion

Both de- and re-socialization give little room for localization based on recognition. At its best de-socialization leads to adaptation and restricted empowerment. Re-socialization has a potential for extended empowerment, provided that the academic subjects are treated according to their genuine characteristics, and that the school helps students to gain confidence in their own rationality and experience by providing clarifying concepts and theoretical perspectives. This will probably not be the case, however, in a unilateral skills approach, as the importance of the external cultural quality of the contents is overlooked. In addition, both de- and re-socialization are fragile courses with a high probability of failure and with shielded socialization (i.e. separation, segregation, or marginalization) as the most probable outcome.

Reinforcing socialization promotes both localization through recognition and optimal conditions for instrumental learning. Within a mainstreaming approach, however, these outcomes are reserved for linguistic majority students. Further, even these students will easily take their cultural background as given, as the academic subjects are hardly treated according to their true nature. Thus intended reinforcing socialization may be reduced to adaptation and restricted empowerment even for linguistic majority students, while intended re-socialization for linguistic minority students is reduced to de-socialization and assimilation through implicit cultural homogenization, a strategy which also seriously weakens the conditions for instrumental learning.

In addition, both re-socialization and reinforcing socialization may overlook or even suppress that any given position – according to the descriptive concept of culture – may have equally valid moral, esthetic, and scientific alternatives. In this way both courses undermine pluralism, as an idea if not as a reality. This is especially serious in the context of modernization and heightened cultural diversity, for, as Goethe once put it, "No person knows his culture who knows only his culture" (as cited in Burtonwood, 1986, p. 160). A more adequate course of socialization requires some comparison and contrasting to secure the external quality of the educational program. But a necessary relativization cannot be stretched to such an extent that all norms and standards align, as the double problem with "easy readers" illustrates. Even if they are redesigned for the purpose of recognition, their justification and design still remain instrumental in character.

This reveals an inherent weakness tied to the descriptive concept of culture, that it may justify any group's claim for a right to practice identity confirmation within its own closed context. In this way, ever-new cultural groups will be constructed that may fight eagerly for their own interests and identity, in perpetual regress. In such a case, no one needs to worry about alternative perspectives on esthetics and moral and scientific truths. Ultimately, not only will the multicultural society dissolve but the concept of a common society as such will be undermined as well (Crittenden, 1982; Engen, 1989; Eriksen, 2002; Popper, 1962).

This is why Baker (2006) agrees with Hoëm's (1978) general position that neither the question of comprehension nor the question of recognition should be determined exclusively in relation to the external quality of the learning material. The internal cultural quality in accordance with the normative cultural concept has to be considered seriously as well. By combining a normative concept of culture with cultural relativism, however, one can secure the external cultural quality of the learning material and at the same time become consciously aware of one's own hierarchy of values, as well as alternative hierarchies, and ultimately also of the normative concept of culture as a social construction (Engen, 1989).

Integrating socialization

As a majority of minority homes are not in a position to compensate for, supplement, and mediate the schools' unilateral influence with home cultural perspectives, the school has to take more responsibility for minority cultural and bicultural matters. A new concept of socialization should therefore exceed the limitations of reinforcing socialization as well as de- and re-socialization. Primarily it should secure optimal conditions for restricted empowerment and instrumental qualification, an outcome that is brought about through a process of localization based on recognition. At the same time, however, socialization should also include a potential for identity expansion, which is a prerequisite not only for extended empowerment but also for optimal instrumental learning. Four characteristics of what has been called *integrating socialization* are:

1 partial and full commonality of values between the home and the school;
2 partial and full commonality of interests between the home and the school;
3 value-oriented factors having an identity-creating function through recognition;
4 instrumental factors being perceived and recognized as instrumental through recognition (Engen, 1989).

Result: Earlier or primary socialization is reinforced and new socialization occurs. Earlier socialization and new socialization enlighten each other mutually.

First, a course of integrating socialization cannot correspond fully with the preferences of any single group as far as instrumental knowledge and skills are concerned if socialization is also supposed to be relevant to other groups in a diverse society. If students, for example, are to be qualified to relate to other world views than their own, only a partial commonality of interests will be functional. If, however, students and their parents through mutual recognition at the same time accept that some expansion of perspectives is favorable for all parties involved, also instrumentally, a full commonality of interests may be established on a meta-level.

Second, if all children are supposed to experience identity confirmation by means of a process of localization based on recognition, a certain minimum commonality of values between the home and the school is essential. But as all groups – majority students included – also need exposure to a multiplicity of perspectives, even the commonality of values will have to be restricted. Localization alone secures only identity confirmation, while identity expansion requires a contrasting and comparison of experiences. By organizing the school's learning program according to a special combination of the external and internal cultural quality of the academic subjects, a potential foundation for integrating socialization and empowerment in both senses of the word may be prepared (Banks, 2008).

Third, there should be a potential for integrating socialization and empowerment in both senses of the word by the way work is implemented in the classroom. On the one hand, the teacher should clarify alternatives for choice, while no definite or ultimate conclusion should be assumed. Tolerance and respect for other world views should also be an inherent and sustained aspect of the approach, while the assumption that all options are equally valuable or tolerable should by no means be the inherent assumption. The capacity to argue for and against different positions should be a central part of the approach. These factors considered together constitute a foundation for a new commonality of values and interests at a meta-conscious and a meta-cultural level.

References

Baker, C. (2006). *Foundations of bilingual education and bilingualism* (4th ed.). Clevedon, UK: Multilingual Matters.
Banks, J. A. (2008). Diversity, group identity, and citizenship education in a global age. *Educational Researcher, 37*(3), 129–139.
Berry, J. W. (2006). *Immigrant youth in cultural transition: Acculturation, identity, and adaptation across national contexts.* Mahwah, NJ: Lawrence Erlbaum.
Bourdieu, P., & Passeron, J. C. (1990). *Reproduction in education, society and culture* (2nd ed.). London: Sage.

Burtonwood, N. (1986). *The culture concept in educational studies.* Windsor, UK: INFR-Nelson.

Carlgren, I., Klette, K., Myrdal, S., Schnack, K., & Simola, H. (2006). Changes in Nordic teaching practices: From individualized teaching to teaching of individuals. *Scandinavian Journal of Educational Research, 50*(3), 301–326.

Collier, V. P., & Thomas, W. P. (2002). Reforming education policies for English learners means better schools for all. *The State Education Standard, 3*(1), 30–36.

Crittenden, B. (1982). *Cultural pluralism and common curriculum.* Melbourne, Australia: Melbourne University Press.

Cummins, J. (2000). *Language, power and pedagogy: Bilingual children in the crossfire.* Clevedon, UK: Multilingual Matters.

Darnell, F., & Hoëm, A. (1996). *Taken to extremes: Education in the Far North.* Oslo, Norway: Scandinavian University Press.

Delgado-Gaitan, C., & Trueba, H. T. (1991). *Crossing cultural borders: Education for immigrant families in America.* London: Falmer Press.

Elsness, T. F. (2003). Nytt årtusen, ny leseopplæring? [A new millennium, new approaches to early reading instruction?] In I. Austad (Ed.), *Mening i tekst: Teorier og metoder i grunnleggende lese- og skriveopplæring* [Meaning in text: Theories and methods for the teaching of fundamental reading and writing] (pp. 167–210). Oslo, Norway: Cappelen Akademisk Forlag.

Engen, T. O. (1975). *Avvikende atferd som sosialt fenomen: Atferdsproblemene i ungdomsskolen under en sosiologisk og sosialpsykologisk synsvinkel: Hovedoppgave* [Deviating behavior as a social phenomenon: Behavior problems in secondary schooling from a sociological and social-psychological perspective: Dissertation]. Oslo, Norway: University of Oslo, Pedagogisk Forsknings Institutt.

Engen, T. O. (1989). *Dobbeltkvalifisering og kultursammenlikning: Utkast til en oppdragelses- lærerplan- og planleggingsmodell* [Double qualification and the comparison of cultures: A model for curriculum planning]. Vallset, Norway: Oplandske Bokforlag.

Engen, T. O. (2003a). De gamle verdier er oprørske kategorier i en verden hvor normen er modsat: Om minoritetsfamiliers utdanningsstrategier [Old values are rebellious categories in a world where the norm is opposite: On minority families' educational strategies]. In C. Horst (Ed.), *Interkulturel pædagogik: Flere sprog – problem eller ressource?* [Intercultural pedagogy: Are many languages a problem or a resource?] (pp. 127–160). Vejle, Denmark: Kroghs Forlag.

Engen, T. O. (2003b). "Sometimes I two-times think . . .:" Competing interpretations of inclusion for language minority students. In T. Booth, K. Nes, & M. Strømstad (Eds.), *Developing inclusive teacher education* (pp. 78–96). New York: Routledge.

Eriksen, T. H. (2002). *Ethnicity and nationalism* (2nd ed.). London: Pluto Press.

Fillmore, L. W. (1986). Teaching bilingual learners. In M. C. Wittrock (Ed.), *Handbook of research on teaching* (3rd ed., pp. 648–685). New York: Macmillan.

Freire, P. (1970). *Pedagogy of the oppressed.* New York: Seabury Press.

Frykman, J., & Löfgren, O. (1994). *Det kultiverte mennesket* [Cultivated man]. Oslo, Norway: Pax.

Gardner, R., & Lambert, W. (1972). *Attitudes and motivation in second language learning.* Rowley, MA: Newbury House.

Gurria, A. (2008). In PISA, PIRLS spotlight global trends [Electronic version]. *Reading Today, 25*(4), 1–4. Retrieved July 15, 2008, from http://www.reading.org/publications/reading_today/samples/RTY-0802-pisa.html

Haug, P., & Bachmann, K. E. (2007). Kvalitet og tilpasning [Quality and adaptation]. *Norsk Pedagogisk Tidskrift* [Norwegian Journal of Education], *91*(4), 265–276.

Hellesnes, J. (1975). *Sosialisering og teknokrati: Ein sosialfilosofisk studie med særleg vekt på pedagogikkens problem* [Socialization and technocracy: A social philosophical study with an emphasis on the problem of pedagogy]. Oslo, Norway: Gyldendal.

Hellesnes, J. (1984). *Farar i metropolis og andre essays* [Menaces in metropolis and other essays]. Oslo, Norway: Gyldendal.

Hoëm, A. (1978). *Sosialisering: En teoretisk og empirisk modellutvikling* [Socialization: The development of a theoretical and empirical model]. Oslo: Norwegian University Press.

Hvistendahl, R., & Roe, A. (2004). The literacy achievement of Norwegian minority students. *Scandinavian Journal of Educational Research, 48*(3), 307–324.

Løvlie, L. (2005). Ideologi, politikk og læreplan [Ideology, politics, and curriculum]. *Norsk pedagogisk tidsskrift* [Norwegian Journal of Education], *89*(4), 269–279.

Organisation for Economic Co-operation and Development (OECD), Directorate of Education. (2008). OECD's PISA survey shows some countries making significant gains in learning outcomes. Retrieved July 15, 2008, from http://www.oecd.org/document/22/0,3343,en_2649_35845621_39713238_1_1_1_1,00.html

Oslo Kommune [Municipality of Oslo]. (2004a). *Språk for felles framtid: Handlingsprogram. Lese-, skrive- og språkopplæring i Osloskolen 2004–2007* [Language for a common future: A program of action concerning reading, writing, and language education in the schools of Oslo 2004–2007]. Retrieved July 15, 2008, from http://www.utdanningsetaten.oslo.kommune.no/getfile.php/Utdanningsetaten/Internett/Dokumenter/handbok/satsningsomrxder/handlingsprog.%20pdf.pdf

Oslo Kommune [Municipality of Oslo]. (2004b). *Tilpasset opplæring med felles læreplan i norsk: Likeverdig opplæring i praksis* [Adaptive instruction with a common curriculum in the Norwegian language: Education for equity in practice]. Retrieved July 15, 2008, from http://www.utdanningsetaten.oslo.kommune.no/getfile.php/Utdanningsetaten/Internett/Dokumenter/dokument/satsningsomrxder/prosjektplan.pdf

Øzerk, K. Z. (2003). *Sampedagogikk: En studie av de norskspråklige og minoritetstospråklige elevenes læringsutbytte på småskoletrinnet i L97-skolen* [Cooperative pedagogy: A study on how linguistic majority and linguistic minority students profit from instruction in the early stages in the 1997 national curriculum school]. Vallset, Norway: Oplandske Bokforlag.

Popper, K. R. (1962). *The open society and its enemies* (4th ed.). London: Routledge & Kegan Paul.

Ricoeur, P. (1973). The model of the text: Meaningful action considered as a text. *Social Research, 38*(3), 529–562.

Ricoeur, P. (2004). *Parcours de la reconnaisance: Trois études* [Ways of recognition: Three studies]. Paris: Éditions Stock.

Roe, A., Linnakylä, P., & Lie, S. (2003). *Northern lights on PISA: Unity and diversity in the Nordic countries in PISA 2000*. Oslo, Norway: University of Oslo, Department of Teacher Education and School Development.

Taylor, C. (1994). The politics of recognition. In C. Taylor & A. Gutmann (Eds.), *Multiculturalism: Examining the politics of recognition* (pp. 25–73). Princeton, NJ: Princeton University Press.

Telhaug, A. O. (2005). *Kunnskapsløftet: Ny eller gammel skole? Beskrivelse og analyse av Kristin Clemets reformer i grunnopplæringen* [The national curriculum of 2006: A new or an old school? A description and an analysis of Kristin Clemets's reforms in elementary education]. Oslo, Norway: Cappelen Akademisk Forlag.

Thomas, W. P., & Collier, V. P. (2002). *A national study of school effectiveness for language minority students' long-term academic achievement*. Santa Cruz, CA: Center for Research on Education, Diversity & Excellence (CREDE).

Undervisnings- og Forskningsdepartementet [Ministry of Education and Research]. (2003). *Gi rom for lesing: Strategi for stimulering av leselyst og leseferdighet 2003–2007* [Make room for reading: Strategy document to stimulate motivation for reading and reading skills 2003–2007]. Retrieved July 15, 2008, from http://www.regjeringen.no/nb/dep/kd/dok/rapporter_planer/rapporter/2003/Gi-rom-for-lesing.html?id=106009

Uppstad, P. H., & Solheim, O. J. (2005). What is reading? A critical account. In P. H. Uppstad (Ed.), *Language and literacy: Some fundamental issues in research on reading and writing* (pp. 125–146). Lund, Sweden: Lund University, Department of Linguistics and Phonetics.

Vygotsky, L. S. (1987). Thinking and speech. In R. W. Rieber & A. S. Carton (Eds.), *The collected works of L .S. Vygotsky: Vol. 1. Problems of general psychology* (pp. 37–241). New York: Plenum Press.

Part 5

The education of indigenous groups

19

Connecting the circle in American Indian education

Donna Deyhle
University of Utah, USA

Karen Gayton Comeau
Haskell Indian Nations University, USA

> Let us put our minds together and see what kind of life we can make for our children.
> (Sitting Bull, Hunkapa Lakota)

The formal education of Indigenous people in the US has a history nearly as long as the American educational system itself – nearly parallel but certainly, in the eyes of White Europeans, not equal. Ignoring American Indians' desires to remain "Indian," from colonial times to the present, the formal education of American Indians has had as its purpose the assimilation of the Indigenous peoples named American Indians by Christopher Columbus in 1492. As Szasz (1988) and other historians have pointed out, education of American Indians by American Indians was the norm long before 1492 and the later arrival of the colonists in the 17th century. Educational models were established by the Cherokees and Choctaws who operated their own schools in the 1840s, educating their citizens in both their Native language and English; both boasted high literacy rates. Consequently, it is ironic that only in the last 40-plus years has the term "Indian self-determination" been used to describe the current policy and philosophical approach employed by tribes and local Indian communities to educate Indigenous children.

In this chapter we will discuss American Indian education or the education of Indigenous people in the United States using the circle as a metaphor to describe what was, what is, and what can be. We believe that, while the circle is not complete, the education of Indigenous people has come nearly full circle – from self-determination pre-Columbus to self-determination and local control in the 21st century. The circle clearly has been disrupted many times throughout the history of relationships between and among the sovereigns in the US – Indian nations, the federal government, and the states. Monumental disruptions in the lives and belief systems of Indigenous people came from federal policies that established boarding schools and the allotment of land. Other federal policies such as termination and relocation in the 1950s, intended to "dissolve Indianness" by moving Indian families from reservations to cities where economic opportunities were theoretically more plentiful, were also disruptive, affecting generations of families and communities. American Indian people, however, maintained their connection to the reservation and their Native identities.

Termination and assimilation as official federal policies ended in the early 1970s when President Nixon set forth a new direction focused on Indian self-determination. Each U.S. president since then has reaffirmed the policy of self-determination.[1]

In order for the reader to understand self-determination in the contemporary context, it is helpful to briefly outline the history of formal Indian education that was for the most part focused on assimilation and paternalistic policies.

What was: An impossibly short history of formal Indian education

The United States government has a unique legal relationship with American Indian tribal governments as set forth in the Constitution of the United States, federal statutes, treaties, and court decisions. The Indian Commerce Clause (Article I, section 8) in the Constitution is generally recognized as acknowledging the broad federal authority and special trust responsibility the United States has over Indian affairs. During the treaty-making period, from 1778 to 1871, in 400 treaties American Indians exchanged nearly 1 billion acres of land for promises of protection against invasion, for education, and for self-government in perpetuity. In more than 100 of these treaties, educational services and facilities were promised, creating moral and legal obligations on the part of the federal government (Tippeconnic & Swisher, 1992, p. 75).

During these two centuries, the goal of civilizing and Christianizing American Indians was pursued through a federally subsidized educational system, with schools operated by churches and later by the federal government itself. As noted by Szasz (1974), children and land were targets of federal policy that forever changed the lives of many Indian people for generations. The educational system, particularly boarding schools, targeted children for assimilation. Children were removed from family, home, and community and taken to boarding schools where assimilation would be hastened once the children no longer had the influences of family, language, and culture. The educational policies and practices in all of these schools were framed by deficit thoughts about Indigenous cultures, and efforts to "Americanize" the youth resulted in strategic policies to eradicate their histories, religions, and languages (Deyhle, Swisher, Stevens, & Galvan, 2008).

The first was the Carlisle Indian School, established by Richard Henry Pratt in 1878. In this and other boarding schools the use of Native languages by children was forbidden under threats of corporal punishment; uniforms were worn; the curriculum included domestic and vocational training; students were placed as laborers and domestic servants in White families' homes during vacation time; Native religions were suppressed; and visits home and from family were not encouraged. American Indian youth did not share their teachers' and school administrators' goals; they resisted (Deyhle et al., 2008). According to several sources, assimilation was "complete" for very few Indians (Archuleta, Child, & Lomawaima, 2000; Lomawaima, 1994; McBeth, 1983; Mihesuah, 1993; Trennert, 1988). Ironically, the boarding school experience for many Indian youth helped create a climate that increased a sense of "Indianness."

In spite of the assimilation policies and practices, Indian identity in the United States is as strong today as it was 100 years ago. American Indians have succeeded in using educational institutions to assert their Indigenous rights of self-determination. Haskell Indian Nations University is one example of a 19th-century residential school that reinvented itself through American Indian leadership.

Established in 1884 as the United States Indian Industrial Training School for the assimilation of young Indian boys and girls into American society, Haskell has evolved into a premier institution of higher education that prepares American Indian and Alaska Native men and women to be scholars and leaders who will carry out the policy of self-determination among their tribes and nations.[2] It is home to one of the first Indigenous teacher training programs in the United States. Over its nearly 125-year history, its purpose has shifted from education for assimilation to education for self-determination. Haskell's student population represents the greatest tribal diversity of any institution in the United States, with an enrollment of 900 students from approximately 130 tribes, nations, pueblos, villages, corporations, or rancherias, and 35 states each semester. A unique curriculum empowers young men and women to complete their education at Haskell knowing more about what it means to be Indigenous than when they entered, regardless of where they fall on the continuum of assimilated to traditional in terms of their identity and upbringing. Funded by the United States Congress through the Bureau of Indian Affairs of the Department of the Interior, Haskell is a unique educational institution in that it is a government institution, and through its history can be traced the history of Indian education policy in the United States. Haskell is viewed as a place where the future of sovereignty is supported and the right to be Indigenous is practiced within a federal bureaucracy that once tried to eliminate it (Deyhle et al., 2008).

What is: Tribal or local control of Indian education

> Self-determination puts Native people in control and uses tribal languages, culture, and values to enhance student work, research, higher education, and other areas related to education. Educators who work from this paradigm face a challenge because a deficit approach, with assimilation as a goal, remains deeply entrenched in schools. The effects of the deficit approach reveal themselves in drop-out rates, attendance rates, academic achievement test scores, and enrollment and graduation rates in colleges and universities.
> (Swisher & Tippeconnic, 1999, pp. 295–296)

Currently 90% of all American Indian and Alaska Native students attend public schools. The Bureau of Indian Education (BIE) has responsibility for 184 elementary and secondary schools and dormitories and two post-secondary institutions, Haskell Indian Nations University and Southwest Indian Polytechnic Institute. These post-secondary institutions, schools, and dormitories are located on 63 reservations in 23 states across the United States, serving approximately 60,000 students representing 238 different tribes. Of the 184 elementary and secondary schools, 122 are operated by tribes through local school boards funded by grants or contracts with the BIE. All schools are empowered through the BIE's policy of local control and the federal government's policy of Indian self-determination.

The paradigm shift toward tribal or local control of Indian education situates education at the local level, similar to the way in which public education operates. Tippeconnic (1999), however, points out that Indian control of education is different from tribal control. Often used interchangeably, the terms *Indian parent involvement, community control, local control,* and *tribal control* are not the same. He states:

> The most significant difference is between tribal control and local or community control, with tribal control meaning that the actual tribal government is in control and local or community control usually meaning that school boards comprise community members. Parent involvement does not mean tribal control. Tribally controlled schools can mean tribal control if schools are sanctioned or chartered by tribal governments. (p. 39)

Despite the strong move to self-determination in education, there are too few positive indicators that schools operated by local boards or organizations are more successful in solving the lingering problems in Indian education. Dropout rates continue to be higher than the national average; graduation rates at both the high school and the college level continue to be lower than the national average; and achievement rates for Native students are not significantly improving. Seventy percent of the BIE schools in 2004–2005 did not make adequate yearly progress (AYP), a metric imposed by the No Child Left Behind Act. The average tenure of a principal in a BIE school is 3.6 years. The turnover in school staff, especially in remote reservation schools, continues to be a problem for the communities they serve.

The U.S. Commission on Civil Rights (2003) reports that the civil rights and cultural identities of American Indian and Alaska Native students are not supported in the classroom. Indian students face racial prejudice in the classroom and school, the low expectations of their teachers, undemanding courses, and vocational tracking. One Indian student sharply criticized his schooling experience:

> The work I am taking now is so simple that it is ridiculous. I took this stuff in about grade four. I look at it now and my mind goes blank. I wasn't dumb before I got here, but I soon will be if I stay in this place.
>
> (Wilson, 1991, p. 378)

These problematic data have led Native practitioners to seriously look at indicators or measures of achievement. Efforts to develop Indigenous evaluation frameworks and culturally appropriate measures or indicators of student success are emerging. A project called American Indian Measures of Success or AIMS was developed in 2004 under leadership of the American Indian Higher Education Consortium (AIHEC). This project at 32 tribal colleges and universities (TCUs) seeks to define relevant indicators of American Indian success as determined by the tribal colleges. The data from these reports present a rich and promising picture of nearly 17,000 students at TCUs.

While effective practices can be cited in a number of schools attended by American Indian and Alaska Native students, those practices are not pervasive enough and are not sustained over sufficient periods of time to produce measurable and generalizable effects (Swisher & Tippeconnic, 1999, p. 299). Clearly, the changes that have promise for best practice must be identified, sustained, and researched over time.

In the next section we will examine how self-determination situated in local or community control is used to strengthen and enhance the future of American Indian and Alaska Native children. Specifically, we identify language programs that are examples of self-determination efforts. Parents and community members are taking the initiative to determine not only how children should be taught, with dignity and respect, but also what they should be taught, their own histories, cultures, and languages, and by whom, Native and culturally knowledgeable teachers. Their demands on their children's schools range from the curriculum to social justice issues. As Swisher (1994) writes, "The voices of Indian people have echoed consistent rhetoric, some of it going back as far as fifty years ago: Indian people want the opportunity to determine all aspects of their children's education" (p. 861).

What can be: Decolonizing the schooling experience

In 1887, the U.S. Commissioner of Indian Affairs articulated a federal policy that prohibited Indian children from studying any language other than English (McCarty, 2003, p. 148). Native languages were outlawed in schools throughout the United States and Canada, and students caught speaking their home languages were punished severely (Lomawaima & McCarty, 2002; McCarty, 2003; Szasz, 1974). Over the next 100 years American Indian people continued to resist these efforts to extinguish who they were by strongly claiming their rights to maintain their languages and cultures. The 1990/1992 Native American Languages Act legally asserted "the right of Indian tribes and other Native American governing bodies to use the Native American languages as a medium of instruction in all schools funded by the Secretary of the Interior" (Reyhner, 1992, p. 622). To lose a language meant to lose a voice to assert one's thoughts. As a Pueblo man explained:

> As you're growing up here [a pueblo community in New Mexico] you will hear things, see things and be involved in activities where the white man's tongue has no place. They can never be explained in English because that language does not have the capacity to explain these things.
>
> (Suina, 2004, p. 289)

The need for language revitalization is critical for many who argue that Indigenous knowledge is embedded in the terms, subtle understandings, ways of talking, and histories inherent in language. Furthermore, something is irretrievably lost when language is not expressed in and through Native culture. As Mary Hermes (2005) explained, "Meaning is more important than words. When the elders say, 'Keep the language,' what they mean is, 'Keep the thought,' because language is the clearest representation of that way of thought" (p. 51). More than 50 Indigenous groups within the United States at the turn of the new millennium were attempting various forms of language revitalization (Hinton & Hale, 2001; Hornberger, 1997).

One of the first and best-known American Indian bilingual programs was the Hualapai project at Peach Springs in northwestern Arizona (Watahomigie & McCarty, 1994, 1997). Started in 1975, this program used thematic curriculum content organized around the local language and social environment, affirmed students' identities as Hualapai, and capitalized on their prior knowledge, specifically their bilingualism, as a means of enhancing their school experience. These instructional changes, in which the Hualapai language and culture were authentic and integral parts of the school, along with an increase of Native teachers that enhanced the integration of the school with the community, resulted in Indian students' increased success at school (Deyhle et al., 2008).

Not only do bilingual and bicultural programs enhance learning of and in the Native language, but they have also been shown to improve American Indian students' proficiency in the dominant societal language. McLaughlin's (1989, 1991, 1992) ethnographic study of one of the first bilingual schools on the Navajo reservation portrays a program successful at serving both objectives. Other ethnographic research suggests that educators need to reinforce, not neglect, the cultural identities of children and that active participation of parents and the use of the Navajo language should be integrated into all aspects of classroom life (Deyhle, 1995; McCarty, 2002).

Holm and Holm (1995) reported positive student gains, when measured against other students on the reservation, in the bilingual program at Rock Point Community School. Leap (1991, 1993) found that the use of the Native language in conjunction with English in the Wykoopah ("two paths") program on the Northern Ute reservation enhanced students' academic opportunities by building a foundation for literacy development in both English and their Native language. On locally developed criterion-referenced measures, students' end-of-the-year scores consistently showed substantial improvements in oral English and reading. Begay et al. (1995) argued that, in addition to enhanced student achievement, the bilingual program at the Rough Rock Community School altered larger power structures by employing local community educators who taught according to community norms and used local cultural and linguistic knowledge.

As opposed to schools with practices that deny or ignore their students' cultural resources, schools that tap into local knowledge and seek the wisdom of the Indigenous community become "wise schools" (Lipka, Mohatt, & the Ciulistet Group, 1998, p. 67). By illustrating that Yup'ik culture, language, and everyday community practices can enhance the teaching of core academic subjects, such as mathematics and science, Lipka and the Ciulistet Group have challenged the devaluation of Indigenous knowledge in schools and have found a culturally relevant way to engage their students.

Other revitalization projects in schools include language classes, after-school programs, and literacy projects. These efforts have also included curricular changes such as the development of authentic texts (McCarty & Dick, 2003; McCarty & Watahomigie, 1998; Sims, 2001), the incorporation of culturally specific hands-on experiences in the classroom, the use of the ceremonial calendar for teaching activities (Benjamin, Pecos, & Romero, 1997; Suina, 2004), and the introduction of special language development sessions for language teachers (Benjamin et al., 1997; McCarty, 2001).

Decisions about language use and measurements of success in its revitalization must lie with American Indian communities. McCarty's (2002) ethnographic study of Rough Rock Demonstration School, the first Navajo-controlled school on the Navajo Nation, is a powerful example of one Indigenous community's efforts at self-determination. By positioning Navajo culture, history, and language as central to the curriculum, Navajo parents, many of whom had struggled with harsh boarding school experiences, argued for the critical importance of local language, knowledge, and control to alter historically framed authority and power relationships. As one parent explained, "My language, to me . . . that's what makes me unique, that's what makes me Navajo, that's what makes me who I am" (McCarty, 2002, p. 179). The move to center Navajo language, as McCarty (2002) points out, is supported by educational research: "Children who learned to read first in Navajo learned how to read (period). That ability aided rather than hindered their English literacy development" (p. 184). And the move to include the "cultural capital" of the Navajo community *in* school enriched and validated students' lives *outside* of the classrooms (Deyhle et al., 2008).

Beyond the assertion of tribal languages in the process of decolonization, tribes have recognized the important role elders can take as mentors, instructors, and cultural keepers of Indigenous knowledge (McCarty, 2001; McCarty & Watahomigie, 1998). Young people serve as language apprentices, and in the Cochiti Pueblo youth and elders are "paired for cultural and work exchanges" (Benjamin et al., 1997, p. 131). Similarly, an inter-tribal language revitalization program in California founded by the Native California Network (NCN) relies on a master–apprentice approach. Older Native speakers of the language are teamed with young tribal members with whom they spend up to 20 hours a week speaking only their heritage language while going about their daily lives. In four years, the program trained close to 50 teams for over 20 different languages. Many new speakers are now quite fluent in their heritage language (Hinton & Ahlers, 1999).

The Navajo Preparatory School, located in Farmington, New Mexico, was established in

1991 by the Education Committee of the Navajo Nation Council as a college preparatory school for Native American students in grades 9–12. This school is an excellent example of community self-determination, racial and cultural respect, and high expectation – resulting in student educational success. It is funded through a grant from the BIE and is governed by a local school board. The school offers students a challenging, innovative curriculum in science, math, computers, and other traditional academic subjects. The curriculum also steeps the youth in a deep appreciation of the Navajo language, culture, and history. The following academic results speak to the wisdom of locating an American Indian presence at the foundation of the school's philosophy. Navajo Prep School has a 91% daily attendance rate, 99% graduation rate, and 0% dropout rate. Nearly 90% of its graduates are enrolled in colleges or universities. The 2005 annual report boasts meeting adequate yearly progress (AYP) since the No Child Left Behind Act was implemented in 2002.

A bold, promising practice that is impacting all of the schools in one state is the example set by the state of Montana. In 1972, Montana rewrote its constitution. Article X, section 1(2) says: "The state recognizes the distinct and unique cultural heritage of American Indians and is committed in its educational goals to the preservation of their cultural integrity." In 1999, the legislature codified the constitutional intent into a law known as American Indian Education for All. The law essentially says:

> Every Montanan ... whether Indian or non-Indian, should be encouraged to learn about the distinct and unique heritage of American Indians in a culturally responsive manner ... all school personnel should have an understanding and awareness of American Indian tribes to help them relate effectively with American Indian students and parents.... Every educational agency and all educational personnel will work cooperatively with Montana tribes ... when providing instruction and implementing an educational goal.
>
> (McCulloch, 2005, p. 2)

According to Denise Juneau, state director of Indian education (2006):

> The twin hopes of Montana's constitutional obligation – Indian Education for All – is that Indian students will feel themselves welcomed when they see themselves reflected in their school hallways and curriculum, and that negative stereotypes will be replaced by an accurate understanding of Indian history and the federal government's trust duty. (p. 3)

The critical question that faced Montana educators following enactment of the law was: "What are the critical facts about American Indians that all Montanans should know?" Juneau (2006) concluded, "When current kindergarten students complete their journey through a public school system that includes the Indian perspective they will be able to see each other beyond preconceived notions and enter into meaningful relations" (p. 4). Workshops and other resources for implementation are readily available from the state Office of Public Instruction. This promising practice in Montana should provide greater understanding about the state's tribal citizens to all of its citizens, and should serve as a model for other states.

The programs and policies highlighted in this section speak to the importance of reclaiming Indigenous languages and cultural knowledge as a critical means to enhance American Indian students' school experiences. And the example from Montana speaks to what American Indian people have also been saying for hundreds of years – non-Native people need to learn about American Indians to become educated citizens. Indian communities have continually asserted the right as distinct peoples to, once again, control all aspects of their children's education. These rights are guaranteed by the sovereignty status of American Indian nations. As Lomawaima and McCarty (2006) explain, "Native communities have persistently and courageously fought for their continued existence as *peoples*, defined politically by their government-to-government relationship with the United States and culturally by their diverse governments, languages, land bases, religions, economies, education systems, and family organizations" (p. 7).

Connecting the circle: Self-determination and Indigenous ways of knowing

American Indian communities have confronted many obstacles in their attempts to revitalize and maintain Native languages and cultures. As discussed earlier, the pervasiveness of assimilationist thinking and efforts to gain control of educational policies and practices in local schools that served Native youth has created a long, uphill battle for tribal peoples. In addition, community disagreement as to the role of the Native language, its place in schools, and the method of its transmission (oral or written) sometimes undermines revitalization efforts. Schools often isolate Native language programs or treat students as second-class citizens (Suina, 2004). The lack of authentic material, trained teachers, resources, or texts and time to create them was another obstacle tribes face (Barnhardt & Kawagley, 2005; McCarty & Watahomigie, 1998; Suina, 2004).

Despite setbacks and challenges, language and cultural revitalization efforts have realized great success in a number of ways. In addition to enhancing learning in both the heritage language and the dominant societal language, of utmost importance has been the fact that many languages have been successfully re-integrated into tribal tradition, great pride has been taken in the effort, and positive dialogue and tribal relations have emerged from the process (Dick & McCarty, 1997). Sims (2001) reports that Acoma Pueblo language camps witnessed increased youth and parent commitment and enthusiasm about not only the Acoma language but community relationships, and that this evidence had in effect prompted parents to make a more conscientious effort to speak the language at home. Others also report that the entire language revitalization process has created a larger awareness as to the importance of reviving their Native language and ultimately of the need for self-governance (Benjamin et al., 1997). As Benjamin et al. (1997) highlight, "This issue has served as a reaffirmation of their efforts to safeguard their religion and culture. Having been on the brink of cultural annihilation, they know how careful they must be about their community's future" (p. 123).

For Indigenous peoples, colonialism has meant the misappropriation and commodification of their traditions and cultural knowledge. Spiritual, medicinal, and philosophical orientations native to the colonized have historically been used by the colonizer to exploit and reap financial benefits. Asserting a resistant stance to this colonialism, Battiste (2002) said:

> Indigenous scholars discovered that Indigenous knowledge is far more than the binary opposites of Western knowledge. As a concept, Indigenous knowledge benchmarks the limitations of Eurocentric theory – its methodology, evidence, and conclusions – reconceptualizes the resilience and self-reliance of Indigenous peoples, and underscores the importance of their own philosophies, heritages, and educational processes. (p. 5)

Consequently, the struggle to reclaim authenticity of, and control over, their own forms of knowledge has occupied a position of political prominence for many American Indian peoples.

One example of this is an epistemological reorientation explored by Barnhardt and Kawagley (2005). At the University of Alaska Fairbanks, they have developed a model of "converging knowledge systems" wherein traditional Native knowledge systems and Western science converge on common ground that reflects both ways of knowing. By linking Western research to the Native knowledge base already established in local communities and organizing core principles that incorporate both world views, "Indigenous communities are more likely to find value in what emerges and to put new insights into practice as a meaningful exercise in self-determination" (p. 21). Barnhart and Kawagley see this as a win–win situation; not only are Native knowledge systems moved from the periphery to the center, thus broadening the scope of knowledge for all, but Native people become more receptive to Western science, which can then be used politically to pursue self-determination.

We began by stating our belief that Indian education has come nearly full circle from its historic, pre-colonial beginnings with Indian parents, family, and community in control of the education and socialization of their children to the contemporary times of self-determination and local control in Indian education. While the circle may not yet be complete, there is certainly a dotted line making the final connection. From practitioners to scholars, leadership is evident in the schools, at the tribal education department level, at the state level, and at the national level. The voices of Indigenous people through organizations such as the National Congress of American Indians, the National Indian Education Association, and the American Indian Higher Education Consortium are resonating in the media and in the halls of Congress. It is appropriate that the voices of Indigenous peoples direct discussions about how best to achieve self-determination. A broadening base of theory by American Indian scholars thrives. It is from this scholarship that models of education designed to best meet the needs of American Indian children will emerge. In the powerful book *Next Steps: Research and Practice to Advance Indian Education*, edited by Karen Gayton Swisher (Standing Rock Sioux) and John W. Tippeconnic III (Comanche) (1999), Native scholars K. Tsianina Lomawaima (Muskogee/Creek), Linda Sue Warner (Comanche), Tarajean Yazzie (Navajo), Linda Skinner (Choctaw), Gregory A. Cajete (Santa Clara Pueblo), Sandra Fox (Oglala Lakota), Deborah Wetsit (Assiniboine), Michael J. Yellow Bird (Sahnish/Hidatsa), Venida Chenault (Prairie Band Potawatomi), D. Michael Pavel (Skokomish), Wayne J. Stein (Turtle Mountain Chippewa), and Clara Sue Kidwell (Choctaw and Chippewa) asserted their voices in the project of reshaping both the curriculum and pedagogies used in the schooling of Indigenous children. Addressing topics from curriculum issues to best practices, the message of self-determination and academic success echoes throughout this collective body of research. We need to listen to the experts – Indigenous teachers, administrators, researchers, parents, community leaders, and youth and children. To connect the circle we need to open the way for the wisdom of generations of Indigenous people to make that closure.

Notes

1 *American Indian and Alaska Native* is the legislative term used to describe Indigenous people as a collective group in the United States. *American Indians* are the Indigenous peoples of the contiguous 48 states. Aleuts, Eskimos (Inupiat and Yup'ik), and Indians (Athabaskan, Tlingit, Haida, and Tsimshian), who are all Indigenous peoples of Alaska, are collectively called *Alaska Natives*. The term *Native American* emerged as ethnic studies programs developed on college and university campuses in the 1960s. The term *Native American* includes Native Hawaiians, who are also Indigenous to the land boundaries of the United States by virtue of statehood.

2 Haskell Indian University is one of the 36 tribal colleges and universities (TCUs) now established in 13

U.S. states and the province of Alberta, Canada. The tribal college movement first began in 1968 with the establishment of the Navajo Community College (now known as Diné College) on the Navajo Nation.

References

Archuleta, M. L., Child, B. J., & Lomawaima, T. (Eds.). (2000). *Away from home: American Indian boarding school experiences.* Phoenix, AZ: Heard Museum.

Barnhardt, R., & Kawagley, A. O. (2005). Indigenous knowledge systems and Alaska Native ways of knowing. *Anthropology and Education Quarterly, 36*(1), 8–23.

Battiste, M. (2002). *Indigenous knowledge and pedagogy in First Nations education: A literature review with recommendations.* Ottawa, Canada: Indian and Northern Affairs Canada.

Begay, S., Dick, G. S., Estell, D. W., Estell, J., McCarty, T. L., & Sells, A. (1995). Change from the inside out: A story of transformation in a Navajo community school. *Bilingual Research Journal, 19*(1), 121–139.

Benjamin, R., Pecos, R., & Romero, M. E. (1997). Language revitalization efforts in the Pueblo de Cochiti: Becoming "literate" in an oral society. In N. Hornberger (Ed.), *Indigenous literacies in the Americas: Language planning from the bottom up* (pp. 115–136). New York: Mouton de Gruyter.

Deyhle, D. (1995). Navajo youth and Anglo racism: Cultural integrity and resistance. *Harvard Educational Review, 65*(3), 403–444.

Deyhle, D., Swisher, K., Stevens, T., & Galvan, R. (2008). Indigenous resistance and renewal. In M. Connelly, M. Fang He, & J. Phillion (Eds.), *The Sage handbook of curriculum and instruction* (pp. 329–349). Los Angeles: Sage Publications.

Dick, G. S., & McCarty, T. (1997). Reclaiming Navajo: Language renewal in an American Indian community school. In N. Hornberger (Ed.), *Indigenous literacies in the Americas: Language planning from the bottom up* (pp. 69–94). New York: Mouton de Gruyter.

Hermes, M. (2005). "Ma'iingan is just a misspelling of the word wolf": A case for teaching culture through language. *Anthropology and Education Quarterly, 36*(1), 43–56.

Hinton, L., & Ahlers, J. (1999). The issue of "authenticity" in California language restoration. *Anthropology and Education Quarterly, 30*(1), 56–68.

Hinton, L., & Hale, K. (2001). *The green book of language revitalization in practice.* San Diego, CA: Academic Press.

Holm, A., & Holm, W. (1995). Navajo language education: Retrospect and prospects. *Bilingual Research Journal, 19,* 141–167.

Hornberger, N. (1997). Quechua literacy and empowerment in Peru. In N. Hornberger (Ed.), *Indigenous literacies in the Americas: Language planning from the bottom up* (pp. 215–236). New York: Mouton de Gruyter.

Juneau, D. (2006). Indian education for all. *Montana's Agenda, 3*(2), 1–4. Missoula, MT: University of Montana Press.

Leap, W. (1991). Pathways and barriers to Indian language literacy-building on the Northern Ute. *Anthropology and Education Quarterly, 22,* 21–41.

Leap, W. (1993). *American Indian English.* Salt Lake City: University of Utah Press.

Lipka, J., Mohatt, G. V., & the Ciulistet Group. (1998). *Transforming the culture of schools: Yup'ik Eskimo examples.* Mahwah, NJ: Lawrence Erlbaum.

Lomawaima, K. T. (1994). *They called it Prairie Light: The story of Chilocco Indian School.* Lincoln: University of Nebraska Press.

Lomawaima, K. T., & McCarty, T. (2002). When tribal sovereignty challenges democracy: American Indian education and the democratic ideal. *American Educational Research Journal, 39*(2), 279–305.

Lomawaima, K. T., & McCarty, T. (2006). *To remain an Indian: Lessons in democracy from a century of Native American education.* New York: Teachers College Press.

McBeth, S. J. (1983). *Ethnic identity and the boarding school experience of West-Central Oklahoma American Indians.* New York: University Press of America.

McCarty, T. L. (2001). Between possibility and constraint: Indigenous language education, planning, and policy in the United States. In J. W. Tollefson (Ed.), *Language policies in education: Critical issues* (pp. 285–307). Mahwah, NJ: Lawrence Erlbaum.

McCarty, T. L. (2002). *A place to be Navajo: Rough Rock and the struggle for self-determination in Indigenous schooling*. London: Lawrence Erlbaum.

McCarty, T. L. (2003). Revitalising Indigenous languages in homogenising times. *Comparative Education*, *39*(2), 147–163.

McCarty, T. L., & Dick, G. S. (2003). Telling the people's stories: Literacy practices and processes in a Navajo community school. In A. Willis, G. E. García, R. Barrera, & V. J. Harris (Eds.), *Multicultural issues in literacy research and practice* (pp. 101–122). Mahwah, NJ: Lawrence Erlbaum.

McCarty, T. L., & Watahomigie, L. J. (1998). Language and literacy in American Indian and Alaska Native communities. In B. Pérez (Ed.), *Sociocultural contexts of language and literacy* (pp. 69–98). London: Lawrence Erlbaum.

McCulloch, L. (2005). *Indian education for all*. Helena: Montana Office of Public Instruction.

McLaughlin, D. (1989). The sociolinguistics of Navajo literacy. *Anthropology & Education Quarterly*, *20*, 275–290.

McLaughlin, D. (1991). Curriculum for cultural politics: Literacy program development in a Navajo school setting. In R. Blomeyer, Jr., & D. Martin (Eds.), *Case studies in computer aided learning* (pp. 151–164). New York: Falmer Press.

McLaughlin, D. (1992). *When literacy empowers: Navajo language in print*. Albuquerque: University of New Mexico Press.

Mihesuah, D. A. (1993). *Cultivating the rosebuds: The education of women at the Cherokee Female Seminary, 1851–1909*. Urbana: University of Illinois Press.

Reyhner, J. (1992). *Teaching American Indian students*. Norman and London: University of Oklahoma Press.

Sims, C. (2001). Native language planning: A pilot process in the Acoma Pueblo community. In L. Hinton & K. Hale (Eds.), *The green book of language revitalization in practice* (pp. 63–73). New York: Academic Press.

Suina, J. (2004). Native language teachers in a struggle for language and cultural survival. *Anthropology and Education Quarterly*, *35*(3), 281–302.

Swisher, K. (1994). Primary and secondary U.S. Native education. In D. Champagne (Ed.), *The Native North American almanac* (pp. 855–868). Detroit, MI: Gayle Research.

Swisher, K., & Tippeconnic, J. W., III (Eds.). (1999). *Next steps: Research and practice to advance Indian education*. Charleston, WV: Appalachia Educational Laboratory. (ERIC Document Reproduction Service No. ED427902)

Szasz, M. C. (1974). *Education and the American Indian: The road to self-determination since 1928*. Albuquerque: University of New Mexico Press.

Szasz, M. C. (1988). *Indian education in the American colonies, 1607–1783*. Albuquerque: University of New Mexico Press.

Tippeconnic, J. W. (1999). Tribal control of American Indian education: Observations since the 1960's with implications for the future. In K. G. Swisher & J. W. Tippeconnic III (Eds.), *Next steps: Research and practice to advance Indian education* (pp. 33–52). Charleston, WV: Appalachia Educational.

Tippeconnic, J. W., & Swisher, K. (1992). American Indian education. In M. C. Alkin (Ed.), *Encyclopedia of education research* (pp. 75–78). New York: Macmillan.

Trennert, R., Jr. (1988). *The Phoenix Indian School: Forced assimilation in Arizona, 1891–1935*. Norman: University of Oklahoma Press.

U.S. Commission on Civil Rights. (2003). *A quiet crisis: Federal funding and unmet needs in Indian country*. Washington, DC: Author.

Watahomigie, L. J., & McCarty, T. L. (1994). Bilingual/bicultural education at Peach Springs: A Hualapai way of schooling. *Peabody Journal of Education*, *69*(2), 26–42.

Watahomigie, L. J., & McCarty, T. L. (1997). Literacy for what? Hualapai literacy and language maintenance. In N. Hornberger (Ed.), *Indigenous literacies in the Americas: Language planning from the bottom up* (pp. 95–114). New York: Mouton de Gruyter.

Wilson, P. (1991). Trauma of Sioux Indian high school students. *Anthropology & Education Quarterly*, *22*(4), 367–383.

20

Indigenous education in Peru

María Elena García
University of Washington, Seattle, USA

In Peru, education was central to the so-called Indian Problem, the post-colonial predicament that elites saw posed by the multiethnic and multilingual nature of Peruvian society. Education was the main process toward fulfilling the promise (progressive to some, ominous to others) of the liberator José de San Martín and generations of statesmen who looked to a future day when there would no longer be "Indians," only "Peruvians." This chapter summarizes some of the key moments in the difficult history of education as a tool for the incorporation of indigenous people and the construction of inclusive models of citizenship. While there have been opportunities and openings, that history has largely been one of disappointment and continuing marginalization for large numbers of indigenous people living in the Andean and Amazonian countryside, as well as the urban margins.

From colonial times to the early 20th century

In the empire the Incas called Tawantinsuyo, which extended roughly from what is today northern Argentina to what is now Colombia, Quechua served as the official language (Cerrón-Palomino, 1989; Mannheim, 1991). As an imperial lingua franca used by local nobility, civil servants, administrators, and traders, Quechua coexisted with various languages and dialects in the region. Bilingualism was an everyday reality in the Tawantinsuyo (Cerrón-Palomino, 1989; von Gleich, 1994). During the Inca-expansion period (1430–1532), a period of intensive military expansion, the Incas executed a policy of language spread that resulted in the widespread diffusion of Quechua throughout their empire. The Incas subjugated over 40 major linguistic groups in about one century, and the empire was estimated at 6 million people (Rowe, 1946). The Incas' language policy was developed in order to maintain control over conquered territories, although the implementation of this linguistic policy has been described as "tolerant and by no means assimilationist" (von Gleich, 1994, p. 83). Though other languages (like Aru, Aymara, Puquina, and Mochica) had also spread, by 1430 Quechua had expanded at the expense of these other languages.

Through conquest and colonialism, Spanish replaced Quechua as the official language in the new viceroyalty of Peru. However, the influence of Quechua not only continued, but even expanded, as it was seen by Spanish colonizers as a useful if transitional lingua franca, especially in areas of extreme linguistic diversity (Cerrón-Palomino, 1989; Heath & Laprade, 1982; Mar-Molinero, 1995). While Spanish became official with the siege of Cuzco in 1533, Quechua was still actively promoted for over 200 years. It was only after the wave of indigenous rebellions of the late 18th century (and especially the Túpac Amaru Rebellion of 1780) that the Quechua language and other indigenous markers such as religion were banned (von Gleich, 1994; Mannheim, 1991).

Quechua prevailed as the language of the colonized peoples, placed unequivocally below Spanish, not only because Spanish was the language of the new rulers, but also because Quechua was an oral language. The imposition of Spanish represented the imposition of writing as a tool of political power and domination. Bruce Mannheim notes three beliefs about the relationship between language, culture, and society that were at the center of this early colonial language ideology: (a) speaking the same language forges bonds among speakers; (b) a language can be imposed on a defeated population by the right of conquest; and (c) language preserves cultural identity (Mannheim, 1991, p. 68). While both Spanish and Quechua were used strategically for the tasks of ruling and proselytizing up until the mid-17th century, in 1770 Charles III declared that compulsory Castilianization should be used to suppress indigenous languages and culture. Despite royal decrees, however, colonial elites continued to communicate with Quechua speakers in Quechua. Landowners and members of the upper classes, concerned about maintaining their dominance, preferred to learn Quechua rather than allow the Indians under their control to learn Spanish. Efforts to promote Quechua also came from elite sectors of indigenous society including the "self-consciously nationalistic cultivation of Southern Peruvian Quechua" (Mannheim, 1984, p. 299) among Cuzco elites, who had been trained in bilingual schools and therefore had knowledge of Spanish.

While compulsory Spanish-language education for most indigenous people remained ineffectual, indigenous nobles (such as the chronicler Garcilaso de la Vega) learned how to read and write in the dominant language. These indigenous elites were also responsible for the beginning of literary production in Quechua. This was a significant development in the history of this indigenous language, and, following Benedict Anderson's insights on the origins of national consciousness (Anderson, 1991), a significant step toward the emergence and manifestation of nationalist sentiment among bilingual elites. One of these bilingual mestizos was a merchant by the name of José Gabriel Condorcanqui (or Túpac Amaru II, as he claimed direct descent from the last Inca, murdered by the Spanish, Túpac Amaru I). Túpac Amaru's revolt against Spanish rule, although brutally crushed less than a year after its inception in 1780, is often cited as the precursor to Peruvian independence (O'Phelan Godoy, 1985).

Because of Túpac Amaru's proclamation of the return of indigenous governance, colonial authorities associated the cultivation of Quechua cultural practices with political nationalism and revolution. After the rebellion failed in 1781, Quechua language, theater, and other cultural expressions were explicitly banned, a prohibition that remained in effect for almost 200 years. As is evident from the large number of Quechua speakers throughout the Americas today (approximately 10 million speakers), attempts to eradicate Quechua failed. Spanish colonizers were successful, though, in relegating it to its current status as an undervalued language, even if it was used (as were other indigenous languages) during Creole[1] independence movements as a symbol of liberation from European control (Cerrón-Palomino, 1989).

The often conflicted and contradictory colonial attitude toward language gave way to new republican complications as the colonies broke away from Spain. While in many ways Benedict Anderson (1991, p. 47) is correct in suggesting that "language was never even an issue in these early struggles for national liberation" since colonies and metropole shared the same dominant language, Quechua was used by liberators such as San Martín to mark a significant difference with Spain (Cerrón-Palomino, 1989, p. 22). Moreover, while Spanish may not have necessarily been "an issue" in Latin American independence struggles, it most certainly played a role – in its written form – in the ensuing process of Latin American nation-building.

Certainly, by the 20th century, language had become a factor in creating national identity. As the language of the ruling classes, Spanish became (and remains) the national and/or official language of the majority of Latin American countries. In Peru, as in other countries, efforts to create a unified nation emphasized the Castilianization of indigenous populations and pointed toward the gradual extinction of indigenous languages. With a few exceptions, Quechua and other indigenous languages have been subordinated to Spanish, which was ratified as the official language in the various constitutions from the time of independence (1821) up to the present day. Nevertheless, the "Indian Problem" was constituted by the tensions between assimilation and cultural preservation. These tensions were at the heart of the political and artistic movement known as *indigenismo*.

A liberal, urban-based movement that emphasized the liberation of the Indian, indigenismo emerged in the early 1900s among middle- and upper-class intellectuals. Though it began in novels, poems, and paintings with romantic literary and cultural representations of Andean peasant and Indian life, indigenista ideology also penetrated state policies and national politics. While mestizaje became the dominant nation-building project of Latin American politicians and intellectuals (Larson, 1995; Stepan, 1991; Vasconcelos, 1925), in Peru it never became an official nation-building "racial project" (de la Cadena, 2000). While favored by some intellectuals from Lima, mestizaje was forcefully rejected by Andean indigenistas who espoused sharp anti-mestizo rhetoric. The central preoccupation of many indigenista intellectuals was the political and economic emancipation of highland Quechua-speaking indigenous communities. These indigenista visions excluded mestizos and Amazonian "savages."

Indigenista ideology informed the constitution of 1920, a document that for the first time gave legal recognition to indigenous communities. During the 1920s, a series of laws and new institutions opened up channels for indigenous demands for education, land, and suffrage. In 1921, President Leguía created the Bureau of Indian Affairs and hosted an Indian congress from which emerged the Comité Pro-Derecho Indígena Tawantinsuyo, the first national indigenista organization that included self-proclaimed indigenous leaders and intellectuals (de la Cadena, 2000; Mallon, 1998).

In the following decades, José María Arguedas, an Andean novelist and anthropologist, was perhaps the most impassioned advocate for the cultural autonomy of indigenous peoples. Well known for his extensive use of Quechua along with Spanish in his poetry, short stories, and novels, Arguedas, like other indigenistas, highlighted the oppression of indigenous peoples, which had distorted the moral economy of communal life. Unlike many indigenistas, though, he also wrote about the new tensions of migration and modernity, and labeled himself a "modern Quechua man." Moving beyond purely historical or utopian accounts of indigenous life, Arguedas began working closely with Peruvian and foreign ethnologists in the 1940s, conducting research into contemporary life in indigenous communities. Indigenismo, then, became infused with a social scientific purpose. Over time, the implementation of any state program targeting indigenous populations required consultation with and the approval of ethnologists working in the designated areas (Valcárcel, 1981, pp. 368–369).

In 1946, the Peruvian Indigenista Institute was founded, and the ministries of education and public works began to promote the "cultural recovery" of indigenous language, art, culture, and religion. During this period, Arguedas worked as folklore curator in the Ministry of Education, working under the Cuzqueño indigenista (and minister of education) Luis Valcárcel. Rejecting assimilationist models, Arguedas stressed the importance of teaching indigenous highland peoples in Quechua. His first-hand experience as a primary school teacher in one of the most desolate regions of Cuzco provided him with a clear understanding of the adverse conditions and difficulties faced by teachers working in indigenous areas. By 1945, the Ministry of Education had begun implementing bilingual education in indigenous schools and teacher-training in bilingual pedagogy (Contreras, 1996; Zavala, 2008).

Bilingual education and indigenous peoples

While the period of the 1940s reflected the Peruvian state's concern over indigenous education, most of the efforts at implementing bilingual indigenous education have come from individuals and organizations independent of the Peruvian state and have been financed primarily with international funding (Pozzi-Escot, 1981). Many of these programs also reflected the Andean bias of indigenismo. In Amazonian Peru, the first attempts at bilingual education came from the Summer Institute of Linguistics (SIL) or the Wycliffe Bible Translators, an organization that began working in Peru in 1946 and began officially working in conjunction with the Peruvian state in the 1950s. A religious organization that operates worldwide, SIL has translated the Bible into indigenous languages and provides literacy training for indigenous groups as part of its mission. Until the early 1990s, the SIL was almost entirely responsible for bilingual education in the Peruvian Amazon region (de Vries, 1990; www.sil.org).

Many bilingual education projects have been temporary and transitional (teaching in the indigenous language only as a way to facilitate learning in Spanish), and most have been funded by private and official international aid agencies such as SIL, the United States Agency for International Development (USAID), and the German Institute for Technological Cooperation (GTZ). Among the best-known programs are: (a) the Bilingual Literacy Program in Quinua, Ayacucho (1964–1970), developed by the SIL and the Institutes for Applied Linguistics Research of San Marcos University and the University of Huamanga (Burns, 1968, 1971; Zuñiga, 1985); (b) the Program for Basic Bilingual Education in Cuzco in 1974 with collaboration from USAID, Cornell University, and the Peruvian National Institute for Educational Research and Development (Weber and Solá, 1980); (c) the Experimental Project of Bilingual Education in Puno (PEEB-P), 1978–1988 (Hornberger, 1988, 1990; Jung, 1992); and (d) the Bilingual and Intercultural Program of the Alto Napo (1975–present), funded primarily by the Peruvian government in its beginning stages, and receiving aid from the GTZ by the 1990s (de Vries, 1990; Fernández, 1985). While the Peruvian government permitted the development and implementation of all of these programs and allowed for the collaboration of regional universities and national education agencies with the groups interested in promoting bilingual education, it provided little, if any, funding toward their maintenance. The 1960s and 1970s, however, did see a period of renewed governmental emphasis on indigenous languages, especially Quechua.

Quechua and revolutionary nationalism: The Velasco period

General Juan Velasco Alvarado's Revolutionary Government of the Armed Forces (1968–1975) emerged in reaction to social unrest and the rise of peasant and guerrilla movements in the highlands in the 1950s and 1960s. Fundamental economic and social structural changes were needed, Velasco argued, to ensure domestic stability. Reflecting an anti-imperialistic, anti-oligarchic, and fervently nationalist ideology, Velasco launched a series of social reforms aimed at improving the conditions of peasants and indigenous peoples. At the heart of these reforms was Velasco's radical agrarian reform, the massive and forceful handover of the land of large estates to former serfs and employees. This reform was officially inaugurated on June 24, 1969, what had been called the national "Day of the Indian." Velasco renamed this day the "Day of the Peasant," officially abolishing the use of the term *Indian*, replacing it with the label of "peasant." Reflecting the enduring Andean-centric nature of social reform, the early official recognition of highland "peasant communities" came years before the 1974 recognition of Amazonian "native communities." Although the idea was simple – distribute land among those who work it – the reform's implementation was largely unsuccessful. While it effectively ended landowners' control over rural workers, it also greatly exacerbated tensions between ethnic groups.

Along with changes in land tenure, Velasco's education reforms were another mechanism of the incorporation of popular sectors. According to Velasco, the education reform (or Inca Plan) would reach "the great masses of [indigenous] peasants, always exploited and always deliberately kept in ignorance" (Velasco, 1972, p. 63). The Inca Plan would change this and address Peruvian "reality" (Zimmerman Zavala, 1974).

While the Education Reform of 1972 was a broad reform addressed to all Peruvians, it targeted primarily indigenous communities. This emphasis was made clear by the National Policy of Bilingual Education of 1972, which called for the implementation of bilingual education in all highland, lowland, and coastal areas where languages other than Spanish were spoken. This was a historically significant step, since the use of native languages for teaching had been prohibited since the 1780s. Adding to the historic revalorization of indigenous languages was a law making Quechua a national language co-equal with Spanish, passed in 1975. The law stated that, after April 1976, the teaching of Quechua would be obligatory at all educational levels. Further, all legal proceedings involving monolingual Quechua speakers would have to be conducted in Quechua (Escobar, Matos Mar, & Alberti, 1975, pp. 61–63; Turino, 1991, p. 274). This law, perhaps more than any other, carried tremendous symbolic importance for both supporters and enemies of Velasco. While many supporters saw it as an appropriately anti-colonial gesture, middle- and upper-class society saw it as symbolizing the retrograde nature of Velasco's government.

By legislating Quechua as a national language equal to Spanish, Peru became the first Latin American country to officialize an indigenous language. By placing Quechua next to the dominant language, however, it also exacerbated prejudices against anyone perceived to be from the Andean highlands. This was one of the factors leading to the overthrow of Velasco and his replacement by General Francisco Morales Bermudez in 1975.

With the change of the president (1975) and of the constitution (1979), the law making Quechua an official language was modified to include Quechua not as an official national language but rather as "a language of official use in the areas and in the way that the Law mandates." However, the law that would mandate where and how Quechua could be considered official was never passed (Pozzi-Escot, 1981; Rojas, 1982). While known as Phase Two of the Revolutionary Government, the new government decrees and laws actually dismantled many of the reforms of the Velasco era, including the emphasis that had been placed on rural and indigenous education. The promises of stability also proved short-lived, as the end of military rule in Peru also coincided with the beginning of a new round of violence between Maoist and Marxist insurgencies and state forces, beginning in 1980, with the attacks of Sendero Luminoso (Shining Path) in Ayacucho.

Education under violence

Sendero Luminoso, a Maoist insurgency group that began its armed struggle in the highlands in 1980, along with smaller Marxists groups, immersed Peru in a bloody civil war for over a decade (Stern, 1998). Fighting between insurgents and state forces and nationwide political and economic chaos devastated the entire country. Indigenous peoples in the highland and in the lowland regions, however, were the most affected by this war, which took close to 70,000 lives. Trapped between two armies, indigenous peoples, and anyone advocating indigenous rights, bore the brunt of political violence. Because Sendero originated in the highlands, indigenous peoples and their advocates were often presumed by government forces to be either subversives or Sendero sympathizers. Thousands of indigenous peasants were tortured, disappeared, or were executed, sometimes only because they could not speak Spanish (Poole & Rénique, 1992). However, by the mid to late 1980s, indigenous peoples had organized into civil defense patrol units, sometimes creating alliances with the military. Some scholars argue that it was indigenous resistance to Sendero that led to the movement's demise (Degregori, 1996; Starn, 1998).

Despite the political dangers, however, there were some developments in language and education policies aimed at indigenous peoples. Anticipating the increased transnational efforts of later decades, the Experimental Project of Bilingual Education in Puno (PEEB-P) ran from the late 1970s until 1988, funded largely by the German Institute for Technical Cooperation (GTZ). This was the only project designed to work towards the maintenance of the native language, as well as the development of Spanish as a second language. Individuals implementing the Puno project faced many of the same problems which challenge education activists today, the principal one being the rejection of the bilingual education proposal by Quechua communities. In the case of the PEEB-P, the project was declared a failure after 11 years, although its legacy among activists as the most successful attempt at bilingual education in the highlands is routinely evoked (Hornberger, 1987).

The state also put forward some notable, if limited, initiatives during the period of political violence. In 1985, for example, the Quechua and Aymara alphabets were officialized, and in 1987, after approximately 10 years of inactivity, President Alan García (1985–1990) reinstated the National Office of Bilingual Education. With the election of Alberto Fujimori as president of Peru in 1990, the country entered a new political stage, one that combined neoliberalism and authoritarian rule. Emergency military control of almost two-thirds of the national territory and the so-called self-coup of April 1992 meant the loss of civil and political rights. A turning point in this adverse political climate came in September 1992 with the capture of Abimael Guzmán, the head of Sendero Luminoso.

By 1993, Peru had begun a slow transition toward democratic rule. This democratizing period produced a new national constitution (1993) designed, among other things, to "recognize and protect the ethnic and cultural plurality of the nation" by guaranteeing the right of all people to use their own language before the state (Article 2). The constitution also highlights "the state's obligation to promote intercultural and bilingual education, depending on the characteristics of each region" (Article 17). Nevertheless, characteristic of the contradictions of Peruvian history, as Fujimori approved progressive changes to the constitution, he simultaneously dissolved the National Office for Bilingual Education, citing lack of funds as his reason for doing so. Owing to international pressure from various organizations, and because of protests by intercultural activists throughout the country, the office was re-established in 1996, but only as a unit (UNEBI) within the National Office of Elementary Education. Even then, most of the UNEBI's funding was cut off during the last months of 1996 and the first months of 1997.

With the re-establishment of the UNEBI in the Ministry of Education in Lima in 1996, the minister of education invited Juan Carlos Godenzzi, an Andean linguist and one of the leading intellectuals advocating intercultural bilingual education, to move from Cuzco (where he was working as program director of an Andean research institute) to Lima and act as its chief. Godenzzi moved to Lima to head the UNEBI in May 1997 and remained in that position until his departure in September 2002. According to Godenzzi, between 1997 and 2001 the UNEBI (made up of only five staff members) produced 94 bilingual teaching manuals (Godenzzi, 2001). With the help of several non-governmental organizations (NGOs), universities, and research institutes, the UNEBI's staff also facilitated bilingual training for over 10,000 teachers working in bilingual areas, and provided enough materials so that all school classrooms in the areas where bilingual intercultural education was implemented could have their own bilingual library (Godenzzi, 2001, p. 6). Despite these achievements, much of the innovation in indigenous education during the neoliberal period, not surprisingly, is due less to the political will of the government and more to the transnational resources and networks of international development.[2]

Intercultural education and indigenous citizenship

Efforts to breathe life into indigenous education were hardly absent even during the difficult moments of the 1980s. The experiences in intercultural education in Puno, though seen as a failure by some, provided a foundation for a new round of policy initiatives. Indeed, many of those who were associated with the PEEB-P in Puno became involved with the implementation of bilingual intercultural education in the 1990s. This project is best known for the pedagogical materials and texts it produced, many still used today (Hornberger, 1988, 1990; Jung, 1992; Jung & López, 1988; López, 1988).

The other notable experience in the 1980s took place in the Amazon and reflected the possible articulation between local, national, and transnational actors. The Program for the Training of Native Bilingual Teachers (FORMABIAP) was a product of the collaboration between the largest Amazonian indigenous federation (AIDESEP, the Inter-Ethnic Amazonian Association for Development in the Peruvian Jungle), the Loreto Pedagogical Institute, the Loreto Departmental Corporation, and the Italian development organization Terra Nuova. FORMABIAP advanced an innovative combination of residential-based education for students in the regional capital city of Iquitos as well as decentralized education in Amazonian indigenous communities. FORMABIAP also seeks to combine "occidental" and "traditional" forms of knowledge in an effort to move beyond Eurocentric models of education (Ames, 2003, pp. 362–363).

Post-authoritarian developments: 2000–2008

The existence of a web of activists, educators, and international supporters provided a promising seed for change that had met a hostile political environment. That environment changed dramatically with the implosion of the authoritarian and corrupt Fujimori administration, and created new opportunities for indigenous education to grow. Valentín Paniagua, president of the Congress when political scandals led then President Fujimori to flee the country, was instituted as president of a transitional government in Peru while new elections were held. Under Paniagua's transitional administration (2000–2001), the UNEBI, for example, increased the number of its staff to 16 and was renamed the National Division of Intercultural Bilingual

Education (DINEBI). The DINEBI was launched on April 5, 2001. Significantly, one of the first actions taken by the DINEBI was to establish a 15-member National Consulting Committee on Intercultural Bilingual Education, 9 of whom were indigenous professionals (Godenzzi, 2001, p. 4). The committee held several national-level meetings with intellectuals, NGO workers, teacher-trainers, and bilingual teachers, and then drafted a report on the *National Politics of Languages and Cultures in Education*. Based on this report, the DINEBI prepared a timeline (Plan Estratégico, 2001–2005) for the future development of bilingual intercultural education in the country.

The 2001 election of Alejandro Toledo as president of Peru provided further evidence of an opening for indigenous rights. Toledo and his Quechua-speaking, Belgian-born wife, Eliane Karp, made much of the presidential candidate's Andean origins on the campaign trail. After defeating Alan García, Toledo inaugurated his presidency with a special ceremony in Machu Picchu and pledged there, along with other South American presidents, to work for the advancement of indigenous people. In the following years, Toledo was in many ways a disappointment to many indigenous leaders who were frustrated by his neoliberal policies and uncomfortable with his decision to appoint his wife as the head of a new state commission for indigenous and Afro-Peruvian affairs (García, 2005; García & Lucero, 2004). Nevertheless, the policies of DINEBI had the backing of the Toledo administration. The funding for DINEBI activities as well as the non-governmental initiatives during this period, however, came less from the Peruvian government than from the agents of international development, including multilateral development agencies and the official aid agencies of Germany, Spain, and Italy, among others.

As the Toledo administration entered office, the Fifth Latin American Conference of Intercultural Bilingual Education was held in Lima, Peru, in August 2002. Participants at the conference drafted a document titled "Multilingual Reality and Intercultural Challenge: Citizenship, Politics, and Education." Of the many challenges described in the document, it is useful to recall one: "The education offered to most [indigenous peoples], particularly that offered to indigenous women and girls, is devoid of quality, and of linguistic, cultural, and pedagogical relevance" (Declaración de Lima, 2002, sections 1.1, 1.5, author's translation). At the end of Toledo's term in 2006, and at the beginning of the presidency of Alan García, that statement continued to be largely true for most indigenous people in the country. By way of conclusion, it is helpful to examine some of the limitations and complications of intercultural bilingual education in contemporary Peru.

Conclusion: Achievements and setbacks

For its advocates, intercultural bilingual education holds the promise of a more equitable, diverse, and respectful society (Godenzzi, 1996; López, 1996). Its proper implementation is a pledge toward eradicating poverty in indigenous communities, while simultaneously promoting indigenous autonomy and cultural pride, and demanding social, cultural, economic, and political rights. Along with the remarkable advances of indigenous movements and political leaders in many Latin American countries, proponents of intercultural bilingual education can claim many victories: constitutional reforms that recognize and legitimize linguistic, cultural, and ethnic diversity; the creation and maintenance of institutes and programs for indigenous students; and the development of educational materials in dozens of indigenous languages.

However, in recent years, those advancements have faced significant challenges. First, there is the danger that even the best-intentioned advocacy can encounter the old problems of paternalism and verticalism that have long haunted indigenous education. NGO and non-indigenous intercultural advocates often complain, for example, of the resistance they find among indigenous parents who are concerned that their children, who often are able to attend formal schools for only a few years, are missing out on opportunities to develop strong Spanish-language skills. Rather than include these parents in curricular planning, many NGO activists find themselves guilty of the very practice they critique: the imposition of education models that do not take into account the demands of local communities. While advocates are certainly correct that bilingual education can often be an effective tool for Spanish-language acquisition, more needs to be done to foster communication between families and educators (García, 2005).

Second, there are the familiar challenges of resource scarcity and distribution. While the DINEBI boasted that every classroom in indigenous schools where bilingual intercultural education is implemented would have its own library, researchers who have visited dozens of bilingual schools in the highlands find that these libraries are few and far between (García, 2005). Similarly, while officially more than 10,000 teachers have been trained in bilingual education methodology, there is little emphasis on evaluation of the training (or the trainers), on follow-ups with individual teachers, or on feedback from teachers about the positive and negative aspects of training sessions.

Third, the design of national education policies still lacks an adequate approach to overcoming dichotomous approaches to education that separate (rural) indigenous and (urban) non-indigenous students. Though the promise of intercultural education is one of dialogue across ethnic and linguistic lines, the reality is a bureaucratic separation that isolates and marginalizes indigenous education. The fusion of indigenous and rural education in a renamed national Directorate of Intercultural Bilingual and Rural Education (DINEIBIR) has increased concern among intercultural education activists that the commitment to intercultural bilingual education is eroding. In the wake of the dismissal of several indigenous professionals from the Ministry of Education and a renewed emphasis on national evaluation exams offered only in Spanish, there is reason to be pessimistic about the place of intercultural bilingual education in the current government's set of priorities (Martínez Perez, 2007).

Yet it is important to put the current climate of anxiety about the future of indigenous education in a broader perspective. Regional programs like FORMABIAP in the Amazon continue their work with the support of international agencies and non-governmental organizations. International programs like the Masters Program for Training in Intercultural Bilingual Education (PROEIB-Andes) in Bolivia have trained dozens of indigenous scholars and leaders who form part of a growing web of transnational activism that remains a resource for local actors who face reluctant and/or hostile national governments. As pointed out by one Peruvian Quechua linguist at the PROEIB who began his work during times of dictatorship and when international agendas barely took notice of the demands of indigenous peoples (cited in García 2007): whatever the current challenges of indigenous education in Peru, it has gone through tougher times before.

Notes

1 Creoles or *criollos* were descendants of Europeans who were born in the Americas.
2 For example, there has been much international support for indigenous literacy and biliteracy programs. For a broader discussion of indigenous literacy and biliteracy, see Hornberger (1997, 2006).

References

Ames, P. (2003). Educación e interculturalidad: Repensando mitos, identidades, y proyectos [Education and interculturality: Rethinking myths, identities, and projects]. In N. Fuller (Ed.), *Interculturalidad y política: Desafíos y posibilidades* [Interculturality and politics: Challenges and possibilities]. Lima: Red para el Desarrollo de las Ciencias Sociales en el Peru.

Anderson, B. (1991). *Imagined communities*. New York: Verso.

Burns, D. (1968). Bilingual education in the Andes of Peru. In J. Fishman, C. Ferguson, and J. Das Gupta (Eds.), *Language problems of developing nations* (pp. 403–414). New York: John Wiley & Sons.

Burns, D. (1971). *Cinco años de educación bilingüe en los Andes del Peru: 1965–1970. Informe final* [Five years of bilingual education in the Peruvian Andes: 1965–1970. Final report]. Lima: Summer Institute of Linguistics.

Cerrón-Palomino, R. (1989). Language policy in Peru: A historical overview. *International Journal of the Sociology of Language, 77*, 11–33.

Contreras, C. (1996). *Sobre los Orígenes de la Explosión Demográfica en el Perú* (Documento de Trabajo No. 61). [About the origins of the demographic explosion in Peru (Working Document No. 61)]. Lima: IEP.

Declaración de Lima. (2002). *Servindi: Servicio de Información Indígena* [Servindi: Indigenous Information Service], No. 13.

Degregori, C. I. (Ed.). (1996). *Las rondas campesinas y la derrota de Sendero Luminoso*. [The rondas campesinas and the defeat of Sendero Luminoso]. Lima: IEP.

de la Cadena, M. (2000). *Indigenous mestizos: The politics of race and culture in Cuzco, 1919–1991*. Durham, NC: Duke University Press.

de Vries, L. (1990). Política lingüística y educación bilingüe en los países Andinos relativas a los Quechua-hablantes [Linguistic politics and bilingual education in Andean countries: The Quechua case]. In L. E. López and R. Moya (Eds.), *Pueblos Indios, Estados y Educación* [Indian peoples, states, and education] (pp. 27–44). Lima: GTZ.

Escobar, A., Matos Mar, J., & Alberti, G. (1975). *Perú país bilingüe?* [Peru, bilingual country?]. Lima: IEP.

Fernández, M. (1985). *Programa de educación bilingüe e intercultural del Alto Napo-Perú. Seminario Subregional, 13–19 Noviembre*. [Intercultural and bilingual education programo for the Alto Napo-Perú. Subregional Seminar, November 13–19]. Lima.

García, M. E. (2005). *Making indigenous citizens: Identities, education, and multicultural development in Peru*. Stanford, CA: Stanford University Press.

García, M. E. (2007, April). *Collaboration in a postcolonial "contact zone": The challenges of intercultural education*. Paper presented at the conference "Indigenous Movements and Intellectuals in the Americas: A Symposium," Tufts University, Medford, MA.

García, M. E., and Lucero, J. A. (2004). Un país sin indígenas? Rethinking indigenous politics in Peru. In N. Postero and L. Zamosc (Eds.), *The struggle for Indian rights in Latin America* (pp. 158–188). Brighton, UK: Sussex Academic Press.

Gleich, U. von (1994). Language spread policy: The case of Quechua in the Andean republics of Bolivia, Ecuador, and Peru. *International Journal of the Sociology of Language, 107*, 77–113.

Godenzzi, J. C. (1996). Introducción: Construyendo la convivencia y el entendimiento: Educación e interculturalidad en América Latina [Introduction: Constructing coexistence and understanding: Education and interculturality in Latin America]. In J. C. Godenzzi (Ed.), *Educación e interculturalidad en los Andes y la Amazonía* [Education and interculturality in the Andes and Amazon] (pp. 23–82). Cuzco: Center for Regional Andean Studies, Bartolomé de las Casas.

Godenzzi, J. C. (2001, September). *Política de lenguas y culturas en la educación: El caso del Perú* [Language politics and cultures in education: The Peruvian case]. Paper presented at the 23rd Meeting of the Latin American Studies Association, Washington, DC.

Heath, S. B. and Laprade, R. (1982). Castilian colonization and indigenous languages: The cases of Quechua and Aymara. In R. Cooper (Ed.), *Language spread* (pp. 118–147). Bloomington: Indiana University Press.

Hornberger, N. H. (1987). Bilingual education success, policy failure. *Language in Society, 16*, 205–226.

Hornberger, N. H. (1988). *Bilingual education and language maintenance: A southern Peruvian Quechua case*. Dordrecht, The Netherlands: Foris.

Hornberger, N. H. (1990). Exitos y desfases en la educación bilingüe en Puno y la política lingüística Peruana [Successes and challenges in bilingual education in Puno and Peruvian linguistic policy]. In L. E. López and R. Moya (Eds.), *Pueblos Indios, Estados y Educación* [Indian peoples, states and education] (pp. 379–410). Lima: GTZ.

Hornberger, N. H. (1997). Quechua literacy and empowerment in Peru. In N. H. Hornberger (Ed.), *Indigenous literacies in the Americas: Language planning from the bottom up* (pp. 215–236). Berlin: Mouton de Gruyter.

Hornberger, N. H. (2006). Voice and biliteracy in indigenous language revitalization: Contentious educational practices in Quechua, Guarani and Maori contexts. *Journal of Language, Identity, and Education*, 5(4), 277–292.

Jung, I. (1992). *Conflicto cultural y educación: El proyecto de educación bilingüe – Puno, Peru* [Cultural conflict and education: The bilingual education project in Puno, Peru]. Quito: Abya Yala.

Jung, I., and López, L. E. (1988). *Las lenguas en la educación bilingüe: El caso de Puno* [Languages in bilingual education: The Puno case]. Lima: GTZ.

Larson, B. (1995). Andean communities, political cultures, and markets: The changing contours of a field. In B. Larson and O. Harris (Eds.), *Ethnicity, markets, and migration in the Andes: At the crossroads of history and anthropology* (pp. 5–54). Durham, NC: Duke University Press.

López, L. E. (1988). Balance y perspectivas de la educación bilingüe en Puno [Evaluation and perspectives of bilingual education in Puno]. In L. E. López (Ed.), *Pesquisas en lingüística Andina* [Inquiries in Andean linguistics] (pp. 79–108). Lima: Universidad Nacional del Altiplano.

López, L. E. (1996). No más danzas de ratones grises: Sobre interculturalidad, democracia, y educación [No more dances of grey mice: About interculturality, democracy, and education]. In J. C. Godenzzi (Ed.), *Educación e interculturalidad en los Andes y la Amazonía* [Education and interculturality in the Andes and Amazon] (pp. 23–82). Cuzco: Center for Regional Andean Studies, Bartolomé de las Casas.

Mallon, F. (1998). Chronicle of a path foretold? In S. Stern (Ed.), *Shining and other paths: War and society in Peru, 1980–1995* (pp. 84–117). Durham, NC: Duke University Press.

Mannheim, B. (1984). Una Nación Acorralada: Southern Peruvian Quechua language planning and politics in historical perspective. *Language in Society*, 13, 291–309.

Mannheim, B. (1991). *The language of the Inka since the European invasion*. Austin: University of Texas Press.

Mar-Molinero, C. (1995). Language policies in multi-ethnic Latin America and the role of education and literacy programs in the construction of national identity. *International Journal of Educational Development*, 15(3), 209–219.

Martínez Perez, R. (2007). *Denuncian desmontaje de la educación intercultural bilingüe (EIB) en Ministerio de Educación* [Denouncing the dismantling of intercultural bilingual education (IBE) in the Ministry of Education]. Retrieved January 3, 2008, from www.servindi.org/archivo/2007/1725

O'Phelan Godoy, S. (1985). *Rebellions and revolts in eighteenth century Peru and Upper Peru*. Cologne, Germany: Bohlau.

Poole, D., and Rénique, G. (1992). *Peru, time of fear*. London: Latin American Bureau.

Pozzi-Escot, I. (1981). La educación bilingüe en el marco legal de la reforma educativa Peruana [Bilingual education in the legal frame of the Peruvian education reform]. In *Acerca de la Historia y el Universo Aymara* [About the Aymara history and universe] (pp. 113–123). Lima: CIED.

Rojas, I. (1982). En torno a la oficialización de las lenguas Quechua y Aymara [About the officialization of Quechua and Aymara]. In R. Cerrón-Palomino (Ed.), *Aula Quechua* [Quechua classroom] (pp. 82–105). Lima: Signo Universitario.

Rowe, J. (1946). Inca culture at the time of the Spanish conquest. In J. Steward (Ed.), *Handbook of South American Indians* (Vol. 2, 183–330). Washington, DC: Bureau of American Ethnology.

Starn, O. (1998). Villagers at arms: War and counterrevolution in the Central-South Andes. In S. Stern (Ed.), *Shining and other paths: War and society in Peru, 1980–1995* (pp. 224–257). Durham, NC: Duke University Press.

Stepan, N. L. (1991). *The hour of eugenics: Race, gender and nation in Latin America*. Ithaca, NY: Cornell University Press.

Stern, S. (Ed.). (1998). *Shining and other paths: War and society in Peru, 1980–1995*. Durham, NC: Duke University Press.

Turino, T. (1991). The state and Andean musical production in Peru. In G. Urban and J. Sherzer (Eds.), *Nation-states and Indians in Latin America* (pp. 259–285). Austin: University of Texas Press.

Valcárcel, L. (1981). *Memorias* [Memories]. Lima: IEP.

Vasconcelos, J. (1925). *La Raza Cósmica: Misión de la Raza Ibero-Americana. Notas de Viaje por la América del Sur* [The cosmic race: The mission of the Ibero-American race. Travel notes from South America]. Barcelona: World Agency of Libraries. (Reprinted in *The complete works*, No. 2, pp. 906–942, México: United Mexican Librarians)

Velasco Alvarado, J. (1972). *La Voz de la Revolución: Discursos del Presidente de la República, General de División, Juan Velasco Alvarado, 1970–1972* (Tomo II) [The voice of the revolution: Presidential speeches, General Juan Velasco Alvarado, 1970–1972 (Vol. II)]. Lima: Ediciones Participación.

Weber, R. M., and Solá, D. F. (1980, December). Developing instructional materials for a bilingual education program in the Peruvian Andes. *Reading Teacher*, 296–302.

Zavala, V. (2008). Teacher training in bilingual education in Peru. In N. V. Deusen-Scholl and N. H. Hornberger (Eds.), *Encyclopedia of language and education. Vol. 4. Second and foreign language education* (pp. 293–308). New York: Springer Science+Business Media.

Zimmermann Zavala, A. (1974). *El Plan Inca, Objetivo: Revolución Peruana* [The Inca Plan, objective: Peruvian revolution]. Lima: Editorial House of the Official Newspaper *El Peruano*.

Zúñiga, M. (1985). *La Educación bilingüe Quechua–Castellano en Ayacucho: Un Programa Experimental de la UNMSM* (Documento de Trabajo No. 52) [Quechua–Spanish bilingual education in Ayacucho: An experimental program of the UNMSM (Working Document No. 52)]. Lima.

21

The struggle to educate the Maori in New Zealand

Wally Penetito
Victoria University of Wellington, New Zealand

Background

Something important is happening in New Zealand today in relations between indigenous (Maori) and European (Pakeha) New Zealanders. Some kind of ambiguous force seems to be operating that is close at hand, yet not quite within reach. Ironically, the major influences seem to be emanating from the collaboration of organic Maori intellectuals with conservative community Maori sources. Peculiarly, the outcomes of these influences are being maintained, if not necessarily advocated, by middle New Zealand. These influences have taken the shape of a cultural movement where questions of indigenous rights, citizenship, and national identity have accomplished a level of relevance usually reserved for times of great stress such as during times of war or economic depression.

Neither of these applies directly to New Zealand society during the period of this writing. At the heart of this movement is what the American philosopher Lear (2006, p. 140) refers to as "the formation of a culturally enriched ego-ideal." In the New Zealand context such an ideal has formed from the emergence of two critical movements. The first of these has been the response to the enormous task of revitalizing an almost moribund Maori language, while the second has been the equally daunting work of redressing and healing past injustices by the Crown against Maori. Whereas the first of these movements focuses on the universal significance of the Maori language (an education system response in the main), the second is much more specifically directed at broader ethical concerns in what the historian Sharp (2004, p. 198) refers to as "reparatory justice," that is, "the righting of the Crown's past wrongs to Maori." Both responses, it is argued, will not only contribute to improved Maori student educational performance but will, more importantly, lead to productive collaborations built on a reciprocal good faith between Maori and the Crown. Within the last quarter-century, evidence suggests that, despite predictable outbursts of exasperation from Maori with regard to breaches of the Treaty, resentment against all forms of racism, disparities of earning power, academic underachievement, unavailability of appropriate housing, and an appalling gap in everyday quality of life, there is a new and refreshing change of attitude or mood that is gently settling across the nation. This chapter identifies some of the more "telling" events that are claimed to be challenging the status quo. The telling events are those activities, episodes, or initiatives that derive from Maori inspiration and, for reasons that can only be inferred at this stage, are "picked up," favored, and as a result popularized universally.

The revitalization of the Maori language and culture and the healing processes generated by the activities of the Waitangi Tribunal have brought about a new generic sense of belonging, an enlivened spirit that draws on the best of both worlds. This spirit of hope is slowly engaging the consciousness of many of New Zealand's citizens, but it is far from being a new phenomenon. Indeed, it has origins in the 1840 Treaty of Waitangi, founding document, evidenced in Governor Hobson's assertion that "He iwi tahi tatou" (We are now one people). It is universally acclaimed in the oft-quoted words coined by Sir Apirana Ngata beginning, "E tipu, e rea, mo nga ra o tou ao" (Grow and branch forth in the days of your world). What marks the contemporary mood as distinctive from that of earlier periods is the mainstream "buy-in" at both symbolic and structural levels. From a Maori point of view there is a need for urgency against insidious influences to inhibit or set limitations on what can be achieved. From a Pakeha perspective, Maori initiatives that looked as though they were challenging mainstream authority would be ignored completely, redefined, or appropriated in some way to fit with the dominant ethos. Of course, a change of mood is nothing more than an ideological shift, perhaps epitomized in the common phrase as a shift in hearts and minds, when what is really desired is a material change in behavior, processes, structures, and outcomes. Using Kuhn's (1962) famous distinction, the question asked in this chapter is: *Can a change of mood* (an emerging consensus) *be sufficient to challenge the veracity of the prevailing consensus* (the status quo) *in order to transform it?* In order to argue the case, the old consensus on Maori education described as the "received view" is measured against the "critical responses to those views."

The education system is playing a central role in supporting and promoting the revitalization and dissemination of *te reo* Maori (the Maori language) as a right for all Maori students and as "knowledge worth pursuing" for all other students. The justice system, through the Waitangi Tribunal, is playing an equally central role in investigating, reporting, and mediating the redress of past injustices caused by the Crown, especially during the period of the settler "land-grab" in the decades immediately following the signing of the Treaty of Waitangi.[1] It is too early, by at least two generations, to say that a more embedded and indigenous-to-New Zealand culture has emerged within society as a whole, but I argue that there is evidence that a "soft revolution" is taking place in the hearts and minds (and in the classrooms, bedrooms, and boardrooms) of New Zealanders right now. There seems to be a tacit acceptance by Pakeha that perhaps a majority of Maori tribes were deeply disadvantaged by an overly zealous colonial power and that a settled future might depend on a public examination of New Zealand's history. Lear (2006) argues that "a crucial aspect of psychological health depends on the internalization of vibrant ideals" (p. 140). This would seem to hold true for aggregations as much as it does for individuals.

The chapter concludes with a discussion of some of the particularly potent critical responses (an emerging consensus) that mark this historic period in the development of New Zealand as an ethnically diverse society founded on the notion of a dual heritage. Some teasing out of the central ideas of "consensus politics" and "being Maori" are made before outlining the evidential approach to the substantive conclusions of the chapter.

Consensus politics and being Maori

Consensus is taken to mean when an agreement or decision is reached by parties after a period of debate and/or discussion where compromises are called for following processes of negotiation. In a modern Western democracy, such as exists in New Zealand, the best decisions are perceived as those that are consensual. This is also true within Maori society. Different views on what constitutes consensus are often compromised in intercultural exchanges. When Maori values, questions about common sense, what counts as reality, and what is reasonable are being debated publicly, they almost always come up against Pakeha cultural, economic, and political hegemony. Pakeha perceptions are presented as universal and immutable views of the way things are. The outcome for Maori is commonly one of frustration, antipathy, and often deep resentment. The peculiar chauvinism of Western thinking is found in the view that espouses compromise as a weakness, and negotiation advisable but only when it is obvious that winning might not eventuate. It is difficult to always be wrong for no other reason than because there are fewer of you to stake your claim.

Consensus is a critical component of praxis, which, according to Shields (1999, p. 62), "is the means of maintaining within oneself the fluid potentiality of 'becoming' while at the same time creating a stable world." A redefinition of consensus that allows for different ways of embodying its principles in the social contract seems a worthy goal for any democracy founded on bicultural principles. This is the praxis currently being enacted in relations between Maori as the *tangata-whenua* (the indigenous people of the land) and Pakeha as *tangata-tiriti* (descendants of European settlers).

There is no one way to be Maori (or anyone else for that matter). But if there is consensus among Maori for one defining characteristic it would be one's claim "to be Maori." Facility in the Maori language says something about the nature of one's claim. For example, the popular aphorism "Toku reo, toku ohooho. Toku reo, toku mapihi maurea" (My language. My awakening) indicates a cultural stance. Place-based knowledge, as in the proverb "Hokia ki nga maunga, kia purea koe e nga hau o Tawhirimatea" (Return to your mountains and there be cleansed by the winds of Tawhirimatea), indicates a position based on a sense of belonging. In New Zealand, one's Maoriness is defined by other Maori on the basis of one's knowledge and affiliation to tribal entities rather than the abstract Maori.

Maori education: The received view

The "received view" and the "critical responses to it" are a strategy used by Slack and Wise (2005) in their discussion of the relationship between culture and technology. The received view refers to those views espoused by the dominant culture through legislation, policies, regulations, and general practice. The authors and researchers listed below are, of course, those reporting on the received view and are not necessarily advocates of those views.

A selection of the more well-known sources that comment on these documents are found in the works of scholars such as the educational sociologist and anthropologist Harker (1971), one of the earlier theorists who attempted to unravel causes behind the disease of continuing Maori underachievement. The research by Barrington and Beaglehole (1974) brought to light the period of the native/Maori school system of 1867–1969. Simon (1998) provided an interpretation of the native/Maori schools' policies from a critical educational anthropologist's perspective, while Simon and Smith (2001) provided a different way again of looking at the native/Maori schools by researching those who were the recipients of the theories, policies, and practices that were enacted during those times. Official reports like those of the Department of Maori Affairs (Hunn, 1960), the Commission on Education in New Zealand (Currie, 1962), and more recently Chapple, Jefferies, and Walker (1997) contributed to the wealth of material that made up the received view, that is, the consensus view on what Maori education was, what defined it, the legal framework in which it operated, its successes and failures, and much more.

Three important components make up the received view. First is the set of commonsense stories the dominant culture tells about Maori education. Education as in mainstream schools is good for everyone. Schools are the best places to receive a formal education. Maori have the potential to achieve as well as anyone. Achievement and success derive from hard work. Maori culture, especially language, is best kept for home. *Matauranga* (Maori knowledge) and *tikanga* (Maori custom) should have a minimal influence in schools. And Pakeha know best what is in the interests of Maori.

The second component that makes up the received view is those stories told of resistance to the received view (Department of Education, 1980; Harker, 1978; Walker, 1985, 1987). The messages conveyed in these stories are that Maori know best what is in their interests and want to exercise greater control over their education. They are adamant that their culture plays a significant contextual role in successful learning. They hold fast to the position that the "problem" of Maori education is systemic rather than cultural. The underlying proposition is that Maori or tribal knowledge is important learning for all New Zealanders.

The third component comprises those new stories informed from critical and/or cultural studies of how the imposed definition of "education" shapes "Maori education." Questions are asked about how change happens, how agency works, and how connections are made and unmade. Qualitatively related are other questions that highlight stories about creating institutional space, identity, politics, and globalization. The sources for these stories are found mainly but not exclusively in contemporary Maori scholarship, especially that originating from the Education Department at the University of Auckland during the 1980s and 1990s. These scholars include, in no particular order, Judith Simon, Tuki Nepe, Cherryl Smith, Graham Smith, Linda Smith, Patricia Johnston, Margie Hohepa, Kuni Jenkins, Jim Marshall, Michael Peters, Elizabeth Rata, and Alison Jones. The enterprise generated by this group of academics is central to developments in Maori education today. The span of influence now extends into the work of government public servants, into the national media, across the political spectrum, and into the sciences and commerce; in fact, it is difficult to ascertain where the demand for a national consciousness does not have Maori aspirations on its agenda.

According to the critique of the system, Maori want an education that begins with their identification as Maori before expanding into the world at large. They want an education that is seen to contribute directly to a national identity, that links formally to all other indigenous peoples, and that is designed to uphold their *mana* (status) as *tangatawhenua* (indigenous or first people) of Aotearoa New Zealand. These stories collectively constitute a "mapping exercise" (Slack & Wise, 2005, p. 5) that contextualizes the practices, questions, contradictions, representations, and effects that accompany the culture of education in New Zealand. Out of this third set of stories arise some penetrating questions, such as: What is Maori about Maori education? What does Maori education mean if the broad underlying philosophy of the education system of Aotearoa New Zealand owes more to ancient Greek scholars and modern British, French, Italian, and American educators than it does to indigenous New Zealanders? What is needed, according to this third group of researchers, is an education that is relevant, appropriate, and right for New Zealand. Maori people have a view about that education, and they have become increasingly informed, vocal, and articulate in expressing it.

The historical foundations underlying Maori education are directly conditional upon a political philosophy of racial and cultural superiority. Ideology, particularly as it is manifested in differential achievement, has developed as a result of successive iterations of policies and practices that assume Maori are dependent on Pakeha goodwill without any reciprocal intention on the part of the mainstream.

What is Maori about "Maori education"?

A preliminary investigation of some of the critical literature in the narrow field of differential achievement in Maori education (Bishop & Berryman, 2006; Department of Education, 1970; Nash, 2001) makes it clear that simplistic, top-down, linear explanations are not helpful in solving this problem. The Maori education field is as diverse and as complex as the people and influences in it. A perusal of the Ministry of Education's Annual Report on Maori Education (2005, or any year) makes this point explicitly. One would expect that analysis and explanation need to at least model that complexity. It is argued that the system is loaded against Maori from the outset. Even the native/Maori school system which lasted for 102 years (1867 to 1969) was in reality a system-in-transition, a place-holder until such time as Maori young people were seen to be sufficiently socialized into the Pakeha world to join the mainstream. Even though Maori students and their home communities were numerically dominant in all these schools, none of the schools exercised a Maori ontological base. They were Pakeha schools, run by Pakeha teachers, implementing a Pakeha curriculum, following Pakeha philosophies of learning and teaching. This is not to say that perhaps even most of the teachers did what they thought was in the best interests of their students.

The system is represented in a "big brother" adversarial role manufactured out of consensus (that is, with apparent mainstream and Maori agreement). The consensus is seen (by the mainstream) as being neither coercive nor oppositional to Maori, but rather "common sense." Maori are left with little choice: they want an education; schools are where one goes to get an education. There is no intention to coerce, but the effect is the same. So long as Maori do not get to exercise their *rangatiratanga* (self-determination) and *mana* (agency) they see themselves caught up in the determinism of victimhood and fatalism. The answer to the question posed in the heading to this section, "What is Maori about 'Maori education'?," is very little up until recent times. In thinking about this problem, accounting for shifts in official definitions of Maori education, and matching those with Maori ways of thinking about their own education, it should be reasonably obvious what is the direction preferred by Maori.

Two political philosophies, two epistemological traditions

The definition of Maori education has seen several shifts over the period of a hundred years plus: as the "civilizing" of the natives in the period 1816–1860, as the "pacification" of the natives in the period 1860–1880, as "assimilation" in the 1880–1930 period, as "cultural adaptation" in 1930–1960, as "integration" in the period 1960–1970, as "taha Maori" and "bilingual education" through the 1970s–1980s, and as "bilingual education" and then "kaupapa Maori" in the period 1980–2008. Each of these periods is also marked with a shift in emphasis in the knowledge base taught in schools. As the British academic Archer wrote, "Education is fundamentally about what people (those in power) have wanted of it and have been able to do to it" (1984, p. 1). What this linear presentation reveals is a gradual move away from the forces for assimilation, a strengthening of a Maori resolve to assert their culture, and an incorporation of the mainstream into the core of Maori culture. Given the 19th-century colonial upheavals and an ongoing cultural hegemony, Maori were by the mid-1990s in the invidious position of losing, probably, the single most significant vestige of their heritage, their language. A comprehensive review of the status of the Maori language by the prominent linguistic researcher Benton (1979a, 1979b) made it crystal clear to *kaumatua* (Maori elders) that unless prompt action was taken the language would die. This realization and the need to act promptly and decisively were sufficient to mobilize Maori communities to take immediate action. The Kohanga Reo (Language Nest) revolution of the 1980s swept through *whanau* (families), *hapu* (communities), and *iwi* (tribes) like wildfire.

The thesis of this chapter is that education through the process of schooling can equip all students in New Zealand into at least two epistemological traditions, one with its roots historically embedded in the West and the other with its origins firmly established in the Pacific and Aotearoa. The mainstream system's response to this notion of dual epistemologies has been to adopt "add-on elements" to a mainstream core curriculum. It has used piecemeal models of intervention, borrowing from a Maori world view and integrated, where overlaps appeared coherent, with mainstream philosophies and practices. Despite the rhetoric of integration, very often what was intended to cohere appeared to some as contradictory.

The European philosopher Popper (1994) argued that there are two components of human reason that help make the universe we live in understandable to ourselves. The first is "storytelling," as when people think they are in the hands of unknown powers and they try to understand the world by inventing stories. The second relates to the invention of "criticism" of the explanatory myths with the aim of consciously improving on them. In Western philosophical terms, Popper continues, storytelling leads to "relativism" (truth can change with context), whereas "criticism" is the task of science and is rational (p. 34). The growth of knowledge, according to this thesis, depends entirely on the existence of disagreement. Popper leaves no spaces for a position between the two doctrines, making his stance typically absolutist.

There is an assumption, because of these priorities, that criticism, science, universalism, and rationality are either not important, do not exist, or cannot coexist because it would be irrational for them to do so in any kaupapa Maori context. According to Maori, what it means to be human is a belief in the dynamic tension that exists in all relationships. It is a Maori "way of being." When analyzing kaupapa Maori in Maori philosophical terms, contradiction and paradox are a part of the philosophical equation. Harvey (2000), a Marxist geographer, denies the choice artificially constructed between particularity and universality. "Within a relational dialectics," he argues, "one is always internalized and implicated in the other." This reasoning also follows for "relativism" and "criticism."

Having an education system based on dual philosophical and epistemological traditions does not seem to me to be in the least bit exaggerated given the ethnic and cultural diversity of most modern states. The majority of New Zealanders prefer to remain closeted in the English language and European philosophical traditions and customs rather than indulge too far in the intricacies of *te ao* Maori (the Maori world). Maori citizens, on the other hand, must acquire a reasonable facility in most things deriving from *te ao* Pakeha (the Pakeha world) merely to move with some comfort in the everyday world of the New Zealander. The Maori language was dangerously close to extinction before it received anything like what was necessary for it to be revitalized. One reason for that is the jaundiced view that, as a minority language, Maori has little or no value outside the confines of a Maori milieu.

For more than a century of formal education, this has been the message to Maori from the dominant monolingual Pakeha society. Maori language revitalization arising out of 1970s research has been the "thin end of the wedge." If the Maori language is resourced so that it can become a fully recognized and used language within New Zealand society, then other aspects of Maori culture will have a much better chance of surviving as well.

Maori education: Critical responses to the received view

In identifying the changing landscape of the culture of education in New Zealand, two particularly potent critical responses are singled out for elaboration: the "kaupapa Maori" movement and the work of the "Waitangi Tribunal." These responses are used to set the stage for what is seen as an emerging consensus.

Kaupapa Maori

In education, the surfacing of kaupapa Maori schools did not come about as some kind of planned, organized, and conscious attempt to provide an alternative to mainstream education (Smith, 1997), at least not initially. The major incentives were present, such as: (a) a lingering dissatisfaction with a mainstream education system that was never going to seriously take the advice of Maori on what Maori wanted and needed; (b) the resounding success of Kohanga Reo in mobilizing Maori families and communities to learn and use the Maori language; (c) the obvious inability of the system to address the persistent academic underachievement of Maori students; (d) a body of well-educated Maori professionals prepared to test the boundaries of the educational provision of pre-service teachers; and (e) Maori community groups with *whanau* (families) who were prepared to take the courageous step of prioritizing the schooling of their own *tamariki* (children) and *mokopuna* (grandchildren) outside the legal framework of the system.

The years between the emergence of kura kaupapa Maori in 1985 and where the system is now in 2008 has had a marked effect on developments in both Maori and mainstream education. In Maori education it is necessary to distinguish at least three major ideals: an established body of knowledge; what would count as standards of excellence associated with that body of knowledge; and the possibility of constituting those who graduate with this body of knowledge as those who embody those ideals as part of education's life-long task. The idea of being a Maori "subject," in the words of Lear (2006, p. 42), "is more demanding than contemporary ideas of cultural identity or identification." The post-modernist philosopher Appiah (2006, p. xviii) suggests that "loyalties and local allegiances determine more than what we want; they determine who we are." Within mainstream education these major ideals have always been present if not always obvious. Overcoming the gap in learning between Maori and Pakeha, where it is seen as significant, means spelling out the same three ideals as above but within Maori terms of reference.

Te kohanga reo (TKR), as seen through Maori eyes, has always been about using the Maori language and culture within the *whanau* (family) context. From the perspective of the mainstream system, TKR is an early childhood education initiative. Kura kaupapa Maori (KKM) schooling has always been about incorporating a totally Maori educational philosophy based on theories of Maori knowledge, learning and teaching, and so forth. All this is evident in the KKM philosophy, named Te Aho Matua. From the perspective of the mainstream system, KKM is an alternative form of primary schooling based on Maori language immersion. Through a Maori lens, TKR focuses on language, family, and community. KKM (primary school level), Wharekura (secondary school level), and Wananga (tertiary level) are all extensions of TKR. Each institution is charged with the responsibility of negotiating and inculcating the three major ideals listed above to constitute what has been referred to earlier as the "culturally enriched ego-ideal." This is what drives the kaupapa Maori movement.

Waitangi Tribunal

According to the historian Belich (1996, p. 196), the influx of settlers into Aotearoa New Zealand in the 19th century was predicated upon Maori consent, a consent premised on general agreement to the Treaty and on welcoming agents of the state, as well as on the selling of land. It came unstuck mainly because the incursion of settlers after 1840 was far in excess of what Maori leadership could manage. That, along with unscrupulous land dealings from both Maori and Pakeha, led to inevitable conflict. The Waitangi Tribunal, established in 1975 with a major amendment made in 1985, has been mandated to investigate breaches of the principles of the Treaty of Waitangi involving actions of the Crown and to recommend to parliament a course of action to redress those breaches. Redress of past injustices can be seen to have at least two major consequences: first, the return of or compensation for something wrongfully taken; and, second, to facilitate processes to help in the healing of those earlier breaches. The treaty claims process addresses the first of these political jurisdictional aspects, while the machinations of the education system play an important role in addressing the second.

The first published report of the Waitangi Tribunal was in 1978. Up to now there are in excess of 90 reports, with an almost equal number of unpublished interim reports, such as *Crown Policy Affecting Maori Knowledge Systems and Cultural Practices* (Williams, 2001). Every report is a potential source of educational knowledge about the people of a particular place and their historical relationship with that place, the changing ecological landscape, and the existing biodiversity that have influenced it over time, as well as the multitude of recorded narratives that specifically and emotionally attach to those places. The education system has yet to explore the possibilities inherent in making use of tribunal reports for the knowledge and pedagogy within them. There is a great wisdom to be tapped when these stories are revealed. The Waitangi Tribunal process has been instrumental in harnessing the methodologies of "storytelling" with "critical science," but now it is time for educationists to follow suit.

The work of the Waitangi Tribunal is complementary to the developments occurring in kaupapa Maori. They both set out to establish a more just society. They both originate out of the notion of a sense of grievance, loss, or separation, and they each focus on one part of the whole while trying to keep connected to the whole. Kaupapa Maori focuses on Maori language revitalization without allowing language to become "detached from the context of social relations" thus losing "its connection to the struggle as a whole" (Harvey, 1996, p. 86). The Waitangi Tribunal focuses on the redress of past injustices on the part of the Crown against tribes, mainly but not exclusively in relation to the transfer of ownership of lands. The process of engagement has had marked effects within tribal communities in terms of being able to restore balance between, for example, losses and gains. Healing is required in order to produce a sense of hope among the people for a future goodness that transcends the current ability to understand the historical legacy. Waitangi Tribunal processes, especially those that occur in the public domain of the *marae* (a Maori traditional forum), are critical spaces for what the Canadian researcher Kirmayer refers to as "the middle-ground between constructivism and realist approaches to meaning" (1993, p. 161). If Maori were not sure about their capacity to know themselves outside Pakeha-centric ways of knowing, the *marae* forum during Waitangi Tribunal hearings extinguished those doubts forever. Storytelling is a healing process. The capacity to adapt and to be positive – at least about the present – is a clear demonstration of Maori and tribal resilience despite the adversities of daily life.

Education: An emerging new consensus

The concluding section to this chapter suggests a way ahead in developing a truly complex education system for Aotearoa New Zealand. Such a system will be based on equality as both a "legal" and an "ethical" activity. It is a system premised on the acceptance of the need for all New Zealand citizens to be able to walk confidently and knowingly in the two cultures that are the founding cultures of the nation. The recent public debacle over claims of "Maori/Tuhoe terrorism" makes the idea of an emerging consensus a deeply flawed argument, nothing more than wishful thinking. However, the fact is that this accusation of terrorism is little more than the most up-to-date episode of Pakeha fear of Maori organizing to assert their self-determination and *mana*. There is a history of such events. Each one has been well documented in New Zealand modern history. They have been variously defined as acts of defiance, as in Hone Heke cutting down the flag-pole, as rebellion among the Hauhau during the period of the Land Wars, as sedition against Rua Kenana at Maungapohatu, and as disobedience from Te Whiti and Tohu Kakahi at Parihaka in standing up against illegal land acquisitions, while in the central North Island *rangatira* (tribal leaders) moved to establish the Kiingitanga in order to halt the loss of land to settlers and, as a consequence, the loss of their own *mana* (power, authority). Through the 20th century and into the 21st there has been a continuous parade of similar events, and without fail they capture the imaginations of a threatened and fearful section of New Zealand society. There are far too many to list, but a few of the more scrutinized are those such as the one led by Eva Rickard at the Raglan golf course over the local council's refusal to return Maori land taken during the Second World War to establish an aerodrome to train pilots. Pakaitore at Whanganui was another site of struggle, led by Tariana Turia, Ken Mair, and others, who squatted on tribal land "illegally" acquired by the Crown. Takaparawha in Auckland city represented generations of Ngati Whatua prime real estate slowly but surely being eroded away from its legitimate guardians until Joe Hawke and his tribal relations said "Enough!" In the mid-1970s Whina Cooper led a land march from the far north to the capital in Wellington to proclaim "not one more acre of land" (to be alienated). The most recent "skirmish" prior to the "Tuhoe terrorism" claims was the foreshore and seabed march on parliament that culminated in the Waitangi Tribunal report (2004).

Whether such episodes as these are labeled forms of resistance or rebellions or whether they are seen as oppositional or confrontational is not really the point. They originate from Maori sources acting out of frustration or a deep sense of injustice against the machinations of Pakeha domination. Both parties have gone to war against each other once (in the 1860s), and since then they have fought as comrades in several wars in a variety of places around the world. There is a sense in which Maori insubordination will always be present so long as Pakeha society remains aloof from Maori aspirations, so long as institutionalized forms of racism continue to be reproduced, and so long as the acceptance of cultural difference is seen as diminishing the social fabric of New Zealand society. Paradoxically it is this insubordination and these acts of resistance to domination that make possible the creation of a new consensus. What is the Pakeha contribution that could be said to have led to a new consensus in relations between Maori and Pakeha? There isn't much, although it could be argued, as they do in France, that "We are in charge. The prevailing consensus is defined by us. If you want to settle in this land, fine, now get on with it – assimilate."

A number of high-profile activities over the last 20 or so years are indicative of Pakeha people's changing mood in accepting elements of Maori culture as part of the indigenous understanding of what it means to belong. Initially, each of these interventions has been treated with caution and sometimes even with resentment but over time has gradually been incorporated as part of Aotearoa New Zealand culture. Separately, these episodes can be accepted as relatively trivial events. Nevertheless, the public furor following each has been considered by Maori to be little more than "Pakeha sounding off again on another guilt trip." These activities are having an effect on relations between Maori and all other New Zealanders in a manner that could not have been anticipated.

The exhibition of Maori artifacts known as "Te Maori," presented in major galleries throughout the United States of America in the early 1980s, was such an extraordinary success that the New Zealand public had to show a renewed interest in its indigenous sense of belonging by supporting the exhibition in a national show of solidarity. Those who can remember the Maori woman telephonist (Naida Pou) greeting someone with the welcome "Kia ora" might also recall the media response that followed that exclamation. The problem wasn't that it was a greeting but that it was a Maori greeting. Today, "Kia ora" is one of the most common expressions heard throughout this country and wherever New Zealanders are in the world. The original name for New Zealand, Aotearoa is now finding favor in the public domain. Even the New Zealand national anthem, "God of Nations," was recently performed publicly and internationally for the first time in the Maori language, again by a Maori woman (Hinewehi Mohi), before a rugby test match at Twickenham, London. Today, there is no quarrel, at least publicly, about the national anthem being performed bilingually at virtually all official events. The *haka* (posture dance) "Kamate! Kamate!" has always been featured with the national rugby team, but now it is performed by almost all national teams, while at the Olympic Games in Greece the *haka* was used as motivation to stir national pride on occasions of special merit. Maori radio operates throughout the country, and no community, remote or inner city, seems exempt from this service. The "News in Maori" has been a less than 15 minute wonder on national television for a number of years, but now there is a specific Maori Television channel where the "Maori News" plays a prominent role.

Two further events are also worthy of mention in this context. The creation of a Maori Party operating successfully in parliament is an enormous achievement. Despite the usual cynicisms that Maori can't make decisions without checking with the *iwi* (tribe), the Maori Party does not operate as a sinecure, and its presence in the debating chamber as well as around the constituencies is adding a new dimension to the political and cultural consciousness of the "ordinary person in the street." One final event for this concluding section will suffice: those who were in New Zealand at the time of the death of the Maori queen, Te Atairangikaahu, will not forget the extraordinary outpouring of grief, respect, and love mixed with liberal doses of curiosity, wonder, and admiration for this remarkable leader and the traditional farewell bestowed on her by her people. The coverage on national television alone, over several days, marked this occasion as a watershed moment for race relations in the country.

The emerging consensus is nothing but a glimmer at this stage, but in the prophetic words of a traditional *matakite* (Maori seer) is the saying "Kei tua te awe mapara, he tangata ke. Mana e noho te ao nei – he ma." The Maori politician and scholar Sir Peter Buck interpreted the prophecy in line with the changing times as "Behind the tattooed face, a different man appears. He will continue to inhabit this land – he is untattooed" (1949/1977, p. 537).

An emerging new consensus does not mean that colonialism or the historical effects of colonialism have ended. It doesn't mean that dominant frameworks for defining agendas or for shaping Maori preferences will cease. Racism does not go away until those who commit these injustices confront them as wrong, unlawful, and unjust and do something to get rid of them. The manufacture of agreements will continue because that is the way things have happened in the past. That is the challenge to mainstream New Zealand. I have argued that there is a sense of some radical hopefulness in the air. "Hope wrestles with despair," according to the American philosopher Cornell West, "but it doesn't generate optimism. It just generates this energy to be courageous, to bear witness, to see what the end is going to be" (cited in Boynton, 2007, p. 116).

For Maori, the emerging consensus is as much about the healing of past and present injustices as it is about forging paths for a new and better future. The Waitangi Tribunal has a role to play in that regard, but as a mechanism for settling grievances it is vulnerable to the whim and fancy of politicians. What might be described as a "radical hope" (Lear, 2006, book title) has developed among Maori. It is a hope that springs from a combination of rational agreements based on the Western mind and what the sociologist Collins (1992, p. vi) refers to as "the deeper emotional processes that produce social bonds of trust," namely, the domain of ritual interactions that play such an important role in Maori culture.

Interventions in education have already been discussed, but perhaps a reminder is appropriate that a total system of institutions, including early childhood (Te Kohanga Reo), primary (kura kaupapa Maori), secondary (Wharekura), and tertiary (Wananga) institutions, has been established where kaupapa Maori (Maori philosophy) is institutionalized. The story behind these developments deserves to be treated independently (see Smith, 1997) but needs to be included in this discussion. Although education through schooling has made a major contribution to the notion of a radical hope, I believe that the much broader approach, witnessed in a Maori revitalization movement and its focus on the rescue mission of the Maori language, opened the possibility of transforming all the major institutions of dominant mainstream New Zealand society. The imminent demise of *te reo* Maori (the Maori language) provided the traditional culturally enriched ego-ideal that forced Maori to "face up to reality." After almost 200 years of colonialism, Maori had learned the ways of the Pakeha, as well as the important lesson of not idealizing them. At last, the traditional visionaries within Maori society lived again through the hope they gave and for the inspiration they provided.

In making a case, the trivial has been confused with the profound, but that should not be a problem; indeed, that seems to be the way of the world. The important point to make about all of these occasions, incidents, or simply moments is that all of them originated from Maori taking direct action, a radical act of resistance. But then all of these "radical actions" have been accepted, adopted, promoted, advanced, encouraged, and in some cases elevated, by Pakeha. This is at least guarded and even tentative evidence of the new and emerging consensus. It simply makes good sense to work together no matter how long it takes. Kia ora – Be of good health.

Note

1 The Treaty of Waitangi was signed by representatives of the British Crown and Maori chiefs from the North Island of New Zealand on February 6, 1840. The treaty recognized Maori land ownership of their lands and extended to the Maori certain rights.

References

Appiah, K. A. (2006). *Cosmopolitanism: Ethics in a world of strangers*. New York & London: W. W. Norton & Company.

Archer, M. S. (1984). *Social origins of educational systems*. London: Sage.

Barrington, J. M., & Beaglehole, T. H. (1974). *Maori schools in a changing society: An historical review*. Wellington: New Zealand Council for Educational Research.

Belich, J. (1996). *Making peoples: A history of New Zealanders from Polynesian settlement to the end of the nineteenth century*. Auckland, New Zealand: Allen Lane, Penguin Press.

Benton, R. A. (1979a). *The Maori language in the nineteen seventies.* Wellington: New Zealand Council for Educational Research, Maori Unit.

Benton, R. A. (1979b). *Who speaks Maori in New Zealand?* Wellington: New Zealand Council for Educational Research.

Bishop, R., & Berryman, M. (2006). *Culture speaks: Cultural relationship and classroom learning.* Wellington, New Zealand: Huia Publishers.

Boynton, R. S. (2007, November 15). Cornell West – professor of religion. *Rolling Stone* (40th anniversary), p. 116.

Buck, P. (1977). *The coming of the Maori – Te Rangi Hiroa.* Wellington, New Zealand: Maori Purposes Board, Whitcoulls. (Original work published 1949)

Chapple, S., Jefferies, R., & Walker, R. J. (1997). *Maori participation and performance in education: A literature review and research programme* (Report for the Ministry of Education). Wellington: New Zealand Institute of Economic Research.

Collins, R. (1992). *Sociological insights: An introduction to non-obvious sociology.* New York: Oxford University Press.

Currie, G. (1962). *Report on the Commission of Education in New Zealand.* Wellington, New Zealand: Government Printer.

Department of Education. (1970). *Report of the National Advisory Committee on Māori Education.* Wellington, New Zealand: Author.

Department of Education. (1980). *He huarahi (A pathway): Report of the National Advisory Committee on Māori Education.* Wellington, New Zealand: Author.

Harker, R. K. (1971). Maori education and research. *The Australian and New Zealand Journal of Sociology, 7*(1), 46–57.

Harker, R. K. (1978). Achievement and ethnicity: Environmental deprivation or cultural difference. *New Zealand Journal of Educational Studies, 13*(2), 107–124.

Harvey, D. (1996). *Justice, nature and the geography of difference.* Cambridge, MA: Blackwell.

Harvey, D. (2000). *Spaces of hope.* Los Angeles: University of California Press.

Hunn, J. K. (1960). *Report on Department of Maori Affairs: With statistical supplement.* Wellington, New Zealand: Government Printer.

Kirmayer, L. J. (1993). Healing and the invention of metaphor: The effectiveness of symbols revisited. *Culture, Medicine and Psychiatry, 17,* 161–195.

Kuhn, T. (1962). *The structure of scientific revolutions.* Chicago & London: University of Chicago Press.

Lear, J. (2006). *Radical hope: Ethics in the face of cultural devastation.* Cambridge, MA: Harvard University Press.

Ministry of Education. (2005). *Nga haeata matauranga* [Rays of light in education]: *Annual report on Maori education 2003/2004 and direction for 2005.* Wellington, New Zealand: Author.

Nash, R. (2001). Models of Māori educational attainment: Beyond the "class" and "ethnicity" debate. *Waikato Journal of Education, 7,* 23–36.

Popper, K. R. (1994). *The myth of the framework: In defence of science and rationality* (M. A. Notturno, Ed.). London & New York: Routledge.

Sharp, A. (2004). The trajectory of the Waitangi Tribunal. In J. Hayward & N. R. Wheen (Eds.), *The Waitangi Tribunal: Te roopu whakamana i te Tiriti o Waitangi* [Empowering the Treaty of Waitangi] (pp. 195–206). Wellington, New Zealand: Bridget Williams Books.

Shields, R. (1999). *Lefebvre, love and struggle: Spatial dialectics.* London & New York: Routledge.

Simon, J. A. (1998). *Nga kura Maori (The Maori schools): The native schools system 1867–1969.* Auckland, New Zealand: Auckland University Press.

Simon, J. A., & Smith, L. T. (Eds.). (2001). *A civilising mission? Perceptions and representations of the New Zealand native schools system.* Auckland, New Zealand: Auckland University Press.

Slack, J. D., & Wise, J. M. (2005). *Culture and technology: A primer.* New York: Peter Lang.

Smith, G. H. (1997). *The development of kaupapa Maori: Theory and praxis.* Unpublished doctoral dissertation, University of Auckland, Auckland, New Zealand.

Waitangi Tribunal. (2004). *Report on the Crown's Foreshore and Seabed Policy* (WAI 1071). Wellington, New Zealand: Legislation Direct.

Walker, R. J. (1985). Cultural domination of Taha Maori: The potential for radical transformation. In J. Codd, R. Harker, & R. Nash (Eds.), *Political issues in New Zealand education* (pp. 73–82). Palmerston North, New Zealand: Dunmore Press.

Walker, R. J. (1987). *Nga tau tohetohe: Years of anger.* Auckland, New Zealand: Penguin Books.

Williams, D. (2001). *Crown policy affecting Maori knowledge systems and cultural practices.* Wellington, New Zealand: Waitangi Tribunal Publications.

Part 6

Citizenship, immigration, and education

22

Diversity, group identity, and citizenship education in a global age

James A. Banks

University of Washington, Seattle, USA

Conceptions of citizenship and citizenship education around the world face challenges from a number of historical, political, social, and cultural developments. Worldwide immigration, globalization, and the tenacity of nationalism have stimulated controversy and new thinking about citizenship and citizenship education (Gutmann, 2004; Koopmans, Statham, Giugni, & Passy, 2005; Torres, 1998).

In this chapter, I describe *assimilationist, liberal*, and *universal* conceptions of citizenship education;[1] state why these concepts should be interrogated; and argue that citizenship and citizenship education should be expanded to include cultural rights for citizens from diverse racial, cultural, ethnic, and language groups. I also state why citizenship education should incorporate recognition of group-differentiated rights (Fraser, 2000; Young, 1989).

Liberal assimilationist notions of citizenship assume that individuals from different groups have to give up their home and community cultures and languages to attain inclusion and to participate effectively in the national civic culture (Greenbaum, 1974; Wong Fillmore, 2005). According to these conceptions of citizenship, the rights of groups are detrimental to the rights of the individual. In contrast, using the Civil Rights Movement of the 1960s and 1970s as an example, I argue that groups can help individuals to actualize their rights and opportunities.

I contend that an effective and transformative citizenship education helps students to acquire the knowledge, skills, and values needed to function effectively within their cultural community, nation-state, and region and in the global community. Such an education also helps students to acquire the cosmopolitan perspectives and values needed to work for equality and social justice around the world (Appiah, 2006; Nussbaum, 2002). In the final part of this chapter, I argue that schools should implement a transformative and critical conception of citizenship education that will increase educational equality for all students. A transformative citizenship education also helps students to interact and deliberate with their peers from diverse racial and ethnic groups. I describe research that illuminates ways in which just, deliberative, and democratic classrooms and schools can be created.

Conceptions of citizenship and citizenship education

A citizen is an individual who lives in a nation-state and has certain rights and privileges, as well as duties to the state, such as allegiance to the government (Lagassé, 2000). Citizenship is "the position or status of being a citizen" (Simpson & Weiner, 1989, p. 250). Koopmans et al. (2005) define citizenship as "the set of rights, duties, and identities linking citizens to the nation-state" (p. 7). These basic definitions are accurate but do not reveal the complexity of citizenship as the concept has developed in modernized nation-states.

Marshall's (1964) explication of three elements of citizenship – civil, political, and social – has been influential and widely cited in the field of citizenship studies (Bulmer & Rees, 1996). Marshall conceptualizes citizenship as developmental and describes how the civil, political, and social elements emerged in subsequent centuries.

The civil aspects of citizenship, which emerged in England in the 18th century, provide citizens with individual rights, such as freedom of speech, the right to own property, and equality before the law. The political aspect of citizenship developed in the 19th century. It gives citizens the franchise and the opportunity to exercise political power by participating in the political process. The social aspect arose in the 20th century. It provides citizens with the health, education, and welfare needed to participate fully in their cultural communities and in the national civic culture. Marshall viewed the three elements of citizenship as interrelated and overlapping and citizenship as an ideal toward which nation-states strive but which they never completely attain.

Cultural rights and multicultural citizenship

Assimilationist, liberal, and universal conceptions of citizenship require citizens to give up their first languages and cultures to become full participants in the civic community of the nation-state (M. M. Gordon, 1964; Young, 1989, 2000). Most cultural, social, and educational policies in nation-states throughout the world, including the United States (Graham, 2005), were guided by an assimilationist policy prior to the ethnic revitalization movements of the 1960s and 1970s. Beginning in the 1600s, missionaries in the United States established boarding schools to assimilate and Christianize Indian youth (chap. 19, this volume). During the 1940s and 1950s, Mexican Americans were punished in school for speaking Spanish (Crawford, 1999). The histories and cultures of groups such as African Americans, Mexican Americans, and American Indians were rarely discussed in textbooks. When they appeared in textbooks, they were most frequently stereotyped (Banks, 1969). Policy and practice in schools, as in other institutions, were guided by Anglo-conformity (M. M. Gordon, 1964).

Since the ethnic revitalization movements of the 1960s and 1970s, marginalized racial, ethnic, and language groups have argued that they should have the right to maintain important aspects of their cultures and languages while participating fully in the national civic culture and community (Carmichael & Hamilton, 1967; B. M. Gordon, 2001; Sizemore, 1973). These groups have demanded that institutions such as schools, colleges, and universities respond to the groups' cultural identities and experiences by reforming curricula to reflect their struggles, hopes, dreams, and possibilities (B. M. Gordon, 2001; Nieto, 1999). They have also demanded that schools modify teaching strategies to make them more culturally responsive to students from different racial, ethnic, cultural, and language groups (Au, 2006; Gay, 2000; González, Moll, & Amanti, 2005).

During the 1960s and 1970s, leaders and scholars in ethnic minority communities in the

United States borrowed some of the concepts and language that had been used by advocates and scholars of White ethnic communities during the first decades of the 1900s, when large numbers of immigrants entered the United States from Southern, Central, and Eastern Europe. Drachsler (1920) and Kallen (1924) – who were advocates for the cultural freedoms and rights of these immigrant groups and who were immigrants themselves – argued that cultural democracy is an important characteristic of a democratic society. Drachsler and Kallen maintained that cultural democracy should coexist with political and economic democracy and that citizens in a democratic society should participate freely in the civic life of the nation-state and experience economic equality. According to Drachsler and Kallen, citizens should also have the right to maintain important aspects of their community cultures and languages, as long as these do not conflict with the shared democratic ideals of the nation-state. Cultural democracy, argued Drachsler, is an essential component of a political democracy.

In the early decades of the 20th century, Woodson (1933/1977) made a case for cultural democracy when he argued that a curriculum for African American students should reflect their history and culture. Woodson harshly criticized the absence of Black history in the curriculum and argued that Black students were being "mis-educated" because they were learning only about European, not African, cultures and civilizations. In the 1970s, Ramírez and Castañeda (1974) maintained that cultural democracy requires teaching methods that reflect the learning characteristics of Mexican American students as well as help them become bicognitive in their learning styles and characteristics.

Kymlicka (1995), the Canadian political theorist, and Rosaldo (1997), the U.S. anthropologist, make arguments today that are similar in many ways to those made by Drachsler and Kallen in the early 1900s and in later decades by Woodson and by Ramírez and Castañeda. Both Kymlicka and Rosaldo maintain that immigrant and ethnic groups should be able to participate fully in the national civic culture while retaining elements of their own cultures. The dominant culture of the nation-state should incorporate aspects of their experiences, cultures, and languages, which will enrich the mainstream culture as well as help marginalized groups to experience civic equality and recognition (Gutmann, 2004).

Expanding Marshall's citizenship typology

The paper in which Marshall (1964) presented his citizenship typology was presented as the Alfred Marshall Lectures at the University of Cambridge in February 1949. The significant post–World War II migrations to the United Kingdom from its former colonies such as Jamaica, India, and Pakistan were just beginning. Marshall was consequently unable to foresee these migrations and their consequences – such as the racialization that occurred in response or the immigrants' quests for equality and inclusion (Solomos, 2008) – and did not incorporate them into his citizenship typology.

Marshall (1964) conceptualizes citizenship as an evolutionary concept that increases equality when it expands. Lipset (1964) states that the "assumption of equality" is perhaps the most important aspect of Marshall's idea of citizenship (p. ix). Marshall viewed citizenship and class as opposing principles and stated that citizenship and the capitalist class system were at war during the 20th century because citizenship and equality expanded simultaneously.

Expanding Marshall's conception of citizenship to include cultural democracy and cultural citizenship is consistent with his view that citizenship evolves to reflect the historical development of the times and expands to increase equality and social justice. Ethnic and language minority groups in societies throughout the world are denied full citizenship rights because of their languages and cultural characteristics, because they regard maintaining attachments to their cultural communities as important to their identities, and because of historic group discrimination and exclusion (Castles & Davidson, 2000; Koopmans et al., 2005; Kymlicka, 1995; Young, 1989). Consequently, the conception of citizenship in a modern democratic nation-state should be expanded to include cultural rights and group rights within a democratic framework.

Multicultural citizenship

Global immigration and the increasing diversity in nation-states throughout the world challenge liberal assimilationist conceptions of citizenship. They raise complex and divisive questions about how nation-states can deal effectively with the problem of constructing civic communities that reflect and incorporate the diversity of citizens and yet have an overarching set of shared values, ideals, and goals to which all of the citizens of a nation-state are committed (Banks, 2007). In the past, the liberal assimilationist ideology guided policy related to immigrants and diversity in most nation-states.

In the liberal assimilationist view, the rights of the individual are paramount, and group identities and rights are inconsistent with and inimical to the rights of the individual (Patterson, 1977). This conception maintains that identity groups promote group rights over the rights of the individual and that the individual must be freed of primordial and ethnic attachments to have free choice and options in a modernized democratic society (Patterson, 1977; Schlesinger, 1991). Strong attachments to ethnic, racial, religious, and other identity groups lead to conflicts and harmful divisions within society. Liberal scholars such as Patterson and Schlesinger also assume that group attachments will die of their own weight within a modernized, pluralistic democratic society if marginalized and excluded groups are given the opportunity to attain structural inclusion into the mainstream society. In this view, the survival of primordial attachments in a modernized democratic society reflects a "pathological condition" in which marginalized groups have not been provided with opportunities that would enable them to experience cultural assimilation and structural inclusion (Apter, 1977). If Mexican Americans are structurally integrated into mainstream U.S. society – argues the liberal assimilationist – they will have neither the desire nor the need to speak Spanish.

A number of factors have caused social scientists and political philosophers to raise serious questions about the liberal analysis and expectations for identity groups in modernized democratic nation-states. These factors include: the rise of the ethnic revitalization movements since the 1960s and 1970s, which demand recognition of group rights as well as individual rights by the nation-state and by institutions such as schools, colleges, and universities (Banks, 2006); the structural exclusion of many racial, ethnic, and language groups in the United States and other Western nations (Benhabib, 2004; Castles & Davidson, 2000; M. M. Gordon, 1964); and increasing immigration throughout the world that has made most nation-states multinational and polyethnic (Kymlicka, 1995). Recent estimates indicate that "the world's 184 independent states contain over 600 living language groups and 5,000 ethnic groups. In very few countries can the citizens be said to share the same language, or belong to the same ethnonational group" (Kymlicka, 1995, p. 1).

Identity groups in a multicultural democratic society

Identity groups can both obstruct the realization of democratic values and facilitate their realization (Gutmann, 2003). Nonmainstream groups, such as Canadian Sikhs and Mexican Americans, and mainstream groups, such as Anglo Canadians and the Boy Scouts of America, are all identity groups. Democracies should treat individuals as civil equals and give them equal freedoms (Gutmann, 2003). Identity groups may try to impose their values on individuals. However, they may also enhance individual freedom by helping individuals to attain goals that are consistent with democratic values and that can be achieved only through group action.

Identity groups provide opportunities for their members to freely associate and express themselves culturally and politically (Gutmann, 2003). Individuals more successfully attain goals through the political system when working in groups than when working alone. Important examples are the political, cultural, and educational gains that African Americans won through their participation in the Civil Rights Movement during the 1960s and 1970s, as well as the momentous changes that the movement initiated in U.S. society as a whole, with significant benefits for other racial, ethnic, and language groups, women, and people with disabilities.

The Immigration Reform Act of 1965 (which became effective in 1968) was a consequence of the Civil Rights Movement. The act abolished the quota system based on immigrants' national origins and liberalized American immigration policy (Bennett, 1988). Immigration to the United States from Asian and Latin American nations increased substantially as a result. Primarily because of the Immigration Reform Act, the racial and ethnic texture in the US has changed significantly. Before 1968, most immigrants to the United States came from Europe. Today, most come from Asia and Latin America. A significant number also come from the West Indies and Africa. The United States is now experiencing its largest influx of immigrants since the late 19th and early 20th centuries. The U.S. Census Bureau (2000) projects that ethnic groups of color – or ethnic minorities – will increase from 28% of the nation's population in 2008 to 50% in 2042.

Marginalized groups have organized and worked for their group rights throughout U.S. history, bringing greater equality and social justice for all Americans. This was the case with the movements for civil rights, women's rights, and language rights (the last promoting the right of all citizens to speak and learn their own languages in the public schools). Groups in the margins of U.S. society have been the conscience of America and the main sites for struggles to close the gap between American democratic ideals and institutionalized racism and discrimination (Okihiro, 1994). Through their movements to advance justice and equality in America, marginalized groups have helped the nation come closer to actualizing the democratic ideals stated in its founding documents – the Declaration of Independence, the U.S. Constitution, and the Bill of Rights (Okihiro, 1994).

Universal and differentiated citizenship

Group differences are not included in a universal conception of citizenship. Consequently, the differences of groups that have experienced structural exclusion and discrimination – such as women and people of color – are suppressed. A *differentiated* conception of citizenship, rather than a universal one, is needed to help marginalized groups attain civic equality and recognition in multicultural democratic nations (Young, 1989). Many problems result from a universal notion of citizenship according to which "citizenship status transcends particularity and difference" and "laws and rules . . . are blind to individual and group differences" (Young, 1989,

p. 250). A universal conception of citizenship within a stratified society results in the treatment of some groups as second-class citizens because group rights are not recognized and the principle of equal treatment is strictly applied.

When universal citizenship is determined, defined, and implemented by groups with power and when the interests of marginalized groups are not expressed or incorporated into civic discussions, the interests of groups with power and influence will determine the definitions of universal citizenship and the public interest. Groups with power and influence often equate their own interests with the public interest. This phenomenon occurs in the debate over multicultural education in the nation's schools, colleges, and universities. Critics of multicultural education such as D'Souza (1991) and Schlesinger (1991) define the interests of dominant groups as the "public" interest and those of people of color such as African Americans and Latinos as "special" interests that endanger the polity.

The challenges of global citizenship

Cultural and group identities are important in multicultural democratic societies. However, they are not sufficient for citizenship participation because of worldwide migration and the effects of globalization on local, regional, and national communities (Banks, 2004a). Students need to develop the knowledge, attitudes, and skills that will enable them to function in a global society. Globalization affects every aspect of communities, including beliefs, norms, values, and behaviors, as well as business and trade. Worldwide migration has increased diversity in most nation-states and is forcing nations to rethink citizenship and citizenship education.

National boundaries are eroding because millions of people live in several nations and have multiple citizenships (Castles & Davidson, 2000). Millions have citizenship in one nation and live in another. Others are stateless, including millions of refugees around the world. The number of individuals living outside their original homelands increased from approximately 33 million in 1910 to 175 million in 2000 (Benhabib, 2004).

National boundaries are also becoming more porous because of international human rights that are codified in the Universal Declaration of Human Rights (1948) and by the European Union. These rights are specified for individuals regardless of the nation-state in which they live and whether they are citizens of a nation or not. Explicated in the declaration are the rights to freedom of expression and religious belief, the right to privacy, and the right for an individual charged with a crime to be presumed innocent until proven guilty (Banks et al., 2005; Osler & Starkey, 2005). Serious tensions exist between the conceptions of international human rights and national sovereignty. Despite the codification of international rights by bodies such as the United Nations, nationalism is as strong as ever (Benhabib, 2004).

Global migration: A challenge to nations and schools

Migration within and across nation-states is a worldwide phenomenon. The movement of peoples across boundaries is as old as the nation-state itself (Luchtenberg, 2004b). However, never before in history has the movement of diverse racial, cultural, ethnic, religious, and linguistic groups within and across nation-states been so extensive, so rapid, or raised such complex and difficult questions about citizenship, human rights, democracy, and education. Many worldwide developments challenge the notion of educating students to function in one nation-state. These developments include the ways that people move back and forth across national borders and the rights of movement permitted by bodies external to nation-states such as the United Nations and the European Union.

Before the ethnic revitalization movements of the 1960s and 1970s, the aim of schools in most nation-states was to develop citizens who internalized their national values, venerated their national heroes, and accepted glorified versions of their national histories. These goals of citizenship education are inconsistent with the citizen's role in a global world today because many people have multiple national commitments and live in multiple nation-states. However, the development of citizens with global and cosmopolitan identities and commitments is contested in nation-states throughout the world because nationalism remains strong. Nationalism and globalization coexist in tension worldwide (Benhabib, 2004; Castles & Davidson, 2000).

When responding to the problems wrought by international migration, schools in multicultural nation-states must deal with complex educational issues in ways consistent with their democratic ideologies and declarations. There is a wide gap between the democratic ideals in Western nations and the daily experiences of students in schools (Banks, 2004a). Ethnic minority students in the United States, Canada, the United Kingdom, Germany, and France – as in other nations throughout the world – often experience discrimination because of their cultural, linguistic, religious, and value differences. Often, both students and teachers perceive these students as the "Other." When ethnic minority students – such as Turkish students in Germany and Muslim students in the United Kingdom – are marginalized in school and treated as the "Other," they tend to emphasize their ethnic identities and to develop weak attachments to the nation-state.

Multicultural democratic nation-states must grapple with a number of salient issues, paradigms, and ideologies as their school populations become more culturally, racially, ethnically, and linguistically diverse. The extent to which nation-states make multicultural citizenship possible, the achievement gap between minority and majority groups, and the language rights of immigrant and minority groups are among the unresolved and contentious issues with which these nations must grapple.

Nation-states throughout the world are trying to determine whether they will perceive themselves as multicultural and allow immigrants to experience multicultural citizenship or continue to embrace an assimilationist liberal ideology (Kymlicka, 1995). In nation-states that embrace multicultural citizenship, immigrant and minority groups can retain important aspects of their languages and cultures while exercising full citizenship rights. Nation-states in various parts of the world have responded to the citizenship and cultural rights of immigrant and minority groups in significantly different ways. Since the ethnic revitalization movements of the 1960s and 1970s, many national leaders and citizens in the United States, Canada, and Australia have viewed these nations as multicultural democracies (Banks, 1986). An ideal exists in these nations that minority groups can maintain important elements of their community cultures and become full citizens of the nation-state. However, there is a wide gap between the ideals of these nations and the experiences of ethnic minority groups. Most ethnic minority groups in nations that view themselves as multicultural – such as the United States, Canada, and Australia – experience discrimination in both the schools and the wider society.

Other nations, such as Japan (Murphy-Shigematsu, 2004) and Germany (Luchtenberg, 2004a, 2004b; Mannitz, 2004), have been reluctant to view themselves as multicultural societies. Citizenship has been closely linked to biological heritage and characteristics in these nations. Although the biological conception of citizenship in both Japan and Germany has eroded within the past decade, it has left a tenacious legacy in both countries. Castles (2004) refers to Germany's response to immigrants as "differential exclusion," which is "partial and temporary integration of immigrant workers into society – that is, they are included in those subsystems of society necessary for their economic role: the labor market, basic accommodation, work-related health care, and welfare" (p. 32).

Since the 1960s and 1970s, the French have dealt with immigrant groups in ways distinct from those of the immigrant nations of the United States, Canada, and Australia. In France the explicit goal is assimilation – called *integration* – and inclusion (Bowen, 2004, 2008; Castles, 2004; Hargreaves, 1995; Scott, 2007). Immigrants can become full citizens in France but are required to surrender their languages and cultures. Integration assumes that cultural and ethnic differences should and will disappear (Hargreaves, 1995; Scott, 2007).

Education for national and global citizenship

Multicultural societies are faced with the problem of constructing nation-states that reflect and incorporate the diversity of their citizens and yet have an overarching set of shared values, ideals, and goals to which all of their citizens are committed. In a democratic society, civic equality and recognition are important values (Gutmann, 2004). These values give ethnic and immigrant groups the right to maintain important elements of their ethnic cultures and languages as well as to participate in the national civic culture.

Nationalists and assimilationists around the world worry that if citizens are allowed to retain identifications with their cultural communities they will not acquire sufficiently strong attachments to their nation-states. Such concerns reflect a "zero-sum conception of identity" (Kymlicka, 2004, p. xiv). The theoretical and empirical work of multicultural scholars indicates that *identity is multiple, changing, overlapping, and contextual, rather than fixed and static* – and that thoughtful and clarified cultural identifications will enable people to be better citizens of the nation-state. Writes Ladson-Billings (2004):

> The dynamic of the modern (or postmodern) nation-state makes identities as either an individual or a member of a group untenable. Rather than seeing the choice as either/or, the citizen of the nation-state operates in the realism of both/and. She is both an individual who is entitled to citizen rights that permit one to legally challenge infringement of those rights [and one who is] acting as a member of a group.... People move back and forth across many identities, and the way society responds to these identities either binds people to or alienates them from the civic culture. (p. 112)

The challenge of unity and diversity

Balancing unity and diversity is a continuing challenge for multicultural nation-states. Unity without diversity results in hegemony and oppression; diversity without unity leads to Balkanization and the fracturing of the nation-state (Banks, 2004b). A major problem facing nation-states throughout the world is how to recognize and legitimize difference and yet construct an overarching national identity that incorporates the voices, experiences, and hopes of the diverse groups that compose it. Many ethnic, language, and religious groups have weak identifications with their nation-states because of their marginalized status and because they do not see their hopes, dreams, visions, and possibilities reflected in the nation-state or in the schools, colleges, and universities (Ladson-Billings, 2004; Osler & Vincent, 2002).

The diversity brought to European nations such as the United Kingdom, the Netherlands, and France by immigrants from their former colonies has increased racial, ethnic, and religious tension and conflict (Koopmans et al., 2005). A bitter controversy arose in France regarding the wearing of the hijab (veil) by Muslim girls in state-supported schools. In March 2004 the French parliament passed a law that prohibits the wearing of any ostensible religious symbol in state schools. Although this law prohibits the wearing of the Jewish yarmulke as well as large Christian crosses, its target was the hijab. The French policy is a contentious and divisive attempt by a nation with a strong assimilationist ideology to deal with religious expression in the public sphere in a way that is consistent with its ideals of equality, liberty, and republicanism (Bowen, 2008). Bowen (2004) describes incisively the different meanings of the headscarf controversy to the mainstream French and to French Muslims:

> For many non-Muslim French, [the headscarves] represent multiple dangers to the Republic; the oppression of women, urban violence, international terrorism, and the general refusal of Muslim immigrants to integrate into the broader society. For many of the five million or so Muslims living in France, the scarves represent the freedom of religious expression guaranteed by French law, the toleration of cultural pluralism, the value of modesty, and the general importance of developing ways to be both good Muslims and good citizens. (p. 31)

As worldwide immigration increases diversity on every continent and as global terrorism intensifies negative attitudes toward Muslims, schools in nation-states around the world are finding it difficult to implement policies and practices that respond to the diversity of students and also foster national cohesion (Banks et al., 2005). The four young Muslim men who are suspected of being responsible for the bombings of the London Underground on July 7, 2005, had immigrant parents but were British citizens who grew up in Leeds. They apparently were not structurally integrated into British mainstream society and had weak identifications with the nation-state and with other British citizens. The immigrant background of most of the suspects and perpetrators of worldwide violence (Suárez-Orozco, 2006) has contributed to the rise of Islamophobia and racial tensions in Europe.

The complicated characteristics of student identifications

Historically, schools in Western democratic nations, such as the United States, Canada, and Australia, have focused on helping students to develop commitments and allegiance to the nation-state and have given little attention to their need to maintain commitments to their local communities and cultures or to their original homelands. Schools assumed that assimilation into the mainstream culture was required for citizenship and national belonging and that students could and should surrender commitments to other communities, cultures, and nations. Greenbaum (1974) states that U.S. schools taught immigrant students *hope* and *shame*. These students were made to feel ashamed of their home and community cultures but were given hope that once they culturally assimilated they could join the U.S. mainstream culture. Cultural assimilation worked well for most White ethnic groups (Alba & Nee, 2003) but not for groups of color, which continue to experience structural exclusion after they become culturally assimilated.

Recent ethnographic research indicates that the narrow conception of citizenship education that has been embraced historically by schools is not consistent with the racial, ethnic, and cultural realities of U.S. society because of the complicated, contextual, and overlapping identities of immigrant students. Research by scholars studying immigrant high school students indicates that these students have complex and contradictory *transnational* identifications. This finding is consistent across studies of Palestinian American youth by El-Haj (2007), of Vietnamese American high school youth by Nguyen (2008), and of working-class Indian American, Pakistani American, and Bangladeshi American youth by Maira (2004). These researchers describe the nuanced and intricate identifications that immigrant youth have with the United States, their countries of origin, and their local communities. This research also indicates that the cultural and national identities of immigrant youth are contextual, evolving, and continually reconstructed.

El-Haj (2007), Nguyen (2008), and Maira (2004) found that the immigrant youths in their studies did not define their national identities in terms of their places of residence but felt that they belonged to national communities that transcended the boundaries of the United States. They defined their national identities as Palestinian, Vietnamese, Indian, Pakistani, and Bangladeshi. They believed that an individual can be Palestinian or Vietnamese and live in many different nation-states. The youth in these studies distinguished between *national identity* and *citizenship*. They viewed themselves as Palestinian, Vietnamese, or Pakistani but also recognized and acknowledged their U.S. citizenship, which they valued for the privileged legal status and other opportunities it gave them. Some of the Vietnamese youth in Nguyen's study said, "I am Vietnamese *and* a citizen of the United States."

Although the immigrant youth in Nguyen's (2008) study viewed themselves as citizens of the United States, they did not view themselves as Americans. They felt that they were not Americans because to be American required an individual to be White and mainstream. Their construction of the criterion for becoming American was a consequence of the racism, discrimination, and exclusion that they experienced in their schools and communities. Both El-Haj (2007) and Nguyen describe how the marginalization that immigrant students experience in schools and in the larger U.S. society reinforces their national identification with distant nations, in which they imagine that they would experience equality and structural inclusion.

Maira (2004) used cultural citizenship to describe the transnational aspects of the citizenship identity held by the South Asian students in her study. These youths maintained contacts and connections with their homeland cultures through popular culture venues, such as websites, films, music, TV serials, cable TV, and DVDs made in their homelands.

Schools and citizenship education in multicultural nations

The nuanced, complex, and evolving identities of the youth described in the studies by El-Haj (2007), Nguyen (2008), and Maira (2004) indicate that the liberal assimilationist notions of citizenship are ineffective today because of the deepening diversity throughout the world and the quests by marginalized immigrant, ethnic, and racial groups for cultural recognition and rights. Schools need to work to implement multicultural citizenship (Kymlicka, 1995), which recognizes the right of and need for students to maintain commitments to their cultural communities, to a transnational community, and to the nation-state in which they are legal citizens.

Citizenship education should also help students to develop an identity and attachment to the global community and a human connection to people around the world. Global identities, attachments, and commitments constitute *cosmopolitanism* (Nussbaum, 2002). Cosmopolitans view themselves as citizens of the world who will make decisions and take actions in the global interests that will benefit humankind. Nussbaum states that their "allegiance is to the worldwide community of human beings" (p. 4).

Cosmopolitans identify with peoples from diverse cultures throughout the world. Nussbaum contrasts cosmopolitan universalism and internationalism with parochial ethnocentrism and inward-looking patriotism. Cosmopolitans "are ready to broaden the definition of public, extend their loyalty beyond ethnic and national boundaries, and engage with difference far and near" (W. C. Parker, personal communication, July 18, 2005). Cosmopolitans view social justice and equality globally and are concerned with threats to the world community such as global warming, the HIV/AIDS epidemic, and war. Students can become cosmopolitan citizens while maintaining attachments and roots to their family and community cultures. Both Nussbaum (2002) and Appiah (2006) view local identities as important for cosmopolitans.

Schools should help students to understand how cultural, national, regional, and global identifications are interrelated, complex, and evolving (Banks, 2004b). These identifications are interactive in a dynamic way. Each should be recognized, valued, publicly affirmed, and thoughtfully examined in schools. Students should be encouraged to critically examine their identifications and commitments and to understand the complex ways in which they are interrelated and constructed.

Citizenship education should help students to realize that "no local loyalty can ever justify forgetting that each human being has responsibilities to every other" (Appiah, 2006, p. xvi). As citizens of the global community, students also must develop a deep understanding of the need to take action and make decisions to help solve the world's difficult problems. They need to participate in ways that will enhance democracy and promote equality and social justice in their cultural communities, nations, and regions, and in the world.

Increasing diversity throughout the world today and increasing recognition of diversity – as well as the intractable problems that the world faces – require a reexamination of the ends and means of citizenship education if it is to promote inclusion, civic equality, and recognition (Gutmann, 2004). Liberal assimilationist conceptions of citizenship education that eradicate the cultures and languages of diverse groups will be ineffective in a transformed "flat" world of the 21st century (Friedman, 2005). Citizenship education in the United States – as well as in other Western nations – should be reinvented so that it will enable students to see their fates as intimately tied to those of people throughout the world. Citizenship education should help students to understand why "a threat to justice anywhere is a threat to justice everywhere" (King, 1963/1994, pp. 2–3).

Mainstream and transformative citizenship education

Citizenship education must be reimagined and transformed to effectively educate students to function in the 21st century. For reform to succeed, the knowledge that underlies its construction must shift from mainstream academic knowledge to transformative academic knowledge. Mainstream knowledge reinforces traditional and established knowledge in the social and behavioral sciences as well as the knowledge that is institutionalized in the popular culture and in the nation's schools, colleges, and universities (Banks, 1993). Transformative academic knowledge consists of paradigms and explanations that challenge some of the key epistemological assumptions of mainstream knowledge (Collins, 2000; Harding, 1991; Homans, 1967). An important purpose of transformative knowledge is to improve the human condition. Feminist scholars and scholars of color have been among the leading constructors of transformative academic knowledge (Collins, 2000; Harding, 1991; Takaki, 1993, 1998).

Mainstream citizenship education is grounded in mainstream knowledge and assumptions and reinforces the status quo and the dominant power relationships in society. It is practiced in most social studies classrooms in the United States (Parker, 2002) and does not challenge or disrupt the class, racial, or gender discrimination in the schools and society. Mainstream citizenship education either does not include each of the four elements of citizenship identified in the first part of this chapter – *civil, political, social,* and *cultural* – or includes them at superficial and limited levels. It does not help students to understand their multiple and complex identities, the ways their lives are influenced by globalization, or what their roles should be in a global world. Instead, the emphasis is on memorizing facts about constitutions and other legal documents, learning about various branches of government, and developing patriotism to the nation-state (Westheimer, 2007). Critical thinking skills, decision making, and action are not important components of mainstream citizenship education.

Transformative citizenship education needs to be implemented in schools if students are to attain clarified and reflective cultural, national, regional, and global identifications and understand how these identities are interrelated and constructed. Transformative citizenship education also recognizes and validates the cultural identities of students. It is rooted in transformative academic knowledge and enables students to acquire the information, skills, and values needed to challenge inequality within their communities, their nations, and the world; to develop cosmopolitan values and perspectives; and to take actions to create just and democratic multicultural communities and societies. Transformative citizenship education helps students to develop the decision-making and social action skills that are needed to identify problems in society, acquire knowledge related to their homes and community cultures and languages, identify and clarify their values, and take thoughtful individual or collective civic action (Banks & Banks, 1999). It also fosters critical thinking skills and is inclusive of what DeJaeghere (2007) calls *critical citizenship education.*

Intergroup relations research and transformative citizenship education

In democratic and transformative classrooms and schools, students from diverse groups interact and deliberate in equal-status situations. They also develop positive racial and ethnic attitudes as well as the knowledge, skills, and perspectives to deliberate with students from diverse groups. Deliberation among citizens from diverse groups is essential for a democratic society (Gutmann, 1987; Parker, 2002). Research indicates that equal status among diverse groups in contact situations is an essential condition for effective intergroup interactions and deliberations. Cohen and Roper (1972) found that White middle-class students dominated classroom interactions with African American students unless interventions increased the status of African Americans. Transformative classrooms create conditions in which students from different groups can interact in ways that enable them to view events from diverse perspectives and to deliberate in equal-status situations.

Allport (1954/1979) theorized that contact between groups will improve intergroup relations if the contact has the following characteristics: (a) The individuals experience equal status; (b) they share common goals; (c) intergroup cooperation exists; and (d) the contact is sanctioned by authorities, such as teachers and administrators, or by law or custom (Pettigrew, 2004). Multicultural textbooks and other materials (Banks, 2007; Takaki, 1993) help to create equal status in classrooms by giving voice to the histories and experiences of all students in the class and by enabling all to experience equality and recognition (Cohen, 1994; Gutmann, 2004).

Students have positive attitudes toward different racial and ethnic groups in transformative classrooms and have equal status in classroom discussions and deliberations. Teachers in transformative classrooms use strategies and materials that help students to acquire democratic racial attitudes and behaviors. Since the 1940s, a number of curriculum intervention studies have been conducted to determine the effects of teaching units and lessons, multicultural textbooks and materials, role-playing, and other kinds of simulated experiences related to the racial attitudes and perceptions of students. These studies indicate that the use of multicultural textbooks, other related teaching materials, and cooperative teaching strategies can enable students from different racial and ethnic groups to develop democratic racial attitudes and to interact in equal-status situations. Such materials and teaching strategies can also result in students choosing more friends from outside their own racial, ethnic, and cultural groups (Slavin, 2001).

These studies provide guidelines that can help teachers to improve intergroup relations, interactions, and deliberations in transformative classrooms and schools. One of the earliest curriculum studies was conducted by Trager and Yarrow (1952), who examined the effects of a democratic multicultural curriculum on the racial attitudes of children in the first and second grades. The curriculum had a positive effect on the attitudes of both students and teachers. The authors gave their study the title *They Learn What They Live* to highlight its major finding: If students experience democracy they will internalize it.

Research indicates that curriculum interventions such as multiethnic readers (Litcher & Johnson, 1969); multicultural television programs (Bogatz & Ball, 1971); simulations (Weiner & Wright, 1973); multicultural social studies materials (Yawkey & Blackwell, 1974); folk dances, music, crafts, and role-playing (Ijaz & Ijaz, 1981); plays (Gimmestad & DeChiara, 1982); discussions about race (Aboud & Doyle, 1996); and discussions combined with antiracist teaching (McGregor, 1993) can have positive effects on the racial attitudes and interactions of students.

Research on cooperative learning and interracial contact

Transformative and democratic classrooms foster cooperation rather than competition among students from diverse racial, ethnic, and cultural groups. Cooperation promotes positive interracial interactions and deliberations. Since 1970, a group of investigators, guided by Allport's (1954/1979) theory, have produced a rich body of cumulative research on the effects of cooperative learning groups and activities on students' racial attitudes, friendship choices, and achievement. Much of this research has been conducted as well as reviewed by investigators such as Aronson and his colleagues (Aronson, 2002; Aronson & Bridgeman, 1979; Aronson & Gonzalez, 1988), Cohen and her colleagues (Cohen, 1972, 1984; Cohen & Lotan, 1995), Johnson and Johnson (1981, 1991), Slavin (1979, 1983, 1985), and Slavin and Madden (1979). Schofield (2004) has written an informative review of this research. Most of it has been conducted using elementary and high school students (Slavin, 1983, 1985).

This research strongly supports the notion that cooperative interracial contact situations in schools – if the conditions described by Allport (1954/1979) are present in the contact situations – have positive effects on both student interracial behavior and student interactions (Aronson & Gonzalez, 1988; Slavin, 1979, 1983). In his review of 19 studies of the effects of cooperative learning methods, Slavin (1985) found that 16 showed positive effects on interracial friendships. In another review, Slavin (2001) also described the positive effects of cooperative groups on racial attitudes and cross-racial friendships. Other investigators have found that cooperative learning activities increased student motivation and self-esteem (Slavin, 1985) and helped students to develop empathy (Aronson, 2002; Aronson & Bridgeman, 1979).

Equal status between groups in interracial situations has to be deliberately structured by teachers or it will not exist (Cohen & Roper, 1972). If students from different racial, ethnic, and linguistic groups are mixed in contact situations without structured interventions that create equal-status conditions, then racial and ethnic conflict and stereotyping are likely to increase. Students from both privileged and marginalized groups are likely to respond in ways that will reinforce the advantage of the higher-status group. In a series of perceptive and carefully designed studies, Cohen and her colleagues consistently found that contact among different groups without deliberate interventions to increase equal-status and positive interactions among them will increase rather than reduce intergroup tensions (Cohen, 1984; Cohen & Lotan, 1995; Cohen & Roper, 1972).

Transformative classrooms and levels of citizenship

Transformative classrooms and schools help students to acquire the knowledge, values, and skills needed to become *deep citizens*. Clarke (1996) states that a deep citizen

> both in the operation of [his or her] own life and in some of its parameters ... [is] conscious of acting in and into a world shared with others ... [and is] conscious that the identity of self and the identity of others is co-related and co-creative, while also opening up the possibility of both engagement in and enchantment with the world. (p. 6)

I have developed a typology designed to help educators conceptualize ways to help students acquire increasingly deeper citizenship that contains four levels (see Figure 22.1). Like the categories in any typology, these levels of citizenship overlap and are interrelated. Nevertheless, differentiating levels of citizenship is useful.

- *Legal citizenship*, the most superficial level of citizenship in the typology, applies to citizens who are legal members of the nation-state and have certain rights and obligations to the state but do not participate in the political system in any meaningful ways.
- *Minimal citizenship* applies to those who are legal citizens and vote in local and national elections for conventional and mainstream candidates and issues.
- *Active citizenship* involves action beyond voting to actualize existing laws and conventions. Active citizens may participate in protest demonstrations or make public speeches regarding conventional issues and reforms. The actions of active citizens are designed to support and maintain – but not to challenge – existing social and political structures.
- *Transformative citizenship* involves civic actions designed to actualize values and moral principles and ideals beyond those of existing laws and conventions.[2] Transformative citizens take action to promote social justice even when their actions violate, challenge, or dismantle existing laws, conventions, or structures.

Rosa Parks refused to give up her seat to a White man on a bus in Montgomery, Alabama, on December 1, 1955. Her action was a pivotal event in the Montgomery bus boycott that ended segregation in transportation in the South and thrust Rev. Martin Luther King Jr. into national leadership. A group of African American college students sat down at a lunch counter reserved for Whites in a Woolworth's store in Greensboro, North Carolina, on February 1, 1960. The students initiated the sit-in movement that ended segregation in lunch counters throughout the South. Both Parks and the students violated existing segregation laws. They were engaging in transformative citizenship because they took action to actualize social justice, even though what they did was illegal and challenged existing laws, customs, and conventions.

The important difference between active and transformative citizens is that the actions taken

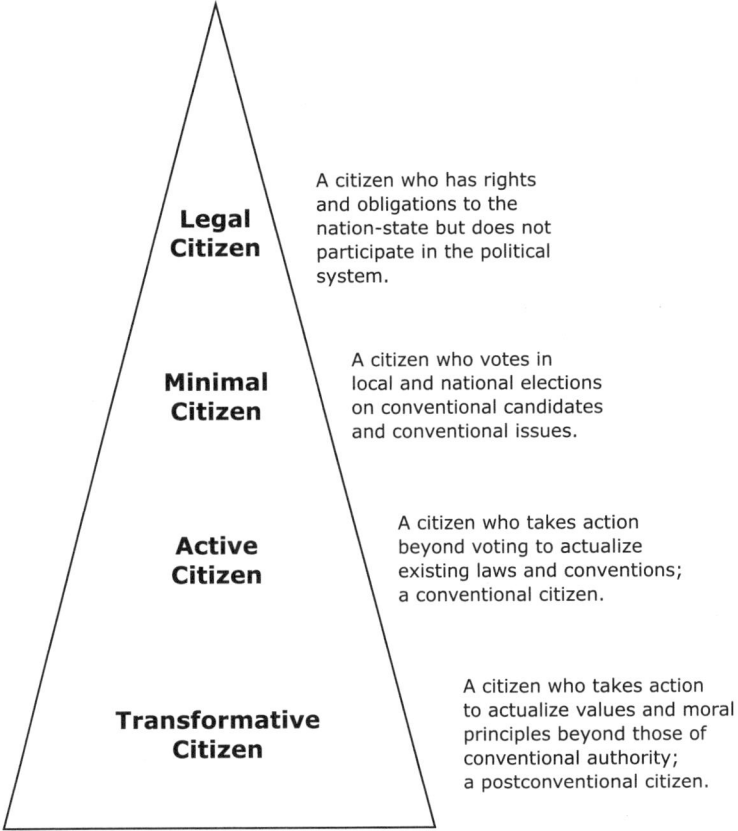

Figure 22.1 Types of Citizens, Defined by Four Levels of Participation. Transformative, or deep, citizenship is exemplified by Rosa Parks and the students who started the sit-in movement in Greensboro, North Carolina, in 1960.

Copyright © 2009 by James A. Banks.

by active citizens fall within existing laws, customs, and conventions, whereas the actions taken by transformative citizens are designed to promote values and moral principles – such as social justice and equality – and may violate existing conventions and laws. Although transformative educators recognize and respect students at all levels of citizenship, their aim is to help students become transformative and deep citizens.

Conclusion

Students experience democracy in classrooms and schools when transformative citizenship education is implemented. Consequently, they are better able to internalize democratic beliefs and values and to acquire thoughtful cultural identifications and commitments. The total school, including the knowledge conveyed in the curriculum, needs to be reformed to implement transformative citizenship education. Inequality and stratification within the larger society are challenged and are not reproduced in transformative and democratic classrooms and schools. Transformative citizenship education helps students to develop reflective cultural, national, regional, and global identifications and to acquire the knowledge and skills needed to promote social justice in communities, nations, and the world.

Reprinted with permission of the American Educational Research Association from *Educational Researcher, 37*(3), pp. 129–139, 2008.

Notes

1 I am using the terms *assimilationist, liberal, liberal assimilationist,* and *universal* as synonyms in describing conceptions of citizenship education.
2 My ideas regarding convention and action beyond conventional levels are adapted from Lawrence Kohlberg's (1971) stages of moral development.

References

Aboud, F. E., & Doyle, A. B. (1996). Does talk foster prejudice or tolerance in children? *Canadian Journal of Behavioural Science, 28*(3), 161–171.

Alba, R., & Nee, V. (2003). *Remaking the American mainstream: Assimilation and contemporary immigration.* Cambridge, MA: Harvard University Press.

Allport, G. W. (1979). *The nature of prejudice* (25th anniversary ed.). Reading, MA: Addison-Wesley. (Original work published 1954)

Appiah, K. A. (2006). *Cosmopolitanism: Ethics in a world of strangers.* New York: Norton.

Apter, D. E. (1977). Political life and cultural pluralism. In M. M. Tumin & W. Plotch (Eds.), *Pluralism in a democratic society* (pp. 58–91). New York: Praeger.

Aronson, E. (2002). Building empathy, compassion, and achievement in the jigsaw classroom. In J. Aronson (Ed.), *Improving academic achievement: Impact of psychological factors on education* (pp. 209–225). San Diego, CA: Academic Press.

Aronson, E., & Bridgeman, D. (1979). Jigsaw groups and the desegregated classroom: In pursuit of common goals. *Personality and Social Psychology Bulletin, 5*(4), 438–446.

Aronson, E., & Gonzalez, A. (1988). Desegregation, jigsaw, and the Mexican-American experience. In P. A. Katz & D. A. Taylor (Eds.), *Eliminating racism: Profiles in controversy* (pp. 301–314). New York: Plenum.

Au, K. (2006). *Multicultural issues and literacy achievement.* Mahwah, NJ: Lawrence Erlbaum.

Banks, J. A. (1969). A content analysis of the Black American in textbooks. *Social Education, 33*(8), 954–957, 963.

Banks, J. A. (1986). Multicultural education: Development, paradigms, and goals. In J. A. Banks & J. Lynch (Eds.), *Multicultural education in Western societies* (pp. 1–29). London: Holt.

Banks, J. A. (1993). The canon debate, knowledge construction, and multicultural education. *Educational Researcher, 22*(5), 4–14.

Banks, J. A. (Ed.). (2004a). *Diversity and citizenship education: Global perspectives.* San Francisco: Jossey-Bass.

Banks, J. A. (2004b). Introduction: Democratic citizenship education in multicultural societies. In J. A. Banks (Ed.), *Diversity and citizenship education: Global perspectives* (pp. 3–15). San Francisco: Jossey-Bass.

Banks, J. A. (2006). *Race, culture, and education: The selected works of James A. Banks.* New York: Routledge.

Banks, J. A. (2007). *Educating citizens in a multicultural society* (2nd ed.). New York: Teachers College Press.

Banks, J. A., & Banks, C. A. M. (with Clegg, A. A., Jr.). (1999). *Teaching strategies for the social studies: Decision-making and citizen action.* New York: Longman.

Banks, J. A., Banks, C. A. M., Cortés, C. E., Hahn, C. L., Merryfield, M. M., Moodley, K. A., et al. (2005).

Democracy and diversity: Principles and concepts for educating citizens in a global age. Seattle: University of Washington, Center for Multicultural Education.

Benhabib, S. (2004). *The rights of others: Aliens, residents, and citizens.* Cambridge, UK: Cambridge University Press.

Bennett, D. H. (1988). *The party of fear: From nativist movements to the New Right in American history.* Chapel Hill: University of North Carolina Press.

Bogatz, G. A., & Ball, S. (1971). *The second year of Sesame Street: A continuing evaluation.* Princeton, NJ: Educational Testing Service.

Bowen, J. R. (2004). Muslims and citizens: France's headscarf controversy. *Boston Review, 29*(1), 31–35.

Bowen, J. R. (2008). Republican ironies: Equality and identities in French schools. In M. Minow, R. A. Shweder, & H. Marcus (Eds.), *Just schools: Pursuing equality in societies of difference* (pp. 204–224). New York: Russell Sage Foundation.

Bulmer, M., & Rees, A. M. (Eds.). (1996). *Citizenship today: The contemporary relevance of T. H. Marshall.* London: UCL Press.

Carmichael, S., & Hamilton, C. (1967). *Black Power: The politics of liberation in America.* New York: Vintage.

Castles, S. (2004). Migration, citizenship, and education. In J. A. Banks (Ed.), *Diversity and citizenship education: Global perspectives* (pp. 17–48). San Francisco: Jossey-Bass.

Castles, S., & Davidson, A. (2000). *Citizenship and migration: Globalization and the politics of belonging.* New York: Routledge.

Clarke, P. B. (1996). *Deep citizenship.* London: Pluto Press.

Cohen, E. G. (1972). Interracial interaction disability. *Human Relations, 25*(1), 9–24.

Cohen, E. G. (1984). Talking and working together: Status, interaction, and learning. In P. Peterson, L. C. Wilkinson, & M. Hallinan (Eds.), *The social context of instruction* (pp. 171–186). New York: Academic Press.

Cohen, E. G. (1994). *Designing groupwork: Strategies for the heterogeneous classroom* (2nd ed.). New York: Teachers College Press.

Cohen, E. G., & Lotan, R. A. (1995). Producing equal-status interaction in the heterogeneous classroom. *American Educational Research Journal, 32*(1), 99–120.

Cohen, E. G., & Roper, S. S. (1972). Modification of interracial interaction disability: An application of status characteristics theory. *American Sociological Review, 37*(6), 643–657.

Collins, P. H. (2000). *Black feminist thought: Knowledge, consciousness, and the politics of empowerment.* New York: Routledge.

Crawford, J. (1999). *Bilingual education: History, politics, theory, and practice* (4th ed.). Los Angeles: Bilingual Education Services.

DeJaeghere, J. G. (2007). Intercultural and global meanings of citizenship education in the Australian secondary curriculum: Between critical contestations and minimal construction. In E. D. Stevick & B. A. Levinson (Eds.), *Reimagining civic education: How diverse societies form democratic citizens* (pp. 293–316). Lanham, MD: Rowman & Littlefield.

Drachsler, J. (1920). *Democracy and assimilation.* New York: Macmillan.

D'Souza, D. (1991). *Illiberal education: The politics of race and sex on campus.* New York: Collier Macmillan.

El-Haj, T. R. A. (2007). "I was born here, but my home, it's not here": Educating for democratic citizenship in an era of transnational migration and global conflict. *Harvard Educational Review, 77*(3), 285–316.

Fraser, N. (2000). Rethinking recognition: Overcoming displacement and reification in cultural politics. *New Left Review, 3*, 107–120.

Friedman, T. L. (2005). *The world is flat: A brief history of the twenty-first century.* New York: Farrar, Straus and Giroux.

Gay, G. (2000). *Culturally responsive teaching: Theory, research, and practice.* New York: Teachers College Press.

Gimmestad, B. J., & DeChiara, E. (1982). Dramatic plays: A vehicle for prejudice reduction in the elementary school. *Journal of Educational Research, 76*(1), 45–49.

González, N., Moll, L. C., & Amanti, C. (2005). *Funds of knowledge: Theorizing practices in households, communities, and classrooms.* Mahwah, NJ: Lawrence Erlbaum.

Gordon, B. M. (2001). Knowledge construction, competing critical theories, and education. In J. A. Banks & C. A. M. Banks (Eds.), *Handbook of research on multicultural education* (pp. 184–199). San Francisco: Jossey-Bass.

Gordon, M. M. (1964). *Assimilation in American life: The roles of race, religion, and national origin.* New York: Oxford University Press.

Graham, P. A. (2005). *Schooling in America: How the public schools meet the nation's changing needs.* New York: Oxford University Press.

Greenbaum, W. (1974). America in search of a new ideal: An essay on the rise of pluralism. *Harvard Educational Review, 44*(3), 411–440.

Gutmann, A. (1987). *Democratic education.* Princeton, NJ: Princeton University Press.

Gutmann, A. (2003). *Identity in democracy.* Princeton, NJ: Princeton University Press.

Gutmann, A. (2004). Unity and diversity in democratic multicultural education: Creative and destructive tensions. In J. A. Banks (Ed.), *Diversity and citizenship education: Global perspectives* (pp. 71–96). San Francisco: Jossey-Bass.

Harding, S. (1991). *Whose science? Whose knowledge? Thinking from women's lives.* Ithaca, NY: Cornell University Press.

Hargreaves, A. G. (1995). *Immigration, "race," and ethnicity in France.* New York: Routledge.

Homans, G. C. (1967). *The nature of social science.* New York: Harcourt.

Ijaz, M. A., & Ijaz, I. H. (1981). A cultural program for changing racial attitudes. *History and Social Science Teacher, 17*(1), 17–20.

Johnson, D. W., & Johnson, R. T. (1981). Effects of cooperative and individualistic learning experiences on interethnic interaction. *Journal of Educational Psychology, 73*(3), 444–449.

Johnson, D. W., & Johnson, R. T. (1991). *Learning together and alone* (3rd ed.). Englewood Cliffs, NJ: Prentice-Hall.

Kallen, H. M. (1924). *Culture and democracy in the United States.* New York: Boni and Liveright.

King, M. L., Jr. (1994). *Letter from the Birmingham Jail.* New York: HarperCollins. (Original work published 1963.)

Kohlberg, L. (1971). *Stages of moral development.* Retrieved February 14, 2008, from http://www.xenodochy.org/ex/lists/moraldev.html

Koopmans, R., Statham, P., Giugni, M., & Passy, F. (2005). *Contested citizenship: Immigration and cultural diversity in Europe.* Minneapolis: University of Minnesota Press.

Kymlicka, W. (1995). *Multicultural citizenship: A liberal theory of minority rights.* New York: Oxford University Press.

Kymlicka, W. (2004). Foreword. In J. A. Banks (Ed.), *Diversity and citizenship education: Global perspectives* (pp. xiii–xviii). San Francisco: Jossey-Bass.

Ladson-Billings, G. (2004). Culture versus citizenship: The challenge of racialized citizenship in the United States. In J. A. Banks (Ed.), *Diversity and citizenship education: Global perspectives* (pp. 99–126). San Francisco: Jossey-Bass.

Lagassé, P. (Ed.). (2000). *The Columbia encyclopedia* (6th ed.). New York: Columbia University Press.

Lipset, S. M. (1964). Introduction. In T. H. Marshall, *Class, citizenship, and social development: Essays of T. H. Marshall* (pp. i–xx). Westport, CT: Greenwood.

Litcher, J. H., & Johnson, D. W. (1969). Changes in attitudes toward Negroes of White elementary school students after use of multiethnic readers. *Journal of Educational Psychology, 60*(2), 148–152.

Luchtenberg, S. (2004a). Ethnic diversity and citizenship education in Germany. In J. A. Banks (Ed.), *Diversity and citizenship education: Global perspectives* (pp. 245–271). San Francisco: Jossey-Bass.

Luchtenberg, S. (Ed.). (2004b). *Migration, education and change.* London: Routledge.

Maira, S. (2004). Imperial feelings: Youth culture, citizenship, and globalization. In M. Suárez-Orozco & D. B. Qin-Hilliard (Eds.), *Globalization, culture, and education in the new millennium* (pp. 203–234). Berkeley: University of California Press.

Mannitz, S. (2004). Collective solidarity and the construction of social identities in school: A case study of immigrant youths in postunification West Berlin. In S. Luchtenberg (Ed.), *Migration, education and change* (pp. 140–166). New York: Routledge.

Marshall, T. H. (1964). *Class, citizenship, and social development: Essays of T. H. Marshall*. Westport, CT: Greenwood.

McGregor, J. (1993). Effectiveness of role playing and antiracist teaching in reducing student prejudice. *Journal of Educational Research, 86*(4), 215–226.

Murphy-Shigematsu, S. (2004). Expanding the borders of the nation: Ethnic diversity and citizenship education in Japan. In J. A. Banks (Ed.), *Diversity and citizenship education: Global perspectives* (pp. 303–332). San Francisco: Jossey-Bass.

Nguyen, D. (2008). *Becoming American: How Vietnamese immigrant youth construct citizenship*. Unpublished doctoral dissertation, University of Washington, Seattle.

Nieto, S. (1999). *The light in their eyes: Creating multicultural learning communities*. New York: Teachers College Press.

Nussbaum, M. (2002). Patriotism and cosmopolitanism. In J. Cohen (Ed.), *For love of country* (pp. 2–17). Boston: Beacon.

Okihiro, G. Y. (1994). *Margins and mainstreams: Asians in American history*. Seattle: University of Washington Press.

Osler, A., & Starkey, H. (2005). *Changing citizenship: Democracy and inclusion in education*. New York: Open University Press.

Osler, A., & Vincent, K. (2002). *Citizenship and the challenge of global education*. Stoke-on-Trent, UK: Trentham Books.

Parker, W. C. (2002). *Teaching democracy: Unity and diversity in public life*. New York: Teachers College Press.

Patterson, O. (1977). *Ethnic chauvinism: The reactionary impulse*. New York: Stein and Day.

Pettigrew, T. F. (2004). Intergroup contact: Theory, research, and new perspectives. In J. A. Banks & C. A. M. Banks (Eds.), *Handbook of research on multicultural education* (2nd ed., pp. 770–781). San Francisco: Jossey-Bass.

Ramírez, M., III, & Castañeda, A. (1974). *Cultural democracy, bicognitive development, and education*. New York: Academic Press.

Rosaldo, R. (1997). Cultural citizenship, inequality, and multiculturalism. In W. V. Flores & R. Benmayor (Eds.), *Latino cultural citizenship: Claiming identity, space, and rights* (pp. 27–28). Boston: Beacon.

Schlesinger, A. M. (1991). *The disuniting of America: Reflections on a multicultural society*. Knoxville, TN: Whittle Direct Books.

Schofield, J. W. (2004). Fostering positive intergroup relations in schools. In J. A. Banks & C. A. M. Banks (Eds.), *Handbook of research on multicultural education* (2nd ed., pp. 799–812). San Francisco: Jossey-Bass.

Scott, J. W. (2007). *The politics of the veil*. Princeton, NJ: Princeton University Press.

Simpson, J. A., & Weiner, E. S. C. (Eds.). (1989). *The Oxford English dictionary* (2nd ed., Vol. 3). New York: Oxford University Press.

Sizemore, B. A. (1973). Shattering the melting pot myth. In J. A. Banks (Ed.), *Teaching ethnic studies: Concepts and strategies* (43rd Yearbook, pp. 72–101). Washington, DC: National Council for the Social Studies.

Slavin, R. E. (1979). Effects of biracial learning teams on cross-racial friendships. *Journal of Educational Psychology, 71*(3), 381–387.

Slavin, R. E. (1983). *Cooperative learning*. New York: Longman.

Slavin, R. E. (1985). Cooperative learning: Applying contact theory in desegregated schools. *Journal of Social Issues, 41*(3), 45–62.

Slavin, R. E. (2001). Cooperative learning and intergroup relations. In J. A. Banks & C. A. M. Banks (Eds.), *Handbook of research on multicultural education* (pp. 628–634). San Francisco: Jossey-Bass.

Slavin, R. E., & Madden, N. A. (1979). School practices that improve race relations. *American Educational Research Journal, 16*(2), 169–180.

Solomos, J. (2008). *Race and racism in Britain* (4th ed.). New York: Palgrave Macmillan.

Suárez-Orozco, M. M. (2006, March 13). Commentary: A question of assimilation. *U.S. News & World Report*, pp. 34, 36.

Takaki, R. (1993). *A different mirror: A history of multicultural America*. Boston: Little, Brown.

Takaki, R. (1998). *Strangers from a different shore: A history of Asian Americans* (Rev. ed.). Boston: Little, Brown.

Torres, C. A. (1998). Democracy, education, and multiculturalism: Dilemmas of citizenship in a global world. *Comparative Education Review, 42*(4), 421–447.

Trager, H. G., & Yarrow, M. R. (1952). *They learn what they live: Prejudice in young children*. New York: Harper & Brothers.

Universal Declaration of Human Rights. (1948). Retrieved December 4, 2007, from http://www.un.org/Overview/rights.html

U.S. Census Bureau. (2000). *Statistical abstract of the United States* (120th ed.). Washington, DC: U.S. Government Printing Office.

Weiner, M. J., & Wright, F. E. (1973). Effects of undergoing arbitrary discrimination upon subsequent attitudes toward a minority group. *Journal of Applied Social Psychology, 3*(1), 94–102.

Westheimer, J. (Ed.). (2007). *Pledging allegiance: The politics of patriotism in America's schools*. New York: Teachers College Press.

Wong Fillmore, L. (2005). When learning a second language means losing the first. In M. M. Suárez-Orozco, C. Suárez-Orozco, & D. Qin (Eds.), *The new immigration: An interdisciplinary reader* (pp. 289–307). New York: Routledge.

Woodson, C. G. (1977). *The mis-education of the Negro*. New York: AMS Press. (Original work published 1933)

Yawkey, T. D., & Blackwell, J. (1974). Attitudes of 4-year-old urban Black children toward themselves and Whites based upon multiethnic social studies materials and experiences. *Journal of Educational Research, 67*(8), 373–377.

Young, I. M. (1989). Polity and group difference: A critique of the ideal of universal citizenship. *Ethics, 99*(2), 250–274.

Young, I. M. (2000). *Inclusion and democracy*. New York: Oxford University Press.

23

Education, integration, and citizenship in France

Eva Lemaire
Université Marc Bloch – Strasbourg II, France

November 2005: pictures of the French suburbs invaded television screens all over the world. For 10 days, the rioters set fire to vehicles and buildings and threw stones at the police. In response, the government declared a state of emergency, an exceptional measure taken by the State in the event of imminent danger to the country. The suburbs of the major French cities, where the immigrant population is concentrated, slipped out of State control. In reaction to this urban violence, extremely rare in France, the French president questioned the failure of the French model of integration:

> The seriousness of this situation testifies to a crisis in direction, in guidelines and in national identity. . . . What is at stake is respect for the law but also the success of our policy of integration. We have to be strict in the application of the rules concerning family regrouping. We have to reinforce the fight against illegal immigration and the trafficking which it engenders.
>
> (Chirac, 2005)

While the president went on to confirm that "children who live in difficult neighborhoods, whatever their origin, are all sons and daughters of the Republic," at the same time he underlined the role immigration played in the risk of disintegration of national identity and its values. In addition, the gravity of the events also gave rise to radical points of view expressing a deep social malaise concerning the immigrant population. The specter of terrorism was not far away from the collective imagination: the Islamists were blamed – albeit wrongly – for the instigation and the spread of such violence. In the same way, some key political figures have suggested that the polygamy practiced by some of the immigrant population is one of the reasons the suburbs flared up in the first place. Such ideas are of course completely far-fetched.

But by burning public buildings like schools, gymnasiums, and libraries, the young rioters seemed rather to be underlining the absence of job opportunities as well as a strong feeling of social exclusion. Is school, as a privileged tool for integration, failing in the mission which is traditionally assigned to it? Since the end of the Napoleonic regime and the emergence of the Third Republic in 1870, school had indeed become the tool par excellence used in the construction of national cohesion. Prior to this date, French society had been divided into different orders, and French territory was made up of different regions on a linguistic and cultural level, the result of conquests, wars, and royal marriages. The role attributed to school, which was made compulsory in 1882, was to impose the exclusive use of the French language as a factor of unification. Refusing to take into account regional languages as well as differences in religion, school as an institution insisted on eliminating all territorial and social differences, in order to create a common identity and to ensure the equality of all citizens. The fundamental basis of this schooling, inherited from the Age of Enlightenment, was also to make it possible for individuals to attain universal knowledge, freed from any of the peer pressure which influential groups could exert on their thinking, and also to further their social advancement.

It is this free, compulsory, and secular school, known as "the school of the Third Republic," which forms the basis of the current French school system. The French republican model of the education system thus rejects any discrimination, each individual having to be treated with the utmost equality. Consequently, cultural differences are not taken into account, in the name of this ideology, and individuals only are recognized in their relation within the school system. Refusing to categorize individuals in a peer group and thus recognize community identities, the French republican model moves away from multiculturalism, a model regarding the irreducibility of each culture as a system of values and beliefs carrying a coherent vision of the world. It invites French citizens to share a common system of values and references and thus to share an identity common to all French citizens. What, however, does being French mean? Here we must examine the concept of national identity and first the concept of identity itself.

If, a few decades ago, a person was born noble, female, or Breton and was expected to remain so, the modern world has largely contributed to making the concept of identity more complex. Nowadays, no one can be categorized in any single peer group, whether it be national, geographical, sociocultural, religious, or even sexual. Identity appears now as a polymorphic and dynamic concept. Collective or individual, identities are no longer permanent, but fluctuate among tensions between continuity and rupture. They are bound to change, through integration, abandonment, and appropriation of patterns based on various subcultures. Each individual does not live within one given culture but within several. The individual incarnates them in a personal, dynamic, and sometimes contradictory way. According to this meaning of identity, "French identity," as a national republican identity, cannot be defined without fixing it in standardized and stereotyped representations. The Ministry of Immigration, Integration, and National Identity, created in 2006 after the crisis which France underwent, seems in any case unable to define what this national identity should be. If the French president recognizes that one cannot envisage French identity without taking into account diversity, his attempts to accurately evoke this "national identity," beyond its effective plurality, amount only to setting out caricatural representations, symbols selected at random as representative. In a speech devoted to culture, Nicolas Sarkozy (2007a) evoked, for example, "The France of the Crusades and the Great Cathedrals, the France of Human Rights and of the Revolution."

Attached to a republican ideal of national unity, the model of French integration must now face up to a pluralism that has become the norm owing to the effects of globalization, European construction, and immigration. "The crisis of the republican model of integration is not a problem which concerns immigrants or those born French as a result of recent immigration," rightly noted Nicolas Sarkozy (2005). "It is a problem which concerns French society as a whole, because it is society as a whole which has trouble finding the meaning of a shared existence and sharing a collective destiny." The model of French integration, where integration means the active and equal involvement of all citizens in society, appears to be in crisis. A taboo has been lifted. School as an institution has been invited "to reinvent itself," a term employed by X. Darcos, minister of education (2007).

The object of this chapter will be thus to question the reorientation of a school system which, in spite of its deep attachment to its founding principles, is trying to adapt itself to the emergence of an increasingly multicultural society.

The teaching of foreign languages and cultures: A notable exception in the school tradition

In the 19th century, school succeeded in homogenizing French society by setting aside regional languages and by imposing French as the common language throughout the whole of France. In the 1970s, France found itself confronted with a new and important challenge: the integration of families joining a husband or a father who had immigrated to France when the mobility of workers was still encouraged to cope with the labor shortage from which the country was suffering. To meet these new demands, a policy relating to the schooling of the children of immigrants was implemented between 1970 and 1984. This differentialist approach constitutes an important exception in the French educational tradition in the way it derogates from the rule of a strictly egalitarian access to education. Specific teaching was offered to these immigrant children from the 1970s: they were able to study their language and culture of origin (*enseignement des langues et cultures d'origine* [ELCO]). This new program aimed first at making it easier for immigrants to return to their native countries. To this effect, along with 10 partner countries from which the immigrants originated, France signed an agreement so that teachers coming from the signatory countries could teach Spanish, Italian, Portuguese, Turkish, Arabic, and Yugoslavian.

This program of teaching, addressed to immigrants, initially replaced for three hours per week the early-learning activities their French classmates, who could not attend the ELCO, attended. The segregation established between French children and immigrant children remains the principal reproach aimed at this teaching: instead of being integrated, the immigrant children were thus segregated. In 2001, Jack Lang, the then minister of education, pleaded in vain for the opening of the ELCO to all pupils without distinction, but the ELCO remained unavailable to children who could not testify that they had a parent or grandparent of foreign origin. The minister not only pointed out the effect of segregation which the ELCO restriction had had on the immigrant children but also wondered about the relevance of continuing to propose this program to second-generation or even third-generation children. In fact most of these pupils, albeit of foreign origin, were nonetheless French. Was it then relevant to continue to distinguish these pupils by offering them these classes, to focus just on these children? In response, some immigrant languages recently became an integral part of the panel of foreign languages on offer for educational training. This measure was taken in response to a preoccupation with diversifying the languages studied at school and corresponded to a recognition of the status of immigrant languages as languages of communication and culture. Nevertheless, this recognition leaves out certain languages. Languages such as Italian, Portuguese, and Arabic actually became more readily available to pupils, but languages like Yugoslavian or Turkish are hardly taught at all. It was especially European and "international" languages which profited from this recognition.

This diversification of the languages offered, to a certain extent, allowed the revalorization of certain immigrant languages but did not put an end to the ELCO, which remained on offer as an extra-curricular activity on a voluntary basis. Nevertheless, the number of pupils in these classes fell significantly for demographic, sociological, and teaching reasons. More and more pupils feel reluctant to be labeled as immigrants, whereas they feel they are fully fledged French citizens. Moreover, certain offshoots contributed to damaging the reputation of the ELCO, courses which sometimes did not correspond to the pupils' way of life or their relationship with France or with their country of origin. The teachers, designated by the governments of the partner countries, were sometimes not very familiar with French language and culture and were unaware of the teaching methods used in France. In spite of the recommendations, emanating in particular from the Council of Europe, to help the missions and the methods of work of the ELCO evolve, intercultural teaching, not always mastered by those teachers, is far from being systematic, and the bilingual-bicultural orientation is not always present.

The French language as a tool for integration

The major element of the educational policy developed with regard to immigrant children remains teaching the language of the host country. Learning French constitutes an absolute priority that justifies the establishment of a differentialist education. From the 1970s onwards, classes specializing in teaching French as a second language have been set up for non-French-speaking children. These classes are called "initiation classes" (*classe d'initiation*) in primary education and "welcoming classes" (*classe d'accueil*) or "adaptation classes" (*classe d'adaptation*) in secondary schools. Teenagers who experience difficulties in reading and writing can be provided with education within classes dedicated to pupils who have not previously had education. If the creation of these measures expresses the desire to take into account the linguistic specificities of immigrant children, it has not been without fierce controversy. How can the integration of these pupils be favorably encouraged while they have been separated, sometimes for several years, from their French classmates who have been following the ordinary school syllabus? In 2002, whereas the number of newcomers increased and the number of specialized classes became insufficient, new, official texts were promulgated which underlined the transitory aspect the schooling of these pupils in specific structures should take. The restriction of the time spent within these particular classes was also justified by pointing out that the teenagers provided with education in these classes were victims, in the long term, of "indirect discrimination." Indeed, they were not an integral part of the ordinary school syllabus, and when they had to leave the specialized classes they were regularly directed towards low-level training or even towards classes dedicated to disabled children.

This evolution of the ELCO corresponded with a change on the political level. From a logic of assimilation, where priority was given, in the 1970s, to an objective of attaining national unity thanks to a common language and culture, emerged a more integrationist model whose aim was above all to allow the involvement of all citizens within French society, whatever their origin. However, if the integration of newcomers into the ordinary curriculum is now facilitated by "bridges" between specific and ordinary classes, there nevertheless remains a problem: that the majority of teachers are not trained for this integration and a lot of them remain reluctant to participate in it.

For adults too, the importance of mastering French for the integration process is clearly stated. Within the framework of the "Welcome and Integration contract" which now links the State and any immigrant admitted legally onto French soil, language training is systematically proposed. After being evaluated, the newcomers are thus directed towards language classes adapted to their level. In a completely new way, with this concept of a contract based on learning French, the dual character of integration is outlined: immigrants are given the responsibility of making the necessary efforts to integrate themselves, but it is also the French State's responsibility to give them the means of reaching that point. However, various associations point to the risk that passing or failing the initial diploma in French language (DILF, new diploma and offshoot of the diploma in French language studies) which concludes this linguistic training could, in the long term, condition the granting of a resident's permit. Language learning, from a tool in favor of integration, would thus become a tool in favor of a policy of immigration control. The law which has just been voted clearly goes in that direction, insofar as it requires future candidates for immigration to learn French before coming to France.

At the moment, the importance for immigrants of being able to speak French is thus strongly reaffirmed. But if learning French constitutes the foundation for integration, the emphasis that it lays on the national language tends to obscure the intrinsic duality of any process of acculturation. Rather than considering the situation of linguistic plurality as a richness making the development of multilingual competence easier for the whole population, whose languages are put into contact, the situation of plurality encounters a strongly monolingual tradition. As in the myth of Babel, languages – at least spoken by immigrants – remain, in the French collective imagination, vectors of separation and discord more than elements to be shared. Since September 2007, foreign languages are certainly taught in primary schools (at elementary level) in order to endow French children with the necessary competence in an increasingly globalized world. But the preliminary disappearance of intercultural education in the academic programs attests to a utilitarian and restrictive vision of multilingual and intercultural competence. In fact, the educational system has deviated from research and practices related to intercultural education, a pedagogy advocated by the Council of Europe and by the European Commission.

Calling into question the intercultural approach

The teaching practices linked to interculturality are likely to vary according to the orientation given to intercultural education. They were introduced into the French educational system in the 1970s to cope with the integration difficulties of immigrant children. The training of teachers in intercultural teaching was consequently developed, in particular by the means of the new Centers for the Formation and Information for the Schooling of Children of Migrants (CEFISEM).

But a discrepancy quickly appeared between research, theory, and classroom practices which makes one wonder whether they really depend on the intercultural approach or not, as these practices contributed to the discrediting of the intercultural approach. Indeed, the experiments, on a professional level, tend to lay more emphasis on the foreign culture of immigrant children than to undertake the real task of accepting diversity. Presumed to be endowed with a different culture, the children are asked to share it with their classmates. Their culture consequently appears most of the time to be folklore in which tradition plays the most important part. A "couscous pedagogy" emerges when the class, invited for example to discover North African culture, shares a traditional meal, possibly accompanied by music and folk dancing. Up to a certain extent, these practices have also contributed to stigmatizing foreign cultures and to establishing them, through their folklore, as distant cultures. This stigmatization proved all the more problematic when the second or third generation of children took part. These pupils and their families saw themselves constantly labeled as different and thereby confronted with their origins. However, intercultural education, as conceptualized by Martine Abdallah-Pretceille (1986) and Louis Porcher (1995) in particular, is not based on the recognition of any differences but rather on the acceptance of diversity. Whereas the paradigm of difference refers to distinct and homogeneous entities which are opposed, the paradigm of diversity refers to heterogeneity as a norm. As Perry Anderson (2005) points out, intercultural education rejects multiculturalism that imperceptibly, ideologically, confines people in a categorization that is above all cultural. Intercultural education thus necessarily supposes a reflection about the very concept of culture, a culture that proves to be multiple and dynamic, and for which there can be no one representation. Consequently, there is no point in learning about "the" Moroccans or "the" Turks. What is at stake is learning to communicate with individuals of whom one of the characteristics is indeed to be Moroccan or Turkish and to learn how to perceive what, to oneself as to others, is relative to cultural, ethnic, social, religious, sexual, or generational aspects. "What is important pedagogically, in intercultural education, is the dynamic dimension, by definition its ever-changing character, the calling in question to which it leads, the questions we are led to ask ourselves," Louis Porcher (1995, p. 60) stresses. After all, is not couscous, together with being a traditional Moroccan meal, also the French people's favorite dish?

Intercultural education thus proves to be an invitation to accept and understand diversity and alterity, and this invitation is relevant only if addressed to all those who live in a situation of plurality. At this time of globalization and European construction, when almost 25% of French people have foreign origins, it is a distorting of intercultural education to reduce this approach to an attempt to valorize immigrant cultures. Not only does it stigmatize the children of immigrants but above all it limits intercultural education to this specific population. In this way, intercultural education was considerably weakened and was consequently removed from official programs by the Ministry of Education in 1984. This indubitably called into question its legitimacy.

Another challenge taken up by a school system deeply attached to the republican ideal was the establishment in French society of the religions which appeared with this immigration. This also brought into question the principle of secularity (*laïcité*). Here again another rift appeared between the partisans of a very strict secularity, in the true French tradition, and a certain number of French intellectuals who defend a more open model of secularity, a model defended by other European countries.

The challenge of the French *laïcité*: Between overture and a retreat behind the values of the republic

La laïcité is one of the founding values of education in France.[1] Indeed the school of Jules Ferry saw the light in a context of separation between church and state. The role of a teacher was then to remove public institutions from the influence of the church. A lot of cinematographic and literary works still feed the collective imagination by opposing the antagonist figures of the teacher and the priest. In a recent speech, President Sarkozy (2007b) contrasted teacher and priest when he declared that, "for the transmission of values and the teaching of the differences between good and evil," the first could never replace the second, "because he will always be lacking the radicality of the sacrifice of his life and the charisma of an engagement carried by hope." This reintroduction of the religious into the field of education by the head of a profoundly secular state provoked a very pointed reaction, in particular within the world of education, part of which felt repudiated in its mission. Indeed, since 1883, it has been up to teachers to instruct and educate children without any form of proselytizing. If it was very quickly made clear that teachers had to free themselves of any trace of religiosity, the form that the *laïcité* had to take within school was nevertheless the object of negotiations. Was it necessary to remove religion from the school syllabus? In fact, the realities referred to by the following expressions – teaching religion, religious teaching, and "teaching religious facts" – are often confused.

In France, teaching religion or religious teaching is propounded in private denominational schools, which is not the case in state schools, by respect for the beliefs of each pupil. It is obvious to French society that religious teaching is part of the private sphere. However, since the Debray report (2002), the question of teaching "religious facts" is now being discussed. This report states that it is necessary to develop a reasoned approach to religion as a fact of civilization. As Daniele Hervieu Leger puts it, worries have indeed appeared about the fact that, "in our countries, the increasing ignorance of religious history takes alarming proportions and creates a vacuum into which all types of esotericisms and integrisms can be poured" (quoted by Delumeau, 2003). The establishment of the Islamic religion, now the second religion in France, is closely linked to the emergence of this new fear, related also to the fear of Islamist terrorism and fundamentalism. What is feared too is the generalization, within French society, of an amalgam of the Islamic religion and its possible offshoots. The aim of teaching religious facts within the educational system is also to reach a better knowledge of religion itself in order to make it easier for all religions to find their place in French society. It aims too at providing all citizens with the intellectual tools that will allow them to practice their religion while respecting the rights and duties of others' religions. In that way, teaching "religious facts" combines with the ideal of *laïcité* insofar as it makes it possible to distinguish between knowledge and belief and contributes to the education of all citizens, whatever their culture or origin.

This "open" framework of *laïcité* converges with the recommendations made by the Council of Europe that secular education should not be conceived without the teaching of religious facts, this training forming an integral part of the intercultural education that all European citizens should receive in this time of pluralism. In French classrooms, however, religious instruction remains largely taboo. The official syllabus does not exclude it. It is found, implicitly or explicitly, in various lessons in primary and secondary education. History, geography, and artistic education in particular seem well suited to the evocation of religion. In practice, however, teachers tend to avoid this theme, for fear of betraying the secular ideal, in a vision of the *laïcité* which conforms to that preached by the black Hussars of the Republic,[2] a secularity which aimed at excluding religion from public education.

The training of primary school teachers prepares them to teach a variety of subjects but not to deal with religion, a subject that is particularly delicate considering the sometimes exacerbated sensibilities of their pupils. There thus remains a gap between the recommendations emanating from the academic world and the European authorities and those at grassroots level who remain strongly attached to the republican ideal of the Third Republic. In addition, the law of 2004, which forbids the wearing of "ostentatious" religious signs, seems to reinforce this inclination. Following the "second Islamic headscarves crisis," when two girls were excluded from school for having refused to remove their headscarves, French legislation called into review a decision by the Council of State (Opinion of the Council no. 346.893), which, in 1989, confronted with the same situation, deemed at the time that the wearing of these religious signs was not "incompatible with the principle of secularity, except if it is an act of pressure, provocation, proselytism or propaganda." Whereas the first opinion resided within the logical acceptance of religious diversity and held its hand out to intercultural education, the return to a stricter notion of *laïcité* went hand in hand with the difficulty the French school system experiences in distancing itself from its founding principles, principles that only rarely refer to heterogeneity and pluralism.

But if, in many instances, intercultural education comes up against some form of opposition, small pockets still remain. It does not always carry this label, but it remains present in both primary and further education, often as concessions made to European authorities.

Pockets of intercultural education

Within the framework of a formal education, the study of diversity, human rights, and citizenship as recommended by the French education system, in accordance with European recommendations, conforms to the principal tendencies of intercultural education: the fight against prejudice and ethnocentrism, an overture towards other cultures and solidarity, and the teaching of democracy and humanistic values.

The study of diversity aims at teaching pupils to be less biased and to open their minds to universal individuality. The objective is to teach them to go beyond the logic according to which each and every one of them belongs to an identifiable cultural group. In other words, the goal is to make pupils aware of the fact that, by identifying or "labeling" people, one generally attributes a ready-made identity.

Educating about human rights makes it possible to teach not only a humanistic content but also the values about which you cannot compromise, whatever your culture. What is at stake within this educational field is that all citizens should learn what ethics are, in opposition to morals, which can vary according to cultural variations. Paul Ricoeur (1990) distinguishes between universal and interrogative ethics and morals which refer to individualities, dictates, and norms. The question of cultural diversity cannot be reduced to the simple management of conflicts and group relationships without the strong assertion of an ethical basis on which to base one's reflexive position. Finally, the educating of future citizens which combines education and human rights is defined by the Council of Europe as "a set of practices and activities designed to help young people and adults to play an active part in democratic life and exercise their rights and responsibilities in society" (Council of Europe, n.d.). A European training program, entitled "Learning and Living: Democracy for All" (covering the period 2006–2009), was implemented for teachers in the European Union. This training program encourages all European citizens to develop a political and civic culture accompanied by critical reflection, values, and attitudes such as solidarity, respect, and the ability to listen to others. Making pupils aware and involving them on various levels (school, local, national, or international) are encouraged at school so that a desire will emerge to take an active part in society as well as a capacity regarding social inclusion.

As a member state of the European Union, France has introduced this measure. But the various forms of teaching are all practiced in primary and secondary education via "educational activities projects" (*projet d'action éducative* [PAE]) and "local education contracts" (*contrat éducatif local* [CEL]). Putting an end to their traditional isolation, state schools, thanks to the CELs, can now engage in and finance projects with an educational vocation by involving partners concerned with the education of children and young people (parents, associations, elected members, regional communities, ministries, etc.). As for the PAE, financed at the European level, they are set up by volunteer educational teams in primary and secondary schools with the aim of giving the necessary tools to children so that they can become complete citizens, able to reflect as citizens of the world. Via an interdisciplinary approach, based for instance on history, geography, civic education, science, and languages, pupils are led to elaborate and carry out projects dealing with "international citizenship" (e.g. joint economies and development of Third World aid). Finally, mobility grants within the European community aim first at developing multilingualism and, at the same time, work towards intercultural openings (for example, the Comenius program for primary and secondary schools or the Erasmus program for higher education).

As for teachers, their awareness about intercultural education stems primarily from training programs about plurilingualism. Insofar as it is now recognized that a purely linguistic ability is not sufficient for communication, the training schemes offered to future teachers now include intercultural skills. However, few hours are allocated, in the initial training of teachers, to questions relating to the integration of children from immigrant backgrounds, for it remains difficult, in France, to stigmatize such children, because theoretically all pupils have to be treated in the same way. Courses devoted, for instance, to the "management of heterogeneity" have been set up so that trainee teachers can reflect upon this important matter within their vocational training. With regard to ongoing training, the same taboo is observed, whereas more and more teachers are confronted by the integration in their classes of immigrant children. For instance, the Centers for the Formation and Information for the Schooling of Children of Migrants (CEFISEM), set up in 1975, became the Academic Centers for the Schooling of Newcomers and Travelers' children (CASNAV) in 2002. The term *migrants* has disappeared. The expression *newcomers*, more neutral on the sociocultural level, makes it possible to name those people who were usually called *immigrants* or *children from immigrant backgrounds*. *Populations with special characteristics* or *populations with specific needs* refer to non-French-speaking newcomers as well as to travelers' children, who are generally native French speakers. These euphemisms do certainly express the intention to avoid stigmatization, but they also express how sensitive a matter this is. The caution with which these people are referred to, in politically correct terms, could eventually mask these realities by refusing to name them. The real difficulty France is facing lies between the will to take account of and recognize diversity and the will not to differentiate, in the name of the strict equality of all citizens.

Equal opportunity: The guiding principle

Following the crisis in the suburbs, in 2005, institutional initiatives were taken in the name of the equal opportunities the State intends to grant all its citizens, regardless of their characteristics. These initiatives were taken when the failure of the model of French integration was admitted for the first time. The very idea of integration was re-endorsed. Whereas in the past it was almost exclusively used when referring to foreigners, immigrants, and second- or even third-generation children of immigrants, the term *integration* is now used when referring to all those people who, although they belong to the same civic community, are ostracized because of their physical appearance or their social and/or cultural origins: women, disabled people, gay people, and so on. A Ministry of Employment, Social Cohesion and Housing, a post of minister delegated to the promotion of equal opportunities, and a High Authority to Combat Discrimination and Favor Equality (HALDE in French) have been created.

However, in an even more paradoxical and ambiguous way, opposed to this egalitarian ideal there is an increasingly marked differentiation between people "having the right" to be integrated and for whom the government confirms it will do its best to integrate and people "having no right" to be integrated: illegal immigrants. According to Brice Hortefeux (2007), the minister for integration and national identity, "the policy of integration applies to the 5 million legal immigrants who are present in France," which excludes 200,000 to 400,000 illegal immigrants.

One marginal but nevertheless representative case illustrates France's ambivalent attitude with regard to its policy of integration: the case of how individual under-age immigrants are dealt with. As they are alone on French soil, without the presence of a responsible adult, these young immigrants are protected by national and international law. Isolated and thus considered "in danger," they are in theory protected by the State until their 18th birthday, the date of their majority. From this date on, the protection these children benefited from becomes null and void. From that moment, these young immigrants generally have to prove that they are well integrated if they want to stay in France on a legal basis. To do so, they have to testify that they speak French, that they are part of the working population, or that they still attend school or are in vocational training. However, in several places, these young people have to cope with the red tape set up by the French administration, which refuses, for example, to deliver work permits to them on the pretext that they did not enter France legally. In addition, a 10-month waiting period is generally observed before these youths can enter school, because of the lack of adapted classes. To a certain extent, the State also requires that these youngsters integrate themselves but does not give them any real means to do so (Lemaire, 2006). This case clearly illustrates the ambiguity of France's attitude, which, on the one hand, intends to solve its problems of integration in favor of a plural and united society, but which, on the other hand, fears and rejects a part of its immigrant population who, if they are indeed illegal, are still part and parcel of the face of French society.

In conclusion, we must thus underline the ambivalence of France towards its policy of integration and the consequences of such an ambivalence on intercultural education. In October 2007, after 20 years of preparation, the National Museum of the History of Immigration opened. This unique venue was supposed to be the first step towards the recognition of the role of colonization and immigration within the construction of a plural French society. But what stands out above all else in regard to this new museum was the total absence of an official inauguration by the president or the minister of immigration. Such an absence cannot but express a certain malaise concerning the question of integration. As far as education is concerned, divided between the founding ideology of the Third Republic and the recommendations thrust upon it, in particular by the European authorities and by the academic world, France tries, sometimes by tacit, sometimes by contradictory, and finally by quite limited ways, to find a place for the cultural diversity so characteristic of French society and also to integrate the idea of an identity and of a citizenship which should not be reduced to a mythical national identity, in which "identity" and "identical" have been confused for so long.

Notes

1 From this point, *laïcité* will be used rather than "secularity," a term that cannot express the notion in its French specificity.
2 The nickname given to teachers at the beginning of the Third Republic.

References

Abdallah-Pretceille, M. (1986). *Vers une pédagogie interculturelle* [Toward an intercultural pedagogy] (3rd ed.). Paris: Anthropos.

Anderson, P. (2005). Le multiculturalisme [Multiculturalism]. In A. Supiot [Ed.], *Tisser le lien social* [Forging social links] (pp. 105–116). Paris: Maison des sciences de l'homme.

Chirac, J. (2005, November). *Declaration from the president to French citizens*. Speech presented at Palais de l'Elysée, Paris.

Council of Europe. (n.d.). Retrieved March 1, 2008, from http://www.coe.int/t/dg4/education/edc/Default_en.asp

Darcos, X. (2007, December). *Programme d'action et de travail pour le deuxième trimestre de l'année scolaire 2007–2008* [Program of action and work for winter term]. Speech presented at Ministère de l'Education Nationale, Paris.

Debray, R. (2002). *L'enseignement du fait religieux dans l'école laïque* [Teaching religious fact in the secular school]. Paris: Odile Jacob.

Delumeau, J. (2003). *L'enseignement du fait religieux, Actes du séminaire des 5, 6 et 7 novembre 2002* [Teaching religious fact, Acts of Seminar of November 5, 6, and 7, 2002]. Paris: Direction générale de l'enseignement scolaire.

Hortefeux, B. (2007, December). *Speech of Brice Hortefeux during the "Assises nationales sur l'intégration* [National Conference on Integration]*."* Speech presented at Ministère de la Santé, de la Jeunesse et des Sports [Ministry of Health, Youth, and Sport], Paris.

Lemaire, E. (2006). L'intégration des mineurs étrangers isolés: l'école, un passeport pour l'intégration socioprofessionnelle? [The integration of unaccompanied immigrant children: school as a passport to socio-professional integration?]. *Ville-Ecole-Intégration Diversité, L'école et l'emploi, 146,* 97–102.

Porcher, L. (1995). *Le français langue étrangère* [French as a foreign language]. Paris: CNDP-Hachette éducation.

Ricoeur, P. (1990). *Soi-même comme un autre* [Oneself as another]. Paris: Seuil.

Sarkozy, N. (2005, June). *Une immigration choisie, une intégration réussie* [Selected immigration, successful integration]. Speech presented at Assemblée nationale, Paris.

Sarkozy, N. (2007a, March). *Besançon speech*. Speech presented at Parc des Expositions de Besançon, Franche-Comté.

Sarkozy, N. (2007b, December). *Lateran speech*. Speech presented at the Lateran Palace, Rome.

24

Citizenship education in France and England

Contrasting approaches to national identity and diversity

Audrey Osler
University of Leeds, UK

Hugh Starkey
Institute of Education, University of London, UK

There is often a perceived tension within education programs between promoting national unity and identity and addressing diversity and the multiple identities of students. The ways in which nation-states address the tension between unity and diversity in the education of citizens (Banks et al., 2005; Parker, 2003) is no longer merely the topic of academic debate but is being discussed by political leaders and policy-makers as they respond to concerns about terrorism and seek to secure political loyalty (Osler, 2008). There is also a tension between the goal of promoting a specific and narrowly defined national identity (which in some cases may imply indoctrination) and the goal of educating for independent, critical thought. This chapter reports on a study of two neighboring European countries, England and France, both of which were introducing new citizenship education programs at the beginning of the 21st century. Drawing on documentary evidence, the study analyzes their contrasting approaches to national identity, social cohesion, and diversity.

The study also examines how French and English citizenship programs address the ongoing challenge which racism and xenophobia pose to democracy in Europe. In 2007, nearly 4 million people in France voted in the first round of the presidential election for the far right *Front national* candidate, Jean-Marie Le Pen, who has an explicitly xenophobic agenda. The political success of the far right has been attributed to feelings of insecurity fueled by the media, which from the mid-1990s has linked urban violence with the presence of minorities (Osler & Starkey, 2005; Wieviorka, 1999).

In Britain, although voter support for far right parties is much less than in France, support for the British National Party increased from just under 50,000 votes at the 2001 general election to nearly 200,000 in 2005 and 238,000 votes in local elections in 2006, resulting in 49 local councilors. Support for racist parties is strong in certain localities. The discourse of far right parties sometimes has an impact on the discourse and behavior of mainstream party candidates in those localities. Institutional racism was identified by the report into the racist murder of Stephen Lawrence (Macpherson, 1999) as pervading British life. Following the attacks of September 2001 in the United States and more particularly the London terrorist bombings in July 2005, there has been a growth in Islamophobic rhetoric in sections of the British media. Racism and political support for racist agendas are thus continuing features of French and British society and a danger to democracy (Osler & Starkey, 2002).

National contexts

A new citizenship education program for England was introduced during a period of constitutional reform, which included: the introduction of the Human Rights Act 1998, incorporating the European Convention on Human Rights into UK law; the establishment of a Scottish Parliament and Welsh Assembly; and a new settlement in Northern Ireland, also involving devolved government. These developments are encouraging public debate about the meanings of nationality, national identity, and citizenship and the extent to which individuals and groups from both majority and minority communities feel a sense of belonging to the United Kingdom and/or its constituent countries of England, Scotland, Wales, and Northern Ireland.

Citizenship education was introduced in England partly in order to counteract disinterest in formal political processes, as expressed by record levels of voter abstentions. The program of study followed the recommendations of the government-commissioned Crick Report, which claimed: "There are worrying levels of apathy, ignorance and cynicism about public life" (Qualifications and Curriculum Authority [QCA], 1998, p. 8). The apparent apathy is seen to threaten democracy itself, with the Crick Report quoting the Lord Chancellor as saying: "Unless we become a nation of engaged citizens, our democracy is not secure" (QCA, 1998, p. 8).

The citizenship education program is described as having three main strands: social and moral responsibility, community involvement, and political literacy (QCA, 1998). As well as a formal brief, and a prescribed program, secondary school teachers have official schemes of work for students (Years 7–11) (QCA & Department for Education and Skills [DfES], 2001, 2002).

However, between the publication of the Crick Report and its implementation, the Stephen Lawrence Inquiry report was published (Macpherson, 1999), which highlighted the institutional racism which pervades the police force and other areas of public life, including education. The report identified the key role which schools can play in challenging racism. The government responded by acknowledging institutional racism and identifying citizenship education as a key means for challenging racism (Home Office, 1999).

In the light of this expectation that citizenship education should challenge racism, the assumptions of the Crick Report may not be well founded. It is not self-evident that voting behavior is an accurate indicator of political interest or engagement. Other evidence suggests increasing levels of political activity, broadly defined, amongst young people in England (Roker, Player, & Coleman, 1999). Although young people from particular minority groups have shown higher levels of abstention than their peers (Commission for Racial Equality [CRE], 1998), this may reflect experiences of exclusion and institutional racism, as reflected in lower educational outcomes and employment rates in these same groups.

The French guidelines and program of study, developed by a working party, the Groupe Technique Disciplinaire, Éducation Civique (Technical subject group for civic education), were introduced in stages, beginning in 1996 with students in Year 7 (*6e*). Teachers were provided with detailed official guidance (Ministère de l'Éducation Nationale de la Recherche et de la

Technologie, 1998), and a number of educational publishers produced textbooks based on the programs of study.

Citizenship education has traditionally been high on the political agenda in France, having its roots in the need to consolidate support for the Third Republic from 1871, when democracy was restored. The first compulsory primary education curriculum statement, published in Article One of the Jules Ferry law 1882, put *instruction morale et civique* (moral and civic training) before reading, writing, and literature among national priorities (Costa-Lascoux, 1998). Government concern that students receive an education that helps them to become good citizens of the French Republic persists to the present day.

Citizenship education from its origins has been intended to help integrate a diverse population into a single national French culture defined as Republican, in other words based on the principles of freedom, equality, and solidarity (*liberté, égalité, fraternité*) and on human rights. It is based on the conviction that the nation-state is responsible for transmitting shared principles for the public sphere.

Citizenship education in France is thus central to publicly funded schooling. The school is the Republic's primary institution for socializing citizens. It is the school, through its curriculum, that is entrusted with the mission of defining what it means to be a citizen and of ensuring that there is a common understanding of the rights and obligations of citizenship. The basis of national education in France is initiation into a common culture through a single curriculum. It does not recognize difference, but starts from the premise that, within the French Republic, all citizens are equal. Inequalities are deemed to stem from family background and therefore are irrelevant to the school, which belongs to the public sphere.

This official French Republican perspective, which finds expression in education legislation, is based on the premise that there is a danger of society fragmenting into ghettos or ethnic minority or religious communities (*communautés*). Such a tendency would undermine the very basis of the nation-state, which is to integrate all citizens into a single Republic founded on common universal values, namely human rights and the rule of law. This reluctance to recognize community identities has engendered conflicts and difficulties for schools, as with the various headscarf affairs since 1989, culminating in the outright ban in schools of all outward and visible signs of religious identity, including the hijab, in 2004 (Gaspard & Khosrokhavar, 1995; Lorcerie, 2005; Starkey, 1999; Tévanian, 2005).

Framework of analysis

This chapter examines the secondary school citizenship education programs in England and France, using 2 of the 18 framing questions from the comparative civic education study initiated by the International Association for the Evaluation of Educational Achievement (IEA). The IEA study (1995) aimed "to explore and clarify how civic education is actually conceptualized and understood within each participating country." Its rationale emphasizes fears for the future of democracy similar to those expressed by Crick: "increasing numbers of adolescents ... are disengaged from the political system.... Polite expressions of opinion ... have little appeal among youth, many of whom distrust government deeply" (Torney-Purta, Schwille, & Amadeo, 1999, p. 14).

The two questions selected for the present study are IEA Core International Framing Questions 2 and 3. These deal respectively with national identity and relations between nations (Table 24.1) and with social cohesion and social diversity (Table 24.2). They do not explore the tension within programs between socialization into a national identity and education for critical thought. They are applied here to documentary evidence from each country, namely, the published programs of study and official guidance to teachers, supplemented, in the case of France, with a citizenship education textbook. In the case of England the examination of the programs of study is undertaken in the light of the government-commissioned Crick Report, which provides a detailed rationale for the specified topics and approach.

The aim of the present study is to highlight similarities and significant differences between the two national programs and identify potential weaknesses. In France, textbooks play an important part in lesson planning for all subjects, including citizenship, and are the main source of teaching material. The same assumption cannot be made for citizenship teaching in England, since schools draw on specific local and topical concerns selected by teachers.

In carrying out this research, we wanted to explore the extent to which these programs of study may be said to be inclusive of all those who may be attending school in each country, particularly minority students. This analysis is original in that France is not included in the IEA survey. Furthermore the IEA data for England (Kerr, 1999) were collected before citizenship curriculum plans were published.

Given that educational institutions in both countries tend to reflect the social structures of the ruling strata of society (male dominated decision-making groups, under-representation of minorities), we pay particular attention to the extent to which the perspectives of minorities are included in citizenship programs. By definition, citizenship is an inclusive concept, and the exclusion of minority perspectives would be a contradiction which would vitiate its effective implementation.

Citizenship education and national identity

This section analyzes the documentation for England and then France using the framing questions in Table 24.1.

England

The program of citizenship education in England, implemented in 2002, consisted of a brief formal list of skills, knowledge, and understanding to be achieved and attainment targets to be met (Department for Education and Employment [DfEE] & Qualifications and Curriculum Authority [QCA], 1999). The Crick Report, from which the program of study was derived, makes references to the changing constitutional context in which citizenship

Table 24.1 Framing Questions on National Identity and Relations between Nations

What expectations are there about acquiring a sense of national identity or loyalty?

How important is sense of belonging to the nation, to communities, to traditions and institutions?

What symbols are introduced?

What documents (e.g. constitution), role models, historical events, ideals are considered important for citizens to know about?

What supranational structures and international organizations and subnational (e.g. ethnic or religious) groups are considered important enough to have a place in the young person's awareness, identity, or loyalty?

Are either supranational or subnational groups thought of as presenting a threat to national identity or loyalty?

education was introduced, arguing that by the end of compulsory schooling at age 16 pupils should:

> know about the changing constitution of the UK, including the relationship between the two Houses of Parliament, the changing role of the monarchy, shifting relationships between England, Scotland, Wales, and Northern Ireland and Britain's relationship with the European Union and the Commonwealth.
>
> (QCA, 1998, p. 51)

Although British citizenship is presented as inclusive of national differences between England, Scotland, Wales, and Northern Ireland, the Crick Report presents visible minorities as "Other." Certainly, the general principle is inclusivity:

> A main aim for the whole community should be to find or restore a sense of common citizenship, including a national identity that is secure enough to find a place in the plurality of nations, cultures, ethnic identities and religions long found in the United Kingdom. Citizenship education creates a common ground between different ethnic and religious identities.
>
> (QCA, 1998, p. 17)

But this spirit of inclusion does not extend to minorities who, it is implied, cannot necessarily be relied upon to conform to the laws, standards, customs, and conventions of our democratic society: "Minorities must learn and respect the laws, codes and conventions as much as the majority – not merely because it is useful to do so, but because this process helps foster common citizenship" (QCA, 1998, p. 18).

Thus the report assumes that minorities (here it is referring to Black British rather than White ethnicities such as Welsh or Scottish) need to change in order to realize a common citizenship. No similar demand is placed on the majority White community, who are simply required to "tolerate" minorities. There is no recognition that minorities also exercise tolerance as part of the everyday experience of living in a multicultural society.

The implied processes of integration require change on the part of minorities, but none in the practices of White British citizens. The report presents a deficit model of minority cultures, which are somehow less law-abiding (and possibly less democratic) than those of Whites, and this is also symptomatic of a colonial approach to Black British communities throughout the report. Such communities have more need of citizenship education than the majority because they are less familiar with and accepting of "laws, codes and conventions." The report itself appears flawed in the way it reflects rather than challenges institutionalized racism in Britain (Osler, 2000).

There is an implicit recognition of the multiple identities held by British citizens. Yet there is also the hint that "national identity" and "common citizenship" may, in fact, be fragile. While there is no direct suggestion that any subnational group may threaten a common British citizenship, the report argues:

> These matters of national identity in a pluralist society are complex and should never be taken for granted. We all need to learn more about each other. This should entail learning not only about the United Kingdom – including all four of its component parts – but also about the European, Commonwealth and the global dimensions of citizenship, with due

regard being given to the homelands of our minority communities and to the main countries of British emigration.

(QCA, 1998, p. 18)

The report implies that some British citizens, those who are not White, cannot really call Britain home.

There is no acknowledgment of racism, but official guidance, published two years later, suggests there should be "consideration of local issues (such as particular manifestations of racism and its removal)" (QCA, 2000, p. 5), though no example is given of how schools might address these manifestations. The guidance recommends seven topics for organizing the study of citizenship, and the first of these is "human rights (including anti-racism)" (QCA, 2000, p. 20). Again, no further explanation is provided.

The Crick Report developed learning outcomes for the lower secondary school (Years 7 to 9), and anticipated that students would study the UN Convention on the Rights of the Child (CRC) (1989), the Universal Declaration of Human Rights (UDHR) (1948), and the European Convention on Human Rights (ECHR) (1950). The context for this learning is framed by concepts such as *discrimination, equal opportunities, tribunal, ballot,* and *trade unions* for the CRC, and *prejudice, discrimination, xenophobia,* and *pluralism* in the section mentioning the other two human rights instruments. Human rights are also linked to *overseas aid, development,* and *charity* (QCA, 1998, pp. 49–52). This guidance fails to stress how ratification of the CRC and of the ECHR places obligations on the government to uphold rights. Instead, the emphasis is on the responsibilities of individual citizens.

The framing questions (Table 24.1) refer to "documents," "role models," or "historical events" which might be used to illustrate the elements of the program of study. In the Crick Report there is little in the way of documents or symbols suggested to reinforce national identity. The only documents cited are international human rights texts. The institutions mentioned in the programs of study include Parliament, the criminal and civil justice systems, the European Union, the Commonwealth, and the United Nations. The Crick Report also included "the changing role of the monarchy" but, along with other national institutions which retain a powerful role, such as the established church and the armed forces, the monarchy is omitted from the programs of study. There is no reference to national symbols such as the national flag or anthem. In this sense, neither the Crick Report nor the programs of study are prescriptive of a national identity.

France

The French documentation, namely the citizenship program of study and official guidance (Ministère de l'Éducation Nationale, 1998), lays considerable stress on national identity and nationality. At the start of secondary school, in Year 7 (*6e*), there is consideration of personal identity, but only in relation to the nation-state (i.e. birth, marriage and death certificates, driving license, or passport). There is an emphasis on entitlement to French nationality and a detailed description of current nationality law. The section on nationality is closely linked to six main national symbols, representing common national values: the Phrygian hat; the national day (14 July); Marianne (personification of the Republic); the flag; the national motto; and the national anthem. The exact same topics have already been covered at primary school and are revisited at the end of the lower secondary school, three years later.

The sections on acquiring French citizenship are addressed essentially to those who may not have it automatically, namely, those whose parents are not French and who were born outside

France. Citizenship is portrayed as a function of nationality, which is in turn defined by commitment to officially recognized shared symbols and values. This is a vertical, rather than horizontal, view of citizenship. A horizontal interpretation does not require either citizenship or citizenship education to be linked necessarily to nationality.

Students in France are expected to study certain key documents, particularly legal and constitutional texts. In Year 7 (*6e*) the program starts with the formal *règlement intérieur*, the text that governs school behavior and procedures, emphasizing that students are in a rule-bound institution. In this school year there are two other national texts and two international. The preamble to the Constitution of the Fourth Republic (1946–1958) refers back to a French tradition of human rights developed at the time of the 1789 Revolution that is maintained in the constitution of the current Fifth Republic and therefore stresses continuity of commitment to these principles.

The other key national document is a letter from the minister of education to teachers dated 1883 setting out the key importance of civic and moral education based on universal principles. These universal principles are set out in the two international texts, the UDHR (1948) and the CRC (1989). The clear implication is that French national values are universal. The principle is evident, but the experience of the way these universal values are embedded or not in the institutions of the French state, including schools, will be perceived differently by different categories of pupil. There is evidence, for instance, of differential treatment by French employers, police, and schools according to perceived ethnic origins (Bataille, 1999; Savidan, 2007).

The study of the French constitution and of international human rights texts, including the ECHR, continues to underpin each year of the secondary program of study. Towards the end of lower secondary school, pupils study the European Union, introduced as a progressive supranational institution of positive benefit to France.

The programs are clear about their purpose, namely, to provide:

> education for human rights and citizenship, through the acquisition of the principles and the values which underpin and organize democracy and the Republic, through knowledge of institutions and laws, through an understanding of the rules of social and political life.
>
> (Ministère de l'Éducation Nationale, 1998, p. 7)

This explicit statement that respect for and knowledge of human rights are a major goal of citizenship education is repeated and emphasized in the official guidance. The UDHR is designated as a "reference document" for each of the four years of lower secondary school, and the whole text or extracts are reproduced in textbooks.

The emphasis on human rights is considerably more developed in the French program than in the English. A very influential report for the minister of education in 1984 and a subsequent action research program ensured that the case for human rights as the fundamental principles underpinning education for citizenship is accepted by all major political parties (Audigier, 1991). In contrast, the Crick Report and the subsequent teacher guidance place human rights in a legal, rather than a broader social or political, framework (QCA, 1998, p. 49, 2000, p. 20). The English formulation of purpose is: "Citizenship gives pupils the knowledge, skills and understanding to play an effective role in society at local, national and international levels. It helps them to become informed, thoughtful and responsible citizens who are aware of their duties and rights" (DfEE & QCA, 1999).

Concepts of community

Citizenship can be understood as belonging to a community. Individuals experience citizenship in local communities, through engagement with others in those communities (Osler & Starkey, 1999, 2005). It is at this level that young people most commonly appear to express their sense of allegiance and belonging (Mitchell & Parker, 2008; Osler & Starkey, 2003). IEA framing questions (Table 24.1) introduce the notion of communities.

The Crick Report gives strong emphasis to the local community and, in particular, ways students can learn about citizenship through "volunteering" (service learning). Crick contends that a key role of citizenship education is to promote political literacy at national, and especially at local or community, level. Citizenship education should encourage "an active and politically-literate citizenry convinced that they can influence government and community affairs" (QCA, 1998, p. 9). Lack of involvement is explained in terms of lack of knowledge or skills, rather than with any disillusionment in political processes arising through structural disadvantage, or through observation of the behavior of certain public figures.

There is an emphasis on rights and responsibilities, which might be construed as implying that citizenship is not an automatic right but must be earned. This raises questions about the citizenship status of those who for whatever reason are not able to take an active part in the community. There is no acknowledgment that experiences such as poverty, unemployment, or disability may lead to social exclusion and prevent full participation.

An understanding of national and ethnic identities and of the UK as a political entity and its relation with other nations does, however, require a study of empire and of independence struggles. From 2008, the history program of study refers to decolonization and resistance to empire. The British government has also approved the recommendation of the Ajegbo Report (DfES, 2007) to add an additional strand to the citizenship curriculum, "Identity and diversity: Living together in the UK." Unfortunately, this report fails to adopt a critical perspective on race or multiculturalism or adequately address the relationship between citizenship and history education (Osler, 2008, 2009).

It is on the question of community that the French program contrasts most starkly with that for England. In France, at the beginning of secondary school, the school as a community is the subject of the first few lessons. The emphasis, however, is on understanding the school as an institution: roles; facilities; the system of governance through class and school councils; and school rules. Elections are held for class representatives, who have a formal role in representing the views of fellow students in the class councils (*conseil de classe*) and on the governing body (*conseil d'administration*).

There is a substantial section on local democracy, including the powers of local councils, and a clear indication of who is eligible to stand for election and who can vote, namely French and EU member state nationals. A further local dimension is the environment and concern to protect local and national heritage, including traditional customs and folklore; food and cooking; art and culture; and historic buildings. This is a conservative agenda in a literal sense. The only indications of cultural diversity relate to regional culinary and folkloric traditions and the collections of local museums.

The work of political parties, unions, pressure groups, and other associations is presented as healthy elements in a democracy. Students are expected to discuss and debate issues these groups raise, and consider ways in which citizens work through them to influence democratic decision-making. What is entirely absent is a consideration of religious groups and structures, in spite of the fact that the Catholic Church, for instance, remains a powerful political force in

France. There is no equivalent to the section of the English program of study which refers to "faith groups."

The missing religious dimension, a function of the French Republic's constitutional commitment to neutrality in education (*laïcité*), is likely to limit the scope of discussions on a number of the issues arising from the program of study, including women in society and issues of social justice. Each of these is potentially the subject of pronouncements by religious authorities, whose views may be important to some pupils' families. However, following the US/UK invasion of Iraq in 2003, there were political concerns about increasingly public assertions of Muslim identities. The 2003 reports of the Stasi and the Debré commissions led to a cross-party consensus to pass legislation to ban visible religious symbols from schools from September 2004 (Lorcerie, 2005).

In contrast to the situation in France, publicly funded schools in England have had an obligation, since 1944, to include a daily act of worship and religious education. From 1997, the Labour government gave an additional impetus to publicly funded faith schools. Although such schools (Christian and Jewish) have been incorporated into the public sector since the 19th-century establishment of a national education system, government support for such schools has extended and now includes a small number of Islamic, Hindu, and Sikh institutions. Many such faith schools have a greater degree of independence in their admissions policies and curricula than other publicly funded institutions (Osler, 2007).

Social cohesion and cultural diversity

This section addresses the second set of IEA framing questions (Table 24.2).

England

The Crick Report gives relatively little attention to the impact of race, ethnicity, home language, social class, religion, or gender on citizenship. There is one passing reference to "an awareness of equal opportunities issues, national identity and cultural differences" (QCA, 1998, p. 19). The only explicit reference to exclusion or discrimination is as follows: "The curriculum should consider the factors that lead to exclusion from society, such as bullying, colour and other forms of 'difference.' It should make students aware of the difficulties such exclusion can have on the individual and society" (QCA, 1998, p. 19). Discrimination is set in the context of

Table 24.2 Framing Questions on Social Cohesion and Social Diversity

---
What do young people learn about those belonging to groups that are seen as set apart or disenfranchised (e.g. by ethnicity, race, immigrant status, mother tongue, social class, religion, gender)?

What groups are viewed as subject to discrimination in contemporary society?

How are instances of past discrimination dealt with?

Are differences in participation rates or leadership roles (e.g. men and women, minorities) discussed or ignored?

Is there tension in the society between perceptions of the need for social cohesion and the need to recognize the cultural, social, political, or economic situation of groups?

How is conflict between groups or between groups and society dealt with?

Are attitudes of respect and tolerance between groups encouraged?

"bullying," which may be interpreted as an interpersonal action rather than structural disadvantage. There are no references to past discrimination; instead, the move towards universal enfranchisement is presented as successful and complete.

There is no sense of historical struggles for social, economic, civil, and political rights. The notion that for some groups this struggle continues is absent. The emphasis is on the need for cohesion, the need to get minorities on board, and the rule of law. Conflict is portrayed as a problem; there are no examples of positive outcomes arising from societal conflict. Although there is concern that the education service be inclusive, it is left to schools and teachers to apply the advice to citizenship education or not.

France

An analysis of a textbook (Lauby, 1999) developed to support the program for students in Year 10 provides evidence on French perspectives on social cohesion and social diversity. Social cohesion is presented in this textbook as shared commitment to the fundamental principles of the Republic: freedom, equality, and solidarity. The program for Year 10 (*3e*) progresses from the individual and individual identity within society to collective citizenship within the nation. The early pages contain several color photographs showing Black people and minorities identifying with the national flag, and proudly representing the nation. The multiethnic French football team's victory in the 1998 World Cup is portrayed as demonstrating the integrative capacity of the Republic.

The Republic is characterized as "indivisible," meaning citizens are guaranteed equality before the law. However, the gap between principles and social reality is explicitly acknowledged. In the textbook, the late President François Mitterrand is quoted as saying in 1988 that "mutual respect is the basis for the pact without which national community would have no meaning. An unjust France is a divided France" (Lauby, 1999, p. 15). In other words, national political action must focus on justice, without which the principle of indivisibility is breached. This statement, although coming from a political figure closely identified with a left-of-center party, is presented as an uncontroversial French Republican statement, rather than a party political claim. It is provided in order to contrast with claims made by "enemies of the [French] Republic," namely, the far right, racist *Front national* party. A section on threats to the Republic highlights the armed Corsican independence movement, racist politicians, and, as in England, voter apathy.

The emphasis, supported by numerous images, is of citizens actively engaged in the French Republic's central task of promoting justice. The book's cover shows young people involved in a demonstration, and there are a further nine photographs of demonstrations and strikes, all presented positively. Active citizenship is linked explicitly to demonstrations, political party membership, and participation in strike action. Striking is described as "one of the great social achievements of workers, it is recognized by the Constitution" (Lauby, 1999, p. 83).

The Republic is portrayed as a "melting pot." France is described as "a country of immigration." People have come to France from all over the world and "accepting the values and the symbols of the Republic they have integrated into French society. Their children have become French citizens" (Lauby, 1999, p. 28). However, it is also pointed out that only French nationals may vote, and so "citizenship is linked to the possession of French nationality" (Lauby, 1999, p. 29). There is little to suggest that minorities may be subject to discrimination, except at the hands of far right political parties. There is a reminder of the 1940 Vichy law excluding Jews from any public office or job, but this is not matched with evidence of current discrimination against minorities in housing, policing, and employment (Dewitte, 1999).

On the other hand there is acknowledgment of social exclusion, represented in the textbook by the homeless and the unemployed. One section is devoted to women's struggle for parity, and one of the illustrations is clearly linked to the communist trade union movement.

While individual members of minorities are welcomed as French citizens, the textbook also makes clear that any attempt to develop a sense of community founded not on citizenship but on ethnic identity or solidarity is alien to the values of the Republic: "The Republic cannot accept an inward-looking communitarianism which is likely to endanger the unity of the nation." Communitarianism is defined as:

> A situation where society is split into inward-looking groups based on ethnicity, culture or religion. This often leads to the setting up of ghettos and sometimes to conflicts between groups. It is the opposite of the French Republic's principle of indivisibility.
> (Lauby, 1999, p. 15)

This tension is demonstrated by a picture of a large number of Muslims praying in a Paris street. The caption is "Exercising fundamental rights." The commentary reads:

> To be a citizen is to be able to exercise one's rights freely. Practicing the religion of one's choice is a fundamental right. However, exercising this right implies not offending other people's religious convictions; there is no place for acts of worship in public places. Consequently all religions should have available properly appointed places of worship.
> (Lauby, 1999)

This implies that those in the picture are at fault and should be inside. It fails to take into account the attitude of local councils, which have frequently denied planning consent for mosques (Hamm & Starkey, 1998).

Compared to the English program of study, the French program is much more ready to take a positive view of political activity and recognize that social conflict can lead to progress. But it is unable to accept notions of personal identity within the Republic, where these identifications are related to ethnicity, culture, or religion. Given that multiple identities are the norm in modern societies, France's failure to recognize the possibility of combining a group identity with a French and Republican identity defines citizenship in exclusive terms (Gaspard & Khosrokhavar, 1995).

Conclusion

A comparative study places national programs of citizenship education in a fresh perspective, allowing readers to reflect on both the countries under discussion and others with which they may be familiar. Any discussion of citizenship education, national identity, and diversity raises questions about the tensions which may be experienced by students between the inclusive ideal and the exclusive (and potentially alienating) reality.

In both England and France, new programs of education for citizenship aim to reinforce and strengthen democracy. The French program is based on Republican values, particularly human rights, and emphasizes the unacceptability of racism and discrimination. The program for England emphasizes social and moral responsibility and active engagement with society. It is therefore more pragmatic and less concerned with core principles.

The French program of study is declarative of its principles of freedom, equality, solidarity, and human rights. These are presented as problematic only in that there is an ongoing struggle for their implementation. Pupils are invited to join that struggle. There is a clear sense of national identity associated with the French Republic.

The English program of study, like the British constitution, relies heavily on the implicit. There is no sense of an existing national identity, which is presented as something yet to be created (QCA, 1998). The very notion of citizenship is relatively new and remains as something to be defined. It is implied that citizenship will develop through consensus rather than struggle. Young people, it is suggested, will grow as citizens through service learning in the local community rather than through participating in strikes, struggles, or demonstrations for change. Local community engagement is presented as equally important to an awareness of national issues. Teachers in England are amazed to hear that French textbooks emphasize the right to strike, and it is difficult to imagine that such a textbook would be well received by British parents.

In both France and England the population is increasingly secular, yet also, paradoxically, increasingly multi-faith. The two countries have adopted different responses to these developments. The French government has taken an approach in which symbols of religion, including the headscarf, which were often in practice tolerated, are no longer permitted. Religion has been pushed, as far as is possible, into the private sphere. By contrast, the British government acknowledges religious diversity and has increased the power and status of religious groups and authorities in schooling. Both approaches bring with them problems. In England, students have the opportunity to study religious identity, although in some schools and some areas students are increasingly segregated by religion. In France, young citizens are expected to ignore their religious identities at school, although these very identities may help shape their public lives as citizens.

Neither program of study gives significant weight to the perspectives or experiences of minorities. The French program roundly condemns racism but fails to explore it. The English program recognizes a range of ethnic groups and expects understanding of diversity. It expects individuals to challenge prejudice and discrimination, but does not consider collective responses or the existence of institutional racism and structural disadvantage. Perhaps the major conclusion that applies to both national programs of study is that there is little evidence that minority groups participated in their formulation. Until national curricula and discourses on citizenship are responsive to minority as well as majority perspectives they are likely to remain exclusive.

References

Audigier, F. (1991). Socialization and human rights education: The example of France. In H. Starkey (Ed.), *Socialisation of school children and the education for democratic values and human rights* (pp. 129–148). Amsterdam: Swets & Zeitlinger.

Banks, J. A., Banks, C. A. M., Cortés, C. E., Hahn, C., Merryfield, M., Moodley, K. A., et al. (2005). *Democracy and diversity: Principles and concepts for educating citizens in a global age*. Seattle: University of Washington, Center for Multicultural Education.

Bataille, P. (1999). Racisme institutionnel, racisme culturel et discriminations [Institutional racism, cultural racism, and discrimination]. In P. Dewitte (Ed.), *Immigration et intégration: L'état des savoirs* [Immigration and integration: The state of knowledge] (pp. 285–296). Paris: La Découverte.

Commission for Racial Equality (CRE). (1998). *The general election 1997: Ethnic minorities and electoral politics*. London: Author.

Costa-Lascoux, J. (1998). L'éducation civique ... trop tard? [Civic education ... too late?]. *La Revue Educations*, *16*, 53–56.
Department for Education and Employment (DfEE) & Qualifications and Curriculum Authority (QCA). (1999). *The National Curriculum for England key stages 3 and 4*. London: The Stationery Office.
Department for Education and Skills (DfES) (2007). *Curriculum review: Diversity and citizenship*. London: Author.
Dewitte, P. (1999). *Immigration et intégration: L'état des savoirs* [Immigration and integration: The state of knowledge]. Paris: La Découverte.
Gaspard, F., & Khosrokhavar, F. (1995). *Le foulard et la République* [The headscarf and the French Republic]. Paris: La Découverte.
Hamm, A., & Starkey, H. (1998). Islamic studies in a French university: Problems, politics and polemics. In K. Chadwick & P. Cooke (Eds.), *Religion in modern and contemporary France: Working papers on contemporary France* (Vol. 3, pp. 58–71). Portsmouth, UK: University of Portsmouth.
Home Office. (1999). *Stephen Lawrence Inquiry: Home Secretary's action plan*. London: Author.
International Association for the Evaluation of Educational Achievement (IEA). (1995). *National case studies final guidelines*. Amsterdam: Author.
Kerr, D. (1999). Re-examining citizenship education: The case of England. In J. Torney-Purta, J. Schwille, & J.-A. Amadeo (Eds.), *Civic education across countries: Twenty-four national case studies from the IEA Civic Education Project* (pp. 203–228). Amsterdam: Eburon/International Association for the Evaluation of Educational Achievement (IEA).
Lauby, J.-P. (1999). *Education civique 3e* [Civic education textbook for age 14/15]. Paris: Magnard.
Lorcerie, F. (Ed.). (2005). *La politisation du voile: En France, en Europe et dans le monde Arabe* [The politicization of the veil: Case studies from France, Europe, and the Arab world]. Paris: L'Harmattan.
Macpherson, W. (1999). *The Stephen Lawrence Inquiry*. London: The Stationery Office.
Ministère de l'Éducation Nationale de la Recherche et de la Technologie. (1998). *Histoire, géographie, éducation civique: Programmes et accompagnement* [History, geography, civic education: Programs of study and guidance]. Paris: Centre National de la Documentation Pédagogique.
Mitchell, K., & Parker, W. C. (2008). I pledge allegiance to ... flexible citizenship and shifting scales of belonging. *Teachers College Record*, *110*(4), 775–804.
Osler, A. (2000). The Crick Report: Difference, equality and racial justice. *Curriculum Journal*, *11*(1), 25–37.
Osler, A. (2007). *Faith schools and community cohesion: Observations on community consultations*. London: Runnymede Trust.
Osler, A. (2008). Citizenship education and the Ajegbo Report: Re-imagining a cosmopolitan nation. *London Review of Education*, *6*(1), 9–23.
Osler, A. (2009). Patriotism, multiculturalism and belonging: political discourse and the teaching of history. *Educational Review*, *61*(1).
Osler, A., & Starkey, H. (1999). Rights, identities and inclusion: European action programmes as political education. *Oxford Review of Education*, *25*(1 & 2), 199–216.
Osler, A., & Starkey, H. (2002). Education for citizenship: Mainstreaming the fight against racism? *European Journal of Education*, *37*(2), 143–159.
Osler, A., & Starkey, H. (2003). Learning for cosmopolitan citizenship: Theoretical debates and young people's experiences. *Educational Review*, *55*(3), 243–254.
Osler, A., & Starkey, H. (2005). *Changing citizenship: Democracy and inclusion in education*. Maidenhead, UK: Open University Press.
Parker, W. C. (2003). *Teaching democracy: Unity and diversity in public life*. New York: Teachers College Press.
Qualifications and Curriculum Authority (QCA). (1998). *Education for citizenship and the teaching of democracy in schools: Final report of the advisory group on citizenship (the Crick Report)*. London: Author.
Qualifications and Curriculum Authority (QCA). (2000). *Citizenship at key stages 3 and 4: Initial guidance for schools*. London: Author.

Qualifications and Curriculum Authority (QCA) & Department for Education and Skills (DfES). (2001). *Citizenship: A scheme of work for key stage 3*. London: Author.

Qualifications and Curriculum Authority (QCA) & Department for Education and Skills (DfES). (2002). *Citizenship: A scheme of work for key stage 4*. London: Author.

Roker, D., Player, K., & Coleman, J. (1999). Young people's voluntary and campaigning activities as sources of political education. *Oxford Review of Education, 25*(1 & 2), 185–198.

Savidan, P. (2007). *Repenser l'égalité des chances* [Rethinking equal opportunities]. Paris: Grasset.

Starkey, H. (1999). Is a threat to *laïcité* in schools a threat to the Fifth Republic? In M. Allison & O. Heathcote (Eds.), *Forty years of the Fifth Republic* (pp. 355–371). London: Peter Lang.

Tévanian, P. (2005). *Le voile médiatique. Un faux débat: L'affaire du foulard islamique* [The veil in the headlines. A false debate: The Islamic headscarf affair]. Paris: Raisons d'Agir.

Torney-Purta, J., Schwille, J., & Amadeo, J.-A. (Eds.). (1999). *Civic education across countries: Twenty-four national case studies from the IEA Civic Education Project*. Amsterdam: Eburon/International Association for the Evaluation of Educational Achievement (IEA).

Wieviorka, M. (1999). *La violence en France* [Violence in France]. Paris: Seuil.

25

Democracy, antiracism, and citizenship education

European policy and political complacency

Hugh Starkey
Institute of Education, University of London, UK

Audrey Osler
University of Leeds, UK

This chapter explores European policies intended to combat racism through education, and it examines the cases of two European countries, England and Sweden. Critical race theory (CRT), developed in the United States (Ladson-Billings, 2004), has aimed to show how race and power are constructed within political culture in such a way as to leave racism untouched and unrecognized. This chapter draws on CRT, and posits the concept of political complacency to explain how, even in policy contexts where racism is acknowledged and policies are introduced ostensibly to challenge racism and address inequality, the effectiveness of such policies is undermined and the direct link between antiracism and democracy neglected.

Racism and antiracism in Europe

The origins of the movement that gave impetus to the creation of powerful European institutions lie in resistance to fascism and Nazism before and during World War II. Given that the Nazi ideology was founded on racism and a denial of the essential equality of human beings, its opponents were, by definition, committed to the promotion of antiracism and racial justice. Following the founding of the United Nations (UN), dedicated to achieving justice and peace in the world through universal respect of human rights (1945–1948), in 1949 European leaders created a regional organization, the Council of Europe, based in Strasbourg, France. Its aim is to foster international cultural cooperation and parliamentary democracy based on respect for human rights and fundamental freedoms (Starkey, 2003).

From the outset, European institutions have been founded on the principle of democracy. As well as practicing democratic governance, member states are committed to equality and non-discrimination in rights, including race equality, through their adherence to the European Convention on Human Rights and Fundamental Freedoms (ECHR) dating from 1950.

This powerful instrument provides a legal mechanism for citizens of member states to claim their rights, including freedom from discrimination on the basis of "sex, race, colour, language, religion, political or other opinion, national or social origin, association with a national minority, property, birth or other status" (ECHR, Article 14).

The two major European institutions are the Council of Europe and the European Union (EU). The Council of Europe is an organization dedicated to promoting cultural cooperation, democracy, and human rights. It represents the founding ideals of postwar Europe, namely the strengthening of democracy and respect for human rights and fundamental freedoms. It is influential rather than powerful. In 2008 there were 47 member states, covering the whole continent from Portugal in the West, to Russia, Georgia, and Turkey in the East. Commitment to the ECHR is a condition of acceptance as a member state. The other, politically more powerful European institution, the EU, was founded in 1957, and in 2008 had 27 member states. All EU members are members of the Council of Europe and thus share the same foundational commitment to equality of rights as the basis of peaceful cooperation. The EU attempts to balance a strong economic agenda, based on free movement of people, goods, and services within member states, with a social agenda that promotes equality and non-discrimination.

The EU has powerful mechanisms such as legally binding directives to ensure compliance by member states. EU directives outlawing discrimination are justified on the basis that racism is antithetical to the fundamental European principles of human rights, dignity, and equality. It threatens the stability of individual states and of the continent as a whole. This was brought sharply into focus with the so-called ethnic cleansing that was both a cause and a result of the wars in former Yugoslavia (1991–1995). European institutions are consequently based on legal frameworks that explicitly acknowledge the importance of antiracism as a feature of democratic life. However, the implementation of effective antiracist initiatives depends on a supportive political climate, and it is this that the chapter now considers.

European policy initiatives on antiracism, 1997–2001

The years 1997–2001 marked a significant period in the promotion of antiracist ideals across Europe. The Treaty of Amsterdam (European Communities, 1997) ensured that antidiscrimination became a basic and fundamental principle of the EU. Article 13 enacted the principle of equal treatment between persons irrespective of "sex, racial or ethnic origin, religion or belief, disability, age or sexual orientation" (European Communities, p. 26). Previous EU legislation introduced in the 1970s and 1980s had addressed discrimination in the labor market based on the grounds of sex, but the new treaty provided the EU with a legal basis to require member states to take action to combat a wide range of discriminations. As a result, in 2000 the EU Commission issued the Race Equality Directive (European Anti-Discrimination Council, 2000), requiring all member states to implement legislative programs at national and/or subnational levels to realize race equality in the field of education.

The EU designated 1997 as the European Year Against Racism and established the European Monitoring Centre on Racism and Xenophobia (EUMC) to provide both the EU and its member states with objective, reliable, and comparable data at the European level on racism, xenophobia, and anti-Semitism. It received a new statute and new title in 2007, becoming the European Union Agency for Fundamental Rights (FRA). In a complementary initiative the Council of Europe in 1997 launched the European Commission Against Racism and Intolerance (ECRI) with a remit to combat racism, xenophobia, anti-Semitism, and intolerance as infringements of human rights. ECRI publishes detailed reports, analyses, and recommendations.

Also in the late 1990s, the EU set up a working group of experts and civil servants to evaluate the extent to which its policies and programs were contributing to antiracism. The group produced an *Action Plan Against Racism* (European Commission, 1998) that was intended to complement specific antiracist measures. The report identified two main means by which racism can be challenged: first, by presenting diversity in a positive light; and, secondly, by creating favorable conditions for a multicultural society.

A further report, *Mainstreaming the Fight Against Racism* (European Commission, 1999), drew together various previous initiatives and emphasized ways in which EU policies and programs can contribute to the fight against racism. Mainstreaming antiracism was defined as integrating the fight against racism as an objective into all EU actions and policies at all levels. This entails actively and visibly considering their impact on race equality when drawing them up.

Citizenship education as a policy response to racism

At the turn of the 21st century, racism was clearly articulated in Europe as a threat to democracy and to peace in the region and the world. In a formal declaration, prepared for the World Conference Against Racism (2001), governments of Council of Europe member states affirmed that:

- Racism and racial discrimination are serious violations of human rights in the contemporary world and must be combated by all lawful means;
- Racism, racial discrimination, xenophobia and related intolerance threaten democratic societies and their fundamental values;
- Stability and peace in Europe and throughout the world can only be built on tolerance and respect for diversity. (Council of Europe, 2000a, p. 3)

The need for antiracism stems from this logic. Racism violates human rights and therefore threatens democracy. Human rights and democracy are the main guarantee of stability and peace.

The strong antiracist rhetoric of European leaders was, at this time, followed by responses in the form of new education policies. Speaking on behalf of the EU at the World Conference, Commissioner Diamantopoulou (2001) emphasized the importance of education in combating racism, arguing that, although the fight against racism was now firmly rooted in European law, experience showed that there are many areas of discrimination that cannot be tackled by law. She suggested that practical action was needed to help change the underlying prejudices that fuel racist attitudes and behavior. She concluded that education has a fundamental role in this endeavor. This is a key analysis, concluding that legislation, while important, needs to be accompanied by a strongly antiracist educational program designed to create a climate of respect for human rights.

In fact antiracism as a European educational policy response took two forms. First, it invested a specific space in the Council of Europe's curriculum development program and, secondly, it was included in the criteria to be addressed by those applying for grants under EU-funded education initiatives.

Rhetorically, the Council of Europe's new curriculum development project of Education for Democratic Citizenship (EDC), launched in 1997 and building on an earlier program of human rights education (Osler & Starkey, 1996), aimed explicitly to develop new models for citizenship education that would be instrumental in the fight against violence, xenophobia, racism, aggressive nationalism, and intolerance (Council of Europe, 2000b). However, in reviewing the initial achievements of the EDC program, the Council of Europe's Committee of Ministers of Education felt obliged to reiterate to their governments that EDC should explicitly support educational approaches aimed at "combating aggressive nationalism, racism and intolerance and eliminat[ing] violence and extremist thinking and behavior" (Council of Europe, 2002, p. 3). The education ministers of the EU subsequently echoed this apparent consensus on the importance of antiracism (Council of the European Union, 2004).

The rhetorical support for antiracism at the highest policy level is not reflected in guidance on particular programs. While the citizenship education project of the Council of Europe moved to a third phase (2006–2009), with a greater emphasis on human rights education (HRE), its terms of reference no longer include combating racism. Rather, it aims to promote EDC/HRE with an emphasis on social cohesion, social inclusion, and respect for human rights. The terms *social cohesion* and *social inclusion*, while sounding positive, reflect a change of focus; effectively the terms of reference allow the issue of racism within formal school education to be ignored. The youth campaign All Different All Equal, addressing non-formal education, remains robustly antiracist (European Minority Youth Network, 2006).

Similarly it was not the Council of Europe's EDC/HRE project, but a separate organization within the Council, the European Commission Against Racism and Intolerance (ECRI), that proposed a general policy recommendation on combating racism and racial discrimination in and through school education (2007).

The recommendation proposes that schools be obliged to incorporate measures to counter racism and to show respect for diversity as an essential element of the school's mission and structures. This includes having a school policy to combat racism, monitoring racist incidents, using strong sanctions against those engaging in serious racist acts, and ensuring that human rights education is integral to the curriculum at all ages.

ECRI reminded governments of the need to finance the policies and to monitor their impact. School inspectors should be required to pay attention to racism and racial discrimination and ensure that schools promote equality in education and implement measures to ensure equal participation for minorities such as the collection of adequate statistics by gender and ethnicity.

Although these unambiguous and robust statements of principle and detailed guidance and recommendations demonstrate that there is a rhetorical consensus at the European level that education should be antiracist, the influence of such recommendations at national and local levels is variable. Education is primarily funded and delivered by national governments and local or regional authorities. European policy can therefore be only advisory with respect to public schooling, and the implementation of antiracist policies depends on the extent to which national and local authorities are prepared to monitor the situation in schools and if necessary sanction non-compliance. The danger of such arrangements is that member states can make a rhetorical commitment to antiracist policies by supporting high-level recommendations without taking steps to address racism within local and national educational structures.

Mainstreaming antiracism in European-funded education programs

Although EU education policy for the most part works indirectly by encouraging governments of member states to enact effective measures aimed at combating racism and its effects, there are spheres where the EU allocates its own resources to educational programs and where it can implement its own policies directly. These include EU-funded research programs and the Lifelong Learning Programme, which funds curriculum development and mobility. This program, known until 2007 as Socrates, annually funds hundreds of transnational cooperation projects involving thousands of students and teachers in schools (Comenius), universities (Erasmus), vocational training (Leonardo da Vinci), and adult learning (Grundtvig).

Applying for these EU funds is a very competitive process, and the EU is therefore in a position to lay down strict criteria and priorities. The drafting of these priorities provides a powerful opportunity to mainstream EU policy. So, for instance, in the program cycle starting in 2000, the published criteria for selection included a statement that projects meeting the following criteria would be given priority: "Emphasis placed by the project on the promotion of *equality between women and men*, equal opportunities for *disabled persons* and contributing to *the fight against racism and xenophobia*" (European Commission, 2000, p. 23, emphasis in original). The Commission noted that almost half the projects in some sections of this complex program addressed these issues specifically (European Commission, 1999). An evaluation of the extent to which EU education programs contributed to promoting European ideals found considerable impact on participants when projects were formulated in a way that emphasized equalities (Osler & Starkey, 1999).

In 2000, the program involving projects between schools, known as Comenius, was explicit in its intentions to support "transnational activities designed to . . . support the fight against racism and xenophobia" (European Commission, 2000, p. 35). Among suggested themes for projects, the Commission proposed: "arts, sciences, environmental education, cultural heritage, European citizenship, use of information and communication technology, fight against racism" (European Commission, 2000, p. 37).

The Commission was thus able to demonstrate that the priorities set for its educational programs support antiracism. However, in the guidance provided for the next generation of projects, starting in 2008, this emphasis on combating racism had disappeared. Indeed, even in publications designed to provide examples of successful projects from the previous funding cycle, there is only one example of a project that addresses racism (European Commission, 2007a).

For the funding cycle from 2008, the emphasis is on making the EU the most competitive knowledge-based economy with sustainable economic development and greater social cohesion. Social cohesion was framed within a concern to promote intercultural dialogue between citizens, conceptualized as individual members of European nations, rather than as an antiracist approach that would directly address institutional and other forms of racism within member states. The program intends to create a sense of European citizenship based on "understanding and respect for human rights and democracy, and encouraging tolerance and respect for other peoples and cultures" (European Commission, 2007b, p. 5).

The strategic perspective within which the Lifelong Learning Programme operates is based on EU citizens and residents acquiring eight key competences for lifelong learning, set out in a formal recommendation (European Commission, 2006). One of these competences is social and civic competence, defined as including intercultural competence and behaviors that enable constructive social and democratic participation "particularly in increasingly diverse societies" (p. 16). While this may include antiracism there is no longer a direct reference to racism or antiracism. Nor is there any explicit encouragement to address discrimination or racial injustice. Instead the extended definition includes a number of related but attenuated terms such as: multicultural; prejudices; equality; democracy; human rights; ethnic groups; shared values; community cohesion; diversity; and respect. The omission of a specific requirement to promote antiracism may be construed as political complacency, taking for granted that previous policies have been internalized. In the preparatory period for the World Conference Against Racism and following the war in former Yugoslavia that highlighted gross abuses of human rights and extreme racist violence which are in direct contradiction to European principles and ideals, political measures were taken to reemphasize the antiracist principles of European institutions. Once new social and educational programs had been put in place, antiracism lost political urgency. Far from being mainstreamed, antiracism became peripheral once racism became invisible to political leaders.

Apart from the EU-funded programs, education in Europe is largely funded and therefore controlled by national, regional, or local administrations. The chapter will now examine two case studies, one from England and the other from Sweden. The first case study, from England, demonstrates the role of community activists in pressurizing government into action.

Antiracist policies in England

Following the election of a Labour government in 1997, antiracist campaigners were effective in persuading the new Home Secretary to set up an inquiry into the failure of the police to investigate competently the murder of Stephen Lawrence, a young Black Londoner. The report of the Stephen Lawrence Inquiry (Macpherson, 1999) identified institutional racism as a major cause of injustice. It led senior politicians from a range of political parties to acknowledge institutional racism as a feature of British society in a range of policy areas including not only the police, but the judicial system, government, and the education service. As a result, the government pledged itself to a program to eradicate racism.

In a now classic formulation, the report of the Stephen Lawrence Inquiry defined institutional racism as:

> The collective failure of an organization to provide an appropriate and professional service to people because of their colour, culture, or ethnic origin. It can be detected in processes, attitudes and behaviour which amount to discrimination through unwitting prejudice, ignorance, thoughtlessness and racist stereotyping which disadvantage minority ethnic people.
>
> (Macpherson, 1999, para. 6.34)

The report effectively made clear that institutional racism is endemic in British society.

A statement by the Home Secretary stressed that institutional racism is not confined to the police force and criminal justice system but has a profound impact across society, affecting everyone. Educational institutions are not exempt from the pernicious effects of racism. For a brief period political leaders in Britain took advantage of the apparent consensus achieved by the Stephen Lawrence Inquiry to express robust support for antiracism. The official government response to the Inquiry included "a commitment to building an anti-racist society" (Home Office, 1999, p. 1).

The Stephen Lawrence Inquiry report recommended that schools play a key role in tackling racism. Of the report's 70 recommendations, 3 address education. As well as proposing amendments to the National Curriculum so that schools might more effectively value cultural diversity and prevent racism, the Inquiry recommended that local education authorities (LEAs) and school governors take a lead in ensuring that racist incidents be recorded and reported. It recommended that schools monitor exclusions by ethnicity and that the school inspection agency, Ofsted, be given a lead role in monitoring how schools are addressing and preventing racism. The government's intention was that this formal monitoring and recording would ensure the compliance of schools with this policy.

In response to the Stephen Lawrence Inquiry the government accepted these recommendations in principle and also identified citizenship education as a key means by which schools would address and prevent racism and encourage young people to value cultural diversity (Home Office, 1999). However, the extent of institutional racism within the education service was made manifest by the refusal of the inspection service, Ofsted, to cooperate (Osler & Morrison, 2000, 2002).

Despite the acceptance in 1999 of the need for schools to prevent and address racism through their curriculum and ethos, education ministers have avoided making positive statements on the role of schools in challenging racism in society. Nor has any education minister acknowledged the existence of institutional racism in the education service. In a parallel development to the attenuation of European statements on antiracism, expressions of commitment to challenging racism have been replaced by requirements to monitor the progress of children from ethnic minorities and to promote community cohesion (Osler, 2002, 2007).

Importantly, in response to the findings of the Stephen Lawrence Inquiry, the British government introduced the Race Relations (Amendment) Act 2000 (RRAA), which places a positive duty on public bodies, including schools, to promote race equality. The Act requires public bodies to introduce policies and practices that actively promote race equality as opposed to simply avoiding discrimination. The Commission for Racial Equality (CRE) was given responsibility for implementation of the Act. It issued a statutory code of practice on the duty to promote race equality (CRE, 2002b) requiring public authorities, including schools, to eliminate unlawful racial discrimination, promote equality of opportunity, and promote good relations between people of different racial groups.

The CRE also issued guidance on this duty for schools, covering issues such as admissions policies and the collection and analysis of data by ethnic group (CRE, 2002a). Schools are expected to set targets for improving the performance of underachieving groups. The guidance stresses that the policy must be applied irrespective of the number of ethnic minority children in the school, noting that "racist acts (such as handing out racist literature) can happen in schools with no pupils from ethnic minorities" (CRE, 2002a, p. 7).

The legislation requires schools to prepare a written statement of policy for promoting race equality and stresses the need for staff training in the implications of such a values statement for their teaching and for the procedures and ethos of the school. The opportunity provided by citizenship education to engage pupils in dialogue about the race equality policy and the values of the school is also clearly signaled.

However, a government report on citizenship education published in 2007, citing figures from the CRE, noted that many schools had not complied with their duty under the RRAA to promote race equality. It observed that only two-thirds had taken the initial step of developing a policy on race equality (Department for Education and Skills [DfES], 2007, p. 34). It would appear that the reluctance of the inspection service to fulfill its role as a monitoring body under the RRAA allows considerable numbers of schools to avoid compliance (Osler, 2008).

In spite of this the government imposed an additional statutory duty, deriving from the Education and Inspections Act 2006, that schools are required to promote community cohesion. Although this new duty may support some schools in predominantly White areas in understanding that questions of racial and social justice are not just the concern of multicultural or inner-city settings, this new duty can be effective only if Ofsted, the school inspection agency responsible for monitoring schools' compliance, prioritizes this issue when inspecting schools.

The past record of the inspectorate provides few grounds for optimism that this will be the case (Osler & Morrison, 2000, 2002).

Democracy and antiracism in Sweden

Sweden provides an interesting example of a nation-state that has conceived and implemented a national action plan to combat racism that attempted to mainstream across all areas of government, giving a significant role to education. The National Action Plan to Combat Racism, Xenophobia, Homophobia and Discrimination was approved by the Swedish government in February 2001, emanating from the Ministry of Industry, Employment and Communications. In other words its primary focus was discrimination in the workplace. The 2001 action plan was followed by two further action plans for human rights covering the period to 2009.

The Swedish government asserted that the national action plan against racism was among its highest priorities. The plan presented antiracism as an essential element in protecting and promoting democracy. It was specifically intended to combat acts of violence and harassment of a racist, anti-Semitic, or homophobic nature, noting that "crimes of this nature are also attacks on democratic governance and the fundamental principle of the equal worth of all people" (Government of Sweden, 2001, p. 6).

The 2001 action plan included references to the 1985 Education Act, which placed an obligation on schools to ensure that educational activities are carried out in accordance with fundamental democratic values. A further Education Act of 1998 strengthened and sharpened this commitment so that everyone in the school system must now work actively to combat all forms of bullying and racist behavior. In 2006, a further statutory measure, the Act Prohibiting Discrimination and Other Degrading Treatment of Children and School Students, included the provision that each school activity should have a specific equal treatment plan to promote the equal rights of children and school students irrespective of sex, ethnic or national origin, religion or other belief, sexual orientation, or disability and to prevent and hinder harassment and other degrading treatment (Government of Sweden, 2007).

Swedish school principals are required to draft, implement, monitor, and evaluate an action plan to prevent and combat all forms of offensive treatment of pupils and their staff in schools. However, as in England, there is evidence in the national action plan that not all schools and local authorities have presented "quality reports" that evaluate the implementation of their antiracism action plan (Government of Sweden, 2001, p. 35, para. 4.6.2).

One principle emphasized in Sweden is the role of the school in promoting common values and directly combating those values that are inimical to democracy. Official guidance insists that schools should not be value neutral but should understand that the concept of tolerance does not extend to racist or homophobic behaviors, for example. The guidance asserts that the principle of the equal worth of all people is a democratic value and attitudes that deny this principle – such as Nazism, racism, sexism, and the glorification of violence – should be actively brought out into the open and combated (Government of Sweden, 2001).

From 2007, to be awarded a degree in education, students must, among other things, demonstrate their knowledge of and ability to convey and embed the basic values of society and democracy as well as regulations that prevent and counteract discrimination and other degrading treatment of children and pupils (Government of Sweden, 2007).

The Swedish policy derives from concerns about the resurgence of neo-Nazi activity among young people. This offends the national tradition of commitment to equality and democracy as the standards for public life. The strength of the Swedish approach is that antiracism is an explicit perspective linked to the preservation and promotion of democracy as a way of life. It also directly engages schools in the mission of combating racist ideologies.

Racism and terrorism

Following the 2005 London terrorist bombings, there was widespread public debate about diversity, integration, and multiculturalism in Britain, including the role of education in promoting national identity and citizenship. In 2006 a small task force, chaired by former school principal Keith Ajegbo, was set up by the Qualifications and Curriculum Authority in England (QCA) to review diversity and citizenship in the curriculum. In the context of government concerns about terrorism, the review panel was invited to consider how ethnic, religious, and cultural diversity might be addressed in the school curriculum for England, specifically through the teaching of modern British social and cultural history and citizenship.

In the context of a changing political climate where British government concerns about racism are trumped by its concerns about terrorism, the new focus of the curriculum moved to combating terrorism rather than promoting race equality. The emphasis became "community cohesion" and promoting a unified national identity (Osler, in press).

The resultant report (DfES, 2007) proposed that a new strand on "Identity and diversity: Living together in the UK" be added to the citizenship education framework. While the report gave impetus to teaching about diversity, it did not strengthen the existing curriculum framework. The report refers to antiracism as something that teachers find difficult and that requires a difficult and fundamental shift in practices and procedures. It scarcely mentions democracy and so fails to argue that racism is an anti-democratic force, thus missing an opportunity to develop a citizenship curriculum that promotes race equality (Osler, 2008).

Comparing England and Sweden

These two case studies illustrate different perspectives on antiracism in education. In Sweden antiracism is linked to preserving and promoting democracy, and its policy of openly confronting expressions of racism and xenophobia contrasts sharply with British approaches. In Sweden, democracy is the fundamental value that underpins the constitution and hence also its schools. It follows that the promotion of antiracism as a measure to promote democracy can be presented as a national policy supported by all democratic parties. In Britain there is no explicit national, formally agreed-upon set of basic principles on which to base education policy and practice. Antiracism was, for a time, promoted as a response to the failure of public services to address the institutional racism embedded in multicultural society. However, political recognition of institutional racism was quickly replaced by a new concern for fighting terrorism. Antiracism was quickly dropped from political discourse.

With respect to education, the National Curriculum for England aims to pass on "enduring values," but these are not made explicit, nor are they linked to human rights and democracy. It is hardly surprising, then, that the subject of citizenship in schools in England is perceived as itself open to accusations of bias and that those drawing up guidelines attempt to depoliticize the subject (Pykett, 2007).

Political complacency

The examples in this chapter provide ample evidence of strategic and detailed policy initiatives to address racism. All such policies have an educational dimension. However, evidence from NGOs and from the European monitoring system (ECRI) suggests that policy implementation within education is largely ineffective. An absence of political leadership may be characterized as political complacency. Unless political leaders continue to articulate the importance of antiracism, and emphasize its importance, those who implement policies assume it is no longer a priority and focus on other concerns.

The failure of political representatives in Britain to engage systematically and consistently with the educational task of promoting democracy, human rights, and antiracism through education reflects a degree of political complacency. Across Europe, the curriculum subjects of citizenship, civic education, and social studies can provide a forum in which anti-democratic values and practices can be, in the words of the Swedish policy, "actively brought out into the open and combated" (Government of Sweden, 2001, p. 36). They can equally lack any antiracist dimension.

Only when racism is actively brought out into the open and combated can antiracism genuinely be mainstreamed within education. The mainstreaming of antiracism requires an understanding that antiracism is essential to democracy. It is by linking antiracism to democracy rather than exclusively to multiculturalism and to minorities that it can start to be understood as an essential feature of democratic society. Antiracism is critical to education policy for all rather than a feature designed to ameliorate disadvantage among minority students.

Critical race theory demonstrates how political cultures fail to recognize and address racism. Avoiding the need to address racism is political complacency. For example, in a major speech, the then British Prime Minister denied the realities of institutional racism, claiming that racism had been largely eliminated from sport and offensive remarks and stereotypes from public discourse (Blair, 2006; Osler, 2008). While at European and national levels there is now powerful legislation to protect against discrimination, this has not been accompanied by public education campaigns to explain and justify these measures. There is scope within programs of citizenship education to promote this awareness, but there is little evidence that it is being achieved effectively.

Following significant examples of political leadership and innovative and powerful legislation in the period 1997–2001, the discourse of combating racism moved to a discourse of tolerance, diversity, and respect for human rights. While the promotion of human rights remains a fundamental principle of European institutions, the avoidance of naming and combating racism may be construed as complacency. Many monitoring bodies continue to report that racism has not in fact been eliminated from public life in Europe. The explicit and crude forms of racism, both personal and institutional, highlighted by the Stephen Lawrence Inquiry have been formally addressed by the Race Relations (Amendment) Act 2000. A legal instrument is used to address the contradiction between racism and democratic principles. While legislation is hugely important, real change in behaviors and attitudes requires a shift in culture. Education is widely acknowledged to have a vital role to play in this respect.

References

Blair, T. (2006, December 8). *The duty to integrate: Shared British values.* Speech presented at 10 Downing Street, London. Retrieved October 20, 2008, from http://www.number10.gov.uk/output/Page10563.asp

Commission for Racial Equality (CRE). (2002a). *The duty to promote race equality: A guide for schools (Non-statutory)*. London: Author.

Commission for Racial Equality (CRE). (2002b). *Statutory code of practice on the duty to promote race equality*. London: Author.

Council of Europe. (2000a, October). *Political declaration adopted by ministers of Council of Europe member states at the concluding session of the European Conference Against Racism*. Strasbourg, France: Author.

Council of Europe. (2000b, October). *Project on "education for democratic citizenship."* Resolution adopted by the Council of Europe ministers of education at their 20th session, Cracow, Poland (No. DGIV/EDU/CIT (2000) 40). Strasbourg, France: Author.

Council of Europe. (2002). *R 2002 12: Recommendation by the Committee of Ministers of Education on education for democratic citizenship*. Strasbourg, France: Author.

Council of the European Union. (2004). *Education and citizenship: Report on the broader role of education and its cultural aspects*. Brussels, Belgium: Commission of the European Communities.

Department for Education and Skills (DfES). (2007). *Diversity and citizenship: Curriculum review (Ajegbo Review)*. London: Author.

Diamantopoulou, A. (2001, September). *Address of European commissioner responsible for employment and social affairs* (Speech presented at the Plenary Session of the World Conference Against Racism, Durban, South Africa). Brussels, Belgium: European Commission.

European Anti-Discrimination Council. (2000, July 19). Council Directive 2000/43/EC: Implementing the principle of equal treatment between persons irrespective of racial or ethnic origin. *Official Journal of the European Communities, L180*, 22. Brussels, Belgium: European Commission. Retrieved October 20, 2008, from http://eur-lex.europa.eu/LexUriServ/LexUriServ.do?uri=OJ:L:2000:180:0022:0026:EN:PDF

European Commission. (1998). *Action plan against racism* (COM (1998) 183). Brussels, Belgium: Author.

European Commission. (1999). *Mainstreaming the fight against racism: Commission report on the implementation of the action plan against racism*. Brussels, Belgium: Author.

European Commission. (2000). *SOCRATES: Guidelines for applicants*. Luxembourg: Office for Official Publications of European Communities.

European Commission. (2006). *Recommendation of the European Parliament and the Council on key competences for lifelong learning (2006/962/EC)* (L394, pp. 10–18). Luxembourg: Official Journal of the European Union. Retrieved October 20, 2008, from http://eur-lex.europa.eu/LexUriServ/site/en/oj/2006/l_394/l_39420061230en00100018.pdf

European Commission. (2007a). *Comenius success stories: Europe creates equal opportunities*. Luxembourg: Office for Official Publications of European Communities.

European Commission. (2007b). *Lifelong Learning Programme: General call for proposals 2008–2010 (Part 1 – Strategic priorities)*. Luxembourg: Office of Official Publications of European Communities.

European Commission Against Racism and Intolerance (ECRI). (2007). *10th general policy recommendation on combating racism and racial discrimination in and through school education*. Strasbourg, France: Council of Europe.

European Communities. (1997). *Treaty of Amsterdam, amending the Treaty of the European Union, the treaties establishing the European Communities and certain related Acts*. Luxembourg: Office for Official Publications of European Communities.

European Minority Youth Network. (2006). *E-newsletter June 2006*. Retrieved October 20, 2008, from http://www.network.ngo.lv/en/e_newsletter/2006

Government of Sweden. (2001). *National action plan to combat racism, xenophobia, homophobia and discrimination* (Written Government Communication 2000/01:59). Stockholm, Sweden: Author.

Government of Sweden. (2007). *Sweden's fourth periodic report to the UN Committee on the Rights of the Child 2002–2007*. Stockholm: Author.

Home Office. (1999). *Stephen Lawrence Inquiry: Home secretary's action plan*. London: Home Office.

Ladson-Billings, G. (2004). New directions in multicultural education: Complexities, boundaries and critical race theory. In J. A. Banks & C. A. M. Banks (Eds.), *Handbook of research on multicultural education* (pp. 50–65). San Francisco: Jossey-Bass.

Macpherson, W. (1999). *The Stephen Lawrence Inquiry.* London: The Stationery Office.

Osler, A. (2002). Citizenship education and the strengthening of democracy: Is race on the agenda? In D. Scott & H. Lawson (Eds.), *Citizenship, education and the curriculum* (pp. 63–80). Westport, CT: Greenwood.

Osler, A. (2007). *Faith schools and community cohesion: Observations on community consultations.* London: Runnymede Trust.

Osler, A. (2008). Citizenship education and the Ajegbo Report: Re-imagining a cosmopolitan nation. *London Review of Education, 6*(1), 9–23.

Osler, A. (in press). Patriotism, multiculturalism and belonging: Political discourse and the teaching of history. *Educational Review, 61*(1).

Osler, A., & Morrison, M. (2000). *Inspecting schools for race equality: OFSTED's strengths and weaknesses: A report for the Commission for Racial Equality.* Stoke-on-Trent, UK: Trentham Books.

Osler, A., & Morrison, M. (2002). Can race equality be inspected? Challenges for policy and practice raised by the OFSTED school inspection framework. *British Educational Research Journal, 28*(3), 327–338.

Osler, A., & Starkey, H. (1996). *Teacher education and human rights.* London: Fulton.

Osler, A., & Starkey, H. (1999). Rights, identities and inclusion: European action programmes as political education. *Oxford Review of Education, 25*(1 & 2), 199–216.

Pykett, J. (2007). Making citizens governable? The Crick Report as governmental technology. *Journal of Education Policy, 22*(3), 301–319.

Starkey, H. (2003). The Council of Europe: Defining and defending a European identity. In M. Pittaway (Ed.), *Globalization and Europe* (pp. 73–105). Milton Keynes, UK: Open University.

26
Diversity and citizenship education in Bulgaria

Hristo Kyuchukov
University of Veliko Tarnovo, Bulgaria

Introduction

Bulgaria is one of the Balkan countries, in which different ethnic minorities have lived together for more than seven centuries. Until about 150 years ago, Bulgaria was a part of the Ottoman Empire, in which different nations lived together under Islamic rule. Because varied ethnic groups live in the territory, Bulgaria's population today includes Armenians, Jews, Roma, Turks, Pomaks, Vlahs, Macedonians, and Greeks. However, the majority of the population as well as the official language of the country is Bulgarian. As a result of the democratic changes in the country in 1989, four minority languages are now officially recognized – Armenian, Hebrew, Romani, and Turkish – and children from these groups can receive instruction in their mother tongue four times per week.

According to the 2001 census, the total Bulgarian population is 7,928,901. Out of this number, 6,655,210 people are of Bulgarian ethnic background, 746,664 are Turks, 370,908 are Roma, 10,832 are Armenians, and 1,363 are Jewish. Of the total population, 6,697,158 speak Bulgarian as their first language, 762,516 speak Turkish, 327,882 speak Romani, and 71,084 speak another mother tongue (Statistika, 2002).

The statistical data show that the two big minority groups – the Turks and Roma – constitute approximately 10% and approximately 5%, respectively, of the overall population. However, other sources suggest different figures, particularly for the Roma population. According to some non-governmental organizations, the Roma also make up about 10% of the Bulgarian population, but most of the Roma prefer not to identify themselves as Roma in order to avoid discrimination. However, if one looks at the number of minority children in the school system, one can easily see that the number of Turkish children is high in comparison with the numbers of other minority children at school.

In 1989 the political system in the country changed from communism to democracy. The new Bulgarian government declared that it would follow principles of democracy, human rights, and freedom of speech. The new political system has influenced all levels of political life, including education. During the communist regime, Roma children were forced to go to school, and this is one of the reasons that today there is a high number of teachers, journalists, physicians, and nurses of Roma origin. They continue fighting for the human, educational, and linguistic rights of the Roma.

In 1990 the National Institute of Education (NIE) surveyed teachers, school principals, scientists, and educators in order to gauge public opinion about the new educational law (Valchev, 2004). The new law focused on the education of minority language students and on issues having to do with the decentralization of the school system. Public reaction to the law was very negative, and there were protests in the streets and at schools. People objected especially to the idea of educating minorities in their mother tongues. In contrast, many minorities in the country supported the new law because it offered them the opportunity to study their mother tongue at school, which was forbidden under communist rule.

One year after the collapse of the communist regime, the educational system had not changed at all. A key issue was the decentralization of the educational system. Forty percent of the people questioned in the NIE survey thought that democratization of education would help decentralize the system; 32% connected democratization with the rights and the freedom of the students; and 15% thought that democratization would bring new choices for developing educational structures. Most people who took part in the survey connected the democratization of the educational system with changes inside it, which shows the isolation of the system. Only 2% connected the democratization of education with the impact of public and economic factors on education.

In the early years of transition, most people opposed the political system influencing the educational system, and 60% of those interviewed indicated that the educational system should be apolitical. However, most of those interviewed believed that the educational system in Bulgaria should be centralized but offer more freedom for teachers and students. Most believed that the curriculum should be the same for all schools, with no variation according to the number of minority children enrolled.

During the past seven years, the negative attitudes towards minority children – and particularly towards Roma – have increased. Interviews with teachers of segregated Roma classes show the very negative attitudes of the teachers towards Roma children and towards their right to be taught in Romani at school (Kyuchukov & Ivanova, 2005). In the Bulgarian school system, there are still segregated schools for Roma children, and most of the teachers and parents resist having Roma children in the same classes with Bulgarian children.

During the last 18 years, the educational system has passed through different stages. Today the educational system is very centralized, and the Ministry of Education controls everything, including the curriculum, the textbooks, the evaluation of students' knowledge, and research.

Citizenship education in Bulgaria

Citizenship education and *intercultural education* are new terms for most educators in Bulgaria. Very few researchers are interested in or work in the fields of interculturalism, human rights education, civic education, and citizenship education. There is no clear understanding of these forms of education, and researchers often mix them. Speaking and writing about one type of education, they will often include another.

In Bulgaria most of the teachers and other educators believe that *intercultural education* helps minority students to acquire knowledge about minority languages, cultures, folklores, songs, and traditions, and that this information has to be learned only by minority students. Majority group students are not at all involved with intercultural education. This is what the majority of the people in Bulgaria think. Intercultural education is often understood as giving minorities the right to study their own language, history, and culture. Although many non-governmental organizations (NGOs) provide training in intercultural education, anti-bias education, and human rights education, there are almost no efforts to implement these concepts in Bulgarian schools. Very often open discrimination and racism exist in Bulgarian schools.

Most Bulgarian teachers and other educators believe that *citizenship education* is for all students from every ethnic group. It includes knowledge about the society in which children live, the structure of the government, the human rights of all citizens, and the freedoms individuals enjoy as human beings. Intercultural education is focused on the language, history, and culture of minority groups, while citizenship education emphasizes the human rights of citizens.

The Bulgarian educational system is trying to implement intercultural and citizenship education. However, it has not been very successful. The challenge is that the two notions are very new for educators, and some of the activities included in intercultural and citizenship education carry negative connotations from the period of communism. Terms like *brotherhood, freedom, equality*, and *rights* were overused by the Communist Party as recently as 20 years ago, and older educators connect these terms with the communist regime. However, Bulgaria's membership in the European Union has had a positive effect on the educational system, because now the country must recognize all international documents on human rights education, minority languages education, and intercultural education.

Minority language education

Minority language education is part of citizenship education. The biggest obstacle is resistance to the idea that minority children have the right to study their own language and culture. Many teachers are still opposed to the idea. In many regions with minority populations, teachers make sure that minority children study Bulgarian rather than their mother tongue. There is a particular bias against Turks and their language. Bulgaria spent approximately 500 years as part of the Ottoman Empire (from 1396 until 1878). Even after the democratic changes, the Turkish political party is the third most powerful party in the country. For the last 18 years, the Turkish party (Movement for Rights and Freedom) has actively participated in the political life of the society, and its members hold a significant number of seats in the Bulgarian Parliament. Most Bulgarians think that the Turks are still ruling the country.

Another minority group that faces negative attitudes from the larger society is the Roma. Although the Roma arrived in the Balkans and in Bulgaria some eight centuries ago, they are still neither accepted nor integrated into mainstream society. In Bulgaria there exist ghetto types of settlements where only Roma live and where Bulgarians and Bulgarian authorities do not go. Unfortunately, discrimination towards the Roma is increasing. Although the Ministry of Education allows Roma children to learn in their mother tongue, most Bulgarians think that such instruction prevents students from gaining fluency in Bulgarian and integrating into society.

There are more than 400 segregated Roma schools in Bulgaria, and their quality of education is very low. Approximately seven years ago, the Roma NGOs started a desegregation process by bringing Roma children from ghetto schools to mainstream schools populated mainly with Bulgarian children. The expectations are that the Roma children in mainstream schools will have access to a higher-quality education and consequently will achieve better in school. Studies of Roma children attending segregated and desegregated schools indicate that those who attend desegregated schools do better in reading, writing, and mathematics than Roma children who attend segregated schools (Kyuchukov, 2006).

Figures 26.1 and 26.2 illustrate the academic performance differences between Roma students who attend segregated and desegregated schools. Figure 26.1 shows that Roma children who attend desegregated schools have higher results in reading comprehension tests than those who attend segregated schools. Figure 26.2 examines spelling mistakes. Again, the Roma children in desegregated classes have much better results than Roma children from segregated schools. Roma children from desegregated schools make fewer spelling mistakes than Roma children from segregated schools.

The Bulgarian Ministry of Education has not closed segregated schools yet, and there are several hundred in the whole country. In 2005 the American billionaire George Soros and the World Bank started an initiative (Decade of Roma Inclusion 2005–2015) in nine East European countries with high Roma populations to help governments to develop policies in 4 priority areas covering health, education, housing, and employment. In education, the recommendations were to focus on specific issues: desegregation of segregated Roma schools; Romani language, culture, and history education; and training young Roma to teach the Romani language, intercultural education, citizenship education, sport, art, and music. Unfortunately, over the last three years there have been no developments in these areas, even though the Bulgarian government had agreed to participate in the initiative.

In the 2003–2004 academic year the University of Veliko Tarnovo started Primary School Education and Romani Language, a new program to train young Roma to be primary school teachers and teachers in the Romani language. After five years and positive results among the students in the program, the National Agency for Accreditation and Evaluation of University Programs recommended that the university close the program because "Roma children who learn Romani as their mother tongue will not be integrated into Bulgarian society" (2007, p. 3). This is an example of discrimination against Roma, which the Ministry of Education is taking no steps to end. The University of Veliko Tarnovo does not accept Roma students into

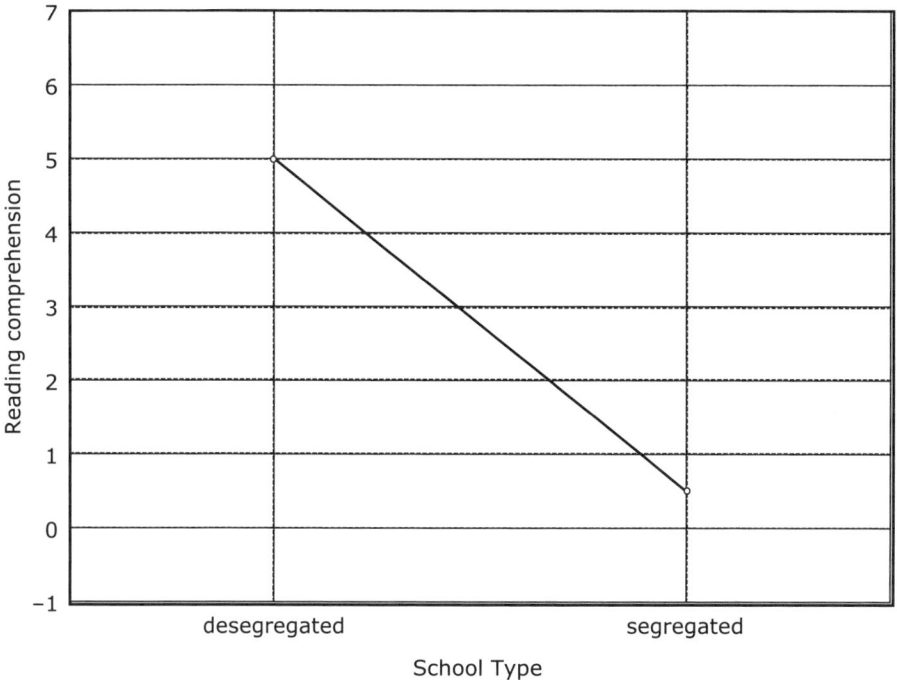

Figure 26.1 Results from Reading Comprehension Test.

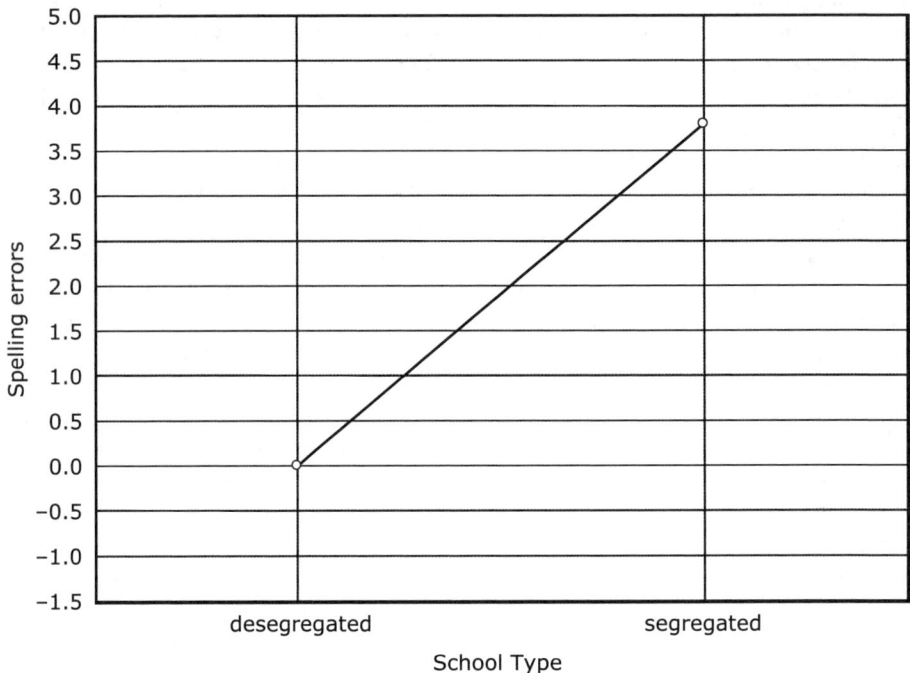

Figure 26.2 Spelling Mistakes Made by Roma Children.

the program because it follows the agency's recommendations. Unfortunately, one hears these types of comments from teachers, from university professors, and from the Bulgarian intelligentsia, none of whom seem aware of the underlying racism which these kinds of comments exemplify.

In Bulgarian society, minorities and minority languages, cultures, and traditions are considered to have little value, and they are not appreciated as rich components of society. Interviews with teachers and school authorities indicate that the bilingualism and biculturalism of minority children are seen not as an advantage but rather as a negative (Kyuchukov & Ivanova, 2005). The status of minority languages – particularly of Turkish and Romani – is very low.

Bulgarian educators do not understand the importance of mother-tongue instruction in the cognitive development of minority children. The research findings about the importance of Romani to the intellectual development of Roma children are not respected (Kyuchukov, 2008a). Most teachers and university professors do not see the connection between mother-tongue instruction and academic success. Fishman (1989) describes the connection between language and culture:

- First, at any given point in time, every language indexes its associated culture more fully than others do;
- Second, at any given point in time, every language symbolizes its associated culture more fully than others do;
- Third, at any given point in time, every language enacts its associated culture more than others do. (p. 54)

The student's home language plays a crucial role in both intercultural and citizenship education. Citizenship education cannot be implemented in a society that ignores and neglects the language and culture of a minority group. The human rights of minorities are often violated because there is no respect for their language and culture. Respect for human rights is part of citizenship education. However, this understanding does not exist in Bulgarian society, even though there are standards for citizenship education developed and accepted by the Ministry of Education. These standards are discussed in the next section.

Standards for citizenship education

Citizenship education in Bulgaria starts in primary classes. There are no standards developed for kindergartens, although there are attempts at citizenship education in kindergarten as well.

Standards for primary school education

The goal of the standards in primary classes is to teach citizenship knowledge and skills in all lessons. There is no such subject as citizenship education. Citizenship education is implemented through all other subjects. The teachers receive some training from different non-governmental organizations such as Diversity – the Balkan Foundation, the Open Society Foundation, the SEGA Foundation, or the three departments for teacher qualifications, which belong to the University of Sofia, Shumen University, and Tracian University in Stara Zagora. However, there is no training for teachers from minority groups. The children in primary classes receive instruction in the following areas:

- knowledge about their personality;
- knowledge about relations with others: friendship, partnership, problem solving;
- knowledge about the family: roles and responsibilities in the family, the social role of the parents, norms in the family;
- knowledge about school: school as an institution, roles and norms in the school;
- knowledge about society: the institutions, the constitution, democratic principles;
- knowledge about the environment: adaptation to the environment, the local institutions and important personalities, how to change the environment, different social groups and the differences in the society;
- knowledge about the world: the Charter of Human Rights, war and peace, the problems faced by children in other parts of the world. (Valchev, 2004)

Together with the above knowledge, children learn skills, including how to do the following:

- take care of themselves, fight for their rights, and make choices;
- assimilate information, use resources, and divide time between tasks;
- communicate with classmates and distinguish a partnership from friendship;
- communicate with adults and with people with disabilities;
- adapt to the school environment, take on responsibilities;
- participate in debates using democratic principles, and communicate with people different from themselves. (Valchev, 2004)

The knowledge and the skills that the children learn are embedded in the subject areas in the primary classes. There are no textbooks or teaching materials for teachers. Teachers who have not received any training in citizenship education cannot teach it to children because they will not be able to familiarize themselves with the material. There are no teachers' manuals or guidelines on the market, there is little research in this area, and there are few scientific educational journals in Bulgaria.

Standards for secondary school education

Citizenship education is also not a separate subject in Bulgarian secondary schools. Knowledge about citizenship is introduced through subjects such as history, geography, biology, and literature. Although education for democratic citizenship is introduced through the subjects mentioned above, in textbooks one rarely finds information about non-Bulgarian ethnic groups. A textbook might include a minority fairytale or a minority song, but this is the extent of the information provided about the diverse groups and cultures in Bulgarian society. Classes in literature, history, and other subjects allow students the opportunity to gain the following:

- knowledge about oneself;
- knowledge about how to contact people and how to communicate;
- knowledge about relations with other people;
- knowledge about one's own family;
- knowledge about school;
- knowledge about small societies;
- knowledge about the country, about law, and about democracy;
- knowledge about the free market. (Valchev, 2004)

Along with knowledge, students have to acquire skills. The skills are interconnected and enable students to understand, analyze, and evaluate information. The first group of skills includes these analytical skills:

- compare similarities and differences in how different groups and cultures fulfill different human needs;
- integrate different opinions on social events;
- identify and use terms such as *chronology, reasoning, change,* and *conflict*;
- develop critical awareness and empathy towards attitudes and values among different people;
- understand public values;
- observe and analyze the social and economic effects on changes in the social environment;
- compare and connect personal changes with the historical context;
- identify and explain examples of stereotypes and prejudices;
- describe the role of institutions in the process of change;
- give examples that show that language, culture, and religion influence the understanding or lack of understanding between people and between social groups;
- identify sources for the rights of citizens;
- collect and analyze information about different social problems in society. (Valchev, 2004)

Knowledge and skills orient young people into the political life of the society and allow them to form attitudes about themselves, positive thinking, active life, cooperation, and solidarity. Citizenship education is developed in primary and secondary classes, but citizenship education in kindergarten is not well developed.

Citizenship education in Bulgarian kindergartens

Fakirska (1998) writes that the aims of citizenship education in kindergarten can be accomplished through various educational activities, such as social life (identity and empathy), living together, and citizenship. Citizenship includes "the attitude towards the mother tongue" (Kyuchukov, 2008b, p. 5). In 1991 Bulgaria ratified the International Convention on the Rights of the Child. In 2000 the Bulgarian government approved a new law for the protection of children (Zakon, 2000). In both documents, it is stated that all children have a right to education in their mother tongue, regardless of their ethnic background, religion, and race. Although the Bulgarian educational law allows students whose mother tongue is not Bulgarian to learn their mother tongue in addition to the obligatory learning of Bulgarian, in kindergartens there are no lessons in a language other than Bulgarian.

Valchev (2004) writes that the goal of contemporary citizenship education is to acquire "the official language of the country – reading, writing, grammar and communicative abilities as well as learning of foreign languages" (2004, p. 5). However, the author does not say anything about the rights of minority children to learn their mother tongues at school or in kindergartens. Many United Nations (UN) documents promote the rights of minorities to be educated in their mother tongue, to develop their own culture, and to practice their religious beliefs (for example, the UN Convention for the Protection of Children's Rights). However, in Bulgaria the international documents ratified by the government are neither widely known nor respected, which results in many violations of the educational human rights of language minority students. These violations are very clear at the kindergarten and preschool levels, where mother-tongue instruction does not exist.

Mother-tongue education at the kindergarten level has two aspects: the *juridical aspect* and the *scientific aspect*. The juridical aspect includes conformance to all international documents signed by the Bulgarian government. Very often the local Bulgarian laws violate the human rights and citizenship rights of students. Not providing minority students with needed facilities to learn their mother tongue is a violation of many international documents. Mother-tongue education for minority students is important for majority students, because it teaches them to respect the languages and cultures of those who are different, which is an important part of citizenship education. Unfortunately, in the Bulgarian educational system this is not a priority.

The scientific aspect means respecting scientific findings. Research in Bulgaria and abroad shows the importance of minority languages in the cognitive development of minority children (Kyuchukov, 2008a). In Bulgaria this research is neither known nor respected. Research findings in Bulgaria indicate that, if the mother tongue of a child is developed, the child will find it much easier to learn Bulgarian as a second language (Kyuchukov, 1997). Taking into consideration the scientific findings, new methods and approaches are needed to teach the mother tongue of the children and the official language of the country in bilingual or multilingual settings. This definitely is a part of the humanistic education that constitutes citizenship and intercultural education.

Conclusions

Citizenship education is one of the most important components in contemporary educational systems around the world. Through citizenship education, students learn to respect each other's rights, to live together, and to value the diversity in society. Citizenship education introduces symbols that are important for a particular country, but it also helps students to learn about human values, the beauty of different cultures, and, most importantly, how to respect other cultures.

In the Bulgarian educational system, citizenship education is still very new and undeveloped. There has been some early success in primary and secondary schools, but in kindergarten much work is required. The educational system is very ethnocentric, and the diversity in mainstream classrooms is not respected as a rich part of society. On the contrary, minorities are seen as people who create problems in society. Bulgarian educators view citizenship education very narrowly – as a way to learn the symbols of the country and the documents important for the majority. There is no emphasis placed on knowledge about minorities, their human rights, and how diverse peoples can live together as citizens of one nation.

Efforts to desegregate Roma students show very positive results. However, the Bulgarian ministry has taken no action toward the desegregation of Roma students from a pilot project to government policy. The Roma children in desegregated classes are well integrated and show high levels of academic success, but segregated Roma schools still exist. Segregated schools are one of the obstacles to establishing intercultural dialogue in the Bulgarian educational system, and are subsequently an obstacle to citizenship education. The Bulgarian educational system still has a long way to go in order to learn how to translate the polite words in the papers and documents into reality. Much work must also be done in Bulgaria to create schools in which all minority children in the country will feel respected for their own cultures and languages and not feel ashamed that they belong to a different ethnic group and culture.

References

Fakirska, J. (1998). Grazhdanskoto obrazovanie v detskata gradina [Citizenship education in kindergarten]. In P. Balkanski & Z. Zahariev (Eds.), *Vavedenie v grazhdanskoto obrazovanie* [Introduction to citizenship education] (pp. 159–164). Sofia, Bulgaria: Laska.

Fishman, J. A. (1989). *Language and ethnicity in minority sociolinguistic perspective.* Clevedon, UK: Multilingual Matters.

Kyuchukov, H. (1997). *Psiholingvistichni aspekti na ranniya bilingvizam* [Psycholinguistic aspects of early bilingualism]. Sofia, Bulgaria: Prohazka & Chakarmazov.

Kyuchukov, H. (2006). *Desegregation of Roma schools in Bulgaria.* Sofia, Bulgaria: SEGA.

Kyuchukov, H. (2008a). *Kognitivni aspekti na obuchenieto po romski ezik* [Cognitive aspects of teaching the Romani language]. Veliko Tarnovo, Bulgaria: Faber.

Kyuchukov, H. (2008b). Myastoto na maychiniya ezik v grazhdanskoto obrazovanie v savremennata detska gradina [The place of the mother tongue in citizenship education in contemporary kindergarten]. *Dom, dete, detska gradina* [Home, child, kindergarten], *12*, 4–9.

Kyuchukov, H., & Ivanova, A. (2005). Otnoshenieto na uchitelite kam obrazovanieto na romskite deca [The attitudes of the teachers towards Roma children]. In H. Kyuchukov (Ed.), *Desegregaciya ili interkulturna integraciya* [Desegregation or intercultural education] (pp. 178–189). Veliko Tarnovo, Bulgaria: Universitetsko Izdatelstvo.

National Agency for Accreditation and Evaluation of University Programs. (2007, April). *Recommendations.* Paper presented to the University of Veliko Tarnovo, Veliko Tarnovo, Bulgaria.

Statistika. (2002). *Statistika na Republika Bulgaria* [Statistics of the Republic of Bulgaria]. Sofia, Bulgaria: National Statistical Institute.

Valchev, R. (2004). *Obrazovatelni iziskvaniya, ocenyavane i grazhdansko obrazovanie* [Educational standards, evaluation and citizenship education]. Sofia, Bulgaria: Centar "Otvoreno Obrazovanie."

World Bank. (2005). *Decade of Roma inclusion 2005–2015*. Sofia, Bulgaria: Government of Romania. Retrieved October 18, 2008, from http://www.romadecade.org/

Zakon. (2000). *Zakon za zakrila na deteto* [Law for protection of the child]. Sofia, Bulgaria: Narodno Sabranie.

Part 7
Language, culture, identity, and education

27

Language, culture, and identity across nations

Suzanne Romaine
Merton College, University of Oxford, UK

Language, culture, and identity

People hold strong beliefs concerning their language, culture, and identity. Although the term *identity* derives from the Latin *idem* ("same"), identity is primarily about constructing differences between ourselves and others. Indeed, it can be seen as the driving force of evolution. For most of human history people lived in small communities quite distinct from their neighbors. Language played a key role in constructing and maintaining distinctive human identities by serving an important boundary-marking function between groups. Someone who does not speak our language is different. The ancient Greeks called those who could not speak Greek properly "barbarians." The more distinct a language or variety is from some other, the more effectively it can serve as an identity marker. Even communities sharing what is ostensibly the "same" language will tend to develop distinctive varieties of it as a way of distinguishing themselves from their neighbors. Thus, the English spoken in England will be different from that spoken in the United States, New Zealand, and South Africa, just as within each country there will be locally distinct varieties tied to specific regions and subcultures.

Languages thus stand in part–whole symbolic relationships with their cultures and come to represent particular ethnic, cultural, and/or national groups that speak them. In this sense they resemble flags, which are emblematic of national identities. Nevertheless, the notion that "language-equals-culture equals identity" is too simple to account for the intricate linkages between languages and cultural identities, especially in view of widespread multilingualism. The once prevailing idea of identities, cultures, and languages as essential, primordial, and natural attributes given from birth and transmitted in stable and unchanging form throughout the lifespan has given way to a different view in which they are seen as constructed, dynamic, and hybrid. As constructed categories, they are subject to change in a never ending process of symbolic boundary construction and reconstruction.

Nation-states, majorities, and minorities

With roughly 6,900 languages in the world, but only about 200 nation-states, there are more than 30 times as many languages as there are countries. Bilingualism or multilingualism is therefore present in practically every nation in the world, whether officially recognized or not (Romaine, 1995). The linguistic heterogeneity of many countries reflects the arbitrariness of shifting political boundaries encapsulating distinct ethnic groups or nationalities with their own languages, cultures, and identities. Language occupies a contested position when nations cannot ground their basis for a common identity on language, religion, or culture. A common national language has been generally seen as inseparably bound to the national culture, a sign of loyalty to the nation itself, and essential for modernization and economic progress. During the late 18th and early 19th centuries new national identities along with the languages and cultures linked to them were created out of the politics of nation building, in which so-called national cultures are in effect the cultures of dominant ethnic groups. The Malaysian constitution (1957), for instance, fuses into one a link between Malay ethnic identity, Malay culture and language, and Islam when it defines a Malay as "a person who professes the religion of Islam, habitually speaks the Malay language, and conforms to Malay custom" (art. 160).

The greatest threat to the languages, cultures, and identities of minority communities is the notion of the nation-state with its official standard language. As the bedrock of the current political world order, the nation-state is the most critical unit of analysis because it is policies pursued within national boundaries that give some languages (and their speakers) the status of majority and others that of minority. Mandarin Chinese with some 900 million speakers is spoken by more people than any other language in the world. Although in China it has the status of majority language, in many other countries it is a minority language, for example Malaysia, where it is spoken by about 25% of the population. Some languages, such as the signed languages used among deaf people, are minority languages in all contexts.

Groups do not normally give up their languages, cultures, or identities willingly, but continue to transmit them, albeit in changed form over time. Not coincidentally, the vast majority of today's threatened languages and cultures are found among socially and politically marginalized and/or subordinated national and ethnic minority groups. Estimates of the number of such groups range from 5,000 to 8,000 and include among them the world's indigenous peoples, who constitute about 4% of the world population but speak up to 60% of its languages (Nettle & Romaine, 2000).

Virtually all nation-states regardless of their political ideology have persecuted minorities in the past, and some continue to do so today. Even if not actively seeking the extermination of minorities, they pursue policies aimed at assimilating them into the dominant culture and language. Most contemporary conflicts in the world are within rather than between states, with more than 80% between nation-states and minority peoples (Clay, 1990). Nevertheless, many ethnic or minority conflicts have a significant international or transnational component because a minority community may be split across one or more countries (e.g. Kurds in Turkey, Iraq, Iran, Armenia, and Syria, or Saami in Russia, Finland, Sweden, and Norway), or because members of the minority community in one state may form part of the majority community in a neighboring one (e.g. Tamils in Sri Lanka, Malays in Singapore). Many regional and immigrant minority languages actually have larger numbers of speakers than the official state languages.

The borders of most nations are often linguistically diverse areas. For various political and historical reasons bilinguals may be concentrated in particular geographic areas constituting regions where use of a language other than the state language is normal. Italy's northeastern corner shares an eastern border with Slovenia and a northern one with Austria. A substantial population speaks either Slovenian, as well as Friulian (more closely related to Provençal than standard Italian), or German. The municipality of Sauris is in effect a German linguistic island severed from the Austrian empire and incorporated into the Italian state. Friulian is one of the largest minority languages of Italy, with over half a million speakers in the Friuli-Venezia Giulia region.

While Finland was part of Sweden, Finnish was a minority language both demographically and functionally. Any Finn wanting to get ahead socio-economically needed to learn Swedish. The linguistic fate of Finnish changed dramatically, however, after independence, when Finnish became the national language. For Swedes in Finland, the result was demotion to minority status. Meanwhile, in the Torne valley retained by Sweden, Finnish speakers ended up on the "wrong" side of the border (as did many Mexicans when the United States annexed Texas in 1846).

The disappearance of a minority language and its related culture and identity almost always forms part of a wider process of social, cultural, and political displacement. Languages of colonial conquest and dominant languages of nation-states penetrate into, transform, and undermine a minority community's ability to maintain its language, culture, and identity in various ways. Usually the dominant language prevails in all areas of official life (e.g. in government, schools, and media), necessitating bilingualism on the part of the minority. Eventually, the dominant language tends to invade the inner spheres of the subordinate language, so that its domains of use become even more restricted. The prestige of the dominant language and its predominance in public institutions lead the community to devalue their own language, culture, and identity as part of a process of symbolic domination.

Global distribution of linguistic diversity and changing patterns of multilingualism

Despite the fact that bilingualism and multilingualism are unremarkable and normal realities of everyday life for most of the world owing to the near universal presence of more than one language in every country, the global distribution of linguistic diversity is strikingly skewed. Papua New Guinea alone contains 13.2% of the world's languages, but only 0.1% of the world's population and 0.4% of the world's land area. The overall ratio of languages to people is about 1 to 5,000. If this ratio existed in the United States, there would be 50,000 languages spoken there (Nettle & Romaine, 2000). Around 80% (N = 5,542) of the world's 6,912 languages are found in just 20 nation-states, among them some of the poorest countries in the world (Gordon, 2005). They include Papua New Guinea (820), Indonesia (742), Nigeria (516), India (427), the United States (311), Mexico (297), Cameroon (280), Australia (275), China (241), the Democratic Republic of Congo (216), Brazil (200), the Philippines (180), Malaysia (147), Canada (145), Sudan (134), Russia (129), Tanzania (129), Nepal (125), Vanuatu (115), and Myanmar (113).

Considerable diversity is also found in some of the most highly developed, industrialized nations. Canada and the United States account for 456 languages or 6.5% of the world's linguistic diversity. Adding Australia with its 275 languages as the other large predominantly Anglophone nation in the list yields a total of 731 languages, amounting to 10.5% of the world's linguistic diversity (Gordon, 2005). The presence of many languages other than English in the United States and Australia often comes as a surprise, because these countries have generally operated and seen themselves as largely monolingual English nations, despite the presence of a considerable number of indigenous and (im)migrant communities using other languages.

The changing character of multilingualism in the world today is manifest in at least three trends. The first is the spread of global languages over the last few centuries. Nine languages have more than 100 million speakers and are spoken by just over 41% of the world's population. Today an Indo-European language (either English, French, Spanish, or Portuguese) is the dominant language and culture in every country in North, Central, and South America (Nettle & Romaine, 2000).

Concomitant with the diffusion of world languages is a second significant trend, namely, increasing bilingualism in a metropolitan language, particularly English, which has become the language of the "global village." No one knows exactly how many people speak English as a first or second language, but some estimates for the former group are 375 million; for the latter, some figures run as high as 1.5 billion (roughly a quarter of the world's population) (Graddol, 1997). As the world's economy has shifted from an industrial base to one based on information, the globalizing new world order is founded on communications technology facilitating linkage of national economies. The role of language and communication is destined to become more critical than ever before. Because the technology facilitating these developments originated largely in the English-speaking world, English is at the leading edge of global scientific and economic development. As much as 80% of the information stored in the world's computers is in English, and 90% of the world's computers connected to the Internet are in English-speaking countries. English is now the most widely used language in publication, with over 28% of the world's books printed in English and over 60 countries publishing books in English. English is also the language of international air traffic control and the basis for Seaspeak used in international maritime communication. Up to 85% of international organizations use English as one of their working languages, among them the United Nations and its subsidiary organs. In this arena French is the only real rival to English, but it has been progressively losing ground. Virtually all major corporations advertise their products in English. English is also the language of international popular culture for today's youth (Romaine, 2006a).

Most people in northern Europe are becoming bilingual in English at an increasingly earlier age through schooling. There will soon be few monolinguals among their school-age populations. English has rapidly become the first preferred foreign language studied at school in the European Union, with nearly 90% of students studying it. Many countries have changed their educational practices regarding the teaching of foreign languages as a response to increasing demand for English. In Iceland, for instance, English has replaced Danish as the first foreign language taught in compulsory education (i.e. primary and lower secondary) in the new national curriculum. Danish is still taught as a compulsory second language to maintain and strengthen ties and cooperation with other Nordic countries. English instruction begins at age 10 (the 5th year of schooling) and is taught for 6 years, while Danish begins at age 12 and is taught for 4 years. During the last 2 years of lower secondary schooling students typically have the option of learning a third foreign language, usually German, but Spanish and French in some cases. In other parts of the world English has rapidly replaced other languages once widely taught as second languages.

Meanwhile, a third trend is the intensification of migration in various positive and negative ways, with more people on the move for various reasons, ranging from those who are refugees from oppressive regimes to those (usually the most privileged) who move for convenience or personal preference. This has brought about increasing linguistic and cultural diversity to much of Europe as well as the United States and other parts of the globe, along with challenges to traditional linkages between languages and identities. Portugal, often cited as an example of a monolingual nation, now has large numbers of immigrants from its former colonies (Angola, Mozambique, Guinea Bissau, Cape Verde, São Tomé and Principe, East Timor, and Brazil).

There may be as many as a quarter of a million "new" immigrants (many of them illegal) from eastern Europe, especially Ukraine and Russia. Immigrants now make up about 5% of the population, one of the highest proportions in the European Union. Iceland too, once regarded as a monolingual nation, has witnessed an influx of immigrants from Asia, especially since the 1990s, in addition to those from European countries. Although only around 3% of the population is non-Icelandic in origin, as many as 40 different languages may be spoken in addition to Icelandic.

By the end of the 20th century, one-third of the urban population in Europe under the age of 35 was composed of ethnic minorities owing to widespread migration in the 1950s and 1960s, when Europe experienced an acute labor shortage. As a result of this migration, about 10% of the school-age population in Europe had a culture and language different from those of the majority of the country in which they resided (Extra & Gorter, 2007). London has become an increasingly diverse city, with as many as 200 languages spoken in its schools as a result of the influx of overseas migrants from the Caribbean and Asia. Similarly, Melbourne, once primarily a monolingual city, now has the largest concentration of Greek speakers in the world.

Over the course of the 20th century in the US the proportion of non-White persons increased from 1 in 8 to 1 in 4. The White population grew more slowly than any other group in the latter half of the 20th century, while from 1980 to 2000 the Hispanic population in the US doubled (Hobbs & Stoops, 2002). The U.S. Census 2000 revealed that persons claiming Hispanic or Latino origin have replaced African Americans as the largest minority group. A third of California's population belong to this minority, and nearly 40% of its population claims to speak a language other than English at home (Hobbs & Stoops, 2002). The United States is now the fifth largest Hispanic country in the world. Cities such as Miami and Los Angeles are now predominantly Hispanophone, and Los Angeles has been Latinized by continuing immigration from Mexico. In three states, California, New Mexico, and Hawai'i, as well as the District of Columbia, minority populations constitute the majority.

Why cultural identities linked to languages matter

Despite the lack of an intrinsic or inevitable one-to-one link between language and identity, or between language and culture, the connections cannot be dismissed as unimportant. Racial, ethnic, and religious identities are bound up with cultural and linguistic identities in exceedingly powerful ways. They engender a potent shared sense of belonging that people are willing to die to defend. In 1980 Plaid Cymru leader Gwynfor Evans vowed to fast to death when Margaret Thatcher's newly elected Conservative government reversed course on its promise to establish a Welsh television channel. In so far as components of cultural identities may become rallying points for furthering the interests (political or otherwise) of a group of people, the very notion of identity has sometimes taken on negative connotations and been referred to as "identity politics." When a group feels threatened, it may try to resist by emphasizing a number of emblematic culture traits (among them language, but also religion, race, and ethnicity) in order to justify its distinctiveness and political claims within the nation-state to which it belongs.

Although language is only one of many features (e.g. dress, behavior patterns, race, religion, nationality, occupation, etc.) that may mark identity, either individually or collectively, many regard languages as a benchmark for cultural diversity because virtually every major aspect of human culture ranging from kinship classification to religion is dependent on language for its transmission. Thus, people feel that an important part of their traditional culture and identity is also lost when that language disappears. Moreover, once lost, a language is far less easily retrievable than other identity markers that might stand in its stead. René Lévesque (1968), former leader of the Parti Québécois and Quebec prime minister, underlined the centrality of French to Québécois identity when he said:

> Being ourselves is essentially a matter of keeping and developing a personality that has survived for three and a half centuries. At the core of this personality is the fact that we speak French. . . . To be unable to live as ourselves, as we should live, in our own language and according to our own ways, would be like living without a heart. (p. 14)

Sir James Henare expressed similar feelings about Maori when he said, "Ko te reo te mauri o te mana Māori" (The language is the essence of Maori identity) (Robust, 2002). Although distinct cultural and ethnic identities can survive language shift, a Québécois or Maori identity expressed through English is not the same as one articulated through French or Maori. To say they are different does not imply that one is necessarily better than the other. It does mean, however, that to argue for the preservation of French in Quebec or Maori in New Zealand is to argue for a people's right to choose the language in which they want to express their cultural identity.

From time to time people may feel conflicting pulls on their attachments to different identities that may be in real or imagined conflict. Circumstances may require people to choose or prioritize one identity, for example nationality, race, religion, gender, and so on over another, or deny choice altogether. The apartheid regime in South Africa classified people primarily into official racial categories of White, Colored, and Black, with the non-White population excluded from citizenship. These classifications determined the language of schooling, residence, access to employment, and so on. In Singapore, a person's mother tongue is automatically defined as identical with the person's race (Chinese, Malay, or Indian), regardless of the language actually spoken. A child's mother tongue is automatically determined by the father's race. Hence, a child born to a Hokkien-speaking father and a Malay-speaking mother will be classified officially as Chinese and have Mandarin Chinese as its mother tongue.

As much as globalization appears to be leading inexorably to homogenization of cultures, at the same time it is creating hybridization. In today's global village we all have overlapping and intersecting identities. Nevertheless, many are still trapped in the mistaken idea that all people have only a single identity—that Kenyans are only Kenyans, Muslims only Muslims, and so on. The presumption that people can be uniquely classified on the basis of religion, culture, or language is a major source of conflict in contemporary society. Sen (2006) observes that "many of the conflicts and barbarities in the world are sustained through the illusion of a unique and choiceless identity" (p. xv). While sharing an identity can be a source of richness and warmth, identity can also kill when it is perceived in terms of a strong and inclusive sense of belonging to only one group. Genocide in Rwanda was premised on classifying people only as Hutus or Tutsis while forgetting their shared identities as Rwandan citizens and Africans, as well as their common humanity. In similar fashion, Albanians and Bosnian Muslims were accorded no place in extreme nationalist visions of an Orthodox Christian "Greater Serbia," where the ethnic identity of a single group became a defining characteristic of nationality. The breakup of established identities, re-emergence and reconstitution of old identities, and creation of new ones all provide ample evidence that identity matters in today's globalizing world. Nevertheless, the varied cultural and linguistic contexts existing in contemporary societies around the globe pose complex challenges for policy makers.

Need for multilingual and multicultural policy and planning

The pervasive presence of some degree of multilingualism indicates a universal need for multilingual and multicultural policy and planning to ensure that members of different language groups within nations have access to and can participate in national affairs without discrimination. Education is among the most critical sites for national planning because schools represent the primary societal institution through which legitimation for the state's dominant language is sought. Formal education is often the first point of contact children have with groups outside their own community and with the national language. Speakers of languages other than the official and national languages recognized for instructional purposes are often at a disadvantage and may come from at-risk populations such as new immigrants, refugees, and so on. Poor school achievement of minority group children due to discontinuities between home and school language is well documented in virtually all nations (Corson, 1990; Tollefson, 1995). Moreover, a minority language that is not taught tends to decline (Allardt, 1979).

Not too long ago minority children in countries like Australia, the United States, Canada, Britain, and Scandinavia were subject to physical violence in school for speaking their home language. Often the education of these children entailed removing them from their parents and their own cultural group. In Canada, the federal government and churches entered into a formal partnership to run a residential school system for Indian and Inuit children as part of the government's assimilation policy. Education in such church-run, government-funded residential schools was supposed to prepare children for life in White society by denying them their native identities, cultures, and languages. The residential school system was in operation for nearly 150 years. In some parts of Canada as many as five generations of children attended, with some communities depopulated of children between the ages of 5 and 20. Such education produced a collective sense of shame about native languages, cultures, and identities.

The varied cultural and linguistic contexts existing in contemporary societies around the globe clearly pose many complex challenges for policy makers. Given the centrality of language to education, policies concerning choice of language(s) as the medium of instruction are essential, even if the need is not always overtly acknowledged. In 2003 the United Nations Educational, Scientific and Cultural Organization (UNESCO) published a new position paper on languages and education in response to its recognition of education as an important tool and as a reflection of cultural diversity in a rapidly changing world. It included a number of recommendations in line with the changing global context for education in a multilingual world, among them the need to preserve the languages and the ethnic identities of small language groups, and the role of English as the lingua franca and the language of instruction in countries where English is not a native language.

Recognizing that issues of identity, culture, power, and nationhood are linked closely to the use of specific languages in the classroom, UNESCO (2003) strongly reaffirmed the value of mother tongues in line with its earlier expert report on the use of vernacular languages in education (UNESCO, 1953). At the same time, however, it stressed the importance of balancing the need for local languages in learning and access to global languages through education. As far as mother tongue teaching is concerned, UNESCO advises that it should cover teaching both of and through this language for as long as possible. Learning through a language other than one's own presents a double burden. Not only must new knowledge be mastered, but another language as well.

Recognition of official and national languages

Many countries codify language policies of one sort or another in their constitutions, laws, or other official documents. The constitutions of 163 countries contain some mention of language; 22 countries either have no constitutions or their constitutions contain no provisions relating to language (UNESCO, 1994–2003). Perhaps the most common provision is declaring a language or languages as official or co-official, or as national language(s). Nevertheless, fewer than 4% of the world's languages have any kind of official status in the nations where they are spoken. The fact that most languages are not recognized officially, restricted to local community and domestic functions, and not written but spoken by very small groups of people reflects the balance of power in the global linguistic marketplace. Around 100 constitutions specify one or more official or national languages with special privileges of use. Seventy-eight mention a single official or national language. The constitution of France says that "the language of the Republic shall be French" (1958, art. 2).

More than 20 countries have more than one official language. India, for instance, has 19, and South Africa has 11. India's constitution (1950) codifies a number of provisions protecting linguistic minorities, including the right to establish and administer educational institutions of their choice, and freedom from discrimination on language grounds. In addition to listing Hindi as the official language, it grants rights to regional state languages, specifies which languages can be used for communication between states, and between states and the national government. Every state is supposed to try to provide adequate facilities for instruction in the mother tongue at primary level to minority language children, and there is a provision establishing a special officer for linguistic minorities. A state or district is recognized as bilingual wherever a language is spoken by 30% or more of the population; the relevant minority language is placed on the same footing as the regional language for use by public authorities.

In practice, no country gives official status to every language spoken within its territory. Where language policies exist, they inevitably privilege a limited set of languages. Even where explicit policies do not exist, governments have to operate in some language(s). This means that policy is implicit even if no specific mention is made of language. The term *de facto* ("by fact") is used for policies that operate covertly, implicitly, without necessarily having any official written support in legal documents. *De jure* ("by law") policies are overt, explicit, officially and legally defined. Probably most majority languages dominate in many domains where they have only de facto and no legal status. English is the dominant de facto or official language in over 70 countries. French has official or co-official status in 29 countries. The majority of countries in the world actually operate either de facto or de jure as monolingual in recognizing only one language for use in education. This does not always mean that no other languages are used in education, but rather that they do not have official status.

This is why an examination of practice is vital. The United States is a classic example of a multilingual country with no official language policy, despite the English-only movement seeking a constitutional basis for recognizing English as sole official language. The idea that linguistic rights need protection has never been part of American culture, and so they have not been seen as central to U.S. courts unless allied with more fundamental rights such as educational equity, and so on (Schiffman, 1996). In India Hindi still has not replaced English as sole official language as the framers of the Indian constitution intended. Article 6 of the Italian constitution (1948) states that the republic protects linguistic minorities by special laws, but discrepancies between policy and practice leave many minorities with no special provisions. Despite the fact that Sardinia is an autonomous region governed by special statutes, Sardinian (spoken by approximately 1 million people) has no official recognition. Sardinian may be used in pre-primary schools if needed for communicating with children. At primary and secondary levels, however, it has recently been introduced as a separate subject on an experimental basis. By contrast, Trentino/Alto Adige (Südtirol), also governed by special statute, gives equal status to German and Italian, and guarantees the right to mother tongue education (from nursery to higher level) for German speakers. Italian is taught as a second language starting from the second year of the elementary cycle. Many other nations are similar to Italy in their incorporation of a number of groups with distinct languages and cultures, and their recognition of only one or a few languages for use within the education system and for other societal institutions.

When a multilingual country uses one or more languages exclusively in public schools, and in the administration of government services and activities, it is making a distinction based on language. In showing a preference for some language(s), whether designated as official or national or not, the state's decision benefits those for whom the chosen language(s) is a primary language, to the detriment or disadvantage of others who either have no or lower proficiency and are denied the benefit or privilege of using their own primary language. The only cases where immigrant and indigenous minorities receive equal treatment are in those countries where neither group is given any special status (Kymlicka & Patten, 2003).

Policies may of course change over time in line with changing circumstances. While in some nations decolonization entailed rejecting colonial languages, globalization has intensified and renewed the need for them. As in India, where shifting from the colonizers' language to the local vernacular(s) was seen as fundamental for building a new nation out of a former colony, Tanzania, Malaysia, and Indonesia pursued supportive polices for their designated national languages (Kiswahili, Malay, and Indonesian, respectively). In 2003, however, the Malaysian government implemented a switch from Malay to English as the medium of instruction in science and mathematics after having spent four decades putting considerable resources into modernizing Malay. Similar shifts toward reinstating colonial languages have affected other countries too. Madagascar, for example, succeeded in having Malagasy as a language of instruction for many years, but in 1988 the government reintroduced French medium education in secondary schools, supported by development aid from France in the form of textbooks. These examples show how difficult it is to break out of the self-reinforcing cycle of increasing intellectual dependency whereby languages such as Hindi and Kiswahili do not develop as languages of science because they are not being used and the argument that they cannot be used because they are not developed (Romaine, 2006b). Many other countries under former colonial rule such as Côte d'Ivoire designated the colonial language as their sole official language for education and government.

In addition, these cases reveal how, in privileging the languages of dominant ethnic groups in multiethnic nations, newly independent countries have followed the same path as in European nation building. Although Kiswahili was officially designated the national language (along with English) when Tanzania became independent in 1962, its spread was strengthened at the expense of the more than 100 indigenous languages spoken by the majority of rural poor. Majority populations have typically shown little enthusiasm for the languages of immigrant minorities either, even when the language concerned is a world language such as Spanish (as in the US) or Arabic (the language of many immigrants in France and the Netherlands). This is due to status differences between the majority and minority populations. Distinctive food, dress, song, and so on are often accepted and allowed to be part of the mainstream, but language much less so. One reason for the general reluctance to view policies of official bilingualism as rights rather than as pragmatic accommodations is that public institutions in the most powerful Western nations (the UK, the US, France, and Germany) have been monolingual for a century or more with no significant movement towards challenging the hegemonic position of the majority language (Kymlicka & Patten, 2003, p. 7). Immigrants have usually assimilated rapidly, and none of these countries has faced the linguistic challenges of Belgium, Spain, Canada, or Switzerland.

In the latter two countries language policy has followed a "personality" or "territory" principle. In Switzerland territorial unilingualism exists under federal multilingualism in the country's four officially declared national languages: German, French, Italian, and Romantsch. Of the 26 cantons, 22 are officially monolingual, with one of the four languages functioning as the dominant language in education. English is much preferred over the other official languages as a second language learned at school. Canada, however, follows the personality principle for its two official languages, French and English, where sufficient numbers warrant. Quebec gives a universal right to French education, but the right to English education is limited to those with at least one parent educated in English.

Linguistic human rights and weak linkages between language policy and planning

Despite evidence of growing rather than decreasing diversity in many education systems, in some countries the trend has been not towards recognition of the need for policy and planning, but towards the imposition of ever more centralized provision and greater intolerance of diversity. There are important differences between "tolerance rights" and "promotion rights." Most democracies provide for freedom from government interference in private language use, but many are reluctant to make legal provision for promotion of languages in the public sector other than the dominant language(s). Some still regard the concept of language rights as "regressive" because they are seen as encouraging the persistence of ethnic differences leading to conflict and divided loyalties. It is an unresolved question whether and when language shift can be required or expected in deliberative democracies. Likewise, one can question whether it is legitimate for the state to insist that all children be schooled in the majority language of the state as the sole or main medium of instruction. National ethnic minorities have many more internationally and nationally coded rights than immigrants.

The linguistic human rights movement has focused on securing a universal right to mother tongue primary education in line with UNESCO's (1953) much cited axiom "that the best medium for teaching is the mother tongue of the pupil" (p. 6). Nevertheless, this declaration did not lead to any widespread adoption and development of vernacular languages as media of education. Despite some encouraging developments in some countries, in most parts of the world schooling is still virtually synonymous with learning a second language. Skutnabb-Kangas (2000) maintains that education for minorities in many parts of the world still operates in ways that contradict best practices, with fewer than 10% of the world's languages being used in education.

UNESCO's (2003) position paper on education in a multilingual world also endorsed many of the recommendations that have emerged from the debate about linguistic human rights, which has become an important topic in the context of the education of linguistic minorities (de Varennes, 1996; Paulston, 1997; Skutnabb-Kangas, 2000). The notion of linguistic human rights attempts to link the debate about language rights with the relatively well-defined international legal framework for human rights. That is, the concept of human rights is invoked as a means of reaching consensus on the rights of linguistic minorities to ensure social justice. These include the rights of indigenous and minority groups to education in their own language, access to the language of the larger community, and that of the national education system, and international languages (King & Schielmann, 2004). Discussion of a Universal Declaration of Linguistic Rights is taking place under the auspices of UNESCO. Such legislation aims at guaranteeing at an individual level that everybody can identify with their mother tongue(s) and have this identification accepted and respected by others, and learn the mother tongue(s) fully, orally (when physiologically possible), and in writing. In most cases, this requires education for indigenous and minority children through the medium of their mother tongue(s); use of the mother tongue(s) in official situations (including schools); and that everybody whose mother tongue is not an official language in the country where they are resident can become bilingual (or multilingual, if they have more than one mother tongue) in the mother tongue(s) and (one of) the official language(s) (according to their own choice).

In practice, this is being achieved to some degree in some contexts, often by means of what has been called a "three language formula" or a "three plus or minus one language formula" in education. In India a three language policy means that children from non-Hindi-speaking areas study their regional language, in addition to Hindi, and English. Hindi speakers, on the other hand, study Hindi, English, and another language. Each state generally has a large population who speak the dominant language of the neighboring state in addition to the dominant language of the state in which they reside. In Andhra Pradesh the dominant language is Telegu, but many speak Kannada, Marathi, and Tamil. Millions of Telegu speakers reside in the states of Karnataka, Orissa, Tamil Nadu, and Maharashtra. Each state is multilingual, and the linguistic majority in one state may be a minority in other states. Each state usually recognizes one official language and restricts the use of other languages to particular districts within the state. Critics of the policy contend that, although it sounds fine in theory, in practice it has not been followed throughout the country.

In Luxembourg, trilingualism in the national language, Luxembourgish (Lëtzebuergesch), French, and German (spoken in the neighboring countries of Belgium, France, and Germany) is encoded in legislation which ensures that all citizens learn all three languages at school. Students begin with their everyday spoken language, Luxembourgish, in compulsory preschool education. German is added in the first year of primary education, and French from the second year of primary school onwards. Over the years, however, and particularly in secondary education, French gets an ever bigger share until it completely replaces German as the language of instruction. English is learned as a fourth compulsory language in secondary education and secondary technical education.

Despite some encouraging developments, weak linkages between policy and planning render many existing policies ineffective (Romaine, 2007). Policies cannot be implemented unless those with the duty to implement them are provided with the necessary resources. Policies cannot be effective unless they are tied to a plan for the monitoring of compliance and the application of sanctions where they are not implemented. Language planning on a regional rather than national basis clearly makes better sense for languages such as Saami, Basque, Catalan, and other languages cutting across national boundaries, but the European Union has generally avoided taking any action which would interfere with national laws or policies concerning linguistic minorities. The result is that many languages are valued only beyond their national borders, while not being recognized for educational or other public purposes even within their own areas of concentration. Despite the spread of global languages, multilingualism will remain a reality for most of the world that must be taken into account in all social, political, economic, and educational policy and planning. A key challenge is to rethink nation-states and their related national identities in more pluralistic and inclusive ways to accommodate new conceptualizations of belonging within culturally and linguistically diverse communities.

References

Allardt, E. (1979). *Implications of the ethnic revival in modern industrialized society: A comparative study of the linguistic minorities in western Europe.* Helsinki: Societas Scientariarum Fennica.

Clay, J. (1990). Indigenous peoples: The miner's canary for the twentieth century. In S. Head & R. Heinzman (Eds.), *Lessons of the rainforest* (pp. 106–117). San Francisco: Sierra Club Books.

Constitution of India (1950). Retrieved July 1, 2008, from http://lawmin.nic.in/coi.htm

Constitution of Italy (1948). Retrieved July 1, 2008, from http://www.vescc.com/constitution/italy-constitution-eng.html

Corson, D. (1990). *Language policy across the curriculum.* Clevedon, UK: Multilingual Matters.

de Varennes, F. (1996). *Language, minorities and human rights.* The Hague: Martinus Nijhoff.

Extra, G., & Gorter, D. (2007). Regional and immigrant minority languages in Europe. In M. Hellinger & A. Pauwels (Eds.), *Language and communication: Diversity and change. Handbooks of applied linguistics* (pp. 15–52). Berlin & New York: Mouton de Gruyter.

Federal Constitution of Malaysia (1957). Retrieved July 1, 2008, from http://www.malaysia-today.net/malaysia_constitution.pdf

French Constitution (1958). Retrieved July 1, 2008, from http://www.assemblee-nationale.fr/english/8ab.asp#TITLE%20I

Gordon, R. G., Jr. (Ed.). (2005). *Ethnologue: Languages of the world* (15th ed.). Dallas: SIL International.

Graddol, D. (1997). *The future of English? A guide to forecasting the popularity of the English language in the 21st century.* London: British Council.

Hobbs, F., & Stoops, N. (2002). *Demographic trends in the 20th century.* Washington, DC: U.S. Government Printing Office.

King, L., & Schielmann, S. (Eds.). (2004). *The challenge of indigenous education: Practice and perspectives.* Paris: UNESCO.

Kymlicka, W., & Patten, A. (Eds.). (2003). *Language rights and political theory.* Oxford, UK: Oxford University Press.

Lévesque, R. (1968). *An option for Quebec.* Toronto, Canada: MacClelland and Stewart.

Nettle, D., & Romaine, S. (2000). *Vanishing voices. The extinction of the world's languages.* Oxford, UK: Oxford University Press.

Paulston, C. B. (1997). Language policies and language rights. *Annual Review of Anthropology, 26,* 73–85.

Robust, T. T. (2002). Ko te reo, te mauri o te mana Māori: The language is the life essence of Māori existence. In J. Burnaby & J. A. Reyhner (Eds.), *Indigenous languages across the community* (pp. 1–16). Flagstaff, AZ: Northern Arizona University.

Romaine, S. (1995). *Bilingualism* (2nd ed.). Oxford, UK: Blackwell.

Romaine, S. (2006a). Global English: From island tongue to world language. In B. L. J. Los & A. van Kemenade (Eds.), *Handbook of the history of English* (pp. 589–608). Oxford, UK: Blackwell.

Romaine, S. (2006b). Planning for the survival of linguistic diversity. *Language Policy, 5*(2), 443–475.

Romaine, S. (2007). The impact of language policy on endangered languages. In M. Koenig & P. De Guchteneire (Eds.), *Democracy and human rights in multicultural societies* (pp. 217–236). Aldershot, UK: Ashgate/UNESCO.

Schiffman, H. (1996). *Linguistic culture and language policy.* London: Routledge.

Sen, A. (2006). *Identity and violence: The illusion of destiny.* New York: W. W. Norton & Company.

Skutnabb-Kangas, T. (2000). *Linguistic genocide in education – or worldwide diversity and human rights?* Mahwah, NJ: Lawrence Erlbaum.

Tollefson, J. (Ed.). (1995). *Power and inequality in language education.* Cambridge, UK: Cambridge University Press.

UNESCO (1953). *The use of vernacular languages in education.* Paris: UNESCO.

UNESCO (1994–2003). *MOST (Management of Social Transformations) clearing house linguistic rights: National constitutions.* Retrieved January 18, 2008, from http://www.unesco.org/most/ln2nat.htm

UNESCO (2003). *Education in a multilingual world.* Paris: UNESCO

28

Language policies and language education in Francophone Africa

A critique and a call to action

Hassana Alidou
Alliant International University, San Diego, CA, USA

Introduction

The purpose of this chapter is to critically assess language education policies and practices in Francophone Africa, using Burkina Faso, Mali, and Niger as case studies. The sociolinguistic character of Francophone Africa has undergone fundamental change since the demise of colonialism. Thus, there is a crucial need to revisit current language policies and pedagogical practices in the so-called "French-speaking" countries and to develop new language education systems and instructional strategies to address the plague of illiteracy and non-education that continues to haunt these nations. The critique presented here calls into question the established philosophical paradigm of "mother tongue" medium of instruction. At the same time, this critique challenges the postcolonial advocacy of "French-only" medium of instruction. Given the diversity of sociocultural, economic, and linguistic conditions throughout Francophone Africa, there is a need to develop forms of education to accommodate this diversity. It is no longer the case (if it ever was) that one size fits all. A serious reevaluation of the status and roles of African languages, and the French language as well, is long overdue. My position is grounded in fifteen years of involvement in international development and in my experience as a first-language speaker of Hausa and Zarma-Songhay, two main languages spoken as national languages in Niger. My work and research in international development involved professional development training for language teachers, extensive observations of primary school classrooms, and policy formulation for governmental institutions and international donors.

It is crucial that linguists, educators, policymakers, and other stakeholders recognize that, since colonization, the role of French has evolved in Africa. Scholars cannot continue to view this sociolinguistic condition as merely reflecting the inherited colonial language or as a case of an oppressive language promoted to official status. On the one hand, it must be acknowledged that African schools designed by French colonial power not only served as a significant space for cultural and linguistic imperialism, but also, in the postcolonial era, have become a large textbook market for French publishing companies, which produce most of the educational materials currently used in Francophone Africa (Alidou-Ngame, 2000). In order to preserve this market, French support for African education is strictly tied to the maintenance of a French-based educational policy from primary school to higher education. Such a policy is an essential factor in the French government's financial and technical support of African education. On the other hand, because of this colonial history, French is becoming the first or second dominant language of a significant number of African children concentrated in urban centers. This sociolinguistic development has implications for the use of French in the classroom. Such an educational consideration was not possible in the 1960s when the acquisition of French was not as widespread. Thus, African scholars such as Bokamba and Tlou (1980) rightfully criticized the use of French as the first language of instruction for African children. However, this critique is not totally applicable today. The teaching and use of the French language in classrooms must be revisited in light of this new sociolinguistic development.

For several decades now, linguists and educators have argued for the use of African languages as media of instruction in schools (Alidou, 1997; Bamgbose, 1997; Fafunwa, Macauley, & Funnso Sokoya, 1989; Mazrui, 2000; Moumouni, 1998). African political leaders have also recommended that these languages be used in education. However, their support for this cause has been more visible in political discourse than in actual policies backed by financial investment. In Francophone Africa, only Guinea Conakry's former president, Seku Toure, fully implemented the use of national languages as the dominant means of instruction in primary and secondary education. Unfortunately, this language education policy ended with his death in 1984. The lack of sufficient financial support from government and private donors has seriously affected corpus planning efforts undertaken by linguists since the 1960s. Consequently, there are very few African languages that have been fully described, updated, and modernized to serve as media of instruction in education. In all Francophone countries the promotion of national languages in education currently remains mainly an educational experiment, rather than a generalized language policy implemented in government schools.

It is my contention that European languages which serve as official languages must be adopted as "African" languages imbued with an African identity. These languages can then be used as effective languages of instruction. By the same token, African languages can and should be used as media of instruction and also taught as a subject in African schools. Governments and the private sector must develop forms of language education that fit the needs of children living in various sociocultural, economic, and linguistic conditions.

Based on the language(s) of instruction, there are three types of formal primary schools in Burkina Faso, Mali, and Niger:

1 French medium only from first to sixth grade; this characterizes mainstream governmental or private schools;
2 French and Arabic as co-equal media of instruction from first to sixth grade; this type of school is the madrasa;
3 experimental bilingual schools that use national languages as media of instruction in the first three years of schooling, with French being introduced as the dominant language of instruction from the fourth grade onward.

The focus of this critique is the government mainstream and experimental bilingual primary schools. The first two sections of this chapter deal with language and curriculum issues in these two types of schools. The third section issues a call to action and provides recommendations to address language education and literacy issues in Francophone Africa.

Educational language policy in Francophone schools: Post-Jomtien conference

In 1990, UNESCO, the World Bank, national ministries of education, and several international organizations gathered in Jomtien, Thailand, to evaluate the state of education in the world. Not surprisingly, the evaluation of the African educational system, as with other socioeconomic sectors and domains in African countries, was depressing. The whole world recognized that Africa is experiencing a serious educational crisis related to the irrelevance of the curriculum, the languages of instruction, and the centralized organizational structures of the educational systems. A call for investments and reforms that take into consideration African people's socioeconomic and cultural backgrounds was made. While most developed countries pledged increased financial and technical support, African governments produced policy papers renewing their interest in designing reforms to influence the adaptation of African curricula to the reality and needs of people and in the use of national languages as media of instruction to promote education for girls.

The use of African languages was particularly viewed as a strategy to promote gender equity and cultural and linguistic diversity in schools. In Burkina Faso, for example, the use of community languages as instructional media facilitates girls' active participation in classroom activities, while the use of French tends to intimidate them. As a secondary school teacher and university lecturer in Niger, I observed that, in the classroom, girls and women were reluctant to speak out because they were afraid to make mistakes in speaking French. (However, they adequately expressed their opinions in writing in French, and in some cases they did better than their male classmates.) Creating a classroom environment in which they were permitted to speak their community languages reduced their level of fear and increased dialogue, interaction, and involvement in the classroom.

After Jomtien, several high-level political gatherings took place to revive the use of African languages for formal basic education. The ministers of education of African states met with linguists and education specialists in Segu, Mali (1992), Mamou, Guinea (1992), Accra, Ghana (1995), and Cape Town, South Africa (1996) in order to produce policy papers related to the use of African languages in education. Each conference ended with a specific declaration favoring the use of African languages as media of instruction in schools. These conferences were supported not only by government agencies but also by the international donor community.

In April 2000, UNESCO and the World Bank organized a ten-year evaluation of the "Education for All by Year 2000" programs. The follow-up meeting that took place in Dakar, Senegal, revealed that in Africa very limited progress had been made. For instance, the implementation, at the grassroots level, of the curriculum and language education reforms designed in the early 1990s by Francophone African countries has been extremely slow. Further, at the end of primary schooling, African students' performance on achievement tests administered in official languages, e.g. French and English, continues to remain far below international standards (UNESCO, 2000a, 2000b).

The question of language of instruction was barely addressed owing to the reluctance of the World Bank and France to support the promotion of national languages in formal education. In fact, since Jomtien, the World Bank and the French government have expressed more resistance to than support for language education reforms proposed by African governments, particularly those of Burkina Faso, Mali, and Niger. However, these governments have endeavored to maintain the momentum and have obtained some technical and financial support from a few international organizations. Currently, only these three Francophone countries have systematically intensified efforts for the creation or revitalization of their experimental bilingual schools. In Burkina Faso, the Ministry of Basic Education (MEBA) and UNICEF created the "Ecoles Satellites" (Satellite Schools). In Mali, the Ministry of Basic Education obtained the support of several international organizations and created "Les Écoles de la Pédagogie Convergente" ("Schools of Convergent Pedagogy") developed by Professor Waumbach from Belgium. This pedagogical approach is based on the oral development of the national language and the inclusion of local performing art (dance and singing). Niger's Ministry of Basic Education received technical and financial support from two German development agencies to revitalize the forty-six bilingual education schools that had been created since 1973. It is in these educational contexts that one can observe pedagogical innovations related to the adaptation of the school curriculum and languages of instruction to students' cultural, linguistic, and economic backgrounds. However, the mainstream schools have remained generally the same, as if the Jomtien Conference had never occurred. Consequently, the current sociolinguistic profile of urban students, particularly as it relates to their proficiency in French, is not taken into consideration by mainstream teachers and curriculum developers specializing in the teaching of French as medium of instruction or subject in the primary school curriculum.

Language issues in mainstream schools

Mainstream primary schools in Francophone Africa are mere copies of colonial schools. The organizational structure of the schools, the curriculum content, and language of instruction policies were modified only slightly after independence, for example simple changes in the names of characters in reading textbooks. "René" is replaced by "Musa" or "Hamidou" and "Mary" by "Mariama." However, there has been no fundamental change in language teaching methods since the colonial era. French is still taught as the exclusive language of instruction, even though for 95% of rural and poor urban children French can be considered a foreign language. In rural settings, particularly, French remains strictly the language of school and homework. Children never use it as the means of communication in their families or communities. In these settings, local languages are the main means of communication.

In urban centers, particularly in the capital cities of Burkina Faso, Mali, and Niger, French is rapidly becoming the first or second language of children from upper- and middle-class families. These children come to school with some oral and written proficiency in French that allows them to understand instruction delivered in this language. They participate actively in class, and the teachers often give them more attention. The educational experience of these children is generally positive, as they achieve academic success. However, these privileged students constitute a minority. The majority of students in both urban and rural schools come from poor, non-literate families where French is not the means of daily communication. Unfortunately, the educational experience of this group of students is characterized by class repetition and a high drop-out rate between fourth and sixth grades. The average rate of dropout in primary schools of French-speaking countries is nearly 25% according to most World Bank and UNESCO annual reports. In Francophone Africa, the majority of primary school students experience exclusion in the classroom. Owing to a lack of proficiency in French, they are silenced and spend most of their time listening to the teacher and the very few students who can speak French. Most of the non-French-speaking students experience academic failure, owing in part to the lack of proficiency in the language of instruction and, in part, to the use of inappropriate language teaching methods by their classroom teachers.

Most of the teachers currently serving in primary schools in Francophone Africa (whether certified or not) do not speak the French language very well. In the sixty schools (half mainstream and half bilingual) I have visited in Burkina Faso, Mali, and Niger since 1990, the majority of teachers have great difficulty teaching in general and using the French language as the means of instruction in particular. Therefore, they frequently code-mix and code-switch. So do their students. This situation is prevalent mainly in rural schools and in schools located in poor urban neighborhoods.

During the colonial era, school teachers used the teaching of grammatical rules, drill repetition, and memorization as language teaching pedagogy. To force pupils to speak the French language, they used drastic physical and psychological measures involving the beating and shaming of students (Mateene, 1985; Moumouni, 1998). Such pedagogical, physical, and psychological methods are still used in Francophone African classrooms, particularly in rural areas. These practices prevail in spite of governments advocating non-violent pedagogy and student-centered and constructivist language teaching approaches.

Teachers construct materials, lessons, and tests that lend themselves to regurgitation. Since most students fear physical punishment, they do their best to memorize the lessons they copied or the reading materials they used in the classrooms. Like parrots, they develop very good repetition skills, but they can barely write their names. Students spend most of their time memorizing lessons for the tests instead of trying to understand the relevance or meaning of what they read. This lack of proficiency in French negatively affects their understanding of knowledge transmitted in that language. Consequently, they perform poorly on achievement tests that require mastery of French and the ability to perform highly cognitive tasks in French.

A review of Burkina Faso, Mali, and Niger Ministry of Education statistics since 1965 shows that 65% of sixth graders annually fail the achievement tests administered in French even though most of them have had six to eight years of instruction in the language. Another problem inherent in mainstream primary schools in poor rural and urban areas in Burkina Faso, Mali, and Niger is the high rate of grade repetition (35%) and the drop-out rate (25%) between fourth and sixth grades (Human Sciences Research Council, 1999; UNESCO, 1990a, 1990b, 2000a, 2000b).

As noted above, the majority of students who experience academic success in Francophone primary schools come from urban middle- and upper-class families, with highly educated parents. In these students' homes, French is the dominant language. A literate culture is also developed in this setting. Children are exposed at a very early age to reading and writing in French. Their parents take them to the local French library, and they are also exposed to television broadcasting in French. TV5, Canal plus, and Antenne 2 are all French channels which are watched daily in these family living rooms. Most of these children also have the chance to attend early childhood education that systematically introduces them to reading and writing in French. In short, these children come to school prepared for instruction delivered in the French language. They represent the majority of students who successfully pass the end of primary school exam. These urban children from the middle and upper classes who are regularly exposed to French represent 70% of the students who graduate from primary school, compared to 30% primary school graduates from poor urban and rural schools. However, the academic success of this particular group of students has nothing to do with governmental education or language policies, but reflects their parents' educational background, social status, and deliberate decision to promote French language and literacy at home.

It is imperative that social class and parental education be carefully analyzed in designing effective educational reforms in Africa. Failure to consider social class as a unit of analysis in educational policy in Africa will contribute to the retention of inadequate educational systems and further promote social inequalities in school and society. In urban settings where more and more children from prominent families come to school with some proficiency in French, it is important to recognize the reality of the sociolinguistic situation by familiarizing teachers with issues of linguistic diversity and equity and the use of pedagogical approaches that will facilitate learning in classrooms where students have various levels of proficiency in the language of instruction. If social class and differential language proficiency are not taken into consideration in the classroom, the learning of the majority of children who come to school without a knowledge of French will be negatively impacted. African classrooms, far from becoming a space for the eradication of societal inequality, will continue instead to serve as a space for maintaining or perpetuating inequality through the promotion of students who have French language competence prior to enrolling in school. Language policies must be sensitive to sociolinguistic transformation in African societies and include language education programs that are socially just.

One would think that in the 1980s and 1990s African educational reformers and policy-makers would have taken into consideration applied linguistic research findings in order to promote the development of adequate language proficiency in primary schools. Krashen's (1976) findings about the significance of meaningful linguistic input in promoting adequate proficiency in a second or foreign language is particularly crucial for addressing language issues in African schools. Identifying appropriate second-language teaching methods that include culturally relevant pedagogy is crucial in promoting language competence in French. Instead of forcing on students the variety of French spoken in France and reading materials produced with French children in mind, it is important to recognize the cultural and social reality of African students in Francophone countries. The teaching – and learning – of French must be organized around what students know already and what they ought to know in order to become effective second-language learners who can understand knowledge acquired in French and use it effectively to further their learning.

The adoption of effective language teaching methods must be accompanied by the development of a literate environment in the community. The language of instruction must be used outside the classroom in order for learners to enhance their proficiency and competence in that language. The creation of community libraries and the promotion of literacy in French and the national languages among adults can provide needed linguistic support for students and teachers. However, such initiatives do not currently exist. In the sixty schools I visited, in almost all cases there was only one source of French language reading material, the official textbook used by the teacher (often produced by French textbook publishers and the ministries of education with World Bank funding). The language teaching methods involved in national reading textbooks used in Burkina Faso, Mali, and Niger are still based on phonics, drills, and memorization. Textbook prefaces commonly suggest the use of active methods, with very limited pedagogical information about the meaning of such methods or how to effectively conduct language lessons using this approach.

A careful analysis of the pedagogical units included in a given text reveals that drills, repetition, and memorization are still the guiding pedagogical principles. These books are not comprised of authentic texts or stories that students can read and enjoy. In this context, reading and writing are never taught as activities that have social and cultural functions. Therefore, very few students develop a desire for reading and writing, and most of them finish primary school with very limited literacy skills in French. In this regard, Mendo (1999) argues that grammatical rules learned during French lessons are never used in natural conversations because, in Cameroon, French is mainly used for specific formal purposes: school and writing letters. Thus children are unable to acquire adequate language proficiency in French. Yet at the end of primary school they are expected to take high-stakes and cognitively demanding tests that assess their mastery of the French language and their ability to solve problems in French. These achievement tests are not only unjust, they are also unreliable indicators of students' abilities.

Specific issues related to experimental bilingual schools

In the early 1970s, a few Francophone countries developed experimental bilingual schools. A review of available data from Burkina Faso, Mali, and Niger Ministry of Education documents indicates that preservation and promotion of African languages and cultures through literacy were the main purposes of the bilingual schools. In that respect, bilingual schools have been part of both nationalization and Africanization of primary schools in the postcolonial period. The second main goal of bilingual education, as stated in Bamgbose's well-known book, *Mother Tongue Education: The West African Experience* (1976), is the acquisition of adequate literacy in both national languages and the dominant languages of instruction, namely French, English, Portuguese, or Spanish, depending upon a country's colonial history.

After twenty to thirty years of experimenting, the use of national languages in primary schools has not been expanded to all primary schools. There are still fewer than 200 bilingual schools (as opposed to more than 3,000 mainstream schools) in each Francophone country. Most of the experimental bilingual schools are marginalized. They are located mainly in poor urban and rural areas. In Burkina Faso, Mali, and Niger, the bilingual schools survive largely because of international development aid. Therefore, depending upon availability of funding, these schools experience short periods of success often followed by long periods of stagnation and academic failure. Demonstration schools (such as the bilingual school located in Segu, Mali) which serve as scientific and pedagogical laboratories for linguists, educators, and policymakers benefit not only from funding and educational materials but also from political attention. They are therefore high-performing schools which produce highly successful students. Indeed, students attending such schools perform far better than mainstream students located in the same geographical area. Of course not all experimental bilingual schools benefit from such attention. However, one can objectively say that, whenever governments and educators invest adequately in bilingual schools, the schools tend to produce better educational outcomes.

In Burkina Faso the Ecoles Satellites were created with the financial support of UNICEF, in Mali, Les Écoles de la Pédagogie Convergente have the technical support of the German Technical Agency (GTZ), and a few international organizations (non-French based) and the Ecoles Expérimentales from Niger are technically and financially supported by the GTZ. In these three countries, the German Foundation for International Development has been contributing to the revitalization program through its professional development training projects for curriculum developers and authors of national language textbooks. I have been involved in these projects as the academy director of the workshops organized by the German Foundation for International Development in Burkina Faso, Mali, and Niger. The account I provide below reflects, therefore, an active participant's perspective.

In the experimental bilingual schools, national languages that serve as regional languages were selected as media of instruction along with French. These languages are used for the first three years of instruction, and French is taught as a subject in the curriculum. In fourth grade, French becomes the main language of instruction even though the use of national languages is acceptable whenever students have difficulty comprehending instruction delivered in French.

For most students attending bilingual schools, national languages used as media of instruction are their dominant languages, and French can be considered a foreign language. The use of these languages as means of instruction in the first three years of education facilitates students' involvement in all classroom interactions.

While most mainstream teachers have at least one year of training in teacher training colleges, teachers serving in bilingual schools have very limited training in teaching French and national languages. In Mali and Niger, bilingual teachers are recruited from among regular schoolteachers. These teachers are identified as enthusiastic volunteers, and they are provided with intensive three-month workshops on national language orthography and transcription in addition to general classroom management workshops. Bilingual teachers from Mali and Niger are civil servants and as such are paid directly by the ministries of education. Their salary is similar to that of teachers serving in mainstream schools. This is not the case in Burkina Faso, where Ecoles Satellites teachers hold a very special position. They are considered not civil servants but community teachers. As such, wherever they serve, the population is responsible for their lodging and salary. Here there are serious teacher turnover problems, owing to the fact that poor rural populations cannot always pay the teachers. Again, poor rural children and parents pay the price for an unsustainable educational reform. By contrast, in mainstream schools, even in rural areas, the government does not expect the population to pay teacher salaries.

Teacher enthusiasm cannot substitute for qualifications required for teaching in national languages and French. Many bilingual teachers face serious professional challenges. They may be able to speak the language of instruction, but they have not mastered reading and writing in that language. Participation in a three-month workshop is not sufficient to master literacy skills. The profile of bilingual teachers described here shows that, from the outset, bilingual school students tend to face serious problems. They are taught by unqualified teachers with very limited knowledge of language pedagogy. "Amateurism" is the best word to describe the situation.

It is important to mention the exceptions to this bleak educational picture: demonstration schools that produce highly successful students. These are the laboratory schools – found in all three countries – that benefit from extensive research, funding, and the involvement of linguists from national universities and international consultants sent by organizations such as GTZ, DSE, USAID, or the Swiss Development Agency (OSEO). In these model bilingual schools, teachers benefit from professional development training related to researchers' interests in mother tongue education. As a result of this pedagogical and linguistic training, teachers in these schools develop transcription skills as well as a stronger knowledge base about teaching in the mother tongue. Their students successfully pass the end of primary school achievement examinations. The performance of bilingual school students attending the demonstration schools is often better than that of students in mainstream schools.

The number of students attending demonstration schools is unfortunately very small in comparison to the overall population of students. Since most African countries rely heavily on international aid, ministries of education and governments in general have very limited power to implement education and language policies not favored by the major donors to a given country's educational programs. It is clear that technical and scholarly arguments in favor of bilingual education and the proven success of demonstration schools are not the only factors influencing the use of research-based results to shape language education policies. While I was conducting research for my dissertation (Alidou, 1997), I interviewed a former secretary of education in a Francophone African country. I posed the question of why the Ministry of Education was not reformulating its language education policy in primary schools, given the positive outcomes of experimental schools with both national languages and French as media of instruction. Although this former secretary was an ardent advocate of national languages, he straightforwardly stated that as long as his country relies on French resources and support, it would never implement such schools on a grand scale. Further, he contended that a direct appeal to the World Bank for resources to expand the use of national languages in primary schools was not a possibility since France remains the main advocate for Francophone African countries at the World Bank. Moreover, he pointed out that the World Bank's lack of support for these demonstration/experimental schools flies in the face of UNESCO's positive evaluation of these schools in the mid-1980s. (The reaction of this former Francophone government official is frequently echoed by other officials if the interviewer promises not to disclose their identity.)

In North America, several studies conducted in bilingual schools indicate that there is a high positive correlation between literacy in one's first language and literacy in one's second language (Cummins, 1979). That is, learning and literacy developed in a student's first language facilitate learning and literacy development in a second language. This correlation is due to the existence of a common underlying linguistic proficiency which allows bilingual learners to transfer linguistic and general knowledge acquired in their first language to their second language. Cummins's argument has become axiomatic, and it is used in several policy papers to argue for the promotion of African languages in formal education (Mazrui, 2000). Indeed, in Africa one could make a similar argument for the promotion of African languages as media of instruction if these languages had the same type of status and development as English, French, or Spanish in the North American context. However, the languages used in bilingual schools in Burkina Faso, Mali, and Niger (as well as in other Francophone countries) have very limited writing and literary traditions. The lack of a literate culture and tradition in these languages impedes the development of adequate literacy skills. It is difficult, therefore, to apply Cummins's (1991) theory of linguistic interdependence between first and second languages in Francophone countries.

In Burkina Faso, Mali, and Niger, bilingual schools also present fundamental equity issues. Students attending these schools who fail to pass the end of primary school achievement tests face serious social problems. They easily relapse into illiteracy, and their access to jobs becomes very limited. Typically, they have not acquired basic literacy and proficiency in French. Owing to underdevelopment in most African villages, there are no paying jobs in rural areas that require literacy skills in national languages, or in French for that matter. Even when there are development projects, if there is a literacy component one or two people from the village can carry out the task. This situation renders bilingual education even less equitable than mainstream education, with its focus on French as the language of instruction. A primary school drop-out from a mainstream/government school will have at least limited proficiency in French which will give him access to working-class positions in urban areas – e.g. gardener, mailman in government or private organizations.

Conclusion and recommendations

This critique of the language education issue in mainstream and bilingual education schools indicates the inadequacy of language education in Francophone Africa, as manifested in the case studies of Burkina Faso, Mali, and Niger. Improvement of the Francophone African educational system, particularly in primary schools, requires an accurate assessment of the situation. As a children's advocate, I strongly believe that parents should have the right to determine the type of school their children attend. Therefore governments should create different types of schools to accommodate the diverse linguistic and cultural needs of the population. Equal financial and technical support should be given to all public schools regardless of the language policy of these schools. I call, therefore, for improvement of language teaching in both mainstream and bilingual schools in Francophone Africa. Governments should encourage competition among schools. This would force schools to improve their performance. Further, governments should develop language teaching/learning programs that take into account both linguistic and socioeconomic diversity.

Intensive workshops organized irregularly, with the support of international donors, cannot be a sustainable strategy for school improvement. Instead of these costly emergency teacher training projects, I call for serious reform of the curriculum in teacher education programs. The teacher training curriculum has not been significantly reevaluated since the colonial period. An analysis of the curriculum content of Ecoles Normales located in Burkina Faso, Mali, and Niger indicates that the courses have not been changed in spite of the various educational reforms undertaken by ministries of education. After each reform, sporadic workshops are organized to familiarize teachers with the policy being implemented and the few pedagogical methods that sustain the reform. Often, these workshops last ten days, and there is no follow-up to determine whether/how teachers are using the new knowledge acquired during the workshops. The serious gap between language education policy and classroom practice must be addressed. Teacher education programs must be redesigned in order to effectively train all new teachers for both mainstream and bilingual classrooms. The ministries of education should make dual teacher certification mandatory for new teachers. Dual certification will allow ministries of education to address teacher shortage problems in both mainstream and bilingual schools.

In the same way that African countries experience food hunger, there is a long-lasting book hunger in Africa. Research has established a high correlation between the availability of books and educational materials and high academic performance. Literacy cannot develop without a literate environment. Such an environment is defined not only by the availability of print material in a community, but also by the use of language in both its oral and written forms for all types of cultural and socioeconomic purposes. It is critical, therefore, that the effort to use national languages and French in schools must be backed up by the promotion of a literate culture in both urban and rural contexts. Availability of libraries that contain reading materials in all languages used in schools and the promotion of literacy among adults and children will provide children with access to meaningful linguistic input both in national languages and in French. Such input is needed in order to develop adequate language proficiency in the languages of instruction (Krashen, 1981).

One of the main problems facing teachers and students in bilingual schools is the lack of uniform orthography for a given African language. National languages used in the bilingual schools have at least two or three orthographies. Teachers are thus confronted with the issue of teaching children literacy skills using several different orthographic representations of their language (Makoni, 2003). This orthographic diversity has a potentially negative impact on students learning to read, because consistency in the representation of the writing system is important to children struggling to develop literacy skills. When the various dialects of a language are mutually intelligible (generally the case), ministries of education should select a single orthographic system to be used by all educational institutions involved in formal basic education. Important also, uniform orthography and textbooks will be cost-effective and answer those critics who charge that the production of educational materials in African languages is costly.

For languages used transnationally, such as Hausa, Fulfulde, and Songhay, which are spoken in several countries in West Africa, regional efforts are needed, involving curriculum developers, linguists, and authors, to identify the dialect in those languages that can be used for educational purposes. Such joint efforts can result in the production of textbooks in national languages that can be used by a significant number of students. This strategy will promote the creation of a large market for reading materials in national languages and lead to investment in local publishing companies specializing in the production of these materials (Alidou-Ngame, 2000).

In conclusion, I call for an accountability system that adequately addresses national and international language education policies in Francophone Africa. Many reforms have been undertaken in Africa. Unfortunately, when these reforms fail, African students end up paying a heavy price: exclusion from the educational system at a very young age, thus limiting their chance for upward mobility in their own society.

Reprinted with permission of the publisher from: Sinfree Makoni, Geneva Smitherman, & Arnetha F. Ball (Eds.). (2003). *Black linguistics: Language, society, and politics in Africa and the Americas* (pp. 103–116). London & New York: Routledge.

References

Alidou, H. (1997). *Education language policy and bilingual education: The impact of French language policy in primary education in Niger.* Unpublished doctoral dissertation, University of Illinois at Urbana-Champaign, Illinois.

Alidou-Ngame, H. (2000). *Stratégies pour le développement un secteur éditorial en langues nationals dans les pays du sahel Burkina Faso, Mali, Niger et Sénégal.* London: Groupe de Travail sur les Livres et le Materiel Educatif.

Bamgbose, A. (1976). *Mother tongue education: The West African experience.* London: Hodder & Stoughton.

Bamgbose, A. (1997). *Language and the nation: The language question in sub-Saharan Africa.* Edinburgh: Edinburgh University Press.

Bokamba, E. G., & Tlou, J. (1980). The consequences of the language policies of African states vis-à-vis education. In K. Mateene, J. Kalema, & B. Chomba (Eds.), *Linguistic liberation and unity of Africa* (pp. 45–66). Kampala, Uganda: OAU Inter-Africa Bureau of Languages.

Cummins, J. (1979). The role of primary language development in promoting educational success for language minority students. In J. Cummins (Ed.), *Schooling and language-minority students: A theoretical framework* (pp. 3–49). Sacramento, CA: California State Department of Education.

Cummins, J. (1991). Interdependence of first- and second-language proficiency in bilingual children. In E. Bialystok (Ed.), *Language processing in bilingual children* (pp. 70–89). Cambridge, UK: Cambridge University Press.

Fafunwa, A. B., Macauley, J. I., & Funnso Sokoya, J. A. (1989). *Education in mother tongue: The Ife Primary Education Research Project (1970–1978).* Ibadan, Nigeria: Ibadan University Press.

Human Sciences Research Council (HSRC). (1999). With Africa for Africa: Towards quality education for all. In V. Chinapah (Ed.), *Education for all: 2000 assessment survey, 1999 MLA Project* (Draft regional report). Pretoria: Author.

Krashen, S. D. (1976). Formal and informal linguistic environments in language acquisition and language learning. *TESOL Quarterly, 10,* 157–168.

Krashen, S. D. (1981). Effective second language acquisition: Insights from research. In M. B. Finocchiaro, J. E. Alatis, H. B. Altman, & P. M. Alatis (Eds.), *The second language classroom: Directions for the 1980s: Essays in honor of Mary Finocchiaro* (pp. 97–109). Oxford, UK: Oxford University Press.

Makoni, S. (2003). From misinvention to disinvention of language: Multilingualism and the South African constitution. In S. Makoni, G. Smitherman, A. Ball, & A. Spears (Eds.), *Black linguistics, language, society, and politics in Africa and the Americas* (pp. 132–153). London & New York: Routledge.

Mateene, K. (1985). Colonial languages as means of domination, and indigenous languages as necessary factors of liberation and development. In K. Mateene, J. Kalema, & B. Chomba (Eds.), *Linguistic liberation and unity of Africa* (pp. 45–66). Kampala, Uganda: OAU Inter-Africa Bureau of Languages.

Mazrui, A. M. (2000). The World Bank, the language question and the future of African education. In S. Federici, G. Caffentzis, & O. Alidou (Eds.), *Thousand flowers: Social struggles against structural adjustment in African universities* (pp. 43–59). Trenton, NJ: Africa World Press.

Mendo, G. Z. (1999). Contextes du français au Cameroun. In G. Z. Mendo (Ed.), *Le français langue africaine: Enjeux et atouts pour la Francophonie* (pp. 45–64). Paris: Editions Publisud.

Moumouni, A. (1998). *L'Education en Afrique*. Paris: Présence Africaine.

UNESCO. (1990a, March 5–9). *World declaration on education for all and framework for action to meet basic learning needs: The Amman Affirmation*. World Conference on Education for All, Jomtien, Thailand.

UNESCO. (1990b). *Compendium of statistics on illiteracy* (1990 ed.), no. 31. Paris: Author.

UNESCO. (2000a). *Global synthesis: Education for all, 2000 assessment*. Paris: International Consultative Forum on Education for All Publications.

UNESCO. (2000b). *Status and trends 2000: Assessing learning achievement*. Paris: International Consultative Forum on Education for All Publications.

29
Language education policy in multi-ethnic Malaysia

Saran Kaur Gill
Universiti Kebangsaan Malaysia

Introduction

Language functions as a powerful symbol both of a supralocal ethnic-cultural identity at the national level and of a community-based ethnic-cultural identity at a smaller group level in many developing nations (Fishman, 1968, p. 6). In Malaysia, as in many other multi-ethnic nations, one of the major ways in which the socio-cultural identities of various ethnic communities are maintained and sustained is through the language of instruction that is selected for the educational systems.

Governments negotiate language medium issues in their attempt to balance national and multi-ethnic community needs. The manner in which the nation, with its political power, makes language-in-education decisions, and the multi-ethnic groups' struggle for their linguistic needs, are described as top-down and bottom-up language planning (Kaplan, 1989, as cited in Kaplan & Baldauf, 1997, p. 196). The description and analysis of the Malaysian language planning and policy journey in this chapter will be contextualized within these two approaches. Top-down language planning is carried out by people with power and authority (many of whom make up the government) who make language-related decisions for the nation, often with minimal consultation with the grassroots language learners and users. Bottom-up language planning is driven by the smaller communities and provides an avenue for individual or community-led decisions to be made for language needs and uses (Kaplan & Baldauf, 1997).

In the Malaysian context, all of these issues will be examined via the evolving dynamics of the national language, Bahasa Melayu, the international language, English, and the significant minority groups' ethnic languages, Mandarin and Tamil. The focus on these languages does not detract from the richness of the diversity of other languages and varying ethnic communities that exist in both West and East Malaysia. Malaysia is a multi-ethnic nation with a rich and colorful multilingual environment, where languages possess multi-functional roles and varying status. The breadth of language variety and spread in Malaysia is discussed in *Language and Society in Malaysia* (Asmah, 1982) and *Language Planning in Southeast Asia* (Abdullah, 1994). Only the above-mentioned languages will be the focus of this chapter for pragmatic reasons.

This chapter will examine language policy and diversity in Malaysia via the linguistic journey of the pre- and post-independence nationalistic period of the 1950s and 1960s, to the period of reassertion of nationalism in the 1970s and 1980s, and to the present period of globalization taking us into the 21st century. As we travel on this journey, we will examine the agendas and linguistic ideologies underpinning the educational linguistic decisions that were made during the entire period of our nation's post-colonial history to present times and how they influenced both the dominant and the minority ethnic communities.

Pre- and post-independence period of nation building and national identity

In this section, we begin with the pre- and post-independence period to examine the history of the emergence of nationalism in Malaysia and the decisions made regarding the selection and institution of the national language, a decision largely spearheaded by Malay political leaders of the dominant community. We will examine the measures that were established to formalize the role of the national language as a unifying factor and signifier of cultural identity for Malaysia, a multi-ethnic nation. In addition, we will examine how the other ethnic communities accepted Bahasa Melayu as the national language – was it by "confrontation, accommodation or benign neglect?" (Beer & Jacob, 1985, p. 1). It is important that these perspectives are considered because "nationalism . . . is best understood by examining the specific conditions under which it arose and developed . . . the historical content and dimension of social and political concepts" (Kamenka, 1976, pp. 3–4).

Pre-independence period

The British, as colonial masters, used their political powers to develop economic wealth in what was then known as Malaya. They did this by influencing the migratory movements of the Chinese and the Tamil communities to provide the human resource needed for their economic ambitions. The Chinese were attracted to the economic potential of Malaya and came as indentured laborers. They worked to pay off their debt to whoever paid for their passage to Malaysia. Having paid off this debt, they worked in mines or opened up shops and businesses. In contrast, massive numbers of laborers from India were recruited by the British under contracts of indentured servitude to work on the rubber plantations in Peninsular Malaysia (Gaudart, 1992).

Given their business skills, most of the Chinese settled in the urban areas where most of the commercial and economic activity took place. The Tamils were split between those who were English-educated and worked in the British administrative service – who migrated to Malaysia attracted by the economic wealth – and those who worked in rubber estates and went to the vernacular schools. The English-educated were in the urban areas; individuals who went to the vernacular schools were on the estates in the rural areas. The Malays were largely located in the rural areas in their villages. They were largely an agrarian community involved in agriculture, fishing, and farming.

In the 1960s, Malaysia had a complex ethnic demographic distribution of almost equal representation of Malays and non-Malays. The population was divided among Malays, constituting 45.9% of the population, Chinese with 35.9%, Indians with 9.6%, non-Muslim natives with 6.6%, and others with 2.2% (Government of Malaysia Department of Statistics, 1965, as cited in Means, 1991).

Under British control, an educational system reflecting the needs of the separate ethnic communities led to the development of four parallel school systems. These were the English, Malay, Chinese, and Tamil medium schools (Philip, 1975). These four school systems varied according to the levels of education: at the primary level there were all four – the English, Malay, Chinese, and Tamil medium system of education. There were two kinds of secondary schools, the English and Chinese medium systems of education. Tertiary or post-secondary education was exclusively in English. This tiered system of schools set the seeds of economic and cultural separatism which has presented challenges to Malaysia that have continued today (Philip, 1975).

Schooling systems in the Chinese and Tamil media of education were set up largely because of indifference on the part of the British. The British felt that, since the immigrants were regarded as birds of passage who would return to their countries of origin after they had accumulated sufficient wealth, they were not inclined to expend money on the Chinese and Indian vernacular systems of education. As a result, the immigrant communities had great freedom to develop their own educational systems. The immigrants spoke their own languages, financed their own schools, and designed their own curriculums (Chai, 1967).

The English schools were set up by mission societies, supported by the British authorities and located in the urban areas. English schools started the tradition of English education in Malaya. These schools required tuition fees and were attended mainly by children whose parents worked in the British civil service and who lived in the urban areas. Most of the students in these schools were Chinese, with smaller numbers of Indians and even fewer Malays. These schools had great social, economic, and educational value, as their students were very much in demand in the civil service and the commercial sectors. Therefore, education in English was extremely attractive to the non-Malays because not only was it the language of the colonizers, but more important it provided social and economic mobility.

The majority of the Malays attended Malay vernacular schools. The British set up Malay vernacular schools near villages that had a significant population so that they would be readily accessible to a number of children. A statement by Frank Swettenham, the resident of the state of Perak, one of the richest states in Malaysia (whose revenues came largely from alluvial tin resources and tin-mining enterprises), sums up the paternalistic attitude the British had towards the Malays that disadvantaged them tremendously. He said:

> The one danger to be guarded against is to teach English indiscriminately. It could not be well taught except in a few schools, and I do not think it is at all advisable to attempt to give to the children of an agricultural population an indifferent knowledge of a language that to all but the very few would only unfit them for the duties of life and make them discontented with anything like manual labour.
> (Perak Annual Report for 1890, as cited in Chai, 1967, p. 241)

The British intended to keep the Malays happy with Malay vernacular education and to keep them in their place in the rural backwaters. The result was

> a philistine educational policy which led the Malays down a blind alley. British paternalism towards the Malays was stultifying and a disservice to the race. While the immigrant races scrambled for a place in the sun, the Malays were kept sheltered in the shade of the British umbrella.
> (Chai, 1967, p. 288)

The hierarchical system of education created the socio-economic and educational cleavages between the Malays and the other ethnic groups – a situation that disadvantaged the Malays so much that it required drastic changes in the educational system and many years of economic and educational assistance from the government before they were able to catch up with the English-educated Chinese and the Indians. These factors contributed to the communal problems of the nation when Malay resentment eventually built up towards the British and the immigrants in the country. Consequently, in the pre-independence period, language planning activities by both the British and the ethnic communities led to the emergence of three sets of vernacular schools – the Malay, Chinese, and Tamil schools. English was heavily utilized in schools in the urban areas. The impact of the tiered education system on post-independence decisions on language policy and planning will be discussed in the section to follow.

Post-independence period

The growth of nationalism and the selection and institution of Bahasa Melayu as the national and official language. During the pre-independence period the Malays felt insecure and threatened. This feeling was largely due to the numerical strength and the social and economic advancement of the immigrant communities. This feeling of marginalization coupled with enforced imperialism resulted in an acute need among the indigenous ethnic group for "their own cultures and histories [to] be restored to a place of honour" (Emerson, 1960, p. 152). The need for cultural empowerment and recognition was essential for the Malay to regain self-respect.

There was thus a strong need for the Malays to legitimize themselves in the land that they considered theirs – calling Malaya *Tanah Melayu* (Land of the Malays) and calling themselves *Bumiputera* (sons of the soil) were part of these efforts. The Malays also reinforced legitimization through symbolic categories like language, religion, and the national anthem, which became very strong signs of identification. Recognition and acceptance of these symbols by other ethnic groups provided the dominant group with a feeling of collective worth and legitimacy. Recognition and equality were what Horowitz (1985) – in his extensive discussion of ethnic group conflicts – refers to as the need for groups, and especially dominant ethnic groups, to establish "relative group worth" and "relative group legitimacy" through political domination and the high symbolic content of politics of ethnic entitlement (p. 185).

One of the strong symbolic claims asserted during this period was that Bahasa Melayu should be the national language, the official language, and the language of education and administration. There was a strong feeling among the Malays that a national language was needed not only to affirm their legitimacy as the dominant group in Malaysia but also as a tool to unify the multi-ethnic citizenry of the nation – to provide a strong sense of cultural identity at the national level. The Malays felt strongly that making Bahasa Melayu the national language and the official language would provide it with the educational and administrative capital needed to give it higher status. Therefore having mastery of this language would provide the Malays with linguistic capital with greater value for economic opportunity, which would lead to social and professional mobility and equality.

In turn, the role and status of English were radically reduced. From being the sole medium of instruction in the education system, English was relegated to being a subject taught in schools as a second language. In the rural areas where there was almost non-existent environmental exposure to English, its role and status were no better than those of a foreign language.

The response of the non-Malay communities to the institution of Bahasa Melayu as the national language. The non-Malays were unhappy with the switch from English to Bahasa Melayu. They did not relate to the language and were dismayed to see that English – which provided opportunities for upward mobility – was being marginalized by Bahasa Melayu. However, there was little resistance, because the Malays used the issue of citizenship as their bargaining tool to establish a dominant role for Bahasa Melayu.

Compromises were made among the leaders of the three ethnic parties that belonged to the umbrella political party known as the Alliance, which later became the United Front (Barisan Nasional). The ethnically aligned political parties were the United Malay National Organization (UMNO), the Malaysian Chinese Association (MCA), and the Malaysian Indian Congress (MIC). Through a process of negotiation and consensus, they developed a compromise known historically as "the bargain" (Asmah, 2007, p. 347). The major concession grained for the non-Malays was the provision of *jus soli*, the right to citizenship based on the principle that the country of citizenship is determined by the country of birth. Writes Mauzy (1985), "This had been the top demand of the non-Malays, and since rigid citizenship provisions were viewed by the Malays as the key to their security, the concession was a considerable achievement" (pp. 154–155). In return for "the relaxation of the conditions for the granting to non-Malays of citizenship, the rights and privileges of Malays as the indigenous people of the country were to be written into the constitution" (Hashim, 1972, p. 207). Other provisions accepted by the non-Malays were that Islam would be the state religion, Malay would be the national and sole official language in 1967 (10 years hence) unless Parliament provided otherwise, and the functions and status of the Malay rulers would be maintained.

Policy for mother-tongue education in the post-independence period. At the same time as energies were focused on instituting Bahasa Melayu as the national language, the government adopted an equitable approach to the maintenance and sustenance of minority mother-language education. This involved combining elements of both the top-down approach, driven by the needs of the dominant group, and the bottom-up approach, considering the needs of the minority communities to language policy and planning.

After independence, the government of Malaya developed Education Ordinance 1957, which was based on the Razak Report (a report by a committee that was formed in 1955 to review the education system and to make recommendations for an education system best suited for an independent Malaysia) (Asmah, 1979). One of the provisions in the Razak Report proved to be beneficial for the development of mother-tongue education and vernacular schools. Provision S3 of the Education Ordinance 1957 stated that

> the educational policy of the Federation is to establish a national system of education acceptable to the people as a whole which will satisfy their needs and promote their cultural, social, economic and political development as a nation, with the intention of making the Malay language the national language of the country whilst preserving and sustaining the growth of the language and culture of peoples other than Malays living in the country.
>
> (Federation of Malaya, 1957, pp. 34–35)

Therefore, the 1956 Razak Report provided for mother-tongue education at the primary school level to be integrated into the national education system. This resulted in the dominant minority communities, like the Chinese and Tamils, setting up what were described as national-type schools, compared to national schools.

Unfortunately, the liberal attitude towards the establishment of vernacular schools was not sustained over time. This was largely for two reasons. These were, first, the anxiety of the Malays over the spirit of gradualism in recognizing and implementing Bahasa Melayu as the language of education by the non-Malays and, second, the development of ethnic polarization among the youth who studied in Chinese and Tamil medium vernacular schools. There was an increasing awareness of the need to establish national unity through an integrated curriculum using the national language, Bahasa Melayu, preferably through the national school educational system. As a result, gradually, changes were made to a number of Education Acts. These have been discussed in detail by Yang (1998). Yang maintains that the various acts culminating in the 1996 Education Act "[do] not guarantee the permanent or continued use of mother tongue as the main medium of instruction in the existing national-type primary schools" (1998, p. 53). The marginalization of mother-tongue education began with the Rahman Talib Committee 1960. The recommendations of their report reversed the liberal approach taken in the Razak Report 1956 (Malaya (Federation), Education Committee, 1956). The recommendations of the Rahman Talib Report were legislated as the Education Act of 1961. It did this by leaving out crucial aspects of the 1957 Ordinance, as underlined below:

> 3. The educational policy of the Federation is to establish a national system of education *acceptable to the people as a whole* which will satisfy their needs and promote their cultural, social, economic and political development as a nation, with the intention of making the Malay language the national language of the country *whilst preserving and sustaining the growth of the language and culture of peoples other than Malays living in the country*.
>
> (Yang, 1998, p. 40, emphasis added)

The authorities were very serious about "the progressive development of an educational system in which the national language is the main medium of instruction" (Ministry of Education Malaysia, 1961, para. 3). As a result, significant resources were used to enhance the status and functional use of Bahasa Melayu in the education system. Consequently, there was a reduction in the budgets for the upkeep of schools that used the vernacular as the medium of education.

Period of modernization of the national language. Malaysia is one of the few nations that has spent 30 years of its post-independence life, with large financial and human resources, planning for and implementing the dominant group's mother tongue, Bahasa Melayu, as the national language and the language of education and administration. This has involved both corpus and status planning, as extensively defined by Cooper (1989). In the Malaysian context, these corpus-planning activities included standardization, codification, and modernization of the language to develop its lexical base for science and technology terminology. In addition, status planning, defined as "deliberate efforts to influence the allocation of functions among a community's languages" (Cooper, 1989, p. 99), had to be undertaken through legislation to ensure that the language had predominant roles in the key domains of education and administration (see Asmah, 1979, for a detailed discussion of these two aspects of language planning in the Malaysian context).

As these issues on national identity were being developed, the world was changing at a rapid pace. Nations around the globe were facing the challenges of globalization and the newly emerging knowledge economy and the impact of these factors on education, language choice, and human resource development. This is one of the major challenges facing many countries around the globe, and has resulted in a drastic change in language policy manifested through a change in medium of instruction from various national languages to that of English.

Period of internationalization and drastic change in language policy: Bahasa Melayu to English

Malaysia is currently undergoing a period that will go down in history as another major change in language policy, from Bahasa Melayu to English. This is a drastic change when examined in the light of its history. Malaysia is a post-colonial nation that, in the fervor of independence and the establishment of national identity, planned extensively over many years for a change in language policy from English – the language of the ruling power – to Bahasa Melayu.

Despite measures taken over a period of 30 years instituting Bahasa Melayu as the language of education, the language policy was reverted in 2003 to provide the English language with a dominant role in the field of science and technology as a medium of instruction. This has meant that there will be further development and use of the English language as the language of knowledge, which is one of the most powerful domains in which a language operates.

One of the main driving forces for this change is the proliferation of knowledge published in English in the field of science and technology. The dominance of English in science and technology publications – and the fact that it had become increasingly difficult for Bahasa Melayu to keep up with translation of these works from English to Bahasa – meant that unless a change was instituted there would be increasing challenges in accessing knowledge and information on the advancements in the fields of science and technology. Also contributing to this decision was Malaysia's need to develop human resources for the knowledge economy. The reasons for the change have been dealt with by Gill (2005) and David and Govindasamy (2005), and are partly explicated by Mahathir, the former prime minister who was largely responsible for the change in the language of education. During an interview, he said:

> Education is for the purpose of acquiring knowledge. The most important thing is the acquisition of knowledge. If you have to use a language which makes the knowledge more easily accessible, you should use that language. . . . Our education system is like any other education system. It's meant to enable us to acquire knowledge. If we have the knowledge available in the national language, by all means, do . . . but the fact is that in science the research that is being done is moving at a very fast pace. Every day literally thousands of papers on new research are being published and practically all of them are in English. To translate English into Bahasa would require a person with three skills, skill in the two languages and skill in the subject that is to be translated, and we don't have very many people who are qualified to do that or who wish to do that. That is why it is easier if you learn English and the students can have direct access to all the knowledge that is available in English.
>
> (Personal communication, June 16, 2005)

Given that this was largely a top-down governmental approach to the shift in language policy, it will be relevant to examine how the dominant ethnic group and the other two significant minority groups responded differently to the change in medium of instruction from Bahasa Melayu, Chinese, or Tamil to English for science and math. The following sections will deal with the contrasting responses of the three communities to this change in language policy.

Malay educators' response to the implementation of change in medium of instruction

The first attempt at change in the language of education was in 1993, but because the political climate did not provide support for this attempt it was not sustained (Gill, 2002). Almost 10 years later, in January 2002, the then prime minister of Malaysia had approximately one and a half years left of his tenure in office. In contrast to the earlier attempt, during this latter period the main Malay political party (UMNO) had greater strength and was more united. The past political divide among the Malays had been overcome, and the majority of them supported the ruling Malay political party. The unity among the Malays provided the much-needed support to institute a change as important and politically charged as a change in language policy.

This is not to say that the Malay intellectuals and particularly Dewan Bahasa dan Pustaka (the agency set up to promote Bahasa) have not raised their disagreements and expressed their disappointment. At the Second Malay Education Congress, held on March 26 and 27, 2005, strong statements were made expressing resistance to a change from Bahasa Melayu to English. Hassan Ahmad, chief executive of Yayasan Karyawan, an organization working to publish great Malay works and the great works of the world's civilizations in Malay, heartrendingly expressed his disappointment when he said:

> What is the point of having an official or a national language when it is not being used for the development of the country in all fields? . . . We will go back to the colonial times when the English language belonged to the elites and those in power.
>
> (Hassan, 2005, pp. 12–13)

There was clearly strong tension between the government's decision and the responses of Malay intellectuals. This cry completely ignores the reality that this time around the change was being instituted because the dominant ethnic group was being disadvantaged by weak competencies in the English language. Any major change from Bahasa Melayu (the national language and the mother language of the dominant ethnic group) would not have been instituted if the dominant ethnic group had not been in a position of disadvantage. The dilemma facing the dominant ethnic group is articulated clearly by Lowe and Khattab (2003) when they say:

> The success in having a national language resulted in the Malays – the race it was designed to help – being disadvantaged. The current policy, therefore, had to be substituted with one which, in fact, was directly opposed to the earlier policy. English now has to be propagated amongst a population schooled only in Malay and with a vested interest in its continued dominance. With English being used as a commercial world language, as well as functioning as a gateway to the Information Communication Technology (ICT) world, large segments of the Malay population which had been insulated from such world changes were being denied access to it. (p. 219)

To understand the development of the disadvantaged position of the dominant ethnic group one needs to appreciate the ways in which globalization is influencing higher education. The re-establishment of English began with the government's wish to develop Malaysia into a regional center of education, which required the liberalization of higher education. Private institutions of higher learning were to use English as the medium of instruction for their various courses. This provision was made to encourage private sector efforts to develop higher education in Malaysia to enable them to attract foreign students to Malaysia as well as provide

Malaysian students – who might instead have gone abroad – with the opportunity to study in English in Malaysia. This dual system of language of instruction eventually led to a bifurcation of higher education, resulting in public universities using Bahasa Melayu and private universities using English as the medium of instruction.

The public universities in Malaysia play an integral social role in the development of human resource for the nation. The government heavily subsidizes the fees of these universities. Government support provides opportunities in the public universities for a large proportion of students who come from the rural areas that are home to the dominant ethnic group. They struggle with English because they come from rural environments that have given them little opportunity to study it. Most of them enroll in the private universities, despite the fact that these universities charge much higher fees. This is mainly because the private universities provide these students with greater flexibility in the choice of programs to study compared to public universities where personal choice is limited and students have to accept the courses that are offered. This situation has led to what is described as "the rural–urban English divide [which] is also a divide between Malays and non-Malays" (David, 2004, p. 5).

These complexities were further compounded by the issue of employment. With the bifurcation of higher education, large numbers of Malay graduates from public universities faced challenges in obtaining employment. Mustapha Mohamed, the then executive director of the government-sponsored National Economic Action Council, articulates the reasons for this problem when he says: "This is basically a Malay problem. . . . It has to do with . . . their poor performances in, and command of, the English language" (Mohamed, 2002, pp. 1, 12). Private sector employers looked for graduates who had English language competency. Consequently, graduates from private institutions of higher learning, who were mainly Chinese, were sought after, as they were more confident and fluent in the English language. If this situation were allowed to continue with no change in language policy, the dominant ethnic group would have experienced negative consequences, which would have led to political and social instability in Malaysia (Gill, 2004).

Chinese educators' response to the implementation of change in medium of instruction

In the Chinese community, the three pillars representing Chinese education, Chinese newspapers, and various guilds, associations, and non-governmental organizations are integral to the culture and identity of the community. These pillars are explicated in an article written by Sim and Soong (2007) (the former is the executive director of Sin Chew Media Corporation and the latter is the director of the MCA's think tank, the Institute of Analysis and Policy Research), who both stress that these three pillars "have evolved because the Chinese community in Malaysia had to defend its own identity, in particular its mother tongue, while negotiating political as well as communal complexities along the way" (p. 24).

The first pillar consists of 1,291 Sekolah Kebangsaan Jenis Cina (SKJC) and 60 independent schools. As for the second pillar, there are six Chinese dailies in Peninsular Malaysia and eight in Sabah and Sarawak. The third pillar is made up of approximately 5,000 associations, ranging from clan-based societies, educationists, and political parties, to trade associations and chambers of commerce. Many date back to the 1800s, and they continue to grow as new industries and community needs arise. The Chinese educational system received and still receives tremendous support both financially and morally from the strong Chinese community.

Given this context, the Chinese educators felt aggrieved that, despite the fact that students in Chinese medium education outperformed students in national schools in the field of science and math, they had to change their medium of instruction. They just could not understand any reason for the need to change, other than the government wanting to change the identity of the national-type schools. Dr. Kua (2005), the former principal of New Era College, a tertiary-level institution that uses Mandarin as the language of education, expresses the community's concerns when he says:

> the Chinese ... education lobbies ... see the teaching of Maths and Science in English as a serious threat to the existence of the mother-tongue education system because at a stroke, it homogenizes all the primary schools. There would be no need for Chinese ... schools when the schools become effectively English schools with a subject in Malay or Chinese. (p. 175)

Describing the context will provide a clearer picture of the Chinese community's concerns. At the Primary School Assessment (this is the level of Primary 6, where students have their first public exam), the change will mean that the subjects will be English, Mandarin, Bahasa Melayu, math in English, and science in English. This means that, if the policy is implemented as is being done in national schools, then everything will be in English except for Mandarin and Bahasa Melayu – both language subjects. Therefore this erases the Chinese make-up of these schools and transforms them into English medium schools with Mandarin and Bahasa Melayu offered as language subjects.

The Chinese educators were extremely unhappy with this situation. But despite their frustrations, this language policy was top-down. These were "policies that come from people of power and authority to make decisions for a certain group, without consulting the end-users of the language" (Kaplan & Baldauf, 1997, p. 196). Despite this, a document drafted by the MCA Central Committee – the MCA is the main Chinese political party in the country – stressed that "an important principle firmly upheld by MCA is that the teaching of mathematics and science in the Chinese primary schools should mainly be in the mother tongue" (MCA 9 Point Party Platform, 2006, p. 30). Therefore, given that it was not possible to avert the directive, they sought to influence the mode of implementation. The strong need to maintain their Chinese identity manifested through mother-tongue education underpinned these efforts. The Chinese community has consistently resisted the change and proposed and implemented modifications to the system of implementation. This has been discussed at length in an article by Gill (2007).

Tamil educators' response to the implementation of change in medium of instruction

The Tamil community in Malaysia forms a smaller percentage of the population than the Chinese. In 2001, Malaysia had a total population of 25 million. The Chinese community makes up 26% of the population, numbering 6,500,000. In contrast, the other significant minority group – the Tamil community – makes up 7.7% (1,925,000) of the population (Department of Statistics, 2001). A larger proportion of the Tamil community belonged to the lower socio-economic group for many years because historically they were brought in by the British to work on rubber estates. A proportion of them gradually climbed up the socio-economic ladder through education, jobs in the civil service, and the traditional mainstays of medicine, engineering, and accounting. But, despite the social class mobility of the Tamil community, it does not sufficiently expend the necessary community-based financial support to Tamil medium education as does the Chinese community to Chinese medium education. The Tamil educational system largely depends on the government for support. How then did the Tamil community respond to the change in medium of instruction? After the announcement for change in language policy in 2002, more than 800 people gathered at a major convention hall in Kuala Lumpur on August 10 to discuss the impact of this change on Tamil schools. Most of the people were head teachers of Tamil schools and chairs of the parent–teacher associations.

Krishnan (2008) states that the major reason for the support of the change was because most of the students came from working-class homes and would not be provided with the opportunity to gain competency in the English language by themselves. Therefore it was felt that this move – particularly in the field of science and technology, which is dominated by English – could only benefit the children.

The Tamil language educators feel strongly that the language, culture, ethos, history, and identity of Tamil students can be safeguarded by the cultural environment of the school, which is mainly Tamil based. Indian parents felt that they get the best of everything in Tamil schools – they have their ethnic cultural identity through the Tamil language as a subject, their national identity through Bahasa Melayu as a subject, and the acquisition of science and math in English, a powerful language.

As a result of these factors and those of improved facilities and performance of Tamil school students, there is greater confidence in the Tamil education system. Consequently, there has been a significant increase in the enrollment in Tamil primary schools in Malaysia, especially since 2003. In 2003, there were 90,127 students. As at January 31, 2007, there were 105,618 students in the 523 Tamil primary schools in Malaysia. This was an increase of 15,491 students (Krishnamoorthy, as cited in Krishnan, 2008, p. 16). Tamil schools have now become more attractive, and more middle-class parents and professionals have started to send their children to Tamil schools.

Conclusion

Despite the challenges and complexities of adopting a bottom-up and top-down approach to language policies, the Malaysian government has over the years maintained a balance between the needs of the dominant ethnic group and those of the minority communities. This balance has resulted in the existence of a vernacular school system existing parallel with the national school system in Malaysian education. Malaysia has the largest number of Chinese medium schools outside of Mainland China. Malaysian educational policies and practices have enabled the major ethnic communities in the nation to maintain and sustain their ethnic linguistic and cultural identities. These policies demonstrate the pragmatism of the Malaysian government and its interest in maintaining and sustaining the ethnic, linguistic, and cultural identities of various ethnic groups.

While the government provides support for ethnic educational systems, one of its biggest concerns is that of developing and enhancing national cultural identity through the national school system. This is why Bahasa Melayu still functions as the main medium of instruction for all subjects except for science and math, which are taught in English. The government is very concerned about ensuring that the majority of Malaysians study in national schools so that they can experience a multi-ethnic educational environment in which they can study, play, grow up, and progress together. Having students experience a multi-ethnic educational environment is essential for the development of national integration and national unity.

One of the biggest challenges facing Malaysia now is that language policy and practices in education have led to "80–90% of ethnic Chinese students attending Chinese schools and about 50% of Indians attending Tamil schools" (Yong, 2003, p. F3). While providing for maintenance and sustenance of ethnic and cultural identity, the "differing language options as medium of instruction may be creating more barriers to national integration than ever before" (David, 2004, p. 11). To attract non-Malays into the national schools systems, efforts are being made to make the national schools the schools of choice so that they will reflect the multi-ethnicity of the nation and provide for plural integration. This is being done by working towards ensuring that there is a greater ethnic mix of teachers in this system and to provide for a plurality of ethnic identity through the provision of mother-tongue languages as subjects. There is also integration into the national milieu through the national system of education, with most subjects still being taught in Bahasa Melayu – the national language – while science and mathematics are taught in English.

References

Abdullah, H. (1994). *Language planning in Southeast Asia*. Kuala Lumpur, Malaysia: Dewan Bahasa dan Pustaka.
Asmah, H. O. (1979). *Language planning for unity and efficiency: A study of the language status and corpus planning of Malaysia*. Kuala Lumpur, Malaysia: Dewan Bahasa dan Pustaka.
Asmah, H. O. (1982). *Language and society in Malaysia*. Kuala Lumpur, Malaysia: Dewan Bahasa dan Pustaka.
Asmah, H. O. (2007). Malaysia and Brunei. In A. Simpson (Ed.), *Language and national identity in Asia* (pp. 337–359). Oxford, UK: Oxford University Press.
Beer, W. R., & Jacob, J. E. (Eds.). (1985). *Language policy and national unity*. Totowa, NJ: Rowman & Allanheld.
Chai, H. C. (1967). *Education and nation building in plural societies: The West Malaysian experience*. Canberra, Australia: Australian National University Press.
Cooper, R. L. (1989). *Language planning and social change*. Cambridge, UK: Cambridge University Press.
David, M. K. (2004). Language policies in a multilingual nation: Focus on Malaysia. In M. K. David (Ed.), *Teaching of English in second and foreign language settings: Focus on Malaysia* (pp. 1–16). Frankfurt, Germany: Peter Lang.
David, M. K., & Govindasamy, S. (2005). Negotiating a language policy for Malaysia: Local demand for affirmative action versus challenges from globalization. In A. S. Canagarajah (Ed.), *Reclaiming the local in language policy and practice* (pp. 123–145). Mahwah, NJ: Lawrence Erlbaum.
Department of Statistics. (2001). *Population and housing census 2000*. Retrieved September 19, 2006, from http://www.statistics.gov.my
Emerson, R. (1960). *From empire to nation: The rise of self-assertion of Asian and African peoples*. Cambridge, MA: Harvard University Press.
Federation of Malaya. (1957). *The Education Ordinance 1957*. Kuala Lumpur, Malaysia: Government Press.
Fishman, J. A. (1968). Sociolinguistics and language problems of developing countries. In J. A. Fishman (Ed.), *Language problems of developing nations* (pp. 3–16). New York: John Wiley & Sons.
Gaudart, H. (1992). *Bilingual education in Malaysia*. Townsville, Australia: Centre for South-East Asian Studies.
Gill, S. K. (2002). *International communication: English language challenges for Malaysia*. Serdang, Malaysia: Universiti Putra Malaysia Press.
Gill, S. K. (2004). Medium of instruction policy in higher education in Malaysia: Nationalism versus internationalization. In J. W. Tollefson & A. B. M. Tsui (Eds.), *Medium of instruction policies: Which agenda? Whose agenda?* (pp. 135–152). Mahwah, NJ: Lawrence Erlbaum.
Gill, S. K. (2005). Language policy in Malaysia: Reversing direction. *Language Policy, 4*(3), 241–260.
Gill, S. K. (2007). Shift in language policy in Malaysia: Unraveling reasons for change, conflict and compromise. *AILA Review, 20,* 106–122.

Hashim, M. S. (1972). *An introduction to the constitution of Malaysia.* Kuala Lumpur, Malaysia: Government Printers.

Hassan, A. (2005, March). *Memartabatkan penggunaan Bahasa Melayu: Dasar, pelaksanaan dan pencapaian* [Ennobling the Malay language: Policy, implementation, and accomplishment]. Paper presented at the Second Malay Education Congress, Kuala Lumpur, Malaysia.

Horowitz, D. L. (1985). *Ethnic groups in conflict.* Berkeley: University of California Press.

Kamenka, E. (1976). Political nationalism: The evolution of the idea. In E. Kamenka (Ed.), *Nationalism: The nature and evolution of an idea* (pp. 2–20). New York: St. Martin's Press.

Kaplan, R. B. (1989). Language planning vs. planning language. In C. N. Candlin & T. F. McNamara (Eds.), *Language, learning, and community* (pp. 193–203). Sydney, Australia: NCELTR.

Kaplan, R. B., & Baldauf, R. B. (1997). *Language planning from practice to theory.* Clevedon, UK: Multilingual Matters.

Krishnan, M. (2008). *Development of Tamil school education in Malaysia: An analysis of achievements and challenges.* Kuala Lumpur, Malaysia: Yayasan Strategik Sosial.

Kua, K. S. (2005). *New era education: Speeches and writings, 1995–2005.* Kajang, Malaysia: New Era College.

Lowe, V., & Khattab, U. (2003). Malaysian language planning and cultural rights in the face of a global world. In A. Goonasekera, C. Hamelink, & V. Iyer (Eds.), *Cultural rights in a global world* (pp. 217–222). Singapore: Eastern Universities Press.

Malaya (Federation), Education Committee (1956). *The Razak Report.* Kuala Lumpur, Malaysia: Government Press.

Mauzy, D. K. (1985). Language and language policy in Malaysia. In W. R. Beer & J. E. Jacob (Eds.), *Language policy and national unity* (pp. 151–177). Totowa, NJ: Rowman & Allanheld.

MCA 9 Point Party Platform. (2006). Retrieved July 30, 2008, from http://www.mca.org.my/Chinese/9%20Point%20Party%20Platform%20pdf/9plans_Eng.pdf

Means, G. P. (1991). *Malaysian politics: The second generation.* Singapore: Oxford University Press.

Ministry of Education Malaysia. (1961). *Education Act 1961.* Kuala Lumpur, Malaysia: International Law Book Services.

Mohamed, M. (2002, March 14). Tailor courses to market needs, NEAC: Institutions must ensure graduates are employable. *New Straits Times*, pp. 1, 12.

Philip, L. F. S. (1975). *Seeds of separatism: Educational policy in Malaya 1874–1940.* Kuala Lumpur, Malaysia: Oxford University Press.

Sim, R., & Soong, F. K. (2007, September 9). 3 pillars of the Chinese community. *New Straits Times*, p. 27.

Yang, P. K. (1998). Constitutional and legal education for mother tongue education. In K. S. Kua (Ed.), *Mother tongue education of Malaysian ethnic minorities* (pp. 26–71). Kajang, Malaysia: Dong Jiao Zong Higher Learning Centre.

Yong, T. K. (2003, February 23). Daunting task to check polarization in national schools. *New Sunday Times Focus*, p. F3.

Part 8
Religion, culture, identity, and education

30

Cultural diversity, Muslims, and education in France and England

Two contrasting models in Western Europe

Nasar Meer
University of Bristol, UK

Valérie Sala Pala
University of Saint-Etienne, France

Tariq Modood
University of Bristol, UK

Patrick Simon
National Demographic Institute, Paris, France

Introduction

It is widely accepted that European nation-states have not subscribed to a common or overarching response to religious minority diversity (Modood, Triandafyllidou, & Zapata-Barrero, 2006). This appears to be particularly evident in educational settings, and may be explained by the heterogeneity of European education systems, as well as the diverging role that religion assumes within different European nation-states (Jackson, Miedema, Weisse, & Willaime, 2007). The most compelling explanation, however, arguably rests in the diverging "philosophies of integration" that have historically shaped these different nation-states' responses to religious minority diversity (Favell, 2003). Indeed, one of the best illustrations of this continuing differentiation may be found in the contrasting interactions between religious diversity and education in France and England.

It is has been argued that the presence of migrant and post-migrant children in France has challenged a model of French republicanism which seeks to educate its future citizens by abstracting them from their cultural, including religious, particularities (Déloye, 1994). This is because the French education system has historically set out to construct a unitary French Republic, one that is characterized by a high degree of uniformity in its *public* identity, culture, and language. It is unsurprising then to learn that the development of multicultural educational policies in France has very effectively been resisted (Lorcerie, 2003; Morel, 2002), though, paradoxically, racial categories clearly operate in schools, where processes of discrimination and segregation are plainly evident (Laforgue, 2006; Payet, 1999; Rinaudo, 1999; Van Zanten, 2006). Conversely, the children of postwar migrants who arrived as citizens of the United Kingdom and Commonwealth (CUKC) have long been recognized as ethnic and racial minorities requiring state support and differential treatment to overcome barriers in their future exercise of citizenship. Indeed, part of the philosophy of integration that this "British multiculturalism" has given rise to frequently emerged from, and therefore attributed great emphasis to, minority particularity in educational policy (Modood & May, 2001). In this chapter we contrast these two national cases by focusing upon examples of "difference" in specific educational accommodation or non-accommodation that have assumed greatest prominence in each country.

These include contestations in France over *laïcité* and the accommodation of Islam and Muslims, especially over the Muslim headscarf, that have emerged in a context marked by an anxiety over the future of the "republican model of integration." Alongside the debates on *laïcité* rest others concerning the development of religious Muslim schools as well as the ways in which "subaltern histories" of immigration and colonialism may or may not be taught. British debates, meanwhile, have long incorporated a dialogue between advocates of antiracist education and multicultural education, with their competing political imperatives and policy implications. While the British approach has historically been marked by a high degree of pragmatic accommodation on the issue of uniforms (including headscarves) and dietary requirements, it is true that this trajectory has been affected by recent policy shifts aimed at a "civic re-balancing" (Meer & Modood, in press; Modood, 2007) that is perhaps epitomized by the introduction of citizenship education, as well as a renewed hesitancy over the issue of religiously specific schools within the publicly funded sector.

The French case: Islam and *laïcité* in public schools

The French system of secularism, which is more widely referred to as *laïcité*, did not find itself in conflict with Islam until the end of the 1980s. This changed when in January 1983 the then prime minister, Pierre Mauroy, problematized the trade union complaints of "Moroccan Muslim" workers during an industrial dispute. At the time, the reference to Islam in an industrial dispute appeared curious, but took a less ambiguous form in the "Muslim headscarf" affair that followed it. This occurred when the school director of a secondary school in Creil (near Paris) invoked the principle of *laïcité* in his decision to exclude three pupils who wore the Muslim headscarf. When in November 1989 the Conseil d'État (the highest administrative court in France) concluded that the wearing of the headscarf is not contradictory to the values of the secular and republican school, it encouraged a liberal reading of *laïcité*. This insisted that the 1905 Act on the separation of the Churches and the State could warrant school exclusions only for proselytism and the disruption of school activities, and school directors were advised to evaluate the situation on a case-by-case basis.

Why, then, did this issue re-emerge 15 years later? Had the wearing of headscarves increased during these years? Were the girls younger and the pressures from their families greater? These are empirical questions that remain unanswered but which were asserted during the decision in July 2003 by Jacques Chirac to set up the Commission of Reflection for the Implementation of the Principle of *Laïcité* in the Republic, known as the Stasi Commission (Stasi, 2004). Following the Commission's main recommendations, the government adopted the March 15, 2004 Act, stating that, "in public primary, secondary and high schools, the wearing of signs or clothes through which the pupils conspicuously display a religious belonging is forbidden" (LOI no. 2004–228, 2004).

This Act was enforced through an administrative regulation on May 18, 2004 which stated that "the prohibited signs and clothes are those by which, whatever they may be called, one is immediately identified by his or her religious beliefs, such as the Muslim headscarf, the kippa or a cross of manifestly excessive dimension" (Ministerial Regulation, 2004). The Muslim headscarf, contrary to a "discreet" Christian cross, was considered to be a conspicuous religious sign.

It is worth remembering that this Act did not stem from a "social demand" but arose from the political sphere itself, emotively relayed by the media (Lorcerie, 2005; Tévanian, 2005). Indeed, public and media discourses tended to reduce the debate to a "clash of civilizations" between an enlightened West and a backward, dangerous, and sexually oppressive Muslim culture. Gender equality was, thus, the second dimension of the controversy, for by invoking the oppression of women, through a strategic use of references to Afghanistan and Iran, the headscarf was frequently characterized as a sign of the subordination of women in "Muslim cultures." In this way the debate on *laïcité* has fostered a sharp return of assimilationism and contributed to a rise in Islamophobia (Geisser, 2003).

Throughout this process a number of other issues were raised which the Stasi Commission recommended government act upon, not least the accommodation of religiously informed dietary requirements as well as the recognition of Kippour and Aïd-el-Kébir as holidays in all public schools. It is worth noting that, since the beginning of the 1980s, there has been provision in school canteens for an optional alternative meal to pork dishes, and more recently Jewish and Muslim minorities have sought the introduction of kosher and halal food. Such provision has faced strong "republican" hostility against adapting a common framework to meet the specific needs of religious minority pupils. Nevertheless, and despite the centralized organization of France's educational system, internal rules for the provision of food within school canteens are issued by local authorities. This means that, while they follow general guidelines, different approaches can in practice be implemented. For example, a recent decision of the Lyon city council to launch a "complete meal without meat" (O. Bertrand, 2007) has been conceived as a compromise to the proponents of *laïcité* and pupils who do not eat pork *without* accommodating the provision of halal or kosher meat. Due to be implemented from September 2008, the decision was taken after intense discussions between the local representatives of the main religions, the main secular organizations, and the city council.

Some Muslim organizations have lobbied for a greater accommodation of religious dietary requirements and have criticized some practices of public institutions. In 2004, the Villefranche-sur-Saône city council sent a letter to all Muslim parents insisting that "all children must eat of each served dish, even in small quantity." Muslim organizations such as the National Council for the Muslim Cult (read as "religion") restated that their demands for halal food in schools were legitimate and complained about the narrow interpretation of *laïcité* evidenced in such attitudes. The official position of the Ministry of National Education proceeded by stating that, although canteens were not obliged to provide substitution meals in order to take into account religious specificities, they were invited to propose diversified meals for health reasons.

One of the most liberal recommendations of the Stasi Commission was the proposal to include the feasts of Aïd-el-Kébir and Kippour in the (long) list of holidays in public schools. This has not been taken up, for President Jacques Chirac rejected the idea by stating that the school calendar already included numerous holidays. Nonetheless, he stated his wish that no pupil would have to apologize for being absent during a religious holiday, and that no important school event should be organized on such days. The interpretation of this benign tolerance is, however, subject to the inclinations of school authorities and the strength of religious communities at the local level.

The British case: Antiracist and multicultural education

In 2002, a British Muslim high school pupil was prohibited from attending her school while she wore a jilbab (a full-length gown). Although the pupil maintained that this garb was prescribed by her religion as she understood it, her school considered it be a contravention of its uniform policy, and feared that other pupils too would be subject to undue pressure to adopt "stricter" forms of Islamic dress if it allowed this pupil to wear hers. On first sight, there appear to be striking similarities between this and other salient cases that have arisen over the issue of *laïcité*. On closer inspection, however, the contrast becomes sufficiently great to discourage any simple parallels. For instance, the British school in question had already accommodated uniform changes that incorporated the wearing of, among others, trousers instead of skirts, shalwar kameez (a tunic and baggy trousers), and headscarves displaying school colors. Just as importantly, however, the school maintained that these accommodations had been made in consultation with the wishes of local parents and communities.

When a resolution to this case was eventually achieved, four years later through judicial means in the House of Lords (Britain's highest court of appeal), Lord Bingham ruled in favor of the school but stressed that:

> This case concerns a particular pupil and a particular school in a particular place at a particular time. . . . The House is not, and could not be, invited to rule on whether Islamic dress, or any feature of Islamic dress, should or should not be permitted in the schools of this country.
>
> (*Begum v. Headteacher and Governors of Denbigh High School*, 2006)

The clear emphasis was, then, on local level pragmatism instead of national level enforcement. Indeed, the jilbab case was settled nearly a quarter of a century after another watershed House of Lords ruling *against* a private school which refused enrollment to an orthodox Sikh boy (who wore long hair under a turban) unless the boy removed his turban and cut his hair (*Mandla v. Dowell Lee*, 1983). The ensuing acceptance that Sikh pupils had the right to wear turbans, because they informed an important part of Sikh identities (mirrored in other spheres beyond education; see Singh, 2005), consolidated the impulse for schools to seek negotiated accommodations of minority differences with a view to incorporating them within the schooling environments. Each case thus suggests that religion has been an important part of the ways in which migration-related diversity has given rise to educational challenges in England. It is perhaps surprising then to note how the most prominent approaches to minority cultural differences, antiracist and multicultural education, have historically had very little to say of religion in education.

For a long time, antiracist education was premised upon the view that education should confront and challenge prevailing societal attitudes and practices marked by racist dynamics (Modood & May, 2001). Throughout the 1980s it was given a sense of urgency in evidence that some minorities were much less likely to achieve the basic qualifications necessary for employment, let alone the social mobility aspired to by their parents (Stone, 1981). Antiracist educators sought to redress these tendencies through an explicit recognition of racism in society, and a greater awareness and sensitivity among educators of racial issues, alongside the promotion of positive images of Black people through the teaching of Black history and promotion of Black role models (Mullard, 1985; Troyna, 1987). It was applied in educational policy when the Inner London Education Authority (ILEA), with the support of some left-wing radicals (including the former mayor of London Ken Livingstone), became receptive to its ideas. Indeed, much of what we know as both antiracist and multicultural education has been enacted at the local education authority level. This is because local education authorities (LEAs) are responsible for education within the jurisdiction of county councils and metropolitan boroughs, which includes responsibility for all state schools with the exception of those that apply for and are afforded "voluntary aided status" (and can therefore opt out) under the terms of the 1944 Education Act (a category of further relevance later in the chapter). Because of these and other powers, including section 11 of the Local Government Act 1966, which afforded local authorities additional funds to support the presence of significant numbers of ethnic minorities requiring language and other access assistance, in many multi-ethnic urban areas LEAs have been able to encourage antiracist and multicultural initiatives in the face of – and at the cost of – some vociferous opposition.

This might be characterized as "municipal drift," a further example of which can be found in one of the earliest adoptions of multicultural praxis. This follows Birmingham LEA's introduction in 1975 of a new school curriculum "which required that pupils learn about and learn from the great world faiths present in the city" (Hewer, 2001, p. 517). Other LEAs promoted innovations including the provision of halal meat and school uniform amendments. Indeed, the guidelines issued by Bradford LEA professed (a) equality of treatment, opportunity, and services in shared educational settings, alongside (b) an equal right to the maintenance of distinctive identities and loyalties of culture, language, religion, and custom. Both of these positions were set out in its LEA policy statement (City of Bradford Local Administrative Memorandum No. 2, 1982), and it is important to emphasize that both antiracist and multicultural education were diffuse conceptions of educational reform, and to that extent it is difficult to present either as entirely distinct from the other (Troyna, 1987, p. 311).

Teaching religions and "subaltern histories" in the French republican school

There is one great exception to *laïcité* in France: the region of Alsace-Lorraine (in the East of France) has had a special status since its annexation by Germany from 1870 to 1918. Owing to this annexation it was not bound by the laws on *laïcité*, and religious education is thus still compulsory in public schools, with teachers appointed by the recognized Churches (that is the Catholic, Protestant, and Jewish religions, but not Islam) and paid for by the State. The content of the curriculum is defined by the Churches, and pupils can be exempted if the parents seek it, but attendance is the rule. In practice about half of the pupils in primary schools, two-thirds in secondary schools, and many in high schools do not attend religious education classes. The continuity of this special status in Alsace-Lorraine more than 100 years after the 1905 Act, despite numerous criticisms, reveals the contradictions of the implementation of *laïcité* in France.

At the national level, there has been a growing call for several years for better teaching of religions in public schools. The idea that religion is a fundamental cultural fact (and not only a belief), and thus that it has to be taught in public schools, was developed between the 1989 Joutard Report (Czajka, Joutard, & Lequin, 1992) and the 2002 Debray Report. During the 1990s, some reforms promoted a better integration of religions into the curriculum, and in 1996 the origin of Christianity was introduced in the history curriculum of the first year of high school, while the origins of Islam were omitted. The 2002 Debray Report recommended integrating the teaching of religion into existing disciplines (starting with history, but also languages or arts), and insisted on the necessity of providing specific training to teachers and school directors.

Issues of national identity are highly politicized in France, and in 2007, for the first time since World War II, a Ministry for Immigration, Integration, National Identity and Co-Development was created with the aim of reinforcing and promoting national identity. This is problematic because immigrants, and more generally ethnic minorities, are conceived of as outsiders who are challenging this national identity and therefore should be required to conform to it (Noiriel, 2007). Alongside this, since 2005, a growing debate has developed over the "colonial fracture" and the debt of the French State towards the people of the former colonies, in North Africa, sub-Saharan Africa, and the West Indies (Blanchard, Bancel, & Lemaire, 2005). The adoption of the February 23, 2005 Act (named the Mekachera Act) sought to recognize the positive contribution of French repatriates from North Africa (*pieds noirs*), but triggered a scandal because its article 4 encouraged the official history curriculum to give "the place that it deserves" to "the positive role played by the French presence overseas, especially in North Africa." This clause was finally revoked after much opposition (R. Bertrand, 2006).

Debates on the contemporary consequences of the past are crucial in the educational system and have been reinitiated by the opening in 2007 of the National Centre for the History of Immigration (Cité Nationale de l'Histoire de l'Immigration), conceived from the 1990s as a project aimed at valorizing immigration as constitutive of the national history. It is leading on the need to teach (and to teach differently) the history of immigration at school, together with the National Institute for Pedagogic Research (Institut National de la Recherche Pédagogique [INRP]), which recently argued that the history of immigration is absent from the curriculum (Falaize, 2007).

Difference and divergence in England: From multicultural to citizenship education

In England, meanwhile, through an elision of political and cultural identities, antiracist and multicultural education became inherently oppositional educational movements. One outcome was that, where multiculturalism was, somewhat erratically, introduced into multi-ethnic British schools, it was regarded by many antiracist educators as "an instrument of control and stability rather than one of change" (Mullard, 1985, p. 50). A recurring antiracist criticism of multicultural education concerned its alleged lack of politics, which related to the antiracist desire to predicate race equality in education on an overarching, oppositional, political identity. Hence groups such as the All London Teachers Against Racism and Fascism (ALTARF), which emerged in the late 1970s, and the publicly funded Constructions of Antiracist Education programs, which developed in the early 1980s through the policies of the ILEA, sought to distance themselves from ethnic or cultural particularity by embracing a singular politics of Black solidarity. In this way they presented their movement as an oppositional pedagogy premised on a political conflict between Black and White interests (Modood, 1988).

The Swann Commission (1985) tried to move beyond this binary logic by promoting and characterizing a multicultural society as one that "values the diversity within it, whilst united by the cohesive force of the common aims, attributes and values which we all share ... diversity within unity" (Swann, 1985, chap. 1, para. 6). In many respects the tension between antiracist and multicultural education are encapsulated in the various dynamics that concerned this report, for, although it was focused upon issues of diversity related to educational settings, its major contribution was that it saw "the issues of ethnic minority children as closely tied up with the basic character of mainstream education" (Verma, 1989, p. 3) and therefore an issue for society as a whole – *just as antiracists had wanted their conceptions of racism to be viewed*. This was nevertheless a limited multiculturalism since it explicitly precluded state support of linguistic pluralism (in terms of "mother tongue" teaching) or the expansion of religious schools, seeking instead to make each matters of private concern. Moreover, its recommendations were not widely adopted, because the Conservative government made radical changes to the autonomy of state schools, previously under greater control of LEAs, with the introduction of the Education Reform Act (ERA) in 1988. This Act required every school to adhere to a curriculum that was centrally defined and *compulsorily* prescribed, and enforced the mandatory testing of pupils at ages 7, 11, 14, and 16 years (with the concomitant publication of school league tables as a measure of school performance and success). The ERA specifically curtailed the powers of the influential Labour-controlled Inner London LEA, which is home to a very large proportion of England's ethnic minority school population.

It is arguable that one policy shift which this earlier centralization has facilitated includes the introduction of citizenship education in England. Citizenship education is a contested idea and set of policies that denote a variety of implications in different contexts (Gutmann, 2003). Its formal introduction into British schools is a recent development, and its late introduction in England, particularly when compared with North America and some European countries, is an interesting anomaly. As Kerr (1999, p. 204) has put it, "The avoidance of any overt official government direction in schools concerning political socialization and citizenship education can almost be seen as a national trait," and indeed can be seen to be paralleled by the equally late adoption in England of the National Curriculum. Similarly, Sir Bernard Crick himself, chair of the Qualifications and Curriculum Authority (QCA) commission into citizenship education, states:

> We were the last civilised country almost in the world to make citizenship part of the national curriculum. I think we thought we didn't need it being the mother of all parliaments and a model to the world of parliamentary government; I think those ideas lingered on and long past reality.
> (B. Crick, personal communication, June 27, 2007)

As his report recommending the introduction of citizenship education put it, part of the groundswell for its recent emergence is undoubtedly a sense of "civic deficit" epitomized by voter apathy among young people, which the report claims "is inexcusably bad and should and could be remedied" (QCA, 1998, sec. 3., para. 10). To this end the QCA, under the commission chaired by Crick, recommended the implementation of a coordinated national strategy for the statutory requirement for schools to spend around 5% of their curriculum time teaching three interdependent elements of citizenship education. These would be (a) social and moral responsibility, (b) community involvement, and (c) political literacy.

While these reiterate elements of the Swann Commission, they perhaps also constitute a modification of earlier approaches. It is noteworthy that there is no explicit reference to antiracism and multiculturalism, confirming to some that citizenship education represents a disengagement from these issues. Osler and Starkey (2001, p. 293), for example, charge the QCA report with "institutional racism" for demanding that "minorities must learn to respect the laws, codes and conventions as much as the majority" (QCA, 1998, pp. 17–18). This they take as evidence of a "colonial approach . . . that runs throughout the report" and which "falls into the trap of treating certain ethnicities as 'Other' when it discusses cultural diversity" (Osler & Starkey, pp. 292–293). Sir Bernard Crick repudiates the view that his committee singled out minorities, saying his committee

> was not willing to give the public the view that the major thrust of citizenship was race relations. We said damn it, it's about the whole population including the majority . . . pupils should learn, respect and have knowledge of national, regional, ethnic, and religious differences. We were simply taking a broader view. We thought that . . . all our nation's children should receive an education that would help them to become active citizens: all our nation's children.
>
> (Personal communication, June 27, 2007)

This need not be evidence of an assimilatory "retreat" from antiracism or multiculturalism, however, but, as Meer and Modood (in press) have argued, something that might be characterized as a "re-balancing" of broader discourses of antiracism and multiculturalism. Indeed, the entire idea of "citizenship education" is in itself surely evidence of this.

Faith schools in England

The issue that really cuts across the development of antiracism, multiculturalism, and citizenship education is that of state-funded faith-based schooling (Meer, in press). It is worth noting that antiracism has often been stridently secularist and implicitly, if not explicitly, ambivalent or opposed to faith-based schooling, and that the multiculturalism of the Swann Commission expressly ruled out the religious schools sought by recent religious minorities such as Muslims and Hindus (but maintained the status quo in respect to more established Jewish and Catholic state-funded faith-based schools). The Crick Report, meanwhile, did not really engage with the issue of faith schooling because it fell outside its remit.

These discursive dismissals and policy oversights are problematic when we recognize that there are currently over 4,700 state-funded Church of England schools, over 2,100 Catholic schools, 35 Jewish schools, and 28 Methodist schools, dwarfing the 7 Muslim schools, or the single Sikh school or Seventh-day Adventist school. It is also indicative of "a modern society which is widely perceived as increasingly secular but is paradoxically increasingly multi-faith" (Skinner, 2002, p. 172). Of all newer minorities that have mobilized for faith schools, Muslims have perhaps been the most vocal. Beyond the issue of parity, Idreas Mears, director of the Association of Muslim Schools (AMS), provides an insight into why this may be:

> I think a general point which is very important to get across is that the state schools do not handle the meaning of Muslim identity well for the children. In actual fact, the way that general society looks at Muslims is as an immigrant minority-ethnic-racial-group and how young people are made to look at themselves through the teaching in state schools tells them "you are this marginal group/minority group and have therefore got to integrate with the mainstream." So there's a process of marginalization and that often leads to resentment. But in a Muslim school that identity is built upon being a Muslim not an ethnic minority.
>
> (Personal communication, April 1, 2006)

Indeed, there are several factors informing Muslim mobilization for faith schools. The first and broadest is paralleled by the interest in other religiously informed faith schooling, and stems from the desire to incorporate more faith-based principles into an integrated education system, so that the "whole person" can be educated in an Islamic environment (Association of Muslim Social Scientists [AMSS], 2004; Hewer, 2001). This would *presuppose* faith rather than treating it as something extraneous to education and external to its major objects (Ashraf, 1990). Second, and through an interpretation of Islam which posits that "after puberty boys and girls should be separated" (Hashmi, 2002, p. 14), there is a concern to develop "safe" environments for post-pubescent children, and in this regard single-sex schooling undoubtedly appeals (Hewer). According to A. Trevathan, however, this need not be an expression of separatism, since "in many ways the community want their children to be raised in a safe environment but still aspire to what successful people aspire to in the West" (personal communication, March 6, 2006), namely social mobility through education. A third factor concerns the current lack of specialist training in the Islamic religious sciences in conjunction with general education, so that young people might "be educated to serve their communities as potential religious leaders" (Hewer, p. 518). This includes the desire to have more British-trained theologians who can discuss theological issues with a contemporary resonance to the lived experiences of being Muslim in England. Fourth, in order to impart more accurate knowledge of Islamic civilizations, literature, languages, and arts (both past and present), there is a desire to see more aspects of Islamic culture embedded within the teaching and ethos of school curricula that are otherwise normatively couched within a Christian-European tradition. Finally, there is the concern over the lower educational attainment of Bangladeshi and Pakistani boys in particular, and the belief that greater accommodation of religious and cultural difference will help address this low achievement and prevent further marginalization.

The debate on the creation of Muslim schools in France

We can contrast this situation with the experience of Muslim schools in France. Private schools include around 2 million pupils, that is, 17% of all pupils, more precisely 13% of the pupils in primary school and 21% of the pupils attending secondary or high school. Almost all these private schools are under contract with the State. The "contract of association" was created by the 1959 Debré Act and at that time involved only Catholic schools. These private schools under contract with the State must respect the national curriculum. Their teachers are paid by the State. These schools also receive a contribution from the local authority, proportionate to the number of pupils. Today, about 95% of the private schools under contract with the State are Catholic, though many Jewish schools have also agreed to enroll about 26,000 pupils. Some schools are open to all denominations, yet to this day there is only one State-sponsored Muslim school: the primary school Taalim-al-Islam located in the French overseas territory La Réunion (opened in 1990). The private Muslim schools in existence are located in Aubervilliers, near Paris (L'école de la Réussite, a secondary school, opened in 2001), Lille (the Averroès high school, created in 2003), and Décines, near Lyon (the Al-Kindi secondary and high school, opened in 2007). An agreement of state sponsorship for these schools is expected in the near future, which would also offer a formal recognition of the legitimacy of Muslim schools among the other faith schools.

Each new Muslim school project is subject to intense debate, and the creation of the first Muslim high school, Averroès, in Lille, offers a good illustration of the symbolic and practical role played by these schools. As summed up on the school's website:

> The idea of the creation of a private Muslim high school was born in 1994 following the exclusion of 19 veiled young girls from the Faidherbe high school in Lille. The mosque Al Imane, located in South Lille, then called the leaders of Muslim organizations to gather in order to cater for these young girls.
>
> (Averroès High School, n.d.)

The school was refused permission three times by the state authorities before being allowed to open. At its opening in 2003, 83 pupils, mostly girls, were enrolled. In the same way, the project of creating a secondary and high school in Décines, near Lyon, faced several refusals from the local state authorities. Finally, the Highest Council for Education (Conseil Supérieur de l'Éducation) made a decision against strong opposition from the local representative of the Ministry of Education, which was using issues such as the security of the building to refuse authorization. The Al-Kindi school finally opened in 2007. Today it enrolls 200 pupils, attending mixed classes. The school's website presents the creation of the school as triggered by a context of "crisis in the public school," crisis in terms of school performance but also because of a "focus on a too narrow conception of *laïcité*." The reasons why some parents want to send their children to Muslim schools are not only the expectation of religious education and the right to wear the Muslim headscarf, but also the most common reasons to avoid public schools, such as performance, security, and discipline.

Conclusion

Religious minorities in England are increasingly seeking an expansion of schools with a religious ethos in the state-maintained faith sector. On the one hand this marks a continuation of the provisions available to earlier religious minorities, while on the other hand the mobilization for Muslim schooling in particular is not premised solely upon the issue of parity, but also upon the recognition of Muslim particularity in pluralizing faith schooling in England. Simultaneously, in the state comprehensive sector, antiracist and multicultural educational concerns have, while sometimes amounting to internally contested debates, had a continuing impact upon educational policy and discourse. These debates have fed ambiguously into the prescribed unity apparent in the recent introduction and mandatory teaching of citizenship education as a core National Curriculum requirement. The case appears to be more conflict driven in France, where the impact of a very rigid conception of *laïcité* and a sort of assimilationist backlash at the turn of the millennium have created an environment that is hostile to the accommodation of religion in the education system. Ethnic diversity itself is seen as a threat against republican values. This context makes it quite difficult to teach issues of immigration and national identity at school in a manner that diverges from the framing encouraged by a prevailing ethno-national ideology. Schools are therefore the main agencies in reproducing an exclusive French national identity. The debates around the history of slavery, colonialism, and immigration have challenged the prevailing republican ideology, but their outcome remains ambiguous. To this end, and despite the recent trends, France and England continue to represent two contrasting cases in Western Europe.

References

Ashraf, S. A. (1990). A suggested common "faith" framework for the curriculum. In S. R. Ameli, A. Azam, & A. Merali (Eds.), *Secular or Islamic? What schools do British Muslims want for their children?* (pp. 27–28). London: Islamic Human Rights Commission.

Association of Muslim Social Scientists (AMSS). (2004). *Muslims on education: A position paper*. Retrieved January 4, 2005, from http://www.amssuk.com/news.htm

Averroès High School. (n.d.). Website. Retrieved November 26, 2007, from http://www.lycee-averroes.com

Begum v. Headteacher and Governors of Denbigh High School, UKHL 15. (2006).

Bertrand, O. (2007, October 2). Lyon lance les cantines œcuméniques: A la prochaine rentrée, un menu "complet sans viande" sera proposé [Lyon launches ecumenical canteens: Next school year, a menu "completely without meat" will be proposed]. *Libération*. Retrieved October 19, 2008, from http://www.liberation.fr/actualite/societe/281969.FR.php

Bertrand, R. (2006). *Mémoires d'empire: La controverse autour du "fait colonial"* [Memories of empire: The controversy surrounding the "colonial"]. Paris: Éditions du Croquant.

Blanchard, P., Bancel, N., & Lemaire, S. (Eds.). (2005). *La fracture coloniale: La société française au prisme de l'héritage colonial* [The colonial fracture: French society under the colonial legacy]. Paris: La Découverte.

City of Bradford Local Administrative Memorandum No. 2. (1982).

Czajka, H., Joutard, P., & Lequin, H. (1992). *Enseigner l'histoire des religions* [Teaching history of religions]. Paris: Centre National de Documentation Pédagogique (CNDP)/Centre Régional de Documentation Pédagogique (CRDP), Besançon.

Debray, R. (2002). *L'enseignement du fait religieux dans l'école laïque* [Teaching religious facts in secular schools]. Paris: Ministère de l'Education Nationale.

Déloye, Y. (1994). *Ecole et citoyenneté* [School and citizenship]. Paris: Presses de la Fondation Nationale des Sciences Politiques.

Falaize, B. (Ed.). (2007). *Enseigner l'histoire de l'immigration à l'école* [Teaching immigration history in school]. Lyon, France: Institut National de la Recherche Pédagogique (INRP).

Favell, A. (2003). *Philosophies of integration: Immigration and the idea of citizenship in France and Britain* (2nd ed.). Basingstoke, UK: Palgrave Macmillan.

Geisser, V. (2003). *La nouvelle Islamophobie* [The new Islamophobia]. Paris: La Découverte.

Gutmann, A. (2003). Unity and diversity in democratic multicultural education: Creative and destructive tensions. In J. A. Banks (Ed.), *Diversity and citizenship education: Global perspectives* (pp. 71–96). San Francisco: Jossey-Bass.

Hashmi, N. (2002). *A Muslim school in Bristol: An overview of the current debate and Muslim school children's views*. Bristol, UK: University of Bristol, Centre for the Study of Ethnicity and Citizenship.

Hewer, C. (2001). Schools for Muslims. *Oxford Review of Education, 27*(4), 515–527.

Jackson, R., Miedema, S., Weisse, W., & Willaime, J. P. (Eds.). (2007). *Religious diversity and education in Europe*. Brussels, Belgium: European Commission.

Kerr, D. (1999). *Citizenship education: An international comparison*. London: Qualifications and Curriculum Authority (QCA).

Laforgue, D. (2006). *La ségrégation scolaire: L'état face à ses contradictions* [Segregation in education: The state facing its contradictions]. Paris: L'Harmattan.

LOI no. 2004-228, March 15. (2004, March 17). Encadrant, en application du principe de laïcité, le port de signes ou de tenues manifestant une appartenance religieuse dans les écoles, collèges et lycées publics [Act regulating, in implementation of the principle of *laïcité*, the wearing of signs or clothes demonstrating a religious belonging in primary, secondary and high schools]. *Journal Officiel, 65*, 5190.

Lorcerie, F. (Ed.). (2003). *L'école et le défi ethnique: Education et intégration* [School and the ethnic challenge: Education and integration]. Paris: European Science Foundation/Institut National de la Recherche Pédagogique (ESF/INRP).

Lorcerie, F. (Ed.). (2005). *La politisation du voile: L'affaire en France, en Europe et dans le monde Arabe* [The politicization of the headscarf: The affair in France, in Europe, and in the Arabic world]. Paris: L'Harmattan.

Mandla v. Dowell Lee. (1983). 2 AC 548 House of Lords transcript. Retrieved September 12, 2007, from www.hrcr.org/safrica/equality/Mandla_DowellLee.htm

Meer, N. (in press). Identity articulations, mobilisation and autonomy in the movement for Muslim schools in Britain. *Race, Ethnicity and Education.*

Meer, N., & Modood, T. (in press). The multicultural state we're in: Muslims, "multiculture" and the civic re-balancing of British multiculturalism. *Political Studies, 56*(3).

Ministerial Regulation. (2004, May 18). Circulaire no. 2004-084, May 15. *Journal Officiel,* 9033.

Modood, T. (1988). "Black," racial equality and Asian identity. *New Community, 14*(3), 397–404.

Modood, T. (2007). *Multiculturalism: A civic idea.* London: Polity.

Modood, T., & May, S. (2001). Multiculturalism and education in Britain: An internally contested debate. *International Journal of Educational Research, 35,* 305–317.

Modood, T., Triandafyllidou, A., & Zapata-Barrero, R. (Eds.). (2006). *Multiculturalism, Muslims and citizenship: A European approach.* London: Routledge.

Morel, S. (2002). *Ecoles, territoires et identités: Les politiques publiques françaises à l'épreuve de l'ethnicité* [Schools, territories, and identities: French public policies facing ethnicity]. Paris: L'Harmattan.

Mullard, C. (1985). *Anti-racist education: The three O's.* Cardiff, UK: National Association for Multicultural Education.

Noiriel, G. (2007). *A quoi sert l'identité nationale?* [What is the use of national identity?] Paris: Comité de Vigilance face aux Usages Publics de l'Histoire (CVUH)/Agone.

Osler, A., & Starkey, H. (2001). Citizenship education and national identities in Britain and France: Inclusive or exclusive? *Oxford Review of Education, 27*(2), 287–305.

Payet, J.-P. (1999). Mixités et ségrégations dans l'école urbaine [Mixes and segregations in the urban school]. *Hommes et Migrations* [Man and Migration], *1217,* 30–42.

Qualifications and Curriculum Authority (QCA). (1998). *Education for citizenship and the teaching of democracy in schools* (Report of the Advisory Group on Citizenship). London: Author.

Rinaudo, C. (1999). *L'ethnicité dans la cité: Jeux et enjeux de la catégorisation ethnique* [Ethnicity in the city: Games and stakes of ethnic categorization]. Paris: L'Harmattan.

Singh, G. (2005). British multiculturalism and Sikhs. *Sikh Formations, 1*(2), 157–173.

Skinner, G. (2002). Religious pluralism and school provision in Britain. *Intercultural Education, 13,* 171–181.

Stasi, B. (2004). *Commission de réflexion sur l'application du principe de laïcité dans la République: Rapport au président de la République* [Commission on the implementation of the principle of *laïcité* within the Republic: Report to the president of the Republic]. Paris: La Documentation Française.

Stone, M. (1981). *The education of the Black child in Britain: The myth of multiracial education.* London: Collins Fontana.

Swann, M. (1985). *Education for all: The report of the inquiry into the education of pupils of children from ethnic minority groups.* London: Her Majesty's Stationery Office (HMSO).

Tévanian, P. (2005). *Le voile médiatique: Un faux débat: "L'affaire du foulard Islamique"* [The mediatic veil: A false debate: "The affair of the Muslim headscarf"]. Paris: Raisons d'Agir.

Troyna, B. (1987). Beyond multiculturalism: Towards the enactment of anti-racist education in policy provision and pedagogy. *Oxford Review of Education, 13*(3), 307–320.

Van Zanten, A. (2006). Une discrimination banalisée? L'évitement de la mixité sociale et raciale dans les établissements scolaires [A banalized discrimination? The avoidance of social and racial mix in schools]. In D. Fassin & E. Fassin (Eds.), *De la question sociale à la question raciale?* [From the social question to the racial question?] (pp. 195–210). Paris: La Découverte.

Verma, G. K. (Ed.). (1989). *Education for all: A landmark in pluralism.* London: Falmer Press.

31

Religion, culture, language, and education in India

Reva Joshee
Ontario Institute for Studies in Education, University of Toronto, Canada

Karen Sihra
Ontario Institute for Studies in Education, University of Toronto, Canada

In India the term *multicultural* gained currency in the 1990s and is linked to demographic realities and long-standing traditions (Bhattacharyya, 2003). *Multicultural education* is a term rarely if ever used, but since the establishment of the post-independence Constitution in 1951 and following two major reports on education in 1953 and 1966, respectively, there has been substantial attention to cultural pluralism and social equality in education. What makes Indian multiculturalism and multicultural education unique is the fact that diversity is considered a defining feature of both Indian identity and Indian democracy. Consequently, the Indian approach to multiculturalism rests on the principles of both unity in diversity and diversity in unity (Alam, 2004). What this means in practice is that diversity is supported not as a necessary evil but as an important ongoing feature of society. Most particularly this approach rests on the twin ideals of autonomy and nondiscrimination as exemplified in article 29 of the Constitution (Protection of interests of minorities), which guarantees linguistic, cultural, and religious groups the right to maintain and develop their distinct identities and forbids discrimination on the basis of race, caste, religion, or language in relation to admission into state-supported educational institutions. This chapter explores how the ideals of autonomy and nondiscrimination have been developed in educational policy and practice in post-independence India, particularly with reference to language, religion, and culture.

Multiculturalism as lived reality

India is arguably the most diverse country in the world. It covers about 3.2 million square kilometers and hosts a population of over 1.1 billion people, making it the second most populous country in the world. In the 2001 national census, about 82% of the population identified as Hindu, 13% Muslim, 2.3% Christian, 1.9% Sikh, 0.76% Buddhist, 0.4% Jain, and 0.01% Zoroastrian. These numbers represent the second largest national Muslim population in the world and the largest Sikh, Jain, and Zoroastrian populations. There are currently

22 languages recognized as official languages, including Hindi and English, which are designated as "national" or "link" languages.

Two communities that are central to discussions of cultural pluralism in India are *dalits* (known officially as scheduled castes) and *adivasis* (known officially as scheduled tribes), which make up 16.2% and 8.2% of the population, respectively (Registrar General and Census Commissioner, India, 2001). The terms *scheduled castes* and *scheduled tribes* are administrative categories; the former used to designate those groups previously know as "untouchables" and the latter, various indigenous groups that for centuries have resisted assimilation into first agrarian and then industrial societies. The members of these two groups themselves use the terms *dalit* (literally translated as "downtrodden") and *adivasi* (literally translated as "original dwellers"). These categories are often grouped with a third category, "other backward classes" (OBC), which is used to encompass a range of groups that have been and continue to be marginalized. The OBC category, which includes lower-caste Hindus and some segments of the Buddhist and Muslim communities, as well as other groups identified on the basis of low economic, social, or educational status, accounts for about 50% of the total population of the country (Government of India, National Commission for Backward Classes, n.d.).

The current approach to incorporating this vast diversity into the daily life of the nation is based largely on an ideal called participatory pluralism (Madan, 1999). Based on the ideas of Mohandas K. Gandhi, this approach simultaneously builds on and challenges older traditions of pluralism that fostered diversity through separation between groups and a hierarchical ordering of society. Participatory pluralism seeks to maintain diversity while breaking down hierarchy and addressing social injustice. Ideally, this form of multiculturalism requires bridging the distance between groups, which must include earnest efforts to celebrate identities other than one's own.

Practicing pluralism within a school may include celebrating holidays associated with all religions in the community. Unlike the practice in Canada, where holidays may be recognized in school announcements or in a display of some kind, this approach necessitates a celebration based on the traditions and practices of the group and encourages all members of the school to participate in the celebration. It also requires an acknowledgment of the pluralism within groups and recognition that cultures are not static; they are constantly being reshaped by their own internal pluralism as well as external forces. Finally, it requires a commitment to addressing inequality between and within groups (for more detailed discussion see, for example, Bhattacharyya, 2003; Madan, 1999; Parekh, 1999; Sangari, 1999). While no one would argue that India has achieved the ideal, it is important to note that, because of this orientation to multiculturalism, state policy flows from the collective lived experience of diversity rather than the other way around (Mishra, Palai, & Das, 2006; Pandey, 2007).

An example of how lived reality influences policy is the development of the Report of the Sachar Committee (Prime Minister's High Level Committee, 2006). In 2005 the Prime Minister's Office recognized that there was a lack of reliable information on Muslim communities in India. The Prime Minister appointed a high level committee headed by Justice Rajindar Sachar to study and report on the lived reality of Muslims in India. The Committee held hearings and conducted investigations that resulted in the preparation of its report, *Social, Economic, and Educational Status of the Muslim Community in India*. Significantly, the report devotes considerable space to the perceptions of non-Muslims as well as Muslims and demonstrates where wider public opinion is at odds with the reality of the lives of Muslims. For example, the report noted that, contrary to popular perceptions, Muslim parents are not reluctant to send their children to schools where they would learn alongside non-Muslim children. Rather there is a lack of adequate and affordable schools, which forces Muslim parents to seek alternatives such as religious-based institutions.

The Committee argued that addressing inequity requires both attending to perceptions of discrimination on the part of minoritized groups and actively fostering diversity. The report recommended both incentives for educational institutions that would create and maintain diversity among their students and an overhaul of textbooks so that they would both reflect reality and foster the creation of values that support diversity. It also advocated support for community-based educational institutions and recommended that they also should have diverse student bodies (Prime Minister's High Level Committee, 2006).

Policy context

India's policies in the area of multiculturalism began before it gained independence from Britain. By the 1920s, policies for what we might now call affirmative action were in place to ensure that minority religious groups were included in the administration of government (Beteille, 2005). While ostensibly these policies were meant to ensure harmony among all groups in the colony, it is widely accepted today that the policies were part of the larger British strategy of "divide and rule" that created new divisions or exploited existing divisions within the indigenous community (Rodrigues, 2005). This legacy continues to taint some of the current policies, especially those for the *dalit*, *adivasi*, and OBC communities.

Today, Indian policies addressing diversity encompass objectives related to secularism, social justice, and the development of a national identity that is inclusive of diversity. The Constitution was cast in the mold of the classical liberal democracy (Beteille, 1998; Hardgrave, 1997) but with what has been called an Indian inflection (Bajpai, 2002). It contains a strong commitment to equality and it seeks to develop an overarching national identity while protecting minority identities based on the premise that strong identification with subgroups is an important building block for identification with the nation as a whole. Yet there is concern among many that the attention to group rights and intergroup equality has come at the price of intragroup inequality, most particularly based on caste, class, and gender (e.g. Hardgrave, 1997; Mahajan, 1999).

At the time of independence, social justice was defined largely in terms of groups that had long suffered economic and social exclusion, namely lower-caste groups, "outcastes," and women. Policies and programs were devised to address what had effectively been centuries of oppression and exclusion based on caste and gender hierarchies. A key policy instrument for addressing social justice has been the Indian version of affirmative action known as the system of reservations. Specific articles of the Constitution mandate the achievement of equality for *dalit* and *adivasi* communities through reservations. This means that a certain number of positions in the public service and in higher education institutions are held for persons from the *dalit* and *adivasi* groups. While this was initially envisioned as a temporary measure, it continues today. Moreover, in the years since independence the system of reservations has been extended to include OBC communities and women in limited ways. Reservations for OBC groups exist only in government employment, although there is currently a lively debate about whether reservations should be expanded to include institutions of higher education.

OBC reservations have been revisited in recent years to reflect the impact of past reservations on future generations. For example, the sons and daughters of OBC reservation "recipients" are exempt from OBC reservations on the grounds that they no longer suffer from the disadvantages of earlier generations. This has, of course, been met with opposition from a variety of groups. However, it is a clear example of how Indian policy evolves to reflect "lived experience" (for more information, see Chalam, 2007; Government of India, Ministry of Human Resource Development, 2008; Government of India, National Commission for Backward Classes, n.d.). In the case of women, reservations exist for elected positions at the local levels but there are no reservations for higher education. In addition to reservations, a bureaucratic infrastructure has been created to safeguard the rights of minoritized groups. Included in the complex of agencies is the National Commission for Scheduled Castes, the National Commission for Backward Classes, the National Commission for Women, the National Commission for Minorities, the National Human Rights Commission, the Ministry of Social Justice and Empowerment, and a host of departments and commissions at the state level.

Secularism in India, unlike the Western versions of this ideal, has meant both that there is no official state religion and that, at least in theory, all religions are equally recognized and valued. In practice this has been translated into several policies and practices, including recognition of a variety of religious holidays as official holidays for everyone, flexible dress codes in schools and other public institutions, and parallel systems of family law based on religious principles. While some of these measures, for example the parallel systems of family law, have been criticized as violating the fundamental principle of gender equality, by and large the recognition of multiple religions has been seen as an important component of Indian society, as well as a contribution India can make to international discussions about interfaith understanding (Bhargava, 2004).

The focus on national identity came out of the acknowledgment that at the time of independence there was no single unified sense of what it meant to be Indian. Instead, people were more attached to ethnic, linguistic, religious, or caste-based identities. Consequently, the Constitution gave due recognition to these identities and – rather than trying to eradicate them – sought to use them as the foundation for a unified national identity. In part this was accomplished by dividing states along linguistic lines and by acknowledging several regional languages as "scheduled" or officially recognized languages. This same value for diversity was evident in Prime Minister Nehru's approach to governing minority cultural groups, which was based on five fundamental principles:

1 People should develop along the lines of their own genius and we should avoid imposing anything on them. We should try to encourage in every way their traditional arts and culture.
2 Tribal rights in land and forests should be respected.
3 We should try to train and build up a team of their own people to do the work of administration and development.
4 We should not over-administer these areas or overwhelm them with a multiplicity of schemes. We should rather work through and not in rivalry to their social and cultural institutions.
5 We should judge results, not by statistics or the amount of money spent, but by the quality of human character that is evolved. (Cited in Bhattacharyya, 2003, p. 157)

In this vision, national identity would be built through active respect for diversity and contact among and between members of the variously constituted cultural groups across the country. While this vision does not reflect the current reality of life in India it does define the fundamental principles on which the approach to multicultural education is based.

Cultural diversity in education

Following from the Constitutional commitments, the three main foci of multicultural education in India have been to address the disadvantages faced by marginalized groups, to encourage the valuing of diversity, and to build a strong national identity. Groups associated with the first focus include particularly girls, *dalits*, *adivasis*, and members of the OBC group. While all three foci address cultural diversity, the first concerns addressing those cultural traditions and structural conditions that have oppressed minoritized groups, and the second and third are linked more directly to issues of religious and linguistic identity.

Minoritized groups

Because the key policies in support of *dalit*, *adivasi*, and OBC communities are connected with affirmative action, it should be no surprise that educational initiatives designed for these groups have generally been linked to access. Programs and initiatives have been developed to provide more schools and teachers in locations where children from these communities can have access to them. Some attention has also been given to developing flexible and alternative educational programs so that children who have other responsibilities (e.g. work, child care) can continue to attend school. Most recently legislation, passed under the title Right to Education, aims to make school attendance mandatory for children ages 6 to 14. The act also mandates that the state provide free education for all students in this age range.

Policy approaches designed to address the inequality of *dalit*, *adivasi*, and OBC groups have been criticized for a variety of reasons. In the first instance, few attempts appear to have been made to ensure that teachers would be respectful of their students. Teachers, who come from upper-caste backgrounds, it is argued, share the same misconceptions of and biases toward members of marginalized groups as others in society. Without adequate attention to issues of teacher attitude, some fear that the existing prejudices and systemic inequalities have been and will continue to be exacerbated. In the case of *adivasi* children, an additional concern has been that their languages and traditions are not valued in the classroom (Dyer et al., 2004; Focus Group on Problems of Scheduled Caste and Scheduled Tribe Children, 2005). At the same time there are few real opportunities for members of minoritized communities to enter into the teaching profession, and there have not been any concerted efforts to build such capacity within minoritized communities.

Specifically with regard to the Right to Education legislation, the central criticism has been that the legislation is not based on a model of rights, which could entail a responsibility on the state to provide quality education for children from marginalized groups. Rather it is a coercive model based on monitoring attendance and punishing parents whose children do not attend school. There is no recognition of the fact that parents might have good reason to keep their children out of school if, for example, the school is doing further damage to their sense of self (Aradhya & Kashyap, 2006).

The Right to Education legislation has also been criticized for not promoting the ideal of the common school system, that is, one in which students of all backgrounds would learn together (Kamat, 2007). It has also been criticized for its lack of focus on children under the age of 6; effectively the state has no responsibility in the provision of preschool. Those parents who have the means will send their children to preschool and those who do not will not. This will perpetuate the distance between the children of the rich and poor. Finally, the legislation does not make adequate provision for the needs of children from particularly disenfranchised groups, including students with disabilities (Madhavan & Manghnani, 2005; Sadgopal, 2001), street and homeless children (DeVenanzi, 2003), and children of sex-workers (Gayen, 2006). A similar initiative has been proposed for the universalizing of secondary education in the proposed 11th Five Year Plan (2007–2012) (Government of India, 11th Five Year Plan Planning Commission, n.d.).

From the early days of independent India one of the roles of education was to bridge the distance between *dalit*, *adivasi*, and OBC groups and the rest of India's communities. And while the Right to Education legislation falls short on this account, the most recent National Curriculum Framework (National Council of Education Research and Training [NCERT], 2005) seeks to address the issue by educating children about the realities of all cultural groups in India as well as presenting information from the perspective of minoritized groups. To this end, the national textbooks produced in 2007 incorporate images and stories of children from a wide variety of backgrounds, use a range of techniques to encourage students to understand the perspective of others, and present information on historical and current forms of exclusion and inequality.

The class VI textbook on social and political life, for example, opens with a story about two boys, one who sells newspapers at a traffic light and the other who rides past that same traffic light on his way to school every day. The two boys strike a friendship and we learn that although both have the same name their lives are vastly different. The boy who sells papers is from a poor Muslim family and the boy on the bicycle is from a middle-class Hindu family. The questions following the story ask the children to examine the differences between the two boys and guides the students to explore the distinction between differences that are valued as part of diversity and differences that are the source of inequality. One of the activities suggested in the book is a discussion of why the boy who sold papers did not go to school, and students are asked to think about whether it is fair that some children do not have the opportunity to go to school (NCERT, 2007c). Although this curriculum intervention does little to address the issues of access and equity for minoritized groups it does begin the process of intergroup understanding.

Religious identity

Over the years many scholars have written about the tradition of tolerance and inclusion inherent in Indian tradition (Jha, 2006). The truth of this claim is debatable, especially in light of the upsurge of Hindu nationalism that developed in the 1980s and 1990s. However, the tolerance of Hinduism was the rhetorical position that allowed the framers of the Constitution to develop their unique version of secularism. The link to Hinduism and early Indian tradition legitimized the view that there are many ways to understand God and therefore all religions should be valued equally. Furthermore, Bhargava (2004) argues that, unlike the more familiar Western version of secularism based on the assumption that religion will be relegated to the private sphere, the Indian version sees religion as a normal part of both the public and the private realms.

This does not mean that there is an official state religion, yet neither is there a strict separation between religion and the state. Instead the state is theoretically in a position to address issues like inequality within religious communities. But, as Bhargava (2004) notes, such intervention is possible only from a position of what he calls "active respect" (p. 4). In other words, the state must actively support a religious community's aspirations in some way in order to have the legitimacy to intervene in its internal functioning. Alam (2004) notes that another important aspect of Indian secularism is that it legitimizes religion in the public sphere so long as it does not interfere with democratic politics. It is on the basis of this version of secularism that religious schools have been allowed to flourish in India.

Like the policies on secularism, the policies on religious education are based in the first instance on a link with early Indian traditions, specifically the fact that in the pre-British period, under both Hindu and Muslim rule, religious instruction formed the core of education (University Commission, 1952). The position during the British colonial period was that government must remain neutral and therefore could not support any religious instruction. Toward the end of the colonial period the Central Advisory Board of Education (CABE) studied the issue of religious education and came to the conclusion that religious instruction should be part of the curriculum of all schools, subject to what was called a "conscience clause" (CABE, 1944, p. 3). This conscience clause would allow any student whose parents were opposed to religious instruction to opt out of such instruction. Rather than take this position, the framers of the Constitution opted for approaches that would be more congruent with the evolving definition of secularism. Specifically, religious instruction would not be part of state-run schools, but the government could provide funding to religious schools run by other bodies (University Commission, 1952). The belief was that the best way to ensure equality among religions was to allow all to develop freely within a united India. Although the state approach to religious education has long been contested (Jahagirdar, 2003), it was not until the late 1990s and early 2000s that it became the topic of a highly charged public conversation.

In 1998 the Hindu Nationalist political party, the Bharatiya Janata Party (BJP), came to power. The BJP is part of a large group of Hindu Nationalist organizations known as the Sangh Parivar (literally "family of organizations"). The Sangh Parivar is based in a philosophy of Hindutva. Hindutva glorifies Hinduism, and its major premise is that the only people who have a right to claim Indian citizenship are those whose ancestors and religious roots originate in India (for a fuller discussion see Thapar, 2004). Muslims and Christians are portrayed at best as outsiders and at worst as the enemy. This philosophy undergirded the National Curriculum Framework for School Education (NCERT, 2000). The curriculum framework and associated textbooks were criticized by many because they violated the principle of secularism both because the state was promoting one religion (Hinduism) and because other religions were not presented respectfully (see, for example, Dhawan, 2004; Thapar, 2004). The issue was taken to the Supreme Court of India, which ruled that it was not unconstitutional for state-run schools to teach about religions.

The National Curriculum Framework adopted in 2005 (NCERT, 2005) permits teaching about religions as well as encourages teachers to find ways to allow students to critically reflect on issues such as human rights, gender, caste, and religion as they influence their everyday lives. The class VI history textbook (NCERT, 2007b), for example, introduces students to important Hindu texts (the *Vedas* and the *Upanishads*) and explores the origins of Buddhism and Jainism. In the explanation of the Hindu texts, the caste system is discussed. Students are told of its origins and of the ways in which it kept certain groups from accessing public opportunities such as education. They are also told that not everyone accepted caste as inevitable and are asked to discuss why people may have been opposed to caste. Thus it provides an historical basis for a critique of caste. The textbooks linked with the 2005 curriculum framework have only recently begun to be used. Consequently, it is unclear what kind of impact they will have on the development of multicultural education in India. What is clear, however, is that without supportive teacher education programs, the full possibility of these texts will not be realized. Although the Right to Education legislation mandates 21 days annually of teacher training, the content and structure of these trainings do not directly address the goal of multiculturalism found in the new textbooks (Ministry of Human Resource Development, 2005).

Linguistic identity

In 1953, the United Nations Educational, Scientific and Cultural Organization (UNESCO) first made its claim that the best medium for teaching children is through their mother tongue. The report cited educational, psychological, socio-political, and historical evidence to support the claim. While the idea resonated with many in India, the challenges of realizing the goal were apparent from the outset (Khubchandani, 2008; Sridhar, 1996). India is home to over 1,600 languages, of which more than 80 are used as languages of instruction at various stages of formal education (Khubchandani, 2008). While it is impressive that 80 languages are in use, this also means that some 1,500 are not. There is concern that the neglect of so many languages is evidence of a devaluing of those communities whose languages are not recognized and will eventually lead to the extinction of most Indian languages (Abbi, 2004). But even the critics recognize that the task India set for itself in terms of languages in education may not be achievable.

Since independence, India has recognized the importance of language in education. The Constitution calls for "adequate facilities for instruction in the mother-tongue at the primary stage of education to children belonging to minority groups" (art. 350A). As early as 1957, India developed the first draft of its official three-language formula, which outlined a way that multiple languages could be incorporated into formal education. Initially the proposal was that children would be instructed in their mother tongue or regional language, Hindi, and one other modern Indian or foreign language.

Currently, the three-language approach generally means that children will be educated in their regional language, a link language (typically Hindi), and a third language (typically English, which is still the dominant language in higher education). For children who live in administrative districts like Delhi where there is no regional language, it was envisioned they would take a regional language from elsewhere. In practice this has not happened, as many students in Delhi have taken Sanskrit as their third language (National Focus Group on Indian Languages, 2005). In this way the language policy is reinforcing the supremacy of Hindi and English without promoting regional languages outside of their geographic areas.

The National Curriculum Framework of 2005 (NCERT, 2005) has reaffirmed the commitment of the state to the three-language formula and has indicated that, where possible, students should be educated in their mother tongue. For students whose mother tongue is not the regional language this has meant that they are often in the position of having to learn four languages instead of three. Also, numerically smaller communities, such as the *adivasi* communities, may not have qualified teachers or an appropriate curriculum available to teach the children in their first language. Thus although this approach clearly signals a value for multilingualism, several minoritized communities continue to be disadvantaged by the three-language formula.

The current National Curriculum Framework has also emphasized that multilingualism is a feature of the collective Indian identity; therefore teaching about linguistic diversity is an important feature of Indian education. For example, the class X textbook on democratic politics (NCERT, 2007a) explicitly discusses the policy of establishing states on the basis of language. It makes the point that, since independence, a number of new states have been created on the basis of either language or ethnicity and puts forth the perspective that this has enhanced Indian democracy and national unity. By comparing the situation in India with the situation in Sri Lanka, the textbook notes that the imposition of a national language and forced assimilation in Sri Lanka have led to civil war. Finally, a section on the number of languages spoken highlights two things: first, that there is considerable subjectivity in determining what constitutes a language (as opposed to a dialect) and that there is no one language that is spoken by a majority of people in India (even Hindi is spoken only by about 10% of all Indians).

Conclusion

As we write this chapter, India is being touted as the upcoming economic powerhouse, and the Indian state is becoming a major player in economic globalization. As elsewhere, this has led to a situation where the goals of education have been closely tied to economic progress. Since the early 1990s, the World Bank and the International Monetary Fund have pushed for a realignment of the goals of Indian education toward a market model (Focus Group on the Problems of Scheduled Castes and Scheduled Tribes, 2005). And while this neoliberal approach to education has been embraced at the post-secondary level, the National Curriculum Framework of 2005 has taken a strong stand against the market model. As the Focus Group on Education for Peace noted:

> Prior to the era of Liberalization, Privatization and Globalization (LPG), we could have taken for granted a reasonable extent of communitarian and citizenship sensitivities from individuals. The consumerist, pleasure-seeking way of life presumed in LPG degrades citizens into consumers. Unilateralism is the essence of consumerism. It erodes reciprocity and makes individuals obsessed with rights to the neglect of duties. They relate to the nation only for what they can get out of it. Educated persons remaining ignorant of, and indifferent to, the duties of citizenship defeats the very purpose of education. (p. 28)

As in the past, policy developers have reached back to Indian tradition, this time calling on Indian traditions of peace to form the basis of elementary and secondary education. This particular vision of peace incorporates a strong commitment to cultural diversity. Cultural diversity is positioned as one of India's greatest treasures, and justice for all individuals is seen as necessarily including active respect for all cultures (National Focus Group on the Aims of Education, 2005). True education, then, is seen as incorporating "values that foster peace, humaneness and tolerance in a multicultural society" (NCERT, 2005, p. 2). As we have seen above, this approach is built on Constitutional commitments to diversity and has been developed though the National Curriculum Framework (NCERT, 2005) and the new textbooks developed to realize the goals of the curriculum framework. While we would not suggest that India has achieved its goals in relation to equality, valuing diversity, or the development of a unified national identity, it is clear that these goals are embedded in the curriculum rather than being an add-on or afterthought.

Real progress in the classrooms will be dependent on reform in the areas of assessment and teacher education. For many years, high stakes tests have been part of the Indian educational system. Like similar tests in other nations these are skewed to content rather than skills like critical or creative thinking. Therefore, if the system of testing remains the same it is likely that both students and teachers will ignore the critical and creative aspects of the new curriculum in favor of a focus on content, that is, memorization of discrete facts that might appear on the exams. Teacher education has also had more of a focus on content, such as subject-based knowledge, than on process. Additionally, teachers in India, like teachers elsewhere, are generally people who did well in their own schooling and therefore may not see a problem with older approaches to education based on strict discipline in the classroom, teacher as expert, and student as empty vessel to be filled with knowledge.

Notwithstanding the above critiques, it is clear that multiculturalists in other countries have much to learn from the Indian example. The notions of participatory pluralism and active respect form a strong foundation for a society that values diversity and social justice. These ideas are only now beginning to inform school curricula. It will be important to continue to study the progress of the new curricula both as a means of resisting the market model in education and as a way of developing a deeply rooted vision of multicultural education.

References

Abbi, A. (2004, May 21). *Vanishing diversities and submerging identities: An Indian case*. Forum Barcelona conference, Barcelona, Spain. Retrieved June 2, 2008, from www.barcelona2004.org/esp/banco_del_conocimento/docs/PO_35_EN_ABBI.pdf

Alam, A. (2004). *Muslim minority, multiculturalism and liberal state: A comparison of India and Europe*. Retrieved January 12, 2008, from http://jmi.nic.in/cwas/anwar_cv_cwas.htm

Aradhya, N., & Kashyap, A. (2006). *The fundamentals: Right to education in India*. Bangalore: Books for Change.

Bajpai, R. (2002). *Minority rights in the Indian Constituent Assembly debates, 1946–1949* (Working Paper Number 30, QEH Working Paper Series). Oxford, UK: University of Oxford, Wolfson College.

Beteille, A. (1998). The conflict of norms and values in contemporary Indian society. In P. L. Berger (Ed.), *The limits of social cohesion: Conflict and mediation in pluralist societies* (pp. 265–292). Boulder, CO: Westview Press.

Beteille, A. (2005). Matters of right and policy. *Seminar Magazine*, 549. Retrieved July 20, 2006, from http://www.india-seminar.com/semframe.htm

Bhargava, R. (2004). India's model: Faith, secularism, and democracy. *Open Democracy*. Retrieved March 12, 2006, from www.opendemocracy.net

Bhattacharyya, H. (2003). Multiculturalism in contemporary India. *International Journal on Multicultural Societies, 5*(2), 148–61.

Central Advisory Board of Education (CABE). (1944). *Report of the Central Advisory Board, 1944–46*. New Delhi: Government of India.

Chalam, K. S. (2007). *Caste-based reservations and human development in India*. New Delhi, India: Sage Publications.

DeVenanzi, A. (2003). Street children and the excluded class. *International Journal of Comparative Sociology, 44*(5), 472–494.

Dhawan, R. (2004). NCERT textbooks: Issues are important and immediate action necessary. *People's Democracy, 28*(26). Retrieved June 2, 2008, from http://cpim.org/pd/2004/0627/06272004_ncert%20text%20books.htm

Dyer, C., Choksi, A., Awasty, V., Iyer, U., Moyade, R., Nigam, N., et al. (2004). Knowledge for teacher development in India: The importance of "local knowledge" for in-service education. *International Journal of Educational Development, 24*(1), 39–52.

Focus Group on Education for Peace. (2005). *Engaging the essence of education: A position paper on education for peace*. New Delhi, India: National Council of Education Research and Training.

Focus Group on the Problems of Scheduled Castes and Scheduled Tribes. (2005). *Position paper*. New Delhi, India: National Council of Education Research and Training.

Gayen, S. (2006). Innovative approaches to combat trafficking of women in the sex trade. *Inter-Asia Cultural Studies, 7*(2), 331–337.

Government of India, 11th Five Year Plan Planning Commission (2007–2012). (n.d.). *Education*. Retrieved May 30, 2008, from http://planningcommission.nic.in/plans/planrel/11thf.htm

Government of India, Ministry of Human Resource Development, Department of Higher Education (2008). *Office Memorandum*. Retrieved May 29, 2008, from www.iitk.ac.in/infocell/iitk/newhtml/officeorders/gois/instructions.pdf

Government of India, National Commission for Backward Classes (n.d). *Persons/sections excluded from reservation which constitute creamy layer of the society*. Retrieved May 29, 2008, from http://ncbc.nic.in/html/creamylayer.html

Hardgrave, R. L. (1997). Dilemmas of democracy in India. In S. N. Sridhar & N. K. Mattoo (Eds.), *Ananya: A portrait of India* (pp. 329–346). New York: Association of Indians in America.

Jahagirdar, R. A. (2003). Secularism in India: The inconclusive debate. *International Humanist and Ethical Union*. Retrieved June 2, 2008, from www.iheu.org/node/298

Jha, D. N. (2006). *Looking for a Hindu identity*. Retrieved January 12, 2008, from http://www.sacw.net/India_History/dnj_Jan06.pdf

Kamat, S. G. (2007). Walking the tightrope: Equity and growth in a liberalizing India. In R. Teese, S. Lamb, & M. Duru-Bellat (Eds.), *International studies in educational inequality, theory and policy*. Retrieved May 30, 2008, from http://www.springerlink.com/content/k67p401866265550/fulltext.pdf

Khubchandani, L. (2008). Language policy and education in the Indian subcontinent. In S. May & N. H. Hornberger (Eds.), *Encyclopedia of language and education* (2nd ed., Vol. 1, pp. 369–381). New York: Springer Science+Business Media.

Madan, T. N. (1999). Perspectives on pluralism. *Seminar Magazine*, 484. Retrieved February 27, 2007, from http://www.india-seminar.com/semframe.htm

Madhavan, M. R., & Manghnani, R. (2005). *Right to Education Bill, 2005* (Legislative brief). New Delhi, India: Parliamentary Research Services.

Mahajan, G. (1999). Rethinking multiculturalism. *Seminar Magazine*, 484. Retrieved February 27, 2007, from http://www.india-seminar.com/semframe.htm

Ministry of Human Resource Development. (2005). *Right to Education Bill 2005*. New Delhi: Government of India.

Mishra, S., Palai, N., & Das, K. (2006, August). *Social cleavages, multiculturalism and emerging space for state in India under globalization regime*. Paper presented at the International Economic History Congress, Session 22, Helsinki, Finland. Retrieved December 12, 2007, from www.helsinki.fi/iehc2006/papers1/Mishra22.pdf

National Council of Education Research and Training (NCERT). (2000). *National Curriculum Framework*. New Delhi, India: Author.

National Council of Education Research and Training (NCERT). (2005). *National Curriculum Framework, 2005*. New Delhi, India: Author.

National Council of Education Research and Training (NCERT). (2007a). *Democratic politics, textbook in politics for class X*. New Delhi, India: Author.

National Council of Education Research and Training (NCERT). (2007b). *Our pasts I, textbook in history for class VI*. New Delhi, India: Author.

National Council of Education Research and Training (NCERT). (2007c). *Social and political life I, textbook for class VI*. New Delhi, India: Author.

National Focus Group on Indian Languages. (2005). *Position paper*. New Delhi, India: National Council of Education Research and Training.

National Focus Group on the Aims of Education. (2005). *Background paper*. New Delhi, India: National Council of Education Research and Training.

Pandey, S. (2007). *Constitutional perspective of multiculturalism in India*. Retrieved January 12, 2008, from http://ssrn.com/abstract=963563

Parekh, B. (1999). What is multiculturalism? *Seminar Magazine*, 484. Retrieved February 27, 2007, from http://www.india-seminar.com/semframe.htm

Prime Minister's High Level Committee (2006). *Social, economic, and educational status of the Muslim community in India*. New Delhi: Government of India.

Registrar General and Census Commissioner, India 2001 Census (2001). Retrieved May 12, 2007, from www.censusindia.net

Rodrigues, V. (2005). Ambedkar on preferential treatment. *Seminar Magazine*, 549. Retrieved July 20, 2006, from http://www.india-seminar.com/semframe.htm

Sadgopal, A. (2001, December). Political economy of the ninety third Amendment Bill. *Mainstream*.

Retrieved March 15, 2006, from www.doccentre.net/docsweb/Education/non_Formal_Education.html

Sangari, K. (1999). Which diversity? *Seminar Magazine*, 484. Retrieved February 27, 2007, from http://www.india-seminar.com/semframe.htm

Sridhar, K. K. (1996). Language in education: Minorities and multilingualism in India. *International Review of Education, 42*(4), 327–347.

Thapar, R. (2004, February 21). *The future of the Indian past*. Seventh D. T. Lakdawala Memorial Lecture delivered at FICCI Auditorium, New Delhi, India, organized by the Institute of Social Sciences.

University Commission (1952). *Report of the University Commission on Religious Education*. New Delhi: Government of India.

32

Islamic religious education and Muslim religiosity in Singapore

Mukhlis Abu Bakar

National Institute of Education, Nanyang Technological University, Singapore

One could almost sense a sigh of relief from among the Malay/Muslim community in Singapore when it was revealed by the authorities that, among the Jemaah Islamiyah (JI) terrorist suspects arrested under the Internal Security Act in 2001 and 2002, none of them were products of the Islamic religious schools, the madrasahs. Such a relief is understandable given that, for a few years prior to the arrests, the madrasah has been the subject of much public debate following criticism of its education system by the Singapore government. Madrasah education was perceived as incompatible within the framework of the national education curriculum and with the needs of a modern economy. The compulsory education policy that followed, which originally required these full-time schools to stop enrolling Primary 1 pupils, drew outcry from the community, with some reading it as a sinister move to close them down. Under these circumstances, any proven connection between the madrasahs and the terrorist group would add pressure on the former and make it much harder for the community to continue defending it.

As it was, the madrasahs went through the JI episode unscathed. That the JI terrorists had all attended mainstream schools put to rest any thoughts that madrasahs in Singapore are copies of their counterparts in neighboring countries, with their alleged roles as training camps for JI recruits. Conversely, in the midst of increased Muslim religiosity, there was growing concern about Islamic radicalism among mainstream students. However, while the pressure on the madrasahs has subsided, the attention on the Malay/Muslim community has intensified, for the arrest of the JI suspects has raised anxieties about the loyalty of an entire community to the state. Additionally, while during the madrasah episode the community took upon itself to "defend" the institution against government criticism, the period following the JI arrests saw the government going all out to "protect" the community from any potential backlash from the rest of society. The primary concern was to ensure that Singapore's national cohesion was not undermined.

Prior to the 1990s, the Singapore government did not pay very close attention to the religious dimension of the Malay/Muslim community life. Problems pertaining to madrasah education were internal to the Malay/Muslim community, engaging the attention of the Malay community and religious leaders and of most Malay political leaders within the government. Today these issues are national concerns because of their impact on economic development, national integration, and security. This chapter examines the tensions between the state and

Islam, focusing on Singapore's Malay/Muslim community and its religious educational institutions at a time of rapid and complex economic, social, and religious developments. It presents a perspective on the connections between education, religion, race, economy, and nation building within the context of Singapore's multi-religious, pluralistic, and modern society.

Singapore

Background

Singapore is a capitalist island city-state of over 4 million people in the middle of the Malay Archipelago. The years immediately preceding and following the separation of Singapore from Malaysia in 1965 were a tumultuous period marked by riots and racial tensions. When it became an independent republic on August 9, 1965, Singapore inherited a population of mixed racial background whose ethnic composition was roughly the same as it is today – Chinese (78%), Malays (14%), Indians (7%), and other races (1%) (Leow, 2001).

The Chinese and Indians can trace their lineage to the immigrant groups that were brought into the Straits Settlements and the Federated Malay States by the British in order to stimulate the colonial economy. The Malays are native to the area, and their ancestors were mostly rural peasants. Almost all Malays profess Islam as their religion. They form the biggest group of Muslims in Singapore, followed by Singaporeans of Arab and Indian descent. The Chinese and Eurasian converts make up the smallest Muslim group. Taoists, Buddhists, Christians, Hindus, Sikhs, and believers of other faiths make up the rest of the population.

Malay is the national language and one of four official languages that also include English, Chinese, and Tamil. English is also the language of administration and is widely used in the professions and in businesses. English is also the primary school language. Along with the primacy of English, the mother tongue languages – Chinese, Malay, or one of several Indian languages, including Tamil – are made a compulsory subject at the primary and secondary school level to safeguard Singaporeans' competence in these languages and their sense of identity with the cultures that their mother tongues represent.

Multiracialism and the place of religion

Singapore is overwhelmingly Chinese, and the governing political party largely depends on the Chinese population for its electoral success. However, Singapore has never been a Chinese state. Nor has Singapore explicitly privileged the biggest minority, the Malays, even though the Malays are recognized in the constitution as the indigenous people of Singapore. Instead, the government declares Singapore a "multiracial" society which safeguards racial tolerance in the law, pushes race out of the front line of politics, and relegates racial cultural practices "to the realm of private and voluntaristic, individual, or collective practices" (Chua, 1995, p. 106).

The political system that emerged thus featured a government that presents itself as working for the interest of the whole country and not for one class, race, or group. Essentially informed and guided by multiracialism, pragmatism, and meritocracy, the government relies on a centralization of authority that is prepared to engage in extensive social engineering to bring about orderly social change. The strategy is to confine politics within the realms of technocratic problem-solving and limit its concerns to issues pertaining to the economy, bring legitimacy to a non-particularistic and achievement-oriented elite, build new institutions and mechanisms to entrench supportive elements, and isolate those seen as overly committed to race or religious-based loyalties (Gopinathan, 1979; Jesudason, 1989).

This pragmatic ideology is best seen at work in education. One of the more important institutions in post-independence Singapore, education is valued both from the government's perspective that stresses the development of human resources and maintenance of cultural and linguistic heritages, and from the individual's perspective of education as an invaluable avenue for social mobility. Education is also considered a key factor in building a national identity and social unity, with national schools providing a common experience for all citizens. The basic governing ingredients are consistently at play, that is, centralization of authority with some measure of autonomy, emphasis on rationalization and cost-effective management, and the steady erosion of the legitimacy of subgroups such as clans and castes (Gopinathan, 1979).

Religion is by far the one major social institution in Singapore that has been treated with much sensitivity. Singapore is constitutionally a secular state, but the constitution upholds the right of groups to adhere to their religious faiths. All religious groups are granted space to engage in their practices at least for as long as religions do not compete with each other and that religious beliefs do not contest the ideological and administrative practices of the government nor its ideological hold on the population (Chua, 1995; Tamney, 1988, cited in Hill & Lian, 1995). Thus religions are openly told to separate themselves from state politics, as evidenced by the institutionalization of the Maintenance of Religious Harmony Act in 1990, which bars religious leaders from commenting on social and political issues in their capacity as preachers.

Precisely because of their ideological appeal, religions were not allowed to play a significant role in the national curriculum. Religion's inclusion in 1984 through a religious knowledge (RK) program was short-lived. Under this program, moral education was taught in secondary schools through courses in Christianity, Islam, Buddhism, Hinduism, and Sikhism, as well as Confucian ethics (C. Tan, 2008). The rationale was that knowledge of religion would provide Singaporeans with the moral ballast to shield them from the supposedly decadent and morally corrosive values of the West. The program was withdrawn in 1989 shortly after the release of the findings of a government-commissioned, social scientific study of religion in Singapore which implicated the RK program in promoting religious proselytization and intensifying religious polarization among students, which, the government feared, could foment social division (Chua, 1995; Hill & Lian, 1995; Tamney, 1992).

Madrasah education

Background

Schools whose educational aims detract from those set by the Ministry of Education (MOE) receive no funding from the government but enjoy significant autonomy in determining their own curriculum. The Chinese medium schools and the madrasahs were such schools, both of which pre-date Singapore's political independence. But unlike the Chinese schools, which were brought into the fold of the Ministry of Education in the 1980s after forgoing their autonomy in setting the curriculum and standards in exchange for financial assistance through the Grant-in-Aid Regulations, the six madrasahs that exist today are still outside the mainstream school system. They offer full-time education at the primary and secondary level, with some extending up to pre-university. They rely on school fees and donations from the Malay/Muslim community to sustain their operations.

Madrasah education is regarded as important and necessary by the government for the cultivation of indigenous Muslim religious elites. They have a significant role to play within the Singapore Muslim community as teachers and scholars on Islam. Traditionally, the primary focus of the madrasahs was on the teaching of religious knowledge and Arabic as well as subjects such as arithmetic and Malay. They provided a convenient and affordable education for students who, apart from obtaining a foundation in religion, were also taught to read, write, and count. Some of the students who completed madrasah education became religious teachers within the community, while those who managed to further their religious studies abroad were appointed to positions as *kadi* (judge), *mufti* (leader in theological matters), and religious officials in various Muslim organizations such as the Islamic Religious Council of Singapore (Majlis Ugama Islam Singapura – MUIS), the Registry of Muslim Marriages, and the Syariah Court (court based on Islamic law with limited jurisdiction over matters, namely Muslim divorce cases).

The historical development of the madrasahs and the challenges they face in multicultural, secular Singapore have been well documented elsewhere (Abdul Rahman & Lai, 2006; Aljunied & Hussin, 2005; C. Tan & Kasmuri, 2007). Some salient points about the madrasahs and the challenges they face in multicultural and multi-religious Singapore are described in this chapter.

Declining enrollment

The 1930s and 1940s were the so-called golden period for the madrasahs, particularly in the case of Madrasah Aljunied, which attracted students from all over Southeast Asia for its high standard of Arabic and vibrant learning environment. In contrast, the period after independence in the 1960s was a downturn for the madrasahs as the pace of industrialization quickened and employment became dependent on educational qualifications. With madrasah education carrying little economic value, enrollment in the madrasahs, especially of boys, declined in favor of the national schools. The expansion of the national education system and the resettlement of villagers into subsidized high-rise public housing in new towns coincided with the further decline of the madrasahs. At their lowest point in the 1970s, the madrasahs became a place of last resort for those who did not make it through the streaming system in the national schools (Abu Bakar, 2006).

Broadening the curriculum

It was in the above context that changes in the objectives of madrasah education – and specifically in the curriculum – were first raised and discussed by Malay political leaders in the late 1960s. The main concerns were to ensure the continued relevance and attractiveness of madrasah education, which would also simultaneously alleviate the problem of poor employment prospects of madrasah graduates. The madrasahs were urged to broaden the emphasis and content of their curriculum by incorporating the teaching of "non-religious" or "secular" subjects such as science, math, and English. Madrasah officials, religious elites, and MUIS also generally supported the proposal affirming the changes that were needed to raise the status of madrasah education and provide students with knowledge related to the economy. By producing not only *ulama* (religious scholars) but also Muslim professionals, it was argued that madrasah education can remain relevant to Singapore's development and attract Muslim parents to send their children to them.

The media consistently ran stories of madrasah students succeeding in obtaining places in or graduating from overseas Islamic universities such as Al-Azhar in Egypt as well as from the local universities such as the National University of Singapore. Such reports appeared to bring home the message that madrasah education was just as good as if not better than that provided by the national schools, and that madrasah graduates have succeeded in obtaining a comprehensive education that is not limited to religious but that also includes secular knowledge.

This was the beginning of a shift in educational emphasis in the post-independence history of the madrasah. While the curriculum changes appeared to be conditioned by the poor job prospects of madrasah graduates, that these changes would save and preserve the Muslim educational heritage was not missed by the madrasah officials and religious elites whose own careers in a sense were also on the line should the madrasahs close. However, as discussed in the following sections, the expansion of the curriculum poses its own problems.

Renewed interest in the madrasah

The efforts discussed earlier increased the demand for madrasah education. Enrollment steadily grew, thereby reversing the trend of previous decades. In 1986, there were 135 Primary 1 pupils enrolled in the six madrasahs. By 1994 and beyond, the figure hovered above the 400 mark, with the year 2000 registering a record of 464 pupils. This represents about 5–6% of the Malay Primary 1 cohort. Every year there were many more applicants than there were places available (Abu Bakar, 2006).

The students' and parents' understanding and expectations of madrasah education increased as enrollment in the madrasahs grew. Alias (1998) found that the majority of parents look to the madrasahs for an encompassing Islamic education that offers both secular and religious knowledge and the freedom to perform religious rituals like *solat* (prayers) and to practice a particular code of modesty such as wearing attire that covers the *aurat* (part of the body that must be covered following a certain standard of decency), which cannot be practiced in the national schools. They subscribe to the idea that religious knowledge should be included in the school curriculum and that Islam as a way of life should not be separated from the rest of a child's education. Indeed, the madrasahs attracted well-educated parents who genuinely value the type of education that madrasahs provide.

The madrasahs' appeal coincides with the perceived encroachment of "undesirable" and "foreign" values that come with the capitalist developments and modernization in Singapore. In the Alias (1998) study, almost half of the parents interviewed expressed the need to equip their children with religious values in the face of modernization, with many citing the madrasah culture as offering an environment in which their children can be insulated from the influence of negative social values associated with modernization such as drug abuse, sexual permissiveness, youth gangsterism, and consumerism. Religion thus became a moral check and the madrasahs a security for their children.

The renewed interest in madrasah education also came at a time of government's emphasis on reviving traditional values and returning to the cultural roots of the respective communities in order to counter the individualism that comes with an increasingly consumerist orientation of Singapore society. While the government has paid lavish attention to the promotion of Chinese culture through initiatives such as the Speak Mandarin Campaign and the Special Assistance Plan schools that provide an intensive Chinese-oriented curriculum to groom the proposed Chinese elite, the Malays have been relatively left to their own devices until recently. Islam, very much entrenched in Malay culture and society, and which has enjoyed a resurgence in Singapore since the 1980s, seems a natural source from which the Muslims can seek moral strength and develop their own identity.

The promise of a balanced education feeds into the Muslims' belief that success is meaningful only if one strives for happiness in this world and the world hereafter. It is a pull factor that many parents find hard to resist, although they are aware that the funds and resources of the madrasahs are severely limited.

Financial constraints

Appealing as it seems, the incorporation of the secular subjects into the madrasah curriculum has aggravated the funding problems that have long beset madrasahs. Financial constraints have meant paying meager salaries to madrasah teachers. This in turn affects the quality of teachers, many of whom have few qualifications and little exposure or training in pedagogy. With the inclusion of secular subjects based on the national curriculum and an increased student enrollment, the problem became critical. Some madrasahs had to turn to volunteer teachers from the national schools to fulfill the new objectives. Others had to dig into their reserves to sustain operating costs.

Facilities such as laboratories, libraries, computer facilities, and suitable premises are also inadequate. There is dire need for the madrasahs to upgrade and renovate their premises and provide infrastructure for the increasing number of students and facilities in view of curriculum expansion. Such projects require herculean efforts and involve substantial sums of money. Madrasahs are constantly appealing for donations from the community, urging people to donate on the grounds that it is a religious obligation to do so (Abdul Rahman, 2006). Many in the community have heeded the call and over the years have contributed tens of millions of dollars to several rebuilding projects.

Poor academic results

Against this backdrop, it is not unexpected that the vast majority of madrasah students do not make it to tertiary levels of education. Malay students in the madrasah perform below their counterparts in the national schools. Between 1996 and 1998, only 35% of Malay students who were in the madrasah from Primary 1 went on to take the national examinations at the end of Secondary 4, compared to 60% from the mainstream schools. Madrasah students' low pass rates for English, math, and science also make it hard for them to move on to post-secondary education. An average of only 9% of such students compared to 29% of Malay students from national schools went on to either the polytechnics or the junior colleges (Osman, 1999). Those who succeeded admitted that they required tremendous outside help to survive and succeed in the system.

In addition to the low quality of teaching in the madrasahs, the poor academic results can also be attributed to the time allotted for the teaching and learning of subjects. A typical madrasah allocates no more than 50% of curriculum time for the teaching and learning of the secular subjects – math, science, English, and Malay – plus a humanities subject such as geography at the secondary level. Any more time than this would mean threatening the madrasahs' identity as educational institutions that teach religious subjects – *Tauhid* (theology on the Oneness of God), *Tafsir* (Quranic exegesis), *Fiqh* (jurisprudence), *Hadith* (collections of sayings of the Prophet), *Nahu* (Arabic grammar), *Tasawwuf* (Islamic mysticism), and *Tarikh* (Islamic history) (Aljunied & Hussin, 2005). In contrast, in the national schools, the secular subjects take up most of the curriculum time (Abu Bakar, 2006). The heavy workload of the students coupled with poor academic results led Abdul Rahman (2006) – an academic – to question the ability of the madrasah to fulfill the dual role of training students to be missionaries and professionals, citing its vision as "utopian" (p. 70).

A national concern

It is in the face of these worrying statistics and the upward trend in madrasah enrollment that madrasah education became a national concern. In 1997, a government minister noted the increasing number of Malays opting out of the mainstream schools, and questioned whether these students receive the quality education necessary for good jobs and to be able to integrate well into the social and economic system. In 1999, a senior minister was more upfront and said that the madrasahs' concentration on religious education would not enable the students to acquire the critical skills that are essential in an economy that gives preference to knowledge workers. The students' identification with their fellow Singaporeans would also be weak, as they would not have shared a common experience in the national schools. Unable to be full participants in Singapore's economy – nor to fit into Singapore's mainstream society – he feared that they would be disadvantaged and become a problem, like the students who had graduated from the now defunct Chinese medium schools. He recommended that Muslim students attend national schools in the morning and madrasahs in the afternoon.

These remarks sparked an emotional outcry from the Malay/Muslim community, who by this time had developed a sense of ownership towards the madrasahs. Many read murky meanings into the minister's statements, and believed that the government was hinting at an impending change in the madrasah system – if not its eventual closure. Others – including madrasah officials – were furious that the government acknowledged neither the madrasahs' efforts to equip students with the knowledge and skills that the ministers mentioned nor their financial struggles. They called for the government to give financial assistance to the madrasahs, citing the Chinese schools as an example. However, madrasah officials forgot that, in the Chinese schools case, the national curriculum had been embraced in exchange for grants, which the madrasahs were not prepared to do.

Compulsory education

The political leadership's interest in the madrasahs continued to be articulated for some years. It culminated in 2000 when legislation on compulsory education (CE) was enacted for implementation in January 2003. At its core, CE is defined as education in the national schools for a duration of six years (from Primary 1 to Primary 6) for Singapore citizens residing in Singapore. It was meant to give Singaporeans "a common core of knowledge" to prepare them for the information age and to build a sense of national identity ("Send Dad to Jail," 1999, p. 25).

It was obvious that the madrasahs would run foul of the CE policy unless they stopped taking in primary students. This prompted fierce rumblings of discontent within the Malay community, which perceived the proposed policy as infringing on their right and freedom to educate their children in ways they viewed as appropriate. Many within the madrasah community were genuinely concerned about the possibility that not many students would be motivated to switch to the madrasah after spending six years in the national schools. Some claimed this would spell the end of the madrasah system and the future supply of the community's religious elites. Moreover, they disputed claims that religious training would be just as effective if it were to start later, at the secondary level.

CE was therefore viewed as a potent threat. The six madrasahs – frustrated with MUIS for its perceived inability to represent their interests to the government – formed the Joint Committee of Madrasahs to develop a collective response to the government's concerns. The influential Singapore Islamic Scholars and Religious Teachers Association (Persatuan Ulama dan Guru Agama Islam Singapura – PERGAS), which spearheaded much of the public protest, quickly dismissed the government's assurance that the madrasahs would not face closure under CE. Such an open and unprecedented protest was a test of the government's treatment of the Muslim minority.

In response to the protest by PERGAS, the government offered a "compromise." In the legislation enacted in 2000, students enrolled in a madrasah are exempted from compulsory attendance in national schools provided that their madrasah's test performance matches the average aggregate score for Malays in the six lowest-performing national schools whose students sit the primary school leaving examination (PSLE) the same year. The madrasahs have to meet this minimum passing standard beginning in 2008. If they fail to meet this standard, they will have to stop providing elementary education. In addition, the six madrasahs' total enrollment of Primary 1 pupils was capped at 400 every year, beginning in 2004.

The compromise appeared to have eased tensions, and the debate ended with what some thought was a "win–win" solution. However, in order to meet the PSLE benchmark, the madrasahs may be forced to reduce teaching time for religious subjects and give more time to secular subjects. However, it may still be an uphill task for the madrasahs to fulfill the new requirement because of their limited resources.

In 2007, a year before the first batch of madrasah pupils were to sit for the PSLE, MUIS announced that three madrasahs had agreed to collaborate within the framework of a joint madrasah system (JMS). In this system, Madrasah Aljunied and Madrasah Al-Arabiah will not enroll primary students so that they can focus on secondary education, while Madrasah Al-Irsyad will close its secondary classes in order to specialize in primary education and serve as a feeder school for Aljunied and Arabiah. At the secondary level, Aljunied will focus on the religious curriculum, offering students intensive religious education at higher levels. Al-Arabiah will provide greater emphasis on the arts and the sciences and cater to students who are more inclined towards a secular education within a madrasah setting.

The collaboration was justified because it enables resources to be shared and optimizes and enables a more focused learning approach to be offered. However, given the madrasahs' past record, the collaboration may be seen as a subtle admission by Aljunied and Al-Arabiah that they are unable to fulfill the PSLE benchmark. In addition, the requirement for Al-Arabiah to duplicate the national curriculum is questionable when vast resources have been set aside by the state for this purpose in the mainstream schools, never mind whether it can mount it successfully without imposing huge costs on the community. At the same time, however, Aljunied's focus on religious education might bring it back to its past glory as the premier Islamic school. The other three madrasahs choose to remain outside the JMS.

Maintaining national cohesion

Background

Just when the debate on madrasah education was showing signs of abating after the "truce" was achieved between PERGAS and the government in 2000, a different kind of debate ensued, triggered by the terrorist attacks on the World Trade Center in New York and the Pentagon in Washington on September 11, 2001, by the radical Islamic group Al-Qaeda. While shock and horror at the atrocities generally typified the immediate reaction of the local public, time since the 9/11 events has muted the response. However, the subsequent arrests in 2001 and 2002 in Singapore of members of the extremist JI group – with alleged links to Al-Qaeda – brought home the message of a terrorist threat from within and catapulted to the forefront not only the Malays but the entire Muslim community. Among the Muslim religious elites, the initial fear was of discovering that among those arrested were graduates of the madrasah. This would tarnish the institution's image further, following challenges to its educational system. Their fears were unwarranted, as it was later revealed that those arrested were neither educated in the madrasah nor possessed of adequate Islamic credentials.

The threat of terrorism in multicultural Singapore and its implications have been reviewed elsewhere (A. Tan, 2002; E. Tan, 2007; Vasu, 2008). Of relevance is the response of the Singapore government to the terrorist threat, in particular its quest to maintain racial and religious harmony and its inclusive approach of actively encouraging the Muslim community to see itself as an integral part of Singapore. The latter is significant, as the terrorist threat from within has created an atmosphere of mutual suspicion and distrust between Muslims and non-Muslims, and leaving this unchecked would serve only to marginalize the Muslim community and jeopardize inter-racial confidence.

Religiosity and religious extremism

One issue that has surfaced from the JI episode is the Muslims' apparent susceptibility to radical and militant Islam. Official reports revealed that most of the local JI detainees had received religious instructions from dubious sources. The religious knowledge they acquired did not come from any recognized programs provided at the mosques, madrasahs, or religious classes or from accredited religious teachers. Some had learned from lone preachers who themselves had no proper religious credentials. Official explanations suggested that many had developed radical ideas based on information they had obtained from the Internet, where an estimated 6,000 websites can be identified as those that set out to abuse Islamic teachings to legitimize terror and espouse extremist and radical ideologies. These websites were believed to have fed on a skewed sense of material injustice that is seen being committed against Muslims in some parts of the world.

Such official articulation of how good sense gets derailed by external influences appears to absolve the Muslim community of any possible wrongdoing. This has generally been the strategy adopted by the government to manage Singapore's multiracial framework, which has been under strain by the terrorist threat. This notwithstanding, there has been the occasional panic – not widely reported – that attempted to link Islamic religiosity and perceived Muslim separateness with increased susceptibility towards terrorism (E. Tan, 2007).

Building inter-racial confidence

That the JI operatives were Muslims and carried out their activities in the name of Islam created the possibility that non-Muslim Singaporeans might overreact and start viewing the entire Muslim community with suspicion. Eager to reassure the government and Singaporeans that Muslims in Singapore are committed to peace and nation building, several Muslim groups issued statements denouncing acts of terrorism and reaffirming their commitment to enlarge the common space of Singaporeans. In particular, PERGAS and its members endorsed a list of guidelines on how Muslim Singaporeans can lead their lives as moderate followers of Islam. In 2003, a group of religious teachers formed a volunteer group – the Religious Rehabilitation Group – to help in the counseling and rehabilitation of the JI detainees.

The government took important steps to strengthen the nation's religious harmony and to ensure that the actions of a minority would not affect the harmonious relations between Muslim and non-Muslim Singaporeans. Through its members of parliament, it intensified the activities of its grass roots via the constituency-based inter-racial confidence circles (IRCC) to strengthen the trust and confidence among the different races and to establish a viable grassroots mechanism to deal with serious racial or religious problems on the ground. Each inter-racial confidence circle comprises leaders of the various racial, religious, social, educational, and business groups, and organizations in the respective constituency (E. Tan, 2007). The government also assigned one of its members of parliament to visit and elicit views from all the national religious bodies and thereafter draft a Code on Religious Harmony, essentially a pledge affirming that groups will practice their respective religions while respecting Singapore's secular and multi-religious context.

The prime minister reminded non-Muslim Singaporeans in his dialogue with community leaders that

> your individual actions have large consequences. You make up the majority of our society. If you let unfounded suspicion affect the way you behave towards Muslim Singaporeans, this will build up resentment among Muslims, and turn even moderate ones against the society. So rein in your emotions and fear, and act rationally.
> (Cited in "Coping With the Terror Threat," 2002, p. 13)

Based on this and the speeches of other ministers over the months subsequent to the arrests, it would appear that there has been an undercurrent of tension and mutual suspicion among ethnic groups. Such tensions were, nonetheless, contained, at least since the anticipated terrorist attack in Singapore has yet to occur.

At a time when national cohesion is critical, it would seem that building Singaporeans' confidence towards each other, particularly that of non-Muslim Singaporeans toward their Muslim counterparts, takes priority even if the government remains concerned over what it perceived as the heightened religiosity and growing separateness of the Muslim community. As late as 1999, Muslims were said to center their social activities in their mosques rather than in multiracial community clubs. They have also been repeatedly told to be "part of the mainstream." At the Singapore21 forum in 1999, senior minister Lee Kuan Yew – responding to a question by a student who asked whether certain instinctive emotional bonds among the ethnic groups could be overcome so that Singapore could truly become a nation – said that a Muslim's religious belief could put him in a position of conflict with the interests of the nation (Ng & Lim, 1999). Then, in 2000, deputy prime minister Lee Hsien Loong admitted the state's concerns regarding the loyalty of the Malay/Muslim community in the event of a war against fellow Malays/Muslims in the region (Kadir, 2006).

Whether these anxieties over the rising influence of Islam and its influence on national integration contributed to the tension in the debate on compulsory education was not very clear. In as far as the JI episode is concerned, the government saw it as convenient to reiterate the need for Muslim Singaporeans not to become exclusive and different and at the same time to call on non-Muslims not to let their emotions and fear overrule their rationality.

During the controversy over the madrasahs, the government presented criticisms and set benchmarks for them without showing interest in knowing how they went about addressing those criticisms and achieving the targets. If the government had acted differently, it would have been viewed as doing a special favor for a particular religious group. In the case of the JI arrests, the government voiced muted concern over the ease with which extremism can grow in the midst of the Muslim community, even as it took pains to show that the radicalization of the JI detainees was the result of their own doing, and not the community's, as they had not obtained proper religious instructions. This was finely balanced with an acknowledgment that community institutions in Singapore are strong, including mosques, well-qualified religious teachers, and a holistic part-time religious education curriculum.

Concluding remarks

By recounting the journey madrasahs have followed over the past half-century, this chapter attempts to offer a perspective on the Malay/Muslim community in Singapore that sometimes was aligned with, and other times was in opposition to, the state within which it holds membership. The push–pull experienced by the community along multiple dimensions – ideological, educational, economic, and social – resulted in the community being faced with numerous decisions and dilemmas that are not easy to resolve. For example, both the leaders of the madrasahs and the government want to equip students with relevant knowledge and skills needed for the economy and to forestall what is perceived as insidious individualism and Westernization. However, the fact that religion is legitimated within a separate system of education that involves a small but significant number of citizens gives the government cause for concern because, in the event of a contest between religious beliefs and government ideology, religion is likely to triumph. The compulsory education policy ameliorates this concern, at least at the level of elementary education.

Government leaders have often highlighted the vulnerability of Singapore as a state with its limited size, lack of natural resources, and diverse population. Since Singapore became independent in 1965, its survival has been the structuring center of reasoning and rationalization for the policies by which Singapore has been governed. While religious and racial tensions are considered major domestic threats to its survival, economic development is seen as a solution to such threats. Political discourse thus frequently underscores economic development, competition, and the meritocratic principle, with the political elite taking a very pragmatic stance (Hill & Lian, 1995). The state's responses to the controversy over the madrasah and the fallout from the arrests of the members of the JI network illustrate the government's intent on managing Singapore for economic development and political stability to ensure its survival.

References

Abdul Rahman, N. A. (2006). The aims of madrasah education in Singapore: Problems and perceptions. In N. A. Abdul Rahman & A. E. Lai (Eds.), *Secularism and spirituality: Seeking integrated knowledge and success in madrasah education in Singapore* (pp. 58–92). Singapore: Singapore Institute of Policy Studies & Marshall Cavendish Academic.

Abdul Rahman, N. A., & Lai, A. E. (Eds.). (2006). *Secularism and spirituality: Seeking integrated knowledge and success in madrasah education in Singapore*. Singapore: Singapore Institute of Policy Studies & Marshall Cavendish Academic.

Abu Bakar, M. (2006). Between state interests and citizen rights: Whither the madrasah? In N. A. Abdul Rahman & A. E. Lai (Eds.), *Secularism and spirituality: Seeking integrated knowledge and success in madrasah education in Singapore* (pp. 29–57). Singapore: Singapore Institute of Policy Studies & Marshall Cavendish Academic.

Alias, Z. (1998). *The goals of madrasah educational system in Singapore: Obstacles and recommendation*. Unpublished honors thesis, National University of Singapore.

Aljunied, S. M. K., & Hussin, D. I. (2005). Estranged from the ideal past: Historical evolution of madrassahs in Singapore. *Journal of Muslim Minority Affairs, 25*(2), 249–260.

Chua, B. H. (1995). *Communitarian ideology and democracy in Singapore*. London: Routledge.

Coping with the terror threat in S'pore. (2002, October 15). *The Straits Times*, p. 13.

Gopinathan, S. (1979). Singapore's language policies: Strategies for a plural society. In K. S. Sandhu, L. Suryadinata, V. Pombhejara, M. Rajaretnam, & C. Tan (Eds.), *Southeast Asian Affairs 1979* (pp. 280–295). Singapore: Institute of Southeast Asian Studies & Heinemann Educational Books (Asia).

Hill, M., & Lian, K. F. (1995). *The politics of nation building and citizenship in Singapore*. London: Routledge.

Jesudason, J. (1989). *Ethnicity and the economy: The state, Chinese business and multinationals in Malaysia*. Singapore: Oxford University Press.

Kadir, S. (2006). Islam, state and society in Singapore. *Inter-Asia Cultural Studies, 5*(3), 357–371.

Leow, B. G. (2001). *Census of population 2000: Education, language and religion* (Statistical release 2). Singapore: Department of Statistics, Ministry of Trade and Industry.

Ng, I., & Lim, L. (1999, September 19). Reality in race bonds exist. *The Straits Times*, p. 26.

Osman, A. (1999, September 5). Malays in mainstream schools doing far better. *The Straits Times*, p. 4.

Send Dad to jail if child doesn't go to school? (1999, October 31). *The Straits Times*, p. 25.

Tamney, J. B. (1992). Conservative government and support for the religious institution in Singapore: An uneasy alliance. *Sociological Analysis, 53*(2), 201–217.

Tan, A. (2002). Terrorism in Singapore: Threat and implications. *Contemporary Security Policy, 23*(3), 1–18.

Tan, C. (2008). The teaching of religious knowledge in a plural society: The case for Singapore. *International Review of Education, 54*(2), 175–191.

Tan, C., & Kasmuri, A. (2007). Islamic religious education: Case study of a madrasah in Singapore. In C. Tan & K.-C. Chong (Eds.), *Critical perspectives on values education in Asia* (pp. 109–123). Singapore: Prentice Hall.

Tan, E. K. B. (2007). Norming "moderation" in an "iconic target": Public policy and the regulation of religious anxieties in Singapore. *Terrorism and Political Violence, 19*(4), 443–462.

Vasu, N. (2008). (En)countering terrorism: multiculturalism and Singapore. *Asian Ethnicity, 9*(1), 17–32.

33

Religion, ethnicity, and identity in Indonesian education

Joel C. Kuipers
George Washington University, Washington, DC, USA

Ella Yulaelawati
Department of Education for the Republic of Indonesia, Indonesia

Introduction

Indonesia has the third largest public school system in the world, with more than 50 million students under its jurisdiction. It also has one of the most diverse student populations, from the standpoint of language and culture. A recent estimate puts the number of distinct, mutually unintelligible languages native to the archipelago at 680; this does not include differences in dialect, accent, and vocabulary that give local color to the fourth largest country in the world. Although its national motto is *Bhinneka Tunggal Ika*, "Out of Many, One," thanks to the successful distribution, acceptance, and use of the national language, Bahasa Indonesia, through its school system – from one end of this 3,500-mile-wide archipelago to the other – this motto has become more than an empty slogan.

From a political and historical perspective, the widespread acceptance, use, and reproduction of the Indonesian national language has been one of the most important products of the Indonesian national education system. The language has been the glue that holds this very diverse nation together in times of crisis, but there are still significant challenges to the management of the nation's dazzling diversity (Table 33.1 shows the ethnic groups in Indonesia). Among these are the overlapping and complex issues of ethnicity, religion, race, and class. The responses of the Indonesian educational system to these difficult issues are themselves complex and diverse, and they have changed over time. While the recognition and management of such social differences in education have been approached in terms of equity (as in Malaysia), they are more recently being approached in terms of equivalencies (*kesetaraan*), a novel approach that seeks to recognize differences at the same time as it seeks translation between domains of experience.

History of education in Indonesia

To comprehend the complex threads of language, religion, ethnicity, and class as they are woven together into the fabric of the current Indonesian educational system, it is useful to provide a

Table 33.1 Ethnic Groups in Indonesia, 2000

	Population (in millions)	Percentage	Main Regions
Javanese	86,012	41.7	East Java, Central Java, Lampung
Sundanese	31,765	15.4	West Java
Malay	7,013	3.4	Sumatra eastern coast, West Kalimantan
Madurese	6,807	3.3	Madura island
Batak	6,188	3.0	North Sumatra
Minangkabau	5,569	2.7	Central Sumatra
Betawi	5,157	2.5	Jakarta
Buginese	5,157	2.5	South Sulawesi
Bantenese	4,331	2.1	Banten
Banjares	3,506	1.7	South Kalimantan
Balinese	3,094	1.5	Bali Island
Sasak	2,681	1.3	Lombok Island
Makassarese	2,063	1.0	South Sulawesi
Cirebon	1,856	0.9	West Java
Chinese	1,850	0.9	Jakarta, West Kalimantan, North Sumatra

Source: Suryadinata, Arifin, & Ananta (2003). Reprinted with permission of the Institute of Southeast Asian Studies, Singapore.

sketch of its history. Characterizing the educational history of this vast archipelago is no easy task given that it encompasses a geographic space larger than that of the continental USA, and it experienced profound influences – across three millennia – from its native Austronesian culture, Hindu-Buddhist culture, Islamic culture, Dutch-European culture, and the contemporary modernist, globalizing culture of national independence. It is possible, however, to glimpse some common themes concerning tensions over sameness and difference, hierarchy, and equality.

Austronesian and Indic culture

From the earliest times, spirituality and learning have had close associations in the Indonesian archipelago. Among the 680 related, but mutually unintelligible, Austronesian languages spoken in the region, there are many similar words that express this relationship. Prominent among these are terms for *source, origin*, and *ancestor*, words which are routinely contrasted with common expressions for *sprout, descendant*, and *offspring* (Fox, 1971, 1994, 1996). These common contrasting vocabulary items not only reflect the common reverence for foundational ancestral wisdom and authority but also harbor tensions arising from the shared desire for independence, innovation, and autonomy.

Even today, one finds great reverence for the knowledge of traditional healers, ancestral wisdom, and conventional sources of information. The languages and cultures are also filled with traditional folktales and verbal expressions that celebrate the exploits of latter-day descendants who, to use a common botanical idiom, "branch off" and "sprout" from the source and develop in new directions. Such botanical metaphors typically represent learning, and indeed cultural reproduction more generally, as a natural and organic process, but one filled with tension between its sources and its offspring.

Judging from the rich legacy of Sanskrit educational terminology currently found in Indonesian languages (Sarkar, 1966; Wirosuparto, 1974), the earliest Indic traders and priests found these preoccupations fertile ground in which to plant the seeds of Hindu beliefs about polity, rank, and cosmos. By the 6th century A.D., there was evidence of centers of learning called *sangraha* in Sumatra. When Marco Polo arrived in what is guessed to be Sumatra in the 13th century, he claims to have visited a residential school for Hindu learning with hundreds of monks.

Islamic schools

According to one popular tradition, the Islamic traders, beginning in the 9th century, made use of these Indic residential schools (also called *pondokan* in Javanese, *langgar, surau*, or *rankang* in Sumatra) for advancing Islamic learning. These developed into the *pesantren* system of Islamic residential schools found in many parts of Indonesia today. Pesantren provided a dormitory environment for boys and girls who were separated from their families as early as age 4. The *santri* (or students) strongly bonded with their teacher, or *kyai*, who taught them *fikih* (laws of ritual obligations), *akhlak* (moral character), *tauhid/aqidah* (belief in the oneness of God), *tafsir* (exegesis), and *hadis* (sayings of Muhammad), as well as core values of sincerity, *tawakal* (submission to God), and loyalty. Today, pesantren provide many important educational services: low-cost traditional religious education, government-recognized curricula (there are two different types to choose from), vocational skills training, and character development.

Dutch colonial education

Initially, the Dutch visits to the Indonesian archipelago were of a largely secular, commercial nature, with little or no "civilizing mission," either religious or educational. Unlike the French, Spanish, or Portuguese travelers to Southeast Asia – who carried with them a religious and educational mandate from the pope – the Dutch harbored no such goals. Until the days of the "ethical policy" in the late 1800s and early 20th century (Penders, 1968), the administration of the Dutch East Indies did not begin to develop a robust system for educating the native populations. When the administration did, however, it had a profound and lasting impact because of the ways in which it recognized – and indeed emphasized – ethnic, religious, and class differences in Indonesian society.

During the so-called liberal period of Dutch policy towards the East Indies (roughly 1840s to 1880), native customs were to be left intact. The Dutch adopted a non-interventionist approach, schooling their own children, but excluding the natives from educational opportunities. An 1849 regulation, for example, forbade entry of Indonesians into European schools (Penders, 1968). By the 1860s, however, pressed by the need for skilled native bureaucrats, a two-tiered system of schools was established – the five-year, Dutch language "first class" schools (*Eerste Klasse School*) and the three-year, Malay language "second class" schools (*Tweede Klasse School*). The former catered to native elites, while the latter were for the children of well-to-do local villagers and notables. However, since the teachers were poorly trained and the dropout rate was high, there were calls for the expansion of missionary schools, which were considered more effective and less expensive to operate. This, however, ran afoul of strong anti-clerical political sentiment in the Netherlands, and so government subsidies for religious schools were not generally permitted until the early 20th century.

In addition to their institutional recognition of social class (by systematically excluding non-elites from educational opportunities), the Dutch system also systematically separated the population in terms of race (*ras*). In 1914, separate Dutch language schools were formally established for the Europeans, Malays, and Chinese, who were considered to be separate races. Thus there were special schools for Europeans (*Europeesch Lagere School* [ELS]), native Indonesians (*Hollandse Inlandse School* [HIS], formerly the *Eerste Klasse School*), and Chinese (*Hollandse Chineesche School* [HCS]).

Linguistic resources were also carefully divided up. The Dutch system reserved access to the Dutch language to Europeans, children of elites, and selected Chinese. The rest of the population was to be taught in the Malay language, which later became the Indonesian language. Although very few children came to the schools speaking either Dutch or Malay, both became important "languages of wider communication" for Indonesians of the 20th century.

Although religious instruction was a much debated issue in Dutch colonial education in the 20th century, ultimately the schools retained an overall secular character. In order to qualify for government subsidies, Christian mission schools had to teach an essentially secular curriculum, and most complied with this requirement. Some Islamic schools in Sumatra established a curriculum similar to that of the HIS Dutch language schools, but they were not considered qualified for subsidies (Penders, 1968).

The Dutch textbooks did not dwell on the pluralistic, but unitary, character of the Indonesian archipelago. In school settings, there was little in the way of civics education other than the occasional ceremony in which students were told to express their loyalty to the queen. The primary context in which local ethnic differences came up in discussion was in the context of understanding and resolving conflict between groups. The Dutch believed that many of the causes of the strife they needed to settle as masters of the archipelago arose from *adat* or "local customs." They focused on mutual respect and recognition, and even developed an *adat* law specialization in law schools to help resolve conflict. Each ethnic group – it was emphasized – was linked to a particular territory, and these in turn were supposed to be linked to a particular language. Some of the merantau (diasporic) groups, for example the Minang, Batak, Bugis, and Bajaw, made this conceptualization problematic, but these cases were dismissed as aberrant.

The Dutch schools eventually came to reproduce a hegemonic ideology that divided the local peoples in terms of class, race, and religion. However, this stratification did not occur without contentious debate within the Netherlands. Serious questions were raised about the policy of *concordantie* (literally, "concordance") by which schooling in the Dutch East Indies was required to be completely congruent with that in the Netherlands. Many believed that Dutch-style education was inappropriate and irrelevant for peoples in the Indies, and served only to alienate the educated from the non-educated. Others raised questions about whether the Dutch had a responsibility to educate the Indonesian population by Westernizing them and aggressively teaching them Western (especially Dutch) ways, or whether they should instead support a nativized system of education that taught students to value their local heritage. Others still argued that any intervention at all in native life was a waste of time.

The debates ultimately did not prevent the heterogeneous peoples of the Indonesian archipelago from seeking an education. Particularly in the diverse outer islands of Indonesia (e.g. Sumatra, Sulawesi, and Kalimantan), students from many different ethnic groups were sometimes brought together in the same classrooms, speaking among themselves and with their teachers using the Malay language. This not only resulted in a greater sense of camaraderie among the different ethnic groups, but they also came to see themselves as roughly equivalent participants (albeit ranking below the Dutch) in a common, Indonesian-speaking collectivity. This embryonic sense of solidarity was partly responsible for the Dutch East Indies' eventual unraveling as a colonial empire and the gradual emergence of a single unitary independent republic of Indonesia after 1945.

Wartime and independence

The humiliating defeat and internment of the Dutch by the Japanese army in 1942 seriously undermined European authority in Indonesian eyes. While the victorious Japanese promised a new era of cooperation among Asians, soon it became clear to Indonesians that the Japanese were merely reproducing many of the same oppressive structures of the Dutch colonial state, only this time with even harsher consequences for non-cooperation. The school system changed little under the Japanese regime, except for mandatory Japanese language lessons, harsher discipline, and ceremonial acts of obedience to show homage to the Japanese emperor.

After the Japanese were defeated by the Allies in 1945, the united struggle of the Indonesian people against the Dutch return led to new appreciation of the ways in which the colonial regime had shortchanged the Indonesian people over the course of its presence in the archipelago, particularly in the realm of education. One of the central goals of the independence movement was to revamp the education system in an equitable manner.

Sukarno era

As the first president of Indonesia, Sukarno focused his energies on remedying the egregious wrongs of the Dutch colonial system, one of the worst of which was the failure to educate the vast majority of the Indonesian people. In the midst of the Indonesian revolutionary struggle in 1947, an Education Plan was developed by the newly established Ministry of Education. The goals of educational reform were the decolonization of the curriculum and the Indonesian mentality, promotion of universal access to education, the promotion of national unity by preventing suspicion and violence, and the development of useful, income-generating skills in students.

By 1964, the goal of national unity was the most prominent item on the agenda of the political leaders. The national educational system sought to integrate the Pancasila national ideology holistically and thematically into a national curriculum. This ideology consists of (a) belief in the one and only God, (b) just and civilized humanity, (c) the unity of Indonesia, (d) democracy led by wise guidance through consultation and representation, and (e) social justice for all Indonesian people.

Hampered by lack of funds and trained teachers and by the general political and economic chaos besetting the national state, implementation of the national curriculum was spotty at best during this period. The massacres following the communist coup attempt in 1965 elevated national allegiance and loyalty to the state as central values to be instilled in all students. The suppression of divisive sentiments of SARA (ethnicity, religion, race, or class) also became a major pedagogical priority.

Suharto's new order

By 1975, the political situation had stabilized and the economy had considerably improved owing to oil revenue windfalls. President Suharto used some of these profits for a massive school building program throughout the archipelago. A new, ambitious national curriculum – developed by Indonesian scholars fresh from studying overseas – resulted in a dizzying array of academic topics teachers had to cover, using elaborate "teacher-proof" lesson plans and worksheets, and often poorly written, decontextualized, and rapidly composed textbooks.

By 1984, this curriculum had been streamlined and simplified and began to recognize the importance of children's "active learning." After years of progressive centralization and consolidation of the national education system, the central government began to recognize the importance of developing "local content" (*muatan lokal*). In this system, up to 20% of curriculum time was allocated to the development of content that was deemed important for schools' own local circumstances. For example, some schools used this time to have teachers instruct students in local literary traditions. Many districts found it difficult, however, to take advantage of these new-found freedoms because of the lack of trained teachers and suitable textbooks. References to religious, ethnic, and class differences were tightly controlled, and carefully interpreted through the lens of the national ideology, Pancasila. Ethnicity was to be appreciated as a matter of heritage and aesthetic interest; religious belief was reduced to a menu of five official "choices" of world religions (Islam, Catholicism, Protestantism, Hinduism, and Buddhism); and the Chinese "race" was aggressively urged to assimilate, acquiring full citizenship in the Indonesian state and forsaking all formal instruction in the Chinese language and writing system.

The era of reform and decentralization

The tremendous growth of the educational system during the New Order resulted in a generation of literate, politically articulate students who were eager to think for themselves and who began increasingly to chafe against dictatorial rule, corruption, and nepotism. When the economy took a sudden turn for the worse in late 1997, students, fearing for their prosperity, began to intensify calls for reform (*reformasi*), and in May of 1998 Suharto stepped down after 34 years in power. As the entire Indonesian system of centralized political authority weakened, new centers of authority began to fill the gap, especially religious authority (Bjork, 2003). Educational authority also became increasingly decentralized, and there was an increased recognition of, and discussion about, religious, ethnic, and racial difference. The following section discusses some of the main dimensions of this current system since 1998.

Social resources for the organization of educational and social identities

In the Indonesian educational system in 2008, the overarching goal is the cultivation of competent, knowledgeable Indonesian citizens who can participate effectively in public and private life. Within that overall framework, however, an important feature of Indonesian identities in educational settings is religion. Other, more subtle factors include language, ethnicity, race, and class.

Agama (*religion*)

Within Indonesia today, the formal definition of religion is simple, because there are six officially recognized religions: Islam (86.1%), Protestantism (5.7%), Catholicism (3%), Hinduism (1.8%), and Buddhism and Confucianism (together making up approximately 3.4%). In practice, the definition is not so easy, because there are various belief systems (*aliran kepercayaan*), especially certain varieties of mysticism (e.g. *kebatinan*) that are related to Islam but are not the same. There are also many tribal groups that practice indigenous forms of spiritual devotion, such as ancestor worship and animism. These latter systems of belief are somewhat problematic, because the official state ideology proclaims a belief in a single Supreme Being. There are also some small, unrecognized Jewish communities in Indonesia, mainly in Jakarta and Surabaya (Museum of the Jewish People, n.d.).

The Indonesian government permits, recognizes, and – to some extent – subsidizes religious education. Recent regulations have clarified – in sometimes controversial ways – the relation between public and religious education. On the one hand, recent rules make it easier for religious and educational institutions to cooperate; places of worship (e.g. mosques) may now be used by public schools in some contexts (e.g. reading and study projects). On the other hand, new rules also support students' right to be instructed about a particular faith by a member of that faith. For example, a Muslim student in a Christian school has the right to be taught about Islam by a Muslim, even though that student is attending a Christian school (Jardine, 2003).

By far the largest system of religious education is Islamic religious education (Azra, Afrianty, & Hefner, 2007). There were 14,796 pesantren (Islamic boarding schools, also known as *pondokan*) scattered throughout the archipelago in 2008, although concentrated mostly in Java. They serve 3,464,334 students in Indonesia, or about 7% of the school-age children. In addition, there are government-run madrasah schools, supervised by the Department of Religion, that offer a standard curriculum in addition to religious instruction. These schools – serving approximately 10% of the school-age population of Indonesia – offer an education parallel to the standard public school education, with primary, middle, and high school levels. While a diploma from a madrasah is currently recognized by public universities, graduates of pesantrens who plan to attend anything other than the IAIN (state institutes of Islamic studies) must take an additional test or equivalency exam (see below).

Since the attacks of September 11, 2001, in the USA, and the various terrorist attacks in Bali and Jakarta, public debate has intensified about the role of Muslim schools, especially pesantren, in fostering anti-Western and anti-modern sentiments. In August of 2004, U.S. President Bush announced the provision of $157 million for the improvement of the quality of religious instruction in Indonesia, presumably as a way of thwarting the development of Islamic radicalism in Indonesia.

Religion is now the greatest single concern in Indonesian life, according to opinion polls (Associated Press, 2005). One of the ways in which religion is manifested is in moral panics about girls' sexuality, particularly as they increasingly interact with non-kin members outside the home in school settings. As Parker (2007) shows, these panics are born out of ambivalence. The perceived trend towards liberal Westernization in Indonesia is regarded as a source of hedonism and evil. However, Westernization is also admired and perceived as a route for economic advancement and improvement in the quality of life.

Other sources of identity in Indonesian educational systems

Bahasa (*language*). On one level, it would appear that language is a powerful unifying factor in Indonesia, with a successful national language spoken in all schools from one end of this heteroglot nation to the other. There is little – if any – resistance to the use of the national language in most educational settings. However, many pesantren (Islamic boarding schools) use only Indonesian when they are studying topics related to the national curriculum. Otherwise they are more likely to use whatever is the local language of the area, for example Javanese, and of course Arabic. In some cases, where the pesantren in question draws students from many different language groups in many different parts of the archipelago, the classical Arabic language of the Qur'an becomes a source of common vocabulary for *santri* who do not share a common language. In these schools, there is little explicit discussion of, or recognition of, the linguistically or ethnically plural nature of the *ummah* (Muslim congregation). The national educational system is the main source of explicit models of linguistic and ethnic diversity.

Recent government regulations explicitly permit the use of the local languages by teachers to orally scaffold student learning, particularly at the lower levels of basic education. Most textbooks, however, do not provide any such scaffolding, as they are exclusively printed in the Indonesian language. Such use of the local language to scaffold learning for students is assumed to be an oral process if done at all. Since 1999, the Chinese language has been permitted as a topic of study, but is not used as a language of instruction.

Suku (*ethnicity*). Since 1998 there has been increasingly explicit recognition of sources of difference among students, particularly in textbooks and government policies. Ethnic stereotypes, once common, are now explicitly avoided in textbooks, and there are areas of the curriculum devoted to exploring communal life in a heterogeneous society (e.g. Pancasila moral education [PMP]). There are no longer any schools that are restricted by ethnicity, although there are many that are ethnically homogeneous by default. For example, in some cities in central Java the students are overwhelmingly from the Javanese ethnic group. Islamic schools – particularly those not following the government curriculum – do not consider ethnicity relevant either, but for different reasons. They tend to minimize the importance of ethnic differences, and emphasize the meaning of shared membership in the *ummah*.

Ras (*race*). The term *race* has diminished as an explicit source of identity in Indonesia over the past 20 years. Few people invoke the category as a way of explaining identity in public settings, especially schools. While in the past it was a way of talking about Chinese and European identity, and indeed the basis for admission to certain schools, most Chinese in Indonesia are more comfortable talking about their identity in "ethnic" terms, congruent with other ethnic groups such as Javanese, Minangkabau, and Batak. In addition, many Chinese use religion as a way of organizing their distinctiveness in educational settings. As Bjork (2002) shows, because some Chinese parents believe that the public schools reinforce patterns of discrimination found in the broader society, they send their children to Catholic schools where they may feel free to resist cultural stereotypes.

Antar golongan (*class*). Perhaps the most subtle, but powerful, dimension of social life in Indonesia today is social class. Sometimes described in terms of *gengsi* (prestige or social status), schools and student identities exhibit marked differences depending on wealth and background. In general, urban is regarded as better than rural, rich better than poor, and inner islands (Java and Bali) are considered superior to outer islands. Within cities, some schools are regarded as more prestigious. For example, within Jakarta, SMA 8 is regarded as the most prestigious high school, reserved for students who are the brightest. Each major city has similar equivalents. The students at these schools tend to come from elite families.

Children from well-to-do families are also able to send their children to private schools. Likewise, within the Islamic school systems, certain pesantren are the most prestigious (e.g. Gontor in East Java is considered one of the elite pesantren, and similar prestige hierarchies exist within Catholic schools). In general, Catholic and Protestant schools are considered more prestigious than Islamic schools. Elite public schools in Indonesia are generally more esteemed than their private equivalents. There is of course considerable variation.

Translating across social categories: Negotiating "equivalencies" (*kesetaraan*)

Faced with a heterogeneous society composed of widely different religious, ethnic, and racial varieties, how does one manage an education system that provides for the whole population? Many nations have resorted to programs that focus on equity, enforcing equal opportunity through quotas and the like. Since the 1990s, in Indonesia, the directorate of equivalency programs (*kesetaraan*) has provided new ways of thinking about the diversity of educational experiences in a multicultural society. Three "packages," corresponding to elementary, middle, and high school levels, have been established as a way of recognizing the informal and non-formal learning that occurs in this vast archipelagic nation, but also permitting a set of common standards for evaluation. These equivalency packages currently provide services to about a half-million learners at the elementary level, 1.5 million at the middle school level, and more than 1 million at the high school level. Among the users of these services are students in religious schools, learners in remote regions of Indonesia, dropouts, migrant workers in foreign countries, home-schoolers, and adult learners.

What makes the equivalency programs unique is that, instead of focusing on "equity" (e.g. through establishment of official racial, ethnic, and social "identities" and rigorous enforcement of quotas), the equivalency program focuses on the relationships among different kinds of educational experiences to common, shared standards of competence (Indonesia, Departemen Pendidikan Nasional, 2006). Thus rather than establishing a fixed set of learning goals associated with a particular national identity (e.g. Chinese, Muslim, or Christian), the emphasis is on negotiating an agreed-upon relation to the national standards of competence. In this way, the equivalency programs are designed to help minimize the perception of elitism, exclusivity, and rigidity sometimes associated with formal education by recognizing a wider range of educational experiences.

For example, when students attending a school that is not part of the national educational system (e.g. a Muslim school) wish to certify that they can meet certain national standards, they receive a "packet" that contains a list of questions requiring them to describe the nature of the educational experiences, and must complete a national test. If the students pass the test and the educational experiences are deemed to be in line with the national standards, the students can then receive certification that their educational level is equivalent with that offered by the national educational system.

The equivalency program provides grants to groups that have not previously participated in the state education system, such as Islamic boarding schools and Christian home-schooling programs. One example of an Islamic boarding school that has benefited from this program is the pesantren Imam Bukhari, the number of whose students participating in the program is rising each year. Another example is the Morning Star Academy, which according to its promotional literature provides a "home school learning environment where the best of Biblically based accredited academia and cutting edge technology are combined to deliver the most relevant and meaningful courses in a user friendly way" (http://www.ms-academy.org). Popular mostly among ethnic Chinese in Indonesia, the Morning Star approach to education can receive recognition by the national educational system through the equivalency program.

The equivalency program also provides ways of translating educational experiences across the vast divides of social class that one finds in Indonesia. For example, while the students from orphanages in Bali and the Muhammadiyah-run orphanages in Java receive recognition from the equivalency program, so also do the students who attend elite international schools. In this way, the national educational system provides a common framework for interpreting otherwise very different educational backgrounds.

Education Act No. 20, 2003, Article 32 (Department of Education, 2003) states that special attention should be given to disadvantaged groups, including those who are members of poor agricultural or fishing communities and those who live in remote areas, including ethnic minorities. Consistent with this act, the equivalency program provides resources to expand the range of delivery methods to reach those populations suffering social exclusion. The equivalency program has promoted the use of mobile classrooms, which involves using converted buses, motorcycles, and boats. The government provides block grants to community groups that engage in outreach programs for disadvantaged learners. It also provides grants to disadvantaged ethnic groups in remote areas, such as the forest peoples of Papua, and to particular coastal communities in Sulawesi whose economic livelihood comes from seafaring and fishing and whose lifestyles severely disrupt the educational opportunities of their children.

A significant number of Indonesians work overseas before completing their formal education, in some cases making it difficult to continue their education upon their return. The equivalency program makes it possible for them to participate in an Indonesian public education, even as they work overseas in countries as distant as Saudi Arabia, Kuwait, Malaysia, Hong Kong, Taiwan, and Singapore. In some cases, this program has not only made it possible for them to continue their education but also qualified them for better-paying jobs.

Critics have argued that the equivalency programs legitimize class and ethnic differences by providing a framework in which such distinctions can be perpetuated, and indeed justified within the context of the Indonesian national department of education. Children of privileged or ethnically isolated backgrounds can thus avoid – it is charged – some of the common experiences provided to other students participating in the national education system. Defenders of the equivalency program respond that, even if these charges are true, the equivalency initiative is still preferable to a system in which multiple educational systems simultaneously operate with little or no central coordination. The challenge is to see equivalency as more than simply a place to deal with the anomalous and marginal cases, but rather an integrating and equitable conception for the education system as a whole.

Conclusions

Indonesia boasts one of the world's largest school systems, serving more than 50 million students. Over the last 60 years since independence, the Indonesian education system has made great strides. The remarkably high literacy rate (90% in 2004), the high rate of participation among girls (99% in 2004), and the spectacular growth of higher education are all remarkable, given Indonesia's breathtaking linguistic and ethnic diversity, the colonial legacy of unfairness and divisiveness, and the overall handicap of third world poverty. All students are now required to attend 9 years of schooling, and the participation rates are high. Facilitated by a successful national language that links every corner of the archipelago, the national school system still faces significant challenges in meeting the needs of one of the world's most heterogeneous societies.

Since the fall of Suharto in 1998, and subsequent decentralization of political and bureaucratic authority, there have been increasing efforts to recognize religious and linguistic difference. While the Suharto regime focused the educational system for over 30 years on creating citizens loyal to a unitary, central state authority, the post-Suharto system has begun to explore local autonomy in decision making with regard to curriculum, financing, and personnel decisions. Some of this "autonomy" was simply a reflection of the monetary crisis of 1998–2000, during which the central government was unable to meet its financial obligations to the provinces. However, in some regions local schools were able to exercise independent judgment in ways that would have been impossible during the previous 30 years (Bjork, 2003).

Since September 11, 2001, and the subsequent bombings in Bali and Jakarta, there has been a new scrutiny of the religious schools in Indonesia, particularly the Islamic boarding schools or pesantren. Only a tiny minority of these schools teaches extremist views, and there is little evidence that their popularity is growing; overall, the number of Indonesian children attending private schools – whether Christian or Muslim – has remained stable or declined over the last 20 years.

Endowed with natural and human resources of spectacular diversity, Indonesia aspires to develop into a society of enlightened tolerance and critical open-mindedness. There is hardly any alternative, because Indonesia has hundreds of languages, many religious traditions, and a long legacy of civilizational mixture, fusion, and synthesis. With a well-established educational system in place, made possible thanks to a widely accepted national language, Indonesia is now in a position to turn its attention from basic issues of national unity and citizenship to more complex educational challenges that recognize differences in religious and ethnic identity.

References

Associated Press (2005, June 6). AP/Ipsos poll: Religious fervor in U.S. surpasses faith in many other highly industrial countries. Retrieved May 10, 2008, from http://www.ipsos-na.com/news/pressrelease.cfm?id=2694

Azra, A., Afrianty, D., & Hefner, R. (2007). Pesantren and madrasa: Muslim schools and national ideals in Indonesia. In R. W. Hefner & M. Q. Zaman (Eds.) *Schooling Islam: The culture and politics of modern muslim education* (pp. 172–198). Princeton: Princeton University Press.

Bjork, C. (2002). Reconstructing rituals: Expressions of autonomy and resistance in a Sino-Indonesian school. *Anthropology and Education Quarterly, 33*(4), 465–491.

Bjork, C. (2003). Local responses to decentralization policy in Indonesia. *Comparative Education Review, 47*(2), 184–216.

Department of Education, Republic of Indonesia. (2003). *Act of the Republic of Indonesia, no. 20*. Jakarta, Indonesia: Author.

Fox, J. J. (1971). Sister's child as plant: Metaphors in an idiom of consanguinity. In R. Needham (Ed.), *Rethinking kinship and marriage* (pp. 219–252). London: Tavistock.

Fox, J. J. (1994). Reflections on "hierarchy" and "precedence." *History of Anthropology, 7*(1–4), 87–108.

Fox, J. J. (1996). The transformation of progenitor lines of origin: Patterns of precedence in Eastern Indonesia. In J. J. Fox (Ed.), *Origins, ancestry, and alliance: Explorations in Austronesian ethnography* (pp. 130–153). Canberra: Australian National University Press.

Indonesia, Departemen Pendidikan Nasional. (2006). *Standar isi untuk satuan pendidikan dasar dan menengah & standar kompetensi lulusan untuk pendidikan dasar dan menengah: Peraturan Menteri Pendidikan Nasional no 22 dan 23, tahun 2006: Dilengkapi lampiran I, standar kompetensi dan kompetensi dasar tingkat SD, MI, dan SDLB, standar kompetensi lulusan (SKL)* [Content standards for elementary and middle school education: Regulations of the National Ministry of Education nos. 22 and 23, year 2006: Supplements attachment I, standards of competence and basic competencies at the SD, MI, and SDLB levels, and the competence standards for graduation (SKL)]. Jakarta, Indonesia: Cipta Jaya.

Jardine, D. (2003). Multi-faith protesters fail to stop religious bill. *Times Educational Supplement, 4537*, p. 20. Retrieved October 27, 2008, from http://search.ebscohost.com/login.aspx?direct=true&db=qeh&AN=BEDI03115698&site=ehost-live

Museum of the Jewish People (n.d.). *The Jewish community of Indonesia*. Retrieved May 11, 2008, from http://www.bh.org.il/communities/Archive/indonesia.asp

Parker, L. (2007). Of faith and feminism: Imagining discursive feminist space for Muslim women. *Outskirts: Feminisms Along the Edge, 17*(1). Retrieved October 27, 2008, from http://www.chloe.uwa.edu.au/outskirts/archive/volume17/parker

Penders, C. L. M. (1968). *Colonial education policy and practice in Indonesia, 1900–1942*. Unpublished doctoral dissertation, Australian National University, Canberra, Australia.

Sarkar, H. B. (1966). The migration of Sanskrit grammar, lexicography, prosody and rhetoric to Indonesia. *Journal of the Asiatic Society, 8*(2), 84, 92–93.

Suryadinata, L., Arifin, E. N., & Ananta, A. (2003). *Indonesia's population: Ethnicity and religion in a changing political landscape*. Singapore: Institute for Southeast Asian Studies.

Wirosuparto, S. (1974). Sanskrit in modern Indonesia. *Studies in Indo-Asian Art and Culture, 3*, 147–159.

Part 9

The education of ethnic and cultural minority groups in Europe

34

Migrant minority groups in Germany
Success and failure in education

Sigrid Luchtenberg
University of Duisburg–Essen, Germany

A recent census in Germany revealed that immigrants make up nearly a fifth of the population, a figure much higher than the 10% cited previously (Federal Statistical Office, 2007). The migrants are not spread evenly throughout the nation. In the eastern states, there are fewer migrants than in the western states, and big cities have a larger migrant population than other places. This chapter focuses on the education of children and youth from immigrant backgrounds, especially second- or third-generation immigrants. The term *minority* refers to migration minorities. Not addressed here are the national minorities, including Sorbs (numbering approximately 60,000), Danes (50,000), Frisians (12,000), and Sinti and Roma (70,000).

Migrant minorities in Germany

There are three relevant migrant groups in the Federal Republic of Germany: work migrants, refugees, and resettlers. Owing to a booming economy, West Germany has had to recruit workers from abroad since the late 1950s. Workers – who were originally called guest workers – came mainly from southern and southeastern European countries such as Turkey, and later Morocco and Tunisia, owing to bilateral contracts. The largest number of work migrants came from Turkey. Some work migrants belong to minority groups in their home country, such as Kurds from Turkey. The guest workers were supposed to stay for a maximum of five years and then be replaced by others. This rotation model turned out to be unacceptable to industry, so workers stayed longer and began bringing their families to Germany. Such settlement increased in 1973, when the government declared a halt to general recruitment, owing to a recession (Hoff, 1995).

At first, work migrants faced substantial work and residential restrictions, but they could apply for greater freedom step by step. Many of them nowadays have an unrestricted residential status (if not citizenship) and full work permission (see Bade & Oltmer, 2004, for the situation in the former German Democratic Republic [GDR]).

The group of refugees in West Germany – and now the unified Germany – is the most heterogeneous group with regard to countries of origin, languages spoken, educational background, and personal migration history, which often includes war memories and worse.

Their number has fallen in recent years owing to new laws that limit opportunities to enter Germany as a refugee. In 1992, more than 400,000 people requested refugee status. By 2000, the number had dropped to 78,564, and in 2006 there were only 21,029 who asked for asylum (Beauftragte, 2007, p. 248). In recent years, the largest number of refugees have come from Iraq, followed by the former Yugoslavia and Turkey (mainly Kurds). Although most of the asylum seekers are not acknowledged as refugees, many of them win the right to stay in Germany as long as the conditions in their home countries remain difficult.

Special laws apply to persons of German origin who lived in the former Soviet Union and its satellites during the fascist period and suffered because they were of German origin. These are the so-called Aussiedler or Spätaussiedler (resettlers), who are descendants of Germans who migrated to Russia, Poland, and Romania during the 17th and 18th centuries. Those who migrated to Germany after 1948 were guaranteed citizenship. After the collapse of the Warsaw Pact system in 1990, the number migrating went up greatly. Regulations since 1993 demand that these migrants show not only proof of their German heritage and discrimination because of this but also competency in German by at least one family member. Furthermore, the number of resettlers – including non-German husbands or wives – is limited to approximately 100,000 per year (in recent years, fewer than that have migrated). More than 2 million resettlers relocated to Germany between 1990 and 2000.

Other groups add to the diversity in Germany, including the Japanese community in Düsseldorf, which encompasses about 11,000 persons. There are also many persons from other countries who work in Germany, mainly with an international firm, with an international authority, or as members of the military.

Owing to labor mobility within the European Union, it is difficult to decide whether someone's stay in a country should be regarded as immigration or as a temporary sojourn, which is often described as transmigration (Pries, 2001). Meanwhile, many countries of origin of the former guest workers are now member states of the EU, so their citizens enjoy the freedom to relocate.

Educational policies

It took the German educational system – which includes schools, administrators, and government officials – a long time to react to the increasing numbers of students from a non-German background in the late 1960s and 1970s. The 16 states control the education of children under 18, and home-schooling is not allowed in Germany. Although children of asylum seekers are not obligated to attend school in Germany, most states allow or even encourage them to go to school. As soon as a family – or a child – receives refugee status, children are required to attend school.

All proposals and measures regarding migrant students in the early period, from the 1960s to the 1980s, can be described as migrant-oriented approaches. They aimed at improving learning conditions for migrant children, teaching German as a second language, and educating teachers about the children's cultures of origin. The description is less positive when it becomes clear that this approach was deficit oriented: the migrant students' inability to speak German and ignorance of German culture and history were the focal point. Instead of acknowledging the development of a migrant culture in Germany, educators focused on the situation in the countries of origin, which often resulted in a rather static concept of a culture. Remigration also had to be considered in developing programs. In many teacher training institutions and universities, early courses and scholarship focused on *Ausländerpädagogik*, or migrant education.

This narrow perspective soon led to criticism of this pedagogical approach and demands for another approach.

Criticism of migrant education led to the development of multicultural education. Multicultural or intercultural education now encompasses all international educational approaches, including the international education proposed by the United Nations Educational, Scientific and Cultural Organization (UNESCO). In Germany, this shift in philosophy has contributed to a better acceptance of multicultural education, especially in administrative circles, even though the main focus in schools and research is on education within a multicultural society. On the other hand, there is a problem when multicultural and international aspects mingle, because many teachers – and students – prefer to deal with international topics such as indigenous people in America and thus tend to neglect the challenges of their own multicultural society. One reason for this tendency could be that it is easier to reflect on distant problems than to tackle your own situation and attitudes.

In 1996 the Standing Conference of the Ministers of Education and Cultural Affairs issued a recommendation on multicultural education that has led to changes in curricula and textbooks in schools, many of which can now be described as open to diversity (Standing Conference, 1996).

Multicultural education focuses on integration and rejects assimilation. This emphasis on integration has called for supporting classes made up of both German and non-German students and rejecting separate classes. Therefore, bilingual education has not been developed to a great extent, though language has always played an important role in multicultural education (Luchtenberg, 2002). The importance of learning German becomes more and more a central point in political policies of multicultural education, with the existence of practices such as testing the linguistic competence of preschool children and teaching German in kindergartens. An old demand from the 1970s and 1980s resurfaces when parents from a non-German background are asked to speak German at home. These requests stem from the political arena, but not from multiculturalists, and have particularly increased after publication of the results of the Program for International Student Assessment (PISA), a project of the Organisation for Economic Co-operation and Development (OECD). The project tested the skills and knowledge of 15-year-old students, and the results were rather disappointing for the German school system. There is a call for improvement in the schools and more efforts from migrants to integrate into German mainstream society. German policy makers have for a very long time neglected both the issue of cohesion in the increasingly heterogeneous society and the challenge of integrating all persons who live in Germany. Instead, a division between the "native German" and the "foreign" population was allowed to grow, with the result that the native German population had no need to deal with the growing multiculturalism, while the foreign population often experienced rejection and non-acceptance, even from many schools and teachers. In 2005, a new immigration law was passed that, together with the new citizenship law from 2000, acknowledges Germany as a country of immigration (Bundesministerium des Inneren [BMI], n.d.). Yet it has to be taken into consideration that this law is intended "to control, regulate and limit immigration" – a somewhat negative approach. Integration is a key concept in this law, and for the first time new (and some not so new) immigrants are required to attend language and information courses. There is a strong focus on the German language, which influences the education of migrant minority children. In 2006 and 2007, "summit conferences on integration" brought together representatives from the federal government, states, and organizations made up of migrants and Germans, such as unions, chambers of commerce, parent associations, charities, and religious groups. A "national integration concept" has been developed that proposes using a variety of activities in many sectors, such as sports and media, to encourage integration. For all these sectors, working groups have been organized in which researchers also participate. The federal government, states, and communities are involved in this effort (Bundesregierung, 2007). Again, the emphasis on learning German is dominant.

Almost no coordinated bilingual education exists. Bilingual students attend German language classes, seek additional support in German as a second language, and can be taught in their mother tongue for up to 5 hours per week, depending on the conditions in their school or school district. Mother tongue instruction has improved in Germany since the 1970s, when it was mainly regarded as a support for remigration. Attending a mother tongue class is not compulsory for the students. Some states now offer a variety of languages, including Kurdish or Farsi, at least in big cities or places with a large community speaking these languages. There are some schools where students can choose to study their mother tongue as a "foreign" language; in most of these cases, Turkish is the language studied. There are only two universities in Germany – Duisburg–Essen and Hamburg – where aspiring teachers can study Turkish in order to teach this subject in primary or secondary schools. Most of these students are second- (or third-)generation Turkish immigrants. Bilingual classes for migrant students, dual immersion classes, and transitional bilingual education are very seldom to be found (Reich & Roth, 2002).

One of the major issues under discussion by administrators, teachers, researchers, and attendees at the first German Islam conference (BMI, 2006) was the organization of Muslim religious education in German schools. According to Remid (2007), there were about 3,300,000 Muslims in Germany in 2006; about one-third had a German passport attained through naturalization.

Religious classes – usually Catholic or Protestant Christian – are organized in Germany in cooperation with the churches, though parents can choose not to have their children attend, which rarely happens. Students older than 14 can decide to withdraw, but then they usually have to attend lessons in ethics or philosophy instead. Muslim students could take remedial courses or ethics instead of religion, but there is a general consensus that Muslim religious education should be available. One of the challenges of offering courses on Islam is finding an institution or group that is authorized to speak for all Muslims. There are other difficulties as well. The lessons are to be given in German in order to allow all Muslim children to participate and to facilitate the control by a school authority, but teacher training does not exist so far (or is just beginning, as it is in the universities of Münster and Osnabrück). Also, all Muslim groups and communities must agree on the curriculum. So far, Muslim religious education is offered in a few cities as an experiment.

Islam has only recently been treated as an issue in schools, though several Christian–Islamic circles have existed since the mid-1990s. These were initiated to counteract the rising xenophobia in the majority society after the reunification of the two German states in the early 1990s. At that time, the biggest Muslim community in Germany, migrants of Turkish origin, was the target of several hostile attacks by groups of right-wing German juveniles. Since September 11 and the following terrorist events, mistrust of Muslims has increased, but on the other hand the need to deal with Islam – not only but especially in educational contexts – has increased as well. Nonetheless, most states in Germany have passed – or will soon do so – a law against wearing headscarves while working in certain fields, including education. State officials argue that a teacher wearing a headscarf would not be an appropriate role model for gender equality or would look strange, especially to younger children. The constitutional court will probably soon have to decide whether all religious symbols have to be banned from schools, instead of the symbol of just one religion.

Hostility against migrants still exists. Therefore, racism is a highly discussed issue. The Standing Conference of the Ministers of Education and Cultural Affairs has given statements on racism several times and has called for tolerance and solidarity. In 2000 the German ministers of the interior and justice founded an organization, Alliance for Democracy and Tolerance, that supports many activities and nonpolitical organizations that fight against racism (Bündnis für Demokratie und Toleranz, n.d.).

Educators – researchers, policy makers, and teachers – have improved their attitude toward the migrant population, but more change is needed. The objectives of preparing all students to live together in a heterogeneous society and of giving migrant students equal educational opportunities cannot be separated from each other. There will be no peaceful society if the rather large group of migrant students is left behind in school and career opportunities. All people need to see value in a multicultural society. In many studies, the attitudes of students and adults toward other ethnic groups have been researched. The results show a certain amount of xenophobia among Germans but also a somewhat negative attitude toward Germany among young immigrants. There is still a great deal of progress to be made in educational politics and research before the German educational system can be described as adequate for the multicultural and multilingual society it has to serve.

Teacher training is a matter of great concern. Although many education students learn about multicultural education and the needs of migrant students, such instruction is still not mandatory in all universities. Many universities offer additional courses for a supplementary qualification in German as a second language and multicultural education. There are very few teachers with a migrant background (about 1% of employed teachers, and 2% of education students).

A recent nationwide project to improve the schooling of students from migrant backgrounds (FÖRMIG) focuses on language improvement in German, the mother tongue, and foreign languages and on professional training and integration in the workforce. Tasks to be addressed include developing language tests, implementing cooperative language training, and increasing support for the concept that all teaching is language teaching. A new and innovative approach is to concentrate on transitions in the educational process, such as the move from primary to secondary school, and to build cooperation among all who are involved, including families, schools, companies, libraries, and clubs (Bundesministerium für Bildung und Forschung, n.d.). The project began in 2004 and will last five years. This is the most advanced project ever implemented in the education of students with a migrant background in Germany, and the minimal expectation is that new concepts and teaching proposals will be gained from it.

Examples of good practice in multicultural education

Despite the fact that overall progress has been slow, there are many examples of good practice. One of the best known examples is School Without Racism, also known as School Without Racism – School With Courage. This European initiative began in Belgium in the 1980s; there are currently more than 700 schools in Europe involved, and about 375 schools in Germany. This is a surprisingly high number, because students have to take the initiative in having their school join the effort, and they must have the support of a majority of students, teachers, and nonacademic personnel in their school. The main focus is on enhancing awareness of discrimination and racism and on enabling students to fight them using the concepts of democracy and human rights (Schule ohne Rassismus, n.d.).

For more than 10 years, the BMW Award for Intercultural Learning has been given mainly to schools or school-related projects. The winners are typical examples of good practice. The prize winner in 2006 was KI-MI-SI, which stands for Kann Ich – Mach Ich – Schaff Ich (I can, I do, I achieve) and is a parent initiative for creating opportunities for meeting and learning outside the school environment. Children between the ages of 8 and 13 and of all nationalities are supervised by parents as they explore cultural diversity, from languages and eating habits to ways of life and work. Another example of good practice is the performance of a Russian fairy tale (*Kolobok*) by two classes in order to gain more understanding between native German children and children of resettlers. The bilingual approach is of special interest: German children were introduced to the Russian language, while the children whose mother tongue is Russian learned to appreciate their bilingualism (BMW Group, 2007).

Another program worthy of mention is Rucksack, in which the language learning of preschoolers with a migrant background is enhanced by including the mothers, who are advised to support children in their mother tongue. Cooperation between the educational personnel and the parents takes center stage (Regionale Arbeitsstelle [RAA], 2007).

Remedial teaching at the University of Duisburg–Essen, in cooperation with the city of Essen, is a successful program. Since 1974 students with a migrant background from all kinds of secondary schools have been able to take lessons in nearly all school subjects. The lessons are given by students of the university and are mostly paid for by the city. The Mercator Foundation sponsors the project (Mercator Stiftung, 2008). The success is remarkable: many of the first children to participate went on to become university students themselves. The university students not only earn some money by giving these lessons, but they also gain teaching experience and intercultural competence (Benholz, 2003). There are many more examples of good practice to be found, though many of them are known only locally.

School results

Although the nationwide discussion about school failure of students with migration backgrounds mainly began after publication of the first PISA results, researchers already knew from yearly graduation statistics that students from migrant backgrounds were struggling. PISA was the first large study in which the classification "student with a migrant background" (one parent born abroad) was used. The main findings follow:

- Nearly 20% of migrant students leave school without any school-leaving certificate.
- Most juveniles with a migrant background attend a *Hauptschule*, a secondary school for the academically less gifted students, which – depending on the state – awards a qualified certificate to students after 9 or 10 years.
- Nearly 40% of migrant students earn the *Hauptschule* certificate, which is insufficient to pursue some professional careers. This certificate has lost much of its value. Although one might have found a satisfactory apprenticeship training position in the 1960s or 1970s with such a certificate, this is far less likely today.
- Only 13% of the migrant students pass the *Abitur*, the final examination in a *Gymnasium* or comprehensive school that allows one to begin university studies.
- Many migrant students attend special schools for disabled or less capable children.
- Many migrant students have to repeat classes.
- More than twice as many migrant students as German students fail at a secondary modern school and have to continue their education in a *Hauptschule*.

- Migrant students stay longer than German students in preschool (in areas where such classes exist).

Table 34.1 shows the "foreign" student population broken down by types of school (Federal Statistical Office, 2005). There are nearly no statistics available that differentiate between students with and without migrant backgrounds (Konsortium Bildungsberichterstattung, 2006, p. 139).

These numbers show that there have been some improvements in the number of foreign students attending secondary schools of a better type than the *Hauptschule*. However, migrant students are still not attending these schools in numbers proportionate to their population. A number of factors account for the fact that some students perform better on tests than others, because there are also students with a migrant background who pass the *Abitur* and attend university. There may be very individual reasons for the variations in student test performance. The results are widely spread, but among the differences there is the education of the parents (Konsortium Bildungsberichterstattung, 2006, p. 148).

The overall lack of educational achievement among migrant students becomes even clearer when school-leaving certificates are considered. Data for Table 34.2 come from the school year 2003–2004 (Federal Statistical Office, 2006).

These poor results are confirmed by recent OECD studies (2001, 2006). They also explain why so many students with a migrant background cannot find an apprenticeship (see also Konsortium Bildungsberichterstattung, 2006, pp. 153ff.).

The OECD studies offer additional findings. The most important one is that the social gap between students is extremely wide in Germany and is by no means closed or even improved in school. Many students from migrant backgrounds come from families with a low social status, and this contributes to their unsatisfactory school careers. Further results show that German teachers lack competence in diagnosing learning difficulties; recognizing such obstacles would be extremely important for helping migrant students to overcome their language and learning

Table 34.1 Percentages of Foreign Students in Types of Schools

Type of School	2001–2002	2002–2003	2003–2004	2004–2005	2005–2006	2006–2007
School kindergartens	25.1	24.2	23.7	23.7	20.7	18.3
Primary schools	12.1	12.0	11.7	11.5	11.2	10.6
Hauptschulen	17.7	18.2	18.6	18.7	18.9	19.2
Secondary modern schools	6.6	6.8	7.0	7.2	7.5	7.7
Gymnasium	3.9	3.9	4.0	4.1	4.2	4.3
Integrative comprehensive schools	12.2	12.5	12.8	13.1	13.5	13.6
Special schools	15.4	15.8	16.0	No data	No data	No data

Table 34.2 Percentages of Germans and Non-Germans Earning Types of School-Leaving Certificates

Result	Germans	Non-Germans
No diploma at all	7.4	18.1
Final exam of the secondary school (*Hauptschule*)	23.5	40.9
Final exam of the secondary modern school	43.7	30.8
Advanced technical college entrance qualification	1.2	1.3
General qualification for university entrance (*Abitur*)	24.3	8.9

problems. The OECD results can also be interpreted as a general lack of support for students with a migrant background in the German school system. It is as a result of these studies that all-day schools are becoming more established in Germany. At most of them, only those students whose parents opt for this opportunity participate in the afternoon program. Regular teaching takes place in the morning, while the afternoon is devoted mostly to mentoring and supervision programs in which more social workers than teachers are involved. These schools are mainly situated in deprived inner-city areas, and participation in these programs could be stigmatizing.

Tables 34.1 and 34.2 offer evidence that German schools have so far failed to promote these students, as well as native German students from lower social classes. The failure to bridge the social gap is without doubt an alarming result, because education and especially a good school-leaving certificate are an essential foundation for any professional or vocational career. It is well known that the need for unskilled labor is decreasing, so a good education plays an increasingly important role in establishing one's starting point into professional life (Heckmann, 2003). For nearly a quarter of young people with a migrant background – especially young men – leaving school without a school certificate or with one from a *Hauptschule* means that there is only a small chance at a regular professional life. Even taking into account certain problems within the migrant group culture – such as preferring jobbing to an apprenticeship, or the negative influence of the social milieu with a high percentage of unemployment, as well as the experience of being stigmatized as "foreigner" or "Muslim" – the educational system in Germany is guilty of not having supported children with a migrant background enough to give them equal opportunities in German society.

After more than 30 years of migrant education in Germany, the results are alarming. Schools and universities must find ways to improve the educational situation of students with a migrant background.

Yet there is another aspect to be discussed in this context: How do these obvious signs of neglect affect the integration of migrants and their offspring? Here, further issues have to be considered:

- The failure to learn German before school starts is publicly viewed as a sign of unwillingness to integrate – disregarding the fact that students with a migrant background have already learned another language.
- Migrant bilingualism is not highly valued in the school system or in society, despite the fact that language competence is generally held in high esteem and is in great demand in fields such as banking, policing, and social work.
- The media still refer to migrants and their offspring mainly in the context of negative events.
- Migrant students' needs and possible contributions in most subjects are not addressed. These facts are very obvious in citizenship education, but are also present in all other subjects (Luchtenberg, 2004).

Male migrant juveniles are statistically more likely to commit a crime than other juveniles. How much of this tendency can be attributed to these youths' exclusion from a satisfying social life and professional possibilities? This possibility was raised in the political and media discourse after the French youth riots in the winter of 2005–2006, but the discussion was brief. The riots did increase German mistrust of ethnic – especially Turkish and thus Muslim – communities. Germans are unhappy that children from these communities cannot speak German when they enter school even though they are born and raised in Germany. It is feared that migrants who live separately from the mainstream society could become radical. Şen (2002) confirms the development of an ethnic infrastructure in Berlin and in big cities in North Rhine-Westphalia, in which nearly all demands of daily life can be fulfilled so that there is no longer any need to mingle with mainstream German society. Members of these communities unite in the face of outside hostility, and leaders fight to keep the local power structure intact.

Conclusion: Proposals for change

As discussed above, there are new insights into the situation of students from migrant backgrounds, mainly owing to OECD studies, and these insights have resulted in some improvement. It is too early to judge the success or failure of these measures, but it is obvious that none of the present proposals tackle the German educational system itself. This is despite the recommendations of international reports such as PISA and the report by the UN commissioner Muñoz, who reported on Germany in 2006 (Human Rights Council, 2007).

There are some conclusions that appear quite often in these reports:

- Forcing 10-year-olds to select secondary schools is regarded as inappropriate.
- The German *Hauptschule* is insufficient to give students a good start in (professional) life.
- The all-day school with its present status is not helpful, especially since many families are unable to pay for their children's lunch.
- The cross-linking between school types and especially between educational sectors is insufficient (kindergarten/preschool – school, school – vocational school).
- Preschool education should be part of the ordinary educational system.
- Social class as a determinant factor of school success is significant and unfortunate.

Klemm (2008) complains that students from migrant backgrounds face a threefold disadvantage: Class and language disadvantages result in achievement differences, which are enlarged by the early (and not even achievement-oriented) distribution of children into different school types, culminating in very different educational outcomes. Bade (2008) notes a further important and alarming aspect: School integration has failed for more than 30 years, and improvement will not come easily, but making up for the years in which school integration has been delayed is essential for social cohesion.

References

Bade, K. (2008). Ein Fremder ist nur ein Freund . . . [A stranger is only a friend . . .] (Guest contribution). *Newsletter BMW Group*, 10–12.

Bade, K. J., & Oltmer, J. (2004). *Normalfall migration* [Migration: A normal case]. Bonn, Germany: Bundeszentrale für politische Bildung.

Beauftragte der Bundesregierung für Migration, Flüchtlinge und Integration. (2007). 7. *Bericht über die Lage der Ausländerinnen und Ausländer in Deutschland* [7. Report on the situation of foreigners in Germany]. Retrieved March 24, 2008, from http://www.bundesregierung.de/Content/DE/Publikation/IB/Anlagen/auslaenderbericht-7,property=publicationFile.pdf

Benholz, C. (2003). Förderunterricht für Kinder und jugendliche Ausländischer herkunft an der Universität Duisburg – Essen [Remedial courses for children and juveniles at the University of Duisburg – Essen]. *ELiSe: Essener Linguistische Skripte – Elektronisch*, *3*(2), 59–68.

BMW Group. (2007). *Ten years BMW Group award for intercultural learning: Jointly learning from diversity.*

Retrieved January 6, 2008, from http://www.bmwgroup.com/bmwgroup_prod/e/0_0_www_bmwgroup_com/verantwortung/gesellschaft/lifeaward/BMWGroupAward_Festschrift_CelebrationPublication.pdf

Bundesministerium des Inneren (BMI). (n.d.). *Gesetz zur Steuerung und Begrenzung der Zuwanderung und zur Regelung des Aufenthalts und der Integration von Unionsbürgern und Ausländern (Zuwanderungsgesetz)* [Law to control and to limit immigration and to regulate the residence and integration of EU citizens and of foreigners (immigration law)]. Retrieved January 5, 2008, from http://www.bmi.bund.de/Internet/Content/Common/Anlagen/Gesetze/Zuwanderungsgesetz,templateId=raw,property=publicationFile.pdf/Zuwanderungsgesetz

Bundesministerium des Inneren (BMI). (2006). Federal minister of the interior Dr Wolfgang Schäuble opens the first German Conference on Islam in Berlin: "Muslims in Germany – German Muslims." Retrieved March 24, 2008, from http://www.bmi.bund.de/nn_148280/Internet/Navigation/EN/Topics/German__Islam__Conference/German__Islam__Conference__node.html__nnn=true

Bundesministerium für Bildung und Forschung. (n.d.). *Förderung von Kindern und Jugendlichen mit Migrationshintergrund (FörMig)* [Affirmative action of children and juveniles with a migration background]. Retrieved January 6, 2008, from http://www.bmbf.de/de/6877.php

Bundesregierung. (2007). *Der nationale Integrationsplan: Neue Wege – neue Chancen* [The national integration concept: New paths – new chances]. Retrieved January 5, 2008, from http://www.bundesregierung.de/Content/DE/Artikel/2007/07/Anlage/2007-10-18-nationaler-integrationsplan,property=publicationFile.pdf

Bündnis für Demokratie und Toleranz [Alliance for Democracy and Tolerance]. (n.d.). *Wir über uns* [We about us]. Retrieved April 27, 2008, from http://www.buendnis-toleranz.de/cms/beitrag/10026563/423673

Federal Statistical Office. (2005). *Bildung – Forschung – Kultur* [Education – research – culture]. Retrieved January 22, 2005, from http://www.destatis.de/

Federal Statistical Office. (2006). *Bildung – Forschung – Kultur* [Education – research – culture]. Retrieved September 14, 2006, from http://www.destatis.de/

Federal Statistical Office. (2007). *Bevölkerung und Erwerbstätigkeit: Bevölkerung mit Migrationshintergrund: Ergebnisse des Mikrozensus 2005* [Population and employment: Population with a migration background: Results of the 2005 micro-census]. Retrieved December 10, 2007, from https://www-ec.destatis.de/csp/shop/sfg/bpm.html.cms.cBroker.cls?cmspath=struktur,vollanzeige.csp&ID=1020313

Heckmann, F. (2003). From ethnic nation to universalistic immigrant integration: Germany. In F. Heckmann & D. Schnapper (Eds.), *The integration of immigrants in European societies: National differences and trends of convergence* (pp. 45–78). Stuttgart, Germany: Lucius & Lucius.

Hoff, G. (1995). Multicultural education in Germany: Historical development and current status. In J. A. Banks & C. A. M. Banks (Eds.), *Handbook of research on multicultural education* (pp. 821–838). New York: Macmillan.

Human Rights Council. (2007). Report of the special rapporteur on the right to education, Vernor Muñoz. Addendum: Mission to Germany 13–21 February 2006. Retrieved January 11, 2008, from http://daccessdds.un.org/doc/UNDOC/GEN/G07/117/59/PDF/G0711759.pdf?OpenElement

Klemm, K. (2008). Dreifach Benachteiligung: Nichts neues: Migranten bleiben in Deutschland's Schulen zurück [Threefold discrimination: Nothing new: Migrants remain behind in Germany's schools]. *Erziehung und Wissenschaft*, *1*, 14–15.

Konsortium Bildungsberichterstattung. (Ed.). (2006). *Bildung in Deutschland: Ein indikatorengestützter Bericht mit einer Analyse zu Bildung und Migration – im Auftrag der Ständigen Konferenz der Kultusminister der Länder in der Bundesrepublik Deutschland und des Bundesministeriums für Bildung und Forschung* [Education in Germany: A report based on indicators with an analysis of education and migration – by order of the Standing Conference of Ministers of Education of the States of Germany and the Federal Ministry of Education and Research]. Bielefeld, Germany: Bertelsmann.

Luchtenberg, S. (2002). Bilingualism and bilingual education and its relationship to citizenship from a comparative German – Australian viewpoint. *Intercultural Education*, *13*(1), 49–61.

Luchtenberg, S. (2004). Ethnic diversity and citizenship education in Germany. In J. A. Banks (Ed.), *Diversity and citizenship education: Global perspectives* (pp. 245–271). San Francisco: Jossey-Bass.

Mercator Stiftung. (2008). *Projekt Förderunterricht* [Remedial courses]. Retrieved March 24, 2008, from http://www.stiftung-mercator.de/cms/upload/pdf/Projektbeschreibung_Forderunterricht.pdf

Organisation for Economic Co-operation and Development (OECD). (Ed.). (2001). *Knowledge and skills for life: First results from PISA 2000*. Paris: Author.

Organisation for Economic Co-operation and Development (OECD). (Ed.). (2006). *Where immigrant students succeed: A comparative review of performance and engagement in PISA 2003*. Paris: Author.

Pries, L. (Ed.). (2001). *New transnational social spaces*. London: Routledge.

Regionale Arbeitsstelle (RAA). (2007). *Rucksack*. Retrieved January 6, 2008, from http://www.raa.de/rucksack.html

Reich, H. H., & Roth, H. K. (2002). *Spracherwerb zweisprachig aufwachsender Kinder und Jugendlicher: Ein Überblick über den Stand der nationalen und internationalen Forschung* [Language acquisition of bilingual children and juveniles: A review on national and international research]. Hamburg, Germany: Behörde für Bildung und Sport.

Remid (2007). *Religionswissenschaftlicher Medien und Informationsdienst* [Media and information service with regard to religious studies]. Retrieved July 23, 2007, from http://www.remid.de/remid_info_zahlen.htm

Schule ohne Rassismus. (n.d.). Homepage. Retrieved January 6, 2008, from http://www.schule-ohne-rassismus.org/the-project.html

Şen, F. (2002). Türkische Minderheit in Deutschland [The Turkish minority in Germany]. *Informationen zur Politischen Bildung, 277*.

Standing Conference. (1996). Empfehlung "Interkulturelle Bildung und Erziehung in der Schule" [Recommendation "Multicultural education in schools"]. Bonn, Germany: Sekretariat der Ständigen Konferenz der Kultusminister der Länder in der Bundesrepublik Deutschland.

35

The education of ethnic, racial, and cultural minority groups in Spain

Teresa Aguado Odina
Distance University (UNED), Spain

The ethnic, racial, and cultural minority groups discussed in this chapter are socially or historically shaped groups or communities whose members share certain cultural, ethnic, or linguistic features that are dynamic and changing. These groups appear in the official discourse, in demographic analyses, and in the images of diversity used to describe Spanish society. The education of members of these groups is influenced by how cultural diversity is understood and dealt with in the educational system. In Spain, attention to cultural diversity oscillates from clear denial, through specific measures for special groups, to the intercultural approach advocated in the most recent academic discourse. The *Roma people (Gypsies), immigrants*, and *linguistic minorities* will be discussed in this chapter. I analyze how national educational policy and legislative regulations have shaped education for these groups. The demographics and the proportion of the Roma, immigrants, and linguistic minorities in the educational system will also be described. Some conclusions will be described regarding the effects of the educational measures reviewed.

Educational policies and legislative regulations

Educational policies are indicated in the principles and objectives of an educational system, as well as in the legal establishment of specific measures and actions designed to achieve those goals. It is a good idea, therefore, to distinguish between "educational policies" (intentions materialized in the legislation and management of these policies) and "real practice," that is, the practical consequences of these policies. Although the laws that regulate Spanish education do not explicitly define cultural diversity, the most relevant legislation regarding the educational measures affecting ethnic, cultural, and linguistic groups is the legislation developed during the so-called educational reform of the mid-1980s and 1990s. The first of these laws was the LOGSE (Ley Orgánica General del Sistema Educativo [General Organic Law of the Educational System]), a significant piece of legislation (Ministerio de Educación y Ciencia [MEC], 1990). It was followed by the Law of Educational Quality in 2002 (MEC, 2002) and then by the legislation contained in the Law of Educational Planning (Ley de Ordenación Educativa [LOE]) (MEC, 2007a).

The LOGSE model addresses the idea of "special educational needs" and extends it to an entire set of collectivities. The law does not stem from an explicit acknowledgment of cultural diversity in society and it does not refer to immigrant students or students from any other minority group; instead, it speaks of autochthonous "linguistic and cultural plurality" and proposes teaching respect for Spain's linguistic and cultural diversity. The educational reform of the 1980s and 1990s, in general, established that interventions to satisfy "special educational needs" should be based on the principles of normalization and school integration (LOGSE, art. 36). The model developed through the LOGSE focuses on three types of programs: compensatory education programs, social guarantee programs, and programs for preserving the language and culture of origin. The compensatory education programs can be permanent or transitory in nature and are based on the use of complementary assistance resources (support teachers, flexible organization formulas, and preferential attention by guidance teams for centers that enroll compensatory education students).

Internal compensation is based on curricular adaptation and diversification; external compensation uses programs that rely on family contact and contact with other agents. Social guarantee programs, in secondary education, are designed for students who do not achieve educational objectives, with the purpose of providing basic and vocational training that will let those students enter the work force or continue studying in different areas, especially in professional training programs. Programs to preserve the language and culture of origin (art. 6.2) are based on the right to linguistic diversity. In 2002, the Law of Educational Quality was passed. In this law, there are elements that reveal a certain continuity with the attitudes that shaped the previous educational reform – the compensatory and deficit viewpoint.

The practical measures proposed to achieve equal results for all students are segregationist in character. One example is the reinforcement and support measures aimed at secondary students (age 12–16) who do not meet educational objectives. For students who, once they have turned 15, opt not to follow any of the curriculum tracks offered (technology, science, or humanities), a different track is established, the so-called professional initiation programs (equivalent to the previous social guarantee programs) that, once completed, allow them to graduate and obtain a mandatory secondary education degree. In practice, these programs have been populated by students who are the children of immigrants or who come from ethnic or linguistic minorities, the students who are deemed to have special educational needs.

The model of the Organic Law of Educational Quality (Ley Orgánica de Calidad de la Educación [LOCE]) (MEC, 2002) originates from an implicitly restrictive concept of diversity by differentiating between three specific groups that require special attention: immigrant students, physically or mentally challenged students, and highly gifted students. Cultural diversity is compared to immigration and educational difficulties, both of which should be dealt with using compensatory measures.

The 2002 Organic Law of Educational Quality expressly acknowledges the cultural and linguistic plurality of the autonomous communities that constitute the Spanish state. Attention to diversity is contemplated for students with special educational needs (physically or mentally challenged students), those who experience late integration into the Spanish educational system (immigrants), those who have specific learning disabilities, and those who are in unfavorable situations. This law expressly uses the term *interculturality* when it alludes to the objectives of the educational system in the first section.

In Spain, the central government is responsible for laws of a general nature, but responsibility for education – that is, the development and application of the national laws – falls to each autonomous community. The different autonomous communities have initiated educational measures intended to implement the national law, measures that range from the adoption of models oriented towards interculturality and inclusiveness to compensatory and segregating models. Most common are special compensatory measures that are, in practice, aimed at three groups: the Roma, the children of immigrants, and linguistic groups.

The Roma: Their presence in society and at school

The Roma have been present in Spain since the beginning of the 15th century. Today, the Roma population is approximately 650,000. The region with the largest number of Roma is Andalusia (about 270,000), followed by Catalonia (80,000), Madrid (60,000), and the Valencian Community (52,000). The Roma population is young when compared with the non-Roma population. In 2008, 45% of the Roma population was under the age of 16; the birth rate is 64 per thousand, while the birth rate for the non-Roma is 14 per thousand. Recently, the Roma marriage rate and the number of children per family have been decreasing gradually. The average age at marriage for women in 2008 was 16 to 20 years of age, and for men 18 to 22 years of age.

The educational level of the Roma population today is lower than that of any other sociocultural group of similar size and composition in Spain. Few Roma in the older generations attended school regularly, and there is a high percentage of Roma women over the age of 18 who are totally or functionally illiterate. According to the Foundation of the Roma Secretariat (Fundación Secretariado Gitano [FSG], 2007), nearly 70% of Roma over the age of 16 have not completed basic mandatory education. Illiteracy is even higher among women. This low level of education has serious social and economic consequences, including (a) limited access to professional or occupational training and, later, to jobs; and (b) the Roma cannot take advantage of social opportunities and programs because they cannot access the information properly.

According to a study carried out by the FSG (2007), "Evaluation of the Educational Normalization of Roma Students in Primary Education," the incorporation of young Roma children into the school system has become standard throughout the state (94% of Roma boys and girls start school at the age of 6 or earlier). Despite this fact, they still have low school attendance rates, low rates of mandatory education completion, and low rates of academic achievement. Even though an increasingly high percentage of Roma families feel that it is important for their sons and daughters to start school early (74% of the children have gone to childcare or nursery school, and 87% of the families have taken the initiative of enrolling children in primary education), there is a very high level of absenteeism and of school failure. The school itself – the way it is organized and the teaching processes – plays a role, as does the need for the children to help and work with their parents (peddling, street sales, etc.) and the need to move the whole family for work-related reasons. However, Roma parents have an increasing understanding of the value of school and education as the basic means of social promotion, as a route to personal development, and as a way to open up possibilities for the future.

Roma students in the educational system

It is nearly impossible to find statistical data on Roma students because it is not gathered in official censuses, because of the stigmatization suffered by this group in Spain. The most recent official data available are from the Ministerio de Educación y Ciencia (MEC) (Ministry of Education and Science), which describe Roma students enrolled in mandatory education in public schools and subsidized schools in Spanish territory, managed directly by the MEC, from the 1995–1996 academic year to the 1999–2000 academic year. Because education is now administered by the autonomous communities, there are no general statistics for the most recent academic years. Most recently, the total number of Roma students enrolled was 23,459, all in public or subsidized schools.

There is evidence that departments paying attention to diversity have data on Roma students who require compensatory attention. This fact gives an idea of how Roma students are perceived and treated. Initially, there seems to be a tendency to consider Roma students to be Spanish, but we find, in practice, a general tendency to give these students compensatory treatment. The rate of absenteeism for Roma students is 60% (Carrasco, 2003).

Educational actions

The Spanish Ministry of Education and Science subsidizes a development program for the Roma people that promotes the publication of specific teaching materials that introduce elements of Roma culture into the curriculum, trains intercultural mediators, and supports initial and ongoing teacher training. These are well-intentioned measures, but they are quite specific and not very significant in the educational system as a whole. Studies carried out in order to diagnose the educational situation of students in mandatory education reveal that there is some progress in access to the classroom, but not in more complex achievements, because the age–grade gap becomes greater in higher grades (Fresno García, 1999). The variables that help or hinder these students have been identified (FSG, 2007; Martínez & Alfageme, 2004):

- Academic preparation is framed as the basis for social and economic mobility in the Roma community. Roma students are at a clear disadvantage compared to other groups and to majority society.
- Integral and interdisciplinary measures are necessary. Greater follow-up and prevention of premature school-leaving as well as alternative training opportunities for Roma students are needed.
- The expectations of teachers and of the family regarding mandatory education as a path leading to training and socialization for children and youth are important.
- The socio-economic level, that is, the degree of precariousness in the Roma families' living conditions, plays an important role.
- The potential of Roma girls is just emerging: higher motivation, better academic results, increased expectations of success, and equal opportunity regardless of gender are necessary.

Emotional and social links must be created between families, students, and the schools. All success in education will go hand in hand with processes for demarginalizing the Roma people socially and with the application of pedagogical models based on affectivity, cooperation, and high expectations regarding the students (Abajo, 1997; Díaz-Aguado, 1991).

Children of immigrants at school

In Spain, it is common to hear the statement that the country has changed from a society that traditionally sent out emigrants to a society that receives immigrants. This differentiation conceals a reality that is not usually mentioned: the large number of Spanish emigrants that, even today, live in other countries. This perception of the presence of immigrants is a reflection of the images used to show immigration in Spain as a problem, an invasion, and a threat (Aguado & Malik, 2008).

Immigration is a dynamic and continuous phenomenon, which makes it hard to prepare reliable statistics that show a detailed description of the foreign population residing in Spain. Most data on the foreign population come from official institutions, which usually count only the number of people who apply for residence or work permits. The number of irregular immigrants, asylum-seekers, and refugees from different countries is difficult to determine, as the resident foreigners who apply for Spanish citizenship are not counted, because they disappear from the statistics as soon as they are granted citizenship (Colectivo Ioé, 2002). The number of work permits given is a reliable indicator of the presence of immigrants. In 1997, 79,832 permits were granted; 254,000 were granted in 2006 (Instituto Nacional de Estadística [INE], 2008).

The presence of immigrants accounts for much of the increase in the Spanish population: in 1998, there were 39.8 million inhabitants; by 2007, that number had reached a little over 45 million. The immigrant population has gone from approximately 1.36% of the total population in 1996 (not counting irregular immigrants or those who had gained Spanish citizenship) to approximately 6% in 2008. If we consider all the people counted as foreigners in the census, the figure rises to 10% of the total population (INE, 2008).

The presence of foreign students in the Spanish education system, even though it does not reach the dimensions found in other European countries, has grown significantly in recent decades (see Table 35.1). This increase has occurred mainly in the public schools and especially since the 2001–2002 school year. The number of immigrant students enrolled decreases from the lower grades to the higher ones and is high in social guarantee programs and in alternative paths for students who fail in the ESO (mandatory secondary education). There were 608,040 immigrant students (8.35% of the total) during the 2006–2007 school year. The percentage has increased nearly one percentage point per year. These students come mostly from South America (259,935), Africa (118,454), non-EU Europe (94,701), and the European Union (77,051). Relatively few come from North America (6,028) and Oceania (309). Of all foreign students, 82.55% are in public schools. The EU, in a recent report on education in member countries (Eurydice, 2007), warns of a situation of "ghettoization" in Spanish education because of the enrollment of immigrants and Roma. The majority of these groups attend public schools located in specific urban areas.

Table 35.1 Non-University Education: Number of Foreign Students According to Origin

Area	1996–1997	2006–2007
European Union	19,170	77,051
Rest of Europe	4,640	94,701
Africa	17,076	118,454
North America	2,008	6,028
Central America	3,161	21,292
South America	10,961	259,935
Asia	5,588	28,626
Oceania	97	309
Other origins	343	1,644
Totals	63,044	608,040

Source: Prepared by author using data from Ministerio de Educación y Ciencia (MEC) [Ministry of Education and Science] (2007b).

The enrollment of foreign students has grown since the 2001–2002 school year. This increase can be explained by the way the LOGSE was applied, by the extension of mandatory enrollment to the age of 16, and by the increasing number of immigrants who came to Spain during this period because of economic growth and immigration policies. Foreigners make up 8.35% of students in the Spanish educational system. Their distribution in the different levels of education is as follows: 6.7% in infant education, 10.32% in primary education, 9.21% in ESO (mandatory secondary education), 4% in non-mandatory higher secondary education, and 12.81% in social guarantee education.[1] There are important differences between the numbers of foreign students enrolled in the different educational levels, differences that increase in the higher levels of education. This fact leads us to ask certain questions. Why does the number decrease as we advance in the educational system? Are the younger students the majority? Do students drop out at the end of primary education, and even more at the end of mandatory secondary education? As time goes by, will the number of students in higher levels increase?

It is interesting to analyze the distribution of foreign students in the different types of schools: public, subsidized, and private. There are three kinds of schools in Spain: public schools, which are publicly owned and financed; private schools, which are privately owned and financed; and subsidized schools, which are privately owned and publicly financed.

Subsidized and private schools are included in a single category (private) in the sources consulted. Most foreign students (80.5%) are enrolled in public schools, while only 66.15% of all students are enrolled in public schools. There are differences if we take the origins of the students into account. According to the Colectivo Ioé (2002), the majority of the students from Africa, non-EU European countries, and Latin American countries (between 80 and 90%) attend public schools, while students from Oceania and North America tend to enroll in private schools.

As we can see, the level of foreigners in the classroom is still low, and they are distributed throughout the Spanish territory, although there are some exceptions where the enrollment of foreign students seems high. This raises some questions. Why are students concentrated in certain schools? To what extent is this reality the result of the social situation (concentration of immigrants in certain areas of certain cities)? What social and educational consequences could these conditions have? Does this situation foster positive relationships between people from different cultural groups?

Ideally, educational administrators would distribute foreign students among different centers, at least among the centers that receive financing from public funds. However, there is a tendency among immigrant families to favor "grouping" their children in certain schools so that they are with other children from the same country and less likely to feel isolated or left out. Also, there is a tendency to believe that the public schools that accept a lot of immigrant students are of lower quality; because of this, non-immigrant families tend to enroll their children in schools with a low immigrant population (INTER Group, 2007). Racist attitudes and fear of difference can be observed in this behavior.

In general, teachers describe the educational situation of the students who are the children of immigrants by using negative characteristics; cultural elements that are obstacles to success in school and to integration are alluded to (Aguado et al., 2007; Carrasco, 2003). A lack of knowledge of the official language is associated with cognitive deficiency and an inability to communicate and to learn. The greatest inequalities appear in the transitions between the educational levels (from primary to secondary school). Some common practices in schools reinforce discrimination against immigrant students: assigning students to support classes, fixed groupings, evaluation criteria, and teaching based on a textbook (Aguado et al., 2007).

Linguistic groups

Spanish schools are monolingual spaces even when students with very diverse mother tongues are enrolled. The education of the linguistic minorities in Spain has concentrated on two linguistic groups, and it has focused on developing clearly differentiated models. One model is based on the autonomous communities with two official languages, that is, Spanish and the community's own language. In the second model, specific programs target speakers of languages that are not official in Spain.

Autonomous communities with two official languages

Some Spanish autonomous communities have a second official language in addition to Spanish. The way linguistic diversity is dealt with in education is different in each community, ranging from the possibility of choosing different linguistic models in communities such as Navarra and the Basque Country to mandatory linguistic immersion in Catalonia, immersion programs in the Valencian Community, and linguistic normalization teams in Galicia. For example, Navarra and the Basque Country offer four different linguistic models for incorporating Euskera, the Basque language, into non-university teaching (see Table 35.2).

- Model A: classes taught in Spanish, with Euskera taught as a subject, on all levels, at all stages, and in all the different trajectories;
- Model B: bilingual teaching in Euskera with Spanish as a subject and as the language used in one or more subjects, depending on the teaching system, the cycle, or the stage;
- Model D: classes taught in Euskera only, except for the subject of Spanish language;
- Model G in Navarra and X in the Basque Country: no classes taught in Euskera and Euskera not taught as a subject.

We see that a minimal number (less than 1%) of the Basque students do not study Euskera; over half of the Basque schoolchildren are taught in Euskera, and the remainder are taught bilingually (some subjects in Spanish and others in Euskera) or have Euskera taught as a subject. This goes a long way to explaining why fluency in Euskera is a basic requirement in the Basque Country for getting a job or continuing to study. Students whose mother tongue is not Euskera must make an extra effort, because having a good command of the language used in the curriculum carries a lot of weight for grades in all the main subjects.

In Catalonia, legal regulations establish Catalan as the language for all instruction levels. Students should not be segregated in different groups or schools because of their language (Linguistic Policy Law, 1998). In the Valencian Community, the linguistic immersion programs

Table 35.2 Distribution of Numbers of Students According to Academic Year and Educational Model in Primary Education in the Basque Country

Academic Year	A	B	D	X	Total
2002–2003	16,935	28,937	50,445	822	97,139
2007–2008	10,541	32,625	63,015	826	107,007

Source: Eusko Jarlaritza (2007).

are oriented to foster Valencian language normalization in the educational system. In Galicia, the linguistic normalization teams are conceived as a tool to promote the use of the Galician language at all educational levels.

Programs for speakers of non-official languages

There are two kinds of educational measures aimed at speakers of languages that are not official in Spain: (a) specific programs for speakers of Arabic and Portuguese derived from agreements signed between the Spanish government and the governments of Morocco and Portugal, respectively, and (b) the "linking" or welcome classrooms for immigrants who enter the Spanish educational system for the first time.

Portuguese and Arabic language and culture programs

Spain has agreements with Portugal and Morocco for carrying out programs to teach Portuguese and Arabic-Moroccan language and culture in Spanish schools. The Portuguese Language and Culture Program works in collaboration with the Portuguese Embassy in Spain. It is organized and functions following instructions approved on October 21, 1996 (MEC, 1997), and it is implemented in centers where students of Portuguese origin are enrolled. Portuguese professors are assigned to the corresponding Spanish schools and they teach subjects in integrated classrooms, in a simultaneous or complementary mode depending on the different organizational forms. The school activities are complemented with student exchanges and field trips to both countries, Portuguese cultural weeks, and teacher training activities. During the 2006–2007 school year, this program was implemented in the majority of the autonomous communities, and 50 teachers, 106 schools, and 8,676 students (5,942 Spanish students and the rest students from Portugal, Brazil, the Azores, and Cabo Verde) participated.

The Program for Teaching the Arabic Language and Moroccan Culture implements the 1980 Agreement on Cultural Cooperation between Spain and the Kingdom of Morocco (Boletín Oficial del Estado [BOE], 1985). The program focuses on students of Moroccan origin enrolled in Spanish public schools, and its main objectives are (a) to foster the teaching of the language and culture of origin, (b) to integrate Moroccan students into the Spanish educational system, and (c) to favor intercultural education. There are two main methods (MEC, n.d.):

- Method A: For schools with few Moroccan students, classes are taught outside of the regular school schedule. One Moroccan teacher covers several schools.
- Method B: For centers with a high number of Moroccan students, classes are given during the normal school schedule.

During the 2007–2008 school year, 102 public schools, 40 teachers, and 2,020 students participated in this program.

Linking classrooms welcome program

Some autonomous communities, Madrid, for example, have programs aimed specifically at immigrants who have only recently entered the educational system. These students are assigned to "linking classrooms." The objective of these classrooms is to integrate students into school and provide them with the linguistic tools they need to take advantage of the educational system. These classrooms are located in some public and subsidized schools, and the children are assigned to them for six months. These classrooms receive specific resources and teachers. At the end of six months, the students are moved to the school where they will continue their education.

One of the aspects of the linking classrooms that has been criticized is their lack of meaningful overlap with the ordinary schools where the students will eventually be enrolled. The result is that the students enjoy a school atmosphere that is very hospitable and warm in many ways for six months, but with no real link to the school that they will experience once this "receiving" period is over (del Olmo, 2007). Some people feel that the ordinary classrooms that already receive recently enrolled students are the ones that should be considered linking classrooms and should be supported with appropriate resources.

Conclusion

The responses of schools to ethnic, cultural, and linguistic groups are modulated by social changes, general policies, the beliefs of professional educators, and the atmosphere of the schools and educational institutions. The education of members of these groups in Spain has oscillated from denying their existence to treating them as students with special needs, as in the case of Roma students and the children of immigrants. Programs such as the cooperation programs aimed at speakers of Arabic and Portuguese are the exception. Regarding the linguistic groups of the Spanish state itself, the measures have been linked to the establishment of specific models, as has been explained.

At present, both in academic discourse and in the discourse of educational policy, the intercultural focus is regarded as the preferred way to respond to linguistic, ethnic, and cultural diversity. The intercultural approach accepts diversity as normal and proposes measures aimed at everyone, not just at some groups as opposed to others (Abdallah-Pretceille, 2003; Aguado, 2003). The intercultural approach is now a rhetorical formula in the Spanish educational system. In practice, the models that have been developed are multicultural models, that is, the groups are defined a priori and then the differences among them are acknowledged: Roma, students who do not speak Spanish, students who have a curricular gap, and students who enter the school system late (immigrants). These practices have exacerbated differences and perpetuated the existence of ghettoes in the Spanish educational system (Eurydice, 2007).

The educational policies have been insufficient, partial, and incomplete. An important cause of this problem has been the lack of sufficient funding and of foresight in such areas as teacher selection and training. The consequence of the "compensatory" and "inclusion" views has been the generalized treatment and consideration of "cultural difference" as a "deficit" that must be "compensated for," encouraging other kinds of inequalities in grade promotion for students from certain cultural groups. In addition, these views have favored the reproduction of stereotypes and have resulted in the students being categorized in a way that has discriminatory effects.

The majority of foreign students have been enrolled, for the most part, in public schools, while only approximately 20% of them are enrolled in private subsidized schools. The public schools with a high concentration of immigrant students have not received sufficient funding to respond to this new challenge. On the contrary, in the schools multiculturalism is experienced as a problem or an undesirable situation. In addition, the acknowledgment and consideration of schools with "students with special educational needs" as "preferred centers" has favored the enrollment of physically and mentally challenged, disadvantaged, and immigrant and Roma students in these schools. Thus, there are two networks, a public one with a very heterogeneous population, and a subsidized one with homogeneous results, the product of a concealed selection system.

Most educational practices reveal an approach that considers linguistic, cultural, and ethnic diversity to be a problem, and so they are associated with specific reinforcement measures. When immigrants or ethnic groups are visibly present, teachers' expectations of their students drop and the teaching and learning experiences that are promoted are less rich and varied. This is true with respect both to the atmosphere of the school and to the teaching methodology used.

Although the academic achievement of students belonging to minority cultures has not been studied and evaluated sufficiently by educators, the statistical data available indicate a greater incidence of "school failure." Similarly, two other important obstacles have been identified: the teaching staff as a whole lacks training for undertaking their teaching tasks and, together with this, adequate didactic resources are not being used. On the whole, the measures adopted for dealing with cultural diversity, because they are aimed almost exclusively at minority cultural groups and not at the student population as a whole, and are not integrated into the curriculum itself, have only a very minor effect on achieving educational equality and social cohesion.

In an isolated fashion, but more and more frequently, so-called learning communities are being developed, particularly in public schools. These learning communities value the cultural, ethnic, and linguistic diversity of the community in which the school is located and reject the idea that differences between individuals and groups constitute a problem. This approach is oriented more toward results and resources than toward deficit or special needs. The purpose is to offer quality teaching for everyone, which implies teaching everyone in diverse ways, not just certain groups that are stigmatized. Learning communities acknowledge that academic learning has its roots both in school and in social processes. The first concern is to introduce teaching that stimulates the students to construct and reconstruct meanings and to seek interpretations of their knowledge within an enriching, compatible school context.

Today, in spite of these examples of integrating, intercultural approaches, Spain has an educational system that is having difficulty teaching students who come to the school with diverse languages, nationalities, beliefs, perspectives, and experiences. The system tends to subordinate the groups that have characteristics defined as special. This happens at both the national level (the Spanish state) and the local level (autonomous communities), although the subordinate groups vary depending on which group is hegemonic and thus defines what is different and what is problematic. In order to achieve a more effective teaching system, political measures need to be oriented toward achieving the best results for everyone, not for just a few, and this necessarily involves taking into account the importance of teachers' beliefs about the meaning of the cultural, ethnic, and linguistic diversity of students and their families.

Note

1 Social guarantee education is an educational program to keep students who fail to get official accreditations in school until they are 16.

References

Abajo, J. E. (1997). *La escolarización de los niños gitanos* [The schooling of the Roma children]. Madrid, Spain: Ministerio de Trabajo y Asuntos Sociales.

Abdallah-Pretceille, M. (2003). *La educación intercultural* [Intercultural education]. Barcelona, Spain: Idea Books.

Aguado, M. T. (2003). *Pedagogía intercultural* [Intercultural pedagogy]. Madrid, Spain: McGraw-Hill.

Aguado, T., Álvarez, B., Ballesteros, B., Castellano, J. L., Gil-Jaurena, I., Malik, B., et al. (2007). *Diversidad cultural logros de los estudiantes en educación obligatoria: Lo que sucede en las escuelas* [Cultural diversity and achievement of students in compulsory education: What is happening in schools]. Madrid, Spain: Ministerio de Educación.

Aguado, T., & Malik, B. (2008). Multicultural and intercultural education in Spain. In C. Grant & A. Portera (Eds.), *Multicultural and intercultural education for the global world: Semantic clarification, good practice and future perspectives in different continents* (pp. 87–115). London: Routledge.

Boletín Oficial del Estado (BOE) [Official bulletin of the state]. (1985). *Acuerdo de cooperación cultural entre España y el Reino de Marruecos* [Agreement on cultural cooperation between Spain and the Kingdom of Morocco]. Madrid, Spain: Author.

Carrasco, S. (2003). La escolarización de los hijos e hijas de inmigrantes y de minorías étnico-culturales [The schooling of immigrant and ethnocultural minorities]. *Revista de Educación* [Review of education], *330*, 99–136.

Colectivo Ioé. (2002). *Immigration, the school and the employment market: An updated X-ray* (Social Studies Collection No. 11) Madrid, Spain: La Caixa Foundation.

del Olmo, M. (2007). La articulación de la diversidad en la escuela: Un proyecto de la investigación en curso sobre las "Aulas de Enlace" [The articulation of diversity in school: A project of the ongoing investigation on the "Linking Classrooms"]. *Revista de Dialectología y Tradiciones Populares* [Review of dialectology and folk traditions], 187–204. Madrid, Spain: Consejo Superior de Investigaciones Científicas (CSIC).

Díaz-Aguado, M. J. (1991). *Escuela y tolerancia* [School and tolerance]. Madrid, Spain: Editorial Pirámide.

Eurydice. (2007). *Eurybase: The information database on education systems in Europe*. Strasbourg, France: Author. Retrieved December 26, 2007, from www.eurydice.org

Eusko Jarlaritza (Gobierno Vasco). (2007). *Datos de la enseñanza no universitaria en el País Vasco 2006/2007* [Data of the non-university educational levels in the Basque Country 2006/2007]. Bilbao, Spain: Viceconsejería de Administración y Servicios. Retrieved December 15, 2007, from http://www.hezkuntza.ejgv.euskadi.net/

Fresno García, J. M. (1999). La comunidad gitana española a las puertas del tercer milenio [The Spanish Roma community at the beginning of the third millennium]. *Cuadernos de Realidades Sociales* [Social Realities Review], *53–54*, 47–74.

Fundación Secretariado Gitano (FSG) [Foundation of the Roma Secretariat]. (2007). *Informe 2006: Discriminación de la comunidad Gitana*. Madrid, Spain: Author.

Instituto Nacional de Estadística (INE). (2008). *Estadísticas sobre inmigración, 2006/2007* [Statistical data about immigration, 2006/2007]. Madrid, Spain: Ministerio del Interior.

INTER Group. (2007). *Racism: A teenager's perspective*. Vienna, Austria: Navreme.

Linguistic Policy Law. (1998).

Martínez, M., & Alfageme, A. (2004). Integración socioeducativa del alumnado gitano en la escuela española [Socioeducational integration of Roma students in the Spanish school]. *Revista Española de Educación Comparada* [Spanish review of comparative education], *10*, 299–323.

Ministerio de Educación y Ciencia (MEC) [Ministry of Education and Science]. (n.d.). Website. Retrieved December 30, 2007, from www.mec.es/cide/innovacion/convenios/hispano/

Ministerio de Educación y Ciencia (MEC) [Ministry of Education and Science]. (1990). Ley Orgánica General del Sistema Educativo [General Organic Law of the Educational System] (LOGSE). Madrid, Spain: Author.

Ministerio de Educación y Ciencia (MEC) [Ministry of Education and Science]. (1997, April 11).

Instrucciones para el Programa de Lengua y Cultura Portuguesa [Instructions for the Portuguese Language and Culture Program]. *Boletín Oficial del Ministerio de Educación y Ciencia* [Official bulletin of the Ministry of Education and Science]. Madrid, Spain: Author.

Ministerio de Educación y Ciencia (MEC) [Ministry of Education and Science]. (2002). Ley Orgánica de Calidad de la Educación [Law of Educational Quality] (LOCE). Madrid, Spain: Author.

36

Educational policies for ethnic and cultural groups in Russia

Isak D. Froumin
The World Bank, Moscow, Russia

Andrei Zakharov
Moscow State Institute for Humanities and Education, Russia

Ethnic and cultural groups in Russia

Ethnic groups

In the course of historical development Russia has taken shape as a multinational and multicultural state with a vast territory. The presence of a large number of different ethnic groups within the boundaries of present-day Russia represents a complicated history of migrations, wars, and revolutions. According to the 2002 census, Russia's territory is inhabited by more than 140 ethnic groups (Goskomstat RF, 2002). The ethnic diversity in Russia has significantly influenced the nature of its development and has had a strong influence on public education policy. These factors determine educational opportunities for different ethnic groups in Russia: (a) political status of an ethnic group, (b) demographic characteristics, and (c) level of development of an ethnic language.

Political status of an ethnic group. According to their political status, ethnic groups who live in Russia can be viewed as either having or not having their own territorial autonomy within the Russian Federation (RF). Based on its territorial arrangement, Russia is an asymmetric state. Of the 83 regions of the Russian Federation, 26 are entities named for one or two ethnic groups. These ethnic groups are called *titular* for the particular region. Under the 1993 Russian Constitution (Konstituciya Rossiskoi Federacii), all citizens of the country enjoy equal rights regardless of their ethnic identity (para. 1–2, art. 19). In reality, titular ethnic groups have more opportunities in the area of education in the regions named for them.

Apart from titular ethnic groups, there are groups that have their own statehood outside the boundaries of the Russian Federation (e.g. Greeks, Germans, Ukrainians, and other ethnic groups). Given the availability of relevant international agreements on cooperation in education, the countries of their ethnic origin may support their educational interests and provide the necessary assistance.

A considerable number of ethnic groups in Russia have no statehood of their own. Some of them have large diasporas outside the Russian Federation (Kurds, Lapps, Roma, and others), and some others live predominantly in Russia (Vepsians, Kets, Siberian Tatars, and others).

Thus ethnic groups have different positions in the Russian political landscape and dissimilar possibilities of influencing an educational strategy.

Demographic characteristics. Among the demographic characteristics of an ethnic group, the most important is the number of people – a factor defining a "national minority" in international law (Kastelajn, Ornelis, Veni, Verbek, & Vlamink, 2003). In 2002, the population of the Russian Federation was 145,167,000 (hereinafter we use the data of National Census 2002 [Goskomstat RF, 2002]). Russians are the most numerous group, constituting 79.8% of the population (115,889,107). Six ethnic groups have 1 million to 6 million people; 33 ethnic groups have 100,000 to 1 million people; 74 ethnic groups have 1,000 to 100,000 people; and 27 ethnic groups have fewer than 1,000 people.

Indigenous minorities of the North, Siberia, and the Far East deserve special mention. There are about 60 such groups in Russia, with a total number of approximately 250,000 people. However, only 40 of them have been granted an official status entitling them to state guarantees of protection of their traditional way of life and education (Stepanov, 2004).

In practice, the population density that influences the enrollment at educational institutions is more important than the total number of the population. Owing to migration, titular ethnic groups were not necessarily predominant in the territories of "their" regions. At the same time Russians – who constitute a majority of the population in the country – are a minority in some ethnic regions. According to the 2002 census, the share of the titular population in the regions of the Russian Federation constitutes less than 30% in 7 regions; from 30% to 50% in 5 regions; and over 50% in 14 regions, including Chechnya (93.5%), Ingushetia (77.3%), Tuva (77.0%), Chuvashia (67.7%), and others.

Each titular ethnic group has a diaspora in other parts of Russia. There exist a few main types of settlement patterns of ethnic groups, which create an important context for educational policy: compact settlements in the titular territory, compact settlements in other parts of Russia, and dispersed settlements. These settlement patterns set forth a wide range of tasks in the area of educational policy at both national and regional levels, from meeting the educational needs of ethnic groups populating a region to supporting the interests of titular ethnic groups in places of their compact settlement outside that region. At present, settlement patterns of ethnic groups have become more complicated because of the increased internal mobility and migration. Russia has become one of the world leaders in the inflow of labor migrants.

Political status and development of the language. About 150 languages are spoken in the territory of Russia (Drofa, 1998). The Russian Constitution guarantees all ethnic groups the right to retain their native tongues and create conditions for studying and developing them (para. 3, art. 68). Russian is the official language in the Russian Federation (para. 1, art. 68). Some ethnic regions (the so-called ethnic republics) have the right to establish their own official languages (Konstituciya, 1993, para. 2, art. 68). In schools these languages are the languages of instruction or are separate compulsory subjects. However, options to use a language other than Russian are determined by the level of development of the language and the level of proficiency of the native population in it. Over 98% (98.2) of Russia's entire population and 92.1% of its non-Russian population speak Russian. Only 3.1% of ethnic Russians speak other languages of the Russian Federation (Goskomstat RF, 2002). A considerable number of languages have fewer than 30,000 speakers. About 60 of them are disappearing languages and have fewer than 3,000 speakers (Woodard, 1996).

The level of development of a written form and literary standards of a language influence its ability to be used in the educational process. The written forms of the languages of most ethnic groups in Russia were developed hundreds of years ago. But more than 50 groups got their written language in the 1920s and 1930s, and some at the end of the 20th century. About

20 languages remain oral (Mikhalchenko & Trushkova, 2003). Languages that have no alphabet cannot be used as a language of instruction even at the elementary school level. Only a few languages in Russia can be used for teaching science and mathematics.

Cultural (religious) groups

Russian ethnic groups historically belong to different religious traditions – Christianity, Islam, Buddhism, Judaism, and some others. The confessional pattern of the country has greatly changed in post-Soviet times. The number of religious organizations has increased. In 2007, 22,956 religious organizations were registered in the Russian Federation. Of this number, 54.4% belong to the Russian Orthodox Church, 1.1% (250) belong to the Roman Catholic Church, and 16.5% belong to Islam (Federal Registration Service, 2007). Other religious groups constitute an insignificant share in the total number of religious organizations. The share of those who consider themselves religious increased from 57% in 1991 to 74% in 2000, and to 82% in 2007 (Federal Registration Service).

Some Russian researchers conclude that, despite an increase in numbers, it would be premature to speak of a religious revival in Russia. Garadzha (2005) states that people often call themselves Orthodox or Muslims, and view these religions as a substantial part of the cultural tradition of their ethnic group. Christianity is more widespread among Indo-European nations, Islam among Turkish and Iberian-Caucasian peoples, and Buddhism among Buryats and Kalmyks, while Tungusic-Manchurian and Finno-Ugric ethnic groups have retained their traditional beliefs (Anikanov, Stepanov, & Susokolov, 1999). Therefore, often the barriers between the religious groups reinforce those between ethnic groups.

Conclusion

A complicated ethnic composition of Russia's population and its multi-confessional nature cause the educational system to fulfill the following functions:

- *Educational function*: providing the universal education to the country's population regardless of ethnic origin and religion;
- *Ethno-cultural function*: disseminating and developing ethnic cultures and languages;
- *Consolidating function*: integrating the ethnically heterogeneous society into a united supranational community – a political nation – with a common system of values.

When formulating its educational policies, Russia has to take into consideration the existing contradiction (as noted by Kuz'min & Artemenko, 2006) between the values embedded in cultures and resulting in multi-directional cultural and educational interests of ethnic groups and a difference in the objectives they can set forth as actors in the educational area.

The implementation of the first two functions objectively requires taking into consideration the ethnic composition of students in the educational process by partially filling the content of education with some components of ethnic culture and arranging education in native (non-Russian) and Russian (non-native) languages, that is, the bicultural and bilingual nature of education (Baker & Jones, 1998). Seeking the balance between various functions of the schooling system for ethnic and cultural minorities, Russian educational policy has experienced multiple changes in its priorities.

Ethnicity and educational policy: Historical perspective

During the pre-Soviet period the public education policy with respect to ethnic minorities was mostly oriented towards the consolidating function. That was prompted by the peculiarities of colonialism. As Grachev (2000) states, expansion of Russia's boundaries in the 16th through the 19th century was objectively of an "incorporating" nature, for its objective was not simply to annex new territories but to incorporate the traditional populations organically into a single supranational community.

The first projects for establishing schools for Oriental non-Russians date back to the beginning of the 18th century when instruction was combined with the teaching of Russian and religious education – conversion to Christianity (Kirzhaeva & Osovskii, 2005). An achievement of the reforms by Alexander I (1804) was the introduction of the native tongue as a language of instruction (Piskunov, 2001). The industrialization of Russia in the mid-19th century made the need for establishing universal primary education an imperative for the nation-state. As a consequence, the educational policy became oriented towards Russification and the assimilation of ethnic groups (Fal'bork & Harnoluskij, 1903).

The above measures were of great practical importance for raising literacy rates. However, an attempt to create a single identity for all ethnic groups that populated the empire failed. The Soviet state used different and contradictory approaches to address the ethnic issue. It proclaimed the right of nations to self-determination, but declared that national differences were of secondary importance to class differences, while at the same time deserving respect and recognition.

In 1926, there were 169 ethnic groups in the Russian Federation (Krasovickaja, 1992). For their education, a new type of public education institution, the so-called ethnic school, was established in 1918. According to the definition of the State Committee on Education, this type of school was oriented towards "population minorities" differing from Russians in "their languages and grassroots specifics" (Krasovickaja, p. 64). Apart from general educational subjects, the content of education included the literature and history of the given ethnic group. But the main criterion of ethnic education throughout the Soviet period was that of the language of instruction, which was supposed to be the native tongue of students (Academy of Pedagogical Sciences, 1980).

Because many ethnic groups did not have written languages, it was the duty of the state to ensure the development of their alphabets. Alphabets for more than 40 ethnic languages were developed between the 1920s and the 1930s. According to 1929 data, 117 colleges in the Russian Federation trained teachers for ethnic schools, and textbooks were published in 56 ethnic languages (Bacyn & Kuz'min, 1995). Instruction in native languages was viewed as an instrument of a universal Communist education rather than one for creating an ethnic and cultural identity. The content of school textbooks was based on Communist ideology and was the same at different ethnic schools.

The establishment of ethnic schools did not conform fully to the tasks of the country's modernization and industrialization goals, which required a good knowledge of Russian. Gradually, the industrialization and unification needs began to prevail. The educational system was re-oriented towards Russian as the language of instruction in the mid-1930s (Kuz'min, 1997). That process was accompanied by reprisals against "ethnic" intellectuals (writers, teachers, and linguists), who were accused of not supporting Russian nationalism.

"Russification" of schooling was the fastest and cheapest means of reforming mass education so that it would promote industrial development. In 1927, as in 1956, instruction in the Russian Federation was carried out in 47 languages, while in 1970–1971 it was conducted in

27 languages, and in 1987–1988 in 22 languages (Bacyn & Kuz'min, 1995). As a result, in 1989, 27.6% of ethnic non-Russians considered Russian to be their native tongue (versus 24.2% in 1970) (Goskomstat RSFSR, 1990).

Communist ideology continued to provide a cultural basis for the integration of the population into a political nation. In the 1970s, it was further developed into the idea of creating an unprecedented "new community – the Soviet people" (an analogue of a political nation). There had to be no real difference between the different nations which formed the Union of Soviet Republics and even between different ethnic groups within the Russian Federation. The role of ethnic culture was officially reduced to the "form" filled with the ideological "content," the same for the entire country. One example is the Tallinn directive announced in 1987, which strictly instructed representatives of Union republics and autonomous republics to view their own history as no more than an illustrative supplement to the state curriculum on the history of the USSR in the ratio of 1 to 10 (Bacyn & Kuz'min, 1995). Since the curriculum at all schools in the Russian Federation was the same, it played a negative rather than a positive role in developing an ethno-cultural identity in ethnic minority children.

Despite the federal system and the declared internationalist ideology, the educational policy in the USSR supported ethnic cultures only to a certain level, restricting its development after that level had been achieved and focusing on the development of a single community described as the "Soviet people." Soviet ideologists proved incapable of rising to the idea of a multiple identity and tried to replace the idea of ethnic identity with that of a political identity.

Nonetheless, as a result of such policies the educational function of schools achieved its peak during the Soviet period; in 2000, literacy among adults reached 99.6% (Bell, 2002). At the same time, the disintegration of the Soviet Union proved the failure of the ambitious policy of assimilation. The Russian Federation was sustained. However, different ethnic groups in Russia (including ethnic Russians) entered a stage of ethnic revival.

Ethnic groups and educational policy in post-Soviet times

The process of democratization, which began in the second half of the 1980s, led to a reform of the educational system that continued through the next decade. The reform involved a number of aspects discussed in this chapter.

Role of ethnic groups in the educational policy

The Constitution of the Russian Federation (Konstituciya, 1993) guarantees the rights of "native minorities" (art. 69) and "minor ethnic communities" (para. 1m, art. 72). Therefore, ethnic groups are viewed as collective subjects possessing needs and rights. The Constitution also grants individuals equal human rights and liberties regardless of race, ethnicity, and language (para. 2, art. 19), and declares such rights as the right to a free choice of the language of education and instruction (art. 26). Rights granted by the new democratic Constitution led to the further revival of ethnic identities, increasing self-organization of ethnic groups, and a growing demand for an education supporting ethnic identity.

In response to this demand, the Law on Education (1992, 1996, and 2007) proclaimed that ethnic groups could be independent actors in the development and implementation of educational policy (Dneprov, 1996). The Law on Education made it possible for ethno-culturally oriented non-governmental organizations to act as founders of non-state educational institutions that address a number of issues related to the content and language of education (para. 4, art. 11). Such organizations exist today, although their influence is insignificant. They operate predominantly in the area of non-formal education – Sunday schools and cultural centers, teaching ethnic history and culture.

The Law on Education (Ministerstvo Obrazovanija i Nauki RF, 2007) also made it possible for "titular" ethnic groups to influence educational policy at the regional level. This sometimes led to unequal opportunities, in which "titular" ethnic groups enjoyed preferences in satisfying their ethno-cultural interests through education. The situation was changed by the Law on Ethnic and Cultural Autonomy of 1996, which granted all ethnic communities – united into organized institutions – the right to submit proposals to executive authorities of all levels to establish public educational institutions with an in-depth instruction of the native language and ethnic culture (Pravitelstvo RF, 1996, art. 11). This mechanism has not been fully used because civil society structures, into which ethno-cultural communities are organized, are weak.

Curriculum policy

The first version of the Law on Education (Ministerstvo Obrazovanija i Nauki RF, 2007) legalized the structure (federal, regional [ethnic-regional], and school-level components) of the state educational standards (para. 1, art. 7). Each component included certain disciplines, for example the federal component included math, physics, biology, and the Russian language; the regional (or ethno-regional) component included local history and geography, and certain other disciplines determined by the regional authorities; and the school components included optional subjects.

There are different assessments of the problems related to this structure of the school curriculum, from recognition of its positive influence on the democratization of education to evidence of its harmful influence on the quality of education (Froumin, 2005). This approach in a number of ethnic republics gave an impetus to defining the objectives and the content of education based on an understanding of the ethnic culture as something that had taken its final shape in the past and was static, and required special measures for its conservation in the present.

An analysis of concepts of the regional (national-regional) component in different regions of Russia (Zakharov, 2007) has shown that there were two main approaches: *mono-ethnic* (or *ethnocentrist*) and *poly-ethnic*. Mono-ethnic approaches are used in some ethnic regions and in the ethnic Russian provinces. Their goal is to integrate students into the culture of the titular ethnic group, while poly-ethnic approaches try to integrate students into the Russian culture.

Decisions taken at the regional level often turned out to actualize the cultural monopoly of the titular ethnic group. That trend resulted in the strengthening of ethno-cultural identity but at the same time led to a decreasing tolerance (and even cases of extremism) and a threat of the disintegration of Russian society. That was proved by tragic inter-ethnic conflicts in the North Caucasus.

In the regions that embrace a poly-ethnic approach, the formation of ethnic identity goes hand in hand with an individual's integration into the multicultural space of the Russian Federation. However, in most cases the implementation of such approaches did not happen successfully because of the lack of expertise and experience in multicultural education in Russia.

The increasing diversity of regional approaches to the objectives and content of education – and the growing ethnic isolation in some regions – have indicated the need for a change in who determines the standards of education. Between 1993 and 1996, the Ministry of Education reformed the basic academic curriculum to ensure "the integration of interests of the federation, the regions, the schools, and the individuals" (Tkachenko, 1994, p. 2). The curriculum reform attempted to find a "balance of ethnic and regional interests and the interests of educational institutions" (Tkachenko, 1996, p. 34). The share of the regional component of educational standards decreased to 10%.

To reinforce control of the federal center over the content of education, the June 2002 amendments to the Law on Education introduced annual appraisal and approval of the federal lists of textbooks recommended (permitted) for use in the educational process (Filippov, 2003). The Federal Ministry of Education justified this move also by the increasing risk of ethnocentrism and nationalism. The final move in the same direction was the abolition of the regional and school components of educational standards. Regions (including ethnic regions) found themselves prohibited from making decisions on these issues. However, such a solution only aggravated the problem.

This structure of the state education standards that ignores ethnic aspects is reinforced by the lack of attention to different ethnic perspectives in traditional school subjects such as history, literature, and geography. The authors of these subject textbooks avoid multiple ethnic perspectives. The government must offer approaches to meet the requirements of ethnic groups related to the content of education. Under the current circumstances, the policy of central government is characterized by duality and ambiguity. A trend towards centralization of education management and the unification of its content was launched in the late 1990s. However, there have also been attempts by the government to find alternative solutions to the problem by applying a multicultural approach to the curriculum. It is not clear which trend will prevail in the state educational policy of the Russian Federation.

Ethnic languages

The Constitution of the Russian Federation and a number of laws guarantee the right to retain native languages and create conditions for their study and development by all ethnic groups. The practical implementation of such a legal framework resulted in an increase in the number of languages taught in schools from 60 in 1990 to 75 in 2006 (in this section we use data received from the Center of Educational Statistics of the Higher School of Economics in Moscow).

Between 1990 and 2006, the total number of people learning their native (non-Russian) languages increased by 59.5%. This trend is consistent with the increase in the total number of students who are learning their native languages, which increased from 5.1% in 1990 to 11.5% in 2006. The share of schools where non-Russian languages are taught (in the total number of general educational institutions) has risen from 12.9% to 18.2%.

The number of languages of instruction and people studying in their native (non-Russian) languages manifested a different dynamic. The number of languages used for instruction decreased slightly from 33 to 32 between 1990 and 2006. The number of schools with instruction in native (non-Russian) languages manifests a persistent trend towards reduction. It dropped by 16.2% from 1990 to 2006. Possibly the reason for these trends is the transition of schools from instruction in native (non-Russian) languages to instruction in the Russian language while retaining native (non-Russian) languages as separate subjects. This is confirmed by a significant increase in the number of teachers of native (non-Russian) languages from 11,700 in 1990 to 26,000 in 2006.

The educational policy in the Russian Federation has created conditions for the study of native (non-Russian) languages in the educational process. This policy indicates the revival of the national languages and the strengthening of ethnic identity. The best opportunities (regulatory, legal, and organizational) in the regions of Russia exist for the languages of titular ethnic groups. The status of official language of a region allows it to be taught as a mandatory course in the ethnic region regardless of the fact that the given ethnic group might not constitute the majority of the population. An increasing number of citizens contact government authorities of the Russian Federation asking the authorities to permit their children who do not belong to the titular ethnic group to avoid study of the titular ethnic language.

The situation resulted in a resolution of the Constitutional Court of the Russian Federation confirming: (a) the status of the Russian language as the universal official language of the Russian Federation; (b) the need to teach the official languages of the Russian Federation without harm to the study of the Russian language; and (c) the need for a differentiated approach in addressing the issues related to the study of languages of titular ethnic groups, with the goal of preventing any abuse of citizens' other rights and liberties (Constitutional Court of the RF, 2004). However, the responses of the regional authorities to language problems in education remain slow; no amendments have been made to relevant regulatory acts of the regions.

In post-Soviet times, ethnic revival is manifested in the expansion of the study of ethnic languages in schools, mostly as separate subjects. This process has so far failed to overcome the Russian national bilingualism policy because of the languages of "titular" ethnic groups.

Education and religious groups

The revival of religious life in post-Soviet Russia led to the increasing importance of education in the formation of religious identity. The relationship between religious organizations and the state in the area of education is regulated by a number of federal legal acts. Their authors were guided by the experience of those Western countries where the church is separated from the state (Hull, 1984). Legally, education in state and municipal educational institutions is of a secular nature (Law on Education, 2007, para. 4, art. 2). Any religious activity is prohibited in schools (Ministerstvo Obrazovanija i Nauki RF, 2008, para. 5, art. 1). Nonetheless, citizens have the right to obtain religious education in the following four ways:

1. by attending religious services as well as classes in Sunday schools;
2. in the family;
3. at non-state educational institutions established by religious organizations;
4. at state and municipal educational institutions if requested in writing by parents and the children's consent is given.

According to data of the Ministry of Education of the Russian Federation (2008), during the 2005–2006 academic year a total of 203 religious educational institutions operated in the Russian Federation, and 61.1% of this number were general (full) secondary education institutions. These educational institutions usually enroll a few dozen students. Besides confessional education whose goal is to introduce students to religious traditions and faith, the Russian law permits religious studies that teach students knowledge about the history of various religions. This approach does not violate the principle of secular education. However, it caused heated public discussions, because purely religious courses were often offered under the guise of the "study of religious culture." In a number of cases, religious organizations participated in the development of courses, and in 20 regions they were taught by clergy (Ministerstvo Obrazovanija i Nauki RF, 2008).

The current policy of the Ministry of Education of the Russian Federation on the study of religion is ambiguous – it periodically supports both multi-confessional and mono-confessional approaches. There is a possibility of the introduction of a compulsory course on World Religions: History, Culture, and Religious Doctrine in September 2008. The course authors emphasize its secular nature because they view religion as a part of culture (Pravoslavie.ru, 2007). State support has been given to the subject Fundamentals of Orthodox Culture. Textbooks for this course have become an object of close attention from both domestic and foreign authors because they do not support a multicultural perspective and often increase ethno-cultural isolation (Willems, 2006).

Interestingly, the introduction of religious subjects has been recently justified by the explanation that students need a spiritual and moral socialization (Moscow Patriarchia, 2007). This kind of approach supports the trend towards the transition from the study of religion to religious education. Under such circumstances, the ambiguous position of the Ministry of Education and Science will increase the influence of dominating religious groups and – considering the multi-confessional composition of the country's population – will be a source of possible religious conflicts.

Problems of educational policy

The above analysis indicates that Russia's current policy on education related to ethnic minorities and small religious groups contains a number of contradictions that require immediate solution:

1. The Law on Education lacks a mechanism for harmonizing the interests of the increased number of stakeholders who participate in the formulation of educational policy. Contradictions that arose in the orientation of the educational policies of the Russian Federation and Russian Federation regions could have been solved by the development of such a mechanism. Instead, the federal center preferred the tactics of limiting the choice of action of the regions. This resulted in an indirect abuse of the interests of the ethnic groups (mostly titular ones) populating those regions. The situation is even more complex in the context of significant differences between various ethnic regions. These differences are manifested in the interconnection between religion and ethnicity, and through the revival of ethnic traditions and language. However, the Russian Federation Constitution treats all ethnic republics equally. The current policy of "one size fits all" cannot be easily changed to a more flexible policy that reflects the different needs and interests of various ethnic groups.
2. The educational policy in the Russian Federation lacks a single strategic orientation. Different and sometimes contradictory tendencies coexist. In the area of the content of education, there is a tendency to deprive the regions of the ability to make decisions (since the late 1990s), while retaining the multi-subject nature of educational policy by basing the content of education on the principle of a dialogue of cultures. In the area of language policy there is a tendency to expand the possibilities for the study of native languages by representatives of titular ethnic groups at the expense of a reduction in the share of other languages – including Russian – in the content of education. In the area of education related to the study of religion there is a tendency to support both courses of a multi-confessional nature and subjects orientated towards the Christianization of students. A result of the above contradiction is that there is no mechanism for the successful simultaneous formation of ethnic and all-Russian (supra-ethnic) personal identity or for

the implementation of an ethno-cultural and consolidating function of education in a multinational society.

3   Education has to play a critical role in the development of values of recognition and tolerance in an intolerant society. However, declarations of an educational policy that supports tolerance are not supported in the Russian Federation by methodologies and substantive innovations in multicultural education. In general, Russian society and the nation are in search of a response to the obvious trend towards an increasing role of education in the formation of ethnic and religious values. So far, neither society nor the state is ready to offer a concept of a truly multicultural education that enables students to develop multiple identities and become tolerant citizens.

References

Academy of Pedagogical Sciences. (1980). *Ocherki istorii shkoly i pedagogicheskoj mysli narodov SSSR (1917–1941)* [Essays on school history and pedagogical ideas of people of the USSR (1917–1941)]. Moscow: Pedagogika Press.

Anikanov, M. V., Stepanov, V. V., & Susokolov, A. A. (1999). *Titul'nye jetnosy Rossijskoj Federacii: Analiticheskij spravochnik* [Titular ethnic minorities of the Russian Federation: The analytical directory]. Moscow: Academic Press.

Bacyn, V. K., & Kuz'min, M. N. (1995). *Rossijskie etnosy i sovremennaja nacional'naja shkola: Shkola i mir kul'tury jetnosov/Uchenye zapiski INPO* [Ethnic minorities in Russia and the modern ethnic school: School and the world of ethnic culture/Scientific notes]. Moscow: Academic Press.

Baker, C., & Jones, S. (1998). *Encyclopedia of bilingualism and bilingual education.* Clevedon, UK: Multilingual Matters.

Bell, I. (Ed.). (2002). *Eastern Europe, Russia and Central Asia 2003.* London: Europa.

Center of Educational Statistics of the Higher School of Economics in Moscow. (n.d.). Unpublished data.

Constitutional Court of the RF. (2004). Resolution No. 16-П. Retrieved December 7, 2008 from http://www.tatar.ru/download_legis.php?DNSID=33912ff5d501667e8b1176726fd2a899&lf_id=838

Dneprov, E. D. (1996). *Shkol'naja reforma mezhdu "vchera" i "zavtra"* [School reform between "yesterday" and "tomorrow"]. Moscow: Academic Press.

Drofa Publishing. (1998). *Rossia: Enciklopedicheskij spravochnik* [Russia: The encyclopedic directory]. Moscow: Author.

Fal'bork, G., & Harnoluskij, V. C. (1903). *Inorodcheskie i inovercheskie uchilisha* [Schools for children of non-Orthodox religion and non-Russian origin]. St. Petersburg, Russia: Academic Press.

Federal Registration Service. (2007). *Rossija v cifrah* [Russia in figures]. Retrieved October 24, 2008, from http://www.gks.ru/bgd/regl/b07_11/isswww.exe/stg/d010/02-07.htm

Filippov, V. M. (2003). *Modernizacija rossijskogo obrazovanija* [Education modernization in Russia]. Moscow: Prosveshenie.

Froumin, I. (2005). Democratizing the Russian school: Achievements and setbacks. In B. Eklof, L. E. Holmes, & V. Kaplan (Eds.), *Educational reform in post-Soviet Russia: Legacies and prospects* (pp. 129–152). New York: Frank Cass.

Garadzha, V. I. (2005). *Sociologija religii: Podavljajuwee bol'shinstvo rossijan schitajut sebja verujuwimi: A tolku?* [Sociology of religion: Vast majority of Russians consider themselves as believers: And does it make sense?]. Retrieved February 9, 2008, from http://wciom.ru/arkhiv/tematicheskii-rkhiv/item/single/3999.html?no_cache=1&cHash=88ccb61c2f&print=1

Goskomstat RF. (2002). *Vserossijskaja perepis' naselenija: Nacional'nyj sostav i vladenie jazykami, grazhdanstvo* [National census: Ethnic composition and language proficiency, citizenship]. Retrieved October 24, 2008, from http://perepis2002.ru/ct/doc/TOM_04_01.xls

Goskomstat RSFSR. (1990). *Nacional'nyj sostav naselenija RSFSR po dannym Vsesojuznoj perepisi naselenija*

1989 [Ethnic composition of the population in RSFSR according to national population census 1989]. Moscow: Author.
Grachev, S. V. (2000). *Geopolitika i prosveshchenie nerusskikh narodov Povolzh'iz (60-e gg. XIX–nachalo XX v.)* [Geopolitics and education of non-Russian people from the Volga region (from 1860 to the beginning of the 20th century)]. Saransk, Russia: Academic Press.
Hull, J. M. (1984). *Studies in religion and education.* London: Falmer Press.
Kastelajn, S., Ornelis, F., Veni, L., Verbek, B., & Vlamink, L. (2003). *Politika v oblasti obrazovanija i nacional-'nye men'shinstva v Rossijskoj Federacii* [Educational policies and ethnic minorities in Russia]. Ghent, Belgium: Ghent University Press.
Kirzhaeva, V. P., & Osovskii, E. G. (2005). *Obuchenie russkomu jazyku vo vtoroj polovine XVIII – nachale XX veka: Politiko-pravovye, sociokul'trnye i lingvokul'turnye apsekty (Monografiia)* [Russian language training of ethnic minorities from the second half of the 18th to the beginning of the 20th century: Legal, political, sociocultural, and linguicultural aspects] (Monograph). Saransk, Russia: Saransky University Press.
Konstituciya Rossiskoi Federacii [Constitution of the Russian Federation]. (1993). Moscow: Yuridicheskaya literatura.
Krasovickaja, T. J. U. (1992). *Vlast'i kul'tura: Istoricheskij opyt organizacii gosudarstvennogo rukovodstva nacional'no-kul'turnym stroitel'stvom v RSFSR* [Authority and culture: Historical experience of the state governance organization by national-cultural construction in RSFSR]. Moscow: Academic Press.
Kuz'min, M. N. (1997). *Nacional'naja shkola Rossii v kontekste gosudarstvennoj obrazovatel'noj politiki* [The Russian ethnic school in a context of state educational policy]. Moscow: Academic Press.
Kuz'min, M. N., & Artemenko, O. I. (2006). Chelovek grazhdanskogo obshestva kak cel' obrazovanija v uslovijah polijetnichnogo rossijskogo sociuma [The person of a civil society as a purpose of education in the multiethnic context of Russian society]. *Voprosy Filosofii* [Philosophical studies], *6*, 40–51.
Mikhalchenko, V., & Trushkova, Y. (2003). Russian in the modern world. In J. Maurais & M. Morris (Eds.), *Languages in a globalizing world* (pp. 260–261). Cambridge, UK: Cambridge University Press.
Ministerstvo Obrazovanija i Nauki RF [Ministry of Education and Science]. (2007). *Zakon ob obrazovanii* [Law on education]. Moscow: Prosvechenije.
Ministerstvo Obrazovanija i Nauki RF [Ministry of Education and Science]. (2008). *Spravka o sostojanii konfessional'nogo obrazovanija v shkolah RF* [Note on religious education in schools in the Russian Federation]. Moscow: MOES.
Moscow Patriarchia. (2007). *Koncepcija vkljuchenija v novoe pokolenie gosudarstvennyh standartov obchego srednego obrazovanija uchebnogo predmeta "Pravoslavnaja kul'tura"* [Concept of inclusion of a discipline of "Orthodox culture" in new state standards of general secondary education]. Retrieved October 24, 2008, from http://www.patriarchia.ru/db/text/358393.html
Piskunov, A. I. (2001). *Istorija pedagogiki i obrazovanija: Ot zarozhdenija vospitanija do konca XX* [History of pedagogy and education: From origins of education up to the end of the 20th century]. Moscow: Academic Press.
Pravitelstvo R. F. (1996). *Zakon o nacilonalnoy i kulturnoi avtonomii* [Law on ethnic and cultural autonomy]. Moscow: Pravo.
Pravoslavie.ru. (2007, August 29). *Predmet: "Istorija mirovyh religij" mozhet byt' vkljuchen v objazatel'nyj uchebnyj plan rossijskih shkol* [Subject: "History of world religions" can be included in the mandatory curriculum of Russian schools]. Retrieved October 24, 2008, from http://www.pravoslavie.ru/news/070829134425
Stepanov, V. (2004). *Rossijskij opyt jetnicheskoj statistiki korennyh malochislennyh narodov Severa* [Russian experience of ethnic statistics of minorities in the North]. Retrieved January 15, 2008, from http://demoscope.ru/weekly/2008/0319/analit03.php
Tkachenko, E. V. (1994). *Reformirovanie obrazovanija v Rossii: Nekotorye itogi, problemy, zadachi* [Educational reform in Russia: Some problems, findings, objectives]. Moscow: APKRO.
Tkachenko, E. V. (1996). *Osnovnye itogi 1994–1995 uchebnogo goda i putiobnovlenija obrazovanija v Rossii* [Key findings of 1994–1995 and the educational renewal in Russia]. Moscow: Prosvechenije.

Willems, J. (2006). *Religiöse Bildung in Russlands Schulen* [Religious education in Russian schools]. Berlin, Hamburg, & Münster, Germany: Academic Press.

Woodard, C. (1996, January 19). Russia debates the future of minority-language education. *The Chronicle of Higher Education, 42*(19), A36.

Zakharov, A. B. (2007). *Regional'nyj (nacional'no-regional'nyj) komponent gosudarstvennyh obrazovatel'nyh standartov* [Ethnic-regional component of the state educational standards]. Kazan, Russia: Kazan University Press.

Part 10

The education of ethnic and cultural minority groups in Asia and Latin America

37

The education of ethnic minority groups in China

Gerard A. Postiglione
University of Hong Kong

Only 10 countries in the world have total populations that surpass that of the ethnic minority population of China. Most ethnic minorities live within China's designated ethnic minority autonomous regions, which cover half the country and provide minority residents with preferential educational policies. Like other multiethnic states, China faces a number of educational challenges: first, ensuring educational access and equity for its 56 officially designated ethnic groups; second, ensuring education that promotes the economic development of its 155 ethnic minority autonomous areas; third, ensuring that schools, colleges, and universities in ethnic minority regions function in accordance with the principle of cultural autonomy as set out in the Chinese constitution; and, fourth, ensuring that education builds interethnic unity. By the start of the 21st century, basic education was popularized in nearly 90% of China's populated regions, including its ethnic minority regions (Ministry of Education, 2006; Xia, Ha, & Abadu, 1999). However, those in remote areas still received only a few years of schooling. At the other end of the system, China's rapidly expanding system of higher education, the largest system in the world, has increased ethnic minority opportunity, yet minority access to the top universities remains a major challenge.

This is not to say that multiethnic diversity is strongly encouraged in schools, only that it is increasingly salient in society and more recognized than in previous decades. While ethnic minority culture is often celebrated by the state at national events, ethnic diversity in schools and society is carefully managed. The current leadership prescribes Chinese ethnicity within the context of its "harmonious society" campaign, and China's ethnicity is viewed as a plurality within the organic unity of the Chinese nation.

Therefore pluralism is as important as harmony in conceptualizing ethnic intergroup processes in China (Gladney, 1991; Mackerras, 1994, 1995). It has been the source of much cultural vitality throughout China's history, though not as conflict free as portrayed, as in imperial times during the Mongol and Manchu eras when intergroup processes included both harmonious acculturation and conflict prone impact integration (Dikotter, 1992). It is helpful to understand the background themes that guide ideology about ethnic minorities in China. For much of its history, China was a highly pluralistic area of the world and guided by a culturalist tradition that assimilated many groups into its cultural center. At about the time of the incursions of the Western powers into China in the 19th century, this began to change, and by the mid-20th century China began to adopt the policies of the former USSR. This amounted to a more politicized set of themes which led to the establishment of nationality autonomous regions. There are a number of scholars in China who now suggest that China draw upon that characteristically culturalist position so as to strengthen national identity among its ethnic minorities (Ma, 2007a, 2007b). In fact, ethnic minority education policies and practices since the founding of the People's Republic of China have paralleled the changing political climate.

After the revolution in 1949, the government worked with ethnic minority elites to integrate diverse territories into the national fabric (Dreyer, 1976). Ethnic minority groups were identified and minority languages were recognized and supported. However, political campaigns that stressed class struggle resulted in destructive policies toward ethnic minority cultural vitality. The Cultural Revolution wrought havoc on the cultural traditions of ethnic minorities. This was followed by a national effort to redress past wrongs, and was accompanied by a resurgence of ethnicity. Since 1978, China's economic reforms and its opening to the outside world have contributed to a critical pluralism in education in which national patriotism and ethnic minority cultural autonomy have to keep pace with market forces and globalization.

As schools work to situate the autonomy of ethnic minority cultural transmission within the national context, the practical challenge is how to make schooling work in ways that bring ethnic minority culture into the national and global or international spheres with the least amount of dislocation to ethnic communities and national unity. The debate over cultural preservation, ethnic autonomy, and state schooling remains complex in China. Schools shape ethnic identity through the values they transmit. Making ethnic minorities into Chinese citizens is an educational task which remains a work in progress. This task cannot remain disconnected from strategies for the improvement of the learning environment and academic achievement of ethnic minorities.

While there may be a variety of perspectives about why minority educational achievement levels are far behind those in the rest of the country, culturally meaningful access to mainstream national education remains the main challenge for improving the quality of ethnic minority community life in China. The notion of cultural backwardness continues to adhere to popular discourse about ethnic minorities, and it is often cited in China as the principal reason for educational underachievement (Harrell, 2001). This notion is not unique to China and was also used by Western nations to stress their cultural superiority, most notably by the British for over a century to the Irish, who they insisted were in need of being civilized, even though Ireland became richer per capita than any other nation in Europe. In fact, about 10 of China's 55 official ethnic minority groups have education levels above the national average. Some, like Chinese Koreans, have earned the status of *youxiu minzu*, a notion similar to a model minority elsewhere.

Thus, a key question concerns the extent to which school norms recognize and encourage diverse cultural groups and create a learning environment that reflects the ethnic diversity of the nation (Banks, 1994). With these themes in mind, this chapter will review the basic situation and policies, research literature, case studies, and debates about China's ethnic minority education.

Basic situation

Ethnic minorities in China are referred to as *shaoshu minzu*, formerly rendered as "national minorities" but more recently as "ethnic minorities" (Bilik, 2000). Their population increases faster than that of the majority Han because of a relaxed birth control policy in the sparsely populated minority areas, but also because of an increased willingness to acknowledge ethnic minority roots, owing in no small part to the preferential policies in family planning, employment, and education. The largest ethnic minority has more than 15 million members and the smallest only about 2,000. While they account for less than 10% of the population, their land contains substantial mineral deposits, forest reserves, and most of the animals that supply milk, meat, and wool. In all, there are 155 nationality autonomous areas (5 autonomous regions, 30 autonomous prefectures, and 120 autonomous counties, including 3 autonomous banners). The main ethnic group in each of these autonomous areas does not usually (about one-third of the time) account for more than half of its population. The law on ethnic regional autonomy adopted in May 1984 includes provisions for autonomous organizations, rights of self-government organizations, help from higher level organizations, training and assignment of cadres, specialists, and skilled workers among the minority peoples, and the strengthening and developing of socialist relations among ethnic groups (Heberer, 1989).

It is virtually impossible to conceptualize China's ethnic minorities as a single entity, owing to cultural, regional, and developmental differences. However, the government's unified set of ethnic minority education policies are intended to be implemented flexibly so as to take account of the unique situation in each ethnic minority region. Ethnic minorities can be differentiated according to many criteria. These include: population size; the nature of the identification of the group; the size, location, and terrain of the region they occupy; the proportion of members of the minority group that inhabit an autonomous province, prefecture, or county; their proximity to and relations with other ethnic groups, including the Han; whether the neighboring Han were migrants or indigenous residents of the region; whether the ethnic minorities are rural or urban groups, agricultural or pastoral groups, border or inland groups, or concentrated or dispersed groups; having a strong religious tradition or none; having a written or spoken language or both; having members of their ethnic group also living across the Chinese border in other countries, either as ethnic minorities or as the major nationality; and, finally, whether they have had a separate tradition of foreign relations with peoples of another region of the world (E. Zhou, 1984).

The educational policies adopted for ethnic minorities since 1979 include the establishment of the Department of Ethnic Minority Education under the State Ministry of Education (which became the State Education Commission from 1985 to 1998), with corresponding organizations and appointments made at the provincial (*minzu jiaoyu chu*), prefecture (*minzu jiaoyu ke*), and county levels (*minzu jiaoyu gu*). Ethnic autonomous regions became authorized to develop their own educational programs, including levels and kinds of schools, curriculum content, and languages of instruction. Special funds for minority education were increased, and a portion of the annual budget for ethnic minority areas could be used for education. Funds for teacher training increased, and various types of in-service training have been set up. Schools can be established according to the characteristics of the ethnic minorities and their regions; in pastoral, frontier, and cold mountainous regions, boarding schools were arranged and stipends provided for students. Special emphasis in education could be placed on ethnic minority language, culture, and historical traditions. Higher education expanded, and cooperation increased between frontier universities and those in the interior. There are 13 designated ethnic minority colleges and universities which have taken on an increasing number of majority Han students in recent years, amid a debate about mainstreaming of ethnic minorities in higher education. Several major universities have special remedial classes for minority students, with preparatory programs in the first year. University admission standards for minority students have been lowered or points added to ethnic minority students' examination scores to make admission easier to attain. Directional admission and work assignments after graduation were arranged so as to build links between ethnic minority areas and the rest of the country.

Of all of the areas of Chinese education, the gaps between policy and practice are probably no more in evidence than in ethnic minority education. In particular, gender disparities persist between the advanced coastal areas and the poor and remote areas of northwest and southwest China where most ethnic minorities reside. Girls constitute 70% of the school-age children under 11 years old who are not in school. They also constitute 75% of the dropouts from primary school. Nine municipalities and provinces had already reached 100% universalization of 9-year compulsory education in 1998, whereas seven provinces and ethnic minority autonomous regions remained below 60% (World Bank, 2004).

Concepts and policies

While China as a nation reacts to the countervailing demands of internationalism, patriotism, and communalism, its education system has to respond to a shifting market of demands. These may include: the demand of individuals for relevant knowledge and practical skills in an increasingly market-oriented economy; the demand of the middle class, ethnic minorities, and other social groups for status culture; and the demand of the state and the national bureaucracy for social control, rationalization, and patriotism. At certain times the state's demands take prominence and exert a strong influence on representations of ethnic minority culture in schooling. At other times, ethnic minority groups demand an improved delivery of practical skills that can aid economic development, even if at some expense to cultural preservation. Whatever the case, the demands of ethnic minority groups for schools to elevate the status of their culture within the national framework are ubiquitous. At times, ethnic minorities see schools as an embodiment of future prosperity but distant from their values and the traditions of their communities. Still, their degree of participation depends to a large extent on the extent to which schooling leads to improved living standards, especially for those minority groups that live in poorer regions of western China.

The Chinese leadership's assumptions about ethnic intergroup processes manifest themselves in the structure and content of schooling, and much can be learned about China by studying how it schools its ethnic minorities, represents their ethnic heritage, socializes them into a national identity, structures their educational opportunities, and links their schooling to economic development.

Social context has a profound influence, especially during the shift from a socialist planned economy (pre-1978) to a market-oriented economy (post-1978) that is more open to the outside world. At the start of the reform period, the Chinese anthropologist Fei Xiaoteng's theory, known as ethnic pluralism within the organic configuration of the Chinese nation, guided much ethnic minority policy (Fei, 1980, 1986, 1991). Since then, market forces have penetrated virtually all ethnic minority communities. This has increased the degree of interethnic contact, especially in the marketplace, and has led to a stage of critical pluralism in which patterns of ethnic interaction enter a tipping point between interethnic conflict and interethnic harmony. It is here that state schools are expected to play a major role in nudging China toward the latter and strengthening a sense of common Chinese nationality, thereby moving China along the path of harmonious multiculturalism.

State schools serve a conservative function by defining and reproducing a national culture that bolsters the social, political, and economic status quo. China's state schools conserve a particular brand of national culture (*zhonghua minzu wenhua*), and are supervised by an authoritarian state weary of outside cultural influences, especially from the West and separatist forces in China's two far western provinces of Xinjiang and Tibet. State schooling is also charged with the responsibility to conserve ethnic minority cultures within a national context in which Han Chinese cultural capital remains dominant.

The Chinese state's approach to ethnic minority education, although highly centralized, has a great deal of flexibility at the local level. Yet the extent to which schools in China create an atmosphere that has positive institutional norms toward diverse cultural groups is limited by notions of cultural backwardness. State education policy accords importance to the special cultural characteristics of ethnic minority regions. However, there is a divide between the national curriculum and ethnic minority community knowledge and values. More research is needed on this issue (Postiglione, 1999).

Research literature

Research literature in English on ethnic minority education access and underachievement in China has moved ahead rapidly, beginning in the 1980s and 1990s. The focus has been on multiple factors, including language and religion, cultural transmission and household finance, migration, social stratification, and employment (Hannum, 2002; Iredale, Bilik, Su, Guo, & Hoy, 2001; C. J. Lee, 1986). Stites (1999), Lam (2005), and M. L. Zhou and Sun (2004) examined China's efforts to develop a viable bilingual policy for the education for ethnic minorities.

With respect to religion, Mackerras (1999) pointed out that state school systems adhere to the principle of secularity, but there are signs of religious revival as a reaction to it. Gladney (1999) examined Chinese Muslims and how religious education and state education provide different representations of minority culture (Yi, 2005b). Sautman (1999) examined preferential access to higher education for ethnic minorities and noted that China is ahead of most countries in the policies and practices of preferential treatment in higher education, but there is also a growing debate about the negative effects of preferential treatment policies.

The question of Chinese education as a civilizing mission is addressed in research by Harrell and Ma (1999) through their study of the Yi minority, who feel that acculturation cannot and should not lead to assimilation. Several similar studies were conducted in China's multiethnic province of Yunnan and nearby Guizhou, including Hansen (1999), who stresses the negative effects of the popular perception about cultural backwardness on the Dai minority. Trueba and Zou (1994) concluded that Miao students' strong sense of belonging to a minority, together with the social support they receive from teachers, administrators, and peers, allows them to surmount obstacles to achieving success in school and university. M. J. B. Lee (2001) pointed out that oppositional identities noted in Ogbu's research (1978, 1981) in the United States do not exist among the ethnic minorities she studied in Yunnan. Also in Yunnan, Tsung (2003) noted the difficulties of basic education conducted in multiple ethnic minority languages. Yu (2008) studied identities of Yunnan Naxi students, who are permitted more curriculum content about their cultural heritage and who outperform most other minorities, and Cheung (2003) analyzed Christianity's role in the education and identity of rural Miao. Also in the south of China, Nam (1996) examined cultural capital as a key element in the academic achievement of the Yao of Guangdong.

Gao (2007, 2008) studied a Korean Chinese school and examined how the model minority stereotype affects the situation of ethnic Korean children in China. Chen (2004, 2008) found that Uyghur minority students bound for universities develop ways to access social capital from their classmate networks to help them adapt to senior secondary schooling in Chinese cities. Zhao (in press) focused specifically on how little universities recognize the cultural distinctiveness of ethnic Mongols at the major universities of China, while Clothey (2003) found how language tracks in a state-sponsored ethnic minority university influence the strength of ethnic identity.

Palden Nyima's research noted how mainstream education leads to a loss of self-esteem and interest in education, particularly in the case of Tibetans, and is reflected in dropout rates (1997, 2000). Upton's research demonstrated how Tibetan language schooling had a major influence on the surrounding community in its role as a training ground for the elite (1999). Bass (1998) provided an overview of educational policies and development in Tibet since 1950, noting that the basis of the Tibetan Autonomous Region (TAR) educational policy is the state's measures to improve educational access for ethnic minorities in China. Zhang, Fu, and Jiao (2008) note that teaching and learning in Tibet University remain relatively conservative because of remoteness, economics, and traditions in monastery education, as well as people's sense of culture preservation.

At the other end of the education system, Bass (2008) points out that the theme of cultural backwardness remains salient. Seeberg (2006, 2008) provides empirical research to explain the struggle of Tibetan girls for education, while noting how they have become part of new social networks that both bind them to their traditional place and create new space for their educational empowerment. Bangsbo (2008) conveys the perspectives of nomadic households about the irrelevance of some school learning to daily life, and the lack of available jobs upon graduation. The Qinghai-based scholar S. Y. Wang (2007) noted the inadequacies of current educational reforms for improving Tibetans' economic survival in a market economy. His 2007 study argued that the present school education failed to equip the Tibetan student for market participation. His study, citing others' research, also found that, across Tibetan regions, Tibetan-owned businesses were estimated as only about 20% of total businesses. This figure could reflect the serious competition in seeking employment by the Tibetan graduates in their home areas. Wang's study concluded that the issue of the language of instruction was one of the key factors that affected the quality of secondary education and further hindered Tibetan students from market participation. Yi's (2005a) research demonstrates how schools in Qinghai can limit Tibetan students' chances of acquiring the kinds of cultural capital that could enable them to progress, and instead cause them to become academic underachievers. C. J. Wang and Zhou (2003) point out the effects of state preferential policies and dislocated boarding schools.

Other research discusses Chinese minority education underachievement in different contexts (Postiglione, 1992a, 1992b, 2000; Postiglione, Teng, & Ai, 1995). Chapman, Chen, and Postiglione (2000) study measures aimed at improving teacher education for ethnic minority regions. With particular reference to Tibet, studies have focused on factors that contribute to school dropouts and measures implemented to raise attendance levels in village and township primary schools in semi-rural and semi-nomadic communities (Postiglione, 1997a, 1997b, 2007; Postiglione, Jiao, & Gyatso, 2005, 2006). The ability of households to access networks of social relationships that stretch from village to county to city is useful for increased educational rewards and becomes a determinant of upward mobility (Postiglione, 2006). The measures that improved school participation rates were qualified teachers, household financial incentives, and curriculum relevance. Studies of elite government secondary schools for Tibetans in urban China examined where the opportunities to attend university would be increased (Postiglione, Zhu, & Jiao, 2004; Zhu, 2007). Students who graduate from the boarding schools for Tibetans that are established in Chinese cities generally feel that they learned to become more independent and self-reliant than their counterparts who stayed in Tibet. However, they report a deterioration of Tibetan language skills and lack of knowledge about their historical and cultural background (Postiglione, Jiao, & Manlaji, 2007).

There has been an increasing amount of research in Chinese on ethnic minority education since the mid-1980s and 1990s by Chinese scholars (Ha & Teng, 2001; Teng, 2002). The study of ethnic minorities in China has been traditionally dominated by the Nationalities Research Institute of the Chinese Academy of Social Science and Central University of Nationalities, both of which were heavily influenced by the work of China's most noted anthropologist, Fei Xiaoteng. Anthropology departments, especially at Zhongshan and Yunnan universities, have also been engaged in the study of ethnic minorities for many years. The study of ethnic minorities' education was not a busy field of study until the 1990s, when Teng Xing of the Central University of Nationalities established a research institute for ethnic minority education, assumed the editorship of the *Journal of Research on Ethnic Minority Education* (*Minzu Jiaoyu Yanjiu*), and spent a Fulbright year studying educational anthropology with Professor John Ogbu at the University of California, Los Angeles. Yet, in recent years, sociology departments, like the one at Peking University led by Ma Rong, have also been taking a role in the study of ethnic minority education. Finally, overseas Chinese students and scholars in America, where ethnicity is well developed as a field, are increasingly focusing their research on ethnicity and education. This group also includes an increasing number of ethnic minority scholars.

Such research partially represents the growing vitality of the sociological study of ethnic minority education in China and the many emerging issues and debates. Nevertheless, they provide a sense of the complex nature of the field as a function of the tremendous diversity of China's ethnic minority communities. It is less probable that research by Chinese sociologists of education will contribute to a one-size-fits-all formula for ethnic minority educational policy. However, through empirical studies, they are bringing more clarity and attention to the educational challenges and dilemmas confronting ethnic minority communities.

The amount and type of research on ethnic minority education in China are a function of the way it is organized. At the national level, the Department of Ethnic Minority Education of the State Education Commission conducts policy-related research, usually commissioned as part of the national 5-year plan. The National Association for Ethnic Minority Education Research organizes conferences attended by scholars and officials on specific themes. The Central University of Nationalities' Institute of Ethnic Minority Educational Research is the only research institute that specializes in research on ethnic minority education. Other units of the Central University of Nationalities and the Chinese Academy of Social Science's Institute of Nationalities Research produce research on ethnic minorities, including education topics. Research is also conducted by other units at the national level, including universities and research institutes (i.e. the National Institute of Educational Research, Beijing Normal University's Institute of Educational Research, and Shanghai Academy of Educational Science's Human Resource Development Institute). Among the journals that publish specifically on minority education are the *Journal of Research on Ethnic Minority Education* (*Minzu Jiaoyu Yanjiu*) and *China's Ethnic Minority Education* (*Zhongguo Minzu Jiaoyu*). Research on ethnic minority education also occasionally appears in other national level journals dealing with minority research, including *Nationalities Research* (*Minzu Yanjiu*) and *Ethnic Unity* (*Minzu Tuanjie*). Other ethnic minority educational research may appear in national level journals such as *Educational Research* (*Jiaoyu Yanjiu*), *Sociological Research* (*Shehui Xue Yanjiu*), and similar journals. The education commissions of ethnic autonomous regions also publish journals, such as *Education in Tibet* (*Xizang Jiaoyu*) or *Education in Xinjiang* (*Xinjiang Jiaoyu*). Finally, the ethnic minority institutes, known as nationalities colleges and universities (*minzu xueyuan, minzu daxue*), and other tertiary level institutions in minority regions also publish journals containing material on ethnic minority education.

Toward harmonious multiculturalism in China?

Ethnic identity in China is still an official category defined by the state and placed on all identity cards. Through state educational institutions, ethnic minority culture becomes transmitted, celebrated, transmuted, truncated, or in some cases eliminated. For example, the language of instruction may send a message to students about their ethnic identity within mainstream society, as well as become an aid or obstacle to gaining equal footing in the job market after graduation. Formal education can become an instrument to broaden cultural sophistication beyond the ethnic community or it can radically intensify ethnic identities and inequalities in cultural capital. In the case of China, the diversity that exists among its ethnic minority population is only partially reflected in the content of school textbooks, even though minority languages are emphasized in many regions. Under the government's new curriculum reforms, schooling could come to more accurately reflect the cultural diversity that characterizes China's ethnic minorities and increase understanding among ethnic groups nationwide, as well as make state schools much more attractive to ethnic communities, thereby promoting a harmonious multiculturalism for a more unified nation (Postiglione, 2008).

References

Bangsbo, E. (2008). Schooling for knowledge and cultural survival: Tibetan community schools in nomadic herding areas. *Educational Review*, *60*(1), 69–84.
Banks, J. A. (1994). *Multiethnic education: Theory and practice* (3rd ed.). Boston: Allyn & Bacon.
Bass, C. (1998). *Education in Tibet*. London: Zed Press.
Bass, C. (2008). Tibetan primary curriculum and its role in nation building. *Educational Review*, *60*(1), 39–50.
Bilik, N. (2000). *Xiandai beijingxia de zuqun jiangou* [The structuring of contemporary ethnicity]. Kunming, China: Yunnan Education Press.
Chapman, D., Chen, X. Y., & Postiglione, G. A. (2000). Is pre-service teacher training worth the money? A study of ethnic minority regions in China. *Comparative Education Review*, *44*(3), 300–327.
Chen, Y. B. (2004). *Uyghur students in a Chinese boarding school: Social recapitalisation as a response to ethnic integration*. Unpublished doctoral dissertation, University of Hong Kong, Hong Kong.
Chen, Y. B. (2008). *Muslim Uyghur students in a Chinese boarding school: Social recapitalization as a response to ethnic integration*. New York: Lexington Press.
Cheung, W. C. (2003, January). *Narrating ethnic identities: A comparative study of education and ethnic identity construction of a minority group*. Paper presented at the meeting on Chinese Education, Chinese University of Hong Kong, Hong Kong.
Clothey, R. (2003, March). *A study of the ethnic identity of students at the Central University of Nationalities*. Paper presented at the annual meeting of the Comparative and International Education Society, New Orleans, LA.
Dikotter, F. (1992). *The discourse on race in modern China*. Hong Kong: Hong Kong University Press.
Dreyer, J. T. (1976). *China's forty millions: Minority nationalities and national integration in the PRC*. Cambridge, MA: Harvard University Press.
Fei, X. T. (1980). Ethnic identification in China. *Social Sciences in China*, *1*, 97–107.
Fei, X. T. (1986). Zhonghua minzu de duoyuan yiti geju [Plurality within the organic unity of the Chinese nation]. *Beijing Daxue Xuebao* [Journal of Beijing University], *4*, 1–19.
Fei, X. T. (1991). *Zhonghua minzu yanjiu xin tance* [New explorations in China's ethnic studies]. Beijing: Chinese Academy of Social Sciences.
Gao, F. (2007). "Koreanness" as a cultural capital: Ethnic educational aspirations of Korean families in

Northeast China. In D. A. Bryant, F. Gao, B. B. Hennig, & W. K. Lam (Eds.), *Research Studies in Education* (Vol. 5, pp. 211–220). Hong Kong: University of Hong Kong Faculty of Education Press.

Gao, F. (2008). What it means to be a "model minority": Voices of ethnic Koreans in northeast China. *Asian Ethnicity, 9*, 55–67.

Gladney, D. C. (1991). *Muslim Chinese: Ethnic nationalism in the People's Republic.* Cambridge, MA: Council of East Asian Studies and Fellows of Harvard University.

Gladney, D. C. (1999). Making Muslims in China: Education, Islamicization and representation. In G. Postiglione (Ed.), *China's national minority education: Culture, schooling, and development* (pp. 55–94). New York: Falmer Press.

Ha, J., & Teng, X. (2001). *Minzu jiaoyu xue tonglun* [A general survey of ethnic minority education]. Beijing, China: Jiaoyu kexue press [Educational Science Publishing House].

Hannum, E. (2002). Educational stratification by ethnicity in China: Enrollment and attainment in the early reform years. *Demography, 39*(1), 95–117.

Hansen, M. H. (1999). *Lessons in being Chinese: Minority education and ethnic identity in southwest China.* Seattle: University of Washington Press.

Harrell, S. (2001). *Ways of being ethnic in southwest China.* Seattle: University of Washington Press.

Harrell, S., & Ma, E. (1999). Folk theories of success: Where Han aren't always the best. In G. Postiglione (Ed.), *China's national minority education: Culture, schooling, and development* (pp. 213–242). New York: Falmer Press.

Heberer, T. (1989). *China and its national minorities: Autonomy or assimilation.* New York: M. E. Sharpe.

Iredale, R., Bilik, N., Su, W., Guo, F., & Hoy, C. (Eds.). (2001). *Contemporary minority migration, education and ethnicity.* Cheltenham, UK & Northampton, MA: Edward Elgar.

Lam, A. (2005). *Language education in China.* Hong Kong: Hong Kong University Press.

Lee, C. J. (1986). *China's Korean minority: The politics of ethnic education.* Boulder, CO: Westview Press.

Lee, M. J. B. (2001). *Ethnicity, education and empowerment: How minority students in southwest China construct identities.* Aldershot, UK: Ashgate Press.

Ma, R. (2007a). Bilingual education for China's ethnic minorities. *Chinese Education and Society, 40*(2), 9–25.

Ma, R. (2007b, November 2). *A new perspective in guiding ethnic relations in the 21st century: "De-politicization" of ethnicity.* Paper read at the Beijing Forum, Beijing, China.

Mackerras, C. (1994). *China's minorities: Integration and modernisation in the 21st century.* Hong Kong: Oxford University Press.

Mackerras, C. (1995). *China's minority cultures: Identities and integration since 1912.* New York: St. Martin's Press.

Mackerras, C. (1999). Religion and the education of China's minorities. In G. Postiglione (Ed.), *China's national minority education: Culture, schooling, and development* (pp. 23–54). New York: Falmer Press.

Ministry of Education (2006). *Zhongguo jiaoyu tongji nianjian 2005* [Statistics on education in China 2005]. Beijing, China: People's Education Press.

Nam, Y. (1996). *A comparative study of Pai Yao and Han Chinese junior secondary school dropouts in Liannan Yao Autonomous County, Guangdong Province, the People's Republic of China.* Unpublished doctoral dissertation, University of Hong Kong, Hong Kong.

Nyima, P. (1997). The way out for Tibetan education. *Chinese Education and Society, 30*(4), 7–20.

Nyima, P. (2000). *Wenming de kunhuo: Zangzu de jiaoyu zhilu* [The puzzle of civilization: The way out for Tibetan education]. Chengdu, China: Sichuan Education Press.

Ogbu, J. (1978). *Minority education and caste: The American system in cross-cultural perspective.* New York: Academic Press.

Ogbu, J. (1981). Education, clientage, and social mobility: Caste and social change in the United States and Nigeria. In G. Berreman (Ed.), *Social inequality: Comparative and developmental approaches* (pp. 277–300). New York: Academic Press.

Postiglione, G. (1992a). China's national minorities and educational change. *Journal of Contemporary Asia, 22*(1), 20–44.

Postiglione, G. (1992b). The implications of modernization for the education of China's national minorities. In R. Hayhoe (Ed.), *Education and modernization: The Chinese experience* (pp. 307–336). New York: Pergamon Press.

Postiglione, G. (Ed.). (1997a). The schooling of Tibetans [Special issue]. *Chinese Education and Society*, *30*(4).

Postiglione, G. (Ed.). (1997b). The schooling of Tibetans [Special issue]. *Chinese Education and Society*, *30*(5).

Postiglione, G. (Ed.). (1999). *China's national minority education: Culture, schooling, and development*. New York: Falmer Press.

Postiglione, G. (2000) National minority regions: Studying school discontinuation. In J. Liu (Ed.), *The ethnographic eye: Interpretive research on education in China* (pp. 51–71). New York: Falmer Press.

Postiglione, G. (Ed.). (2006). *Education and social change in China: Inequality in a market economy*. New York: M. E. Sharpe.

Postiglione, G. (2007). School access in rural Tibet. In E. Hannum & A. Park (Eds.), *Education and reform in China* (pp. 93–116). New York: Routledge.

Postiglione, G. (2008). Making Tibetans in China: The educational challenges of harmonious multiculturalism. *Educational Review*, *60*(1), 1–20.

Postiglione, G., Jiao, B., & Gyatso, S. (2005). Education in rural Tibet: Development, problems, and adaptations. *China: An International Journal*, *3*(1), 1–23.

Postiglione, G., Jiao, B., & Gyatso, S. (2006). Household perspectives on school attendance in rural Tibet. *Educational Review*, *58*(3), 317–337.

Postiglione, G., Jiao, B., & Manlaji. (2007). Language in Tibetan education: The case of the Neidiban. In A. W. Feng (Ed.), *Bilingual education in China: Practices, policies and concepts* (pp. 49–71). New York: Multilingual Matters.

Postiglione, G., Teng, X., & Ai, Y. (1995). Basic education and school discontinuation in national minority border areas of China. In G. Postiglione & W. O. Lee (Eds.), *Social change and educational development: Mainland China, Taiwan and Hong Kong* (pp. 186–206). Hong Kong: Centre of Asian Studies.

Postiglione, G., Zhu, Z. Y., & Jiao, B. (2004). From ethnic segregation to impact integration: State schooling and identity construction for rural Tibetans. *Asian Ethnicity*, *5*(2), 195–217.

Sautman, B. (1999). Expanding access to higher education for China's national minorities: Policies of preferential admissions. In G. Postiglione (Ed.), *China's national minority education: Culture, schooling, and development* (pp. 173–211). New York: Falmer Press.

Seeberg, V. (2006). Tibetan girls' education: Challenging prevailing theory. In G. Postiglione (Ed.), *Education and social change in China: Inequality in a market economy* (pp. 75–110). New York: M. E. Sharpe.

Seeberg, V. (2008). Girls first! Conditions for promoting education in Tibetan areas of China. *Educational Review*, *60*(1), 51–68.

Stites, R. (1999). Writing cultural boundaries: National minority language policy, literacy planning, and bilingual education. In G. Postiglione (Ed.), *China's national minority education: Culture, schooling, and development* (pp. 95–130). New York: Falmer Press.

Teng, X. (2002). *Zuqun, wenhua yu jiaoyu*. [Ethnicity, culture, and education]. Beijing, China: Minzu Press.

Trueba, H., & Zou, Y. (1994). *Power in education: The case of Miao university students and its significance for American culture*. Washington, DC: Falmer Press.

Tsung, L. (2003, January). *Language policy and minority education in China: The case of the Yi, Naxi, Dai and Tibetan schools in Yunnan*. Paper presented at the Meeting on Chinese Educational Research, Chinese University of Hong Kong, Hong Kong.

Upton, J. (1999). The development of modern school based language education in the PRC. In G. Postiglione (Ed.), *China's national minority education: Culture, schooling, and development* (pp. 281–342). New York: Falmer Press.

Wang, C. J., & Zhou, Q. H. (2003). Minority education in China: From state preferential policies to dislocated Tibetan schools. *Educational Studies*, *29*(1), 85–104.

Wang, S. Y. (2007). The failure of education in preparing Tibetans for market participation. *Asian Ethnicity*, *8*(2), 131–148.

World Bank. (2004). *Basic education in poor/minority areas*. Retrieved December 24, 2007, from www.worldbank.org.cn/English/content/683u1148366.shtml

Xia, Z., Ha, J. X., & Abadu, W. (1999). Xizang Zizhiqu Minzu Jiaoyu 50 Nian [50 years of ethnic education in the Tibetan Autonomous Region]. *Zhongguo minzu jiaoyu 50 nian* [50 years of ethnic education in China] (pp. 45–74). Beijing, China: Hongqi Chubanshe [Red Flag Press].

Yi, L. (2005a). Choosing between ethnic and Chinese citizenship: The educational trajectories of Tibetan minority children in northwest China. In V. L. Fong & R. Murphy (Eds.), *Chinese citizenship: Views from the margins* (pp. 41–67). London & New York: Routledge.

Yi, L. (2005b). Muslim narratives of schooling, social mobility and cultural difference: A case study in multi-ethnic northwest China. *Japanese Journal of Political Science, 6*(1), 1–28.

Yu, H. B. (2008). *Schooling and identity among the Naxi*. Unpublished doctoral dissertation, University of Hong Kong, Hong Kong.

Zhang, L. F., Fu, H., & Jiao, B. (2008). Accounting for Tibetan university students' and teachers' intellectual styles. *Educational Review, 60*(1), 21–37.

Zhao, Z. Z. (in press). *Am I privileged? Minority Mongol students and cultural recognition in Chinese universities*. New York: Lexington Press.

Zhou, E. (1984). Guanyu woguo minzu zhengce de jige wenti [A few questions concerning our country's nationality policy]. In Zhou Enlai (Ed.), *Zhou Enlai xuanji* [Selected works of Zhou Enlai] (Vol. 2, pp. 247–271). Beijing, China: People's Press.

Zhou, M. L., & Sun, H. K. (Eds.). (2004). *Language policy in the People's Republic of China: Theory and practice since 1949*. Norwell, MA: Kluwer Academic Press.

Zhu, Z. Y. (2007). *State schooling and ethnic identity: The politics of a Tibetan neidi school in China*. New York: Lexington Press.

38

Social inequality as a barrier to multicultural education in Latin America

Martin Carnoy
Stanford University, USA

Discussions of multicultural education are usually set in particular nations' economic, social, and political context. That context influences how different groups in the society participate in the distribution of resources. It also influences ethnic and race relations that set the tone for tolerating cultural differences among the diverse groups that make up most societies. In turn, distribution of resources and tolerance for cultural and social differences define who gets how much education and the nature of the education they get.

This chapter argues that the conditions for multicultural education in Latin American societies are particularly difficult because of the great economic and social inequalities characteristic of these societies. To make the analysis in the chapter more concrete, it compares educational delivery and the conditions for racial and ethnic minorities in two highly unequal societies, Brazil and Chile, with one economically and socially much more equalized Latin American country, Cuba. It provides additional examples from countries with relatively large Indigenous populations such as Mexico, Peru, and Central America. Chile is an interesting example of a highly stratified society, because for the past 17 years its education policy has, under the same rather progressive political party, been consistently oriented to improve student performance and to stress education equity, but the policy has had only some success. Brazil is another interesting example, since it has until quite recently claimed to be a raceless society, when in fact it is marked by great disparities between African Brazilian people and those of European origin.

We begin with some stylized facts: Empirical evidence shows that most Latin American countries are characterized by some of the highest levels of income inequality in the world (World Bank, n.d.). Many are almost archetypes of what a traditional class society might look like in 21st-century trappings. In this context, even when socioeconomic differences are accounted for, European-origin Latin Americans do much better economically than Latin America's Indigenous peoples and those of African origin (for Mexico, see Carnoy, Santibañez, Maldonado, & Ordorika, 2002; Psacharopoulos & Patrinos, 1994; for Ecuador, see Garcia Aracil & Winkler, 2004; for Brazil, see Arias, Yamada, & Tejerina, 2004). Further, it appears that, in most countries, much of the wage gap for disadvantaged minorities is related to their large gap in educational opportunities (Garcia Aracil & Winkler; Psacharopoulos & Patrinos).

Based on these stylized facts, the chapter starts out by suggesting that high levels of income inequality in Latin America tend to lower the quality of education for all groups, and have a particularly negative relation with the academic achievement of lower social class students. Further, we try to make the case that high levels of socioeconomic disparity serve to increase greatly the distance of ethnic minority groups from the mainstream, and that this has an especially adverse impact on the quality of disadvantaged minorities' schooling and access to higher levels of education.

The chapter suggests some reasons why general forms of economic and social inequality contribute to worsening educational conditions for ethnic/racial minorities and increasing the barriers to multicultural education. We argue that, in highly unequal societies, ethnic/racial minorities tend to get fewer resources, and that, in this context, separating them into their "own" schools almost guarantees that their (lower-quality) education will provide them with less access to upper secondary and tertiary education and hence to "good" jobs.

The chapter contends that Chile's and Brazil's extreme social class segregation of pupils in different schools probably contributes to its difficulties in improving average student performance and the overall quality of educational delivery and that this extends to its disadvantaged minority groups – in Chile's case, the Mapuche Indians, and in Brazil's, the African Brazilians. Cuban society is also marked by racial disparities, but, in contrast with Brazil and Chile, greater overall economic and social equality in Cuba has gone far toward reducing these disparities. African Cubans, we argue, appear to be in a far better situation today to contest racism than are Blacks in Brazil and Indigenous peoples in the rest of Latin America.

Student performance and income inequality

It is widely accepted that the level of parents' education and family economic and social resources are important indicators of how well individual students perform in school (Rothstein, 2004). On an international level, this translates into the well-known proposition that student performance on international tests is generally higher in countries with higher average levels of parent education and higher gross domestic product per capita (Figure 38.1[1]). However, as Figure 38.1 shows, there is considerable variation around the trend line that relates students' test scores to a country's level of economic resources. Figure 38.1 also shows that students in Latin America score below the trend line and, in some cases, far below the line. Thus one important reason that Latin American students may not do as well academically as students in countries with about the same level of resources (gross domestic product [GDP] per capita) is the high level of economic and social inequality in most Latin America societies.

Elsewhere, we tested the proposition that student performance may be related to income inequality at the national level (Carnoy, Beteille, Brodziak, Loyalka, & Luschei, 2008). We used the reported results of two international tests of mathematics in 2003 – TIMSS (Third International Mathematics and Science Study), administered by the International Association for the Evaluation of Educational Achievement (IEA), and the Programme for International Student Assessment (PISA), administered by the Organisation for Economic Co-operation and Development (OECD)[2] – to estimate the relationship of the average test score to income inequality, controlling for gross domestic product per capita.[3] We found that the more equal the income distribution and the higher the GDP/capita in a country, the higher students' average test scores.

One reason that average test scores might be higher in countries with more equal income distribution is that students from low-income families are relatively better off economically than in countries with similar GDP per capita but greater inequality. If, as suggested by

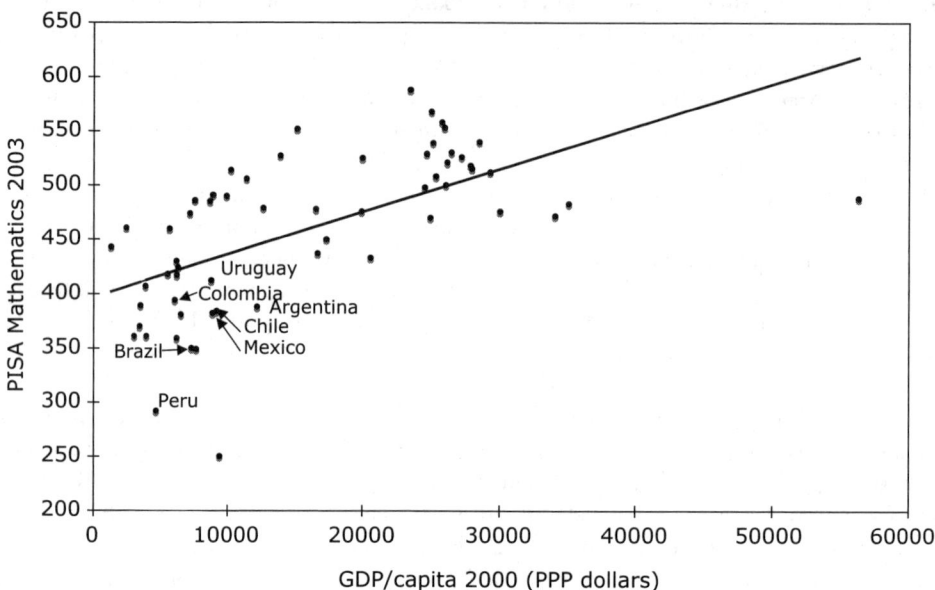

Figure 38.1 Trend Line of PISA 2003 and Imputed PISA 2003 Mean Mathematics Scores with Gross Domestic Product per Capita and Location of Latin American Students' Performance Relative to the Trend Line.

Source: Programme for International Student Assessment (PISA) (2004).

Chiu and Khoo (2005), income inequality is positively correlated with inequality in the distribution of teacher qualifications and school resources among schools, shifting teacher skills from higher- to lower-income schools could have a substantial impact on lower-income students in countries with greater income inequality. High-income students' performance should be less affected by income distribution differences among countries.

We also found that the relation between test score and income inequality is stronger across countries for lower-scoring students than for higher-scoring students. The larger impact of income inequality on lower-scoring students may represent a resource allocation effect: in societies with greater income equality, the lowest-scoring students may be more likely to be getting poorer resources (teacher quality, for example) in their schools than in societies with greater income equality. Furthermore, lower-scoring students may be more negatively affected than higher-scoring students when the quality of schools is lower, compounding the negative impact of poorer resources allocated to schools with lower-scoring students.

Considering that extreme income inequality has been a persistent feature of most Latin American economies for as long as income data have been recorded, we would expect that factors associated with greater inequality could be a major reason that average student performance is relatively low in Latin American societies. In contrast, one Latin American country with a very equal income distribution but a relatively low income per capita is Cuba. Cuban GDP/capita was about 4,000 purchasing power parity (PPP) dollars in 1998, as compared with 7,300 $PPP in Brazil in 2000 and 9,000 $PPP in Chile in 2000. Cuban students have never participated in a PISA or TIMSS test but did participate in a 1997 United Nations Educational, Scientific and Cultural Organization (UNESCO) test of third and fourth graders in 13 Latin American countries (Laboratorio Latinoamericano de Evaluación de la Calidad de la Educación [LLECE], 1998). Students in Cuba scored more than one standard deviation higher in both mathematics and language than the mean score for the region. Rural students in Cuba scored at about the same level in mathematics as elite private school students in Brazil and Chile. The average score in mathematics for the lowest quintile of Cuban students was higher than the mean score in Brazil or Chile (Carnoy & Marshall, 2005).

This is not to suggest that equalizing income distribution by itself would increase the performance of students in a country or a state; rather, it seems that there are factors associated with more equal income distribution likely to make education better for most students, not just those from low-income families. These factors are the following:

1 In countries with more equal income distribution, family and community resources related to children's academic performance are more equally distributed, making children more alike socially and academically, and therefore more likely to be treated more equally by institutions such as the health care system and the schools.
2 In countries with more equal income distribution, the variation in school resources, such as teacher education and the quantity of school supplies going to schools with children of lower and higher social class, is smaller than in countries with more unequal income distribution – that is, the distribution of human capital is likely more equal, so that the availability of human capital (more able teachers) is greater across schools. This implies that schools in countries with more equal income distribution catering to lower-income students are more likely to have more equal school resources compared to schools catering to higher-income students (Chiu & Khoo, 2005, Table 2).
3 In countries with more equal income distribution, students are less likely to be clustered in school with students like them socioeconomically. That is, student bodies are more likely to be mixed socioeconomically, with a higher percentage of disadvantaged students mixed in with students from more advantaged families in the same school (Chiu & Khoo, 2005, Table 2).
4 Because of the previous three conditions, countries with more equal income distribution are likely to provide more school resources to students from disadvantaged backgrounds, both because they are more likely to be mixed in with students from higher socio-economic (SES) backgrounds and because school resources (mainly human capital) are distributed more equally across schools.
5 Because of conditions 1 and 2, it could be easier politically for governments to convince higher-income taxpayers to spend public revenue on the education of lower-income students in more economically equal societies, since spending on disadvantaged students is more closely related to the spending required to improve the education of higher-income taxpayers' own children.

Evidence on the distribution of students and resources among schools in Latin America

The way that students and school resources are distributed across schools in various countries has not been a major concern of policy makers until very recently. It is difficult to say whether the distribution of resources has a major impact on average school quality, or whether the distribution reflects more generally how societies are organized to maximize human potential through public institutions such as schools, and that organization impacts school quality. The human capital model would argue that more equal distribution of investment in human capital should result in more equal distribution of income. But the relationship may go in the opposite direction – that is, the underlying historical, social, and political conditions that produced more unequal income distribution may have a powerful influence over the distribution of access to resources by lower and higher social class groups. Hence, human capital formation may be more the result of historical conditions related to the distribution of income and wealth rather than a major influence on that distribution.

Nevertheless, the distribution of students and school resources across schools provides an overall indicator of social values in various countries and, in some sense, the kind of educational and economic outcomes that might result from a continuation of such policies. Two reasonable indicators for these purposes are the concentration of students by social class in schools and the distribution of teachers' education (one measure of teaching capacity) across schools. Assuming that these two variables are also related to test score differences among students, they could be important in helping understand why students do less well academically when children and teachers are distributed unequally across schools. In a highly unequal society, when Indigenous students are clustered in schools and Indigenous groups have relatively little economic and political power, their schools get fewer resources, including less well-prepared and less experienced teachers.

The social class distribution of students in schools

Indicators of the distribution of students in school were taken from UNESCO's survey of Latin American third- and fourth-grade student performance in 13 countries in 1997 (LLECE, 1998).[4] Table 38.1 shows the mean fourth-grade mathematics score and the mean and variance of the average of schools' socioeconomic index in each of six Latin American countries – Argentina, Brazil, Chile, Colombia, Cuba, and Mexico. The school's socioeconomic index is measured here as an average of a principal component factor analysis using students' parental education, number of books in the household, and student reported frequency of work outside the home as factor loadings.[5] Because of the way the index is constructed (factor analysis), countries such as Brazil, with low average socioeconomic background (SES), have negative average school SES, and Argentina and Cuba, where parents' education is relatively high, have positive average school SES. Of particular interest to us is the standard deviation of school average SES in each country. The higher the standard deviation, the greater the variance of average school SES among schools in that country. Table 38.1 suggests that all the countries shown except Cuba have a high variation in average school SES. Chile's is somewhat lower than Argentina's, Brazil's (the highest), Colombia's, and Mexico's. Thus, most Latin American school systems are characterized by large variances among schools in the average socioeconomic background of the students attending them.

The variance of SES among schools in Cuba is much lower than in the other countries. One reason that this may be so is that in Cuba there is lower variation in individual students'

Table 38.1 Latin America: Average Fourth-Grade Mathematics Score, School Average Socioeconomic (SES) Index, and SES Index Standard Deviation, 1997

	Argentina	Brazil	Chile	Colombia	Cuba	Mexico
Mean fourth-grade mathematics score	286	278	269	261	358	266
SES index mean	0.47	−0.47	0.12	−0.37	0.90	−0.22
Standard deviation	0.82	0.85	0.75	0.83	0.49	0.81

Source: Carnoy, Gove, & Marshall (2007, Table 4.1a, SES factor).

socioeconomic background than in other countries. When there are smaller differences in SES among children in a country, schools are more likely to be similar, SES-wise, even when little attention is paid to where children from different social class groups go to school.

Furthermore, even when we control for individual students' socioeconomic background, the school average SES is significantly related to individual student performance and contributes in a major way to explaining the variation in individual student performance in Argentina, Brazil, Chile, and Mexico, but not in Cuba (Carnoy & Marshall, 2005).

A more vivid way of showing how concentrated students are by social class in the schools they attend in Latin America is to estimate the distribution of students by their SES in schools by their average student SES. We have these data for basic education (K–8) in Chile in the late 1990s (Table 38.2). The data in this table show that 90% of students whose families are in the top 10% socioeconomically attend schools whose students, on average, are in that same social group. More than 90% of students in the top 20% socioeconomically attend schools whose students, on average, are in the same social group. At the bottom of the social ladder, the numbers are not quite as stark, but more than 60% of students whose families are in the bottom 10% socioeconomically attend schools where the average social class is in the bottom 20%. Thus, at the bottom most of the lowest-income children attend schools with a high fraction of very low-income students, and, at the top, essentially all high SES students attend schools that have only high SES students.

School systems in most countries of the world are marked by concentrations of students with similar socioeconomic background across schools. Nevertheless, in Latin America, students are even more segregated into socially homogeneous schools than in developed countries or in places such as Asia, where students are more likely to attend more socially heterogeneous schools. In addition, in Latin American countries where there are important ethnic and racial minorities, these, too, tend to be concentrated in certain regions and towns and, therefore, schools. Many members of these minority groups live in large cities, but because of social class segregation, even in cities, their children tend to attend schools with children from the same ethnic/race group.

Social segregation under conditions where there is a relative scarcity of high-quality

Table 38.2 Chile: Distribution of Students Across Schools, by Socioeconomic Class of Students and Average Socioeconomic Class of Students in Schools, 1998

School SES Decile	Student's Socioeconomic Class Decile									
	I	II	III	IV	V	VI	VII	VIII	IX	X
I	38.0	19.8	16.1	9.2	6.5	4.3	3.0	1.9	1.1	0.2
II	23.4	18.0	17.5	12.7	10.3	6.8	6.0	3.0	1.9	0.5
III	16.4	14.5	15.7	14.3	12.9	8.8	8.9	5.3	2.5	0.7
IV	11.5	10.9	13.6	14.3	14.6	11.5	12.3	7.0	3.4	0.7
V	6.6	8.7	10.6	12.5	14.5	12.1	15.9	11.1	6.4	1.7
VI	3.4	4.2	5.5	9.0	12.7	12.2	19.1	17.7	12.8	3.5
VII	1.2	1.7	2.4	4.2	7.2	8.6	18.5	22.9	24.6	8.7
VIII	0.4	0.7	0.9	1.6	3.1	4.2	10.9	20.6	34.4	23.1
IX	0.0	0.1	0.0	0.3	0.6	0.9	2.2	8.9	28.9	58.0
X					0.1	0.0	0.5	1.2	8.2	89.9
Missing data	6.0	5.6	7.5	9.7	9.9	8.9	13.1	12.1	12.3	14.8

Source: González (2001).

teaching and other high-quality school resources means that students from low socio-economic/disadvantaged minority background families are likely to attend schools staffed by teachers with lower capacity and fewer non-teaching resources at their disposal. In contrast, places such as Cuba and South Korea have both better-developed teaching capacity relative to countries such as Mexico, Brazil, and Chile (see Schmidt et al., 2007, on the Korea–Mexico comparison, and Carnoy, Gove, & Marshall, 2007, on the Cuba, Brazil, and Chile comparison) and much less socially segregated school systems, which means that it is much more likely in those countries that students from different social classes attend the same school. The end result is that lower social class students in Cuba (this includes African Cuban children in Cuba) and Korea are much more likely than those in Argentina, Brazil, Chile, and Mexico to have well-prepared teachers and attend well-equipped schools.[6]

Race/ethnicity, class, and education

In addition to extreme class stratification, Latin American societies are marked by important race/ethnic divisions, which are partly reflected in the educational system even beyond the obvious connections between race/ethnicity and class. We have increasing evidence of educational race and ethnic gaps in Latin America, mainly in terms of educational attainment and of the relative achievement on tests of ethnic minority students in various Latin American countries.

Data for Indigenous groups throughout Latin America and for African Brazilians show that they have lower educational attainment than European-origin Latin Americans (Winkler & Cueto, 2004). This is the case even when controlling for socioeconomic background (SES), including rural location, although SES is a very important indicator of attainment differences even for disadvantaged minorities.

An exception to this norm is Cuba. Data are limited, but a comparison of education in the population older than 25 years in Brazil, Cuba, and the United States shows that, in Brazil in 1987, only 1% of Blacks, 2% of Mulattos, and 9% of Whites had completed college, compared to 11% of Blacks and 20% of Whites in the United States, and 3.5% of Blacks, 3.2% of Mulattos, and 4.4% of Whites in Cuba in 1981. The high school completion rates for Whites, Blacks, and Mulattos were equal at 10–11% in Cuba in 1981, compared to 14% for Whites, 5% for Blacks, and 8% for Mulattos in Brazil in 1987 (de la Fuente, 1998, Table 1). Similarly, equal proportions (22%) of the different race groups in Cuba were employed as professionals in the civilian labor force in the 1980s (Blacks constitute a high proportion of doctors, for example), whereas in Brazil Blacks and Mulattos were about one-third as likely to be professionals as Whites (3% versus 9%) (de la Fuente, Table 2).

Indigenous and Black students also score significantly lower on national tests. Using basic education test data in Chile, McEwan (2004) shows that Mapuche Indian students score 0.3–0.4 standard deviations lower than non-Indigenous students in the fourth grade and 0.4–0.5 standard deviations in the eighth grade. To put this in perspective, this gap is somewhat higher than the Indigenous–non-Indigenous gap in Bolivia (McEwan) and is less than the Black–White test score gap in the United States (Rothstein, 2004). McEwan estimates that about one-half of the fourth-grade test score gap for Mapuche students is attributable to their parents' lower SES, but that one-half can be attributed to differences in school and classroom characteristics (including average class/school SES). School/class differences are more important than parental characteristics in accounting for the lower Mapuche test scores in the eighth grade.

Many Mapuches live in Santiago, but many are still concentrated in and around Temuco, in Chile's Araucania region. A 2003 OECD report discusses the unequal treatment of Mapuches in that region, suggesting that vocational high schools there tend to prepare young Indians for low-wage service jobs even as they provide them with courses that focus on Mapuche history and identity (OECD, 2003).

We do not have data on test scores by race in Cuba, but, in Brazil, Mulattos, Blacks, and Indigenous peoples score lower on the national test (SAEB) applied to samples of fourth, eighth, and third-year secondary graders (Rosemberg, 2004). Black students score the lowest among these three groups, and the higher the grade the larger the test score gap between all three minority groups and White Brazilians. This is true despite a decline in the percentage of the sample represented by each minority group in the higher grades. That means that, even as lower-scoring (and poorer) minorities drop out of school, the achievement gap increases, suggesting that, as in Chile and Bolivia, the role of school quality differences in Brazil in the minority achievement gap increases with more years of schooling. One likely explanation for the gap is that African Brazilians are concentrated in low-income states with, on average, lower-quality public schools (as measured by the lower percentage of university-educated teachers) (Kotani, 2004; World Bank, 2001). As discussed below, there is solid evidence in Brazil that the proportion of university-educated teachers in basic education schools has a positive effect on student achievement.

In addition, a number of studies show that students in Indigenous schools score lower than Indigenous students in rural, non-Indigenous schools. Thus, concentrating Indigenous students with other Indigenous students may have a negative impact on their academic performance, perhaps because, as Kudó (2004) argues for Peru, the teachers sent to these schools are expected to deliver a bilingual, bicultural curriculum but are so poorly prepared that students end up learning little or nothing. In Mexico, the average on a national test of Spanish language for third-grade students in Indigenous schools in two states with large Indigenous populations – Chiapas and Guerrero – was 445, versus 489 scored by students in rural public schools. In Mexico as a whole, students in Indigenous schools scored 25 points lower in Spanish than third graders in rural public schools. However, in mathematics, the difference was much larger – 80 points less in Chiapas, 50 in Guerrero, and 45 in Mexico as a whole (422, versus 469 for students in rural public schools). Only 28% of students in Indigenous schools achieved the basic level or above compared to 49% in rural public schools (Backoff, Andrade, Sanchez, & Peón, 2007).

A recent study of Indigenous education in Mexico shows that, even within matching socio-economic class groups in rural areas, students in Indigenous schools score lower on a sixth-grade test and that one of the most important correlates of that lower score is teacher quality (Instituto Nacional de Evaluación Educativa [INEE], 2007). The study also shows that higher teacher quality has a bigger impact in Indigenous schools than in rural non-Indigenous schools.

Similarly, in Panama, in 2005, third-grade students in Indigenous schools scored 5 points lower in Spanish and 12 points lower in mathematics on a national test than students in rural public schools – this was about 0.4 to 0.75 standard deviations difference, respectively (Carnoy, Luschei, et al., 2007).

Student social class and the distribution of teacher capacity

In Latin America there may be considerable variation in teacher education. Teachers at the elementary level many be *normalistas* (high school graduates from normal high school plus a year of teacher certification, as in Panama), or graduates of pedagogical institutes (not universities) or graduates of universities. At the middle school level (basic secondary) or upper secondary levels, teachers usually have university education, but many older teachers do not, and many do not have subject matter degrees even at the upper secondary level. There is some evidence that teachers with university education (particularly with specialization in a subject matter, such as math) are better prepared to teach in middle and secondary grades (Carnoy, Luschei, et al., 2007), and even in primary school (Carnoy & Marshall, 2005). A detailed empirical study of the second phase of public primary schooling (fifth to eighth grades) in Brazil shows that the proportion of university trained teachers in a school has a positive, statistically significant effect on test score gains (Carnoy, Gove, Loeb, Marshall, & Socias, 2004).

Data on the distribution of teacher skills across schools with higher and lower SES students are hard to come by in Latin America, but we do have some indication that more skilled teachers generally teach higher SES students. For example, in Panama, in the lowest poverty quintile schools, only 46% of primary teachers had less than a university degree in 2005, whereas in the highest poverty quintile schools 70% had no university training (Carnoy, Luschei, et al., 2007). Teachers teaching in Panama's Indigenous schools have lower levels of education and are less experienced than teachers in rural schools (Carnoy, Luschei, et al., 2007). Seventy percent of teachers in Indigenous schools have no university training compared with 58% in rural schools as a whole. Sixty percent of third-grade teachers in Indigenous schools have only 1–5 years of experience compared to 21% low-experienced teachers in the third grades of rural schools. As mentioned earlier, a study of Indigenous education in Peru claims that teachers lack the training to teach in such schools (Kudó, 2004, p. 127).

Of course, teacher formal education does not fully measure quality differences among teachers. There is reason to believe that, beyond formal teacher education, teacher subject knowledge is also distributed unequally in Latin America. Studies in Mexico and Panama show that teachers who score lower on subject knowledge tests are more likely to teach in schools with students from low-income families (Carnoy, Luschei et al., 2007; Luschei, 2005).

One of the main problems in distributing teacher quality among schools is that most teachers want to teach near where they themselves grew up (Lankford, Loeb, & Wyckoff, 2002). If a local area produces very few or low-quality teachers, some new graduates must be assigned to schools in localities where they do not particularly want to teach. If the locality is low-income and Indigenous, with poorly prepared students who do not speak the dominant language and are difficult to teach, it makes it all the more complicated to retain young teachers from higher-income or urban localities. In most Latin American countries, teachers compete in *concursos* (job competitions) to move from one school to another, and there are few incentives for teachers to teach in difficult-to-reach or low-income localities. There, conditions in schools are poor and there is a strong likelihood that the least capable teachers end up teaching children who need the best-prepared teachers to acquire middle-class academic skills.

The argument that students from lower-income families are more likely to be in schools where teachers are less educated and have lower subject content knowledge extends to an even greater degree in Latin America when it comes to disadvantaged minority groups, such as Indigenous peoples and Blacks. This happens partly because they are most likely to be in the lowest income groups. But it is also because minority race/ethnic groups are the most socially marginalized in Latin America and hence have the least access to high-quality public resources, such as good schools and health care services. The history of African or Native American education in the United States has its parallels in African Latin American and Indigenous education in Latin America, despite the greater frequency there of intermarriage between those groups and Europeans.

Three features of post-1959 Cuban society worked to mitigate the differences between Blacks and Mulattos and Whites in the labor market and in schools much more than in Brazil.

The first is that the monetary rewards to most jobs in the Cuban economy vary little, so that the differences between high- and low-paying jobs are not great. In Brazil, income differences are large. Thus Cuba probably has reduced racial/ethnic differences by reducing *all* differences between social class groups. Blacks might still be at the bottom of the economic and social totem pole in Cuba, but the totem pole is very short.

The second is that from the beginning of the Revolutionary period in Cuba

> Manifestations of racism became socially unacceptable: they were both anti-national and anti-revolutionary.... Revolutionary Cuba was envisioned as a raceless society, one in which the color of one's skin would have no influence on one's opportunities. This was not merely rhetoric. For the most part, the government's social policies were color-blind and did open significant opportunities for all sectors of the population, regardless of race.
> (de la Fuente, 1998, p. 2)

This did not cleanse Cuban society of racism, which is apparently on the rise as the dollar economy and tourism have increased in the past 20 years. But 50 years of greater equality has permanently changed the racial discourse in Cuba.

Most important for this change was and is the equalizing force of Cuban education. The organization of Cuba's education system forms a sharp contrast to the types of teacher distributions in other Latin American countries (Carnoy, Gove, & Marshall, 2007). For the past 30–40 years, Cuba has had a highly trained teacher labor force that has met its teaching needs. Indeed, Cuba exports teachers for temporary assignments in other countries, including large numbers to Venezuela. Because the central government assigns teachers to schools, and there are many young teachers who come from rural areas and lower social class ex-urban areas, rural and ex-urban primary schools in Cuba are staffed with teachers who teach with similar skills to those teaching in urban Havana (Carnoy, Gove, & Marshall). The government is able to provide almost the same-quality schooling to rural and ex-urban students as to the children of university-educated urban dwellers.

Thus, even if a disproportionate number of Blacks in Cuba are likely to have gone to low-income schools in post-Revolutionary Cuba (because before and after 1959 they lived in the lowest-income housing), the quality of those schools in terms of teacher quality and the quality of facilities would not be very different than in an "upscale" urban school (Carnoy, Gove, & Marshall, 2007). The key is that the teachers teaching Black, low-income students are part of a well-trained teacher labor force and very similar to teachers in schools attended by children with highly educated parents. In addition, if African Cubans were more likely to have less-educated parents, the Cuban state would be more likely to intervene and compensate through extra-familial activities to offset the possibly less academically enriching conditions of their family life. In effect, a well-organized teacher training and teacher management system sets the context in which even the most marginalized children get education more equal to the children of economically and socially dominant groups than in societies such Brazil's or Chile's. Differences still persist in Cuba, but the most reliable studies of discrimination in Cuba suggest that they are greatly reduced (see de la Fuente, 1998, for a review of such studies). This has the effect of reducing variation in academic performance, educational attainment, and the type of jobs held by disadvantaged minorities compared to other Latin American countries, and, we believe, also enhances the average academic performance of all children in Cuban society.

Implications for multicultural education

Multicultural education, where it exists in Latin America, has generally provided schooling for Indigenous peoples, sometimes in their native language (Maya, Quechua, or Mapuche, for example). History and social studies courses in most Latin American countries emphasize their people's Indigenous, European and, in the Caribbean and Brazil, African roots. In the best of cases, such multicultural education can empower these ethnic groups and help them sense their importance in the national culture. It may also make learning in school easier for the children from these groups. Through empowerment, children and teachers should have more confidence in their "right" to do well academically and to be full participants in economic and social progress.

Nevertheless, this process is much more successful in a context where resources are made available to ensure that the children actually do learn more in school and that their communities participate in the country's economic progress. Thus, the main lessons of comparing the high degree of inequality and educational stratification in most Latin American societies with the much greater equality and reduced stratification in Cuba are two:

1. It is difficult to realize the positive effects of multicultural education when the society is highly stratified – pupils in marginalized Indigenous schools taught by teachers with low capacity, provided with few resources, and learning in settings that underscore their marginality to the rest of national society cannot hope to feel a sense of inclusion or potential success. Of course, rapid economic growth can facilitate social and economic mobility even in highly stratified societies, and students from poor families attending low-resource schools may still succeed academically and economically. But the probability of success is low even when the students are provided with multicultural education aiming to provide a well-developed sense of self to disadvantaged ethnic minorities.
2. In societies such as Cuba, which greatly reduce the differences in the quality of education provided to students from families with differing human, social, and cultural capital, and also reduce the differences in economic outcomes for individuals with different academic achievement, lower social class and disadvantaged minority students are much more likely to achieve relative success. In objective terms, they probably also gain a greater sense of inclusion in their national society, which, in turn, makes *their* children better learners. Even if such societies were without multicultural programs, disadvantaged minorities would do relatively better because of the national strategy of reducing differences between social class groups and reaching all children with high-quality education.

Communist societies have generally not made an effort to deal with racial and ethnic intolerance. Post-Tito Yugoslavia and the Bosnian war are just one example of this failure; others are continued discrimination against the Roma in Slovakia and continued anti-Semitism throughout Eastern Europe. Yet, according to several writers, overcoming racism has been part and parcel of Cuba's Revolutionary ideology, and, thanks to concrete economic and social gains for African Cubans, the efforts have had moderate success in overcoming deep-seated racism in Cuban society (see www.afrocuba.com).

All Latin American societies promote an ideology of meritocracy, social mobility, and equality for all, regardless of race, ethnicity, or social class background. Many promote multiculturalism. Brazil's face to the world for years had been one of a nation devoid of racism, where intermarriage created a mulatto society, and Brazil is now implementing affirmative action policies in university admissions. Yet extreme social class differences and educational systems that reflect these differences make the realization of these ideals difficult in practice. This chapter suggests that, for multiculturalism to work, socioeconomic differences and their expressions in the educational system need to be considerably smaller than they are. Reducing them will require much more than some quick fixes to the educational system – governments in these societies need to attack economic and social inequalities directly and with them the low quality and unequal distribution of resources to education.

Notes

1 The regression line in Figure 38.1 has a slope of 3.71 PISA mathematics points for every $1,000 of GDP/capita. To construct the database for Figure 38.1, we took the mean mathematics scores by country for the PISA 2003 test for all countries where students took that test. In addition, we added in the PISA 2000 scores for countries that took the 2000 test but not the 2003 test, and we imputed a PISA score for countries that took the TIMSS 2003 test but not the PISA 2000 or PISA 2003 test. The imputed PISA score was based on a regression of PISA 2003 mathematics scores on the TIMSS 2003 test score.
2 TIMSS has been administered to fourth and eighth graders in many countries, in 1995 (also to seventh graders in 1995), 1999, 2003, and most recently in 2007. TIMSS focuses on mathematics and science. PISA has also been administered in many countries – in this case to 15-year-olds – in 2000, 2003, and most recently in 2006. PISA focuses on mathematics, science, and reading. The tests have somewhat different purposes – TIMSS is more interested in assessing the effect of curriculum differences among countries, whereas the PISA is more concerned with how well students are learning the critical thinking skills needed for working in the 21st-century labor market.
3 For our estimates, we used a popular measure of income inequality named the Gini coefficient (after its originator, the Italian statistician Corrado Gini). The more equal the income distribution, the smaller the Gini coefficient, which varies between 0 and 1.
4 UNESCO Santiago, Chile, did a second survey of student achievement (third and sixth graders) in 2006. Students in the six countries performed similarly in relative terms, except that students in Chile and Mexico did relatively better in mathematics compared to 1997. Cuban students continued to outperform the others by a large amount (LLECE, 2008).
5 Average school SES is constructed by averaging individual student components of SES in each school.
6 Even with equal salaries and class sizes, when teachers can choose where they teach, they tend to be less attracted to remote poorer areas with few cultural attractions and fewer prospects of marriage. Further, teachers around the world prefer to teach more capable students who come from homes with more academic resources.

References

Arias, O., Yamada, G., & Tejerina, L. (2004). Education, family background, and racial earnings inequality in Brazil. *International Journal of Manpower, 25*(3/4), 355–374.
Backoff, E., Andrade, E., Sanchez, A., & Peón, M. (2007). *El aprendizaje del español, las matemáticas, las ciencias naturales, y las ciencias sociales en la educación básica en México: Tercero de primaria* [Student achievement in Spanish, mathematics, natural sciences, and social sciences in basic education in Mexico: Third grade]. Mexico, DF: Instituto Nacional de Evaluación Educativa (INEE).
Carnoy, M., Beteille, T., Brodziak, I., Loyalka, P., & Luschei, T. (2008). *Do countries paying teachers higher relative salaries have higher student mathematics achievement?* Amsterdam: International Education Association (IEA).
Carnoy, M., Gove, A., Loeb, S., Marshall, J., & Socias, M. (2004). *How schools and students respond to school*

improvement programs: The case of Brazil's PDE. Unpublished manuscript, Stanford University, School of Education, Stanford, CA.

Carnoy, M., Gove, A. K., & Marshall, J. (2007). *Cuba's economic advantage*. Stanford, CA: Stanford University Press.

Carnoy, M., Luschei, T., Lynch, D., Marshall, J., Naranjo, B., Ruby, A., et al. (2007). *Improving Panama's educational system for the 21st century economy and society*. Unpublished manuscript, University of Pennsylvania, Graduate School of Education, Philadelphia.

Carnoy, M., & Marshall, J. (2005). Cuba's academic performance in comparative perspective. *Comparative Education Review, 49*(2), 230–261.

Carnoy, M., Santibañez, L., Maldonado, A., & Ordorika, I. (2002). Barreras de entrada a la educación superior y a oportunidades profesionales para la población indígena Mexicana [Barriers to entry in higher education and professional job opportunities for Mexico's indigenous population]. *Revista Latinoamerica de Estudios Educativos* [Latin American Journal of Educational Studies], *32*(3), 9–43.

Chiu, M. M., & Khoo, L. (2005). Effects of resources, inequality, and privilege bias on achievement: Country, school, and student level analyses. *American Educational Research Journal, 42*(4), 575–603.

de la Fuente, A. (1998). *Recreating racism: Race and discrimination in Cuba's "special period"* (Cuba Paper Briefing Series, No. 18). Washington, DC: Georgetown University, Center for Latin American Studies, Caribbean Project. Retrieved October 22, 2008, from http://www.cubastudygroup.org/index.cfm?FuseAction=Experts.Detail&Expert_id=34

Garcia Aracil, A., & Winkler, D. (2004). Educación y ethnicidad en Ecuador [Education and ethnicity in Ecuador]. In D. Winkler & S. Cueto (Eds.), *Ethnicidad, raza, género, y educación en América Latina* [Ethnicity, race, gender, and education in Latin America] (pp. 55–92). Washington, DC: Programa de Promoción de la Reforma Educativa en América Latina y el Caribe (PREAL).

Gonzalez, P. (2001). *Estructura institucional, recursos, y gestión en el sistema escolar chileno* [Institutional structure, resources, and management in the Chilean education system]. Santiago, Chile: Ministerio de Educación.

Instituto Nacional de Evaluación Educativa (INEE). (2007). *La educación para poblaciones en contextos vulnerables: Informe anual, 2007* [Education for disadvantaged populations: Annual report, 2007]. Mexico, DF: Author.

Kotani, K. (2004). *Growing together: Regional disparities in primary education in Brazil* (Monograph). Unpublished master's thesis, Stanford University School of Education, Stanford, CA.

Kudó, I. (2004). La educación indígena en el Perú: Cuando la oportunidad habla una sola lengua [Indigenous education in Peru: When opportunity speaks a single language]. In D. Winkler & S. Cueto (Eds.), *Ethnicidad, raza, género, y educación en América Latina* [Ethnicity, race, gender, and education in Latin America] (pp. 93–132). Washington, DC: Programa de Promoción de la Reforma Educativa en América Latina y el Caribe (PREAL).

Laboratorio Latinoamericano de Evaluación de la Calidad de la Educación (LLECE). (1998). *Primer estudio internacional comparativo sobre lenguaje, matemática y factores asociados en tercero y cuarto grado* [First international comparative study on language, mathematics, and related factors in the third and fourth grades]. Santiago, Chile: UNESCO.

Laboratorio Latinoamericano de Evaluación de la Calidad de la Educación (LLECE). (2008). *Segundo estudio regional comparativo y explicativo (SERCE)* [Second comparative and explanatory regional study]. Santiago, Chile: UNESCO.

Lankford, H., Loeb, S., & Wyckoff, J. (2002). Teacher sorting and the plight of urban schools: A descriptive analysis. *Educational Evaluation and Policy Analysis, 24*(1), 37–62.

Luschei, T. (2005). *In search of good teachers: Patterns of teacher quality in two Mexican states*. Unpublished doctoral dissertation, Stanford University School of Education, Stanford, CA.

McEwan, P. J. (2004). La brecha de puntajes obtenidos en las pruebas por los niños indígenas en Sudamérica [The test score gap for indigenous children in South America]. In D. Winkler & S. Cueto (Eds.), *Ethnicidad, raza, género, y educación en América Latina* [Ethnicity, race, gender, and education in Latin America] (pp. 283–313). Washington, DC: Programa de Promoción de la Reforma Educativa en América Latina y el Caribe (PREAL).

Organisation for Economic Co-operation and Development (OECD). (2003). *Reviews of national policies for education: Chile*. Paris: Author.

Programme for International Student Assessment (PISA). (2004). *Learning for tomorrow's world: First results from PISA 2003*. Paris: OECD.

Psacharopoulos, G., & Patrinos, H. A. (1994). *Indigenous peoples and poverty in Latin America*. Washington, DC: World Bank.

Rosemberg, F. (2004). Desigualidades de raza y género en el sistema educacional Brasileno [Race and gender inequalities in the Brazilian educational system]. In D. Winkler & S. Cueto (Eds.), *Ethnicidad, raza, género, y educación en América Latina* [Ethnicity, race, gender, and education in Latin America] (pp. 239–282). Washington, DC: Programa de Promoción de la Reforma Educativa en América Latina y el Caribe (PREAL).

Rothstein, R. (2004). *Class and schools*. Washington, DC: Economic Policy Institute.

Schmidt, W. H., Tatto, M. T., Bankov, K., Blömeke, S., Cedillo, T., Cogan, L., et al. (2007). *The preparation gap: Teacher education for middle school mathematics in six countries (MT21 report)*. Retrieved October 22, 2008, from http://usteds.msu.edu/MT21Report.pdf

Winkler, D., & Cueto, S. (Eds.). (2004). *Ethnicidad, raza, género, y educación en América Latina* [Ethnicity, race, gender, and education in Latin America]. Washington, DC: Programa de Promoción de la Reforma Educativa en América Latina y el Caribe (PREAL).

World Bank. (n.d.). *World development indicators*. Retrieved December 12, 2007, from http://devdata.worldbank.org/dataonline

World Bank. (2001). *Brazil: Teachers, development and incentives. A strategic framework* (Report No. 20408 BR). Washington, DC: World Bank, Human Development Department.

39

Achieving quality education for Indigenous peoples and Blacks in Brazil

Petronilha Beatriz Gonçalves e Silva
Federal University of São Carlos, Brazil

Sonia Stella Araújo-Olivera
Autonomous University of the State of Morelos, Mexico

When Brazilian Indigenous and Black descendants of Africans ask for the teaching of their respective histories and cultures throughout the educational system and demand that education be made accessible for their people, they are thinking of more than recognition and reparations. They would like to affect and to influence the education of all Brazilians by adding a multicultural perspective to Brazilian education. The purpose of this chapter is to describe the struggles and achievements of Indigenous peoples and Blacks for educational opportunities and a high-quality education.

Whether or not educators are aware of the demands of Indigenous peoples and Blacks, they face problems related to approximately 50% of the Brazilian population, which consists of 49.5% Blacks[1] and approximately 0.4% Indigenous peoples. Educational policies directed towards these groups have implications for the education of all citizens because any measure that focuses on one group affects all the others.

Education is a fundamental tool for full citizenship in a multiethnic and multiracial nation such as Brazil. Educated citizens are prepared to participate in decisions concerning society and are able to articulate and negotiate the desires, interests, and needs of their own social, ethnic, and racial groups as well as those of others.

When the 1988 Brazilian Constitution was written, the earliest constitutional determinations to correct educational inequalities and to recognize the value of the history and cultures of all Brazilian ethnic and racial groups[2] were established. This legislation – enacted in response to the demands of Blacks and Indigenous peoples – supports national policies for curriculum reform. In the 1990s, the Ministry of Education implemented measures to respond to the ethnic, social, and historical needs of the 220 different Brazilian Indigenous groups. The first policy addressing the Black population, which is made up of descendants of enslaved Africans who were brought forcibly to Brazil from the 16th to the 19th centuries, was not issued until 2003.

To understand the context for the formulation of these policies, it is important to focus on the proposals and initiatives of the Black and Indigenous peoples' movements, which use different approaches to guarantee quality education for youth and adults (Gonçalves e Silva, 2003). The struggle of Indigenous peoples and Blacks is a continuing resistance against the dehumanization they have experienced since the 16th century.

The colonization process initiated by the Portuguese and the Spanish in Latin America during the 16th century – imposing what they called civilization – still has severe physical and mental consequences. The invasion of the territory the Europeans called the Americas, the genocide inflicted, the cultures violated, and the attempts to dehumanize the Indigenous peoples and Blacks continue to damage identities, which is reinforced by the nation's tacit or explicit policies. These continuing injuries displace peoples from their ancestral homelands, destabilize social and political organizations, and deprive individuals of the knowledge needed to construct their future. It is within this context that readers should situate the long struggle by Indigenous and Black Brazilians for education and the other rights which are due to all citizens.

It was through forceful encounters and shocks with the Indigenous peoples and with the Africans whom they enslaved – and through repeated attempts to destroy them – that the Europeans discovered ways of being human that were very different from their own (Lazo, 1989; Ortiz, 1942). The Europeans could not easily understand the ways of being which they observed among Indigenous peoples and Africans. Consequently they believed that Africans and Indigenous peoples were different and exotic. The Europeans couldn't imagine that Africans and Indigenous peoples shared worldviews.

The desire to transform the worlds they tried to dominate into European constructions led the colonizers to force Indigenous peoples and Africans to relinquish their cultures and identities. However, they were not as successful as they had envisioned. The Europeans then started to demean Indigenous peoples and Blacks and to consider their characteristics invisible. Incapable of making Indigenous peoples and Black Brazilians disappear physically and culturally, the colonizers put forth – according to the "tale of miscegenation" – the myth of social democracy in Brazil, intending to make cultural characteristics that did not have European roots disappear.

Today society still tries to validate the claim that *mestizos* erased a part of their original ethnic-racial roots, those considered to be inferior by the society's dominant groups and by those who assimilated its ideas and ideals. However, as Picotti (1989) observes, the history and culture of the different peoples who live both in Brazil and in other Latin American nations open up spaces for exchanges and the re-creation of cultures, in spite of ideological and political efforts to establish the belief that "all are one and the same thing" (pp. 142–146). This occurs because history always develops within cultures by cultivating, recognizing, and cherishing roots, establishing links with the primordial matrices, and re-creating meanings and ways of being and living.

The history of Latin America and its nations – in which different cultures have experienced conflict and communicated – has been constructed in the midst of the re-creation of what it means to be human and within diverse ways of living. The history of these nations is the result of exchanges among different cultures. According to Gonçalves and Gonçalves e Silva (2006), the history of each particular social and ethnic-racial group results, among other processes, in the interaction with other peoples and their unique characteristics. Their common history is generated by the intersection of different ways of being and living.

The history of each Latin American people is manifested in the tension with the European-rooted civilization, which sees itself as universal and primordial. A host of other possible ways of being human, of thinking, acting, making things, living together, and struggling together, interact with European culture. In this interplay, one common history has emerged, one that does not erase the unique characteristics of different racial and ethnic groups.

It is in this interplay involving impositions, resistances, re-creations, and communication that the Latin American *pedagogica* has developed. It is a set of relationships in which educational processes are devised, working within the tension between domination and liberation, abrogation and recognition of identities, and education for citizenship or for submission – processes in which the oppressed confirm their humanity before those who attempt to dehumanize them (Dussel, 1987; P. Freire, 1978). It is in this interplay that curriculum policies have been formulated in Brazil. The goal of these policies is to recognize the historical and political development of Indigenous and Afro-Brazilians as they overcome social, ethnic, and racial inequalities, obtain cultural and identity rights, and reverse the mutual lack of knowledge as well as the tense relationships among groups.

Indigenous peoples' history and culture in Brazilian education

Since the 1990s, when the Ministry of Education established a national Indigenous education educational policy, the Indigenous peoples' demands and proposals have begun to be recognized in Brazil. This policy was conceived as a kind of education based on principles such as bilingualism, specificity, and interculturality aiming, among other things, to guarantee the physical, linguistic, and cultural survival of Indigenous peoples, to support their exercise of rights, and to make it possible for them to communicate and interact with other ethnic, racial, and social groups.

Nevertheless, there is a risk in carrying out homogenizing measures and of implementing actions that will continue to convert schooling among Indigenous populations into an instrument of oppression in the transition from local experiences to a national policy supported by government funding and organized by technicians or bureaucrats. These initiatives do not reflect knowledge of the diversity and characteristics of Indigenous peoples, as has been pointed out by Indigenous activists and their allies in their struggle (see, among others, Aiwa, 1997; J. Freire, 2004; Grupioni, 1997, 2004, 2007).

The success of legal measures that take into account the rights of marginalized groups is influenced by the prejudices and representations which underestimate and demean them. Thus, municipal and state powers responsible for implementing the law often fail to generate the necessary conditions for the objectives that it is proposed should be attained, even though Bill 9394/1996 of the National Education Guidelines and Principles (Brazil, 1996) complies with the demands of the Indigenous Movement for elementary public Indigenous schools, the National Council of Education defines the guidelines to implement them (Brazil, 1999), and the National Plan for Education establishes clear goals.

In order to correct possible distortions and to support the implementation of legal measures, the Ministry of Education has been circulating informative guidelines, such as the Parameters in Action: Indigenous School Education (Ministério da Educação, 2002), References for the Training of Indigenous Teachers (Monte & Grupioni, 2002), National Curriculum Reference for Indigenous Schools (Ministério da Educação, 1998), and Materials for the Training of Indigenous Teachers in the Field of Language (Maia, 2006). Indigenous organizations, research institutions, and universities concerned about the training of Indigenous teachers have also helped with the development and dissemination of information and orientation through different channels. Among them are the Notes on Indigenous School Education (UNEMAT, 2005–2008), which publishes papers by Indigenous teachers, instructors, and researchers.

These works are designed to fill a gap in the literature dealing with specific topics of Indigenous education, such as the need for schools to be shaped by Indigenous populations and not imposed on them, bilingual teaching, the fostering and encouragement of Indigenous forms of wisdom and knowledge and everyday practices of each group, and concern for the preservation of cultural practices and natural resources. The other important topics are introduction to scientific knowledge (recognized by society at large and indispensable for the formation of full citizens); the need for a mediating space between communities and the political-social system of the Brazilian nation; the creation of a space for learning to communicate with different social, racial, and ethnic groups; and teaching methodologies for intercultural education.

The expectations for teacher training courses for Indigenous education are very high. These courses are expected to encourage research and studies of topics such as literacy in the native language, the meaning of infancy and of being a child among Indigenous groups, cooperation, sustainable land work, traditional sports, medicinal herbs, and rituals and spirituality. Teachers are also expected to develop teaching materials in native languages, teach bilingually, develop methodologies to work with Indigenous families and communities, be knowledgeable about sustainable development, and know about the ancient practices of the communities and contemporary agribusiness demands (Januário, 2004; Mendonça, Zorrthea, & Torres, 2005; Reider & Gestera, 2005).

Programs responsible for the education of Indigenous teachers are also expected to encourage pedagogical and political debates and interchanges that strengthen Indigenous teachers' organizations. An important goal of these organizations is to influence the policies and implement dialogue with non-Indigenous organizations and make alliances with them. These organizations have already accomplished several achievements, such as the establishment of Indigenous education councils at local levels, whose goal is to inform the general population about and to provide leadership for Indigenous education. The establishment of a national council for Indigenous education and the ongoing discussions and initiatives on affirmative action for Indigenous peoples in higher education are among recent efforts undertaken by these organizations (Grupioni, 2007; Mendonça et al., 2005; Paresi, 2005).

Indigenous organizations have taken an active role in monitoring student progress since the adoption of affirmative action policies for Indigenous peoples. They also participated in evaluations of the experiences of public universities that adopted quotas for Indigenous people to determine whether these universities have high academic standards and attain the standards established by Indigenous peoples.

For Indigenous people, high-quality education in primary and secondary schools and in higher education means allowing for the appropriation and production of scientific knowledge, fostering citizenship skills needed to act in society, cherishing Indigenous identity and ways of life, and respect for and support for Indigenous historical projects. It is an education that reflects the realities of different communities, discusses controversial topics related to life in society, creates conditions for interchange between Indigenous wisdom and other forms of knowledge, and produces and disseminates knowledge for society at large in the critical interchanges among academic exigencies and Indigenous peoples' expectations (Grzybowski et al., 2004; Universidade do Estado de Mato Grosso, 2005).

There is still much work to be done by educational institutions in order for them to offer the education required by Indigenous peoples, taking into consideration the available literature and reports on their school and college experiences. To attain excellence, educational institutions must: (a) recognize the diversity of Brazilian Indigenous peoples and recognize the weakness and limitations of the representations by non-Indigenous perspectives of Indigenous worlds; (b) understand that the destruction of cultures and the disappearance of Indigenous languages jeopardize identities, including the national identity; (c) learn to integrate oral and written discourse pedagogically; (d) create means to produce and disseminate Indigenous knowledge in collaboration with Indigenous organizations; (e) facilitate dialogue among cultures; and (f) search for ways to address the numerous questions, interests, desires, and needs of an ethnically diverse society.

High-quality education of Indigenous groups in Brazil is still hindered by the consequences of the destruction and oppression which began with the colonizing process in the 16th century. Education is seen by Indigenous people as a way to overcome this legacy. This is not a point of view exclusive to Brazil; it is shared by Indigenous peoples throughout Latin America as well as people who live on other continents. Since the 1970s, Indigenous teachers and their non-Indigenous allies have worked to create and consolidate basic principles for Indigenous education. The importance of learning with one another is among these principles (Garcia, 2005; Grupioni, 2007; Winkler & Cueto, 2004).

International support has been very important for initiatives designed to improve education for Indigenous groups in Latin America, including Brazil. In 1989, Convention 169 on Indigenous and Tribal Peoples of the International Labour Organization consolidated Indigenous rights and recognized their collective rights and the individual rights of Indigenous people. Indigenous people also have benefited from the initiatives of the United Nation's Working Group on Indigenous Populations. In September 2007, the United Nations also approved a declaration of the rights of Indigenous peoples. Anaya (2007) states that different agreements and international rules have proved essential for all Indigenous peoples, and are central for their growth as citizens and for attaining rights related to self-determination, cultural integrity, possession of their lands and natural resources, social well-being and development, and self-government.

The Ford Foundation program "Pathways to Higher Education" has been another international source of support for university education for Indigenous populations in Mexico, Peru, Chile, and Brazil. This program offered financial support for higher education designed for Indigenous students and produced positive results. Most Indigenous students involved in it have strived to attain knowledge that will benefit and empower their communities. Some institutions that formally recognize Indigenous goals in their public values and plans face strong resistance from teachers and professors who fail to integrate Indigenous knowledge into the curriculum. This resistance has harmed intercultural dialogue, which recognizes the value of Indigenous perspectives on knowledge and is fundamental for effective Indigenous education (Paiva & Fonseca, 2006).

As Brazilian Indigenous leaders point out, as long as Brazil does not recognize itself as a pluralistic or multicultural society, it runs the risk of developing educational programs that suppress Indigenous identities by considering their cultures inferior, educating them to defend interests that are inconsistent with their own, and opposing Indigenous ownership of traditional lands (de Souza Lima & Barroso-Hoffmann, 2004).

Da Silva (1987) and da Silva and Grupioni (1995) have written valuable work on Indigenous education. They state that success in Indigenous education depends upon the successful education of non-Indigenous students. Non-Indigenous students must interact with Indians regarding issues such as matters of citizenship and the need to know that Indians are not fated to disappear, as some people continue to think. In addition, non-Indigenous students must learn about and value Indigenous cultures, history, and contributions to the Brazilian nation.

In 1987, in partnership with the São Paulo Pro-Indian Commission, da Silva examined criticism and negative images in classroom materials, and put forth a proposal for reforming elementary education, with the goal of overcoming stereotyped views of Indigenous peoples. Realizing that in order to know reality in all its dimensions it is necessary to include the point of view of the oppressed, several scholars point out that Indigenous problems concern all citizens. Consequently, the entire population must become familiar with their social organizations and rights and participate in their defense. For that reason, Indigenous peoples' organizations proposed the introduction of the study of the history and cultures of Brazilian

Indigenous peoples in the entire Brazilian educational system. Recently this demand has been addressed by the legislation enacted in Bill 11.465/2008 (Brazil, 2008).

In 1995, da Silva and Grupioni organized a collaborative publication that, in the words of the Ministry of Education, "resets Indigenous populations in the course of history" (p. 8). Twenty-two authors addressed the question of living together with difference from a multidisciplinary and multicultural perspective. The objectives of the publication were to make information on Indigenous societies available in order to create conditions for cross-cultural communication among Native Brazilians and non-Indigenous groups to reinforce the concept that difference means wealth and that the coexistence of differences is essential in a democratic nation. This book has become an important reference for teachers, professors, educators, and researchers about Indigenous worlds and multiculturalism. The key idea in this publication is that the problems faced by a segment of the population do not concern that part only, but involve other groups as well. This same position is taken in the demands and proposals by the Afro-Brazilian population.

Afro-Brazilian and African history and culture in Brazilian education

This section of this chapter discusses ways in which the Black Movement attempts to influence education in Brazil. Ninety million Black people live in Brazil, the largest Black population outside the African continent. The presence of their ways of being, of living, thinking, and celebrating their African roots, is evident in Brazilian history and is undeniable in the everyday life of the nation. According to Araújo (1986, pp. 68–69): "In all levels of existence, even though they are geographically Latin American, [Brazilians are] much more African than one may at first realize. . . . The Brazilian way of being, in its originality, represents one more of the ways of being African." Nevertheless, economic and educational inequalities have negatively affected Black Brazilians and placed them at a serious disadvantage.

These inequalities are the result of a society which – although characterized by ethnic and racial diversity – values its European roots above others, and which basically sees itself as White (Carone & Bento, 2002). This self-image and these feelings have led to strategies that tried to eliminate Blacks physically, morally, and culturally. Indigenous peoples have had a similar experience in Brazil. But, since this is impossible, an effort has been made to assimilate Blacks into the physical and intellectual White-European patterns, and to the interests and ethics of a segment of the population whose goal is to be dominant (Carone & Bento; Gonçalves & Gonçalves e Silva, 2000, 2006).

The introduction of Afro-Brazilian history and culture into Brazilian schools as part of a state curriculum policy, in the view of the Black Movement, could be a way to change this situation. That's why Federal Bill 10639/2003 (Brazil, 2003), which introduced the mandate to teach Afro-Brazilian history and culture in the elementary and middle schools, has been so well received by Blacks.

In 2004, the National Council of Education (CNE) interpreted, regulated, and introduced the addenda to the Guidelines and Principles for National Education so that they could be implemented by the educational system. The goals of the Guidelines and Principles are to recognize and cherish the participation of enslaved Africans and their descendants in the making of the Brazilian nation, to combat racism and all kinds of discrimination, and to educate Brazilians so they will support positive ethnic and racial relations. The Report CNE/CP 3/2004 (Brazil, 2004a) and the Resolution CNE/CP 1/2004 (Brazil, 2004b), which deal with the National Curriculum Guidelines for the Education of Ethnic-Racial Relations and for the

Teaching of Afro-Brazilian History and Culture, were then approved (Ministério da Educação, 2004).

Without state intervention, Afro-Brazilians – as well as Indigenous peoples – would face extreme difficulties trying to change the patterns of inequality that affect them, given the conditions of exclusion imposed on them by a discriminatory and racist society. The struggle of the Black Movement for an education that recognizes and cherishes Black people's history and their ethnic and racial cultures is a movement for positive social and ethnic-racial relations that empower each Brazilian citizen to participate on an equal footing in decisions that concern all citizens.

Since the beginning of the 20th century, the distorted view of ethnic-racial relationships – perpetuated by the myth that Brazil was a racial democracy – has been criticized by Black Movement organizations. Throughout this century, the kind of education envisioned by Afro-Brazilians is expressed in their various initiatives, especially in teacher education courses offered both to members of the movement and to other teachers. The Black Movement's ideas and ideals have been defended by activists, manifested in pedagogical experiences, and documented by researchers. Members of the Black Movement, in their organizations and as students or instructors in schools and universities, have generated initiatives that offered theoretical and practical references that supported the formulation of curriculum policies.

The ongoing and progressive action of Black activists has developed principles that affect the national project of education, which has finally resulted in the acknowledgment of the diversity within Brazilian society. By participating in political meetings and courses, organizing alternative instructional materials and texts, and addressing demands to educational authorities, Blacks educated themselves politically and received support to develop studies at all levels of the educational system (dos Santos, 2007; Gonçalves, 1994; Pinto, 1993). According to Gonçalves e Silva (2004) these educational principles are: facing and overcoming forms of racism and intolerance; rejecting the homogeneity of forms of knowledge believed to be superior; recognizing of values, ways of reasoning, and specific behaviors of different ethnic and racial groups; special treatment in specific situations; and recognizing of the unique conditions of different ethnic, racial, and social groups. Since 2003, these principles have been present in affirmative action policies, which assign quotas to Blacks in the majority of the 50 public universities that adopted the policy. These policies complement Report CNE/CP 3/2004, and are often articulated in relationship to it.

In the 1990s, the Ministry of Education began to mention the diversity of the Brazilian population in documents addressed to school teachers. Between 1996 and 2002, the Ministry circulated the National Curriculum Parameters (PCNs), which clearly discuss cultural pluralism. The PCNs have offered for the first time guidelines for the introduction of classroom materials that originated from different Brazilian ethnic and racial groups (Ministério da Educação, 1997, 1998). However, the PCNs have failed to analyze the tense ethnic and racial relations in Brazil, especially those involving Blacks and Whites, which has led some observers to believe that intergroup problems are limited to the educational setting, thus contributing to the ideology of racial democracy (Munanga, 1996).

In 1998, the Inter-Ministry Working Group on the Situation of Blacks asked the Ministry of Education to publish additional materials for schools and teachers. Professor Munanga and 11 other educators and researchers from the Black Movement were invited to develop a book on the Afro-Brazilian racial question and culture (Munanga, 1999). This book – titled *Overcoming Racism at School* – emerged from the protests and proposals from the Black Movement, particularly those put forth in 1995 during the celebrations of the 300th anniversary of the death of Zumbi, the last leader of the Quilombo Palmares. These protests may be summarized as: fighting against the centuries-old exclusion of the Black population from schools; condemning humiliations and outrages suffered by Black students at all levels of teaching because of racist biases, attitudes, texts, and pedagogical materials; the urgent necessity for re-education about ethnic and racial relations; ignorance among different ethnic/racial groups about other groups and their own heritage; and the necessity of overcoming such ignorance in order to create a democratic, egalitarian society. As Munanga (1999) observes in the introduction:

> Recovering the collective memory and the history of the Black community is not only of interest to students of Black origin [for] the culture we feed on every day is the result of all ethnic groups which, in spite of the unequal conditions in which they have developed, have contributed each in its own way to the accumulation of economic wealth and the making of society and the national identity. (p. 16)

With the publication of *Overcoming Racism at School*, the Ministry of Education has assumed the responsibility to fight racism at school and in pedagogical relationships. The president of the Republic himself,[3] when presenting the book's second edition, said: "There is no racial prejudice that can resist the light shed by knowledge and objective study" (Munanga, 2000, p. 3). He stressed that it is imperative that "education be of quality, that it may open minds and promote respect for cultural differences; [and] it is indispensable that curricula and textbooks be free of any racist contents or intolerant stances" (p. 9).

With the publication of *Overcoming Racism in School*, the requirements of international agreements that Brazil had signed with organizations, such as the UNESCO 1960 Conventions and the World Conference Against Racism, Racial Discrimination, Xenophobia and Related Intolerance of 2001, were met. A similar initiative was made in 2002 with the appointment by the president and the minister of education of Indigenous and Black members to the CNE, both of which were nominated by the Indigenous and Black movements.[4] In 2003, these actions reached a high point when the newly elected Brazilian president[5] signed his first law, the previously mentioned Bill 10639/2003. Another high point was reached when the CNE argued that the study of Afro-Brazilian history and culture should be articulated with the study of African history and culture, and that these two subjects should become mandatory throughout Brazil (Ministério da Educação, 2004).

The goal of curriculum reform was not to make Brazilians more erudite, but rather to encourage them to re-educate themselves about ethnic and racial relations in Brazil. The CNE also stated that studying ethnic and racial relations is essential for fulfilling the constitutional requirements and the National Education Guidelines and Principles regarding rights to citizenship, and the right for all citizens to know the people responsible for the making of the nation. Consequently, the CNE has concluded that the Guidelines for Teaching Afro-Brazilian History and Culture and for the Education of Ethnic-Racial Relations have to be implemented in all levels of teaching, from preschool to the tertiary level, if their objectives are to be achieved.

Fulfilling these requirements has not been easy. Teachers initially complained about the lack of adequate school materials. The Education Ministry has tried to fill this gap with publications, debate forums, seminars, and teacher education courses. Most state and city councils of education have not yet changed their practices to make them consistent with the social realities of their educational systems. Believing that Brazil is a racial democracy, many educators and researchers, such as Maggie (2005–2006), argue that this curriculum policy promotes racism.

It is within this framework that teachers committed to the struggle for a just society for Blacks and other groups – based on previous experiences, especially in the 1970s, 1980s, and

1990s – conceptualize educational projects to implement Report CNE/CP 3/2004. Several other projects have been put into practice, supported by courses offered by universities, government education departments, and Black Movement groups. These activities focus on what has been called *Africanities*, that is, forms of knowledge and meanings generated within the African continent, during the Middle Passage, in the transference of thoughts and technologies to non-African territories, and in Black people's fight for liberation and against racism.

What is the meaning of Africanities in the education of Brazilian citizens? Answers include: to overcome ideologies that assign a superior position to civilizations rooted in Europe and an inferior one to African, Indigenous, and Aboriginal civilizations; to identify and disseminate information regarding the impact and significance of the contributions of Africa on the other continents by means of specific forms of knowledge, technologies, and values produced by the enslaved and their descendants; and to encourage students to know and cherish the history and dignity of all human groups that make up the Brazilian nation, including immigrants. The goal is not to replace an ethnocentric, Eurocentric view with an African one, but to widen the focus of curricula to encompass Brazilian cultural, racial, social, and economic diversity. In order to achieve these goals, educators must work cooperatively with, and not apart from, social movements. The educational system and educational establishments have to engage in a dialogue with the Black Movement and with organizations that study and disseminate Black history and culture[6] so that antiracist pedagogies can be properly developed, applied, and evaluated.

What is required for educational excellence within the framework of antiracist pedagogies? In the first place, changes "in the discourses, reasoning, logic, gestures, postures, and ways of dealing with Black people" are required (Gonçalves e Silva, 2004, p. 390). Also required are strategies that will guarantee equal rights for all, as well as teaching strategies and activities that value the diversity of the characteristics that distinguish each ethnic and racial group from others. It is essential that the history and culture of all groups be recognized and appreciated, including those of Black people, which have been rejected rather than devalued (Ministério da Educação, 2004). The history and heritage of White Brazilians also has to be rewritten from a truthful standpoint that does not perpetuate a false superiority.

In order to offer high-quality education and to define the criteria to evaluate it in the perspective of participatory citizenship, the Report CNE/CP 3/2004 establishes the following principles: "political and historical awareness of diversity; strengthening of identities and rights; [and] educational actions fighting racism and discriminations" (Brazil, 2004a, pp. 18–19). The mandate to teach Afro-Brazilian and Indigenous peoples' history and culture, established by the Federal Bills 10639/2003 and 11465/2008, and the experiences of Indigenous education and the Black Movement initiatives for the education of Blacks are important contributions to Brazilian education.

Contributions of Blacks and Indians to national education

The Brazilian state has begun to take measures to establish a just society by considering the demands of Indigenous peoples and Blacks, who constitute almost half of Brazilians. However, some segments of society are resistant to change, including educational systems and institutions that frequently organize their work as if the nation were monocultural and all of its inhabitants should adapt a single worldview, namely that of an excluding society.

Meanwhile, Blacks and Indigenous groups make activism a space for the exercise of freedom and criticism in which they produce knowledge about and for their peoples and for society. For Blacks and Indigenous groups, attending school is not just an individual achievement; it is a practice of activism which brings with it academic performance and participation in society with autonomy, social commitment, and freedom to express their identities.

Advanced scientific and technical knowledge, while necessary, is not sufficient for Indigenous groups or Blacks to become students or scholars and to be trained as professionals and to exercise citizenship in the interest of the well-being of their people. In addition, it is necessary that one's own ethnic and racial roots be valued and cherished without undervaluing or belittling those of other groups. Opportunities to get to know other groups, to engage in dialogue with them, and to respect their identities are required.

The presence of Blacks and Indigenous groups in educational institutions, monitored even if at a distance by the Black and Indigenous peoples' movements, constrain institutional political plans, curricula, and pedagogical relationships. This constraining dynamic, however, is based on the belief that all, without distinction, must be educated, so that they may interact with one another with commitment, competence, and freedom in a multicultural and pluralistic society. This constraining occurs so that omissions, distortions, and inequalities vis-à-vis challenging identities are corrected for the benefit of humankind (King, 1999), and so that racism, the ideology of Whitening, and other oppressive supremacies are finally overcome.

Intercultural educational processes, as proposed by Indigenous peoples, and the dialogue among cultures – emphasized by groups of the Black Movement – make clear that dialogue is the fundamental practice for comprehending and dealing with or interacting with people who are different. For these processes and dialogues to take place, educational institutions must be willing to practice non-discrimination, and educators and students must be willing to stand up against inequalities. They must also be willing to overcome ethnocentrisms, deconstruct prejudices, and learn from and exchange knowledge with people of Indigenous, Black, European, and Asian roots. This kind of learning reaches far beyond the interpersonal relationships upon which it is based, and the social and pedagogical practices that it unleashes. It may influence cultures and policies of globalization, which very often become hegemonic, thus ignoring the diversity of peoples and nations (Banks, 2004).

We want to close this chapter by synthesizing what has been discussed by highlighting one of the most decisive contributions of Brazilian Blacks and Indigenous people to national education. This is by discussing what criteria high-quality education in multicultural societies should fulfill.

The demands and proposals by Blacks and Indigenous peoples indicate that high-quality education hinges on learning and teaching processes that value the interaction of individuals, situated historically and socially within the environment in which they live and act, with other individuals from different ethnic and racial backgrounds – namely their schoolteachers, classmates, and staff. These are learning and teaching processes that create the conditions in which different worldviews and life perspectives enrich each other. These pedagogical processes must encourage minority groups, as citizens, to participate in governing society. It is important to stress that the analysis of the complexity of ethnic and racial relationships in Brazil, particularly in education, requires more than one chapter to discuss it comprehensively. In addition, we should mention that the positions described in this chapter are those expressed by Blacks and Indigenous peoples fighting for equal rights in a discriminatory and non-egalitarian society.

Notes

1 In the Brazilian census the Instituto Brasileiro de Geografia e Estatística (IBGE) classifies the population by color as *brancos* (Whites), *pretos* (dark-skinned people), *pardos* (Mestizos), *amarelos* (descendants of

such peoples as the Japanese, Chinese, and Korean), and *Indígenas* (Indigenous peoples). In order to know the color of a person, the auto-classification is adopted. Those who classify themselves as *pardos* are in the great majority, the children of parents one of whom is Black and the other White. Many of the *pardo* classify themselves as "Blacks with *light skin*." In social sciences and education, analyses of the population are done for each group separately, and, in order to know the total of Blacks, the sum of *pretos e pardos* is calculated.

2 Indigenous people, and African, European, and Asian descendants.
3 Namely, President Fernando Henrique Cardoso.
4 The representative appointed by the Indigenous Movement was Professor Francisca Novantino Paresi; the representative appointed by the Black Movement was Professor Dr. Petronilha Beatriz Gonçalves e Silva.
5 President of the Republic Luiz Inácio Lula da Silva.
6 For example, the Afro-Brazil Museum in the city of São Paulo (www.museuafrobrasil.com.br.) or the Centers of Afro-Brazilian Studies (www.udesc.br/neab.htlm).

References

Aiwa, G. M. (1997). Escola apurinã: Uma experiência de revitalização da língua indígena [Apurinã school: An experience for the revitalization of the Indigenous language]. In W. D'Angelis & J. Veiga (Eds.), *Leitura e escrita em escolas indígenas* [Reading and writing in Indigenous schools] (pp. 209–220). Campinas, Brazil: Associação de Leitura do Brasil, Mercado de Letras.

Anaya, S. J. (2007). Cenário internacional: Os direitos humanos dos povos indígenas [International scenario: Human rights of Indigenous peoples]. In A. V. Araujo (Ed.), *Povos indígenas e a lei dos "brancos": O direito à diferença* [Indigenous peoples and the law of "White": The right to difference] (pp. 167–194). Brasília, Brazil: Ministério da Educação.

Araújo, A. (1986). Por um pensamento negro-brasileiro [Black-Brazilian thought]. *Estudos Afro-Asiáticos* [Afro-Asian Studies], *12*, 63–80.

Banks, J. A. (Ed.). (2004). *Diversity and citizenship education: Global perspectives*. San Francisco: Jossey-Bass.

Brazil. (1996). *Bill 9394/1996 of the National Education Guidelines and Principles*.

Brazil. (1999). *Resolução CNE/CEB no 03/99: Fixa Diretrizes Nacionais para o Funcionamento de Escolas Indígenas* [Resolution CNE/CEB no 03/99: National guidelines for Indigenous peoples' schools]. Brasília, Brazil: Conselho Nacional de Educação.

Brazil. (2003). *Federal Bill 10639/2003: Establish mandatory teaching of Afro-Brazilian history and culture in the elementary and middle schools*.

Brazil. (2004a). *Parecer* [Report] *CNE/CP 3/2004: Guidelines for education of ethnic-racial relations and for the teaching of Afro-Brazilian history and culture*. Brasília, Brazil: Conselho Nacional de Educação.

Brazil. (2004b). *Resolução* [Resolution] *CNE/CP 1/2004: Guidelines for education of ethnic-racial relations and for the teaching of Afro-Brazilian history and culture*. Brasília, Brazil: Conselho Nacional de Educação.

Brazil. (2008). *Bill 11. 465/2008: Establish mandatory teaching of Indigenous cultures and history in the elementary and middle schools*.

Carone, I., & Bento, M. A. S. (2002). *Psicologia social do racismo: Estudos sobre branquitude e branqueamento no Brasil* [Social psychology of racism: Studies on whiteness and whitening in Brazil]. Petrópolis, Brazil: Vozes.

da Silva, A. L. (Ed.). (1987). *A questão indígena na sala de aula: Subsídios para professores de 1° e 2° graus* [The Indigenous question in the classroom: Materials for primary and secondary teachers]. São Paulo, Brazil: Brasiliense.

da Silva, A. L., & Grupioni, L. D. B. (Ed.). (1995). *A temática indígena na escola: Novos subsídios para professores de 1° e 2° graus* [Indigenous topics at school: New materials for primary and secondary teachers]. Brasília, Brazil: Ministério da Educação e Cultura, Mari, UNESCO.

de Souza Lima, A. C., & Barroso-Hoffmann, M. (2004). *Desafios para uma educação superior para os povos indígenas no Brasil: Políticas públicas de ação afirmativa e direitos culturais diferenciados* [Challenges for

Indigenous higher education: Affirmative action and cultural rights public policies]. Rio de Janeiro, Brazil: Museu Nacional.

dos Santos, S. A. (2007). *Movimentos Negros, educação e ações afirmativas* [Black movements, education and affirmative actions]. Unpublished doctoral dissertation, Universidade de Brasília, Instituto de Ciências Sociais, Brasilia, Brazil.

Dussel, E. (1987). *Para uma ética da libertação latino-americana III: Erótica e Pedagógica* [Ethics for Latin American liberation: Erotica and pedagogy]. São Paulo, Brazil: Loyola, &Piracicaba, Brazil: UNIMEP.

Freire, J. R. B. (2004). Trajetória de muitas perdas e poucos ganhos [A trajectory of several losses and few achievements]. In C. Grzybowski, S. Correa, F. L. de Carvalho, J. E. Durão, G. Oleveira, & I. Pietricovsky (Eds.), *Educação escolar indígenas em Terra Brasilis, em tempo de novo descobrimento* [School education in Indigenous Terra Brasilis: Time for new discovery] (pp. 11–32). Rio de Janeiro, Brazil: Instituto Brasileiro de Análises Sociais e Econômicas.

Freire, P. (1978). *Pedagogia do oprimido* [Pedagogy of the oppressed]. São Paulo, Brazil: Paz e Terra.

Garcia, J. (2005). Experiências de enseñanza superior para pueblos indígenas em América Latina: Proyecto de la universidad intercultural Amawtay Wasi [Experiences of higher education teaching for Indigenous peoples in Latin America: The project of the Amawtay Wasi University]. *I Conferência Internacional sobre Ensino Superior Indígena: Construindo Novos Paradigmas* [First international conference on Indigenous higher education: Building new paradigms] (pp. 49–64). Barra dos Bugres, Mato Grosso, Brazil: Universidade Estadual de Mato Grosso.

Gonçalves, L. A. O. (1994). *Le movement noir au Brésil: Représentation social et action historique* [The Black Movement in Brazil: Social representation and historical action]. Lille, France: Presses Universitaires du Septentrion.

Gonçalves, L. A. O., & Gonçalves e Silva, P. B. (2000). Movimento negro e educação [Black Movement and education]. *Revista Brasileira de Educação* [Brazilian Journal of Education], *15*, 134–158.

Gonçalves, L. A. O., & Gonçalves e Silva, P. B. (2006). *Jogo das diferenças, o: O multiculturalismo e seus contextos* [Game of differences: Multiculturalism and its contexts] (4th ed.). Belo Horizonte, Brazil: Autêntica.

Gonçalves e Silva, P. B. (2003). Citizenship and education in Brazil: The contribution of Indian peoples and Blacks in the struggle for citizenship and recognition. In J. A. Banks (Ed.), *Diversity and citizenship education: Global perspectives* (pp. 185–218). San Francisco: Jossey-Bass.

Gonçalves e Silva, P. B. (2004). Projeto Nacional de Educação na perspectiva dos Negros Brasileiros [National Education Project in the perspective of Black Brazilians]. *Conferências do Fórum Brasil de Educação* [Brazilian Conference of the Forum on Education] (pp. 385–395). Brasília, Brazil: Conselho Nacional de Educação, UNESCO.

Grupioni, L. D. B. (1997). De alternativo a oficial: Sobre a (im)possiblidade da educação escolar indígena no Brasil [From alternative to official: On the (im)possibility of Indigenous school education in Brazil]. In W. D'Angelis & J. Veiga (Eds.), *Leitura e escrita em escolas indígenas* [Reading and writing in Indigenous schools] (pp. 184–201). Campinas, Mercado de Letras, Brazil: Associação de Leitura do Brasil.

Grupioni, L. D. B. (2004). Um território ainda a conquistar [A territory yet to be conquered]. In C. Grzybowski, S. Correa, F. L. de Carvalho, J. E. Durão, G. Oleveira, & I. Pietricovsky (Eds.), *Educação escolar indígenas em Terra Brasilis, em tempo de novo descobrimento* [School education in Indigenous Terra Brasilis: Time for new discovery] (pp. 33–50). Rio de Janeiro, Brazil: Instituto Brasileiro de Análises Sociais e Econômicas (IBASE).

Grupioni, L. D. B. (2007). *Educação indígena e diversidade* [Indigenous education and diversity]. Symposium conducted at a colloquium on Indigenous school education, Universidade de São Paulo, São Paulo, Brazil.

Grzybowski, C., Correa, S., de Carvalho, F. L., Durão, J. E., Oleveira, G., & Pietricovsky, I. (Eds.). (2004). *Educação escolar indígena em Terra Brasilis: Tempo de novo descobrimento* [School education in Indigenous Terra Brasilis: Time for new discovery]. Rio de Janeiro, Brazil: Instituto Brasileiro de Análises Sociais e Econômicas (IBASE).

Januário, E. (2004). Entrevista com Rony Walter Azoinayce Paresi [Interview with Rony Walter Azoinayce Paresi]. *Cadernos de Educação Escolar Indígena* [Indigenous Studies School of Education], *3*(1), 160–163.

King, J. E. (1999). In search of a method for liberating education and research: The half (that) has not been told. In C. A. Grant (Ed.), *Multicultural research: A reflective engagement with race, class, gender and sexual orientation* (pp. 101–119). Philadelphia: Falmer.

Lazo, J. L. (1989). Celebremos los 500 años de la resistencia anticolonial [We celebrate 500 years of anticolonial resistance]. In A. Colombres (Ed.), *1942–1992: A los 500 años del choque de dos mundos: Balance y prospectiva* [1942–1992: After 500 years of the clash of worlds: Balance and foresight] (pp. 51–56). Buenos Aires, Argentina: Ed. Del Sol.

Maggie, Y. (2005–2006). Uma nova pedagogia racial? [A new racial pedagogy?]. *Revista da USP, 68*(22), 112–129.

Maia, M. (2006). *Manual de Lingüística: Subsídios para a formação de professores indígenas na área de linguagem* [A manual of linguistics: Materials for the training of Indigenous teachers in the field of language]. Brasília, Brazil: Ministério da Educação.

Mendonça, T. F., Zorrthea, K. S., & Torres, M. (2005). Política indígena nos cursos de formação de professores indígenas [Indigenous politics in Indigenous teacher training courses]. *I Conferência Internacional sobre Ensino Superior Indígena: Construindo Novos Paradigmas* [First international conference on Indigenous higher education: Building new paradigms] (pp. 161–167). Barra dos Bugres, Mato Grosso, Brazil: Universidade Estadual de Mato Grosso.

Ministério da Educação. (1997). *Parâmetros curriculares nacionais* [National curriculum parameters]. Brasília, Brazil: Author.

Ministério da Educação. (1998). *Referencial curricular nacional para as escolas indígenas* [National curriculum reference for Indigenous schools]. Brasília, Brazil: Author.

Ministério da Educação. (2002). *Parâmetros em ação: Educação escolar indígena* [Parameters in action: Indigenous school education]. Brasília, Brazil: Author.

Ministério da Educação. (2004). *Diretrizes curriculares nacionais para a educação das relações étnico-raciais e para o ensino de história e cultura Afro-Brasileira e Africana* [National curriculum guidelines for the education of ethnic-racial relations and for the teaching of Afro-Brazilian history and culture]. Brasília, Brazil: Author.

Monte, N., & Grupioni, L. D. B. (2002). *Referências para a formação de professores indígenas* [References for the training of Indigenous teachers]. Brasília, Brazil: Ministério da Educação.

Munanga, K. (1996). *Parecer ao PCN: Pluralidade cultural* [Report to the PCN: Cultural plurality]. São Paulo, Brazil: Universidade de São Paulo.

Munanga, K. (1999). *Superando o racismo na escola* [Overcoming racism at school]. Brasília, Brazil: Ministério da Educação.

Munanga, K. (2000). *Superando o racismo na escola* [Overcoming racism at school] (2nd ed.). Brasília, Brazil: Ministério da Educação.

Ortiz, F. (1942). Por colón se descubrieran dos mundos [The mutual discovery of two worlds]. *Revista Bimestre Cubana, 40*(2), 180–190.

Paiva, V., & Fonseca, A. (2006). *Relatório de pesquisa sobre "The pathways to higher education" a educação superior indígena no Brasil.* [Unpublished research report about "The pathways to higher education" on higher education for Indigenous peoples in Brazil]. Fundação Ford, Rio de Janeiro, Brazil.

Paresi, F. N. (2005). Perspectiva para a normatização do ensino superior indígena no Brasil [Perspective for the regulation of Indigenous higher education in Brazil]. *I Conferência Internacional sobre Ensino Superior Indígena: Construindo Novos Paradigmas* [First international conference on Indigenous higher education: Building new paradigms] (pp. 129–134). Barra dos Bugres, Mato Grosso, Brazil: Universidade Estadual de Mato Grosso.

Picotti, C. D. V. (1989). El descubrimiento de América y la otredad de las culturas [The discovery of America and the otherness of cultures]. In A. Colombres (Ed.), *1942–1992 a los 500 años del choque de dos mundos: Balance y prospectiva* [1942–1992: After 500 years of the clash of worlds: Balance and foresight] (pp. 141–151). Buenos Aires, Argentina: Ed. Del Sol.

Pinto, R. P. (1993). *O movimento negro em São Paulo: Luta e indentidade* [Black Movement in São Paulo: Struggle and identity]. Unpublished doctoral dissertation, Universidade de São Paulo, São Paulo, Brazil.

Reider, A., & Gestera, K. (2005). Perspectivas de novos cursos para a habilitação de indígenas em nível superior [Perspectives for new courses for graduating Indians in higher education]. *I Conferência Internacional sobre Ensino Superior Indígena: Construindo Novos Paradigmas* [First international conference on Indigenous higher education: Building new paradigms] (pp. 169–174). Barra dos Bugres, Mato Grosso, Brazil: Universidade Estadual de Mato Grosso.

UNEMAT. (2005–2008). Notes on Indigenous school education. *Cadernos da Universidade do Estado de Mato Grosso/UNEMAT* [Journal of the State University of Mato Grosso].

Universidade do Estado de Mato Grosso (2005). *I Conferência Internacional sobre Ensino Superior Indígena: Construindo Novos Paradigmas* [First international conference on Indigenous higher education: Building new paradigms]. Barra dos Bugres, Mato Grosso, Brazil: Universidade Estadual de Mato Grosso.

Winkler, D., & Cueto, S. (Eds.). (2004). *Etnicidad, raza, género y educación em América Latina* [Ethnicity, race, gender, and education in Latin America]. Santiago, Chile: Programa de Promoción de la Reforma Educativa en America Latina y Caribe.

40

The education of ethnic minority groups in Mexico

Sonia Stella Araújo-Olivera
Autonomous University of the State of Morelos, Mexico

Petronilha Beatriz Gonçalves e Silva
Federal University of São Carlos, Brazil

Introduction

This chapter focuses on and analyzes education policies in Mexico, where the ethnically diverse population includes White, Mestizo, and Indigenous peoples. Even though the official language is Spanish, more than 50 Indigenous languages are spoken. Among these, Nahuatl, Mixteco, Tseltal, Hñahñu, Mazateco, Zapoteco, and Chol are the most common languages spoken by students. Despite this diversity, interethnic relations in Mexico are conditioned by a dominant Eurocentric rationality and by economic cycles that began during 16th-century colonial expansion, continued during the 19th-century Industrial Revolution, and persist in today's neoliberal and globalization processes.

Some groups in Mexico, products of these hegemonic models, were privileged in their abilities to reproduce themselves, to affirm their identity, and, most importantly, to exercise their rights, while many members of the larger society were marginalized. For Indigenous peoples, the discrimination resulted in their exclusion from common social benefits and limited development of their own identities (Secretaria de Desarrollo Social [SEDESOL], 2005). This domination created – both in the culture and in individuals – a system that allowed racist practices that denied Indigenous peoples the complete exercise of their human rights and that served as an impediment for the country's democratic development and consolidation. Within such a frame, intercultural education becomes an ethical imperative, for it can reaffirm those marginalized populations and bring about meaningful and innovative changes in the educational and political spheres.

Consequences of Eurocentric rationality on the Indigenous world

In Article 2 of its 1917 Constitution, Mexico defines itself in the following terms:

> This nation has a pluricultural composition, originally sustained by its Indigenous peoples, who are those descendants from the populations that inhabited the Country's

territory when Colonization began, and who still keep their own social, economic, and political institutions, or part of them.

(Constitución Política de los Estados Unidos Méxicanos, 1917)

This declaration in favor of plurality is repeated in the 1994 General Law for Education (Ley General Educación, 1994), Article 38:

> Basic education, at its three levels, will procure the required adjustments to respond to the linguistic and cultural characteristics of each and every one of all the diverse Indigenous groups in this country, as well as those of dispersed, rural populations, and migrating groups.

The relatively recent recognition of the country's cultural diversity as one of the nation's most important features, particularly in respect to its Indigenous groups, demands special actions from various and different fields. In the political milieu it means that society must guarantee to all Indigenous peoples the full practice of their rights. To do so, we need to understand the factors that have kept and maintained this large group at the margins of society, making them invisible, disqualifying their vision of the world, and thus eliminating their chances to perpetuate their own ways of life with dignity. We must first understand the effects caused by European expansion and colonization of these societies four centuries ago.

It is well known that the region named Latin America – *Abya Yala* for the Kuna, the original inhabitants of today's Panama – was invaded and colonized in the 16th century, mainly by the Spanish and Portuguese. The newcomers brought a European way of life and their own political objectives. They became rich quickly, by conquering the new territories, and then transferred their riches to Spain (de las Casas, 1552, p. 17). Mexico experienced both a military and a cultural invasion (Freire, 1972). Through the former, the Spanish sought to own the newly discovered territory, to apply their own forms of government, to introduce their own structures of economic transactions, to control all rebellions, and to subdue Indigenous people and rapidly turn them into slaves to exploit their labor. At the same time, the Spanish imposed their own Eurocentric rationality and established it as the region's one and true rationality. Supported by the compulsory teaching of Spanish and the Catholic religion, the Spanish forced the Indigenous peoples of the Americas to accept their lifestyles, beliefs, rituals, and values.

It was by such means that the Indigenous person came to be seen as the "other" – primitive, barbarian, and savage: in short, not a whole human being (Dussel, 1995). It is worth remembering the controversy between Juan Ginés de Sepúlveda and Bartolomé de las Casas, together with the Papal Bull of 1537 (B. Hernández, n.d.), which tried to determine if those Indigenous individuals in the newly found territories had a soul and, if so, if it was equal in rank to a European's soul. In this context, to be considered human Indigenous peoples had to become European, or something close to it. Some adapted by building an Indigenous elite that linked itself with the privileges and interests at the center of power. Others, those who resisted colonization, became marginalized. Since then, the relationships between Europeans and "Indians" have been marked by the violent and excluding logic of domination, generating victims through the practice of oppression, which "reduced Indian peoples to the lowest ways of servitude" (Dussel, 1995, p. 159). Simultaneously their identity, their cultural values, their language, and their vision of the world were negated.

If we search for the reasons why the name "Latin America" was granted to this part of the planet, we also learn more about the consequences that resulted from discrimination and the imposition of Eurocentric rationality. According to Saint-Geours (2007), it was convenient for

French political interests, in 1860, for the continent to be known as Latin America. The term induced all to think of its population as "Latin," and hence the one and only ethnic group of its social configuration. The new name, then, not only made Indigenous peoples invisible but also contributed to the establishment of a European way of life.

According to this way of life, ethnic differences constituted an excuse for segregation. The Indigenous biological, somatic, and genetic attributes were linked with racial, moral, aesthetic, and intellectual characteristics that generated disqualifying stereotypes. The conjunction of all these factors generated a social system and a scheme of representations guided by principles of an instrumental rationale that, in varied magnitudes, created adverse conditions for the survival of those groups that were able to escape the trend towards homogenization.

Cultural resistance

Indigenous peoples resist homogenization until this very day, but – as Fiori (1986) notes – not even the fiercest of dominations could turn them into "things." They still hold an array of knowledge acquired through oral transmission and related to survival in such fields as astronomy, botany, medicine, and agriculture. Just as their languages do, this knowledge builds and rebuilds itself based on its own models. This process of knowing builds itself any time a conversation takes place, that is, wherever everyday knowledge becomes processed as a community affair. This practice of oral communication is necessarily linked to the community's political-pedagogical efforts. From such activity it may be gathered that education occurs in everyday action, as it is connected to other people's rights to belong to various spheres of economy, culture, and society. On the other hand, the school is not the only place to acquire knowledge and develop human dignity. In consequence, the Indigenous peoples' right to education cannot be restricted to their participation in the public school system but must include their active participation in the community's life as a whole.

For centuries, Indigenous peoples were – and they still are – excluded from the exercise of their rights, and by the same token they are placed in asymmetrical conditions in relation to other Mexicans. Consequently, to implement intercultural education requires first the full exercise of Indigenous cultural and citizenship rights.

Indigenous education in Mexico: Asymmetry and exclusion

Since pre-colonial times, the Indigenous peoples of Mexico, like others in this world, had a system of educational practices through which older generations passed their knowledge to younger ones. Archaeological and historic sites provide evidence for the existence of buildings where formal education was provided. Even so, the history of Mexican education states that "Indigenous systematic education as such began in New Spain during the Colonial Period" (Bertely, 2002, p. 5).

Indigenous education in Mexico: From colonial times to the present

"The Indigenous education delivered in Mexican schools since the Spanish Conquest still is a process of assimilation that reproduces discrimination, economic exploitation, and political manipulation" (N. Hernández, 2003, p. 1). In effect, all Indigenous groups are placed into extreme situations (Freire, 1972). Through social practices and schooling processes established by the Spanish, Indian communities have always been confronted with the difficulty of adjusting to another way of life. They needed to understand other ways of behavior, to develop other forms of cognitive abilities, and to learn other symbolic codes. All these processes became implanted through physical and symbolic violence by "oppressing these peoples with the hardest, most horrible, and roughest servitude that any, men or beast, could ever have experienced" (de las Casas, 1552, p. 17). Indigenous peoples were forced to learn and then labor in activities unknown to them, and under conditions of extreme exploitation. Simultaneously, their customs, religious conceptions, and ways of transmitting all kinds of knowledge were dislocated by military and European domination. The result was a disarrangement of their social life and of the material and spiritual referents that guided and organized their lives.

The 1572 Indian Laws granted rights, obligations, and legal status to peoples culturally and linguistically different from the Spanish. These laws were eliminated in the 19th century, following Mexican independence. During this period of time all educational institutions offered a great variety of options to Spanish and Mestizo students, but the Indigenous agenda was not granted a specific place. According to Beltrán (1992), the national effort disregarded all linguistic and cultural diversity that resulted in the term *Indian* disappearing from official documents. At the end of the century, the main interest of the State was to consolidate itself and to encourage the country's industrialization; it thus paid little attention to the need to increase all education services. In some states it was believed that, for people to accept the hegemonic model of progress and consequently raise their intellectual, moral, and aesthetic level, it was necessary to maintain the schools' important functions, although it was judged necessary to divide them into two categories: those strictly urban and those peripheral to it. Consequently, an unequal distribution of the budget for education became evident in the better material conditions for schools in state capitals and district heads, in contrast to those located at the periphery. To these problems must be added the unfavorable conceptions most teachers held about Indigenous peoples and their ability to learn. Such prejudice justified a reduction in the programs' contents and a biased adaptation of methodologies and school schedules. Moreover, the system emphasized the teaching of Spanish as a base for learning all subject matter, an approach detrimental to the pupils' native language and culture. The "mestizaje myth" worked in Mexico in the same way that racial democracy did in Brazil. It concealed ethnic inequalities and discrimination behind the idea that all Mexicans were Mestizos.

In 1948, as a result of the activities undertaken by the Bureau of Indian Affairs [*Departamento de Asuntos Indígenas*], the *tarascan* project in the state of Michoacán, the Institute for the Alphabetization of Monolingual Indigenous Peoples [*Instituto de Alfabetización para Indígenas Monolingües*], and the National Indigenous Institute [*Instituto Nacional Indigenista* (INI)] were created. The latter introduced into Oaxacan, Chiapas, and Chihuahua schools people known as bilingual cultural promoters, who used the Indians' own languages to teach Spanish and subjects such as health, farming, and animal husbandry. These promoters were Indigenous youths with an elementary school education who received training to work in the areas just mentioned. After 1964, and as a consequence of such activities, the National Service of Bilingual Cultural Promoters [*Servicio Nacional de Promotores Culturales Bilingües*] became part of the Public Education Bureau [*Secretaría de Educación Pública* (SEP)].

Other types of organizations may be added to the above, as indicative of the movement generated from issues concerning Indigenous peoples in Mexico: in 1973, the Organization of Naua Indigenous Professionals [*Organización de Profesionistas Indígenas Nauas, A.C.*]; in 1974, the Chiapas Indigenous Congress [*Congreso Indígena de Chiapas*]; in 1975, the National Congress of Indigenous Peoples [*Congreso Nacional de Pueblos Indígenas*]; and, in 1977, the National Alliance of Bilingual Indigenous Professionals [*Alianza Nacional de Profesionistas Indígenas Bilingües, A.C.* (ANPIBAC)].

In 1979, ANPIBAC was characteristic of bilingual-bicultural education as taught by Indigenous peoples, grounded in their own conceptions of the world. The learning process was oriented to teach the linguistic structure and grammar of each group's own language, to make students competent in speaking, reading, and writing it. Spanish was taught as a second language. In addition, ANPIBAC tried to foster Indigenous culture and philosophies, as well as some universal values originating in other world cultures. In spite of this effort, the students' qualitative progress was limited and insufficient. For example, completion rates did not exceed 65%. N. Hernández (2003) lists some of the shortcomings of the program: educators had a poor understanding of Spanish and a limited command of their own language; they lacked the proper educational materials; and the quantity, quality, and diversity of those materials were rather poor. Also, the methods used were inadequate for teaching Spanish as a second language. In short, the government had little comprehension of the objectives, content, and special methods for teaching in a bilingual environment.

Still, even at the end of the 20th century, references to intercultural education rarely appeared in the official Mexican discourse: the 1995–2000 Program for Educative Development [*Programa de Desarrollo Educativo*] does not mention it; neither does it appear in teaching plans, nor in the programs for educating new teachers. The General Office for Indigenous Education [*Dirección General de Educación Indígena*], created in 1978, initially proposed the bilingual and bicultural model, preserving the criteria of first teaching in the Indigenous mother tongue to later learn Spanish. According to Bertely (2002) and Aguilar (2004), in this century the Mexican State on one hand made progress by recognizing the nation's ethnic and linguistic diversity, as well as admitting the economic, political, and social state that Indigenous peoples still had to endure. On the other hand, through the implementation of some of the policies mentioned, the government kept on institutionalizing a homogeneous identity for all Indigenous groups, and therefore the education programs geared to them were practically all the same. In addition, most programs were characterized by their precariousness and segregating character, rendering cultural differences invisible while ignoring cultural diversity. The result was that Indigenous peoples' expectations about school diminished, again fostering inequalities based on education, or lack of it. It is fair to recognize that the national education system, particularly at the level of basic teaching, did attempt to reduce the gap between Indigenous and mainstream groups. In practice, however, the former were still expected to renounce their culture to adopt that of the latter. Accordingly, and in general, Mexican society thinks that what "Indigenous peoples need to do to leave poverty behind is to behave like non-Indians," and that Indigenous peoples "always will have a social limitation due to their racial [physical] characteristics" (SEDESOL, 2005, p. 49).

Bertely argues that, in effect,

> all through the last century, Indigenous peoples have been considered incapable of making a decision, together with their families and community, about what a quality and pertinent education means to them. Consequently, educational policies for Indigenous peoples have not resulted from a democratic dialogue with them.
>
> (2002, p. 10)

Within this scenario it is not surprising to see the extreme poverty in which Indigenous peoples still find themselves, not only in relation to excessively high rates of illiteracy, failure to be promoted, and school leaving, but also in showing low employment rates and precarious health, holding low-paying jobs, and experiencing great difficulties in accessing preventive medicine. The search for better life conditions caused both individuals and entire groups to migrate to Mexico's urban centers. The mixture of different cultures thus generated further complicated the search for solutions to the problem of intercultural education. Simultaneously, these phenomena strengthen the hypothesis that respect for cultural diversity is not limited to a pedagogical intervention. It rather constitutes an ethical dimension that demands specific actions in the political arena, actions that must be implemented to institute deep structural changes to guarantee diversity as a positive value for turning all members of Mexican society into citizens of a democratic nation.

Affirmative actions and interculturality

One could share Muñoz's (1998, 1999, 2002) affirmation that proclaims, explicitly or implicitly, that Indigenous education has not yet reached a status of primary concern in today's Mexico, particularly when one considers the actions the state implemented within the frame of affirmative action policies. According to Sverdlick, Ferrari, and Jaimovich (2005), in their origin these policies pretended to enforce the constitutional principle of material equality while they tried to reverse the effects of different types of discrimination. In the field of politics, the idea of *equality* has been considered a sine qua non condition to develop democracy in everyday endeavors, not to mention in the full exercise of personal and cultural rights. To guarantee the access, permanency, and completion rates of students belonging to groups or sectors disfavored by society's mainstream, the scope of the education offered by the state must be widened. Access is also conditioned by each home's economic possibilities, particularly relevant when it comes to Indigenous peoples, given that poverty and ethnic affiliation are factors that usually come together. Procedures and actions organized by the state, aimed at reversing a deeply rooted, adverse, and unequal access to education as a human right, allowed the government to offer increased educational opportunities. Nonetheless, such actions still do not guarantee equal access to knowledge or a quality education for all, at each and every level of the education system. Such a situation does not guarantee a higher level of self-esteem in Indigenous peoples in comparison with that held by the rest of the population.

Schmelkes (2003, p. 5) recognizes that "few Indigenous peoples leaving high school, mostly from rural zones, may succeed in passing the admission exams at the University level," a fact that demonstrates the double exclusion exercised by most universities, where academic selection is made from groups of students who have already successfully navigated similar processes. Throughout the series of selection, different factors beyond school training play a role, for example the student's social and cultural capital and his/her socioeconomic level. Free remedial courses at all school grades, together with the granting of scholarships, could possibly start to mitigate the effect of these negative social factors and improve Indigenous students' access to public universities. Among the actions undertaken to encourage Indigenous students to attend university, the Mexican government created "intercultural universities" in zones where these groups are concentrated: Estado de México, Chiapas, Yucatán, Quintana Roo, San Luis de Potosí, Oaxaca, Guerrero, and Tabasco.

Economic aid programs were established for the least favored sectors of society. Sverdlick et al. (2005, p. 102) analyze those programs and identify "policies where the target population is more diffuse, in general determined by their income level, together with other policies aimed at specific groups, like those groups speaking an Indigenous language." They also warn that "many times, and given the poverty characteristics of Indigenous populations . . . this difference [in economic income] may be used only analytically, given that, when particular policies are implemented, one group is not distinguished from the other" (Sverdlick et al., p. 102). After analyzing the programs, the authors discovered the existence of two models: those that simply provide some kind of financial aid to sectors with low income, and those that combine this kind of aid with the transformation of the institutions that provide services to these groups. An example of the first model is the National Program of Scholarships for Higher Education [*Programa Nacional de Becas de Educación Superior* (PRONABES)], which provides grants to low-income students enrolled in technical studies, associate professional, or bachelor programs at public universities. PRONABES grants priority to institutions located in or near Indigenous communities or in rural or marginal urban areas, or to cases where the student belongs to families registered in the family census called OPORTUNIDADES. Another example is the National Program of Scholarships for Academic Excellence and School Development [*Programa Nacional de Becas para la Excelencia Académica y el Aprovechamiento Escolar*], aimed at students with socioeconomic disadvantages and living in Indigenous towns, or individuals with different capacities who earned a minimum average of 8.0 during the previous five school terms. A third program is the Relief Program for Indigenous Youths in Higher Education [*Programa de Auxilio para la Educación Superior de Jóvenes Indígenas*], administered by the INI of Mexico, which provides economic assistance specifically for Indigenous people with low incomes who have earned a minimum school average of 8.5, in order for them to remain in the country's system of public universities. The fourth and last is the Program in Support of Indigenous Students in Higher Education Institutions [*Programa de Apoyo a Estudiantes Indígenas en Instituciones de Enseñanza Superior*], supported by the Ford Foundation and the National Association of United Institutions of Higher Education [*Asociación Nacional de Unión de Instituciones de Educación Superior* (ANUIES)]. This program combines economic support to the students with demands for change in the institution that receives them. These changes are necessary to establish supportive academic mechanisms (remedial and leveling courses, tutoring, and individual attention to students, among others). These should encourage optimal performance in school, better completion rates, and entry into graduate school, as well as fostering the student's return to his/her community as a qualified professional, while encouraging in the academic milieu recognition and respect for human diversity.

In spite of all these efforts, the National Survey of Discrimination in Mexico [*Encuesta Nacional sobre Discriminación en México*] reports:

> Three of four Indigenous peoples interviewed judge they have fewer opportunities of going to school than other people; ... two of every three judge they have few, or no, possibilities for improving their lives; ... 45% affirm that their rights have not been respected owing to their [Indigenous] condition; ... 40% of all Mexicans favor organizing themselves with other persons in their communities to avoid an Indigenous group establishing residence close by.
>
> (SEDESOL, 2005, p. 50)

The education of Indigenous students, just like that of the professors that cater to them, even though it gained presence in political and cultural scenarios, is not thought of as a central mission in education, nor are the pertinent structural changes inside the state that are supposed to coherently assume a commitment to its ethnic diversity. This fact notwithstanding, at the beginning of this millennium some advances have occurred, and some institutional spaces have opened gradually. An example is the General Coordination of Bilingual and Intercultural Indigenous Education [*Coordinación General de Educación Indígena Intercultural Bilingüe* (CGEIB)], dependent on the SEP. However, this proposal still remains conditioned by the current homogenizing national curriculum, at all levels of the education system. This, among other facts, compels us to agree with N. Hernández that:

It is necessary to modify the country's Constitution to include in it an education congruent with the country's cultural and linguistic diversity. Within this basic tenet an inclusive education program must be developed, one that could offer an intercultural education for all Mexicans.

(2003, p. 15)

It is crucial to insist that, in these much needed reformulations (organization, study plans, and curricula), all those concerned must participate as major protagonists, particularly those Indigenous communities that have been long and largely ignored; this inclusion is necessary in order to guarantee the Chiapanec demand: *"que todos quepan"* ("that all may fit").

Intercultural education from "below": Challenges for the third millennium

Even while living in substandard conditions, and even if "made to believe that as Indigenous peoples we had no culture, that our language was inferior to Spanish, and that it was shameful to speak it" (N. Hernández, 2003, p. 18), Indigenous peoples continued their struggle in the last decade of the 20th century. During the process of globalization, diverse social restraints worsened and brought with them a renewed fight against problems such as racism, discrimination, nationalism, and all other biases with roots in Eurocentric positions.

In 1992, after 500 years of resistance, the Indigenous people fought for the idea of "never again a Mexico without us" by promoting reforms in specific constitutional articles. In 1994, the Zapatista Army of National Liberation [*Ejército Zapatista de Liberación Nacional* (EZLN)], from southeast Mexico, attacked the country's political structure with their liberating cry of *"Ya Basta!"* ("Enough!"). These protestors questioned all kinds of institutions, political, social, and ideological, while demanding their rights to justice, democracy, education, social peace, and life itself.

The public eruption of the EZLN reactivated old demands that propitiated the development of new pedagogical alternatives in the region, together with various projects to be managed within the Indigenous communities, oriented toward a bilingual and intercultural education for all people, Indigenous and non-Indigenous. The aim was to prepare everyone to know, understand, respect, and live in conditions of equality in the midst of difference. Also new was the diversity of actors in education, even if each one held dissimilar or contrasting interests and beliefs: governmental institutions, religious associations, non-governmental organizations, and Indigenous groups.

Research and reports in the field of education reveal that, with the objectives mentioned above, regional and community endeavors are nourished to the point that those same Indigenous communities, in several Mexican regions, are developing their own new projects: Chiapas (Avila Naranjo, Micalco Méndez, Saldívar Moreno, & Santos Baca, 2004; CGEIB, 2006; Gutiérrez Narváez, 2006; Saldívar Moreno, 2001), Puebla (CGEIB, 2006), Chihuahua (CGEIB, 2006), Veracruz (CGEIB, 2006), Michoacán (CGEIB, 2006; García Segura, 2004), and Oaxaca (Vázquez & Gómez, 2006), among others. After analyzing these studies, it becomes clear that those teaching proposals introduced before the Zapatista movement were characterized by the same ideas of cultural assimilation and homogenization as those introduced at the beginning of the 20th century: for example, the use of mother tongues at school while using the same nationwide school plans and programs. Facing the lack of alternative proposals that would promote changes in the quantity and quality of education, many communities created their own. Within these proposals diverse principles intermingled, whether they were autochthonous, Zapatistas, national, or universal. Besides allowing more people to participate in formulating the basic concepts for the creation of a community school, these programs introduced different kinds of actors as teachers, sometimes to the point of substituting official teachers with their own community-trained youths, who had, nonetheless, some training from their courses in official elementary and junior high schools.

In summary, the Indigenous communities reject the educational offer made by the national government, for they consider that it still does not thoroughly acknowledge or solve their own problems. As a consequence they have taken the initiative to train their own teachers and to demonstrate that they can build a different kind of quality education, open to all, and consistent with their own ways of organizing communal life in their own towns.

Some final thoughts

The authors of this article share Zarco's (2004, p. 12) affirmation:

> A pedagogy geared towards interculturality implies the construction of knowledge and sensibilities that would help us transcend that which is ours, and savor that which is different, to recognize our own from the unfamiliar, to appreciate, and esteem the other's reasons for happiness, and to become critical of all attitudes that are unfavorable to the exaltation of life, or that inhibit or deny human dignity.

The cultural, economic, social, and political effects of centuries of domination persist in the exclusion and marginalization that Indigenous peoples have endured throughout their lives. These groups confront neoliberal globalization in asymmetrical conditions and with great disadvantages in comparison with the country's non-Indigenous populations. Everyday life in these (and in those considered) "Mestizo" populations is still conditioned by recurrent notions of the Eurocentric model, imprinted and transmitted by education systems that keep reproducing the homogenizing conceptions of the majority. The status of these different populations, cultures, and languages, even though they share a single territory and participate in one single "National Project," is still a cause for conflict. This is so because the "difference" is constructed through an artificial value of inferiority, applied to one group by the other, mainly to prohibit the former's participation in decision-making processes of all kinds, affecting their basic human rights, be they educational, political, or plainly human. Historically, this difference turned into one of weakness, and the different into an inferior person, and the idea of interculturality has not yet overcome the ideology of subordination.

The idea of interculturality that prevails in public policy, including the national education system, still derives from those groups in power and is still sustained by their own particular conceptions. Indigenous communities and towns do not recognize themselves in those policies, and this will continue to be the case as long as hegemonic activities and interests establish, from a point of view external to native cultures, what Indigenous peoples need to learn in a multi-cultural society. To have respect for that which is different in terms of equality and human rights implies to put into practice differentiated cultural and education policies (that is, affirmative action policies) to compensate for adversity in human conditions. For example, Indigenous communities must be participants and collaborators in the creation of teaching plans and programs; their worldviews, their processes of learning and teaching, and their own curricula must be included. They must also intervene to control and evaluate their own learning processes.

Today's challenge for intercultural education is to foster an authentic and reciprocal knowledge between Indigenous and non-Indigenous peoples, one that encourages reciprocal understanding, solidarity, and sensitivity to each other. Such an attitude would cultivate what Freire (2001) terms "unity in diversity." In order to achieve such a state of social harmony, people must transcend preconceptions and representations about the other's inferiority, which still lurk in many members of most societies, consequently interfering with intercultural living. The challenge to build bridges towards transculturality is by no means a minor one, since the education process may not be thought of as *for* Indigenous peoples but as *with* them. Accordingly, a system like this may stimulate the critical reflection of Indigenous and non-Indigenous peoples, oriented to the evaluation of one's own tradition from one's own cultural resources (Dussel, 2005).

In contrast, terms like *dialogue between cultures* and *recognition of the differences* seem not to possess the necessary strength to modify realities if they are not accompanied by legitimate exercises in autonomy and the full participation of all citizens in everyday living and in mutual interaction within all aspects of society. The legalization, actualization, and full exercise of ethnic rights remain an eagerly desired and socially valuable good, one for which all concerned populations still fight. Nonetheless, these struggles develop within a swamp of contradictions that hinder their full implementation. First, education must provide opportunities for face-to-face interactions and sharing in intercultural environments in order for non-Indigenous groups to become acquainted with the "Other" (Dussel, n.d.). Only then can ruptures occur in universalizing and homogenizing postures that will allow one to welcome the "Other." Without such ruptures no dialogue, negotiation, or democratic life will be possible.

The authors would like to thank Elena Bernal Garcia for translating this chapter.

References

Aguilar, J. (2004). Hacia una memoria argumental sobre la educación intercultural en México [Towards an argumentative memory about intercultural education in Mexico]. *Revista Mexicana de Investigación Educativa* [Mexican Journal of Educational Research], 9(20), 39–59.

Avila Naranjo, R., Micalco Méndez, M. M., Saldívar Moreno, A., & Santos Baca, E. (2004). Retos en la formación de maestros en educación intercultural: La experiencia de la Casa de la Ciencia en Chiapas [The challenges of training teachers in intercultural education: The experience of the House of Science in Chiapas]. *Revista Mexicana de Investigación Educativa* [Mexican Journal of Educational Research], 9(20), 109–128.

Beltrán, G. A. (1992). Conferencia con motivo del primer aniversario de la muerte de Lázaro Cárdenas [Conference to mark the first anniversary of the death of Lázaro Cárdenas]. In G. A. Beltrán (Ed.), *Obra antropológica XI: Obra polémica* [Anthropological work XI: Controversial work]. Mexico: Universidad Veracruzana, Instituto Nacional Indigenista, Fondo de Cultura Económica.

Bertely, M. B. (2002). Panorama histórico de la educación para los indígenas en México [Historical overview of education for Indigenous people in Mexico]. In L. E. Galván (Ed.), *Diccionario de historia de la educación en México: Siglos XIX y XX* [Dictionary of history of education in Mexico, 19th and 20th centuries]. Retrieved October 24, 2008, from http://biblioweb.dgsca.unam.mx/diccionario/htm/articulos/sec_5.htm

Constitución Política de los Estados Unidos Méxicanos [Political Constitution of the United States of Mexico]. (1917). Retrieved November, 13, 2007, from http://www.ordenjuridico.gob.mx/constitucion.php

Coordinación General de Educación Indígena Intercultural Bilingüe (CGEIB). (2006). *Experiencias innovadoras en educación intercultural, 2* [Innovative experiences in intercultural education, 2]. Mexico: Secretaría de Educación Pública (SEP).

de las Casas, B. (1552). *Breve relación de la destrucción de las Indias Occidentales* [A brief relation of the destruction of the Occidental Indies]. Retrieved February 20, 2007, from Biblioteca Virtual Cervantes, http://www.cervantesvirtual.com/servlet/SirveObras/12479514321225063632457/index.htm

Dussel, E. (n.d.). *Para uma ética da libertação Latino-Americana* [Towards an ethic of liberation for Latin America]. São Paulo, Brazil: Loyola-UNIMEP.

Dussel, E. (1995). *Introducción a la filosofía de la liberación* [Introduction to a philosophy of liberation] (5th ed.). Bogotá, Colombia: Nueva América.

Dussel, E. (2005). *Transmodernidad e interculturalidad* [Transmodernity and interculturality]. Retrieved October 24, 2008, from http://www.afyl.org/transmodernidadeinterculturalidad.pdf

Fiori, E. M. (1986). Conscientização e educação [With awareness and education]. *Educação e Realidade* [Education and Reality], *11*(1), 3–10.

Freire, P. (1972). *Pedagogía del oprimido* [Pedagogy of the oppressed]. Montevideo, Uruguay: Tierra Nueva.

Freire, P. (2001). *Política e educação* [Politics of education] (5th ed.). São Paulo, Brazil: Cortez Editora.

García Segura, S. (2004). De la educación indígena a la educación bilingüe intercultural: La comunidad p'urépecha [From Indigenous education to bilingual intercultural education: The p'urhépecha community]. *Revista Mexicana de Investigación Educativa* [Mexican Journal of Educational Research], *9*(20), 61–81.

Gutiérrez Narváez, R. (2006). Impactos del zapatismo en la escuela: Analisis de la dinamica educativa indigena en Chiapas (1994–2004) [Impacts of *zapatismo* in school: Analysis of the dynamics of Indigenous education in Chiapas (1994–2004)]. *Revista Liminar* [Liminar Journal], *4*(1), 92–111. Retrieved October 24, 2008, from http://redalyc.uaemex.mx/redalyc/src/inicio/ArtPdfRed.jsp?iCve=74540108&iCveNum=5094

Hernández, B. L. (n.d.). *The Las Casas–Sepúlveda controversy: 1550–1551*. Retrieved May 13, 2008, from http://userwww.sfsu.edu/~epf/2001/hernandez.html

Hernández, N. (2003). De la educación indígena a la educación intercultural: La experiencia de México [From Indigenous education to intercultural education: The Mexican experience]. *School of International Training Occasional Papers Series, 4*, 15–24. Retrieved July 1, 2008, from http://www.sit.edu/publications/docs/ops04mexican.pdf

Ley General Educación [General Law for Education]. (1994). Retrieved October 24, 2008, from http://www.ordenjuridico.gob.mx/Federal/PE/R/Leyes/13071993(1).pdf

Muñoz, H. (1998). Los objetivos políticos y socioeconómicos de la educación intercultural bilingüe y los cambios que se necesitan en el currículo, en la enseñanza y en las escuelas indígenas [The political and socioeconomic objectives of intercultural and bilingual education, and the changes curricula and teaching need for teaching in Indigenous schools]. *Revista Iberoamericana de Educación* [Ibero-American Journal of Education], *17*, 31–50.

Muñoz, H. (1999). Política pública y educación indígena escolarizada en México [Public politics and Indigenous education at school in Mexico]. *Cadernos Cedes, 19*(49), 39–61.

Muñoz, H. (2002). La diversidad en las reformas educativas interculturales [Diversity in the intercultural education reforms]. *Revista Electrónica de Investigación Educativa* [Electronic Magazine of Educational Research], *4*(2). Retrieved October 24, 2008, from http://redie.uabc.mx/vol4no2/contenido-cruz.html

Saint-Geours, Y. (2007). L'Amérique Latine est le laboratoire du monde [Latin America is the world's laboratory]. *L'Histoire* [History], *322*, 6–11.

Saldívar Moreno, A. (2001). Diseño de estrategias socioeducativas para el desarrollo: Acercando la educación al desarrollo de Chiapas [Design for sociological education strategies for development: Closing the gap between education and development in Chiapas]. *Cultura y Educación* [Culture and Education], *13*(1), 17–36.

Schmelkes, S. (2003, November). *Educación superior intercultural: El caso de México* [Intercultural higher education: The case of Mexico]. Lecture at the International Exchange of Educational Experience, organized by the Ford Foundation, the Support Unit Indigenous Communities of UdG and

ANUIES, Paris. Retrieved October 24, 2008, from http://www.anuies.mx/e_proyectos/pdf/La_educ_sup_indigena.pdf

Secretaria de Desarrollo Social (SEDESOL). (2005). *Primera encuesta nacional de discriminación en México 2005* [National survey of discrimination in Mexico 2005]. Mexico: Consejo Nacional para Prevenir la Discriminación (CONAPRED) [National Council to Prevent Discrimination].

Sverdlick, I., Ferrari, P., & Jaimovich, A. (2005). *Desigualdade e inclusão no ensino superior: Um estudo comparado em cinco países da América Latina* [Inequality and inclusion in higher education: A comparative study in five countries of Latin America]. Buenos Aires, Brazil: Laboratorio de Políticas Públicas [Laboratory of Public Policies]. Retrieved October 24, 2008, from http://www.lpp-uerj.net/olped/documentos/1523.pdf

Vázquez, S., & Gómez, G. (2006). Autogestión indígena en Tlahuitoltepec Mixe, Oaxaca, México [Self-management in Tlahuitoltepec Indigenous Mixe, Oaxaca, Mexico]. *Ra Ximhai, 2*(1), 151–169.

Zarco, C. (2004). Presentación. *Reflexiones de Raúl Fornet-Betancourt sobre el concepto de interculturalidad* [Reflections of Raul Forner-Betancourt regarding the concept of interculturalism]. Mexico: Coordinación General de Educación Indígena Intercultural Bilingüe [General Coordination of Indigenous and Bilingual Education] (CGEIB). Retrieved July 1, 2008, from http://eib.sep.gob.mx/files/reflexiones_fornet.pdf

Index

Abdallah-Pretceille, Martine 327
Aboriginal Australians 9, 12, 13, 115, 223, 230
Aboud, Frances E. 188, 199–209, 229, 230
Abu Bakar, Mukhlis 437–448
accommodation 28
acculturation 27, 28, 253, 258, 327
achievement gap 3, 13, 66, 469
additive approach 81
affirmative action 33
    Brazil 522–523, 529, 532
    India 427–428, 429
    Mexico 545, 548
Africa: decolonization 13
    destruction of Indigenous culture 3
    Francophone 385–396
    immigrants from 63–64, 122
African Americans 33, 43, 186, 194, 304
    assimilation 12
    Civil Rights Movement 1, 9, 82–83, 84, 135, 178, 307
    classroom interactions 314
    cultural democracy 305
    cultural ecology 24
    ethnic studies 84
    linguistic practices 245
    mathematics 241
    multicultural education 82–83
    see also Black students
African Brazilians 512, 513, 518, 519, 526–528, 531–535
African Caribbeans 4, 13
    see also Black students
Africanities 534
Afrikaans 152, 153, 154
Afrocentrism 38
Ahmad, A. 40
Ajegbo Report (2007) 125, 131, 341, 356
Alaska 242, 273n1
Algebra Project (AP) 242
Alidou, Hassana 385–396
Allemann-Ghionda, Cristina 134–145
Allport, G.W. 16, 87, 203, 212, 314, 315
Alsace-Lorraine 417
Althusser, Louis 181
American Association of Colleges for Teacher Education (AACTE) 88–89
Anderson, Benedict 277
Anderson, Perry 327–328
Anglican Church 149
Ansley, F.L. 177
anti-oppressive education 80
antiracist education 14, 20, 59, 81, 135
    Australia 115–116
    Brazil 534
    Canada 103
    early childhood 225
    Europe 348–359
    South Africa 152
    Sweden 355–356
    United Kingdom 127, 131, 353–355, 356, 416–417, 418–419, 420, 422
    United States 80
antiracist theory 25, 26, 35, 36, 45
anti-Semitism 349, 355, 522
apartheid 147, 148, 150, 155, 378
Appiah, K.A. 294, 313
Apple, Michael 124, 175, 176
Apter, D.F. 12

Arab countries 4, 512
Arabic 217, 481
Araújo, A. 531
Araújo-Olivera, Sonia Stella 526–539, 540–551
Archer, M.S. 292
Argentina 516, 517, 518
Arguedas, José María 278–279
Aronson, E. 315
Asia: decolonization 13
　diversity 9
　immigrants 51, 63–64
Asians: United Kingdom 23, 123, 128, 203
　United States 69
assimilation 3, 11–12, 27–28, 45, 49, 311
　Australia 110, 111, 115
　Canada 379
　citizenship 303, 304, 306, 309, 312, 313
　Europe 136, 141
　France 310, 326
　Japan 23, 159
　linguistic minorities 253, 254
　Maori 292, 296
　Mexico 542, 547
　migrants 56, 57, 58, 59, 60
　Native Americans 266, 267, 272
　South Africa 150, 152, 155
　United Kingdom 122, 126
asylum seekers 123, 464
　see also refugees
Au, K.H. 245
Australia: Aboriginal Australians 9, 12, 13, 115, 223, 230
　assimilationism 11, 12
　citizenship education 3
　destruction of Indigenous culture 3
　diversity 9–10
　early childhood education 230
　ethnic revitalization movements 1, 9
　languages 375
　migrants 54, 56
　multicultural education 2, 13, 109–120
　multiculturalism 57, 309
Austria 53, 54, 57
Austronesian culture 450
authenticity 41
autonomy 425, 501, 502, 503, 549

Bahasa Melayu 398, 400–402, 403, 404, 406, 407
Baker, C. 259
Balkanization 11
Ball, A.F. 245
Bamgbose, A. 391
Bang, M. 244
Banks, James A. 1–5, 9–32, 80–81, 84, 91, 303–322

Barnhardt, R. 273
Bar-On, D. 214
Barry, B. 33
Basque separatism 11
Battiste, M. 272
Begay, S. 270
Begum v. Headteacher and Governors of Denbigh High School 416
behavioral engagement 68–69
behavior-change interventions 200, 204–206
Bekerman, Zvi 210–222
Belgium 53–54, 382
Bell, Derrick 177, 178
Benjamin, R. 272
Bennett, Christine 81, 87
Berlak, A. 35
Bernal, Dolores Delgado 87
Berry, J.W. 258
Bertely, M.B. 544
Bhabha, H. 38, 39, 44
Bigler, Rebecca S. 186–198, 200, 201, 205, 206
bilingual education 13, 84, 85
　Africa 386, 388, 391–393, 394
　Australia 113
　Brazil 528, 529
　children's racial attitudes 204
　Europe 138
　Germany 465, 466, 468
　Israel 215–218
　literacy 245–246, 252
　Maori 292
　Mexico 543, 544
　Native Americans 269
　Peru 279, 280, 281, 282–284
　Russia 488
　Spain 480–481
　United States 23, 33
　see also mother-tongue language learning
bilingualism 374, 375, 376, 381
　Germany 468, 470
　Russia 493
　see also multilingualism
Black feminism 174
Black Movement (Brazil) 531–532, 534, 535
Black students: South Africa 148, 150–151, 152, 153, 154
　United Kingdom 124, 128, 129, 130
　see also African Americans
　　African Brazilians
Blair, Tony 125, 129, 130, 179
BMW Award for Intercultural Learning 467–468
Bolivia 518
"border crossing" 39
Bourdieu, P. 42, 43, 257

Bowen, J.R. 311
Bowles, S. 25
Boykin, Wade 87
Brah, A. 37
Brazil 4, 513, 526–539
    higher education 530
    income inequalities 521
    mathematics 241
    race 512, 518, 519, 522–523, 531–535, 535n1
    social class 516, 517, 518
    teacher capacity 520
Brazilian immigrants in Japan 160, 164
Britain *see* United Kingdom
British National Party (BNP) 131, 334
Brown v. Board of Education (1954) 83, 178
Buck, Peter 297
Buddhism 9, 425, 439, 454, 488
Bulgaria 360–369
bullying 101, 161, 204–205, 206, 342–343
Buraku people 160, 162, 167
Burkina Faso 387–388, 389, 390, 391–392, 393, 394
Burstein, M. 99
business case discourse 98, 99
Butler, Judith 181, 182

Cahill, D. 117, 118
Cameroon 390
Canada: assimilationism 11, 12, 379
    children's racial attitudes 203
    citizenship education 3
    critical race theory 35, 36
    cultural deprivation paradigm 22
    destruction of Indigenous culture 3
    diversity 9–10
    ethnic revitalization movements 1, 9
    French separatism 11
    holidays 426
    languages 375, 382
    migrants 53, 54, 56
    multicultural education 2, 13, 96–108
    multiculturalism 57, 309
    PISA 118
    policy discourses 97–101
candy sellers 241
capitalism 43, 174, 226
Caribbean: destruction of Indigenous culture 3
    migrants to the UK 122
Carnoy, Martin 512–525
Carraher, D.W. 241
Carrim, N. 154
Castañeda, A. 22–23, 87, 305
caste 426, 427, 429, 430, 431
castelike minorities 24

Castles, Stephen 49–61, 309–310
categorization 192–194, 212
Catholic Church 130, 149–150, 341–342, 488, 541
    see also Christianity
Chai, H.C. 399
Cheche Konnen Project 243
Chile 512, 513
    higher education 530
    race 518
    social class 516, 517, 518
    student performance 523n4
China 4, 9, 51, 71, 374, 501–511
Chinese people: Indonesia 454, 456, 457
    Japan 159, 160, 164, 167
    Malaysia 9, 398, 399, 400, 401, 405–406
    Singapore 438, 441, 443
Chirac, Jacques 323, 414, 415
Christianity: China 505
    faith schools 130, 420, 421
    France 417–418
    Germany 466
    India 425, 431
    Indonesia 454, 455
    Malaysia 9
    Russia 488, 489
    Singapore 439
    see also Catholic Church
cities 52, 70
    education action zones 129
    Model Schools for Inner Cities program 104–106
citizenship 3, 303–322
    active 316–317
    Canada 98, 100, 102
    conceptions of 304
    cosmopolitanism 312–313
    differentiated 307
    Europe 137, 139, 352
    France 324, 332, 336, 339–340, 343, 344
    global 308
    India 433
    international 330
    legal 316, 317
    Malaysia 401
    migrants 53, 57
    minimal 316, 317
    multicultural 306, 309, 312
    United Kingdom 124, 129–130, 131, 338–339
    universal 307–308
citizenship education 3, 303, 310
    antiracism 350–351, 354, 357
    Australia 115
    Bulgaria 361–362, 365–368

conceptions of 304
cosmopolitanism 312–313
Eastern Europe 139
Europe 140, 141
France 334–337, 339–342, 343–345
goals of 309
mainstream 313–314
student identifications 311–312, 313
transformative 303, 313, 314, 316–318
United Kingdom 3, 122, 129, 334–339, 340, 341–343, 344–345, 354, 356, 414, 419–420
Civil, Marta 242
Civil Rights Movement 1, 9, 82–83, 84, 135, 178, 307
civil war in Peru 81
Clark, K. 203
Clarke, P.B. 316
class *see* social class
Cochran-Smith, Marilyn 89
coexistence 212, 219
cognition 240
cognitive engagement 68, 69
cognitive-developmental theory 187, 188
Cohen, Elizabeth G. 87, 314, 315, 316
collaborative skills 72
Collins, P.H. 183
Collins, R. 298
Colombia 516
colonialism 3, 43, 136
Africa 385–386, 389
India 431
Indonesia 451–452, 453
Latin America 527, 541
Malaysia 398–399
Mexico 541
Native Americans 272
New Zealand 297
Peru 276–277
South Africa 148
colorblindness 44, 178, 192, 229
Comeau, Karen Gayton 265–275
Commission for Racial Equality (CRE) 121, 126, 354
communication skills 71–72
communism 490, 522
communitarianism 38, 344
community 12, 29, 335
Canada 104
France/England comparison 341–342, 344, 345
community agency 69
community cohesion 121, 122, 124–125, 129–130, 131, 354, 356
see also social cohesion

community languages 112, 113
compensatory education programs 19, 475, 476, 477, 482
comprehension 246, 254–255
Confucianism 454
consensus politics 289–290
conservatism 38–39, 137
constructivism 152, 154, 187, 188
consumerism 226, 433, 441
contact models 87, 203–204, 206, 212
content integration 15–16, 81
contributions approach 81
controversies 86–87
Cope, B. 35
cosmopolitanism 14, 312–313
"cosmopolitan alternative" 40–41, 43
South Africa 155
Council of Europe 139, 330, 349, 350–351
Council of Ministers of Education for Canada (CMEC) 97–98, 101
Crenshaw, Kimberlé 177, 183
Crick, Bernard 419, 420
Crick Report 335, 337–338, 339, 340, 341, 342
critical multiculturalism 34, 35–36, 41–45
critical pedagogy 43, 44, 82, 88, 165, 176
critical race theory (CRT) 25, 35, 36–37, 176, 177–179, 183
children's racial attitudes 225
critical multiculturalism 42, 44
methodologies 88
political complacency 348, 357
critical theory 25, 26, 173, 174, 175–176, 183
critical thinking skills 71, 105, 226, 227, 230–231, 314
criticism 293
Cross, William 87
cross-cultural competency 26, 72
Cuba 513
race 518, 520–521
social class 516–517, 518, 522
student performance 514–515, 523n4
teacher capacity 518, 521
cultural assumptions 16, 20
cultural backwardness 502, 505, 506
cultural capital 14, 255, 505, 506, 508
cultural democracy 22–23, 305
cultural deprivation paradigm 17, 19, 21–22, 26
cultural difference 3, 14, 19, 21, 22–23, 26
critical multiculturalism 43
cultural racism 37
diversity distinction 44
equity pedagogy 17
Europe 136, 137
France 324

Japan 161
multiculturalism 35, 38
Spain 482
United Kingdom 124
see also diversity
cultural difference paradigm 22–23
cultural dominance 151–152
cultural ecology 19, 24, 162
cultural hybridity 38–40
cultural modeling 244–245
cultural pluralism *see* pluralism
cultural racism 36–37, 39
culturally responsive pedagogy 17, 89, 227–228
culture 34–37, 135
Australia 113, 114
"cosmopolitan alternative" 40–41
critical multiculturalism 43
descriptive concept of 256–257, 259
early childhood education 227
Goethe 259
Gramsci 175
hybridity theory 39
influence on learning 239–251
intercultural education 328
languages 373
Maori 291, 292, 296–297, 298
Palestinian-Jewish schools 217
Cummins, J. 393
curriculum: Australia 112, 113–114, 117
Brazil 531, 533
democratic multicultural 315
early childhood education 223–224
EDC program 350–351
ethnic additive paradigm 19, 21
India 431, 433, 434
Indonesia 453–454
intercultural education 138, 142
Israel 211, 217
madrasahs 440–441, 442
Native Americans 267, 270, 271
racism 178
Russia 490, 491–492
South Africa 152, 153
United Kingdom 126, 127, 128, 129, 131

Da Silva, A.L. 530–531
Darder, A. 36
de la Fuente, A. 521
decentralization: Bulgaria 361
Indonesia 454, 458
South Africa 153, 155
decoding 246, 254, 255
decolonization 13, 341, 381, 453
deconstruction 182

deep citizens 316
deficit orientation: Germany 464
Native Americans 267
Spain 482
United Kingdom 338
United States 240
Delgado, R. 177, 179
democracy: Bulgaria 360, 361
Europe 348–349, 350, 352, 357
Sweden 355–356
democratic racial attitudes 16
demographic divide 3
Denmark 53–54
Derman-Sparks, Louise 205, 225
Derrida, Jacques 182
desegregation 83, 178
de-socialization 257, 258, 259
developmental intergroup theory (DIT) 187–195
developmental psychology 223
Deyhle, Donna 265–275
dialogue 214, 217, 256, 535, 549
differential exclusion 56, 58
disability 14, 84, 85–86, 352, 365
discourse 180–181, 182
discrimination 4, 11, 309
anti-bias approach 225
Australia 115–116
behavior-change interventions 205, 206
Bulgaria 362, 363–364
citizenship education 345
critical race theory 42
early childhood education 231
European law 349
France 343, 344, 414
immigrants 49
India 425
institutional 138
Israel 211
Japan 159, 160, 162, 163, 167, 168
Mexico 540, 542, 543, 546, 547
South Africa 152, 154, 155
Spain 479
structural paradigm 20, 25
Sweden 355
United Kingdom 122, 342–343
United States 307
see also racism
segregation
diversity 9–10, 310–311, 382
Australia 109–111, 116, 118
Brazil 532, 534
Bulgaria 360
Canada 96, 101–102, 104, 106
China 501, 508

citizenship education 313, 334, 342–344
difference distinction 44
Europe 136–137, 138–139, 140, 141–142, 310–311, 350
France 330, 332
India 425–426, 427, 429–433, 434
Indonesia 449
intercultural education 327–328
Japan 166, 168
languages 377–378
Mexico 541, 544, 545, 547
migrants 55–58
religious 413–424
Russia 486
social activism 231
South Africa 147
Spain 474, 475, 483
United Kingdom 122, 125, 129, 131, 356, 419
United States 79, 89, 186
unity in 549
dolls 230
Dowa education 162
Drachsler, J. 305
D'Souza, D. 308
Du Bois, W.E.B. 82–83, 178

Earls, Felton 69
early childhood education 223–235
  Bulgaria 367
  Germany 465, 468, 471
  purpose and goals 226–231
  trends 224–226
Eastern Europe 53, 135, 139, 377, 522
economic assistance 545–546
Education for Democratic Citizenship (EDC) 350–351
El-Haj, T.R.A. 312
empathy 201, 203, 205, 213
empowering school culture 15, 17, 81
empowerment 252, 254, 256, 258, 259, 260
enculturation 150
engagement 68–69
Engen, Thor Ola 252–262
England: antiracist policies 353–355, 356
  citizenship education 334–339, 340, 341–343, 344–345, 419–420
  faith schools 420–421
  multicultural education 418–420
  see also United Kingdom
English as a second language (ESL) 85, 242
  Australia 111, 113, 114
  United Kingdom 125, 126, 129
  see also non–English-speaking backgrounds
English language 67, 375, 376, 380, 402

African American 245
Australia 110, 111, 117
faith schools 422
Malaysia 399, 400, 401, 403–407
New Zealand 293
Singapore 438
South Africa 153, 154
UNESCO report 379
United Kingdom 124
see also languages
environmental issues 226, 230
equal opportunity: France 331
  United Kingdom 123, 128
equality 14, 59, 310
  Canada 98, 101, 104
  citizenship 305
  Europe 348, 349, 352
  France 324, 331, 336, 343, 344–345
  India 427, 433
  Mexico 545
  New Zealand 296
  structural paradigm 25
  United Kingdom 354
  United States 79, 307
equity: Africa 393
  Canada 104, 105
  equity pedagogy 15, 16–17, 81
  Japan 165
equivalency programs 456–458
essentialism 36, 37–38, 43, 136, 137, 138
  definition of 45n2
  developmental intergroup theory 189, 192–193
  hybridity theory 39
  South Africa 147, 151
  "strategic" 182
ethnic additive paradigm 18, 19, 21
ethnic conflict 374, 378
ethnic group status 486–487, 491
ethnic revitalization movements 1, 9, 11–13
  group rights 306
  multicultural citizenship 304–305, 309
  response paradigms 17–21
ethnic separatism 58
ethnic studies 81, 84
ethnicism 37
ethnicity: critical multiculturalism 42, 44
  hybridity 38, 39
  Indonesia 454, 456
  "left-essentialist multiculturalism" 38
  Russia 489–490, 494
  situatedness 174
  see also race
ethnomathematics 241

Eurocentrism 527, 534, 540, 541–542, 547, 548
Europe: antiracism policies 348–359
  assimilationism 11
  colonialism 3
  diversity 9, 310–311
  English language 376
  intercultural education 134–145
  migrants 53–54, 377
  multiculturalism 33
  religious minority diversity 413
  see also European Union
European Commission Against Racism and Intolerance (ECRI) 349, 351
European Convention on Human Rights and Fundamental Freedoms (ECHR) 335, 339, 340, 348–349
European Union (EU) 123, 125, 134, 139–140
  antiracism policies 349–350, 351–353
  citizenship education 340
  linguistic minorities 383
  teacher education 330
Evans, Gwynfor 377
exams: Africa 389, 392
  immigrants 66
  Singapore 444
  see also high-stakes testing
expectations 104
explicit attributions 189, 193
explicit labeling 189, 192

faith schools 124, 129, 130, 342, 420–422
Fakirska, J. 367
family 65–66, 69, 224
Feagin, J.R. 225
feminism 88, 174, 183, 313
Feuerverger, G. 216
fictive kinship 24, 29n2
Fillmore, L.W. 254
Finland 375
First Nations 12, 99, 100
Fishman, J.A. 364
Folb, P. 151
Ford Foundation 530
Foster, M. 175
Foucault, Michel 180, 181, 182
France: Algerians 13
  assimilationism 11, 57, 58, 141, 310
  citizenship education 334–337, 339–342, 343–345
  diversity 310–311
  integration and citizenship 323–333
  language issues 23, 380
  migrants 54, 56, 58, 59
  Muslims 4, 311

political belonging 56
  religion 414–416, 417–418, 421–422
  resistance to multicultural education 413–414
  see also French language
Francophone Africa 385–396
Freire, Paulo 82, 175, 549
French language 326–327, 380
  Africa 385–396
  Madagascar 381
  Quebec 378, 382
Friedman, J. 39, 40
friendship 203, 204, 206, 213–214
Froumin, Isak D. 486–497
Fujimori, Alberto 281, 282
Fukuoka, Y. 163
funding: Africa 391
  Australia 112, 114, 118
  China 503
  early childhood education 232
  EU 351–352
  madrasahs 442
  United Kingdom 128
funds of knowledge 88, 242

Gandhi, Mohandas K. 426
García, María Elena 276–287
Gardner, Howard 71
Gates Foundation 70
Gavison, R. 216–217
Gay, Geneva 80, 89, 90
gender: African language 387
  behavioral engagement 69
  boys' literacy skills 102
  China 504, 506
  early childhood education 227
  equality 352
  Indonesian moral panics 455
  intersectionality 183
  migrants 54, 55
  Muslims 415
  performativity 181
  Roma students 477
  United States 14, 135
gender studies 84, 85
Germany 463–473
  assimilationism 11
  citizenship 309–310
  difference-oriented pedagogy 136
  ethnic belonging 56
  migrants 53, 54, 56, 57, 58
  Turks 4, 309
Gibson, Margaret 81
Gill, Saran Kaur 397–409
Gillborn, David 173–185

Gilroy, P. 38
Gintis, H. 25
Glazer, Nathan 19, 33
Glazier, J.A. 217
globalization 88, 308, 378
    Australia 116–117, 118
    Canada 99
    knowledge-intensive work 70–71
    migrants 50–51, 59, 62–64
    nationalism tension with 309
    skills 70
Godenzzi, Juan Carlos 282
Goethe, J.W. von 259
Gonçalves e Silva, Petronilha Beatriz 526–539, 540–551
Gonzales, N. 242
Gotanda, N. 177
Gramsci, Antonio 175–176
Grant, Carl A. 82, 86, 151
Greenbaum, W. 311
group work 72, 87
group-attribute covariation 189, 193–194
Grupioni, L.D.B. 530–531
Guinea Conakry 386

Habermas, Jürgen 45
habitus 42, 257
Hall, S. 38, 44
Hammack, P.L. 215
Hanson, Pauline 116
Hargreaves, David H. 128
Harley, K. 153–154
Harper, Stephen 99
Harvey, D. 293
Haskell Indian Nations University 266–267, 273n2
Hassan Ahmad 404
Hatcher, R. 35
headscarves (hijab) 311, 329, 336, 414, 422, 466
Hellesnes, J. 256
Helman, S. 214
Helms, Janet 87
Henare, James 378
Hermes, Mary 269
Hernández, N. 542, 544, 546–547
hidden curriculum 113, 115
higher education: Brazil 529
    Bulgaria 363–364
    China 501, 503, 505–506
    Latin America 530
    Malaysia 404–405
    Mexico 545, 546
    Native Americans 266–267, 268
    Spain 479

high-stakes testing 67, 224, 391, 433
    see also exams
hijab *see* headscarves
Hilliard, Asa 87
Hindus: faith schools 130, 420
    India 425, 430, 431
    Indonesia 450–451, 454
    Malaysia 9
    Singapore 439
Hirasawa, Yasumasa 159–169
Hirschfeld, L.A. 193
Hispanics 59, 377
    see also Latinos
Hoëm, A. 254, 255–256, 257, 258
holidays 13, 21, 415, 426, 428
holistic paradigm 26–27
Holm, A. 269
Holm, W. 269
homophobia 355
    see also sexual orientation
Hong Kong 51–52
Horowitz, D.L. 400
Hortefeux, Brice 331
Howard, John 110, 115, 116
Hughes, Julie Milligan 186–198
Hugonnier, Bernard 71
human capital 515–516
human rights 10, 308
    Bulgaria 367
    Canada 103
    citizenship education 339, 340, 357, 362, 365
    Europe 349, 350, 351, 352, 357
    France 330, 336, 340, 344–345
    Japan 162, 165, 166–168
    linguistic 382–383
    Mexico 548
    see also rights
Huntington, S. 33
hybridity 38–40, 42, 43
    globalization 378
    structural approaches 174
    United States 88, 91

Iceland 376, 377
identity: Canada 98, 99, 100, 102–103
    China 508
    choices 43
    critical multiculturalism 42, 44, 45
    de-socialization 257
    early childhood education 227, 228
    European 140
    France 324, 332, 344
    group-based 37–38, 39, 41
    hybridity 38, 39, 40, 88, 91

India 430–431
Indonesia 455–456, 459
integrating socialization 260
intergroup encounters 213
intergroup theory 187
Israel 218
languages 373, 377–378, 397
linguistic minorities 253
Maori 291
Mexico 540
multiple identities 36, 310
Muslim 420
Native American 266
politics of 219
research 87
Russia 490
structural approaches 180
United Kingdom 129–130, 131
see also national identity
identity groups 306, 307
ideology 291–292
immigrants 3, 49–61, 62–76
    academic outcomes 64–70
    Australia 109–110, 111–112, 113, 116, 118
    citizenship 306
    culturally responsive pedagogy 227
    diversity and belonging 55–58
    educational challenges 58–60
    Europe 136, 139–140, 141, 142, 310–311
    family background 65–66
    France 323, 324, 325–326, 327, 328, 331–332, 343, 418
    Germany 309–310, 463–473
    globalization 62–64
    illegal 331–332
    Japan 159–160, 163–165
    labor issues 53–55
    language issues 23, 67
    Malaysia 399
    school contexts 66–67
    skills 70–72
    social supports 69–70
    Spain 475, 477–479, 481–482, 483
    student engagement 68–69
    student identifications 311–312
    United Kingdom 122–125, 126
    United States 10, 176, 307
    voluntary/involuntary 24
    see also migration
        refugees
implicit attributions 189, 193–194
implicit labeling 189, 192
inclusiveness 104, 153–154, 230, 338
    see also social inclusion

income inequalities 512–516
India 2, 425–436
    languages 380, 381, 383, 425–426, 428, 432–433
    migrants to the UK 122
    religion 4, 430–431
Indic culture 450–451
indigenismo 278, 279
Indigenous peoples 3, 4, 10
    assimilation 12
    Australia 115, 116, 118, 119n1
    Brazil 526–527, 528–531, 533, 534–535
    cultural ecology 24
    Japan 160
    languages 374
    Latin America 512, 518, 519, 520, 522, 541–542
    Maori 227, 288–300
    Menominee Indians 244
    Mexico 13, 540–541, 542–549
    Peru 276–287
    Russia 487
    see also Aboriginal Australians
        Native Americans
Indonesia 449–459
inequality 4, 13, 43, 58
    Africa 389–390
    African Americans 82–83
    African Brazilians 531, 532
    Australia 118
    critical race theory 178
    critical theory 175, 183
    Europe 141
    intergroup encounters 214
    intersectionality 183
    Israel 211
    Latin America 512–516, 523
    Marxism 174
    Mexico 543
    school contexts 66
    United States 135
informal employment 55
Inglis, Christine 109–120
ingroup preference 189, 193, 194
institutional racism: antiracist theory 20
    cultural ecology 24
    definition of 353
    New Zealand 296
    QCA report 419–420
    structural paradigm 25
    United Kingdom 334–335, 338, 353, 354, 356, 357
    United States 307
integrated schooling 200, 203–204

integration 45, 56–57, 58
   Australia 110
   Europe 136, 142
   France 310, 324, 326–327, 331, 332
   Germany 465–466, 471
   linguistic minorities 253
   Malaysia 408
   Maori 292, 293
   South Africa 149–152, 154
   United Kingdom 123
intercultural communication 113
intercultural competence 352
intercultural education 14, 80, 83–84
   Brazil 535
   Bulgaria 361–362
   criticisms of 137–138
   Europe 134–145
   France 326, 327–328, 330–331
   implementation 141–142
   Mexico 540, 544, 547, 548–549
   national interpretations 139–141
   origin of 135–137
   Peru 282, 283–284
   Spain 475, 482
   see also multicultural education
interest convergence 178
intergroup encounters 16, 87, 315–316, 549
   China 504
   identity and identification 213
   Israel 211–212, 213–215, 216–218, 219
   racially integrated schooling 203–204, 206
intergroup theory 16, 187–188
International Association for the Evaluation of Educational Achievement (IEA) 336, 337, 513
international institutions 137
International Monetary Fund (IMF) 433
inter-racial confidence 445–446
intersectionality 173, 174, 183
Irvine, Jacqueline Jordan 88, 89
Islam 4, 57–58
   faith schools 420–421
   France 329, 414–416, 417–418
   Germany 466
   Indonesia 451, 454, 455, 457
   Malaysia 374, 401
   radical 3
   Russia 488
   Singapore 437–448
   see also Muslims
Islamophobia 4, 311, 335, 415
Israel 210–222
Italy 374–375, 380–381

Jaber-Massarwa, D. 214
Jains 425
James, A. 131
Japan 2, 3, 159–169
   citizenship 309
   Dowa education 162
   human rights-oriented approach 166–168
   immigrants 9, 51
   Indonesia 453
   Koreans 4, 163
   languages 23
   multicultural living-together 165
   Newcomer students 159–160, 163–165
   returnee students 160, 161–162
Jemaah Islamiyah (JI) 437, 444, 445, 446, 447
Jencks, C. 25
Jews: faith schools 130, 420, 421
   Indonesia 454
   Israel 210–222
   Russia 488
   see also anti-Semitism
Johnson, D.W. 315
Johnson, R.T. 315
Jones, E. 224
Jones, S. 175, 176
Joshee, Reva 96–108, 131, 425–436
Juneau, Denise 271
justice 288, 289, 295, 343
   see also social justice

Kalantzis, M. 35
Kallen, H.M. 305
Kamehameha Elementary Education Project (KEEP) 227
kaupapa Maori 292, 293, 294, 295, 298
Kawagley, A.O. 273
Kenworthy, J.B. 204
Kerr, D. 419
Khattab, U. 404
Kincheloe, J. 36
kindergartens 367
   see also early childhood education
King, Martin Luther, Jr. 316
knowledge: children's racial attitudes 188
   citizenship education 365, 366
   commonality of interests 257
   critical multiculturalism 43
   Indigenous 244, 270, 272–273, 529, 530, 542
   knowledge construction 15, 16, 81
   learning processes 239
   literacy 254
   mainstream/transformative 313, 314
   Maori 290, 291, 294
   power relationship 42

scaffolding 243–244
situated 240
knowledge economy 403
Kobayashi, T. 161
Koopmans, R. 304
Koreans 4, 159–160, 161, 163, 166, 167–168, 502
Kuhn, T. 17–18, 20–21, 289
Kuipers, Joel C. 449–459
Kymlicka, W. 41, 305, 306
Kyuchukov, Hristo 360–369

labeling 189, 192
labor: Japan 160
  migrants 50, 53–55, 62–63
  skills 70–72
Ladson-Billings, Gloria 83, 86, 176, 177, 310
Lakey, J. 224
language paradigm 19, 23–24
language skills 72
languages 3–4, 13, 373–384
  Africa 385–396
  African Americans 245
  Australia 10, 110, 112–113, 114, 116–117
  Brazil 529
  Bulgaria 360, 361, 362–365, 367
  Canada 103
  China 506, 508
  citizenship education 367
  Europe 138, 139–140, 142
  France 324, 325, 326–327
  Germany 465, 466, 467, 470
  immigrants 66, 67
  India 425–426, 428, 432–433
  Indonesia 449, 450, 451, 452, 455–456
  Israel 215, 217
  Japan 160, 163–164
  Latin America 519
  literacy 245–246, 252
  Malaysia 397–409
  Maori 288, 289, 290, 292–293, 294, 295, 298
  Mexico 540, 543, 544
  Native Americans 265, 266, 268, 269–270, 272
  Peru 276–279, 280, 281, 282, 283, 284
  plurilingualism 330–331
  Russia 487–488, 489–490, 492–493
  Singapore 438
  South Africa 153, 154
  Spain 475, 480–482
  Type I monolingual society 215
  United Kingdom 126
  see also bilingual education
    English as a second language
    English language
    linguistic minorities
    mother-tongue language learning
Latin America 512–525
  colonialism 527, 541
  destruction of Indigenous culture 3
  income inequalities 513–516
  Indigenous education 530
  race 518–519
  social class 516–518
  teacher capacity 519–521
  use of term 541–542
Latinos 33, 64, 69, 83, 186, 377
Lau v. Nichols (1974) 85
Lauby, J.-P. 343, 344
law 178
Lawrence, Stephen 124, 128, 129, 178–179, 334–335, 353
Le Pen, Jean-Marie 334
Leap, W. 269–270
Lear, J. 288, 289, 294
learner-centeredness 152
learning: cooperative 203, 315
  core propositions on 239–240
  cultural influences on 239–251
  instrumental 259
  learning styles 87–88
  literacy 244–246
  mathematics 241–242
  science 243–244
learning communities 483
learning disabilities 469–470, 475
Lee, Carol D. 239–251
the Left 86–87, 127
"left-essentialist multiculturalism" 38
legal cases: *Begum v. Headteacher and Governors of Denbigh High School* 416
  Brown v. Board of Education 83, 178
  Lau v. Nichols 85
  Mandla v. Dowell Lee 416
  Mikro v. the State 153
Leger, Daniele Hervieu 329
legislation: bilingual education 85
  Brazil 526, 528, 533
  Bulgaria 361
  disability rights 86
  European 349
  France 414–415, 418
  India 429
  Indonesia 457
  Japan 166
  Malaysia 401, 402
  Mexico 541, 543
  Native Americans 269, 271
  Peru 280
  Russia 490–491, 492, 493, 494

Singapore 439, 443
South Africa 148, 152, 153
Spain 474–475, 480
Sweden 355
United Kingdom 121–122, 124, 127–130, 335, 354, 357, 417, 419
United States 307
Lemaire, Eva 323–333
Lévesque, René 378
Lévi-Strauss, C. 39
Levy, F. 71
Li, G. 228
Liben, L.S. 188, 194, 200, 201
liberal assimilationism 11, 12, 303, 306, 309, 312, 313
Lifelong Learning Programme 352
linguistic minorities 252–262, 374–375, 382–383
Bulgaria 360, 361, 362–365
citizenship rights 305–306
Spain 480–482
linguistics 174, 181
"linking classrooms" 481–482
Lipka, Jerry 242, 270
Lipset, S.M. 305
literacy 244–246, 252–262
Africa 391
Indonesia 458
Russia 490
second language learning 393
local education authorities (LEAs) 125, 128, 353, 417, 419
localization 256, 259–260, 453–454
Lomawaima, K.T. 272
Longitudinal Immigrant Student Adaptation (LISA) 65, 66, 67, 68
Lowe, V. 404
low-income students: African Brazilians 519
Cuba 521
cultural deprivation paradigm 17, 19, 21–22
early childhood education 224
environmental issues 226
income inequalities 515
Latin America 517–518, 520
Mexico 545–546
structural paradigm 25
see also poverty
social class
Lucas, Tamara 89
Luchtenberg, Sigrid 463–473
Luxembourg 53–54, 383
Lyotard, J.-F. 38

Madagascar 381
Madden, N.A. 315
madrasahs 437, 439–444, 446, 447, 455
Mahathir Mohamad 403
mainstreaming skills approach 253–254, 259
Maira, S. 312
Major, John 128
Malaysia 9, 374
immigrants 51–52
language 381, 397–409
Singapore independence from 438
Mali 387–388, 389, 390, 391–392, 393, 394
Mandla v. Dowell Lee 416
Mann, Horace 79–80
Mannheim, Bruce 277
Maori 227, 288–300, 378
Maoz, I. 213, 214, 219
Mapuche Indians 512, 518–519
Margalit, A. 41
marginalization 4
Marshall, T.H. 304, 305
Marxism 174, 175, 182–183
mathematics 241–242, 513
Mauzy, D.K. 401
May, Stephen 33–48
McCarty, T.L. 270, 272
McGurk, Brother 150, 153
McLaren, P. 36, 175
McLaughlin, D. 269
Mears, Ideas 420
media: children's racial attitudes 201–203, 206
France 415
Germany 470
mediators 201
Medin, D.L. 244
Meer, Nasar 413–424
Menominee Indians 244
mentors 69–70
meritocracy 178
metacognition 239
Mexican Americans 4, 13, 83, 224, 304, 307
cultural democracy 305
cultural ecology 24
ethnic studies 84
language issues 23
liberal assimilationist view 306
Mexico 4, 540–551
higher education 530
Indigenous schools 13, 519
migrants 53
social class 516, 517, 518
student performance 523n4
teacher capacity 520
Michael, Sister 149–150
Middle East 51–52
migration 3, 10, 49–61, 308–310

diversity and belonging 55–58
educational challenges 58–60
Europe 136, 137
globalization 50–51
intercultural education 138
internal 50–51
labor issues 53–55
languages 376–377
Malaysia 398
Russia 487
second-generation migrants 54–55
United Kingdom 122–125
see also immigrants
refugees
Mikro v. the State 153
Mitterand, François 343
Model Schools for Inner Cities program 104–106
Modood, Tariq 413–424
Mohamed, Mustapha 405
Mohan, R. 36
Moll, L. 242
mono-ethnic approach 491
Montana 271
Montgomery bus boycott 316
Moodley, K.A. 14
Morocco 481
Moses, Robert 242
mother-tongue language learning 19, 361, 362, 364
   Australia 112
   Bulgaria 367
   France 325–326
   Germany 466
   India 380, 432
   Malaysia 401, 402, 406, 408
   Mexico 547
   Russia 489, 492
   UNESCO 379, 382, 383, 432
   United Kingdom 126
   see also bilingual education
languages
Moyenda, S. 35
multicultural education 2, 9–32
   Australia 109–120
   Canada 96–108
   children's racial attitudes 200, 201–203
   critiques of 86–87, 308
   definitions of 80–82
   dimensions of 15–17, 81–82
   Germany 465, 467–468
   goals of 14
   India 425, 429–433, 434
   intercultural education distinction 134–135
   Japan 159–169
   Latin America 512, 522–523
   migrants 49–50, 59–60
   multi-factor paradigm 26–29
   practice 90
   rise and characteristics of 13–15
   Russia 495
   South Africa 146–158
   Spain 482
   teacher education 88–89
   theory and research 87–88
   United Kingdom 121–133, 417, 418–420, 422
   United States 79–95
   young children 223–235
   see also intercultural education
multicultural living-together 165, 167, 168
multiculturalism 2, 13, 33–48
   Australia 110–111, 114
   backlash against 57
   Canada 97, 98–100, 102
   China 504, 508
   culturalist critique 34, 35–37
   Europe 350
   immigrants 57
   India 425, 426, 427
   Latin America 522, 523
   postmodernist critique 34, 37–38
   Singapore 438
   South Africa 151, 154, 155
   United Kingdom 121, 125, 131, 414, 418–419, 420
multilingualism 373, 374, 375–377, 379–382, 383
   Europe 138, 140, 142
   India 432
   Malaysia 397
   South Africa 245–246
   see also bilingualism
Munanga, K. 533
Murnane, R. 71
Muslims 4
   Australia 116
   Bosnian 378
   faith schools 130, 420–421
   France 311, 329, 342, 344, 414–416, 421–422
   Germany 466, 470
   India 425, 426–427, 431
   Indonesia 455
   Malaysia 9
   Russia 488
   Singapore 437–448
   United Kingdom 123, 124–125, 128, 129–130, 309, 416, 420–421
   see also Islam
Myrdal, Gunnar 79

name-calling 200, 204–205
Nandy, D. 126
narrative approaches 212–213, 216
Nasir, N. 241, 242
National Assessment of Educational Progress (NAEP) 67, 245
National Association for Multicultural Education (NAME) 86, 90
national culture 11, 28, 374, 504
National Curriculum (UK) 123–124, 128, 129, 131, 353, 356, 419, 422
National Curriculum Statements (NCS) (South Africa) 152, 153–154
national identity 23, 38, 58, 310, 312
   China 502
   citizenship education 334, 335, 337–340, 345
   France 324, 332, 339–340, 345, 418, 422
   India 427, 428
   Israel 218
   language 374
   linguistic minorities 253
   Malaysia 402
   Peru 278
   United Kingdom 337–339, 345, 356
   see also identity
nationalism 39, 308, 309, 310
   aggressive 351
   Japan 161
   Malaysia 398, 400
Native Americans 16, 83, 265–275, 304
   conversation rules 245
   definition of 273n1
   ethnic studies 84
Navajo Preparatory School, Inc. 270–271
Nazism 348, 355
neoconservatism 18–19, 21
   Canada 96–97, 99, 101–102, 106
   Japan 166
neoliberalism 55, 58
   Canada 96, 98, 99, 100, 101–102, 106
   India 433
   Japan 166
neo-Marxism 25, 35
Netherlands: assimilationism 11
   colonial Indonesia 451–452
   diversity 310–311
   ethnic revitalization movements 9
   migrants 54, 56
   multiculturalism 57
   Muslims 4
Neubert, K. 224
New Right 39
New York City 55, 70
New Zealand: Maori 227, 288–300
   migrants 56
Nguyen, D. 312
Nieto, Sonia 79–95, 227
Niger 385, 387–388, 389, 390, 391–392, 393, 394
non–English-speaking backgrounds (NESB) 110, 111, 112, 114, 117
   see also English as a second language
Northern Ireland 229–230
Norway 252–253
Nunes, T. 241
Nussbaum, M. 312, 313

Odina, Teresa Aguado 474–485
Ofsted 353–355
Ogbu, J.U. 24, 29n2, 162
Ohta, H. 164
orthography 394
Osler, Audrey 334–347, 348–359, 419–420

Pala, Valérie Sala 413–424
Palestinians 210–222
Panama 519, 520, 541
Pancasila 453, 454
Paniagua, Valentín 282
Papua New Guinea 375
paradigms 17–21
parents: Australia 113, 117
   children's racial attitudes 199
   early childhood education 224
   education level of 65, 513
   immigrants 65
   Israel 217–218
   linguistic minorities 253–254
   madrasahs 441
   Peru 284
   South Africa 151
Park, R. 11
Parker, B. 153–154
Parker, Rosa 316
"Pathways to Higher Education" 530
peace education 214, 218, 219
peers 69, 200
Peller, G. 177
Penetito, Wally 288–300
perceptual discriminability 189, 191, 195
performativity 181, 182
Peru 4, 276–287, 519, 520, 530
Peruvian immigrants in Japan 160, 164
Phillips, C.B. 205
Piagetian theory 188
PISA *see* Programme for International Student Assessment
play 224
pluralism 11, 81, 259

China 501, 502, 504
France 324
India 426, 434
Mexico 540–541
United Kingdom 123, 126
United States 79
plurilingualism 330–331
political literacy 335, 341
politics: Bulgaria 360, 361
  consensus 289–290
  Malaysia 404
  New Zealand 297
  Peru 279–280, 281, 282–283
  Singapore 438, 439
poly-ethnic approach 491
Popper, K.R. 293
Porcher, Louis 327, 328
Portugal 376, 481
postcolonialism 88
Postiglione, Gerard A. 501–511
postmodernism 34, 37–38, 39, 40, 45, 88
post-structuralism 173–174, 180–182, 183
poverty: culturally responsive pedagogy 227
  immigrants 65, 66
  Indigenous peoples 544, 545
  learning research 240
  minorities 58
  Model Schools for Inner Cities program 104
  see also low-income students
power 35, 176, 308
  critical multiculturalism 42–43, 45
  post-structuralism 180–181, 183
prejudice: children's racial attitudes 186–187, 188–194, 199, 200, 202, 204–205, 206
  early childhood education 230–231
  Mexico 543
  prejudice reduction 15, 16, 20, 81
  young children 223
  see also racism
private schools: Indonesia 456, 458–459
  Spain 479, 482
problem solving 241, 242, 243
Programme for International Student Assessment (PISA) 67, 252, 513, 523n2
  Australia 118
  Germany 465, 468
  intercultural education 142
  Latin America 523n1
  migrants 54
proportional group size 189, 191
protective disidentification 20, 24–25
psychodynamic theory 212
psychological salience 188, 189, 191–192, 195, 229

Puerto Ricans 23, 84

Qualifications and Curriculum Authority (QCA) 129, 335, 338–339, 356, 419–420
Quebec 378, 382
Quechua 276–279, 280, 281, 283
queer studies 85, 88

race 2–3, 36–37
  Brazil 512, 531–535, 535n1
  children's racial attitudes 186–198, 199–209, 229, 315
  critical pedagogy 176
  Cuba 521
  early childhood education 227, 230–231
  Europe 136
  immigrant segregation 66
  Indonesia 451–452, 456
  intersectionality 183
  Latin America 518–519, 520
  Marxism 175, 182–183
  post-structural theory 180–182, 183
  South Africa 146, 147, 148, 151, 153, 155
  structural approaches 174
  United Kingdom 124, 126, 128
  see also critical race theory
    ethnicity
racism 3, 36, 43, 297, 535
  African Brazilians 531, 532, 533, 534
  Australia 115–116
  Bulgaria 362
  bullying 101
  Canada 100, 103
  citizenship education 339, 344, 345
  critical race theory 177–178, 179
  Cuba 521, 522
  culture of 58
  European antiracism policies 140, 348–359
  France 334, 344, 345
  Germany 467
  hybridity theory 39
  Mexico 540, 547
  multiculturalism 35
  New Zealand 296
  police 179
  South Africa 151, 153
  structural paradigm 20, 25
  United Kingdom 123, 131, 334–335, 339
  see also antiracist education
    institutional racism
    prejudice
Ramírez, M. 22–23, 87, 305
Ramsey, Patricia G. 223–235
Raz, J. 41

567

recognition discourse 103, 104, 255–256, 258
Reconceptualizing Early Childhood Movement 225
reductionism 137, 138
reflexivity 44
refugees 65, 227, 308
    Germany 463–464
    United Kingdom 123, 128
relational engagement 68, 69
relativism 136, 138, 259, 293
religion 413–424
    citizenship education 341–342, 345
    Europe 138
    France 328–329, 341–342, 344, 345, 414–416, 417–418, 421–422
    fundamentalism 4
    Germany 466
    India 425, 428, 430–431
    Indonesia 454–455
    Israel 218
    Russia 488, 493–494
    Singapore 437–448
    United Kingdom 345
    see also Christianity
        Hindus
        Islam
        Jews
religious education: France 417
    Germany 466
    India 431
    Indonesia 452, 455, 458–459
    Russia 493–494
    Singapore 437, 439–444, 446, 447
    United Kingdom 131
remedial teaching 468
research: China 505–507
    multicultural education 87–88
researchers 16
resettlers 464, 468
resistance 296, 298, 542
re-socialization 257, 258, 259
resources 515–516
Rethinking Schools 90
Ricoeur, Paul 255–256, 330
the Right 33, 34, 37–38, 86
    Canada 96
    United Kingdom 127, 131
rights: actualization of 549
    Canada 98, 102, 103, 104
    citizenship 304, 305–306, 310
    France 344
    group 11, 37, 40, 41, 303, 306
    Indigenous 530, 542
    individual 306
    linguistic 380, 382–383
    movement 10
    Native Americans 268, 271–272
    Russia 490
    see also human rights
Roma: Bulgaria 360, 361, 362–364, 368
    Slovakia 522
    Spain 476–477, 483
Romaine, Suzanne 373–384
Rosaldo, R. 305
Rosen, Y. 214
Russia 486–497
Rwanda 378

Said, Edward 38, 181
Sami 255
Sánchez, George 83
Sardinia 380–381
Sarkozy, Nicolas 324, 328
Saturday schools 113, 126
Saussure, F. de 174
Saxe, G. 241
Sayed, Y. 152, 154
scaffolding 243–244, 456
Schlesinger, A.M., Jr. 19, 308
Schliemann, A.D. 241
Schofield, Janet Ward 87, 315
school culture 15, 17, 27, 28, 81
School Without Racism 467
schools: acculturation 27, 28
    Africa 386, 388–389, 391–392, 393–394
    antiracism 351, 353–354, 355
    Australia 111–112, 113, 114
    Canada 97–98, 100–101
    China 504–505
    cultural difference paradigm 22–23
    empowering school culture 15, 17, 81
    Europe 136
    France 324, 328
    Germany 468–470
    immigrants 66–67
    Indonesia 451–452, 455, 456, 457, 458–459
    Japan 164, 167
    Malaysia 399, 405–406, 407–408
    Maori 292, 294
    Model Schools for Inner Cities program 104–106
    Palestinian-Jewish 210, 215–218
    racially integrated schooling 203–204
    Russia 489
    South Africa 148–149, 150, 151, 152–154, 155
    structural paradigm 25, 26
    total school environment 26–27
    United Kingdom 124

science 71, 243–244
second language learners 67
segregation: Bulgaria 361, 362–363, 368
    developmental intergroup theory 192, 195
    France 325, 414
    immigrants 49
    Israel 211
    Latin America 513, 517–518, 542
    linguistic minorities 253
    schools 66–67
    Spain 475
    triple 66
    United Kingdom 121, 123, 124, 127, 130
    United States 83, 178, 316
self-concept development 18, 19, 21, 228
self-determination 12–13, 216–217
    Indigenous peoples 530
    Native Americans 265, 266, 267, 268, 273
    Russia 489
self-efficacy 68, 69, 206
self-esteem 104, 187
    Australia 113
    cooperative learning 315
    Indigenous peoples 545
    social supports 69
Sen, A. 378
Sendero Luminoso 280, 281
Serbia 378
sexism 43, 355
    anti-bias program 205, 206
    bullying 101
sexual orientation 14–15, 86, 355
Sharp, A. 288
Shields, R. 290
Shohamy, E. 215
signifying 245
Sihra, Karen 425–436
Sikhs: faith schools 130, 420
    India 425
    Singapore 439
    United Kingdom 416, 420
Silin, J.G. 225
Simon, Patrick 413–424
Sims, C. 272
Singapore 9, 51–52, 378, 437–448
skills 70–72
Slaby, R.G. 205
slavery 148
Slavin, R.E. 203, 315
Sleeter, Christine 82, 87, 89
Slovakia 522
social action approach 81
social activism 227, 231
social class: Africa 389–390

    citizenship 305
    Cuba 518, 522
    Germany 471
    income inequalities 515
    Indonesia 456, 457, 458
    intersectionality 183
    Latin America 513, 516–518, 520, 522
    Marxism 174, 175
    structural paradigm 25
    United Kingdom 127
    see also low-income students
social cohesion 3, 57, 60
    Canada 98, 99, 100–101, 104
    citizenship education 342–344
    Europe 142, 351, 352
    Germany 471
    see also community cohesion
social exclusion 58, 341, 344, 457
social guarantee programs 475, 483n1
social identity theory 187
social inclusion 59, 351
    see also inclusiveness
social justice 80, 82
    Canada 96, 97, 98, 100, 102–103, 104, 105–106
    cosmopolitanism 313
    India 427, 434
    Indonesia 453
    Japan 165
    linguistic rights 382
    United States 79
social support 69–70
socialization 254, 256, 257, 258, 259–260, 336
solidarity 227, 228–229
    France 336, 343, 344–345
    Indonesia 452
Soudien, Crain 146–158
South Africa 2, 146–158, 378
    Constitution of 147
    integration periods 149–152
    languages 380
    multilingualism 245–246
    school responses to policy change 152–154
South Asians 13, 203
South Korea 51, 518
Spain 11, 382, 474–485, 541
Spivak, Gayatri Chakravorty 182
Spolsky, B. 215
Sri Lanka 432
standards: Bulgaria 365–367
    Indonesia 457
Starkey, Hugh 334–347, 348–359, 419–420
Steele, C.M. 24–25
Stefancic, J. 177, 179
Steinberg, S. 36

stereotyping: Canada 103
  children's racial attitudes 187, 188–194, 199, 200
  Indonesia 456
  Israel 213
  protective disidentification 20, 24–25
  South Africa 155
  Spain 482
Stone, M. 21
storybooks 201–202, 227, 229
Stovall, D. 182, 183
structural paradigm 20, 25–26, 45, 174
structuralism 173, 180
student engagement 68–69
Suárez-Orozco, Carola 62–76
Suárez-Orozco, Marcelo 62–76
subjectivity 180, 181, 182
Subrahmanian, R. 154
Suharto, President 453, 454, 458
Sukarno, President 453
Swann Commission 418–419, 420
Sweden 53–54, 57, 355–356, 375
Swisher, K. 267, 268, 273
Switzerland 53, 54, 57, 382

Taiwan 51–52
talk story 245
Tamils 398, 399, 400, 401, 406–407, 438
Tanzania 381
Tate, William 151, 177, 178
Tatum, Beverly Daniel 87
Taylor, C. 135, 255–256
Taylor, E. 179, 241
Te Atairangikaahu 297
Te Kohanga Reo (TKR) 294, 298
Te Maori 297
teacher education 88–89
  Africa 392, 394
  Brazil 528, 529
  China 503, 506
  EU program 330
  France 327, 330–331
  Germany 464, 467
  India 431, 433
  intercultural education 142
  Latin America 519–520
  Peru 282, 284
  Spain 483
  United Kingdom 128, 129
teachers: Africa 389, 392
  culturally responsive education 227–228
  dimensions of multicultural education 15–17
  early childhood education 223–224, 230
  France 330–331

income inequalities 515
India 429
Latin America 519–521
madrasahs 442
Palestinian-Jewish schools 217, 218
racism 177
school culture 27, 28
South Africa 154
United Kingdom 122
Teaching for Change 90
Teaching Tolerance 90
technology 70, 71, 72, 403
television 201, 205, 230
terrorism 4, 57–58, 311, 323, 335, 437
  Australia 116
  Indonesia 455
  racism 356
  Singapore 444–445
  United Kingdom 121, 124, 125, 129
textbooks 314, 315
  Africa 385, 390, 394, 395
  citizenship education 337, 343, 345
  India 427, 430, 431
  Indonesia 452, 456
  Russia 492, 494
Thatcher, Margaret 127–128
Third International Mathematics and Science Study (TIMSS) 513, 523n1, 523n2
Thomas, K. 177
"three Rs" 70
Tibet 504, 506
Tippeconnic, J.W. 267, 273
Toledo, Alejandro 283
tolerance: children's racial attitudes 199
  Europe 350, 352, 357
  integrating socialization 260
  Russia 495
  South Africa 151
  United Kingdom 338
Tomlinson, Sally 121–133
Toronto District School Board (TDSB) 104–105
Torres, C. 34
Torres, R.D. 36
Toure, Seku 386
traditionalism 11, 12, 38
Trager, H.G. 315
transformative approach 81, 91, 313, 314–315, 316–318
tribal control 267
Tropp, L.R. 204
Troyna, B. 35
Turks: Bulgaria 360, 362
  Germany 4, 309, 463, 466, 470

United Kingdom (UK): African Caribbeans 4, 13
  antiracism 115, 353–355, 356, 416–417
  assimilationism 11, 141
  children's racial attitudes 203
  citizenship education 3, 334–339, 340, 341–343, 344–345, 419–420
  cultural deprivation paradigm 22
  diversity 310–311
  ethnic revitalization movements 1, 9
  faith schools 420–421
  language issues 23
  migrants 56, 305
  multicultural education 2, 13, 121–133, 418–420, 422
  multiculturalism 57, 414
  Muslims 4, 309, 311
  political belonging 56
  political complacency 357
  race relations legislation 179
  terrorism 356
  see also English language
United Nations Educational, Scientific and Cultural Organization (UNESCO) 137, 465
  African schools 387, 393
  languages 379, 382–383, 432
  Latin America 514, 516
United States (US): assimilationism 11, 12, 56, 304, 311
  children's racial attitudes 192
  citizenship education 311–312, 313
  Civil Rights Movement 1, 9, 82–83, 84, 135, 178, 307
  community-based organizations 69
  critical race theory 35
  cultural deprivation paradigm 21
  destruction of Indigenous culture 3
  diversity 9–10, 186
  ethnic revitalization movements 1, 304–305, 306
  Hispanics 377
  immigrants 53, 55, 56–57, 59, 63–65, 176, 307
  influence on Europe 135–136
  language issues 23, 375, 380
  Latin America comparison 518, 520
  learning 240
  literacy 244
  mathematics 242
  Montgomery bus boycott 316
  multicultural education 2, 13, 14–15, 79–95
  multiculturalism 33, 35, 309
  religious fundamentalism 4
  second language learners 67

  see also African Americans
    Mexican Americans
    Native Americans
Universal Declaration of Human Rights (UDHR) 10, 308, 339, 340

Valchev, R. 367
values 257, 260, 310
  France 330, 336, 340, 344
  madrasahs 441
  Russia 495
Van Ausdale, D. 225
Velasco Alvarado, Juan 279–280
Villegas, Ana María 89
violence 116, 123

Waitangi Tribunal 289, 295, 298
Waldron, J. 40–41
Wasson-Ellam, L. 228
Werbner, P. 39
West, Cornell 297–298
West Indians 23
  see also African Caribbeans
White supremacy 79, 147, 155, 177, 179, 183
Whiteness 44
women: Black feminism 174
  India 428
  migrants 55
  see also gender
Woodson, Carter 82–83, 305
World Bank 387, 393, 433
World of Difference (WOD) 90
Wright, S.C. 204

xenophobia: Europe 140, 349, 350, 352
  France 334
  Germany 466, 467

Yamawaki, K. 166
Yang, P.K. 402
Yarrow, M.R. 315
York, Darlene Eleanor 88
Youdell, Deborah 173–185
young children see early childhood education
Yulaelawati, Ella 449–459

Zakharov, Andrei 486–497
Zapatista Army of National Liberation (EZLN) 547
Zarco, C. 548
Zeichner, Kenneth 89
Zhou, Min 69
Zoroastrians 425